25 Dictionaries *di* 393

26 Vocabulary *voc* 402

27 Diction *d* 413
a. Appropriateness
b. Denotation, connotation
c. General and specific
d. Figurative language

28 Language Variety *lv* 432
a. Varieties of English
b. Standard varieties
c. Ethnic varieties
d. Occupational varieties
e. Regional varieties
f. Other languages
g. In academic writing

29 Building Common Ground *cg* 445
a. The golden rule
b. Taking time to listen

VI PUNCTUATION

30 Commas , 460
a. Introductory elements
b. Compound sentences
c. Nonrestrictive elements
d. Series
e. Parenthetical, transitional elements
f. Other uses
g. Dates, titles, etc.
h. Quotations
i. For understanding
j. Unneeded commas

31 Semicolons ; 480
a. To link clauses
b. In a series
c. Overused
d. Misused
e. With quotation marks

32 End Punctuation . ? ! 487
a. Periods
b. Question marks
c. Exclamation points

33 Apostrophes ' 493
a. Possessives
b. Contractions, etc.
c. Plurals, words as words

34 Quotation Marks " " 499
a. Direct quotations
b. Dialogue
c. Titles, definitions
d. Irony, coinages
e. Misused
f. With other punctuation

35 Other Punctuation ( ) [ ] — : / . . . :-) 508
a. Parentheses
b. Brackets
c. Dashes

d. Colons
e. Slashes
f. Ellipses
g. Emoticons

VII MECHANICS

36 Capitals *cap* 522

37 Abbreviations, Numbers *abb/num* 529

38 Italics *ital* 538

39 Hyphens - 544

VIII RESEARCH

40 Becoming a Researcher *res* 552
a. Assignments, topics
b. Narrowing a topic
c. Investigating a topic
d. From hypothesis to working thesis

41 Conducting Research *res* 562
a. Primary, secondary sources
b. Library, database sources
c. Computer databases
d. Field research

42 Using Sources *res* 586
a. Choosing sources
b. Reading sources
c. Taking notes
d. Plagiarism
e. Interpreting sources

43 Research Essays *res* 607
a. Refining plans
b. Organizing
c. Drafting
d. Incorporating sources
e. Reviewing a draft
f. Revising, editing
g. Preparing references
h. Proofreading

44 MLA Documentation *MLA* 623
SAMPLE ESSAY 645

45 APA, CBE, and Chicago Documentation *APA/CBE/CMS* 665
APA Style
SAMPLE ESSAY 678
CBE Style
SAMPLE ESSAY 712
Chicago Style
SAMPLE ESSAY 719

IX ACADEMIC WRITING

46 Understanding Disciplinary Discourse *dis* 698
a. Assignments

d. Evidence
e. Formats

47 Writing in the Disciplines *dis* 707
a. Writing to learn
b. Learning to write
c. Social sciences
SAMPLE ESSAY 709
d. Natural sciences
SAMPLE ESSAY 712
e. Applied sciences
SAMPLE ESSAY 716
f. Humanities
SAMPLE ESSAY 719

48 Writing about Literature *lit* 723
a. Literary language
b. Reading literature
c. Considering the assignment
d. Developing a critical stance
TEXT-BASED ESSAY 729
CONTEXT-BASED ESSAY 734
READER-BASED ESSAY 737

49 Essay Exams *exam* 740

X ACCESSING, PRESENTING TEXT

50 Working On-Line *com* 750
a. Writing with a computer
b. Getting on-line
c. Using the Internet
d. Accessing information

51 Designing Documents *doc* 758
a. Visual structure
b. Consistency
c. Headings
d. Visuals

52 Professional Business Formats *bus* 767

53 Oral Presentations *oral* 777

54 Writing Portfolios *port* 784

XI FOR MULTILINGUAL WRITERS

55 Nouns 788

56 Verbs, Verb Phrases 798

57 Prepositions 810

58 Clauses, Sentences 816

Glossaries 827

Selected Answers 857

Index *Index–1*

Third Edition

THE ST. MARTIN'S HANDBOOK

<>

Andrea Lunsford

OHIO STATE UNIVERSITY

Robert Connors

UNIVERSITY OF NEW HAMPSHIRE

with a new section
for multilingual writers by

Franklin E. Horowitz

TEACHERS COLLEGE
COLUMBIA UNIVERSITY

ST. MARTIN'S PRESS

NEW YORK

Senior Editor of The St. Martin's Handbook   Marilyn Moller
Senior Acquisitions Editor   Karen Allanson
Managing Editor   Patricia Mansfield Phelan
Senior Project Editor   Erica Appel
Associate Editor   Steven Kutz
Editorial Assistants   Susan Cottenden, Jennifer Valentine
Production Supervisor   Joe Ford
Text Design   Anna George
Cover Design   Sheree Goodman

Library of Congress Catalog Card Number: 94–65181
Manufactured in the United States of America.
9 8 7 6 5
f e d c b

For information, write:
St. Martin's Press, Inc.
175 Fifth Avenue
New York, NY 10010

ISBN: 0-312-10212-7

ACKNOWLEDGMENTS

Gwendolyn Brooks. "We Real Cool" from *Blacks,* published by Third World Press: Chicago. Copyright © 1991 by Gwendolyn Brooks.
"Chicken Soup: It Might Help Your Memory" from *Newsweek,* December 1986. Copyright © 1986, Newsweek, Inc. All rights reserved. Reprinted by permission.

Acknowledgments and copyrights are continued at the back of the book.

Preface

The story of *The St. Martin's Handbook* stretches back to 1983, when, in the course of investigating the history of writing instruction, we came across some information that led us to a series of compelling questions. We discovered, for example, that in the late nineteenth century, professors at Harvard perceived that their students had great difficulty distinguishing between the use of *shall* and *will,* and that in the 1930s, American students persistently misused *would* for the simple past. How quaint, we thought; look at how much student writing problems have changed, and at how our notions of what is or is not an "error" have changed too.

But what exactly were some of these changes? This question took on greater significance as we focused our investigation on the history and development of composition textbooks. As part of that research, we found that the first edition of John C. Hodges's *Harbrace College Handbook* (1941) was based on an analysis of over twenty thousand student papers written in the 1930s. So, we reasoned, that book reflected the writing problems of students of the time, problems that were decidedly different from how to use *shall* and *will.* How might the problems faced by our students have changed?

With something of a shock, we realized that we didn't know. Further investigation showed us not only that Hodges's research seemed to be the last serious effort of that kind but that his handbook was still organized exactly as it had been in 1941. Since subsequent college handbooks had necessarily responded to that book, we realized with some surprise that the world of composition handbooks was still being tacitly guided by conceptions of error patterns that were half a century old.

We set out, then, to discover what patterns of error actually characterize student writing today, and which of these patterns seem most important to their instructors. To answer this question, we gathered a nationwide sample of over twenty thousand marked student essays and carefully analyzed a scientifically stratified sample of them, eventually identifying the twenty

v

error patterns most characteristic of student writing today. We got some provocative results.

Most intriguing was how many of these errors related in some way to visual memory—wrong words, wrong or missing verb endings, missing or misplaced possessive apostrophes, even the *its/it's* confusion—which suggests that students today are less familiar with the visible aspects of writing than students once were. One effect of an oral, electronic culture seems to be that students do not automatically bring with them the visual knowledge of writing conventions that text-wise writers possess and use effortlessly.

This problem of visualization was most pronounced in terms of spelling errors, which occur—by a factor of 300 percent—more frequently than any other error. Interestingly enough, the words students most often misspell are homonyms, thus further suggesting that the visual aspect of spelling is particularly important, that in a world of secondary orality we need to find ways to help students visualize their language.

Our research also revealed that many errors are governed not so much by hard and fast rules as by rhetorical decisions involving style, tone, and rhythm. Among others, such errors include omitted commas after an introductory element, inappropriate shifts in verb tense, and misused commas with restrictive and nonrestrictive elements. This finding suggested to us that students need help writing prose that is not only mechanically correct but rhetorically effective as well. Doing so, we believe, demands that they view the tools of writing—grammar, punctuation, mechanics—as having rhetorical force and as being based on choices they must learn to make.

If we could say with some assurance what errors characterize student writing today, what could we say about student use of larger rhetorical elements? To put our question in the discourse of rhetoric, having focused so intently on the third rhetorical canon—style—what could we discover about the first and second canons—invention and arrangement? We turned back to the twenty thousand essays, looking this time at content and organization. Again, we got some provocative results. We found, for instance, that these aspects of the composing process are as important to readers today as they were over two thousand years ago, when Aristotle said that the two responsibilities of any orator were to state a claim clearly and to prove it. The use of good reasons, proof, evidence, and examples—the rhetorical tools of invention—elicited the most consistent commentary from teachers, followed by commentary on the ways in which such materials were arranged or organized.

These findings strongly suggest that readers are interested in the *what* as well as the *how* of student writing. More specifically, they suggest that student writers need to master traditional methods of analysis and patterns of development not simply to demonstrate that they can recognize the difference between classification and division, for example, but rather to gain the understanding and assent of their readers. In fact, 77 percent of the papers we examined contained comments about large rhetorical issues, a finding that in itself challenges the claim sometimes heard that teachers do little with student papers except mark errors.

Distinguishing features

Attention to good writing, not just to surface correctness. Our research and experience convince us that students need extensive practice in *writing,* and in writing that is compelling and powerful. Like all composition handbooks, this book provides guidance in checking and revising for correctness. Unlike most others, however, it also offers *ample opportunity for student writing,* in guided-writing and imitation exercises that get students to stretch their writing muscles as well as in revision exercises that send them back into their own writing.

This attention to rhetorically effective writing informs every chapter in the book, including those dealing with grammar and mechanics. The chapter on adjectives and adverbs, for instance, asks students to focus not only on how to use adjectives and adverbs correctly but also on the more compelling question of why and in what circumstances to use them at all. The end punctuation chapter provides rules for using periods, question marks, and exclamation points, and, in addition, it asks students to try revising a piece of their own writing for sentence variety, using declarative, interrogatory, and exclamatory structures. In other words, we have tried to present grammar and mechanics as tools to use for a writing purpose, not simply to use "correctly."

Systematic attention to reading. Because we see writing and reading as inextricably linked, we have included reading instruction throughout the text. Not only do we offer extensive guidance to help students read observantly and critically—whether evaluating a draft, an argument, a paragraph, or a source—but we also present reading as one more tool that can help improve writing and research skills. The first chapter offers explicit guidelines for reading, as do the chapters on research, on the disciplines, and on literature. In addition, almost every other chapter includes a special exercise asking students to "read with an eye for" some structure or element they are learning to use as writers. These exercises ask them to study passages from published essays (and sometimes, poems) or from drafts of their own work. In addition to the benefits of studying expert use of basic rhetorical elements, such exercises will, we hope, help build students' visual knowledge of writing and writing conventions. Many of these exercises then ask students to imitate something in the passage—in other words, to step from their reading into writing.

And since many of you use a handbook along with a reader, we have deliberately taken many passages from essays often included in composition readers—that is, from the essays your students are likely to be reading. These examples serve as models for imitation, as prompts for writing, or as occasions for readerly response. Such passages will of course serve as memorable examples; more important, however, they will provide the larger rhetorical context so often missing in most other handbooks.

The *common ground chapter* rests on two major assumptions: that writers will wish to address readers whose backgrounds, values, and perspectives will be different from their own and will also vary widely from reader to reader; and that language offers a primary means of acknowledging and respecting such differences and of bridging them by establishing common ground among readers and writers. Based on Kenneth Burke's theories of identification and division in language use, this chapter asks students to take a close look at how the words they use can help them work to include— or exclude—their readers. Special guidelines help students think carefully and concretely about the language they choose to refer to others and to recognize that these choices have very real consequences. Emphasis throughout the chapter is on how such language choices can help them make connections with others.

The *chapter on audience and purpose* asks students to consider what they know—and need to know—about their readers and about their own purposes and rhetorical stances. In short, the chapter asks students to gather available information about "real-life" audiences—where they come from, how old they are, and so on—*and* to examine their own assumptions about an audience as they *imagine* them to be—that they are all middle-class, say, or all of one race. Such assumptions are often revealed in and shaped by language. For example, use of the pronoun *we* assumes that an imagined audience will identify with this "we." If they do not, however, the writer is likely to exclude—in other words, lose—them as readers. Thinking about audience in this dual way helps students determine whether their writing is likely to achieve its purposes and reach its intended readers.

Practical guidelines for recognizing, understanding, and revising the most common errors. We try to give a clear message about the role of "correctness" in standard academic English *along with* realistic discussion of actual usage. Without oversimplification, our goal is to help students make effective choices. Most important, we present errors as opportunities for improving skills, as something to be examined in rhetorical context and learned from rather than as blots to be eradicated. We ask students not simply to amass information about errors but to analyze the sources and consequences of those errors in their own writing—to build, if you will, a theory about how to improve their writing.

A look at language in everyday use. Our experience as teachers tells us that students use most of the patterns and structures discussed in this text intuitively in their everyday discourse. To help students see language in this way, each chapter includes a brief boxed vignette on the everyday use of that chapter's subject—agreement, say, or adjectives—and asks them to look for additional examples, providing, we hope, another opportunity for them to become keen observers of language. Used systematically, these brief studies of everyday language use offer students and teachers a way to build a bridge between the conventions of college writing and the broader communities in which we all live.

Six chapters on research writing. Nowhere do students need more thorough instruction in how to move back and forth between reading and writing than in the writing they do based on sources. For this reason, *The St. Martin's Handbook* concentrates not simply on helping students produce a "research paper," but on *how they might use research for many writing purposes,* showing students how to approach all sources with a questioning eye and how to assess source materials critically, not just to find them and use them. Step-by-step guidelines on synthesizing data and drawing inferences are designed to help students use their research in support of their own written arguments.

Attention to the needs of basic writers. Several features of this edition are especially appropriate for basic writers. The focus on reading not only provides instruction and practice in critical reading but also offers practice drawing conclusions or inferences from their reading—practice that is particularly valuable for basic writers. In addition, the focus on their own writing and on their own writing development helps basic writers to make a crucial link between their first-year writing course and the academic writing they must master for all their college work. Finally, the use of actual student sentences and essays throughout the book and the emphasis on everyday uses of language in every chapter invite students—and particularly basic writing students—to link the language of this handbook and the classrooms it is used in with their experiences outside of school.

New to this edition

For the third edition, we sought to build on our base of research and teaching practice, and thus turned to the students who have been using *The St. Martin's Handbook.* In a nationwide survey to which 287 students replied, we sought to find out how students actually use our book and what we could do to make it more useful. Their astute judgments, their suggestions, and their complex realization that *good writing means more than just following the rules* inform this edition at every turn. In particular, students told us

they are assigned to give oral presentations in many classes—
and need help with this assignment
they speak less "correctly" at home than in class—
and need help "shifting language gears" for academic writing
they use the handbook most often for writing research papers—
and need help using and documenting electronic sources
they write on a computer—
and want more in the handbook about working on-line
they use the handbook in all their classes—
and want more models of writing in other disciplines

Many of the new features respond directly to these student concerns.

A unique chapter on oral presentations. Chapter 53 provides guidelines on preparing and delivering oral presentations. Ninety-five percent of our student respondents asked for this chapter, clearly recognizing the importance of speaking in their academic and professional lives. This chapter builds on other connections between oral and written discourse found throughout the book—in the Everyday Use vignettes in every chapter, in a new chapter on language variety, and in a new section on talking and listening in Chapter 1.

A new section for multilingual writers. Written by Franklin Horowitz of Teachers College, Columbia University, Part XI covers grammatical and rhetorical issues of concern to multilingual writers, including ESL writers. Chapter 55 offers help with nouns and noun phrases; Chapter 56 covers verbs and verb phrases; Chapter 57 focuses on adverbs and prepositions; and Chapter 58 gives advice on clauses and sentences. There are also special pointers throughout the book that offer advice on topics where ESL writers need extra help. A quick reference chart of all the materials for multilingual writers can be found at the back of the book.

A unique chapter on language variety. Chapter 28 discusses standard, regional, ethnic, and occupational varieties of English, showing students how different varieties of English (and of other languages as well) can be used appropriately and effectively in their academic writing. This chapter provides a series of explicated examples, exercises, and guidelines to help students "shift language gears" as needed between community, workplace, and school.

Expanded attention to electronic textuality. More than 75 percent of our student respondents said they do all their writing on a computer.

Indeed, from word-processing their essays to conducting research on-line to communicating with teachers and other students via E-mail, students are working on computers. We address this reality in a number of new features: increased attention to using electronic databases (Chapter 41); up-to-date advice on citing and documenting electronic sources (Chapter 44); and especially in new chapters on working on-line (Chapter 50) and designing documents (Chapter 51).

More coverage of writing across the curriculum. Chapter 46 provides guidelines to help students understand and use the discourse of any discipline; and Chapter 47 introduces some of the writing typical of the humanities, social sciences, natural sciences, and applied sciences (with examples of student writing in history, psychology, biology, and engineering).

A new chapter on writing about literature. Chapter 48 presents three critical approaches to interpreting a literary work—text-based, context-based, and reader-based—and includes examples of student writing about fiction, drama, and poetry. The chapter also includes a glossary of literary terms and new guidelines on reading a literary work.

Increased emphasis on critical thinking. Beginning with the Introduction, "Thinking Critically about Your Own Writing," this book focuses on critical thinking in every chapter. The Introduction provides a framework to help students approach their writing with a critical eye, including guidelines to help them check for the most common errors. This framework carries through every subsequent chapter, with editing guidelines to help students think about and revise their drafts and end-of-chapter activities that guide them in thinking critically about issues in each chapter and applying what they learn to their own writing. The Introduction also includes an index to nine other chapters with explicit critical thinking and reading guidelines, including Chapter 5, "Thinking Critically: Constructing and Analyzing Arguments." Together, the Introduction and Chapter 5 might serve as a unit on critical thinking.

A unique chapter on writing portfolios. Chapter 54 provides guidelines to help students select the best examples of their own writing and assemble a portfolio.

Attention to the role of narrative and personal experience in academic discourse. Recognizing the vital place of narrative in helping us to understand and identify with others, this edition aims to get students thinking about how and when they can use brief narratives and anecdotes, including those from personal experience, to bring vivid examples and description into their writing (Chapter 3), to develop paragraphs (Chapter 6), and to support arguments (Chapter 5).

Throughout, this edition of *The St. Martin's Handbook* seeks to provide students with a ready reference that will help them make appropriate grammatical and rhetorical choices. Beyond this immediate goal, we hope to guide students in understanding and experiencing for themselves the multiple ways in which truly good writing always means more than just following the rules. Truly good writing, we believe, means applying those rules in specific contexts for specific purposes and with specific audiences in ways that will bring readers and writers, teachers and students, to spirited conversation as well as to mutual understanding and respect.

An expanded ancillary program. Several useful resources accompany *The St. Martin's Handbook.* All have been revised for this third edition and are available free of charge to instructors. The workbook is available for students to purchase. Instructors are authorized to make copies of the software for their students and may order the CLAST and TASP guides and the *Pocket Guide to Research and Documentation.*

CLASSROOM RESOURCES
Annotated Instructor's Edition, by Cheryl Glenn
The St. Martin's Guide to Teaching Writing, Third Edition
   by Robert Connors and Cheryl Glenn
Assigning, Responding, Evaluating: A Writing Teacher's Guide, Third Edition
   by Edward M. White
The St. Martin's Sourcebook for Writing Tutors
   by Christina Murphy and Steve Sherwood
The St. Martin's Manual for Writing in the Disciplines, by Richard Bullock
Transparency Masters

STUDENT RESOURCES
The St. Martin's Workbook, Third Edition, by Lex Runciman
The St. Martin's Pocket Guide to Research and Documentation
An ESL workbook: *Grammar Troublespots,* Second Edition,
   by Ann Raimes
Preparing for the CLAST with The St. Martin's Handbook
Preparing for the TASP with The St. Martin's Handbook

SOFTWARE
Writer's Prologue
Grammar Hotline
Documentation Hotline
Exercise Tutor
Diagnostic Exercises
MicroGrade

Acknowledgments

The St. Martin's Handbook remains a collaborative effort in the best and richest sense of the word. We are particularly indebted to Marilyn Moller of St. Martin's Press, whose efforts as editor on this edition—as on all others—have been above and beyond the call of any duty we have ever known; for her friendship, guidance, and sheer intellectual verve, we are deeply grateful. We thank Karen Allanson for her enthusiastic support of our work and for her efforts on behalf of the entire project at St. Martin's. Erica Appel has managed the entire handbook from manuscript to bound book with skill and grace—and together with Joe Ford has made an enormously complex project run smoothly. Scott Poston has developed the excellent electronic ancillaries. Susan Cottenden, Christine Kline, and Jennifer Valentine offered thoughtful assistance in many matters, large and small. For the elegant and accessible design, we are indebted to Anna George, and for the handsome new cover design, we thank Sheree Goodman. And for providing us with careful response to the text and astute analyses of its usefulness to teachers, we are grateful to the St. Martin's sales representatives; they are, in our experience, simply the best.

The St. Martin's Handbook is accompanied by an imaginative and highly practical set of ancillary materials. For their assistance in editing these materials, we are most grateful to Amy Horowitz, Steven Kutz, Clare Payton, Diana Puglisi, and especially Kristin Bowen, who has worked so hard and on so many aspects of the project that we simply could not get along without her.

From its inception, *The St. Martin's Handbook* has had the benefit of the meticulous, insightful, and enormously helpful reviews of Franklin Horowitz, Teachers College of Columbia University. For this edition, our debt to Frank is far greater still, for he has provided a superb new section for multilingual writers. His erudition and keen wit are evident on every page.

Special thanks to colleagues Richard Bullock, Christina Murphy, Lex Runciman, Steve Sherwood, and Ed White, who contributed uncommonly innovative books that accompany the handbook; to Cheryl Glenn for her outstanding work on both *The St. Martin's Guide to Teaching Writing* and *The Annotated Instructor's Edition;* and to Dr. Edward Huth, who graciously shared information about the new CBE reference style.

As always, we feel extremely fortunate to have had the contributions of a group of very fine student writers, whose work appears throughout this text: Kelly Barr, Laura Brannon, Leah Clendening, Tisha Clevinger, Amy Dierst, Sean Finnerty, Jennifer Georgia, Jennifer Gerken, Amy Lewis, Faye Purol, Chris Reeves, Daniel Taffe, Leslie Shaffer, and Tamara Washington. We are also grateful to the many instructors who generously shared their assignments with us, and particularly to Karen Burke LeFevre and Kenneth

A. Connor of Rensselaer Polytechnic Institute; to Richard Shiels, Ray Jazerinak, and Louis Ulman of Ohio State University; to Keith Walters of the University of Texas; and to Tom Bredehoft of the University of Northern Colorado. In addition, Beverly Moss and Nathan Gray of Ohio State University have helped us to think about student research in more inclusive and expanded ways, and Jenell Reed has offered fine advice about making our text easier for students to use.

For this edition, we wish to give special thanks to those teachers and students whose campuses we have visited for their generous criticism of our work; this text owes a great deal to their wise advice and counsel. In addition, we are most appreciative of the colleagues who have painstakingly reviewed our manuscript and its several revisions and shared their thoughts on our efforts. Their incisive comments, queries, criticisms, and suggestions have improved this book immeasurably: Valerie Balester, Texas A & M University; Arnetha Ball, The University of Michigan; Diane Belcher, The Ohio State University; Maria Bridges, Miami-Dade Community College; Avon Crismore, Indiana University-Purdue at Fort Wayne; Michel de Benedictis, Miami-Dade Community College; Marcia Farr, University of Illinois, Chicago; Christine Francisco, City College of San Francisco; Judith Gardner, University of Texas at San Antonio; Keith Gilyard, Syracuse University; Angeletta Gourdine, Oregon State University; Juan Guerra, University of Washington; Andrew Harnack, Eastern Kentucky University; Shirley Brice Heath, Stanford University; Van Hillard, Duke University; Judith Kohl, Dutchess Community College; Ellen Lange, University of California at Davis; Mike Moran, University of Georgia; Deborah Raphan, Brooklyn College; Mary Shapiro, University of Texas at Austin; Keith Walters, University of Texas at Austin; Walt Wolfram, North Carolina State University.

We also wish especially to thank the hundreds of students who responded so thoughtfully, thoroughly, and helpfully to our request for criticism and advice about their use of our handbook. The marks of their work are everywhere evident in this edition. Their names are far too numerous to list here, but we would like to thank the instructors who distributed questionnaires among their students: Norbert Artzt, Miami-Dade Community College; Charles Boyd, Genesee Community College; Ray Foster, Scottsdale Community College; George Gopen, Duke University; Maureen Hardigree, University of Georgia; Andrew Harnack, Eastern Kentucky University; Judith Kohl, Dutchess Community College; Ken Risden, University of Minnesota at Duluth; Elisa Sparks, Clemson University; Gwen Stanford, Georgia College.

We also wish to acknowledge and express our gratitude to the many users of the second edition who took the time to respond to a detailed questionnaire and whose many comments and criticisms helped us see what to expand and what to trim, what to fix and what to leave alone as we revised this book. We thank L. R. N. Ashley, Brooklyn College; Susie Barrett,

Point Loma Nazarene College; Debra Boyd, Winthrop University; David Brailow, McKendree College; Oscar Budde, Case Western Reserve University; Anne Carmody, City University of New York, Lehman College; Timothy Clark, Ohio State University; Thomas Condon, Curry College; Professor Congdon, University of Connecticut; Gail Corso, Neumann College; Robert Crooks, Bentley College; Marlene Davis, College of William and Mary; Robert DeGise, Bradley University; Judy Doenges, Pacific Lutheran University; Joan Draper, University of Colorado; Chris Ellery, Angelo State University; Charles Etheridge, McMurry University; Jessica Freedman, American University and George Mason University; Chris Gordon, St. Cloud State University; Lee Haring, Brooklyn College; Daniel Harrison, University of Rochester; Kim Hughes, University of Pennsylvania; Mike Johanyak, Kent State University; Donald Johns, University of California at Davis; Ralph Johnson, Western State College; Judy Karmiohl, Schenectady Community College; Elaine Kauvar, Baruch College; Mark Koch, St. Mary's College, Orchard Lake; Ronald Kovach, Illinois Benedictine College; Faye Kuzma, Ferris State University; Virginia LaGrand, Trinity Christian College; R. Lawton, Linfield College; Ken Letko, College of the Redwoods, Del Norte; Carol Long, Willamette University; Dandi Markall, Ashland University; Eric Marshall, Kansas Wesleyan; Marilyn Mayer, Morningside College; John McCauley, Ohio State University; Joseph Mills, University of California; John Mitchell, Ohio University; Mike Moran, University of Georgia; Sandra Muirhead-Gould, Kent State, Stark Campus; William Northcutt, Miami University; Suzanne Owens, Lorain County Community College; Claire Pedretti, Berea College; John Piller, University of Richmond; Eugene Policelli, Central Connecticut State University; M. J. Robinson, Loyola Marymount University; Cary Ser, Miami-Dade Community College; Thomas Sharpe, Washington State Community College; Alice Sink, High Point University; Margaret Sokolik, University of California at Berkeley; Elizabeth Stolarek, Ferris State University; Michael Strickland, Guilford College; Elaine Supowitz, Community College of Allegheny County, Allegheny; Lynn Sykes, Purdue University, Calumet; David Turner, Illinois Benedictine College; Anthony Tyler, State University of New York, Potsdam; Marilyn Valentino, Lorain County Community College; Sarala Van Dover, Lincoln University; James Varn, Morris College; Joseph Wagner, Kent State University; Mary Louise Willey, University of Massachusetts, Boston; Kim Wolfe, Cuyamaca College and Palomar College; Linda Woodson, The University of Texas at San Antonio; David Zauhar, University of Illinois, Chicago; Sharon Zuber, College of William and Mary.

Finally, we wish to say thanks to some very special friends: Keith Walters, whose keen eye and brilliant teacherly insights continue to challenge and instruct us; Lorraine Carlat, whose organizational skill and infinite patience continue to amaze and gratify us; Suzanne Clark, whose theoretical and practical insights have continued to help us think more imaginatively about students writing about literature; Suellynn Duffey, Amy Goodburn, Sherri Helsley, Donna LeCourt, Carrie Leverenz, Beverly Moss, Aneil Rallin, and Patrick McSweeney, who have cheerfully provided more support than we have had any right to expect; and—always—Lisa Ede, our critical reader and friend extraordinaire.

We could go on and on and on and on, for we are fortunate (beyond our wildest dreams, as our mentor Ed Corbett would say) to be part of a unique scholarly and academic community, one characterized by compassion, by commitment to students, by a celebration of learning. We are grateful to be among you.

Andrea Lunsford
Robert Connors

A Note to Students

Our goal in writing *The St. Martin's Handbook* has been to produce a book that will help you become competent and compelling writers, a book that you can use easily throughout—and beyond—your college years.

The introductory chapter of this book, "Thinking Critically about Your Writing," is our attempt to provide you with a tool for analyzing your use of the writing patterns and strategies most college students need to practice. The introduction—and indeed, the entire book—offers a critical thinking program for building on strengths and eliminating weaknesses in your own writing.

Throughout this text, we thus ask that you become accustomed to carefully analyzing your own prose. In almost every chapter, we will not only provide explanations and opportunities for practice but also ask you to apply the principles presented directly to your own writing. If you follow our directions, they will guide you in becoming a systematic self-critic—and a more effective writer. And since writing and reading in many ways go hand in hand, many chapters will also offer you a chance to read with an eye for various logical or stylistic or conventional aspects of writing, often in the work of some of the finest writers in English. Sometimes you will be asked to try to imitate their sentences. As your writing improves, so will your reading.

Chapters 1–6 will guide you through the process of expository and argumentative essays—from your first choice of a topic to your final typed essay. Chapters 7–39 provide thorough discussion of writing conventions—grammar, word choice, punctuation, and mechanics. These chapters provide examples and practice to guide you in mastering such conventions and in learning to use them appropriately and effectively.

Next come chapters that will help you carry out and use research in your writing and examine the writing of your chosen discipline. Then come chapters that focus on accessing and presenting texts: working on-line, designing documents, using professional and business formats, making oral presentations, and developing a writing portfolio. Finally, there is a section for multilingual writers.

Using The St. Martin's Handbook

This book has been designed to be as easy as possible to use. You can find what you are looking for by consulting the table of contents or the index. Once you find the correct chapter, you can skim the many headings. If your instructor uses our codes in marking your essays, you can find the code symbols on the inside back cover and at the top of each page. Even the exercises are easy to use, for at the end of the book we include answers to many of them, to allow you to check your understanding as you work.

Because we assume you will be consulting this book regularly when you are revising your drafts, we wish to call to your attention the many guidelines to help you check and edit your own drafts; to make these easy to find, they are in light blue boxes marked with a blue arrow.

For those who use a computer, we offer two quick-reference software programs, *Grammar Hotline* and *Documentation Hotline*, along with *Writer's Prologue*, a word processor with integrated drafting and revision guidance. Each is available for DOS/Windows and Macintosh systems. These programs may be available on campus networks or purchased at bookstores.

Finally, we call your attention to a feature you might use in thinking critically about your writing: a writing log. We urge you to keep a log as a repository of materials from and for your writing—notable anecdotes, exemplary phrases, memorable images, troublesome words or structures. Procedures for keeping a log are described on p. I-4, and exercises at the end of every chapter suggest materials to add to it. Keeping a log can help you to examine and contemplate—and thus improve—your own writing.

A *tutorial on using* The St. Martin's Handbook

For this book to serve you well, you need to get to know it—to know what's inside and how to find it. The following tutorial is designed to help you familiarize yourself with *The St. Martin's Handbook*; the answers are on p. 857.

Starting with the table of contents

1. Where will you find advice on revising a draft?
2. Where will you find quick information on checking verbs for -*s* and -*es* endings? on checking subject-verb agreement in general?
3. Where will you find guidelines on documenting sources?

4. Is there any help in the handbook for multilingual students, including those who speak English as a second language?

For planning and drafting

5. It's the first week of class, and you are at work on your first essay. Where in the handbook can you find general guidelines on planning and drafting an essay?

6. Assigned to write an essay that argues a claim, you've been warned to be very careful about using any personal narratives as support for your argument. Does the handbook offer any advice about how to use narrative appropriately in college writing?

7. In an essay arguing for "equal pay for equal work" addressed to members of your writing class, you want to avoid any language that stereotypes members of any group. Where in the handbook can you find advice about using considerate rather than hurtful language?

8. You've been assigned to give an oral presentation. Is there anything different you need to do in writing that will be heard rather than read? Where does the handbook offer advice on writing and giving oral presentations? How did you find this information?

For editing

9. As you edit a final draft, you stop at the following sentence: *Winning may be the name of the game but it isn't a name I care for very much.* You can't decide whether to put a comma before *but.* What does the handbook recommend that you do? How and where do you find this answer?

10. You speak several languages, and you still confuse the prepositions *in* and *on.* Where in the handbook can you find help?

11. Does the word *none* take a singular or plural verb? You can't decide. Where in the handbook can you find a quick answer to this question? How did you find the answer?

12. Your teacher has written *ref* next to this sentence: *Transmitting video signals by satellite is a way of overcoming the problem of scarce airwaves and limiting how they are used.* Where do you look in the handbook for help responding to your teacher's comment?

For doing research

13. You need help getting started with library research. Where can you find help in the handbook?

14. Should you quote, paraphrase, or summarize? Are there any guidelines in the handbook to help you decide? How do you find these guidelines?

15. You're required to use something called APA style in a psychology paper. Where in the handbook can you find this information?

16. Using MLA style, how do you document information obtained from a CD-ROM source?

For all your college courses

17. A take-home exam in political science asks you to compare Marx's and Lenin's theories of revolution. You've never before written a political science paper, and so you're not sure how to proceed. Do you need to cite sources—and if so, do they need to be primary? Do political science papers follow any set format?

18. You need to write an abstract as part of a biology report. Are there guidelines for doing so in the handbook? Is there a model?

19. For a literature course, you're writing an essay interpreting a poem by Emily Dickinson. Where can you find help in the handbook?

20. A report you're working on must include both tables and figures. You aren't sure of the difference, nor do you know how to set them up. Where in the handbook can you get help?

We hope that this book will prove to be a useful reference. But in the long run, a book can be only a guide. You are the one who will put such guidance into practice, as you work to become a precise, powerful, and persuasive writer. Why not get started on achieving that goal right now?

Andrea Lunsford
Robert Connors

Contents

Preface   v
A Note to Students   xvii
Introduction: Thinking Critically about Your Writing   I–1

PART ONE · THE WRITING PROCESS   1

1 Writing, Reading, and Research   2

   a Considering the process of writing   2
   b Considering the process of reading   8
   > *Some guidelines for reading*   9
   c Doing research   11
   d Talking and listening   12
   e Taking notes   14
   f Benefiting from collaboration   15
   > *Some guidelines for collaborating with others*   16

2 Considering Purpose and Audience   18

   a Deciding to write   18
   b Identifying a problem   19
   c Understanding writing assignments   19
   > *Analyzing an assignment*   20
   d Deciding on your purposes   22
   > *Considering purposes*   22

*The > symbol marks quick-reference guidelines.

e Considering genre   *24*
f Considering language   *24*
g Considering your rhetorical stance   *25*
> *Considering your rhetorical stance*   *26*
h Focusing on your audience   *26*
> *Considering your audience*   *27*

3 Exploring, Planning, and Drafting   32

a Exploring a topic   *32*
b Establishing a working thesis   *38*
c Gathering information   *40*
d Organizing information   *41*
e Writing out a plan   *46*
f Producing a draft   *48*
> *Some guidelines for drafting*   *49*
  A sample first draft   *49*
g Reflecting on your writing process   *52*
> *Thinking critically about your own writing process*   *52*

4 Revising and Editing   54

a Getting distance before revising   *55*
b Rereading your draft   *56*
c Collaborating: getting response to your draft   *57*
> *Reviewing a draft*   *58*
d Evaluating the thesis and its support   *62*
e Analyzing organization   *63*
f Reconsidering title, introduction, conclusion   *64*
g Examining paragraphs, sentences, words, tone   *65*
h Determining format   *71*
i Editing   *71*
j Proofreading the final draft   *73*
  A sample essay   *73*

5 Thinking Critically:
  Constructing and Analyzing Arguments   78

a Thinking critically   *79*
b Recognizing argument   *80*
c Formulating an argumentative thesis   *84*

d Formulating good reasons   *86*
e Using narratives to support an argument   *86*
> *Checking your use of narrative*   *87*
f Establishing credibility   *87*
g Appealing to logic   *91*
h Appealing to emotion   *100*
i Organizing an argument   *105*
   A sample essay   *107*
j Analyzing an argument   *113*
> *Analyzing an argument: the classical system*   *113*
> *Analyzing an argument: the Toulmin system*   *114*

6 Constructing Paragraphs   *116*

a Paragraphing for readers   *116*
b Constructing paragraphs   *118*
c Making paragraphs unified   *119*
d Making paragraphs coherent   *123*
> *Commonly used transitions*   *131*
e Developing paragraphs fully   *133*
f Composing special-purpose paragraphs   *144*
g Linking paragraphs   *150*
> *Editing the paragraphs in your writing*   *151*

PART TWO ▪ SENTENCES: MAKING GRAMMATICAL CHOICES   *155*

7 Constructing Grammatical Sentences   *156*

a Understanding basic sentence grammar   *158*
b Recognizing the parts of speech   *159*
c Recognizing the parts of a sentence   *170*
> *Basic sentence patterns*   *171*
d Classifying sentences   *188*
> *Editing the sentences in your own writing*   *191*

8 Understanding Pronoun Case   *193*

a Subjective case   *194*
b Objective case   *195*

c Possessive case   *196*
d *Who, whoever, whom,* and *whomever*   *198*
e Case in compound structures   *201*
f Case in appositives   *202*
g Case in elliptical constructions   *202*
h *We* and *us* before a noun   *203*
> *Editing case*   *204*

9 Using Verbs   *206*

    Verb Forms   *206*
> *Editing -s and -es endings*   *208*
a Auxiliary verbs   *210*
b Regular and irregular verbs   *211*
> *Editing for -ed or -d endings*   *211*
> *Some common irregular verbs*   *212*
c *Lie* and *lay, sit* and *set, rise* and *raise*   *215*
    Verb Tenses   *217*
d Present tense forms   *218*
e Past tense forms   *219*
f Future tense forms   *220*
> *Editing verb tenses*   *220*
g Verb tenses in sequences   *222*
    Voice   *224*
    Mood   *226*
h The subjunctive   *227*
> *Editing the verbs in your own writing*   *230*

10 Maintaining Subject-Verb Agreement   *232*

a Third-person singular subjects   *232*
b Making the subject and verb agree   *233*
c Compound subjects   *236*
d Collective-noun subjects   *236*
e Indefinite-pronoun subjects   *237*
> *Common indefinite pronouns*   *237*
f Relative-pronoun subjects   *238*
g With subjects, not complements   *238*
h Subjects plural in form but singular in meaning   *239*
i Subjects following verbs   *239*
j With titles and words used as words   *240*
> *Editing for subject-verb agreement*   *240*

11 Maintaining Pronoun-Antecedent Agreement   243

   a Compound antecedents   244
   b Collective-noun antecedents   245
   c Indefinite-pronoun antecedents   246
   d Checking for sexist pronouns   246
   > *Avoiding generic use of* he, his, *or* him   246
   > *Editing for pronoun-antecedent agreement*   247

12 Using Adjectives and Adverbs   249

   a Adjectives distinguished from adverbs   249
   b Adjectives after linking verbs   252
   c Adverbs to modify verbs, adjectives, and adverbs   252
   d Comparatives and superlatives   255
   e Nouns as modifiers   257
   > *Editing adjectives and adverbs*   258

PART THREE ▪ SENTENCES: MAKING CONVENTIONAL
          CHOICES   261

13 Maintaining Clear Pronoun Reference   262

   a Clear antecedents   263
   b Close antecedents   264
   c Troublesome pronoun reference   266
   > *Editing for clear pronoun reference*   268

14 Recognizing Shifts   271

   a In tense   272
   > *Editing unnecessary shifts in tense*   272
   b In mood   273
   c In voice   274
   d In person and number   275
   > *Editing unnecessary pronoun shifts*   276
   e Between direct and indirect discourse   276
   f In tone and diction   278

15 Identifying Comma Splices and Fused Sentences   281

   > *Checking for comma splices and fused sentences*   282
   a Revised as two sentences   283

b Revised with comma and coordinating conjunction   *284*
c Revised with semicolon   *285*
d Recast as one independent clause   *286*
e Recast as one independent clause, one dependent clause   *286*

16 Recognizing Sentence Fragments   *290*

> *Checking for sentence fragments*   *291*
a Phrase fragments   *292*
b Compound-predicate fragments   *294*
c Dependent-clause fragments   *295*

17 Placing Modifiers Appropriately   *297*

a Misplaced modifiers   *298*
b Disruptive modifiers   *301*
c Dangling modifiers   *303*
> *Editing misplaced or dangling modifiers*   *306*

18 Maintaining Consistent and Complete
Grammatical Structures   *307*

a Consistent grammatical patterns   *307*
b Subjects and predicates   *309*
c Elliptical structures   *311*
d Missing words   *312*
e Comparisons   *313*
> *Editing comparisons*   *313*

PART FOUR ▪ SENTENCES: MAKING STYLISTIC
CHOICES   *317*

19 Constructing Effective Sentences   *318*

a Emphasizing main ideas   *319*
> *Editing for sentence emphasis*   *321*
b Being concise   *322*
> *Editing for conciseness*   *326*

20 Creating Coordinate and Subordinate Structures   *328*

a Coordination to relate equal ideas   *330*
> *Editing for coordination*   *332*

b Subordination to distinguish main ideas   *334*
> *Editing your use of subordination*   *338*

21 Creating and Maintaining Parallel Structures   *340*

a In a series   *340*
b With pairs   *342*
c With all necessary words   *344*
d For emphasis and effect   *345*
> *Editing for parallelism*   *346*

22 Varying Sentence Structures   *349*

a Sentence lengths   *350*
> *Editing to vary sentence length*   *353*
b Sentence openings   *354*
> *Editing to vary sentence openings*   *356*
c Sentence types   *357*
> *Editing to vary sentence types*   *360*

23 Creating Memorable Prose   *362*

a Strong verbs   *364*
> *Editing verbs and nouns*   *366*
b Active and passive voice   *367*
c Special effects   *369*

PART FIVE · SELECTING EFFECTIVE WORDS   *373*

24 Mastering Spelling   *374*

a The most commonly misspelled words   *375*
> *The fifty most commonly misspelled words*   *375*
b Homonyms   *377*
> *The most troublesome homonyms*   *377*
c Spelling and pronunciation   *381*
d Spelling rules   *382*
e Plurals   *387*
f A personal spelling inventory   *389*
> *Using a spell checker*   *390*

25 Using Dictionaries 393

    a Exploring the dictionary 394
    b Distinguishing among dictionaries 396
    c Consulting specialized dictionaries 399

26 Enriching Vocabulary 402

    a Considering your vocabulary 402
    b Recognizing word roots 405
    c Recognizing prefixes and suffixes 406
    d Building a word hoard 409

27 Considering Diction 413

    a Choosing appropriate language and register 413
    b Denotation and connotation 421
    > *Checking for wrong words* 422
    c Balancing general and specific diction 424
    d Using figurative language 425
    > *Editing for diction* 430

28 Considering Language Variety 432

    a Recognizing different varieties of English 433
    b Standard varieties of English 434
    c Ethnic varieties of English 435
    d Occupational varieties of English 437
    e Regional varieties of English 438
    f Bringing in other languages 440
    g Varieties of language in academic writing 442
    > *When you might shift among languages* 443

29 Considering Others: Building Common Ground 445

    a Remembering the golden rule: considering stereotypes about gender, race, and other things 446
    > *Editing out sexist language* 450
    b Taking time to listen 455
    > *Editing for language that builds common ground* 455

PART SIX · UNDERSTANDING PUNCTUATION CONVENTIONS   459

30 Using Commas   460

   a Introductory elements   *462*
   b Compound sentences   *463*
   c Nonrestrictive elements   *464*
   d Items in a series   *468*
   e Parenthetical and transitional expressions   *470*
   f Contrasting elements, interjections, direct address, tag questions   *470* ·
   g Dates, addresses, titles, numbers   *471*
   h Quotations   *473*
   i To facilitate understanding   *474*
   j Unnecessary commas   *475*
   > *Editing for commas*   *476*

31 Using Semicolons   480

   a To link independent clauses   *480*
   b To separate items in a series   *483*
   c Overused semicolons   *483*
   d Misused semicolons   *484*
   > *Editing for effective use of semicolons*   *485*
   e With quotation marks   *486*

32 Using End Punctuation   487

   a Periods   *488*
   b Question marks   *489*
   c Exclamation points   *490*
   > *Editing for end punctuation*   *491*

33 Using Apostrophes   493

   a Possessive case   *493*
   > *Editing for possessive apostrophes*   *495*
   b Contractions and other omissions   *496*
   > *Editing for misuse of* its *and* it's   *496*
   c Plurals and words used as terms   *497*

34 Using Quotation Marks   499

   a Direct quotations   *499*
   b Dialogue   *502*
   c Titles and definitions   *502*
   d Irony and coinages   *503*
   e Misused quotation marks   *504*
   f With other punctuation   *504*
   > *Editing for quotation marks*   *505*

35 Using Other Punctuation Marks   508

   a Parentheses   *509*
   b Brackets   *510*
   c Dashes   *512*
   > *Editing for effective use of dashes and parentheses*   *513*
   d Colons   *514*
   e Slashes   *516*
   f Ellipses   *517*
   g Emoticons   *518*

PART SEVEN • UNDERSTANDING MECHANICAL CONVENTIONS   521

36 Using Capitals   522

   a To begin a sentence or a line of poetry   *522*
   b Proper nouns and proper adjectives   *523*
   > *Some commonly capitalized terms*   *524*
   c Titles of works   *526*
   d *I* and *O*   *526*
   e Unnecessary capitalization   *527*

37 Using Abbreviations and Numbers   529

   Abbreviations   *529*
   a Titles and academic degrees   *529*
   b Years and hours   *531*
   c Acronyms and initial abbreviations   *531*
   d Other kinds of abbreviations   *532*
   > *Editing for appropriate use of abbreviations*   *533*
   Numbers   *534*

e Numbers expressed in one or two words   *534*
f Numbers expressed in more than two words   *534*
g Numbers that begin sentences   *535*
h Conventional uses of figures   *535*

38 Using Italics   *538*

a Titles   *538*
b Words, letters, numbers referred to as words   *540*
c Foreign words and phrases   *541*
d Names of vehicles   *541*
e Special emphasis   *542*

39 Using Hyphens   *544*

a To divide words at the end of a line   *544*
b With compound words   *546*
c With prefixes and suffixes   *547*

PART EIGHT ▪ DOING RESEARCH AND USING SOURCES   *551*

40 Becoming a Researcher   *552*

a Understanding research assignments and topics   *555*
> *Scheduling a research project*   *557*
b Narrowing and focusing a topic   *558*
c Investigating what you know about your topic   *560*
d Moving from hypothesis to working thesis   *560*

41 Conducting Research   *562*

a Using primary and secondary sources   *562*
b Exploring library and database resources   *564*
> *Directory of library resources*   *565*
c Searching computer databases   *577*
d Conducting research in the field   *580*
> *Conducting observation*   *582*
> *Planning an interview*   *583*
> *Designing a questionnaire*   *584*

42   Using Sources   586

   a Choosing sources   *586*
   > *Keeping a working bibliography*   *587*
   b Reading sources with a critical eye   *590*
   c Taking notes   *593*
   > *Taking accurate notes*   *593*
   > *Deciding whether to quote, paraphrase, or summarize*   *594*
   > *Quoting accurately*   *596*
   > *Paraphrasing accurately*   *599*
   > *Summarizing accurately*   *600*
   d Recognizing plagiarism, acknowledging sources   *602*
   > *Recognizing plagiarism, acknowledging your sources*   *604*
   e Interpreting sources   *605*

43   Writing a Research Essay   607

   a Refining your plans   *607*
   b Organizing information   *610*
   c Drafting your essay   *611*
   d Incorporating source materials   *613*
   > *Signal verbs*   *616*
   > *Incorporating quotations, paraphrases, and summaries*   *618*
   e Reviewing your draft   *619*
   f Revising and editing your draft   *620*
   g Preparing a list of works cited or your references   *621*
   h Preparing and proofreading your final copy   *621*

44   Documenting Sources: MLA Style   623

   > *Directory to MLA style*   *624*
   a Parenthetical citations   *625*
   b Explanatory and bibliographic notes   *629*
   c List of works cited   *630*
   d A sample research essay, MLA style   *645*

45   Documenting Sources: APA, CBE, and Chicago Styles   665

   APA Style   *665*
   > *Directory to APA style*   *666*
   a Parenthetical citations   *667*
   b Content notes   *670*

c List of references   *671*
d A sample research essay, APA style   *678*
    CBE Style   *689*
e In-text citations and reference lists   *689*
    Chicago Style   *691*
> *Directory to Chicago style*   *691*
f In-text citations and notes   *692*
g Bibliography   *695*

PART NINE • ACADEMIC WRITING   *697*

46 Understanding Disciplinary Discourse   *698*

a Analyzing assignments and expectations   *699*
> *Analyzing an assignment in any discipline*   *700*
b Understanding disciplinary vocabularies   *701*
c Identifying the style of a discipline   *703*
d Understanding the use of evidence   *704*
e Using conventional patterns and formats   *705*

47 Writing in the Disciplines   *707*

a Writing to learn   *707*
b Learning to write   *708*
c Writing in the social sciences   *708*
    A sample psychology essay, excerpted   *709*
d Writing in the natural sciences   *711*
    A sample biology lab report, excerpted   *712*
e Writing in the applied sciences   *715*
    A sample engineering report, excerpted   *716*
f Writing in the humanities   *718*
    A sample history paper, excerpted   *719*

48 Writing about Literature   *723*

a The language of literary interpretation   *724*
> *A glossary of literary terms*   *724*
b Becoming a strong reader of literature   *727*
> *For reading literature*   *727*
c Considering your assignment, purpose, and audience   *728*

d Developing a critical stance   *729*
   A sample essay on a work of fiction   *730*
   A sample essay on a drama, excerpted   *734*
   A sample journal entry on a poem   *737*
   > *Editing your writing about literature*   *739*

49 Writing Essay Examinations   *740*

   a Preparing for essay examinations   *740*
   b Analyzing questions   *742*
   > *Common strategy terms*   *742*
   c Thinking through your answer and taking notes   *743*
   d Drafting your answer   *744*
   e Revising and editing your answer   *744*
   f Considering a sample essay answer   *745*
   g Analyzing and evaluating your answer   *747*

PART TEN ▪ ACCESSING AND PRESENTING TEXT   *749*

50 Working On-Line   *750*

   a Frequent questions about writing with a computer   *750*
   b Getting on-line   *753*
   c Communicating via the Internet   *754*
   d Accessing information via computer   *755*

51 Designing Documents   *758*

   a Creating a visual structure   *758*
   b Using consistency to guide readers   *760*
   c Using headings   *761*
   d Using visuals   *763*
   > *Some guidelines for using visuals*   *764*

52 Using Professional and Business Formats   *767*

   a Writing for readers   *767*
   b Using conventional formats   *768*
   c Applying for a job   *770*

53 **Making Oral Presentations** .777

  a Considering the assignment, purpose, and audience   777
  b Writing to be heard   778
  c Sample text for oral presentation   780
  d Using visuals   781
  e Practicing the presentation   782
  f Making the presentation   782
  > *Editing text for oral presentation*   783

54 **Assembling a Writing Portfolio** 784

  a Considering purpose and audience   784
  b Selecting work   785
  c Thinking about the writing you include   786

PART ELEVEN ▪ FOR MULTILINGUAL WRITERS: MASTERING THE NUANCES OF ENGLISH 787

55 Understanding Nouns and Noun Phrases 788

  a Distinguishing count and noncount nouns   788
  > *Some general patterns for using count and noncount nouns*   790
  b Maintaining singular and plural   790
  c Using determiners   791
  d Working with articles   793
  e Arranging modifiers   796

56 Understanding Verbs and Verb Phrases 798

  a Forming verb phrases   798
  b Using present and past tenses   801
  c Understanding perfect and progressive verb phrases   802
  d Distinguishing stative and dynamic verbs   804
  e Using modals   805
  f Using participial adjectives   808

57 Understanding Prepositions
and Prepositional Phrases 810

   a Using prepositions idiomatically 810
   > *Strategies for using prepositions idiomatically* 811
   b Using two-word verbs 813

58 Forming Clauses and Sentences 816

   a Expressing subjects explicitly 816
   b Expressing objects explicitly 817
   c Using English word order 817
   d Recognizing the sentence nucleus 818
   e Using noun clauses, infinitives, and gerunds 819
   f Using adjective clauses 822
   g Understanding conditional sentences 824

Glossary of Grammatical Terms 827
Glossary of Usage 841
Answers to Even-Numbered Exercise Items 857
Index *Index–1*

Thinking Critically about Your Writing

What do Bill Clinton, Oprah Winfrey, and Pat Riley all have in common? Stop to reflect a moment, and you may note that each is at the center of a very complex situation—in government, television, and sports. Moreover, all must find ways to manage enormous amounts of information if they are to retain a presidency, maintain a top Nielsen rating, and win an NBA championship. Their commonalities go even further, however, for these public figures are all known to be very quick on their mental feet. Each is able to grasp complex organizational structures and problems quickly, to hold a great deal of information in their heads, and to see patterns in ways that help them stay on top of their fields. A shorthand way of naming the common characteristic they share is to say they are all very good at **critical thinking**, that quality most often identified as necessary not only to economic success but also to personal fulfillment in an age as complex as ours.

As a college student, you share with Clinton, Winfrey, and Riley a need for critical thinking skills. Throughout your college years, you too will be at the center of a complex situation, one that calls on you to absorb and analyze vast amounts of information across a broad range of fields and to identify and pursue a course of study that will in some ways define your future, one that can launch you on a path of lifetime learning, work, and personal fulfillment. One way to make the most of these college years is to consciously strive to improve your critical thinking abilities, to be one of those who can look at a body of diffuse and often conflicting information and identify where a problem lies, one who can cut through reams of red tape to get to the heart of a matter.

Your writing course is in many ways a foundation course in critical thinking, providing guidance and practice in figuring out what you think about particular topics and issues, in articulating your thoughts, and in then convincing others that your ideas are reasonable ones, worthy of consideration. With research essays in particular, you will be challenged to work with many other people's ideas—to think critically about what they claim and whether they convince you to accept their claims; to sift through many diverse, often conflicting claims; and finally to move from considering other people's ideas to determining and articulating your own.

Using *The St. Martin's Handbook* to practice critical thinking

Every chapter in *The St. Martin's Handbook* offers guidance and practice to help you think critically about your writing. Most chapters include editing guidelines to help you check and revise—that is, to think about—your drafts. (See the guidelines for editing verbs, for example, on page 230.) And every chapter concludes with guided practice in critical thinking to help you think hard about issues raised in the chapter. In most chapters, this practice is in two parts—first, asking you to read a passage written by someone else with a critical eye; then, leading you to think critically about your own writing. (See "Thinking Critically about Verbs," for example, on p. 231.)

In addition, you will find explicit guidance in building critical thinking skills in the following chapters:

- **Chapter 1** calls attention to the ways talking, listening, reading, and writing all work together to foster strong critical thinking and offers specific guidelines for listening and reading critically.

- **Chapter 2** guides you in analyzing audiences and purposes, while **Chapter 29** helps you to think hard about the language you use and how it can build common ground with others.

- **Chapter 4** provides extensive guidelines for reviewing texts, your own as well as those of others.

- **Chapter 5** takes you through the process of developing a critical stance on an issue and analyzing and arguing for that stance. The chapter includes a sample student essay and practical guidelines to help you analyze arguments using two different systems of argument: classical and Toulmin.

- **Chapter 27** includes advice about analyzing denotative and connotative meanings of words for the agendas or biases they may reveal.

- **Chapter 42** provides concrete guidelines to help you think critically about any sources you read as a researcher and about how to move from those sources to your own ideas.

- **Chapter 46** guides you in thinking critically in all the disciplines across the curriculum—to consider and recognize their expectations, conventions, and constraints—with special attention to disciplinary ways of reading.

- **Chapter 48** provides guidelines for reading literature with a critical eye.
- **Chapter 53** helps you prepare for real thinking on your feet, giving oral presentations.
- **Chapter 54** asks you to step back and think critically about a large body of your written work in order to build a writing portfolio.

What we mean by critical thinking, then, is pretty straightforward: it calls for stepping back from your own work and taking a good, hard, close look at it, getting down to the fine details as well as examining the big picture of how well your writing works to achieve your purposes. But critical thinking only begins with this close-up look; as a critical thinker, you can use the information you gain by examining your writing very closely to draw a series of conclusions about how to strengthen your writing, how to make it work better and more effectively for you.

Every chapter in *The St. Martin's Handbook* adds to your ability to think critically about your own writing by asking you to reflect on and articulate what you have learned from that chapter and to apply those lessons to your own writing. As you work through this book and as you consult it as a reference, then, you will be practicing critical thinking at almost every turn. Eventually, this way of thinking critically—of stopping to identify what you are doing and trying to make these processes of analysis as systematic and effective as possible—will become habitual with you. In the meantime, you can speed that process along by analyzing how you use this book as well as by analyzing your own writing through taking a writing inventory.

Taking a writing inventory

What is a writing inventory? How can taking one help you develop critical thinking abilities? The word *inventory* comes from a Latin word meaning "find," and in reference to writing, taking inventory carries the familiar meaning of taking stock—finding and looking closely at items in your stock of writing, cataloging, and describing those items—much as you might take inventory of the records in your old LP collection or as a store manager might take inventory of items on hand. But taking inventory also carries another sense of "find," one we more often associate with the words *invent* and *invention*. In this sense, taking inventory means to discover new things about your writing and to use your discoveries to articulate the strengths and weaknesses in your own writing as well as to build a plan for improvement.

This dual sense of taking inventory runs throughout *The St. Martin's Handbook,* asking you to think critically and analytically about your own writing. This process will help you produce stronger and stronger pieces of new writing, which you can then use as material for further analysis. How might you identify those features of your writing most important for such an inventory? That question, a crucial one for thinking critically about your writing, has been one of many questions guiding research conducted for this book. In an analysis of a representative sample taken from twenty thousand first- and second-year essays from colleges and universities across the United States, we did some critical thinking of our own. In doing so, we found that the features readers most often comment on fall into three categories:

1. Broad content issues
2. Organization and presentation
3. Surface errors

These research findings suggest that readers evaluate the effectiveness of your writing by how well you use and control these features of it and that you can benefit from organizing an inventory of your own writing according to these three major categories. Following are some guidelines for doing so.

≫ Taking a writing inventory

1. If you are using this chapter in a writing course, assemble copies of the first two or three pieces of writing you do, making sure to select pieces to which either your instructor or other students have responded.
2. Read through this writing, adding your own comments about its strengths and weaknesses.
3. Examine the instructor and peer comments very carefully, and compare them with your own comments.
4. Group all the comments into the categories discussed in this chapter—broad content issues, organization and presentation, and surface errors.
5. Make an inventory of your own strengths and weaknesses in each category.
6. Identify the appropriate sections of this book for more detailed help in areas where you need it.
7. Make up a priority list of three or four particular problems you have identified, and write out a plan for eliminating them.
8. Note at least two strengths you want to build on in your writing.

Keeping a writing log

One very good way to keep track of your writing strengths and weaknesses is by establishing a **writing log**, a notebook or folder in which you can record observations and comments about your writing—from instructors, other students, or yourself. This book will offer you frequent opportunities to make entries in a writing log, beginning with this chapter. As you take inventory of some of your writing, you will be gathering information about how readers respond to various features of it—broad content issues, organization and presentation, and surface errors. This information can serve as the data for an opening entry in your writing log. Here is an example of one such entry, made by Tamara Washington, an undergraduate at Ohio State University.

ENTRY 1 WRITING INVENTORY

I've taken a first look at the essay I wrote on the second day of class, one my response group and the teacher read. Here's what I've found so far:

	Strengths	Weaknesses
Broad content issues	lots of good examples	ideas not in logical order
Organization, presentation	great title! (Everyone loved it.)	paragraphs too short to make my points (Two are only one sentence long.)
Surface errors	semicolons used correctly—I was worried about this!	one unintentional sentence fragment an *its/it's* mistake(!) (See p. 496, and *never* make this mistake again!!)

ASSESSING BROAD CONTENT ISSUES

As a writer, you are in some ways like the supervisor of a large construction job or the conductor of an orchestra: you must orchestrate all the elements of your writing into a persuasive performance, assemble all the ideas, words, evidence, and so on into one coherent structure. Doing so calls on you to attend carefully to several big questions: what is the purpose of your writing? what points does it make? does it fully develop, support, or prove those points? to whom is it addressed? does this writing reflect your full powers as a writer? Answering such questions as part of your writing inventory is important, for readers expect your purpose to be clear, your points to be fully established, and so on. They expect, in short, that you are a good writer, and they look to you to guide them skillfully to an understanding of your meaning.

Our research indicates that readers comment most often on the following broad content issues in student writing:

1. Use of supporting evidence
2. Use of sources
3. Achievement of purpose
4. Attention to audience
5. Overall impression

Use of supporting evidence

According to Aristotle, an effective speaker needs to do two basic things: make a claim and prove it. Readers, too, expect that a piece of writing will make one or more points clearly and illustrate or support those points with ample evidence—good reasons, examples, or other details. Effective use of such evidence helps readers understand a point, makes abstract concepts concrete, and offers "proof" that what you are saying is sensible and worthy of attention and assent. In fact, this element is the one readers in our research commented on *most often,* accounting for 56 percent of all comments we analyzed. These readers tended to make statements like these:

This point is underdeveloped.

I like the way you back this claim up.

The details here don't really help me see your point.

Good use of proofs.

I'm not convinced—what's your authority?

The three reasons you offer are very persuasive.

Good examples.

Any inventory of your writing should include a close look at how well you use supporting evidence.

> For more discussion of the use of good reasons, see 5d; of examples and details, see 5g–i. For more on providing such support in paragraphs, see 6e.

Use of sources

One special kind of supporting evidence for your points comes from source materials. Choosing possible sources, evaluating them, and using the results of your research effectively in your writing not only supports your claim but also builds your credibility as a writer, demonstrating that you understand what others have to say about a topic and that you are fully informed about varying perspectives on the topic. But finding enough sources, judging their usefulness, and deciding when to quote, when to summarize, and when to paraphrase—and then doing so accurately and working the results smoothly into your own writing—is a skill that takes considerable practice, one you should develop throughout your college writing career. You can begin sharpening that skill now by taking a close look at how well you use sources in your writing. The readers whose responses we studied commented regularly on such use of sources. Here are some of their remarks:

> Your list of sources is extraordinarily thorough—impressive reading!
>
> Only two sources? You need at least several more.
>
> Who said this?
>
> Nice use of Sagan's main argument!
>
> One of the clearest paraphrases I've seen of this crucial passage.
>
> Your summary leaves out three of the writer's main points.
>
> Your summary is just repetition—it doesn't add anything new.
>
> This quotation beautifully sums up your argument.
>
> Why do you quote at such length here? Why not paraphrase?
>
> You cite only sources that support your claim—citing one or two with differing views would help show me you've considered other opinions.

≫ For more discussion of choosing, reading, and evaluating sources, see 42a–b; of quoting, paraphrasing, and summarizing, see 42c; and of incorporating source materials in your text, see 43d.

Achievement of purpose

Purposes for writing vary widely—from asking for an appointment or a job interview to sending greetings or condolences to summarizing information for a test to tracing the causes of the Second World War for an essay. In college writing, your primary purpose will often be directly related to the assignment you receive. As a result, you need to pay careful attention to what an assignment asks you to do, noting particularly any key terms in the assignment such as "analyze" or "argue" or "define" or "summarize." Such words are important in meeting the requirements of the assignment, staying on the subject, and thus achieving your purpose.

Readers' responses can often reveal how well you have achieved your primary purpose. Here are some comments responding to purpose:

> Why are you telling us all this?
>
> What is the issue here, and what is your stand on it?
>
> Very efficient and thorough discussion! You explain the content very clearly and thus reveal your understanding of the article.
>
> What is your purpose here? What do you want to happen as a result of your argument?
>
> You simply give a plot summary here, one that does little to analyze character development.

Your writing will profit from some time spent identifying the purposes of several pieces of writing you have done and thinking about how well you achieved those purposes.

≫ For guidelines on considering purposes, see 2d.

Attention to audience

All writing is written to be read, if only by the writer. Most college writing is addressed to instructors and other students, though you may sometimes write to another audience—a political figure, a prospective employer, a campus administrator. The most effective writing is that which is sensitive to readers' backgrounds, values, and needs. Such writing, for example, takes time to define terms readers may not know, to provide necessary background information, to consider readers' perspectives on and feelings about a topic. Here are some reader comments on audience:

> This doesn't sound like something written for fourth-graders.
>
> Careful you don't talk down to your readers.
>
> You've left me behind here. I can't follow.
>
> Your level of diction is perfect for relating to the Board of Trustees.
>
> I'm really enjoying reading this!
>
> Don't assume everyone shares your opinion about this issue.

≫ For guidelines on considering your audience, see 2h and 29b.

Overall impression

When friends or instructors read your writing, they may often give you information about the overall impression it makes, perhaps noting the ways in which it seems to be improving or in which you may be lapsing back into bad habits. As a writer, you will do well to note such responses carefully. In particular, you need to make such comments as concrete as you can by trying to determine, for instance, exactly what has caused some improvement or weakness in your writing. Setting up a conference with the instructor is one way to explore these general responses. Before doing so, however, carry out your own analysis of what the comments mean, and then find out what your instructor thinks.

In the sample of twenty thousand essays we examined, readers tended to give their overall impression most often in a note at the very beginning or the very end of an essay, saying things like the following:

> I was looking for more critical analysis from you, and I've found it!
>
> Much improved over your last essay.
>
> Your grasp of the material here is truly impressive.
>
> What happened here? I can't understand your point in this essay.
>
> I know you can do a much better job of summarizing than this shows.
>
> You have the capacity to become a fine writer. I'm pleased with this!

For more specific ways of assessing the overall impression your writing creates, see the final exercise in every chapter of this book. These exercises are set up to help you take inventory of your use of the topics in each chapter.

EXERCISE I.1

Begin your writing inventory by recording the results of a careful look at broad content issues in at least one piece of your own writing. (1) First, list all comments your instructors and classmates have made about your use of supporting evidence, use of sources, achievement of purpose, attention to audience, and overall progress. If you find other large-scale issues referred to, include them in your list. (2) Then, look over your writing with your own critical eye, using the guidelines in this introduction to evaluate your handling of broad content elements. (3) After examining the lists, summarize your major areas of strength and those areas in which you need to improve. (4) If you are keeping a writing log, enter this inventory there.

ASSESSING ORGANIZATION AND PRESENTATION

The most important or brilliant points in the world will have little effect on readers if they are presented in a way that makes them hard to recognize, read, or follow. Indeed, research for this book confirms that readers depend on writers to organize and present their material—sections, paragraphs, sentences, arguments, details, source citations—in ways that provide aids to understanding. After use of supporting evidence, the features of student writing most often commented on had to do with organizational issues. In addition to clear and logical organization of information, readers appreciate careful formatting and documentation of sources. Although you can't always "tell a book by its cover," our research suggests that the "cover" of your writing—its physical format—can offer an important aid to readers and help to establish your credibility as a conscientious writer. Careful attention to the conventions of source documentation can produce the same result. Because organizational and presentational features of writing give important signals to your readers, they are well worth including in your writing inventory. Here are those features most often commented on in the student writing we examined:

1. Overall organization
2. Sentence structure and style
3. Paragraph structure
4. Format
5. Documentation

Overall organization

Readers expect a writer to provide organizational patterns and signals that will help them follow the thread of what the writer is trying to say. Sometimes such organizational cues are simple. If you are giving directions, for example, you might give chronological cues (first you do A, then B, and so on), and if you are describing a place, you might give spatial cues (at the north end is A, in the center is B, and so on). But complex issues often call for complex organizational patterns, and you might find yourself needing to signal readers that you are moving from a problem to several possible solutions, for example, or that you are moving through a series of comparisons and contrasts. Because the organizational patterns you choose provide crucial signals for readers, you can profit by taking a close look at the organizational strengths and weaknesses of some of your writing. Readers responded in the following ways to organizational features:

I'm confused here—what does this point have to do with the one before it?

Your most important point is buried here in the middle. Why not move it up front?

Organization here is chronological rather than topical; as a result, you write synopsis, not analysis.

How did we get here? You need a transition.

Very clear, logical essay. A joy to read.

I'm lost: this sentence seems totally out of place.

You need to reorganize the three details: son, friend, *then you.*

For more discussion of overall organization, see 4e and 5i. For more on organizational methods of development, see 3d; on transitional signals that aid organization, see 6d; and on ways of linking paragraphs, see 6g.

Sentence structure and style

Effective sentences form the links in a chain of writing, guiding readers in ways that aid reading and understanding. If you have never taken a close look at how your sentences work (or don't work) to help organize your writing and guide readers, a little time and effort now will provide an overview. How long do your sentences tend to be? Do you use strings of short sentences that make the reader work to fill in the connections between them? Do any long sentences confuse the reader or wander off the topic? How do your sentences open? How do you link them logically? Answering these questions provides additional data for your writing inventory. Here are some comments the readers in our research made about sentences:

The pacing of your sentences here really keeps me reading—excellent variation of length and type.

Combine sentences to make the logical connection explicit here.

Your use of questions helps clarify this complex issue.

This is not effective word order for a closing sentence—I've forgotten your main point.

These sentences all begin with nouns—the result is a kind of dull clip-clop, clip-clop, clip-clop.

Too many short, simple sentences here. This reads like a grocery list rather than an explanation of a complex issue.

This sentence goes on forever—how about dividing it up?

For guidelines on editing sentences, see p. 191. For detailed discussion of sentence types, see 7d; of sentence effectiveness, see Chapter 19; and of sentence variation, see Chapter 22.

Paragraph structure

Just as overall organization can help readers follow the thread of thought in a piece of writing, so too can paragraph structure. You may tend to paragraph by feel, so to speak, without spending much time thinking about structure. In fact, the time to examine your paragraphs should generally be *after* you have completed a draft. Since paragraphs play such a major role in making your writing coherent and clear, however, you can profit by examining them carefully now. Begin by studying any readers' comments that refer to your paragraphs. Here are some of the kinds of comments you might find:

> The sentences in this paragraph don't follow in a logical order.
>
> Why the one- and two-sentence paragraphs? Elaborate!
>
> Your introductory paragraph immediately gets my attention and gives an overview of the essay—good!
>
> I can't follow the information in this paragraph.
>
> This paragraph is not unified around one main idea.
>
> Very effective ordering of details in this paragraph.
>
> This paragraph skips around two or three points. It has enough ideas for three paragraphs.

For guidelines on editing paragraphs, see p. 151. For detailed information on paragraph development in general, see Chapter 6.

Format

Readers depend on the format of a piece of writing to make their job as pleasant and efficient as possible. Therefore, you need to pay very close attention to how your materials are physically presented and to the visual effect they create. Because format guidelines vary widely from discipline to discipline, even from assignment to assignment, part of your job as a writer is always to make certain you know what format is most appropriate for a particular course or assignment.

In the research conducted for this book, readers made the following kinds of comments about format:

> You need a title, one that really works to get across your meaning.
>
> This tiny single-spaced type is almost impossible to read.
>
> The table of contents here is very clear and helpful.
>
> Number pages—these were not in the right order!
>
> Your headings and subheadings helped me follow this report.
>
> Never turn in a computer-printed essay without separating the pages and tearing off the tractor holes.

For more thorough discussion of format, see Chapter 51.

Documentation

Any writing that uses source materials requires careful documentation—parenthetical citations, endnotes, footnotes, lists of works cited, bibliographies—to guide readers to your sources and let them know you have carried out accurate research. A close look at your writing may reveal that you have internalized certain documentation rules—listing an author's last name first, for instance—but that you don't understand others at all. While very few writers, even strong writers, carry all these documentation guidelines around in their heads, they do know where to look to find them. Here are some readers' comments that focus on documentation:

> I checked my copy of *Emma* and this quotation's not on the page you list.
>
> Footnote numbers should come at the *end* of quotations.
>
> What are you paraphrasing here? Your introduction merely drops readers into the middle of things. *Introduce the material paraphrased.*
>
> What are you summarizing here? Where do these ideas come from?
>
> I can't tell where this quotation ends.
>
> Keep your parenthetical citations as simple as possible—see 44a.
>
> Why aren't works listed in alphabetical order?
>
> This is *not correct* MLA citation style. Check your book!
>
> What is the date of this publication?

≫ For more information on documenting sources, MLA style, see Chapter 44; APA, CBE, and Chicago styles, see Chapter 45.

EXERCISE I.2

Continue your writing inventory by analyzing the five features of organization and presentation described above in at least one piece of your writing. (1) Chart your instructor's comments, and consider asking a classmate whose opinions you value to comment on your use of these features. (2) Then, add your own observations about your use of these features. (3) On the basis of these analyses, summarize what you take to be your major areas of strength as well as those areas in which you need to improve. (4) If you are keeping a writing log (see pp. I-4 and I-5), enter the results of your analysis there.

LEARNING FROM YOUR SURFACE ERRORS

Whereas readers may notice your handling of broad content issues and your organization and presentation either because these provide stepping stones for following your meaning or because they create stumbling blocks to such understanding, your spelling, grammar, punctuation, word choice, and other small-scale matters will seldom draw attention unless they look wrong. Because such surface errors disrupt communication between writers and readers, they are an important source of information about your writing.

What can we tell you about the kinds of surface errors you are likely to find in your writing and the response they elicit from readers? Our study of student writing reveals, first of all, that—even with word processors and spell checkers—spelling errors are *by far the most common,* by a factor of more than three to one. (A list of the words most often misspelled can be found in Chapter 24.) Second, readers are not disturbed by all surface errors, nor do instructors always mark all of them. In fact, whether your instructor comments on an error in any particular assignment will depend on his or her judgment about how serious and distracting it is and what you should be dealing with at the time. Finally, not all surface errors are even consistently viewed as errors. In fact, some of the patterns identified in our research are considered errors by some instructors but stylistic options by others.

While many people may tend to think of "correctness" as absolute, based on hard and fast, unchanging "rules," instructors and students know better. We know that there are "rules," all right, but that the rules change all the time. "Is it okay to use *I* in essays for this class?" asks one student. "My high school teacher wouldn't let us." "Will more than one comma error flunk an essay?" asks another. These questions show that rules clearly exist, but they also suggest that these rules are always shifting and thus constantly need to be explored.

Our research shows some of the shifts that have occurred in the last century alone. Mechanical and grammatical questions that no longer concern most people used to be perceived as extremely important. In the late nineteenth century, for instance, instructors at Harvard said that the most serious writing problem their students had was an inability to distinguish between the proper uses of *shall* and *will.* Similarly, split infinitives seemed to many instructors of the 1950s a very serious problem, but at least since the starship *Enterprise* set out "to boldly go" where no one has gone before, split infinitives have wrinkled fewer brows.

These examples of shifting standards do not mean that there is no such thing as "correctness" in writing—only that *correctness always depends on some context.* Correctness is not so much a question of absolute right or wrong as it is a question of the way the choices a writer makes are perceived by readers. As writers, we are all judged by the words we put on the page. We all want to be regarded as competent and careful, and errors in the writing we produce work against that impression. The world judges us by our control of the conventions we have agreed to use, and we all know it. As Robert Frost once said of poetry, trying to write without honoring the conventions and agreed-upon rules is like playing tennis without a net.

A major assumption this book makes is that you want to understand and control not only the broad content issues and organizational features of writing but the surface conventions of academic writing as well. Since you already know the vast majority of these conventions, the most efficient way to proceed is to focus on those that are still unfamiliar or puzzling. Achieving this practical focus means identifying, analyzing, and overcoming patterns of surface error in your writing.

Why not decide right now to take charge of your own writing by charting and learning from your errors? This effort need not mean becoming obsessed with errors to the exclusion of everything else in your writing. Perfectly correct writing is, after all, a limited and limiting goal. You want to aim for a perfectly persuasive and enlightening piece of writing—that also happens to be correct.

To aid you in producing writing that is conventionally correct, we have identified the twenty most common error patterns (other than misspelling) among United States college students in the late 1980s. Here they are, listed in the order of occurrence.

≫ *The twenty most common errors*

1. Missing comma after an introductory element
2. Vague pronoun reference
3. Missing comma in a compound sentence
4. Wrong word
5. Missing comma(s) with a nonrestrictive element
6. Wrong or missing verb ending
7. Wrong or missing preposition
8. Comma splice
9. Missing or misplaced possessive apostrophe
10. Unnecessary shift in tense
11. Unnecessary shift in pronoun
12. Sentence fragment
13. Wrong tense or verb form
14. Lack of agreement between subject and verb
15. Missing comma in a series
16. Lack of agreement between pronoun and antecedent
17. Unnecessary comma(s) with a restrictive element
18. Fused sentence
19. Misplaced or dangling modifier
20. *Its/it's* confusion

Statistically, these twenty are the errors most likely to cause you trouble. A brief explanation and examples of each one are given in this chapter, and each error pattern is cross-referenced to at least one place elsewhere in this book where you can find more detail or additional examples.

1

Missing comma after an introductory element

When a sentence opens with an introductory word, phrase, or clause, readers usually need a small pause between the introductory element and the main part of the sentence. Such a pause is most often signaled by a comma.

INTRODUCTORY WORD

Frankly, we were baffled by the committee's decision.

INTRODUCTORY PHRASE

In fact, the Philippines consist of more than eight thousand islands.

To tell the truth, I never have liked the Mets.

Because of its isolation in a rural area surrounded by mountains, Crawford

Notch doesn't get many visitors.

INTRODUCTORY CLAUSE

Though I gave detailed advice for revising, his draft became only worse.

Short introductory elements do not always need a comma. The test is whether the element seems to need a pause after it. The following sentence, for example, would at first be misunderstood if it did not have a comma— readers would think the introductory phrase was *In German nouns,* rather than *In German.* The best advice is that you will rarely be wrong to add a comma after an introductory element.

In German, nouns are always capitalized.

For guidelines on editing for commas after introductory elements, see p. 477. For more on commas and introductory elements in general, see 7c, 22b, and 30a.

2

Vague pronoun reference

A pronoun like *he, she, it, they, this, that,* or *which* should refer clearly to a specific word (or words) elsewhere in the sentence or in a previous sentence. When readers cannot tell for sure whom or what the pronoun refers to, the reference is said to be vague. There are two common kinds of vague pronoun reference. The first occurs when there is more than one word that the pronoun might refer to; the second, when the reference is to a word that is implied but not explicitly stated.

POSSIBLE REFERENCE TO MORE THAN ONE WORD

Before Mary Grace physically and verbally assaulted Mrs. Turpin, ~~she~~ *the latter* was a judgmental woman who created her own ranking system of people and used it to justify her self-proclaimed superiority.

Transmitting radio signals by satellite is a way of overcoming the problem of scarce airwaves and limiting how ~~they~~ *the airways* are used.

REFERENCE IMPLIED BUT NOT STATED

The troopers burned an Indian camp as a result of the earlier attack. This *destruction of the camp* was the cause of the war.

They believe that a zygote, an egg at the moment of fertilization, is as deserving of protection as the born human being, but ~~it~~ *such an assertion* cannot be proven scientifically.

⟫ For guidelines on editing for clear pronoun reference, see 13c. For more on pronoun reference, see Chapter 13.

3

Missing comma in a compound sentence

A compound sentence is made up of two (or more) parts that could each function as an independent sentence. If there are only two parts, they may be linked by either a semicolon or a coordinating conjunction (*and, but, so, yet, nor, or, for*). When a conjunction is used, a comma should usually be placed before it to indicate a pause between the two thoughts.

> The words "I do" may sound simple, but they mean a complex commitment
>
> for life.

> We wish dreamily upon a star, and then we look down to see that we
>
> have stepped in the mud.

In *very* short sentences, this use of the comma is optional if the sentence can be easily understood without it. The following sentence, for example, would be misunderstood if it did not have a comma—readers would think at first that Meredith was wearing her feet. The best advice is to use the comma before the coordinating conjunction because it will always be correct.

> Meredith wore jeans, and her feet were bare.

➤ For guidelines on editing for commas in compound sentences, see p. 477. For further discussion and examples, see 7d1 and 30b.

4

Wrong word

"Wrong word" errors range from simple lack of proofreading, like using *should* for *would*, to mistakes in basic word meaning, like using *prevaricate* when you mean *procrastinate*, to mistakes in shades of meaning, like using *sedate* when you mean *sedentary*. Many errors marked "wrong word" are *homonyms*, words that are pronounced alike but spelled differently, like *their* and *there*.

> A knowledge of computers is ~~inherent~~ *assumed* in his office.

> Mark noticed the ~~stench~~ *fragrance* of roses as he entered the room.

> *Paradise Lost* contains many ~~illusions~~ *allusions* to classical mythology.

➤ For guidelines on checking a draft for wrong words, see 27b. For additional, more detailed information about choosing the right word for your meaning, see Chapter 27. For discussion of choosing respectful words, see Chapter 29.

5

Missing comma(s) with a nonrestrictive element

A nonrestrictive element is a word, phrase, or clause that gives additional information about the preceding part of the sentence but does not restrict or limit the meaning of that part. A nonrestrictive element is not essential to the sentence; it can be deleted without changing the sentence's basic meaning. As an indication that it is not essential, it is always set off from the rest of the sentence with a comma before it and, if it is in the middle of the sentence, after it as well.

Marina, who was the president of the club, was first to speak.

Louis was forced to call a session of the Estates General, which had not met for 175 years.

The bottom of the pond was covered with soft brown clay, a natural base for a good swimming hole.

≫ For guidelines on editing for commas with nonrestrictive elements, see p. 477. For additional explanation, see 30c.

6

Wrong or missing verb ending

The verb endings -s or (-es) and -ed (or -d) are important markers in standard academic English. It is easy to forget these endings in writing because they are not always pronounced clearly when spoken. In addition, some varieties of English do not use these endings in the same way as standard academic English.

Eliot ~~use~~ feline imagery throughout the poem.

uses

I runs a mile every morning before breakfast.

The United States ~~drop~~ *dropped* two atomic bombs on Japan in 1945.

Nobody ~~imagine~~ *imagined* he would actually become president.

An *-s* (or *-es*) ending must be added to present-tense indicative verbs whose subjects are singular nouns; *he, she,* and *it;* and most indefinite pronouns (such as *anyone, each, everybody, nobody, nothing, someone*). The ending is not added to verbs whose subjects are plural nouns; *I, you, we,* and *they;* and indefinite pronouns that have a plural meaning (such as *both* and *few*). The past-tense and past-participle forms of most verbs must end in *-ed* (or *-d*).

> For guidelines on editing for verb endings, see pp. 208 and 211. For more on verb endings, see pp. 206–210, 9b, 9c, and 10a.

7

Wrong or missing preposition

Many words in English are regularly used with a particular preposition to express a particular meaning; for example, throwing a ball *to* someone is different from throwing a ball *at* someone. The first ball is thrown to be caught; the second, to hurt someone. Using the wrong preposition in such expressions is a common error. Because most prepositions are so short and are not stressed or pronounced clearly in speech, they are also often left out accidentally in writing.

The bus committee is trying to set a schedule that will meet the needs of most people who rely ~~in~~ *on* public transportation.

Nixon compared the United States ~~with~~ *to* a "pitiful, helpless giant."

Finally, she refused to comply ~~to~~ *with* army regulations.

In his moral blindness, Gloucester is similar ~~with~~ *to* Lear.

Hilary is absolutely enamored ~~with~~ *of* Barbie.

> For guidelines on checking for prepositions, see 56b. For additional information about choosing the correct preposition, see 7b6.

8

Comma splice

A comma splice occurs when two (or sometimes more) clauses that could each stand alone as a sentence are written with only a comma between them. Such clauses must be either clearly separated by a punctuation mark stronger than a comma—a period or semicolon—or clearly connected with a word like *and* or *although*, or else the ideas they state should be combined into one clause.

Westward migration had passed Wyoming by; even the discovery of gold in nearby Montana failed to attract settlers.

I was strongly attracted to her, ^for^ she had special qualities.

~~They always had~~ ^Having^ roast beef for Thanksgiving, ~~this~~ was a family tradition.

For guidelines on checking for comma splices, see p. 282. For additional information about ways to avoid or revise comma splices, see Chapter 15.

9

Missing or misplaced possessive apostrophe

To show that one thing belongs to another, either an apostrophe and an *-s* or an apostrophe alone is added to the word representing the thing that possesses the other. An apostrophe and *-s* are used for singular nouns (words that refer to one thing, such as *leader* or *Chicago*); for indefinite pronouns (words like *anybody, everyone, nobody, somebody*); and for plural nouns (words referring to more than one thing) that do not end in *-s*, such as *men* and *women*. For plural nouns ending in *-s*, such as *creatures* or *fathers*, only the apostrophe is used.

Overambitious parents can be very harmful to a ~~childs~~ ^child's^ well-being.

Ron Guidry was once one of the ~~Yankee's~~ ^Yankees'^ most electrifying pitchers.

For discussion and guidelines on editing for possessive apostrophes, see 33a.

10

Unnecessary shift in tense

An unnecessary shift in tense occurs when the verbs in a sentence or passage shift for no reason from one time period to another, such as from past to present or from present to future. Such tense shifts confuse the reader, who must guess which tense is the right one.

Joy always laughs until she ~~cried~~ ^cries^ at that episode of *Dynasty*.

Lucy was watching the great blue heron take off when she ~~slips~~ ^slipped^ and ~~falls~~ ^fell^ into the swamp.

Each team of detectives is assigned to three or four cases at a time. They ~~will~~ investigate only those leads that seem most promising.

The senator had begun his speech when a young man in jeans ran up to the podium. He ~~shoves~~ ^shoved^ a cream pie in the senator's face.

>> For guidelines on editing unnecessary shifts in tense, see 14a. For more on using verb tenses in sequences, see 9g.

11

Unnecessary shift in pronoun

An unnecessary pronoun shift occurs when a writer who has been using one kind of pronoun to refer to someone or something shifts to another for no reason. The most common shift in pronoun is from *one* to *you* or *I*. This shift often results from an attempt at a more formal level of diction, which is hard to maintain when it is not completely natural.

When one first sees a painting by Georgia O'Keeffe, ~~you are~~ ^one is^ impressed by a sense of power and stillness.

If we had known about the ozone layer, ~~you~~ ^we^ could have banned aerosol sprays years ago.

>> For guidelines on editing unnecessary pronoun shifts, see 14d.

12

Sentence fragment

A sentence fragment is a part of a sentence that is written as if it were a whole sentence, with a capital letter at the beginning and a period, question mark, or exclamation point at the end. A fragment lacks one or both of the two essential parts of a sentence, a subject and a complete verb; or else it begins with a subordinating word, which means that it depends for its meaning on another sentence.

LACKING SUBJECT

Marie Antoinette spent huge sums of money on herself and her favorites. *Her extravagance helped* ~~Helped~~ bring on the French Revolution.

LACKING COMPLETE VERB

The old aluminum boat *was* sitting on its trailer.

BEGINNING WITH SUBORDINATING WORD

We returned to the drugstore*, where* ~~Where~~ we waited for the rest of the gang.

≫ For guidelines on checking for sentence fragments, see p. 291. For more detailed information on sentence fragments, see Chapter 16.

13

Wrong tense or verb form

Errors that are marked as being the wrong tense or verb form include using a verb that does not indicate clearly that the action or condition it expresses is (or was or will be) completed—for example, using *walked* instead of *had walked* or *will go* instead of *will have gone*. In some dialects of English, the verbs *be* and *have* are used in ways that differ significantly from their use by most native speakers; these uses may also be labeled as the wrong verb form. Finally, many errors of this kind occur with verbs whose basic forms for showing past time or a completed action or condition do not follow the regular pattern, like *begin, began, begun* and *break, broke, broken*. Errors may occur when a writer confuses the second and third forms or treats these verbs as if they followed the regular pattern—for example, using *beginned* instead of *began* or *have broke* instead of *have broken*.

Ian was shocked to learn that Joe ^had died only the day before.

The poet ~~be~~ ^is looking at a tree when she ~~have~~ ^has a sudden inspiration.

Florence Griffith Joyner has ~~broke~~ ^broken many track records.

The Greeks ~~builded~~ ^built a wooden horse that the Trojans ~~taked~~ ^took into the city.

> For guidelines on editing verb tenses, see p. 220. For more detailed information about verb tenses and forms, see 7b1 and Chapters 9 and 10.

14

Lack of agreement between subject and verb

A subject and verb must agree, or match. In many cases, the verb must take a different form depending on whether the subject is singular (one) or plural (more than one): *The old man is angry and stamps into the house* but *The old men are angry and stamp into the house.* Lack of agreement between the subject and verb is often just a matter of leaving the -s ending off the verb out of carelessness and failure to proofread, or of transcribing a dialect form that does not have this ending (see Errors 6 and 13). Sometimes, however, it results from particular kinds of subjects or sentence constructions.

When other words come between subject and verb, a writer may mistake a noun nearest to the verb for the verb's real subject. In the following sentence, for example, the subject is the singular *part,* not the plural *goals.*

A central part of my life goals ~~have~~ ^has been to go to law school.

Other problems can arise from subjects made up of two or more parts joined by *and* or *or;* subjects like *committee* or *jury,* which can take either singular or plural verb forms depending on whether they are treated as a unit or as a group of individuals; and subjects like *mathematics* and *measles,* which look plural but are singular in meaning.

My brother and his friend Larry commutes every day from Louisville.

The committee ~~was~~ *were* taking all the responsibility themselves.

Measles ~~have~~ *has* become much less common in the United States.

Pronoun subjects cause problems for many writers. Most indefinite pronouns, like *each, either, neither,* or *one* take a singular verb. The relative pronouns, *who, which,* or *that* take verbs that agree with the word the pronoun refers to.

Each of the items in these designs ~~coordinate~~ *coordinates* with the others.

Johnson was one of the athletes who ~~was~~ *were* disqualified.

Finally, some problems occur when writers make the verb agree with a word that follows or precedes it rather than with the grammatical subject. In the following sentences, for example, the subjects are *source* and *man.*

His only source of income ~~were~~ *was* his parents.

Behind the curtains ~~stand~~ *stands* an elderly man producing the wizard's effects.

> For guidelines on editing for subject-verb agreement, see p. 240. For additional information about subject-verb agreement, see Chapter 10.

15

Missing comma in a series

A series consists of three or more parallel words, phrases, or clauses that appear consecutively in a sentence. Traditionally, all the items in a series are separated by commas. Many newspapers and magazines do not use a comma before the *and* or *or* between the last two items, and some instructors do not require it. Check your instructor's preference, and be consistent in either using or omitting this comma.

Sharks eat mostly squid, shrimp, crabs, and other fish.

You must learn to talk to the earth, smell it, squeeze it in your hands.

> For guidelines on editing for series commas, see p. 477. For more on parallel structures in a series, see 21a, or on using commas in a series, see 30d.

16

Lack of agreement between pronoun and antecedent

Most pronouns (words like *I, it, you, him, her, this, themselves, someone, who, which*) are used to replace another word (or words), so that it does not have to be repeated. The word that the pronoun replaces or stands for is called its antecedent. Pronouns must agree with, or match, their antecedents in gender—for example, using *he* and *him* to replace *Abraham Lincoln* and *she* and *her* to replace *Queen Elizabeth*. They must also agree with their antecedents in referring to either one person or thing (singular) or more than one (plural)—for example, using *it* to replace *a book* and *they* and *them* to replace *fifteen books*.

Most people have few problems with pronoun-antecedent agreement except with certain kinds of antecedents. These include words like *each, either, neither,* and *one,* which are singular and take singular pronouns; antecedents made up of two or more parts joined by *or* or *nor*; and antecedents like *audience* or *team,* which can be either singular or plural depending on whether they are considered a single unit or a group of individuals.

Every one of the puppies thrived in ~~their~~ *its* new home.

Neither Jane nor Susan felt that ~~they~~ *she* had been treated fairly.

The team frequently changed ~~its~~ *their* positions to get varied experience.

The other main kind of antecedent that causes problems is a singular antecedent (such as *each* or *an employee*) that could be either male or female. Rather than use masculine pronouns (*he, him,* and so on) with such an antecedent, a traditional rule that excludes or ignores females, a writer should use *he or she, him or her,* and so on, or else rewrite the sentence to make the antecedent and pronoun plural or to eliminate the pronoun.

Every student must provide his *or her* own uniform.

~~Every student~~ *All students* must provide ~~his~~ *their* own ~~uniform~~ *uniforms*.

Every student must provide ~~his own~~ *a* uniform.

For guidelines on editing for pronoun-antecedent agreement, see p. 247. For additional information about pronoun-antecedent agreement, see Chapter 11.

17

Unnecessary comma(s) with a restrictive element

A restrictive element is a word, phrase, or clause that restricts or limits the meaning of the preceding part of the sentence; it is essential to the meaning of what precedes it and cannot be left out without changing the sentence's basic meaning. Because of this close relationship, it is *not* set off from the rest of the sentence with a comma or commas.

An arrangement⁄ for orchestra⁄ was made by Ravel.

Several groups⁄ opposed to the use of animals for cosmetics testing⁄ picketed the laboratory.

People⁄ who wanted to preserve wilderness areas⁄ opposed the plan to privatize national parks.

The vice president succeeds⁄ if and when the president dies or becomes incapacitated.

Shakespeare's tragedy⁄ *Othello*⁄ deals with the dangers of jealousy.

In the last example above, the appositive is essential to the meaning of the sentence because Shakespeare wrote more than one tragedy.

For guidelines on editing out unnecessary commas with restrictive elements, see p. 478. For additional information about restrictive phrases and clauses, see 30c and 30j1.

18

Fused sentence

Fused sentences (sometimes called run-on sentences) are created when two or more groups of words that could each be written as an independent sentence are written without any punctuation between them. Such groups of words must be either divided into separate sentences, by using periods and capital letters, or joined in a way that shows their relationship, by either adding words and punctuation or by rewriting completely.

The current was swift ~~he~~ could not swim to shore.
. He

Klee's paintings seem simple they are very sophisticated.
, but

She doubted the value of meditation she decided to try it once.
; nevertheless

≫ For guidelines on checking for fused sentences, see p. 282. For more information about ways to revise fused sentences, see Chapter 15.

19

Misplaced or dangling modifier

A misplaced modifier is a word, phrase, or clause that is not placed close enough to the word it describes or is related to. As a result, it seems to modify some other word, phrase, or clause, and readers can be confused or puzzled.

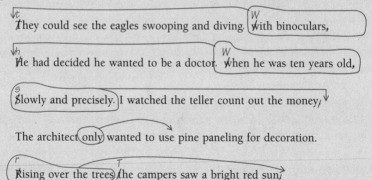

t
They could see the eagles swooping and diving. With binoculars,
W

h
He had decided he wanted to be a doctor. When he was ten years old,
W

S
Slowly and precisely. I watched the teller count out the money,

The architect only wanted to use pine paneling for decoration.

r   *T*
Rising over the trees the campers saw a bright red sun,

A dangling modifier is a word, phrase, or elliptical clause (a clause from which words have been left out) that is not clearly related to any other word in the sentence. The word that it modifies exists in the writer's mind, but not on paper in the sentence. Such a modifier is called "dangling" because it hangs precariously from the beginning or end of the sentence, attached to nothing very solid.

you are
A doctor should check your eyes for glaucoma every year if over fifty.

Looking down the stretch of sandy beach, *one sees* people ~~are~~ lying face down trying to get a tan.

As a male college student, *a* ~~M~~ many people are surprised ~~at my~~ *that I,* support ~~for~~ the draft.

⟫ For guidelines on editing misplaced and dangling modifiers, see p. 306. For additional information, see 17a and c.

20

Its / It's confusion

The word *its,* spelled without an apostrophe, is the possessive form of *it,* meaning "of it" or "belonging to it." The word *it's,* spelled with an apostrophe, is a shortened form of *it is* or *it has.* Even though with nouns an apostrophe often indicates a possessive form, the possessive form of a pronoun in this case is the one *without* the apostrophe.

The car is lying on it's side in the ditch.

It's a white 1986 Buick.

It's been lying there for two days.

⟫ For guidelines on checking *its* and *it's,* see 33b.

EXERCISE I.3

Continue your writing inventory by analyzing the surface errors (and strengths) in one piece of your writing. (1) Go through your writing, noting all comments, positive or critical, in such areas as spelling, grammar, punctuation, capitalization, and other issues like those discussed in the section above. (2) Then go through once more, using the guidelines on the twenty most common errors in this introduction, to add your own observations about strengths and areas that need improvement. (3) Finally, compile a list of both strengths and weaknesses, and decide which areas you plan to work on first. (4) If you are keeping a writing log, enter the results of your writing inventory there.

Part One

The Writing Process

$$\Longleftrightarrow$$

1. Writing, Reading, and Research   2

2. Considering Purpose and Audience   18

3. Exploring, Planning, and Drafting   32

4. Revising and Editing   54

5. Thinking Critically: Constructing and Analyzing Arguments   78

6. Constructing Paragraphs   116

1

Writing, Reading, and Research

CHANCES ARE THAT YOU HAVE BEEN A WRITER, reader, and researcher since you were a small child. When you first began trying to write your name, for instance, you were also learning to read what you had written. And you were, in addition, doing research—making observations, asking questions, proceeding by trial and error, and probably also taking cues from the response your newfound skills evoked from admiring relatives. In fact, throughout your life, whether you've been aware of it or not, the processes of writing, reading, and researching have been closely interrelated. Certainly, a significant part of your college education will involve these activities, for they are the primary means of creating and sharing academic knowledge.

1a

Considering the process of writing

No one can complete college without doing a lot of writing, and more and more people in business and the professions now realize the crucial importance of being able to write effectively. In fact, research shows that writing encourages and enhances certain kinds of learning and even that some kinds of complex thinking are extremely difficult without it. Writing, then, is not a mysterious artistic talent that only a lucky few are born with but an essential and powerful means of discovering what you know and communicating that knowledge to others. As one author says:

> Writing is foremost a mode of thinking and, when it works well, an act of discovery. I write to find out what I believe, what seems logical and sensible to me, what notions, ideas, and views I can live with.
>
> – JOSEPH EPSTEIN

Writers, then, are people who create and explore observations and ideas on paper and care about the ways that their readers respond to their written words. In order to write successfully, however, it helps to understand how the writing process works and how to develop a method that works for you. Looking carefully at the way you go about writing, at your processes of writing, should help you view your own writing with a critical eye and determine how to make the kinds of changes that will lead to better writing and greater intellectual rewards. Because the writing process is directly related to the quality of the finished piece of writing, the next several chapters will focus on the various parts of that process.

The mental activities that actually accompany the writing process are tremendously complex. They are, moreover, so subtle and so lightning fast that we are only now beginning to learn how they all interact. But we do know that writers always set and shift and reset a series of goals as they write. These goals range from those as large as "try to make the reader laugh here" or "explain this concept" to those as small as "use a semicolon instead of a period here to make this section flow more smoothly."

Researchers often describe the process of writing as seamless and **recursive**, meaning that its goals or parts are constantly flowing into and influencing one another, without any clear break among them. This shifting set of goals may focus one moment on deciding how to organize a paragraph and the next moment on using knowledge gained from that decision to revise the wording of a sentence. Repetitive, erratic, and often messy, writing does not proceed in nice, neat steps: first an idea; then a plan; then an introduction, body, and conclusion. In fact, these "steps" often take place simultaneously, in a kind of spiraling sequence, with exploring, drafting, and revising all taking place throughout the process of writing. A writer may get an idea for a conclusion while drafting the introduction or may plan one paragraph while revising the previous one.

Everyday Use

Deciding which college to attend and going through the process of applying and enrolling called on you to do some important reading, writing, and researching. You may remember doing some research on possible colleges, poring over catalogs to determine which schools would be appropriate, and writing up the final applications. Think for a moment about how you have used reading, writing, and research in other decisions you've made recently—what computer to buy, where to vacation, and so on.

In any case, writers seldom pay attention to these constantly shifting goals and recursive patterns. Ideally, writing can be a little like riding a bicycle; with practice, the process becomes more and more automatic. As you become more practiced as a writer, more and more of the goal juggling you do will become automatic. Like an experienced cyclist, you will be able to pay attention to the big things—oncoming traffic, the view, the route you're taking—without thinking too consciously about changing gears or moving your feet.

It is useful to think of the writing process as a series of recursive activities: **considering purpose and audience**, during which the writer determines the purposes the piece of writing is intended to accomplish and thinks carefully about the persons to whom it is addressed; **exploring, planning, and drafting**, during which the writer gathers information, develops a tentative thesis and organization, and puts down on paper a version of the piece of writing; **revising, editing, and proofreading**, during which the writer works with the draft to improve it and polishes it to its final form. But these activities seldom if ever occur in a linear sequence, with one completed step rigidly following another. Rather, most writers move back and forth—considering the assignment, exploring the topic, thinking about audience, gathering more information, planning, drafting, revising, drafting another section, revising again, planning a little more, focusing more sharply on audience, revising yet again, editing, and proofreading—until the writing is complete. Though the following sections discuss the various parts of the process in the order presented above, in any actual writing task these activities are almost always interwoven.

1

Considering purpose and audience

In most of your college work, the writing process will begin with an assignment for a course. Whether the topic is specified by the instructor or left up to you, you will do well to begin by thinking carefully about the assignment itself, making sure you understand what it is asking you to do and, if necessary, clarifying it with your instructor.

As you think about the assignment carefully, you will want to decide what major purposes you hope to accomplish in the piece of writing. In addition to presenting yourself well and demonstrating your skill as a writer, you will want the writing to accomplish some goal—to persuade your readers to take a certain action, to explain some event or phenomenon to them, and so on. And because specific purposes can be fulfilled only in relation to specific readers, you will want to think carefully about your audience, those readers to whom your piece of writing is addressed. (See Chapter 2.)

2

Exploring

Writing worth reading usually starts with a nagging question or puzzle or idea that calls for some exploration—thinking about what you already know, coming up with a working thesis, gathering information if necessary. While this kind of exploring continues throughout the writing process, it is often the way a writer begins.

Depending on the writing task, exploring can last a few minutes or several months. If you have to write a one-page essay in class about your family, you will probably jot down a few notes and start writing very quickly. If, on the other hand, you have six weeks to prepare a fifteen-page paper on U.S.-Japanese relations, you need to do some research and explore the topic thoroughly before planning what you want to say. (See 3a.)

3

Planning

Planning involves deciding how to organize your writing. Sometimes an organizational plan will occur to you at an early stage and help shape your thesis and direct any research you need to do. More often, perhaps, a plan will grow out of the thesis or your search for information. However your plan develops and however tentative it is, it will act as a guide as you produce a first draft. Your thesis and organization may shift as you draft, but just having them will help you keep on course or at least help you remember where you are headed. (See 3d and 3e.)

4

Drafting

Drafting is the central part of writing—the one element in the process that can never be skipped or avoided. As one student put it, drafting is that point "where the rubber meets the road," the time when you try your ideas out in writing. As much as anything, drafting serves as a continuation of the process of exploration. The British writer E. M. Forster once wrote, "How can I know what I think until I see what I say?" Indeed, no matter how thoroughly you may already have explored your topic, you will discover more about it while drafting. Sometimes these new insights will cause you to turn back—to change your organizational plan, to bring in more information, to approach the subject from a new angle, to rethink the way you appeal to your audience, or even to reconsider your purpose. Drafting, then, is *not* just putting your ideas down on paper. More often than not, it also involves coming up with new ideas or completely reshaping your concept of what you are trying to achieve in the essay.

Because writing the actual draft is just one part of this recursive activity, many experienced writers report that they rarely try to make their writing come out perfectly the first time. Rather, they view drafting as just that—the process of working out a *first draft*, during which they explore thoughts and try out arguments. The goal of drafting is not to produce a final copy or even a version good enough to show anyone else. Smooth sentences, the ideal word choice, and the right punctuation can come later; in your first draft, just get your thoughts down until you run out of ideas to explore. (See 3f.)

5

Revising

With your first draft, you have a version of your essay before you, and the rest of your work will be devoted to making sure it says what you want it to say. Doing so requires careful rereading and analysis of the draft with an eye toward establishing a systematic plan for revising.

Re-vision means literally "seeing again." It means looking at a draft with a critical eye—seeing it anew and deciding if it accomplishes your original goals. You may have assumed before now that revising is simply a matter of correcting misspellings, inserting missing commas, and typing up the result. Although such tasks are important, true revision is something more. It means examining the draft to reassess the main ideas, the organization, the structure of paragraphs, the variety of sentences, the choice of words, the attitudes toward the topic and the audience, the thoroughness with which the topic is developed. It means polishing to achieve smooth phrasing and memorable prose. It may mean writing new sentences, moving paragraphs, eliminating sections, doing additional research, or even choosing a new topic and starting over. In fact, because it can be extensive, revising often closely resembles drafting.

Getting responses from others

In addition to your own analysis of the draft's strengths and weaknesses, you may want to get responses from other people. The analysis you do on your own is important, of course, because no one knows as well as you what you are trying to say. But most writing assumes an audience larger than the writer alone; and revising can be made easier and more productive if you can actually make use of such an audience, be it your friends, your classmates, or your instructor. Getting comments and criticisms from others is a way of seeing your work through new eyes, and it is a helpful part of any writer's revision process. (See 4c.)

6

Editing and proofreading

After you have received any critical responses to your draft and have revised thoroughly, the tasks of editing and proofreading begin. Editing involves making what you have written ready for the world, which means making it meet those conventions of written form known as correctness. Sentence structure, spelling, mechanics, punctuation—all must meet conventional standards. Editing, too, may lead you to reconsider an idea, a paragraph, a transition, or an organizational pattern—and you may find yourself planning or drafting once again. When all editing is complete and you have produced a final manuscript, you then must proofread to catch and correct any typographical errors. (See 4i and 4j.)

7

Thinking critically about your own writing

Although you may not have thought very much about how you go about producing a piece of writing, you probably already have your own characteristic writing process. One of the best ways to improve this process is to make the effort to analyze it from time to time. You can do this most systematically by keeping a **writing log**, a notebook in which you jot down your thoughts about a writing project while you are working on it or after you have completed it. Studying these notes will help you identify patterns of strength and weakness in your writing, and sharing the writing log with your instructor or your classmates may yield some helpful advice on how you can write more efficiently and more effectively. (For more on keeping a writing log and for a sample entry from one student's log, see p. I-4.)

To get started thinking critically about and evaluating your own writing process, answer the following questions. If you are keeping a writing log, record your answers there.

Examining your own process of writing

1. How do you typically go about preparing for a writing assignment? Describe the steps you take, including rereading the assignment, asking questions about it, talking to instructors or friends, jotting down ideas, gathering information, and so on. How far in advance of the due date do you usually begin working on the assignment?

2. When and where do your best ideas often come to you?

3. Where do you usually do your writing? Describe this place. Is it a good place to write? Why, or why not?

4. When you write, are you usually physically alone? Is there usually music, conversation, or other sounds in the background?

5. What materials do you use? pen or pencil, note pad, loose-leaf paper, index cards, typewriter, word processor? What do you find most (and least) helpful or appealing about these materials?

6. What audience do most assignments ask you to address? the instructor? classmates? a wider audience? How much thought do you typically give to the audience as you work on the assignment?

7. What strategies do you typically use to explore a topic?

8. How do you typically go about writing a first draft? Do you finish it in one sitting, or do you prefer to take breaks?

9. How do you typically go about revising, and what does your revision process include? Do you write out complete revised drafts or simply insert, delete, or move material in the draft you are revising? How many drafts or stages of revision do you usually go through before the final version? Why? What are the things you think about most as you revise?

10. If you get stuck while writing, what do you usually do to get moving again?

11. What would you say is most efficient and most effective about your writing process? What is most enjoyable? What is least efficient and least effective about your writing process? What is least enjoyable?

12. What specific steps could you take to improve your writing process?

EXERCISE 1.1   Thinking Critically about Your Writing Process

Take a few moments to remember all the writing you did when you were applying to college: the letters you wrote, the forms you completed, and so on. In a brief paragraph, describe this writing, and speculate on how it may have helped you to be accepted by the college(s) that did accept you. Using the guidelines in 1a7, try to recall the process you followed.

1b

Considering the process of reading

If you have ever read a book or seen a movie about Helen Keller, you will remember the electrifying moment when she first learns to "read," when she first realizes that the symbols traced in her palm contain meanings. Through these symbols, she begins to "see" a new world in her imagination. And so it is with all readers, for all of us build imaginative worlds of meaning, "virtual realities," from words. The words themselves, after all, are just marks on a page; it takes an active reader to construct meaning from them. You will recognize this principle if you think of a time when you were reading along and suddenly realized that you were not getting any meaning, that you were just looking at words. Only when you went back, engaged those words actively, and puzzled them out were you really reading.

1

Reading to write

Reading is closely related to writing, if only because writers need to be able to read their own work with a careful eye. Indeed, one good way to improve your writing is by paying close attention to what you read, taking tips from writers you especially admire. In the words of William Faulkner, "Read, read, read. Read everything—trash, classics, good and bad, and see how they do it." Throughout this handbook, we will be examining the work of well-known writers to "see how they do it," to see what they do with the strategies and structures you yourself will be practicing.

In addition, most chapters include exercises asking you to read a passage with an eye to some element—adjectives, subordination, dashes, and so on. These exercises are designed to help you learn to use these elements in your own work—and they can lead you to insights about how you can make your own writing more accurate and more powerful.

2

Reading with a critical eye

The writer Anatole Broyard once cautioned readers about the perils of "just walking through" a book. A good reader, he suggested, "stomps around" in a book—underlining passages, scribbling in the margin, noting any questions or comments. The following are some guidelines that can help you do more than just "walk through" your reading:

≫ *Some guidelines for critical reading*

PREVIEWING

- Determine your purpose for reading. Is it to gather information for a writing assignment? to determine whether a source will be useful for a research project? to study for an examination? to prepare for class discussion?
- Consider the title. What does it tell you about what is to come?
- Think about what you already know about the subject. What opinions do you hold on this subject? What major topics do you anticipate? What do you hope to learn? *(Continued)*

- What do you know about the author? What is the author's purpose? his or her rhetorical stance? What expertise does he or she have in this subject? What biases might he or she have?
- Look at how the text is structured. Are there subdivisions? Read over any headings. Skim the opening sentences of each paragraph.
- Decide what you think the main point or theme of the text will be.

READING AND ANNOTATING

- Read carefully, marking places that are confusing or that you want to reread.
- Identify key points or arguments, important terms, recurring images, and interesting ideas, either by underlining them in the text or by making notes in the margin.
- Note any statements that you disagree with or question and any counterevidence or counterarguments that occur to you.
- Note any sources used in the text.

SUMMARIZING

- Summarize the main points. Do they match your expectations? (See 42c3.)
- Jot down any ideas you want to remember, questions you want to raise, and ideas for how you may use this material.

ANALYZING

- Identify evidence that supports the main argument or illustrates the main point, as well as any that seems to contradict it.
- Decide whether the sources used are trustworthy.
- Identify the writer's underlying assumptions about the subject as well as any biases revealed in the text. (See 42b.)

TALKING WITH OTHERS

- Compare your understanding of the reading with that of several classmates.
- Pinpoint any differences between your interpretation of main points or your interpretation of the author's effectiveness and that of your classmates.
- Take turns saying what is most memorable about the reading, what is most confusing or unclear about it, and what you would like to know more about.

REREADING

- Reread quickly to be sure you have understood the reading, keeping in mind any alternative views offered by your classmates.
- Identify the author's purpose. Was that purpose accomplished?
- Determine whether all the questions you had during the first reading have been answered.

RESPONDING

- Think about the reading as a whole. What did you like best about it? What puzzled or irritated you? Were your expectations met? If not, why not? What more would you like to know about the subject?
- Note what you have learned about effective writing from this reading. If you keep a writing log, record your notes there.

EXERCISE 1.2   Thinking Critically about Your Reading Process

Following the guidelines in 1b2, read one of the assigned essays from your course text, or if you are not using a text, read the student essay in Chapter 4 or Chapter 5 of this book. Summarize the reading briefly, and note any thoughts you have about your critical reading process (in your writing log, if you keep one).

1c

Doing research

The reading and writing you do in college are part of what we broadly think of as research: your own *re*-curring search, that is, your own ongoing search for knowledge. In fact, much of the work you do in college turns this ongoing and sometimes informal search into various kinds of more formal research. An idea that comes to you over pizza, for example, may lead you to conduct a survey that in turn becomes an important piece of evidence in a research project for your sociology class. Or a question your instructor asks leads you to a late-night discussion with a roommate and then to a number of reference books, which serve as sources for your response to a question on a take-home examination.

For many writing assignments, of course, you will need to do even more extensive or formal research and for broader purposes: to get a better understanding of the topic, to see how your thoughts and perceptions about it compare with those of others, to determine which aspects of it you can and would like to investigate or discuss, to find evidence or examples by carrying out either field-based or library-based research. Even if you know the topic very well, your research will be an important tool for establishing credibility with your audience and thus gaining their confidence in you as a writer. (See Chapters 40–45.)

1d

Remembering the importance of talking and listening

For a number of reasons, the arts of language—reading, writing, speaking, and listening—are often treated separately in school. In fact, as the printed page has taken on more and more importance in our society, reading and writing have come to take precedence over talking and listening. As a result, you can probably remember lessons in reading and writing from the first grade on, whereas you may have had lessons in speaking only infrequently or as "electives," and you may never have had a lesson in listening.

Recent developments in media and technology, however, have led educators and researchers to pay attention to the ear and the mouth (the organs of listening and talking) as well as to the eye and the hand (those of reading and writing). Today it seems both practically difficult and theoretically unwise to draw strict boundaries among these arts. After all, as noted above, writers are always readers of their own texts; they may also hear their texts read aloud, and they may read or speak them aloud themselves. To take a familiar example, when we watch the presentation of a presidential State of the Union Address, we appear to be listening. But we are also "reading" the appearance; and if we go on to think about or otherwise interpret the address, then in some sense we may be said to be "writing" as well. Moreover, while the president is speaking, he is almost always reading a carefully crafted written text, and he is listening to the response of the live audience and perhaps even to electronic cues from his advisors in order to make minute changes in his delivery.

1

Talking to learn

In your college work, you will do plenty of talking and listening, and those activities will add immeasurably to the quality of the thinking and learning you do. Throughout, this text encourages you to talk over your work with others, to engage in collaborative learning. Talking in this way can help you to

- Practice making points you will need to use later.
- Explain your ideas to others and get immediate feedback.
- Work through with others problems with writing and with other assignments.
- Put what you learn into your own words.
- Warm up for writing or reading assignments.

2

Listening to learn

The flip side of talking is **listening,** an art that is of tremendous importance to success in college. You can maximize the value of listening if you

- *Really* listen—consistently and attentively. Practicing this kind of concentration will yield surprisingly quick results.
- Try to listen purposefully. Concentrate on the big points and on what you most need to know.
- Ask questions that will yield answers worth listening to. Set yourself to get the information you need.
- Take notes. Try to repeat information in your own words.

3

Using spoken and written language appropriately

It might seem obvious that talking and writing are different acts. Yet talking is very important to writing, as the previous section suggested. And writing is increasingly linked to talking in important ways, particularly if the speaker is a political leader speaking on television or a talk-show host working on television or radio or any one of us using various other technologies that tend to merge speech and writing (such as a voice-mail message you might write out carefully before recording). So it seems important to consider not only the important link between talking and writing but also what distinguishes the two media and when each one—or a mixture of both—is most appropriate.

Some would say that talk is informal, spontaneous, immediate, ephemeral, and often free-form; whereas writing is formal, planned, distanced, lasting, and standardized. Recent philosophers and linguists have helped us understand that such a distinction is too rigid, that speech is, in fact, planned and distanced: we don't speak randomly or without thought. The differences, in short, are ones of degree, not kind.

In spite of their close connection, mixing spoken and written forms is not always appropriate—as you will no doubt notice if you complete the following exercise. In most college writing you do, you will stick primarily to written forms of standard academic English, inserting spoken forms to quote others, to capture the sounds and rhythms of speech, or to create other special effects. Even in making oral presentations (see Chapter 53), you will probably want to write out your presentation and practice it a number of times to make sure it is clear and accessible.

EXERCISE 1.3   Thinking Critically about Spoken and Written Language

One good way to recognize differences in degree between spoken and written language is to record yourself and a friend in casual conversation for half an hour or so. Listen to the tape, choose a five-minute segment, and transcribe it word for word, trying to get down exactly what you said. You may have to invent some spellings to capture your speech most closely. Then choose a two-page sample of your writing that you feel represents some of your best work. Compare the two samples, noting differences in the occasion or purpose for writing or speaking, in content, in sentence types, and in word choice. What differences can you note between your own speaking and writing?

1e

Taking notes

In much college work, good note-taking is a kind of survival skill, one that helps you manage the mountains of information coming your way. You may in fact already have perfected a note-taking system of your own. Whatever the case, considering how to take notes most effectively will add to your success as a critical reader, writer, and listener. Here are some guidelines to help you review your own note-taking processes. (See 42c on note-taking while doing research.)

- *Consider your purpose.* Are you taking down a quotation that you intend to use in an essay? recording key words and phrases in outline form during a lecture to use when you study for an exam? recording the major points in a reading assignment, using your own words, paraphrases, or summaries in preparation for a class discussion? noting your personal responses and reactions to something you are reading, looking for an idea you may turn into the beginning of an essay? Knowing your purpose in note-taking can help you decide exactly what you should take down.

- *Consider your own style.* Do you think best with pencil in hand, stopping often as you read to jot down an idea, or writing notes almost continuously as you listen to a lesson or lecture? Or does the act of writing distract you, so that you lose track of what you are reading or hearing? Thinking about these questions can help you decide whether you should take notes while reading and listening—or whether it is more effective for you to listen or read first and then take notes soon thereafter.

- If you are taking notes while reading or attending a lecture, *look for the major points, and note their relationships to one another.* When you want to recall information from a reading or a lecture, a series of random jottings is usually less helpful than a series of clearly related points.

- *Label your notes* so that you can remember where they came from. If you are taking notes in class, simply head the sheet of paper with the course title and date. If you are taking notes from a reading, note the book's or the article's author, title, and place and date of publication. If you are taking personal notes, consider heading the page with a label reminding you of the purpose for the notes.

1f

Benefiting from collaboration

The philosopher Hannah Arendt once remarked that "for excellence, the presence of others is always required." Nowhere is Arendt's observation more accurate than in the college community. Your college course work will call on you to do much reading, writing, research, talking, listening, and note-taking. And as you probably have already realized, you will not—or need not—always carry out all these activities in solitude. Far from it. Instead, you can be part of a broad conversation that includes all the texts you read; all the writing you produce; all the talks you have with teachers, friends, family members, and classmates—whether in person or electronically; all the observations and interviews you conduct; all the discussions, lectures, and conversations you listen to. It is this broad conversation we have in mind when we stress the importance of collaboration to you as a student seeking to achieve excellence in college and throughout your life.

Collaboration can play an important part in all the writing you do, first if you talk with others about your topic and your plans for approaching it and then if you seek responses to your draft and gather suggestions for revising and improving it. In much the same way, reading can be done with others—first by entering into a mental conversation with the author and then by comparing your understanding of the text with that of other readers and using points of agreement or disagreement as the basis for further analysis.

For this term at least, the most immediate and valuable of your collaborators may be the members of the class in which you are using this book. Indeed, you can learn a great deal by listening carefully not only to your instructor but to all your classmates. You can profit even more by talking over issues and comparing ideas with them, and by using them as a first audience for your writing; for they will inevitably offer you new perspectives, new ways of seeing and knowing. Here are some guidelines on working with others:

≫ *Some guidelines for collaborating with others*

1. Your instructor may well assign groups of students to work together in class. If not, remember that the smaller the group, the better your chances of finding meeting times in common. Consider setting up a group of between three and five members.

2. Trade phone numbers and schedules, and set a regular time for meetings.

3. Set an agenda or a to-do list for each meeting. If, for instance, you need to work on introductions to an essay you have been assigned, agree to bring several versions for each member of the group to evaluate and respond to. If you intend to read and critique entire drafts, make arrangements to distribute copies to each member ahead of time. If you are assigned to do a *group* project or report, divide up the work fairly, and set up a time line to guide each person's work.

4. Use the meetings not only to discuss assignments the instructor may give but also to work together on difficult readings, assignments, or problems—or to prepare for an examination. If an assignment is long, ask each member to explain one section to the others. If the group has trouble understanding something, ask your instructor for help.

5. Establish ground rules for your group work. The first might be that every member have an equal opportunity to contribute to the group. Consider assigning (and sharing) duties at each meeting: one person acts as general notetaker, for instance, and another keeps the discussion on the topic at hand.

6. Listen carefully to what each person says. If discussion lags or disagreements arise, try paraphrasing what each person has said to see if everyone is hearing the same things.

7. Before any conflicts arise, decide on a means of resolving them. Will the group work by majority rule? If so, all members must have an opportunity to state their positions and reasons clearly and fully before a vote is taken. Remember that creative and constructive conflict is desirable in group discussions: if everyone just agrees to go along, the result is usually a watered-down effort. The trick is to get a really spirited debate going, to listen to all perspectives, to argue out all possibilities—without being hostile. If you keep your goal in mind—the best possible presentation, for example—you should be able to maintain the necessary balance between debate and consensus.

8. Establish periodic times at which to assess the group's effectiveness, with all group members making notes on the following questions and sharing their responses with one another: What has the group accomplished so far? What has it been most helpful with? What has it been least helpful with? What has each member contributed to the group? What about the group is not working well? How can we make the group more effective?

9. If the group will be making a presentation, be sure you know exactly what the assignment calls for and exactly how much time you will have. Divide the preparatory work fairly, and complete it some days *before* the formal presentation, leaving time for at least two practice sessions. Then decide how each group member will contribute to the presentation, making sure that everyone has a role—especially if individual grades will be assigned. (See Chapter 53.)

10. If you are preparing a group-written essay or document, consider dividing up the drafting duties among all group members. Then schedule at least two meetings to hammer out the draft *together*, reading it aloud and working for clarity and consistency of tone as well as for strong organization and plenty of supporting detail. When the final draft is ready, have every member proofread, and assign one member to make last-minute corrections.

2

Considering Purpose
and Audience

Effective writers share at least one thing in common with *expert jugglers: they are able to attend to a number of important elements at once, to keep, as it were, a lot of balls in the air. Among the most important and pervasive of the elements a writer must juggle are those concerning* purpose *and* audience. *As a writer, you will have occasion to write for many purposes and to address many audiences—to amuse your friends, to reassure your parents that you are still alive and well, to inform a credit-card company about an error in your bill, to explain a sales campaign to employees, to persuade your local government to lower its assessment of the value of your house, and so on. As a careful and effective writer, you will want to understand as much as possible about your purposes for writing and about the readers you are addressing. This chapter will get you started thinking about these crucial elements in any writing process.*

2a

Deciding to write

Because purpose and audience are such important considerations in effective writing, you should start thinking about them at an early stage, as soon as you make the decision to write.

In a general sense, of course, this decision is often made for you. You must take an essay examination at ten in the morning; your editor sets a Tuesday deadline for your newspaper story; a professor announces that a research paper will be due next month; your employer asks for a full report on a complex issue before the next management meeting.

But even in such situations, consciously *deciding to write* is important. Experienced writers report that making up their minds to begin a writing task represents a big step toward getting the job done. You can use this insight to your advantage, determining not to put off a writing assignment but to meet it head-on by consciously deciding to get to work on it.

2b

Identifying a problem

When a topic is left open, many writers put off getting started because it is difficult thinking of or deciding on the topic. Experienced writers say that the best way to choose a topic is literally to let the topic choose you. That is, the subjects that compel you—that puzzle, intrigue, irritate, or in some way pose a problem for you—are likely to engage your interests and hence evoke your best writing. Even with assigned topics, by asking yourself what is most problematic about the topic, you can often find some aspect that is particularly compelling. Once you start to *wonder* about a topic, to see it in terms of the problems it raises, you are at the point of having something to think—and write—about. You can begin to identify a problem by thinking through the following questions:

- What topics do you wish you knew more about?
- What topics are most likely to get you fired up?
- What about one of these topics is most confusing to you? most exciting? most irritating? most tantalizing?
- What person or group might this topic raise problems for?

EXERCISE 2.1

Think back to a recent writing assignment. What helped you finally decide to write? Once you had decided to write, what exactly did you do to get going? In a paragraph or two, describe your situation, and answer these questions. Then compare your description with those of two or three classmates.

2c

Understanding writing assignments

Most on-the-job writing addresses specific purposes, audiences, and topics: a group of scientists produces a report on food additives for the federal government; an editorial assistant composes a memo for an editor,

> **Everyday Use**
>
> You can probably remember a time when something you wrote failed to achieve your purpose or, worse yet, backfired on you. Even a fairly routine thank-you note calls for careful thinking about its audience and its purpose—such a note sent to a grandparent in response to a birthday present will differ considerably from a letter thanking a prospective employer for an interview or a club for help on a group project. Take a moment now to think about thank-you letters you have either sent or received. How did these letters differ according to their different purposes and audiences?

summarizing the problems in a new manuscript; a team of psychologists prepares video scripts intended to help companies deal with alcoholism among their employees. These writers all have one thing in common: specific goals. They know why, for whom, and about what they are writing.

College writing assignments, in contrast, may seem to appear out of the blue, with no specific purpose, audience, or topic. In extreme cases, they may be only one word long, as in a theater examination that consisted of the single word *Tragedy!* At the opposite extreme come assignments in the form of fully developed cases, often favored in business and engineering courses. Such cases are very specific: you could, for example, be asked to assume the role of a civil engineer who is to evaluate various proposals for constructing a bridge and report the results to your superiors.

In between the one-word exam and the fully developed case lies a wide spectrum of assignments. You may get assignments that specify purpose but not audience—to write an essay arguing for or against capital punishment, for example. Or you may be given an organizational pattern to use—to compare and contrast two of the novels you have read in a course—but no specific topic. Because each assignment is different and because comprehending a topic is crucial to your success in responding to it, you should always make every effort to understand the assignment fully.

⫸ Analyzing an assignment

- *What exactly does the assignment ask you to do?* Look for words like *analyze, classify, compare, contrast, describe, discuss, define, explain,* and *survey.* These are key terms, and you should be sure you understand what task they require. Remember that these words may differ in meaning among disciplines—*analyze* might mean one thing in literature and something rather different in biology.

- *What knowledge or information do you need?* Do you need to do any research? (See 3a and 3c.)

- *How can you limit—or broaden—the topic or assignment to make it more interesting?* Do you have special interest in or knowledge about any particular aspect of the topic? Be sure to check with your instructor if you wish to redefine the assignment in any way.

- *What problem(s) does the topic suggest to you?* How might the problem(s) give you an interesting angle on the topic?

- *What are the assignment's specific requirements?* Consider genre, length, format, organization, and deadline. Being sure of such things will help you know the scope expected. Your instructor is not likely to expect extensive library research for a paper due in twenty-four hours, for example. If no length is designated, you should ask for some guidelines. (See 2e.)

- *What is your purpose as a writer in this assignment?* Do you need to demonstrate knowledge of a certain body of material, or do you mainly need to show your ability to express certain ideas clearly? (See 2d.)

- *Who is the audience for this piece of writing?* Does the task imply that you will *assume* a particular readership besides your instructor? (See 2h.)

Throughout the next two chapters, we will follow the work of Jennifer Gerkin on an essay for her first-year English course at Ohio State University. Her class was given the following assignment: "Examine the effects of prejudice on your life, and discuss your efforts to deal with those effects."

Jennifer saw that the assignment was broad enough to allow her to focus on something that interested her, and she knew that the key word *examine* invited her to describe—and analyze—situations concerning prejudice in her life. Her instructor said to assume that he and members of the class would be the primary audience.

EXERCISE 2.2

The following assignment was given to an introductory psychology class: "Discuss in an essay the contributions of Jung and Freud to modern clinical psychology." What would you need to know about the assignment in order to respond successfully? Using the questions in 2c, analyze this assignment.

2d

Deciding on your purposes

The writing of college essays, reports, and other assignments almost always involves multiple purposes. On one level, you are writing to establish your credibility with your instructor, to demonstrate that you are a careful thinker and an effective writer. Fulfilling this purpose means considering your instructor's expectations very carefully, a concern addressed in detail in 2h. But good college writing also accomplishes some other, more individual purposes that the writer has in mind. In fact, the best writing you do in college will be writing that in some way achieves a goal or goals of your own, that says as clearly and forcefully as possible what you think about a topic and what you have to say to readers about the topic.

For example, if you are writing an essay about abortion, your purposes might be to inform your readers, to persuade them to support or oppose legalized abortion, or even to clarify in your own mind the medical information about abortion or the moral debate over it. If you are writing a profile of your eccentric grandfather, you might be trying to amuse your readers and to pay tribute to someone who has been important to you.

In ancient Rome, the great orator Cicero noted that a good speech generally fulfills one of three major purposes: to delight, to teach, or to move. Although the world has changed mightily in the two thousand years since Cicero's time, our purposes when we communicate with one another remain pretty much the same: we seek to *entertain* (delight), to *inform and explain* (teach), and to *persuade or convince* (move).

Most of the writing you do in college will address one or some combination of these purposes, and it is thus important for you to be able to recognize the overriding purpose of any piece of writing. If, for example, a history professor asks you to explain the web of events that led up to the 1964 Civil Rights Act (primary purpose: to explain) and you write an impassioned argument on the need for the act (primary purpose: to persuade), you have misunderstood the purpose of the assignment.

For most college writing, you should think in terms of *purposes* rather than one single purpose. Specifically, you should consider purpose in terms of the *assignment,* the *instructor's expectations,* and *your own goals.*

≫ *Considering purposes*

- *What is the primary purpose of the assignment?* to entertain, to explain, to persuade—or some other purpose? What does the primary purpose suggest about the best ways to achieve it? If you are unclear about the primary purpose, have you talked with your instructor or classmates about it? Are there any secondary purposes to keep in mind?

- *What are the instructor's purposes in giving this assignment*—to make sure you have read certain materials? to determine whether you understand certain materials? to evaluate your thinking and writing abilities? to determine whether you can evaluate certain materials critically? How can you fulfill these expectations?

- *What are your goals in carrying out this assignment*—to respond to the topic adequately and accurately? to meet the instructor's expectations? to learn as much as possible about a new topic? to communicate your ideas as clearly and forcefully as possible? How can you achieve these goals?

As she considered the assignment, Jennifer Gerkin saw that her primary purpose was to explain the effects of prejudice on her life, but she recognized some other purposes as well. Because this essay was assigned early in the term, she wanted to get off to a good start; thus one of her purposes was to write as well as she could, to demonstrate her ability to her classmates and her instructor. In addition, she decided that she wanted to find out something new about herself and to use this knowledge to get her readers to think about themselves.

EXERCISE 2.3

Choose one of the following assignments, and describe its various purposes. If your instructor chooses, this exercise may be done in small groups, with one member taking notes and reporting to the rest of the class.

1. Compare two book-length studies of Malcolm X.
2. Discuss the controversies surrounding the use of genetic engineering to change characteristics of unborn children.
3. Write about a person who has been important in your life, and describe why he or she has affected you strongly.
4. Support or attack proposals for a national health plan.
5. Analyze the use of headlines in a group of twenty advertisements.
6. Describe a favorite spot in your hometown.
7. Explain the concept of virtual reality.
8. Read two poems by e. e. cummings, and decide which one you like better. Write an essay explaining why you prefer the one you do.

2e

Considering genre

Most of the writing you do in college will fall into the broad genre of academic discourse. Thus you can benefit from considering what distinguishes academic discourse from other **genres**, or kinds, of writing, such as poetry, drama, fiction, business correspondence, or advertising copy, to name but a few examples. The **academic writing** you do most often will have the following characteristics:

- *standard academic English,* characterized by conventional use of grammar, spelling, punctuation, and mechanics
- *reader-friendly organization,* which introduces and links ideas clearly so that readers can easily follow the text
- *a clearly stated claim supported by various kinds of information,* including examples, statistics, personal experiences, anecdotes, and authority
- *conventional academic formats,* among them lab reports, literature reviews, and research essays

Knowing the characteristics of academic discourse can help you produce the kind of writing that will be expected of you. As you begin any writing task, then, it is wise to ask, "What kind of writing does this assignment ask for?" and to stop and think about how you can meet these expectations.

2f

Considering language

Most of your college work will be done in writing—and in writing in standard academic English. Some of the writing you do may demand that you use some specialized occupational or professional variety of English—those characteristic of medicine, say, or science or law or music. Similarly, you may wish to use regional or ethnic varieties of English to represent particular speech patterns, perhaps to catch the rhythm and sound of someone's spoken words. You may even find that you need to use words from a language other than English—in quoting someone, perhaps, or in using certain technical terms. In considering your use of language, you need to think about your audience and overall purpose; what languages and varieties of English will be most appropriate for reaching that audience and accomplishing those purposes? (See Chapter 28.)

p/a

▶ *FOR MULTILINGUAL WRITERS*
Bringing in Other Languages

Consider your audience's knowledge of language. Even when you write in English, you may want or need to include words, phrases, or even whole passages in another language. If so, you need to consider whether your readers will understand that language and whether you need to provide a translation.

Sometimes the meaning of the other language will be clear from the context, as in the following sentence:

> On the gulf where I was raised, *en el valle del Rio Grande* in South Texas—that triangular piece of land wedged between the river *y el golfo* which serves as the Texas-U.S./Mexican border—is a Mexican *pueblito* called Hargill. . . .
> – GLORIA ANZALDÚA, "Entering into the Serpent"

In this passage, Anzaldúa gives enough surrounding information and uses Spanish words that are close enough to English equivalents (*valle,* valley; *golfo,* gulf) for readers unfamiliar with Spanish to follow her meaning.

Other times you will need to translate, as in the following example:

> Listen to the air. You can hear it, feel it, smell it, taste it. *Woniya waken*—the holy air—which renews all by its breath. *Woniya, woniya waken*—spirit, life, breath, renewal—it means all that.
> – JOHN (FIRE) LAME DEER, "Talking to the Owls and Butterflies"

In this instance, translation is especially necessary because the phrase Lame Deer is discussing has multiple meanings in English.

You should italicize or underline any foreign words (38c). See 28f for details about how to provide translations in your text.

EXERCISE 2.4

Consider a writing assignment you are currently working on. What are its purposes in terms of the assignment, the instructor, and you, the writer? What genre, or kind of writing, does it call for?

2g

Considering your rhetorical stance

"Where do you stand on that?" is a question often asked, particularly of those running for office or occupying positions of authority—a police chief, a college president, a company manager. But as writers, we must ask the question of ourselves as well. Where you stand on your topic, your **rhetorical stance**, is important to your writing; and an understanding of this stance is closely related to an understanding of both your purposes for writing and your intended audience. Thinking about your stance will help you examine the feelings you have on any topic and where those feelings come from and thus help you address the topic fully. And knowing your own stance well will help you see how that stance might differ from the stances held by members of your audience.

A student writing a proposal for increased services for the disabled, for instance, knew that her stance on this topic was profoundly influenced by her having a brother with Down's syndrome. She knew, therefore, that she brought an intense interest to this topic that she couldn't count on her audience having. She would need to work hard, then, on finding ways to get her audience to understand—and share—her stance.

Considering your rhetorical stance

- What is your overall attitude toward the topic? approval? dislike? curiosity? indifference? How strong are your feelings?
- What social, political, religious, personal, or other influences have contributed to your attitude?
- How much do you know about the topic? What questions do you have about it?
- What interests you *most* about the topic? Why?
- What interests you *least* about it? Why?
- What seems important—or unimportant—about the topic?
- What preconceptions, if any, do you have about it?
- What do you expect to conclude about the topic?

2h

Focusing on your audience

Understanding others means being able to "talk their language" or "walk a mile in their shoes." The philosopher Kenneth Burke notes that language is our primary means of making such a meeting of minds possible, of identifying with other people. We know that skilled writers consider their audiences carefully; in fact, one of the characteristic traits of a mature writer is the ability to write for a variety of audiences, using language, style, and evidence appropriate to particular readers.

The key word here is *appropriate:* just as a funeral director would hardly greet a bereaved family with "Hi, there! What can I do for you?" neither would you be likely to sprinkle jokes through an analysis of child abuse written for a PTA. Why not? Because such behavior would be wildly inappropriate in that context, and your good sense would lead you to consider the nature of your audience and to address them appropriately.

Although an instructor may serve as the primary audience for much of your college writing, you may sometimes find yourself writing for others: lab reports addressed to your class, business proposals addressed to a hypothetical manager, or—in an American history class—a letter to a seventeen-year-old living in the year 1775. Every writer can benefit from thinking carefully about who the audience is, what the audience already knows or thinks, and what the audience needs and expects to find out.

⫸ Considering your audience

- What person or group do you most want to reach? your boss? other college students? scientists? people already sympathetic to your views? people unsympathetic to your views? potential voters? members of a group you belong to—or don't belong to?

- How much do you know about your intended audience? In what ways may its members differ from you? from one another? Think in terms of level of education, geographical region, age, gender, occupation, social class, ethnic and cultural heritage, politics, religion, marital status, sexual orientation, and so on. (See Chapter 29.)

- What assumptions can you make about your audience? What might they value? Think in terms of qualities such as brevity, originality, conformity, honesty, security, adventure, wit, seriousness, thrift, generosity, and so on. What goals and aspirations do they have?

- What languages and varieties of English does your audience know and use? What special language, if any, will they expect you to use? (See Chapter 28.)

- What is your audience's stance toward your topic? That is, where do you think your audience is coming from in terms of your topic? What are they likely to know about it? What preconceived views might they have?

- What do you need to be sensitive to in your audience's background?

- What is your relationship to the audience? Is it student to instructor? friend to friend? subordinate to superior? superior to subordinate? citizen to community? something else? *(Continued)*

- What is your attitude toward the audience? Is it friendly? hostile? neutral? one of admiration? of impatience?
- What attitudes will the audience expect you to hold? What attitudes might disturb or offend them?
- What kind(s) of response(s) do you want to evoke?

In addition to her instructor, Jennifer Gerkin's audience included the members of her writing class. Thinking about her classmates, she saw that they were mostly her age; that they were almost all the same race, Caucasian; that they were all from the Midwest.

1

Addressing specific audiences

Thinking systematically about your audience can help you in a number of ways in making decisions about a writing assignment. For example, it can help you decide what sort of organizational plan to follow (you might choose one that would be easiest for a particular audience to understand), what information to include or exclude, and even what specific words to choose. If you are writing an article for a journal for nurses about a drug that prevents patients from developing infections from intravenous feeding tubes, you will not need to give much information about how such tubes work or to define many terms. But if you are writing about the same topic in a pamphlet for patients, you will have to give a great deal of background information and define (or avoid) technical terms.

EXERCISE 2.5

To experiment with how considerations of appropriateness for a particular audience affect what you write, describe one of your courses to three audiences: your best friend, your parents, and a group of high school students attending an open house at your college. Then describe the differences in content, organization, and wording that the differences in audience led you to make.

2

Appealing to your whole audience

All writing aims to appeal to some audience, and all writers need to pay very careful attention to the ways in which their writing can either invite readers to participate as part of the audience or leave them out. One small example may help illustrate this important point. Look at the following sentence:

> As every schoolchild knows, the world is losing its rain forests at the rate of one acre per second.

The writer here gives a clear message about who is—and who is not—part of the audience: if you know what "every schoolchild knows," you can consider yourself part of this audience. But what if you don't know this fact or have reason to suspect it is not true? Then you may feel that you are not part of this writer's audience: the writing does not invite you to participate.

There are various ways you, as a writer, can help make readers feel they are part of your audience. Things to be especially careful with include the pronouns you use, the assumptions you make, and the kind of support you offer for your ideas.

Using appropriate pronouns

The pronouns you use can include or exclude readers. Writers sometimes use *we,* for example, in a way that asks readers to join or identify with a particular group. Study the following example:

> As all of us are quick to agree, we have an absolute constitutional right to bear arms.

In this case, notice how the language either allows you or does not allow you to become part of the audience. The sentence implies that all of "us" agree that "we" have the right to carry guns. But what if you are not in favor of this proposition? Then you are excluded from this writer's audience, and you may feel irritated or antagonistic, or that the writer is speaking for you in ways you don't like.

As a writer, if you use *we* to include your readers, make sure that those you are addressing really fall into the group you are implying.

Making no unfounded assumptions

Be careful about any assumptions you make about your readers and their views, especially in the use of language that may unintentionally exclude readers you want to include. Use words like *naturally* and *of course* carefully, for what seems natural to you—that English should be the official U.S. language, for instance, or that smoking should be outlawed—may not seem at all natural to those you may wish to include in your audience.

The best advice about any audience you wish to address is to take nothing about them for granted. Think as carefully as you can about the individuals whom you wish to be part of your audience, and use language that includes rather than excludes them. (See also Chapter 29.)

Offering appropriate evidence

The examples and other evidence you offer in support of your arguments can help draw in your readers. The student mentioned in 2g, for example, who was writing about services for the disabled, might find that personal anecdotes about a particular disabled person could bring the topic to life for readers who have no personal experience with or interest in the topic. By asking readers to imagine themselves "in a wheelchair, trying to enter a building with steps but no ramp," she would be clearly inviting them to be part of her audience and would be helping them accept her ideas. Such strategies can also, however, leave readers out. Complex statistical evidence might well appeal to public-policy planners but may not appeal to—or could even leave out—ordinary citizens. The point is that you should carefully choose the supporting evidence that is most likely to invite your readers to see themselves as part of your audience.

USING SOURCES
Thinking Critically about Their Purpose and Stance

Awareness of purpose and audience can help you evaluate sources, from the textbooks you are assigned to the materials you may draw on in doing research. You can begin to examine sources carefully by asking questions such as these:

> What does the writer want to accomplish here?
> Why does the writer want to accomplish this purpose?
> What does the writer believe about this topic?
> What should I take the writer's word about?
> What should I be skeptical about?
> Whom does the writer seem to be addressing?
> What does the writer want readers to do, and why?
> What social, religious, political, personal, or other institutional influences may have led the writer to choose this purpose? to assume this stance?

(See 42b for more information on evaluating sources.)

THINKING CRITICALLY ABOUT PURPOSE AND AUDIENCE

Reading with an Eye for Purpose and Audience

Advertisements provide good examples of writing that is tailored carefully for specific audiences. Find two ads for the same product that appeal to different audiences. You might compare ads in a men's magazine to those in a women's magazine to see what differences there are in the message and photography. Or you could look at products that seem to appeal to men (Marlboro cigarettes, perhaps) next to those that are marketed to women (such as Virginia Slims). What conclusions can you draw about ways of appealing to specific audiences?

Thinking about Your Own Attention to Purpose and Audience

Consider something you have written or are working on right now.

1. Can you state its purpose(s) clearly and succinctly? If not, what can you do to clarify its purpose(s)?

2. What other purposes for this piece of writing can you imagine? How would fulfilling some other purpose change the writing?

3. Can you tell from reading the piece who the intended audience is? If so, what in your text clearly aims to relate to that audience? If not, what can you add that will strengthen your appeal to this audience?

4. What other audiences can you imagine? How would the writing change if you were to address some different audience?

5. Does your writing follow the conventions of standard academic discourse— and if not, how should you revise so it will?

If you are keeping a writing log, enter any conclusions you can make about purpose and audience in your own writing.

3

Exploring, Planning, and Drafting

THE LATE LEWIS THOMAS, one of America's most celebrated essayists, began writing essays when he was invited to contribute a monthly column to the New England Journal of Medicine. A scientist and medical doctor, Thomas at first tried various methods of planning and organizing, including making meticulous outlines. Nothing seemed to work. After producing several of what Thomas himself considered "dreadful" essays, he shook off all attempts at detailed planning and just plunged right in, thinking about and developing his ideas by simply writing as fast as he could.

Like Thomas, you may do your best by diving right into your writing projects, exploring your topics as you draft. Or you may work more effectively by doing extensive exploration and producing detailed blueprints before you ever begin drafting. As this example suggests, there are many productive ways to go about exploring, planning, and drafting. This chapter takes a close look at some of the ways these activities work in practice.

3a

Exploring a topic

The point is so simple that we often forget it: we write best about topics we know well. One of the most important parts of the entire writing process, therefore, is exploring your topic, surveying what you know about it and then determining what you need to find out about it.

You may already have a good system for exploring topics you wish to write about. If so, use it, and share it with friends and members of your class. If you have no particular personal system, however, this chapter's brief description of strategies may be very useful in getting you to think about a

> *Everyday Use*
>
> If you have ever written a love letter, you probably know all about exploring a topic and working hard on a draft. You might have spent days, weeks, even months, exploring the ideas you wanted to convey, thinking over what exactly to say and considering the effects your language will have. And you may have drafted, torn up the draft, and then drafted some more, searching for just the right words to express something deeply felt and equally difficult to put into words.
>
> Thank goodness few writing tasks are as demanding as a love letter, but most of the writing you do will call on you to give some serious thought to what you want to say and how you want to say it. Take a moment to think of other occasions outside of school when you have had to think long and hard about something you needed to write—a letter to a friend asking for a special favor, a personal statement to accompany a job application, or something else. How exactly did you go about exploring your topic and planning what to say?

topic and in helping you determine what you already know—and indeed in helping you solve problems that may crop up later, in the actual writing. The strategies include brainstorming, freewriting, looping, clustering, and questioning.

1

Brainstorming: talking with others

The most immediate way to begin exploring a topic is also the most simple and familiar: *talk it over* with others. This exploratory talk can work effectively for you in two distinctly different ways: (1) As you talk about your topic, you can hear your mind at work, articulating what you think about the topic and what you most need to know about it. (2) You can also seek out those who know about your topic and talk with them, listening carefully and taking notes.

One excellent way to talk with others about your topic is in a brainstorming session. Used widely in business, industry, and engineering, **brainstorming** means tossing out ideas—often with several others, either in person or via computer—in order to discover new ways to approach a topic. If you don't have others to talk or brainstorm with, however, you can still easily brainstorm. All you need is a pen, pencil, or computer keyboard and some blank paper, and you are ready to carry out the following steps:

1. Give yourself a time limit—five or ten minutes, perhaps—and write down in list form *every* word or phrase that comes into your mind about your topic. Just put down key words and phrases, not sentences. No one has to understand the list but you. Don't worry about whether something will be useful or not. Just get it *all* down.

2. If nothing much seems to occur to you, try thinking the opposite. If you are trying, for instance, to think of reasons to reduce tuition at your college and are coming up blank, try concentrating on reasons *to increase* tuition. Once you start generating ideas in one direction, you can move back to exploring the other side of the topic.

3. When the time is up, stop and read over your list. If anything else comes to mind, add it to the list. Then reread the list, looking for patterns, clusters of interesting ideas, or one central idea.

2

Freewriting

Freewriting is a method of exploring a topic by writing about it—or whatever else it brings to mind—for a period of time *without stopping*. Here is the way to do it:

1. Set a time limit of no more than ten minutes. Begin by thinking about your topic, and then simply let your mind wander, writing down everything that occurs to you, in complete sentences as much as possible. Don't stop for anything; if necessary, write "I can't think of what to write next" over and over until something else occurs to you.

2. When the time is up, look at what you've written. You are sure to find much that is unusable, irrelevant, or nonsensical. But you may also find important insights and ideas.

3

Looping

Looping is a form of directed freewriting that narrows or focuses a topic in five-minute stages, or loops. As in freewriting, you write whatever comes to mind about your topic, following the free flow of your thoughts. Then you identify a central thread in those thoughts and follow it wherever it leads you. Here is how to do looping:

1. With your topic in mind, spend five minutes freewriting *without stopping*. This is your first loop.

2. Look back at what you have written. Find the strongest or most intriguing thought. This is your "center of gravity," which you should summarize in a single sentence; it will become the starting point of your next loop.

3. Starting with the summary sentence from your first loop, spend another five minutes freewriting. This second loop circles around the center of gravity in the first loop, just as the first loop circled around your topic. Look for a center of gravity within this second piece of freewriting, which will form the basis of a third loop.

4. Keep this process going until you have discovered a clear angle on your topic or something about it you can pursue in a full-length essay.

▶ *FOR MULTILINGUAL WRITERS*
Using Your Native Language to Explore Ideas

For generating and exploring ideas—the work of much brainstorming, freewriting, and looping—you may be most successful at coming up with good ideas quickly and spontaneously if you work in your native language. Later in the process of writing, you can choose the best of these ideas and begin working with them in English.

4
Clustering

Clustering is a way of generating ideas using a visual scheme or chart. It is especially useful for understanding the relationships among the parts of a broad topic and for developing subtopics. Clustering is done as follows:

1. Write down your topic in the middle of a blank piece of paper and circle it.

2. In a ring around the topic circle, write down what you see as the main parts of the topic. Circle each one, and draw a line from it to the topic.

3. Think of any ideas, examples, facts, or other details relating to each main part. Write each of these down near the appropriate part, circle it, and draw a line from it to the part.

4. Repeat this process with each new circle until you can't think of any more details. Some trails may dead-end, but you will still have various trains of thought to follow and many useful connections among ideas. (See 3a7.)

5
Questioning

The strategies presented thus far for exploring topics are all informal and based on the freewheeling association of ideas. There are also more formal, structured strategies, which involve asking—and answering—questions. The following are several widely used sets of questions designed to help you explore your topic, either on your own or with one or two others. You may also make up your own questions.

Questions to describe a topic

Originally developed by Aristotle, the following questions can help you explore any topic by carefully and systematically describing it:

1. *What is it?* What are its characteristics, dimensions, features, and parts? What does it look like?
2. *What caused it?* What changes occurred to create your topic? How is it changing? How will it change? What part of the changing process is involved with your topic? What may it lead to in the future?
3. *What is it like or unlike?* What features differentiate your topic from others? What analogies does your topic support?
4. *What larger system is your topic a part of?* How is your topic related to this system?
5. *What do people say about it?* What reactions does your topic arouse? What about the topic causes those reactions?

Questions to explain a topic

This is the well-known question set of *who, what, when, where, why,* and *how.* Widely used in news reporting, these questions are especially useful to help you explain a topic.

1. *Who* is doing it?
2. *What* is at issue?
3. *When* does it begin and end?
4. *Where* is it taking place?
5. *Why* does it occur?
6. *How* is it done?

Questions to persuade

When your purpose is to persuade or convince, answering the following questions, developed by the philosopher Stephen Toulmin, can help you think analytically about your topic. (See 5i2.)

1. What *claim* are you making about your topic?
2. What *good reasons* support your claim?
3. What *underlying assumptions* support the reasons for your claim?
4. What *backup evidence* do you have or can you find to add further support to your claim?

5. What *refutations* of your claim can be made?
6. In what ways is or should your claim be *qualified*?

6

Trying other genres

One good way to get yourself thinking in a fresh, new way about a topic, to get a new angle or a different take on it, is to try translating your subject into a different **genre**, or kind of writing. If, for example, you have been assigned to write an essay on the Wife of Bath's character in *The Canterbury Tales*, why not try writing some rap lyrics that she might have come up with—or country blues or fifties rock-and-roll? If you are working on a history assignment, try writing a poem or limerick about your subject. The idea is to jog your customary thinking patterns, to try seeing your subject from a new perspective and thus to find something new and compelling to say about it. In addition, you may have some fun experimenting with and mixing genres.

7

Looking at one student's exploratory work

Jennifer Gerkin, the student whose work we began following in Chapter 2, tried two strategies to explore her topic: brainstorming and clustering. Since she was already part of a peer group in her class, she turned to her group members for a brief discussion of the general topic the class was working on: the effects of prejudice on their lives. After the group brainstormed for half an hour, they made separate notes. Here are some of Jennifer's:

> *Some* prejudice in everyone
> Where does it come from?
> Learned—we aren't born with it
> Examples: against some races or other groups
>   against some ways of thinking
>   against some ways of dressing

Talking and brainstorming helped her get an idea of what she might have to say about prejudice. In order, then, to find out whether she really wanted to pursue this angle on her topic, she decided to try clustering. What she produced is shown at the top of p. 38.

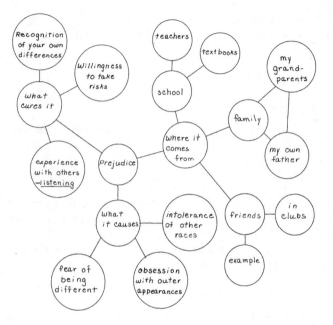

EXERCISE 3.1

Choose a topic that interests you, and explore it by using two of the strategies described in 3a. When you have generated some material, you might try comparing your results with those of other members of the class to see how effective or helpful each strategy was. If you have trouble choosing a topic, use one of the preliminary working theses in Exercise 3.2.

3b

Establishing a working thesis

A **thesis** states the main idea of a piece of writing. Most kinds of college writing contain a thesis statement, often near the beginning, which functions as a promise to the readers, letting them know what will be discussed. Though you will probably not have a finished thesis when you begin to write, you should establish a tentative **working thesis** early on in your writing process.

The word *working* is important here, as the working thesis may well be clarified or otherwise changed as you write. Even though it will probably change, a working thesis is important for two reasons: (1) it focuses your thinking, research, and investigation on a particular point about the topic and thus keeps you on track; and (2) it provides concrete questions to ask about purpose, audience, and your rhetorical stance (helping you see, for example, what you must do to design a thesis for a particular audience).

A working thesis should have two parts: a **topic** part, which states the topic, and a **comment** part, which makes an important point about the topic. Here are two examples.

┌────────── TOPIC ──────────┐┌────────── COMMENT ──────────┐
Recent studies of depression suggest that it is much more closely related
──
to physiology than scientists had previously thought.
┌────────── TOPIC ──────────┐┌────────── COMMENT ──────────┐
The current health care crisis can be traced to three major causes.

A successful working thesis has three characteristics. It should

1. Be potentially *interesting* to your intended audience
2. Be as *specific* as possible
3. Limit the topic enough to make it *manageable*

You can evaluate a working thesis by checking it against each of these criteria. The following example is for a working thesis on global warming:

PRELIMINARY WORKING THESIS

Theories about global warming are being debated around the world.

INTEREST The topic itself holds interest, but it seems to have no real comment attached to it. The thesis merely states a bare fact, and the only place to go from here is to more bare facts.

SPECIFICITY The thesis is fairly clear but not specific. Who is debating these theories? What is at issue in this debate?

MANAGEABILITY The thesis is not manageable: it would require research on many countries and in many languages.

ASSESSMENT This thesis needs to be narrowed with the addition of a workable comment before it can be useful. Also, the field for investigation is too large and vague. This preliminary thesis can be narrowed into the following working thesis.

WORKING THESIS

Scientists from several countries have challenged global-warming theories and claimed that they are more propaganda than science.

For her essay, Jennifer Gerkin produced this preliminary working thesis: "Prejudice is learned." When Jennifer subjected this thesis to the criteria of interest, specificity, and manageability, she decided that it was interesting but not very specific or manageable. After further discussion with her peer group and a conference with her instructor, she decided to focus on a specific kind of prejudice and to adopt this working thesis: "Obsession with appearances has been part of my life since the day I was labeled 'the smart one.'"

EXERCISE 3.2

Choose one of the following preliminary working theses, and after specifying an audience, evaluate the thesis in terms of interest, specificity, and manageability. Revise it as necessary to meet these criteria.

1. Drug abuse presents the United States with a big problem.
2. Abortion is a right.
3. Othello is a complex character whose greatest strength is, ironically, also his greatest weakness.
4. White-collar crime poses greater danger to the economy than more obvious forms of street crime.
5. An educated public is the key to a successful democracy.

EXERCISE 3.3

Using the topic you chose in Exercise 3.1, write a preliminary working thesis. Evaluate it in terms of interest, specificity, and manageability. Revise it as necessary to create a satisfactory working thesis.

3c

Gathering information

Many of your writing assignments will call for some research. Your instructor may specify that you research your topic and cite your sources, or you may simply find that you do not know enough about your topic to write about it effectively without doing some research. You may need to do research at various stages of the writing process—early on, to help you understand or define your topic, or later on, to find additional examples in support of your thesis. But once you have defined a working thesis, consider what additional information you might need.

If you find it necessary to do research, you should probably begin with those resources closest to hand: your instructor, who can help you decide what kind of research to do, and your textbooks, which may include a bibliography or list of references. Basically, you can do two kinds of research: **library research,** which includes nonprint sources as well as books and periodicals, and **field research,** which includes personal observation, interviews, surveys, and other means of gathering information directly. A detailed discussion of how to conduct both kinds of research appears in Chapter 41.

3d

Organizing information

Exploring a topic and gathering information can provide essential data for an essay, but the data are raw—and not very helpful—until they have been organized. Even as you are finding information on your topic, therefore, you should be thinking about how you will group or organize that information so that it will be accessible and persuasive to your readers.

The ways you group your information will ultimately depend on your topic, purpose, and audience. At the simplest level, however, writers most often group information according to three principles:

1. Space—*where* bits of information occur
2. Time—*when* bits of information occur, usually chronologically
3. Logic—*how* bits of information are related logically

1

Organizing information spatially

If the information you have gathered is *descriptive,* you may choose to organize it spatially (see 3a5 for questions that help you describe a topic). Using **spatial organization** allows the reader to "see" your information, to fix it in space. A report on a college library's accessibility to students in wheelchairs, for example, might well group information spatially. In describing the spaces in the library that are most often used and then evaluating their accessibility to a student in a wheelchair, the writer would surely present information spatially—one room or space or area at a time. In this case, the description of the student's progress through various library spaces might even be accompanied by a map. (See 6c for examples of information organized spatially.)

2

Organizing information chronologically

You are probably already very familiar with **chronological organization**, since it is the basic method used in stories, cookbooks, and instruction manuals. All of these kinds of writing group information according to when it occurs in some process or sequence of events. Reports of laboratory studies and certain kinds of experiments also use chronological order.

A student studying the availability of motorcycle parking in a campus lot ordered his information chronologically to show the times when motorcycles entered and exited the lot and thus identify peak periods of demand for parking spaces. This student chose to present this information in narrative (story) form, using chronological order to build tension as the minutes tick by and the lot gets more and more crowded, the cyclists more and more frustrated. If you choose to present information in a narrative, or story, form, you will probably use chronological order. But reversing that order—starting in the middle or at the end and then skipping back to the beginning using a kind of flashback technique—can also provide effective methods of organizing.

Chronological order is especially useful in **explaining a process**, step by step by step. A biology report might require describing the process of circulation in a frog. An anthropology essay might include an explanation of the initiation rituals in a Native American culture. If you decide to organize information about a process in chronological order, you can test whether your explanation is clear and precise by asking a fellow student to read it over and report how easy (or hard) it is to follow the steps of the process.

3

Organizing information logically

In much of the writing you do in college, you will find it appropriate to organize information according to some set of logical relationships. The most commonly used **logical patterns** include *illustration, definition, division and classification, comparison and contrast, cause and effect, problem and solution,* and *narration.* (See 6c for examples.)

Illustrating a point

Often much of the information you gather will serve as examples to **illustrate a point.** An essay discussing how one novelist influenced another might cite a number of examples from the second writer's books that echo themes, characters, or plots from the first writer's works. An appeal for donating money to the Red Cross might be organized in a series of examples of how donations are used. If you illustrate a point in writing intended to persuade or convince, arrange the examples in order of increasing importance, for maximum effect.

Defining terms

Many topics can be developed by **definition:** by saying what something is—or is not—and perhaps by identifying the characteristics that distinguish it from things that are similar or in the same general category. A magazine article about poverty in the United States, for example, would have to define very carefully what it means by poverty—what level of personal income, household assets, or other measure defines a person, family, or household as "poor." An essay about Pentecostalism for a religion class might develop the topic by explaining what characteristics separate Pentecostalism from related religious movements.

Dividing and classifying

Division means breaking a single item into its parts; **classification** means grouping many separate items according to their similarities. Dividing a topic involves beginning with one object or idea and discussing each of its components separately. An essay about the recruiting policies of the United States military, for instance, might be organized by dividing the military into its different branches—army, air force, and so on—and then discussing how each branch recruits volunteers. Classifying involves putting items or pieces of information into categories. If you have been reading histories of the eighteenth century in preparation for writing an essay on women's roles in that time and you have accumulated dozens of pages of notes, you could begin to organize this mass of undigested information by classifying it: information related to women's education, women's occupations, women's legal status, and so on.

Comparing and contrasting

Comparison focuses on the similarities between two things, whereas **contrast** highlights their differences, but the two are often used together.

Asked to read two chapters in a philosophy text (one on Plato and the other on Aristotle), to analyze the information, and to write a brief response, you might well use an organizational framework based on comparison and contrast. You could then organize the response in one of two ways: by presenting all the information on Plato in one section and all on Aristotle in another *(block comparison)* or by alternating between Plato and Aristotle, looking at particular characteristics of each *(alternating comparison)*.

Analyzing causes and effects

Cause-effect analysis either examines why something happens or happened by looking at its causes, or it looks at a set of conditions and explains what effects result or are likely to result from them. An environmental-impact study of the probable consequences of building a proposed dam, for instance, suggests moving from causes to effects. On the other hand, a newspaper article on the breakdown of authority in inner-city schools might be organized by focusing on the effects of the breakdown and then tracing those effects back to their causes.

Considering problems and solutions

Moving from a **problem** to a **solution** presents a natural and straightforward way of organizing certain kinds of information. The student studying motorcycle parking decided to structure the overall organization of his data in just this way: he identified a problem (the need for more parking) and then offered two possible solutions. Many assignments in engineering, business, and economics call for a similar organizational strategy. One economics professor asked students to gather information on the latest slide in the stock market and to use that information to give advice to investors who lost money. The information students gathered first defined the problem the investors faced and then formed the basis for potential solutions.

Narrating

Narration involves telling a story of some kind, whether it is about something that happened in your life or about a historical event that you wish to explain. You might, for example, choose to tell the story of your first day on campus as a way of illustrating some of the challenges new students face. Or you might choose to tell the story of the 1992 Los Angeles riots in a way that highlights the tensions between the ethnic communities there in order to explore the causes and effects of those tensions.

Narrating calls on the writer to set the story in a context readers can understand, providing any necessary background, descriptive details, and time markers and transitions ("later that day," "following," and so on) to guide readers through the story.

Combining organizational patterns

You may want to combine organizational patterns, as is suggested above, using narration in writing about the causes and effects of ethnic tensions in Los Angeles. Or you might combine several passages of narration with vivid descriptive illustrations so as to make a striking comparison, as one student recently did in an essay about the dramatic differences between her life on her Native American reservation and her life as a teacher in a predominantly Anglo school. The possibilities for combining patterns in this way have increased considerably with the advent of electronic forms of text production; soon such combinations may include not only pictures but sound and other multimedia effects as well.

One common way of combining organizational patterns is with a series of anecdotes and snapshots. **Anecdotes** are brief stories, usually about a particular event; **snapshots** are brief descriptions. Both can offer concrete support for a point and help readers to visualize or recognize a situation. A student who had worked in a nursing home used just such a technique in writing about patient abuse, presenting several snapshots of those living in the home and anecdotes about her own experiences on the job as a support for her major point: that her readers should thoroughly investigate such a facility before allowing any relative to be left there.

Jennifer Gerkin, for example, begins by narrating an important personal experience and then uses that story as a means of illustrating her tentative thesis—the problem that her excessive concern with appearances poses for her. She follows the narrative with several paragraphs that consider the effects of that problem, and she closes the essay by offering some possible solutions to the problem. Thus her essay, which is based on personal experience, combines the patterns of narrative, cause-effect, and problem-solution.

EXERCISE 3.4

Using the topic you chose in Exercise 3.1, identify the most effective means of organizing your information. Write a brief paragraph explaining why you chose this particular method (or these methods) of organization.

EXERCISE 3.5

Identify which method or methods of organization you would recommend for students who are writing on the following topics, and explain why.

1. The need for a new undergraduate library
2. The autobiographical elements in Virginia Woolf's *To the Lighthouse*
3. Why voting rates in U.S. elections are declining
4. Education to prevent the spread of AIDS
5. The best contemporary rap artist or group

3e

Writing out a plan

A writer who has organized information carefully is one who already has a plan for a draft, a plan that should then be written down. The student who wrote about the motorcycle-parking shortage organized all his data and developed the following plan. Notice that his plan calls for several organizational strategies within an overall problem-solution framework.

INTRODUCTION
give background on the problem (use *chronological order*)
give overview of the problem (use *division*)
state purpose—to offer solutions

BODY
describe the current situation (use *narrative*)
present proof of the problem in detail (use *illustration*)
present two possible solutions (use *comparison*)

CONCLUSION
recommend against first solution because of cost and space
recommend second solution, and summarize benefits of doing so

Preparing a formal outline

You may wish to prepare a more formal outline. A formal outline is a double-edged sword. On the one hand, it allows you to see before drafting exactly how the parts of your essay will fit together—how your ideas relate, how abstract your ideas are, what the overall structure of your argument will be. On the other hand, a full, formal outline can be devilishly hard to write before you've considered your material in a less formal way.

Most formal outlines follow a conventional format of numbered and lettered headings and subheadings, using Roman numerals, capital letters,

Arabic numerals, and lowercase letters to show the levels of importance of the various ideas and their relationships. Each new level is indented to show its subordination to the preceding level. The following is an example:

Thesis statement
  I. First main topic
     A. First subordinate idea
        1. First supporting idea
        2. Second supporting idea
        3. Third supporting idea
     B. Second subordinate idea
        1. First supporting idea
        2. Second supporting idea

 II. Second main topic
     A. First subordinate idea
        1. First supporting idea
        2. Second supporting idea
     B. Second subordinate idea
        1. First supporting idea
        2. Second supporting idea
           a. First supporting detail
           b. Second supporting detail

Each level contains at least two parts, so there is no A without a B, no 1 without a 2. Comparable items are placed on the same level—all capital letters, for instance, or all Arabic numerals. Each level develops the idea before it—1 and 2 under A, for example, include the points that develop, explain, or demonstrate A. Headings are stated in parallel form—either all sentences, or all grammatically parallel statements.

Formal outlining requires logical thought and careful evaluation of your ideas, and this is precisely why it is valuable. Charting out such an outline allows you to see the skeleton of an essay, making sure that all the bones are in the right and logical places, that all the relationships make sense. A full-sentence outline will make those relationships most clear; so if you want to give your organization the most rigorous test of its structure, try working it into a full-sentence outline. If the logical relationships seem fully established, a topic outline will provide the necessary test of coherence. Remember, however, that an outline is at best a means to an end, not an end in itself. New ideas will almost surely occur as you write; you should not feel bound to the ideas on your outline. Though an outline serves on one level as a plan for your essay, it can also serve to stimulate altogether new thoughts and plans, ones you should feel free to consider and pursue. Many instructors require a formal outline, particularly with a research essay. An example of a formal outline appears in 44d.

Whatever form your plan takes, you may want or need to change it as you begin drafting. Writing has a way of stimulating thought, and the process of drafting may bring up new ideas. Or you may find that you need to reexamine some information or gather more information.

EXERCISE 3.6

Write out a plan for an essay supporting the working thesis you developed for Exercise 3.3.

3f

Producing a draft

Most of us are in some sense "producing a draft" the moment we begin thinking about a topic. One writer reports that his best ideas for opening essays almost always come to him in the shower, another that she "practices" writing versions of paragraphs or sentences in her head while driving to and from work. At some point, however, we sit down with pen, typewriter, or word processor to attempt an actual version of a draft.

1

Be flexible

No matter how good your planning, investigating, and organizing have been, chances are you will need to do more of them as you draft. This fact of life leads to the first principle of successful drafting: be flexible. If you see that your organizational plan is not working, do not hesitate to alter it. If some information now seems irrelevant, leave it out, even if you went to great lengths to obtain it. Throughout the drafting process, you may need to go back to points you have already been through. You may learn that you need to do more research or that your whole thesis must be reshaped or that your topic is too broad and should be narrowed. The writing process is primarily a learning process, and you will continue planning, investigating, and organizing throughout that process.

2

Know your best writing situation

Definite principles of drafting are hard to come by because we know very little about how writers produce drafts. What we do know suggests that there may be almost as many ways to produce a successful draft as there are people to do it. Nevertheless, you can profit by learning as much as possible about what kind of situation is likely to help you produce your best writing. *Where* and *when* are you most comfortable and productive writing? *What conditions* do you prefer—complete quiet? music? Do you have any *rituals* that help—exercising beforehand? making a pot of coffee? Once you determine the atmosphere most conducive to your best writing, make every effort to do your drafting in that atmosphere.

>> *Some guidelines for drafting*

- *Have all your information close at hand and arranged according to your organizational plan.* Stopping to search for a piece of information can break your concentration or distract you.
- *Try to write in stretches of at least twenty minutes.* Writing can provide momentum, and once you get going, the task becomes easier.
- *Don't let small questions bog you down.* As you write, questions will come up that need to be answered. But unless they are major ones, just make a note of them or a tentative decision and move on.
- *Remember that a first draft need not be perfect.* In order to keep moving and get a draft done, you often must sacrifice some fine points of writing at this stage. Concentrate on getting all your ideas down on paper, and don't worry about anything else.
- *Stop writing at a place where you know exactly what will come next.* Doing this will help you start easily when you return to the draft.

Here is Jennifer Gerkin's first draft.

Prejudice in My Life

"Your daughter is absolutely beautiful!" the woman   1
gushed as she talked to my father. She was a friend of
his from work, and had heard much about my sister Tracy
and I, but had never met us before. I could tell that
she was one of those blunt, elderly ladies, the type that
pinches cheeks, because as soon as she finished appraising my sister, she turned to me with a deductive look in
her eye. Her face said it all. Her beady brown eyes
traveled slowly from my head to my toe as she sized me up
and said rather condescendingly, "Oh, and she must be the

smart one." I looked down at my toes as I rocked nervously back and forth. Then, looking at my sister I realized for the first time that she was very pretty, and I
was, well, the smart one.

The incident, which occurred when I was six and my   2
sister was seven, has changed me in many ways. Primarily, as a result of the harsh appraisal my father's
acquaintance gave me, I have always been very concerned
about my appearance. Conceivably, a concern about my
appearance can be beneficial, however, at times it is a
bit of an obsession. I have become overly critical of my
own appearance, but even more critical of the appearance
of those around me. I instantly judge a person by the
way he or she looks, a prejudice that includes everyone,
not just minorities.

Certainly, there are many men and women who are ob-   3
sessed with their appearance. Although my obsession over
my own appearance has relaxed dramatically over the past
few years, especially since I've been in college, it is
still a problem that affects my life in many ways. I can
remember exactly what I wore for every first day of
school since eighth grade, or on any other important day
of my life. Granted, this simply may mean that I have a
good memory, but I can also remember what a majority of
my friends wore on the first day of school, and describe
each garment with amazing speed and accuracy, right down
to the last accessory.

Similarly, I used to take two to two and a half   4
hours to get ready for school, church, shopping, or simply to walk the dog. Fortunately, I have cut my "primping time" down and can now get ready in a thrifty half an
hour.

My obsession with my appearance is something I can   5
overcome, or at least control, but as I mentioned before,

my critical eyes are always turned towards others. The minute I see someone, I assess them by their appearance. For example, if I see a person who is dressed shabbily, I instantly assume they are poor and unintelligent. If I see someone with fancy clothes and nice jewelry, I usually assume that they are rich and snobbish. For a more concrete example, on one of the first few days of class, a young man walked into my English class with a bandanna on his head and blue lipstick on his lips. I immediately thought, "What a weirdo!" Later, after talking to this classmate, I found that he was a very interesting, intelligent member of society that I respect very much. I am ashamed that I judge people so hastily, and I try very hard to overcome my prejudice.

I include everyone in my hasty assessment of people 6 by their appearance. So in a way, I guess I am extremely prejudiced. The only difference between my assessment of whites and of ethnic minorities is that the latter includes a few stereotypes, as well as "surface judgments." Hence, I have two hurdles to overcome; traditional stereotyping, and my own "personal stereotyping."

I have taken major steps to overcome my harsh judge- 7 ment of people. Several years ago, I would have let the fact that a classmate had blue lipstick and a bandanna on deprive me of meeting an interesting individual. Now I never let my first judgement of people be the one that counts; I find out how the person really is inside. This has widened my horizons to include many people that I may have never had the pleasure to meet had I maintained my original judgement.

I feel that many people are preoccupied with appear- 8 ances. When we overcome this shallow perception of our brothers and sisters, prejudice will vanish. I am waiting anxiously for the important day when we will no

```
longer judge each other according to what is on the out-
side, but for what is on the inside. And when this day
finally arrives, I promise to all mankind that I will not
remember what I was wearing.
```

EXERCISE 3.7

Write a draft of an essay from the plan you produced for Exercise 3.6.

Reflecting on your writing process

Once you finish a draft, make a point of reflecting a bit on your writing process and of noting your thoughts in your writing log if you are keeping one (see 1a7). With the experience of writing still fresh in your mind, you can note down what went well, what gave you problems and why, what you would like to change or improve.

When Jennifer Gerkin reflected on her writing process, she discovered that brainstorming with her classmates and clustering had been the most fruitful methods for generating ideas and examples and that answering questions to explain the topic hadn't added much. She also recognized that she felt very comfortable with her classmates and her professor (her audience), which made writing about something personal relatively easy. In addition, she saw that she'd worked extra hard to make her essay interesting, wanting to impress an audience she liked and respected so much. The main weaknesses, she decided, were in grammar, punctuation, organization, and diction. As for the strengths, Jennifer saw that by using her personal experiences, she made a serious topic quite approachable, even entertaining.

≫ *Thinking critically about your own writing process*

1. How did you arrive at your specific topic?
2. When did you first begin to think about the assignment?
3. What kinds of exploring or planning did you do?

4. How long did it take to complete your draft (including the time spent gathering information)?
5. Where did you write your draft? Briefly describe the setting.
6. How did awareness of your audience help to shape your draft?
7. What have you learned from your draft about your own rhetorical stance on your topic?
8. What did you learn about your ideas for this topic by exploring, planning, and talking to others about it?
9. What do you see as the major strengths of your draft?
10. What do you see as the major weaknesses of your draft?
11. What would you like to change about your drafting process?

THINKING CRITICALLY ABOUT YOUR OWN WRITING PROCESS

Using the preceding critical thinking guidelines, reflect on the process you went through as you prepared for and wrote the draft of your essay for Exercise 3.7. Make your answers an entry in your writing log, if you are keeping one.

4

Revising and Editing

There's only one person a writer should pay attention to. . . . It's the reader. And that doesn't mean any compromise or sell-out. The writer must criticize his or her own work *as a reader.*

— WILLIAM STYRON

Learn to trust your own judgment, learn inner independence, learn to trust that you will sort the good from the bad. . . .

— DORIS LESSING

THESE TWO EXPERIENCED WRITERS know firsthand the power that self-criticism and self-confidence bring to the task of revising. If you have analyzed your own process of writing, you probably know whether you tend to revise extensively and when you tend to make revisions. Perhaps you also know what kinds of revisions you typically make. And a careful look at any piece of writing you have submitted to an instructor will reveal how well you edited the paper. You may, however, have thought of revising and editing as the same thing; after all, both involve changes in a draft. The distinction between the processes of revising and editing, however, will be useful as you become a more powerful and more efficient writer.

Revising involves re-envisioning your draft—taking a fresh look at how clearly your thesis is stated and how persuasively it is developed, how effective your organization is, how varied your sentences are, how appropriate and memorable your choice of words is. In each case, you will be rethinking your aims and methods in terms of your original purpose and audience. Revising may call for changes both large and small. You may need to reshape sentences, rethink sections, gather more information to support a point, perhaps even do some further exploratory writing.

Editing, on the other hand, involves fine-tuning your prose, attending to details of grammar, usage, punctuation, and spelling. You might think of editing as the dress rehearsal for a written performance, making your writing ready for public presentation. This chapter will explore the processes of revising and editing and provide you with a systematic plan for making the best use of these processes in your own writing.

4a

Getting distance before revising

The ancient Roman poet Horace advised aspiring writers to get distance from their work by putting it away for nine years. If such advice seemed impractical to the Romans, it seems just about impossible to those writing in the late twentieth century. You have schedules to follow, deadlines to meet, examinations to take, graduation requirements to fulfill. Nevertheless, Horace's advice holds a germ of truth: the more time and distance you give yourself between the writing of a draft and its final revision, the more objectivity you will gain and the more options you will have as a writer. Even putting the draft away for a day or two will help clear your mind and give you some distance from your writing.

Everyday Use

We revise and edit all the time, even in our conversations. Directions to a child on how to measure ingredients for cupcakes may have to be revised on the spot, for instance, if the child isn't understanding, or a story may be revised in the telling to get the sequence of events right. You may well remember a time when you consciously edited what you were saying in order to be tactful or considerate of someone's feelings. For example, a woman seeing a new baby for the first time was stuck for what to say to the proud parents—for the baby struck her as anything but cute. Revising and editing rapidly in her head, she stumbled on what she hoped was a tactful as well as an honest response. "What a baby!" she exclaimed. "What a baby!"

For a portion of a day, listen carefully for revising and editing in conversations you hear or take part in. Then analyze what kinds of revisions you heard and what seemed most interesting about them.

4b

Rereading your draft

After giving yourself—and your draft—a rest before revising, review the draft by rereading it carefully for meaning, by recalling your purpose, and by considering your audience.

1

Rereading for meaning

Effective writers are almost always effective readers, particularly of their own writing. You can best begin revising, then, by rereading your draft carefully. For this reading, don't worry about small details. Instead, concentrate on your meaning and how clearly you have expressed it. If you see places where the meaning seems unclear, note them in the margin.

2

Remembering your purpose

After rereading, quickly note the main purpose of the piece of writing, and decide whether it matches your original purpose. You may want to go back to your original assignment to see exactly what it asks you to do. If the assignment asks you to prove something, make sure you have done so. If you intended to propose a solution to a problem, make sure you have indeed set forth a well-supported solution rather than, for instance, an analysis of the problem. (See 2c and 2d.)

3

Reconsidering your stance

Before or during the revision process, you can profit by taking time to look at your draft with one central question in mind: where are you coming from in this draft? That is, you should articulate the rhetorical stance you take in the draft and inquire what factors or influences have led you to that position. Early on in her revision process, Jennifer Gerkin noted that she felt she took a somewhat defensive stance in her draft, and she wondered what was making her feel and sound defensive. After brainstorming with her group and talking with her instructor, she decided that some of her feeling of defensiveness came from her growing recognition of how she had become prejudiced in ways that she had never before thought about and that frankly she did not like. She then decided to try to incorporate this insight into her revision.

4
Considering your audience

How appropriate is the essay for your audience? Think carefully about how your audience's experiences and expectations may be different from yours. (See 2h.) Will they be interested in and able to follow your discussion? Is the language formal or informal enough for these readers? Have you defined any terms they may not know? What objections might they raise?

▶ *FOR MULTILINGUAL WRITERS*
Asking a Native Speaker to Review Your Draft

One good way to make sure that your writing is well developed and easy to follow is to have someone else read it. You might find it especially helpful to ask a native speaker to read over your draft and to point out any words or patterns that are unclear or not idiomatic.

EXERCISE 4.1

Take twenty to thirty minutes to look critically at the draft you prepared for Exercise 3.7, rereading it carefully, checking to see how well the purpose is accomplished, and considering how appropriate the draft is for the audience. Then write a paragraph about how you would go about revising it.

4c

Collaborating with others: getting response to your draft

In addition to your own critical appraisal, you may want to get responses from friends or classmates. Although you may trust them to do a thorough job for you, remember that they probably don't want to hurt your feelings by criticizing your writing. You can help by convincing them that constructive criticism is what you need and that trying to "protect you" by not mentioning problems does you no good.

But even honestly critical readers need to know where to focus their responses. In some cases, you may get exactly the advice you need by asking a quick, direct question: "What do you see as my thesis?" Be sure to pose questions that require more than yes/no answers. Ask readers to tell you in detail what they see, and then compare their reading to what you see. Merely asking, "Is my thesis clear?" will not tell you nearly so much as, "Would you paraphrase my thesis so I can see if it's clear?"

The following are some questions for evaluating a draft. They can be used to respond to someone else's draft or one of your own. When you ask someone to evaluate your draft, be sure that person knows your assignment, intended audience, and major purposes.

≫ *Reviewing a draft*

1. *The assignment.* Does the draft carry out the assignment? What could the writer do to better fulfill the assignment?

2. *The title and introduction.* Does the title tell the reader what the draft is about? Does it catch the reader's interest? How? What does the opening accomplish? How else might the writer begin? (See 4f1 and 4f2.)

3. *The thesis and purpose.* Paraphrase the thesis as a promise: "In this paper I will . . ." Does the draft fulfill that promise? Why, or why not? Does it fulfill the writer's major purposes? (See 4b2 and 4d.)

4. *The audience.* How does the draft capture the interest of and appeal to the intended audience? (See 4b4.)

5. *The rhetorical stance.* Where does the writer stand on the issues involved in the topic? Is the writer an advocate or a critic? What words or phrases in the draft indicate the stance? Where does the writer's stance come from—that is, what influences have likely contributed to that stance? (See 4b3.)

6. *The supporting points.* List the main points in order of presentation. Then number them in order of interest to you. Review them one by one. Do any need to be explained more or less fully? Should any be eliminated? Do any seem confusing or boring? Do any make you want to know more? How well are the main points supported by evidence, examples, or details? (See 4d.)

7. *The organization.* What kind of overall organizational plan is used— spatial, chronological, logical, or some other plan? Are the points presented in the most useful order? What, if anything, might be moved? Can you suggest ways to make connections between paragraphs clearer and easier to follow? (See 4e.)

8. *The paragraphs.* Which paragraphs are clearest and most interesting to read, and why? Which ones are well developed? How are they developed? Which paragraphs need further development? What kind of information seems to be missing? (See 4g1.)

9. *The sentences.* Choose the three sentences you consider the most interesting or the best written—stylistically effective, entertaining, or otherwise memorable. Then choose three sentences you see as weak—confusing, awkward, or uninspired. Are the sentences varied in length, structure, and openings? (See 4g2.)

10. *The words.* Mark words that are particularly effective, that draw vivid pictures or provoke strong responses. Then mark words that are weak, vague, or unclear. Do any words need to be defined? Are the verbs active and vivid? Are any words potentially offensive, to the intended audience or to anyone else? (See 4g3.)

11. *The tone.* What dominant impression does the draft create—serious, humorous, satiric, persuasive, passionately committed, highly objective? Mark specific places where the writer's voice comes through most clearly. Is the tone appropriate to the topic and the audience? Is it consistent throughout? If not, is there a reason for its being varied? (See 4g4.)

12. *The conclusion.* Does the draft conclude in a memorable way, or does it seem to end abruptly or trail off into vagueness? If you like the conclusion, tell why. How else might it end? (See 4f3.)

13. *Final thoughts.* What are the main strengths and weaknesses of the draft? What surprised you, and why? What was the single most important thing said? What do you want to know more about?

Following are some responses Jennifer Gerkin got from three classmates, Tisha Clevinger, Chris Reeves, and Sean Finnerty:

1. *The assignment.* You do what we were asked to do: "Investigate the effect of prejudice on your life." (Clevinger)

2. *The introduction.* I like it . . . It's a dramatic scene that catches the reader's interest. Also, it makes the reader feel for the author. (Clevinger) Another way to begin would be with your first encounter with the young man in the bandanna and then use a flashback to give the cause of your prejudice. (Finnerty)

3. *The thesis.* No apparent thesis statement. (Finnerty) "In this paper I will describe how this incident has caused me to be very critical of myself and those around me, solely on the basis of looks." The essay fulfills the thesis by showing specific examples to illustrate the point. (Clevinger)

4. *The audience.* Well, we are your audience, along with Professor Walters. You got my attention right away. . . . I didn't feel like you ever talked down to us. (Clevinger)

5. *The rhetorical stance.* You take a very strong stand against prejudice, especially your own. It's clear that you are mostly criticizing yourself. Does this change a little at the end, though? (Reeves)

6. *The supporting points.* (1) Original cause of obsession, (2) obsession over your own appearance, (3) obsession and judgment of others' appearances, (4) realization of the ramifications of such judgments, (5) benefits. All these points are necessary. Each was interesting, but I'd like to see the part about the classmate with blue lipstick developed more. (Reeves)

7. *The organization.* The essay is organized in a cause-effect analysis. You show what causes your obsession with appearance and its effect on you. This is a good way to organize. The transitions are smooth. (Reeves)

8. *The paragraphs.* Paragraphs 1 and 5 are the most interesting because you tell the reader about your own experiences; paragraphs 3 and 4 are a close second; 5 and 6 might be stronger combined as one paragraph. (Clevinger) Paragraph 1 is the clearest, but 3 and 4 are the most interesting to read; 3 begins awkwardly, however: How about saving the statement about how you relaxed your prejudice until 7, where it would fit in better? (Finnerty)

9. *The sentences.* I like sentence 3 because it is very descriptive; I can picture the lady standing there. The last sentence is interesting and made me remember the essay. Sentence 29 could be reworded so that it reads more smoothly. (Reeves)

10. *The words.* The words *beady, harsh appraisal, thrifty,* and *horizons* are effective; I had difficulty with *deductive.* How about looking for some other words for *appearance?* You use it excessively. (Clevinger) I like the descriptive words in the first paragraph, except for *deductive; primarily* might be unnecessary in paragraph 2; paragraph 3 would be better without *dramatically* (*relaxed some* sounds more genuine). (Finnerty)

11. *The tone.* Serious and objective. This tone is appropriate because prejudice is a serious topic, and it's important to try to be objective about oneself. The last sentence is humorous in tone, which shows you are taking the topic seriously but taking yourself lightly. (Reeves)

12. *The conclusion.* The final sentence is memorable. (Clevinger, Reeves) Glad the paper ends humorously. (Clevinger) It could have ended by saying something about the woman in paragraph 1. (Reeves)

13. *Final thoughts.* The main strength of the paper is the way it keeps the reader's attention.

As these responses demonstrate, different readers may react in very different ways to the same piece of writing. They do not always agree on what is strong or weak, effective or ineffective; they may not even agree on what the thesis is. In addition, you may find that you simply do not agree with their advice. As the author, the authority on what you want to say, you must decide what advice to follow and how best to do so. In examining responses to your writing, you can often proceed efficiently by looking first for areas of agreement ("everyone was confused by this sentence—I'd better revise it") or strong disagreement ("one person said my conclusion was 'perfect,' and someone else said it 'didn't conclude'—better look carefully at that paragraph again").

THE INSTRUCTOR'S RESPONSE

Jennifer Gerkin also got some advice from her instructor, Professor Keith Walters, in the form of marginal comments on her draft. Here are excerpts from these comments.

The incident, which occurred when I was six and my   2
sister was seven, has changed me in many ways. Primarily ⟨,⟩
as a result of the harsh appraisal my father's
acquaintance gave me, I have always been very concerned
about my appearance. Conceivably, a concern about my *?*
appearance can be beneficial, however, at times it is a
bit of an obsession. I have become overly critical of my
own appearance, but even more critical of the appearance
of those around me. I instantly judge a person by the
way he or she looks, a prejudice that includes everyone,
└─────→ *Such judgments are not a prejudice*
not just minorities.   *but a practice that may be a basis for*
for   *prejudice.*
parallelism
    Similarly, I used to take two to two and a half   4
hours to get⟩ready for school, church, shopping, or
          ↓*ing*
simply t̶o̶ walk the dog. Fortunately, I have cut my
               ⌒
"primping time" down and can now get ready in a thrifty
half an hour. *Why a 2-sentence paragraph?*
    I feel that many people are preoccupied with   8
appearances. When we overcome this shallow perception of
our brothers and sisters, prejudice will vanish. I am

eagerly?

waiting <u>anxiously</u> for the important day when we will no

longer judge each other according to what is on the

by?

outside, but ⟨for⟩ what is on the inside. And when this day

finally arrives, I promise to all <u>mankind</u> that I will

Many writers now use

not remember what I was wearing. *humankind or people.*

<u>humankind</u> or <u>people</u>.

a great ending!

In addition, he suggested that she reconsider how well her examples work and that she add more concrete detail to make it easier for readers to imagine the examples. Based on all the responses she received, she decided to (1) state her thesis more explicitly, (2) provide concrete examples of her own biases, and (3) reconsider individual word choice as well as her conclusion.

EXERCISE 4.2

Using the questions listed in 4c as a guide, analyze the draft you wrote for Exercise 3.7.

4d

Evaluating the thesis and its support

Once you have received advice on your draft from all available sources and have studied the responses, reread the draft once more, paying special attention to your thesis and its support. Make sure your thesis sentence contains a clear statement of the *topic* that you will discuss and a *comment* explaining what is particularly significant or noteworthy about the topic. As you continue to read, ask yourself how each paragraph relates to or supports the thesis and how each sentence develops the paragraph topic. Such careful rereading can help eliminate irrelevant sections or details or identify sections needing further details or examples.

Be particularly careful to note what kinds of evidence, examples, or good reasons you offer in support of your major points. If some points need more support, look back at your exploratory work and at suggestions from your readers. Jennifer Gerkin, for example, saw that one of her readers had asked for further development of paragraph 6, and so she added two examples. If necessary, take time to gather more information and do further exploration (see 3a and 3c).

EXERCISE 4.3

After rereading the draft you wrote for Exercise 3.7, evaluate the revised working thesis you produced for Exercise 3.3, and then evaluate its support in the draft. Identify points that need further support, and list those things you must do to provide that support.

4e

Analyzing organization

One good way to check the organization of a draft is by outlining it. By drawing up an outline *after* the draft is finished, you can evaluate the organizational plan as it actually exists in the draft. After numbering the paragraphs in the draft, read through each one, jotting down its main idea or topic. Then examine your list and ask yourself the following questions:

What organizational strategies are used? spatial? chronological? logical? Are they used effectively? Why, or why not?

Do the main points clearly relate to the thesis and to one another? Are any of them irrelevant?

Can you identify any confusing leaps from point to point? Do you need to provide additional or stronger transitions?

Can you identify clear links between paragraphs and ideas? Do any others need to be added?

Have any important points been left out?

EXERCISE 4.4

Draw up a brief outline of Jennifer Gerkin's first draft (in 3f), and evaluate its organization. Begin by answering the questions in 4e.

EXERCISE 4.5

Check the paragraph transitions in Jennifer Gerkin's first draft (in 3f). Did you find any others that were weak or missing? If so, suggest at least two ways of strengthening them or adding some.

4f

Reconsidering the title, introduction, and conclusion

First and last impressions count. In fact, readers remember the first and last parts of a piece of writing better than anything else. For this reason, it is wise to pay careful attention to three important elements—the title, the introduction, and the conclusion.

1

The title

A good title gives readers information, draws them into the piece of writing, and even indicates the writer's view of the topic. It is an important device for defining what the writer is seeking to do. The title of Jennifer Gerkin's draft, "Prejudice in My Life," was accurate enough but not vivid or intriguing. Following a discussion of this draft, she produced a new draft and titled it "The Smart One." This revision piques readers' curiosity and leads up to the startling statement that ends paragraph 1, though it does not really let readers know the essay's topic.

2

The introduction

A good introduction accomplishes two important tasks: first, it draws readers into the piece of writing, and second, it presents the topic and makes some comment on it. It contains, in other words, a strong lead, or hook, to attract readers' interest and often an explicit thesis as well. One common kind of introduction opens with a general statement about the topic and then goes into more detail, leading up to a statement of the specific thesis at the end. A writer can also begin an introduction effectively with a *vivid statement* of the problem that led to the thesis or with an *intriguing quotation,* an *anecdote,* a *question,* or a *strong opinion.* The rest of the introduction then develops this beginning item into a more general or detailed presentation of the topic and the thesis. (See 6f.)

In many cases, especially when the writer begins with a quotation or an anecdote, the introduction consists of two paragraphs, the first providing the hook and the second, an explanation of its significance. Jennifer Gerkin followed this pattern in her introduction, whose first paragraph contains a very strong hook: a narrative anecdote from her childhood that immediately appeals to readers. The second paragraph then explains how this experience led to the obsession with appearance that is her topic. Although she considered the suggestion of one of her respondents that she shift the order of paragraphs and open with paragraph 2 in order to make the topic clear immediately, she decided that the dramatic opening paragraph makes the introduction more effective.

3

The conclusion

Like introductions, conclusions present special challenges to a writer. A good conclusion leaves readers satisfied that a full discussion has taken place. Often a conclusion will begin with a restatement of the thesis and end with more general statements that grow out of it; this pattern reverses the common general-to-specific pattern of the introduction. Writers can also draw on a number of other ways to conclude effectively, including a *provocative question*, a *quotation*, a *vivid image*, a *call for action*, a *warning*, (See 6f for a fuller discussion and examples of various kinds of conclusions.)

Jennifer Gerkin's concluding paragraph clearly restates her thesis, and the final sentence packs just the punch she wanted. But the first three sentences are general, and two of her respondents described them as "too idealistic" and "righteous and heavy." She decided to qualify her statements in the second sentence and thus make the conclusion more realistic.

When we overcome this shallow perception of our brothers
                          may not disappear but will certainly diminish.
and sisters, prejudice ~~will vanish.~~
                        ∧

EXERCISE 4.6

Review Jennifer Gerkin's draft in 3f, and compose an alternative conclusion, perhaps taking the advice of one of her respondents to "end by saying something about the woman in paragraph 1." Then write a paragraph commenting on the strengths and weaknesses of the conclusion she used.

4g

Examining paragraphs, sentences, words, and tone

In addition to the large-scale task of examining the logic, organization, and development of their writing, effective writers look closely at the smaller elements: paragraphs, sentences, and words. Many writers, in fact, look forward to this part of revising because its results are often dramatic. Turning a bland sentence into a memorable one—or finding exactly the right word to express a thought—can yield great satisfaction and self-confidence.

1

Examining paragraphs

Paragraphing serves the reader by visually breaking up long expanses of writing and signaling a shift in focus. Readers expect a paragraph to develop an idea or a topic, a process that almost always demands several sentences or more (see 6a). The following guidelines can help you evaluate your paragraphs as you revise:

1. Look for the topic or main point of each paragraph, whether it is stated or implied. Then check to see that every sentence expands, supports, or otherwise relates to the topic.
2. Check to see how each paragraph is organized—spatially, chronologically, or by some logical relationship. Then determine whether the organization is appropriate to the topic of the paragraph and whether it is used fully to develop the paragraph. (See 6c and 6d.)
3. Count the number of sentences in each paragraph, noting paragraphs that have only a few. Do these paragraphs sufficiently develop the topic of the paragraph? See also the guidelines for editing paragraphs at the end of Chapter 6.

In paragraph 4 of her draft, Jennifer Gerkin had only two sentences, and these actually illustrate a point made in paragraph 3. She decided, therefore, to combine the two paragraphs and elaborate on the first sentence in the original paragraph 4.

> . . . Similarly, I used to take two to two and a half
>
> hours to get ready for school, church, shopping, or
>
> simply to walk the dog. Fortunately, I have cut my
>
> "primping time" down and can now get ready in a thrifty
>
> half an hour. *For example, I might try on five different outfits (and five different shades of lipstick), none of which would satisfy my demanding eyes.*

EXERCISE 4.7

Choose two other paragraphs in Jennifer Gerkin's draft in 3f, and evaluate them using the guidelines listed above. Write a brief paragraph in which you suggest ways to improve the development or organization of these paragraphs.

2

Examining sentences

Good sentences operate like a well-practiced marching band, each one moving forward in an orderly and impressive way that keeps readers engaged and ready for more. As with life, variety is the spice of sentences. You can add variety to the life of your sentences by looking closely at their length, structure, and opening patterns. (See the guidelines for editing sentences at the end of Chapter 7.)

Varying sentence length

Too many short sentences, especially one after another, can sound like a series of blasts on a car horn—or like an elementary school textbook—whereas a steady stream of long sentences may tire or confuse readers. Most writers aim for some variety of length, then, breaking up a series of fairly long sentences with a very brief one, for example.

In looking at paragraph 2, Jennifer Gerkin found that all of its five sentences were almost exactly the same length: nineteen, twenty-two, nineteen, twenty, and twenty words. In revising, she decided to shorten the second sentence (to make the comparison more dramatic) and to extend the last sentence to thirty-six words.

The incident, which occurred when I was six and my
sister was seven, has changed me in many ways.
~~One~~ that has been an
~~Primarily as a~~ result of ~~the~~∧harsh appraisal ~~my father's~~
extreme concern for
~~acquaintance gave me, I have always been very concerned~~

~~about~~ my appearance. Conceivably, a concern about my

appearance can be beneficial; however, at times it is a

bit of an obsession. I have become overly critical of my

own appearance, but even more critical of the appearance

of those around me. I instantly judge a person by the
practice that is the basis for prejudice and one that limits my
way he or she looks, a∧~~prejudice that includes everyone,~~
appreciation of myself as well as of others.
~~not just minorities.~~

Varying sentence structure

The simple sentence is the most common kind of sentence in modern English, but using only simple sentences can be very dull. On the other hand, overusing compound sentences may result in a singsong or repetitive rhythm, and strings of complex sentences may sound, well, overly complex. It is best to vary your sentence structures (see 22c).

Varying sentence openings

If anyone has ever noted that your writing seemed choppy, the cause of the problem probably lay in unvaried sentence openings. Most sentences in English follow subject-predicate order and hence open with the subject of an independent clause, as does the sentence you are now reading. But opening too many sentences in a row this way results in a jerky, abrupt, or choppy rhythm. You can vary sentence openings by beginning with a dependent clause, a phrase, an adverb, a conjunctive adverb, or a coordinating conjunction. (See 22b.)

Jennifer Gerkin's opening paragraph provides vivid description and imaginative use of dialogue, but it can be improved by varying the sentence openings. Note how revising some of the openings improves the flow and makes the entire paragraph easier to read and more memorable.

"Your daughter is absolutely beautiful!" the woman
gushed as she talked to my father. ~~She was a~~ [A] friend of
his from work, ~~and~~ [she] had heard much about my sister
Tracy and I, but had never met us before. I could tell
that she was one of those blunt, elderly ladies, the type
that pinches cheeks, because as soon as she finished
appraising my sister, she turned to me with a deductive
look in her eye. Her face said it all. [B] ~~Her b~~eady brown
eyes ~~traveled~~ [traveling] slowly from my head to my toe, ~~as~~ she sized
me up and said rather condescendingly, "Oh, and she must
be the smart one." I looked down at my toes as I rocked
nervously back and forth. Then, looking at my sister I

realized for the first time that she was very pretty, and

I was, well, the smart one.

Checking for sentences opening with it and there

As you go over the sentences of your draft, look especially carefully at those beginning with *it* or *there* followed by a form of *be*. Sometimes such a construction can create a special emphasis, as in "It was a dark and stormy night." But such structures can also easily be overused or misused. You don't know what *it* means, for instance, unless the writer has already pointed out exactly what the word stands for (see 13c). A more subtle problem with these openings, however, is that they may be used to avoid taking responsibility for a statement. Look at the following two sentences:

It is necessary to raise student fees.

The university must raise student fees.

The first sentence avoids responsibility by failing to tell us *who says* it is necessary. (See 23a1.)

EXERCISE 4.8

Here are two sentences from Jennifer Gerkin's draft that feature *it is* or *there are*. Make at least two revisions that eliminate these constructions.

1. Certainly, there are many men and women who are obsessed with their appearance.

2. Conceivably, a concern about my appearance can be beneficial; however, at times it is a bit of an obsession.

EXERCISE 4.9

Find a paragraph in your own writing that lacks variety in sentence length, sentence structure, or sentence openings. Then write a revised version.

3

Examining words

Even more than paragraphs and sentences, **word choice**, or diction, offers writers an opportunity to put their personal stamp on a piece of writing. As a result, writers often study their diction carefully, making sure they get the most mileage out of each word. Because word choice is highly individual, general guidelines are hard to define. Nevertheless, the following questions should help you become aware of the kinds of words you most typically use:

1. Are the nouns primarily abstract and general or concrete and specific? Too many abstract and general nouns can create boring prose. To say that you bought a new car is much less memorable and interesting than to say you bought a new convertible or a new Nissan. (See Chapter 27c.)

2. Are there too many nouns in relation to the number of verbs? The *effect* of the *overuse* of *nouns* in *writing* is the *placing* of too much *strain* on the inadequate *number* of *verbs* and the resultant *prevention* of *movement* of the *thought*. In the preceding sentence, one tiny form of the verb *be* (*is*) has to drag along the entire weight of all those nouns. The result is a heavy, boring sentence. Why not say instead, *Overusing nouns places a big strain on the verbs and consequently slows down the prose?*

3. How many verbs are forms of *be?* If *be* verbs account for more than about a third of your total verbs, you are probably overusing them. (See Chapter 9.)

4. Are verbs *active* wherever possible? Passive verbs are harder to read and remember than active ones. Although the passive voice has many uses (see Chapter 9), often your writing will be stronger, more lively, and more energetic if you use active verbs.

5. Are your words *appropriate?* Check to be sure they are not too fancy— or too casual. (See Chapter 27.)

Jennifer Gerkin made a number of changes in diction on the basis of her classmates' responses, her instructor's comments, and her own critical analysis. In paragraph 1, for example, her use of *deductive* puzzled several people. After checking the dictionary, she decided she had chosen the wrong word and substituted *judgmental*. In addition, she replaced overly general words in several places, changing *looked* to *stared* in paragraph 1 and *fancy* to *stylish* and *nice* to *expensive* in paragraph 5. Finally, in the last sentence, she took her instructor's suggestion and substituted *humankind* for *mankind,* which many people object to as sexist.

4

Examining tone

Word choice is closely related to **tone,** the attitude toward the topic and the audience that the writer's language conveys. In examining the tone of your draft, you need to consider the nature of the topic, your own attitude toward it, and that of your intended audience. Check for connotations of words as well as for slang, jargon, emotional language, and the level of formality to see whether they create the tone you want to achieve (humorous, serious, impassioned, and so on) and whether that tone is an appropriate one, given your audience and topic. You may even discover from your tone that your own attitude toward the topic, your rhetorical stance, is different from what you originally thought. (See Chapter 27.)

Since Jennifer Gerkin's respondents and instructor praised her draft highly for its combination of humor, seriousness, and objectivity, she felt that her general tone needed no major changes. As mentioned earlier, however, she did revise her conclusion somewhat to tone down its excessive idealism and "righteous and heavy" quality.

EXERCISE 4.10

Turn to 3f, and read Jennifer Gerkin's paragraphs 3, 4, and 5. Describe the tone you think she achieves. Does it seem appropriate to the audience she was writing to—her professor and classmates in a first-year college writing course—and to her topic? Assume these paragraphs are intended instead for a group of third-graders. What would you do to alter the tone for this audience?

4h

Determining format

Before you produce a copy for final editing and proofreading, take the time to consider issues of format. It will be obvious to you whether you are working with handwritten, typed, or word-processed copy, of course. But particularly in the latter case, you have many helpful formatting options. You can easily insert headings in a larger size type or in bold type, for instance. You can consider using a different font for examples. If you have a graphics program, you can easily include charts or other illustrations. Whatever your final decisions, now is the time to think carefully about the overall visual appearance of your final draft. (See Chapter 51.)

4i

Editing

Because readers expect, even demand, a final copy that is clean and correct in every way, and because you want to put your very best foot forward in any formal writing you do, you need to make time for thorough and careful editing. You can make editing somewhat systematic by keeping a personal checklist of editing problems. All writers have personal trouble spots, problems that come up again and again in their writing. You may already be aware of some of your own trouble spots and will probably have others pointed out to you. Paying attention to the *patterns* of editing problems you find in your writing can help you overcome errors.

An editing inventory

After identifying any typical trouble spots in your writing and getting advice on editing from this handbook, organize the information you have gathered in a systematic way. To begin, list all the errors or corrections marked on the last piece of writing you did. Then note the context of the sentence in which each error appeared. Finally, try to derive a guideline to spot future errors of the same kind. You can broaden these guidelines as you begin to find patterns of errors, and you can then add to your inventory every time you write and edit a draft. Here is an example of such a checklist.

MARKED ERRORS	IN CONTEXT	LOOK FOR
wrong preposition	*to* for *on*	*to*
spelling	*to* for *too*	*to* before adjectives and adverbs
fragment	starts with *when*	sentences beginning with *when*
spelling	*a lot*	*alot*
missing comma	after *however*	sentences opening with *however*
missing apostrophe	*Michael's*	all names
missing apostrophe	*company's*	all possessive nouns
tense shift	*go* for *went*	use of present tense
spelling	*sacrifice*	*sacrafice*
comma	after *for example*	use of introductory elements

This writer has begun to isolate patterns, like her tendency to write sentence fragments beginning with subordinating conjunctions (*when* and *while*) and her tendency to leave out apostrophes in possessives (*company's* and *Michael's*) and commas after introductory elements.

Some errors, such as the use of wrong words and misspellings, may seem so unsystematic that you are unable to identify patterns in them. If spelling presents a special problem for you, try keeping a spelling checklist (24f), or getting a spelling checker as part of a word-processing program. Keeping an editing checklist will gradually allow you to identify most of the problems that regularly trouble you.

EXERCISE 4.11

Using several essays you have written, establish your own editing checklist based on the one shown in 4i.

4j

Proofreading the final draft

As a writer, you need to make your final draft as free from error as possible. You can do so by taking time for one last, careful proofreading, which means reading to correct any typographical errors or other slips, such as inconsistencies in spelling and punctuation. To proofread most effectively, read through the copy aloud, making sure that punctuation marks are used correctly and consistently, that all sentences are complete, and that no words are left out. Then go through it again, this time reading backwards so that you can focus on each individual word and its spelling. This final proofreading aims to make your written product letter-perfect, something you can be proud of.

You have already seen and read about a number of the revisions Jennifer Gerkin made in her first draft. The following is the edited and proofread version she turned in to her instructor. If you compare her final draft with her first draft, you will notice a number of additional changes made in editing and proofreading. For example, she corrected *I* to *me* in the second sentence, made the spelling of *judgment* consistent, made several pronouns singular in new paragraph 4 to agree with their antecedents, and deleted unnecessary commas. What other improvements can you spot?

```
Jennifer Gerkin
Professor Walters
English 110
October 18, 1991

                    The Smart One

     "Your daughter is absolutely beautiful!" the woman      1

gushed to my father. A friend of his from work, she had

heard much about my sister Tracy and me but had never met

us before. I could tell that she was one of those blunt,

elderly ladies, the type that pinches cheeks, because as
```

soon as she finished appraising my sister, she turned to
me with a judgmental look in her eye. Her face said it
all. Beady brown eyes traveling slowly from my head to my
toes, she sized me up and said rather condescendingly,
"Oh, and she must be the smart one." I stared down at my
toes and I rocked nervously back and forth. Then, looking
at my sister, I realized for the first time that she was
very pretty, and I was, well, the smart one.

This incident, which occurred when I was six and my   2
sister was seven, has affected me in many ways. One
result of that harsh appraisal has been an extreme concern for my appearance. Although some concern about how
one looks can be beneficial, at times it has become a bit
of an obsession with me. I have become not only overly
critical of my own appearance but even more critical of
the appearance of those around me. I instantly judge a
person by the way he or she looks, a practice that is the
basis of most kinds of prejudice and one that limits my
appreciation of myself and of others.

Although many men and women are preoccupied with   3
their appearance, my particular obsession has affected my
life to an extent that now seems incredible to me. I can
remember exactly what I have worn on the first day of
school every year since eighth grade and on every other
important day of my life. Often, I attempt to attribute
these amazing recollections to the fact that I have a
good memory. However, additional evidence confirms that
an obsession with appearance better accounts for my
behavior. I can also recall what a majority of my friends
wore on the first day of school and describe each garment
with amazing speed and accuracy, right down to the last
accessory, whereas I remember almost nothing about the
day's events. Similarly, I used to take more than two
hours to get ready for school, church, shopping, or even
walking the dog. I would, for example, frantically try

on five different outfits and five different shades of
lipstick, none of which would satisfy my demanding eyes.
Fortunately, since coming to college, I have cut down my
"primping time" and can now get ready in a thrifty half
hour.

My obsession with my own appearance is something I   4
have managed to overcome or at least control, but it
affects my relationships as well: my critical eyes are
always turned toward others. The minute I see someone, I
assess him or her on the basis of appearance. For example, if I see a person who is dressed shabbily, I instantly assume that she is poor and unintelligent. If I
see someone with stylish clothes and expensive jewelry, I
usually assume that he is rich and snobbish. More specifically, on one of the first few days of this quarter, a
young man walked into my English class wearing a bandanna
on his head and blue lipstick. I immediately thought,
"What a weirdo!" Later, after talking to this classmate,
I have come to realize that he is a very interesting, intelligent person whom I respect very much.

I include everyone in my hasty assessment of people   5
by their appearance. The only difference between my
assessment of my fellow whites and that of other ethnic
groups is that my assessment of minorities includes a few
traditional stereotypes, as well as "surface judgments"
based on appearances. For example, when I see a woman
wearing the traditional Muslim veil, I instantly assume
she is meek and subservient to men; when I see an Amish
family in a black horse-drawn buggy, I assume that their
lives are dull and emotionally repressed. Hence, I have
two hurdles to overcome: traditional stereotyping and my
own "personal stereotyping."

I am ashamed that I judge people so hastily, and I   6
try very hard to overcome my prejudice because I realize
it limits me. Several years ago, I would have let the

fact that a classmate wore blue lipstick and a bandanna
deprive me of meeting an interesting individual. Now, I
try never to let my first judgment of people be the one
that counts; I make the effort to find out how the person
really is inside. I have widened my horizons to include
many delightful people whom I might never have had the
pleasure to meet had I maintained my original judgment.

I know, however, that many people in our society   7
remain preoccupied with appearances. When this shallow
perception of our brothers and sisters is overcome, prejudice may not disappear, but it will certainly diminish.
Eagerly, I await the important day when we no longer
judge each other according to what is on the outside but
pay attention instead to what is on the inside. And when
this day finally arrives, I promise all humankind that I
will not remember what I--or anyone else--was wearing.

EXERCISE 4.12   Reading with an Eye for Revision

Using the guidelines in 4c, read the draft you wrote in Exercise 3.7 with an eye
to revising. Try to do this at least a day after the time you finished the draft.
List the things you need or want to address in your revision. At this point, you
may want to exchange drafts with some classmates and share responses.

EXERCISE 4.13

Revise, edit, and proofread the draft you wrote for Exercise 3.7.

THINKING CRITICALLY ABOUT YOUR OWN REVISING PROCESS

1. How did you begin revising?
2. What kinds of comments on or responses to your draft did you have?
   How helpful were they, and why?
3. How long did revising take? How many drafts did you produce?

4. Were the revisions that you tended to make mostly additions? deletions? replacements of one word, one example, and so on by another? transfers of material from one place to another?

5. What kinds of changes did you tend to make? in organization, paragraphs, sentence structure, wording, adding or deleting information?

6. What gave you the most trouble as you were revising?

7. What pleased you most? What would you most like to change about your process of revising, and how do you plan to go about doing so?

5

Thinking Critically: Constructing and Analyzing Arguments

*H*OW DO WE COME TO MAKE UP OUR MINDS *about something? What causes us to give our assent to some ideas and people and yet withhold them from others? And how do we seek—and sometimes gain—agreement from others? These are questions that thinkers have pondered down through the ages, from Plato, Confucius, Mohammed, and the Apostle Paul to Joan of Arc, Mahatma Gandhi, Václav Havel, Nelson Mandela, and Rigoberta Menchú. The need to explore such questions, however, has never been more pressing than it is today, as language intended to persuade us—to gain our assent (and often our souls, our bank accounts, and our votes as well)—surrounds us more than ever before. This language—in advertisements, news stories, textbooks, reports, and electronic media of all kinds—not only competes for our attention but argues for our agreement as well.*

In fact, even supposedly abstract and seemingly objective subjects like mathematics depend to a large extent on successful **argument***: language whose purpose is to persuade. As two professors have pointed out, the common idea that mathematics represents some unchanging and absolute truth is in fact a myth. "Mathematics in real life is a form of social interaction," they note, in which "proving" anything involves a mixture "of calculations and casual comments, of convincing argument and appeals to the imagination."* As in mathematics, issues in medical and other scientific research often are resolved more through argumentation and interpretation of data than through reference to just "the facts."*

Since argument so pervades our lives, we need to understand and be able to recognize and use it effectively—and to question our own arguments as well as those put forth by others. This chapter offers practice in the survival arts of recognizing, understanding, questioning, and using written arguments.

---

*Philip J. Davis and Reuben Hersh, *Descartes' Dream: The World According to Mathematics* (Boston: Houghton, 1988).

5a

Thinking critically

Although **critical thinking** may be given a number of fancy or complex definitions, one good way to assign meaning to this term is to say that it is the process by which we make sense of all the information around us. As such, critical thinking is a crucial component of argument, for it guides us in recognizing, formulating, and examining the arguments that are important to us. For the purposes of considering such arguments, several elements of critical thinking are especially important:

Taking a questioning stance. Rather than accepting your own ideas and beliefs as true, and rather than accepting what you read, see, and hear at face value, you should approach all ideas with a potentially critical eye.

Asking pertinent questions. Concentrate on asking questions that will get to the heart of the matter at hand, questions that will yield a path for exploration or pave the way for answers. Whether you are thinking about ideas put forth by others or about those you yourself hold, you will want to ask the following kinds of questions:

- What is the writer's agenda?
- Why does he or she hold these ideas or beliefs?
- What larger social, economic, political, or other conditions may have influenced these ideas?
- What does the writer want readers to do—and why?
- What reasons does the writer offer in support of his or her ideas? Are they good reasons?
- What sources does the writer rely on? How reliable are they? What agendas do these sources have?
- What objections might be made to the argument?
- What are the writer's underlying or unstated assumptions? Are they acceptable—and why, or why not?

Getting necessary information. Often you will need to find additional data to help you decide whether to accept or reject an argument. Consider the need for *more information* on the topic as well as for *other perspectives;* both will be of value. (See Chapters 41 and 42.)

Interpreting and assessing information. No information that comes to us in language is neutral. Just like a photograph that presents one view of the world by focusing on a tiny tree-lined park instead of on a dingy high-rise right down the street, all information has a perspective, an interpretation. Your job as a critical thinker is to identify the perspective or interpretation—to *assess* that interpretation, examining its sources and finding out what you can about its context. Asking the kinds of pertinent questions suggested above will help you examine the interpretations and conclusions drawn by others. **Making and assessing your own arguments.** The ultimate goal of all critical thinking is to construct your own ideas, reach your own conclusions. These too you must question and assess. The rest of this chapter will guide you in the art of making and assessing your own arguments.

5b

Recognizing argument

In one important sense, all language use has an argumentative edge. Even when you greet someone warmly, you wish to convince the person that you are genuinely glad to see him or her, that you value his or her presence. In this sense, we are immersed in argument the way we are immersed in air. Advertisements argue that we should buy certain products; clothing argues that we should admire or respect the people inside; our friends argue—through their actions, their language, even their personal style—that we should accept and value them.

Even apparently objective news reporting has strong argumentative overtones. By putting a particular story on the front page, for example, a paper argues that this subject is more important than others; by using emotional language and focusing on certain details in reporting an event, a newscaster tries to persuade us to view the event in a particular way. What one reporter might call *a massive demonstration,* for example, another might call *a noisy protest,* and yet another, *an angry march.* We can find this argumentative edge, therefore, wherever we find meaning in language. The pervasiveness of language used in these ways led one language philosopher to define human beings as "wordlings" and another to note that the words we use are already full of the meanings other users have given them. To get in on the conversation, we have to join in the argument over what words mean.

Jennifer Gerkin's primary purpose in her essay "The Smart One" (in 4j) is to explain the roots of her own prejudice. Yet her essay clearly has an argumentative edge: to persuade readers to guard against their own biases. In this essay, therefore, explanation plays the major role and argument, a secondary role. This chapter, in contrast, will look at writing whose primary purpose is argument and, specifically, at ways to provide convincing support for a claim.

Everyday Use

Perhaps the most pervasive form of argument we face in our everyday lives is advertising. From the cereal box at breakfast to the posters on the bus to a few minutes of television before bed, advertisements call out to us to buy some product, vote for some candidate, behave in some particular way. To get a sense of how much advertising comes into your everyday life, keep a notebook with you for one day and put down a mark every time you see or hear an advertisement. Count up your total at the end of the day, and compare your count with those of others in your class. Where did you encounter advertising most often? Which of the advertisements were particularly powerful, and why?

1

Understanding the purposes of argument: personal style and the question of gender

If all language is in some sense argumentative, then it goes almost without saying that the purposes of argument will vary widely. For many, many years, however, traditional notions of argumentation tended to highlight one purpose—winning. While winning is still one important purpose of argumentation, studies of the argumentative strategies of people from groups historically excluded from public debate—including women and citizens of color—have demonstrated that conquest is by no means the only purpose of argument. Nor may it be the one you may most often wish to use. For instance, if you are trying to decide whether to major in business or in chemistry, you may want to consider, or "argue," all sides of the issue. Your purpose is hardly to win out over someone else, however. Instead, your purpose is to understand your choices in order to make a wise decision.

This chapter cannot provide a full description of all the purposes of argument. A brief overview of the major purposes of argument, however, will help you examine your own purposes for arguing:

To win or conquer

The most traditional purpose of academic argument, arguing to win is used in campus debating societies, in political debates, in trials, and often in business. The writer or speaker aims to control the audience, to present a position that prevails over or defeats the positions of others. Presidential debates, for example, aim to produce a winner. Like other arguments whose purpose is to win, such debates are focused most often not on changing the opponent's mind but on defeating him or her in order to appeal to another party—in the case of presidential debates, the voting public. In the case of a trial, two lawyers attempt to defeat each other in order to appeal to a third party, either the judge or the jury.

To convince

More often than not, out-and-out defeat of another is not only unrealistic but undesirable. Rather, the goal is *to convince* another person to change his or her mind about an issue. Doing so calls on a writer to provide reasons so compelling that the audience willingly agrees with the writer's conclusion. Such is the goal of Dr. Jack Kevorkian, who knows he cannot conquer or defeat those who oppose assisted suicide. Rather, Kevorkian realizes he must provide reasons compelling enough to change people's minds. And such would be your purpose if you were asked to prepare a report on the major causes of the Civil War: your job would be to convince your readers that you have identified the major causes.

To reach a decision or explore an issue

This purpose often calls on the writer to enter into conversation with others, to collaborate in seeking the best possible understanding of a problem, exploring all possible approaches, and choosing the best alternative in a particular context. Argument *to decide or explore* seeks not to conquer or control others or even to convince. Rather, it seeks a sharing of information and perspectives in order to make informed political, professional, and personal choices. This is the purpose you will probably have in many situations—from trying to decide which computer to buy to exploring the best health care system for an elderly relative. Such situations, and many others like them, are ones that are not combative or competitive but are instead based on collaborating with others to reach the best possible decision.

2
Knowing when argument is appropriate

Of course, argument is not always necessary. If everyone can agree on the truth of a statement, no argument is needed. For instance, saying that personal ownership of computers in North America has increased in the last twenty years is a factual statement that should not produce an argument. On the other hand, saying that computers pose dangers to mental health is an arguable assertion that must be convincingly supported before readers will accept it.

In many important areas of our lives, widespread agreement seldom exists. Is nuclear-power generation necessary? Should we take one job or another, live in one location or another, marry one person or another, or marry at all? Should our town increase taxes for schools? Should we risk job security by protesting a policy we feel to be unethical? Is a new building an architectural masterpiece or an eyesore? Is the use of pesticides threatening the lives of farm workers? Such arguable questions are often at the center of our lives, and in most instances they fall into that area where absolute knowledge or truth is simply unavailable.

To acknowledge that we can seldom find absolute answers to personal, political, and artistic questions, however, is not to say that we cannot move toward agreement on such questions by thinking clearly about them. In fact, this is precisely the way we gain most human knowledge: by arguing through and, sometimes, coming to agreement on crucial issues.

In much of your work in college, you will be asked to participate in this process by taking a position and arguing for that position—whether to analyze a trend or explain a historical event or prove a mathematical equation. Such work will usually call for you to convince or decide and will therefore require you to make an arguable statement, to make a claim based on the statement, and finally to present good reasons in support of the claim.

3
Checking whether a statement can be argued

An early step in the process of argument to convince or decide is to make a statement about a topic and then check to see that the statement can, in fact, be argued. An arguable statement should have three characteristics:

1. It should attempt to convince readers of something, change their minds about something, or urge them to do something—or explore a topic in order to make a wise decision.
2. It should address a problem for which no easily acceptable solution exists or ask a question to which no absolute answer exists.
3. It should present a position that readers might realistically have varying perspectives on.

EXERCISE 5.1

Using the three characteristics in 5b3, decide which of the following statements are arguable and which are not.

1. *Schindler's List* was the best movie of the last twenty years.
2. The climate of the earth is gradually getting warmer.

3. The United States must further reduce military spending in order to balance the budget.
4. Shakespeare died in 1616.
5. Marlowe really wrote the plays of Shakespeare.
6. Water boils at 212 degrees Fahrenheit.
7. Van Gogh's paintings are the work of a madman.
8. The incidence of lung cancer has risen in the last ten years.
9. Abortion denies the fetus's inherent right to life.
10. The fifty-five-mile-per-hour speed limit lowers accident rates.

5c

Formulating an argumentative thesis

Once you have an arguable statement, you need to make a claim about it, one you will then ask readers to accept. Your claim becomes the working thesis for your argument. For example, look at the following statement:

The use of pesticides endangers the lives of farm workers.

This statement is arguable—it aims to convince, it addresses an issue with no easily identifiable answer, and it can realistically be disputed.

Although it does make a kind of claim—that pesticides threaten lives—the claim is just a factual statement about *what is*. To develop a claim that can become the working thesis for an argument, you usually need to direct this kind of statement toward some action; that is, your claim needs to move from *what is* to *what ought to be*.

STATEMENT ABOUT WHAT IS	Pesticides endanger the lives of farm workers.
CLAIM ABOUT WHAT OUGHT TO BE	Because pesticides endanger the lives of farm workers, their use should be banned.

This claim becomes your argumentative thesis. Like any working thesis, it contains two elements: a topic (the statement about what is), and a comment (the claim about what ought to be). See 3b for more discussion of how to formulate a thesis.

```
                    ┌──────────── TOPIC ────•─────────────┐
Because  pesticides endanger the lives of farm workers,
         ┌────── COMMENT ──────┐
         their use should be banned.
```

Recognizing implied theses

In some fields, such as literature or history, you will usually be making a claim that urges readers not to take action but to interpret something in a certain way, to see certain information as you see it. Doing so calls on you first to offer readers your interpretation as clearly as possible and then to support your interpretation in a way that will bring readers to share your view.

In such cases, the claim about what ought to be is usually implied rather than stated. For example, a history report making the claim that moral opposition to slavery was the major cause of the Civil War is in effect arguing that readers should view the Civil War in this light—that they should accept this particular interpretation of its cause—rather than seeing the cause as a constitutional struggle over states' rights or an economic conflict between northern industrialists and southern planters. Or if you are asked on an art history exam to argue the claim that van Gogh's paintings are the works of a madman, you are in effect trying to persuade your instructor to view van Gogh's works as unconscious products of a disordered mind rather than the result of conscious, rational artistic decisions.

EXERCISE 5.2

Using two arguable statements from Exercise 5.1 or two that you create, formulate two working argumentative theses, identifying the topic and the comment of each one.

EXERCISE 5.3

Formulate an arguable statement, and create a working argumentative thesis, for two of the following general topics.

1. The Bosnian conflict
2. Mandatory testing of prison inmates for HIV
3. Free access to computers for all students on campus
4. A new federal student-loan program
5. Surrogate motherhood

Formulating good reasons

In his *Rhetoric,* Aristotle discusses the various ways one can argue a point. Torture, he notes, makes for a very convincing argument, but not one that reasonable people will resort to. As our increasingly violent society may be coming to realize, a pointed gun is no substitute for good reasons. In effecting real changes in minds and hearts, we need instead to rely on *good reasons* that establish credibility, that appeal to logic, and that appeal to emotion.

5e

Using narratives to support an argument

Because storytelling is universal, narratives can be very persuasive in helping readers understand and accept an argument. In arguing for increased funding for the homeless, for instance, you might include a brief narrative about a day in the life of a homeless person, to dramatize the issue and help readers *see* the need for more funding.

1

Using personal stories

Stories drawn from your own experience can exert great appeal to readers, for they can help make your point in true-to-life, human terms and establish your credibility by helping readers know you better and therefore identify with you more closely. In arguing that health care should be universal in the United States, President Clinton often draws on personal stories of his own family's experience with the current system. In much the same way, the writer bell hooks tells the story of her own experience with elitist educational institutions as a way of arguing for changes in those institutions.

2

Taking care to use narrative appropriately

As with all other appeals, make sure that any stories you relate are used not merely to tell a story but rather to support your thesis. Be sure as well that you do not rely solely on the power of stories to carry your argument, since doing so can make you seem focused too much on yourself (and perhaps not enough on your readers).

arg

In writing the essay at the end of this chapter, Jennifer Georgia began by reflecting on her own experiences with her topic, choosing a major field of study. As a result, her first draft rested heavily on her own story about why she designed her own major. Readers liked hearing her story, but they told her that for her argument to be convincing, she needed to go beyond the story of her own experience, to give other reasons as well. In revising, she thus condensed the story of her own search for a major and used that story as only one of a number of good reasons in support of her thesis.

Checking your use of narrative

- Does the narrative support your thesis?
- Will the story's significance to the argument be clear to your readers? Don't leave them to figure it out for themselves.
- Is it one of several good reasons?

▶ **FOR MULTILINGUAL WRITERS**
Counting Your Own Experience

You may have learned that your own personal experience doesn't count in making academic arguments. If so, reconsider this advice, for showing an audience that you have personal experience with a topic can carry strong persuasive appeal with many English-speaking audiences. As with all evidence used in an argument, however, evidence based on your own experience must be pertinent to the topic, understandable to the audience, and clearly related to your purpose.

5f

Establishing credibility

To make your argument convincing, you must first gain the respect and trust of your readers, or **establish your credibility** with them. Your character is embodied in your words, and the way this character is perceived by others largely influences how credible you and your arguments will be. The ancient Greeks called this particular kind of character appeal *ethos* and valued it highly. The little boy who cried "Wolf!" when there was no wolf approaching was very quickly mistrusted by his townspeople. His was essentially a problem of *ethos*: he lost credibility because he could not be trusted to tell the truth. In general, writers can establish credibility in three ways:

1. By being knowledgeable about the topic at hand
2. By establishing common ground with the audience in the form of respect for their points of view and concern for their welfare
3. By demonstrating fairness and evenhandedness

1

Demonstrating knowledge

A writer can establish credibility first by establishing his or her credentials. You can, for instance, show that you have some personal experience with the subject, as Jennifer Georgia does in the opening of her essay (see 5i3). In addition, if you show that you have thought about the subject carefully or researched it, you can establish a confident tone. In doing so, your point is not to boast or show off but to assure your audience that your position is based on adequate knowledge and has been systematically thought out.

To determine whether you can effectively present yourself as knowledgeable enough to argue an issue, consider the following questions:

- Can you provide information about your topic from sources other than your own knowledge?
- What are the sources of your information?
- How reliable are your sources?
- Do any sources contradict each other? If so, can you account for or resolve the contradictions?
- If you have personal experience relating to the issue, would telling about this experience help support your claim?

These questions will help you probe your own stock of knowledge and assess your own credibility in making a claim, and they may help you see what other work you need to do to establish credibility. They may well show that you must do more research, check sources, resolve contradictions, refocus your working thesis, or even change your topic.

2

Establishing common ground

Many arguments between people or groups are doomed to end without resolution because the two sides occupy no common ground, no starting point of agreement. They are, to use an informal phrase, coming from completely different places. Such was often the case, for example, in Arab-Israeli talks, in which the beginning positions of each party were so far apart that no resolution could ever be reached.

Lack of common ground also dooms many arguments closer to our everyday lives. If you and your roommate cannot agree on how often to clean your apartment, for instance, the difficulty may well be that your definition of a clean apartment conflicts radically with your roommate's. If you and a classmate cannot agree on how to work together on a joint assignment, you may find that your different backgrounds lead you to approach the job in two different ways. You may find, in fact, that you will not be able to resolve such issues until you can establish common definitions on which to base the arguments. Thus, common ground provides a necessary starting point, one that can turn a futile quarrel into a constructive argument. (See Chapter 29.)

Common ground is just as important in written arguments as it is in diplomatic negotiations or personal disputes. Because topics and writers and audiences are so individual and varied, no foolproof or absolute guidelines exist for a writer wishing to establish common ground with an audience. The following questions, however, can help you find common ground in presenting an argument:

- What are the differing perspectives on this issue?
- What common ground can you find—aspects of the issue on which all sides agree?
- How can you express such common ground clearly to all sides?
- How can you discover—and consider—opinions on this issue that differ from your own?
- How can you use language—occupational, regional, or ethnic varieties of English, or languages other than English—to establish common ground with those you address?

If you turn to Jennifer Georgia's essay in 5i3, you will see that she attempts to establish common ground with her readers by relating her experience in focusing on a course of study to theirs. If you can establish common ground on an issue, you will have taken a giant step toward demonstrating goodwill toward your readers. We are inclined, after all, to listen with interest and attention to those we believe to have our best interests at heart. On the other hand, we are naturally suspicious of those who seem to want to further only their own interests.

3

Demonstrating fairness

In arguing a position, writers must demonstrate fairness toward opposing arguments. Audiences are more inclined to give credibility to writers they believe to be fairly considering and representing their opponents' views than to those who seem to be ignoring or distorting such views. We have all experienced unfair arguments: a co-worker loses his temper and blames you for a decision that was largely his idea, or a clever politician avoids a tough question at a news conference by giving an answer that ignores the questioner's point and then calling on someone else. Such tactics seem unfair, and to the extent that we recognize them, we condemn them. It goes without saying, then, that to be an effective writer, you need to avoid such tactics and establish yourself as open-minded and evenhanded. The following questions can help you discover ways of doing so:

- Can you show that you are taking into account all significant points of view? How?
- Can you demonstrate that you understand and sympathize with points of view other than your own? How?
- What can you do to show that you have considered evidence carefully, even that which does not support your position?

4

Recognizing ethical fallacies

Some arguments focus not on establishing the credibility of the writer but on destroying the credibility of an opponent. At times, such attacks are justified: if a nominee for the Supreme Court has acted in unethical ways in law school, for example, that information is a legitimate argument against the nominee's confirmation. Many times, however, someone attacks a person's character in order to avoid dealing with the issue at hand. Be extremely careful about attacking an opponent's credibility, for doing so without justification can harm your own credibility. Such unjustified attacks are called **ethical fallacies**. They take two main forms: ad hominem charges and guilt by association.

Ad hominem (Latin for "to the man") charges directly attack someone's character rather than focusing on the issue at hand, suggesting that because something is "wrong" with this person, whatever he or she says must also be wrong.

Molly Yard is just a hysterical feminist. We shouldn't listen to her views on abortion. [Labeling Yard *hysterical* and linking that label with *feminist* focuses on Yard's character rather than on her views on the issue at hand.]

Guilt by association attacks someone's credibility by linking that person with a person or activity the audience considers bad, suspicious, or untrustworthy.

Senator Fleming does not deserve reelection; one of her assistants turned out to be involved with organized crime. [Is there any evidence that the senator knew about the organized-crime involvement?]

EXERCISE 5.4

Study carefully the following advertisement for a mutual fund, and then list the ways in which the copywriters demonstrate knowledge, establish common ground, and demonstrate fairness. Do you think they succeed or fail in establishing credibility?

Is Your Money Where Your Heart Is?

It is important to invest your money in companies that have proven themselves to be responsible both financially and socially. It is important for you and it is important for the world.

At Working Assets Common Holdings we invest your money in companies that are successful, stable, and have a positive history of caring for people and the planet.

• Working Assets is one of the oldest and largest socially responsible mutual fund families in the US.

• Working Assets has seven mutual fund portfolios to meet a range of investment objectives.
• IRAS, 403B7 Plans, and Automatic Investment programs are available.
• Our minimum investment is $250.

Please call us for a no-obligation prospectus with complete details of fees and expenses. Please read it carefully before you invest or send money.

800-223-7010

Secure the future with socially responsible investing.

WORKING ASSETS®
COMMON HOLDINGS
111 Pine Street • SanFrancisco, CA 94111
©1993. Distributed by Working Assets Capital Management.

EXERCISE 5.5

Using a working argumentative thesis you drafted for Exercise 5.2 or 5.3, write a paragraph or two describing how you would go about establishing your credibility in arguing that thesis.

Appealing to logic

While the character we present in writing always exerts a strong appeal (or lack of appeal) in an argument, our credibility alone cannot and should not carry the full burden of convincing a reader. Indeed, many are inclined to view the **logic of the argument**—the reasoning behind it—as more important than the character of the person presenting the case. In truth, the two are usually inseparable and thus of equal importance. Nevertheless, strong logical support characterizes most good arguments. This section will examine the most effective means of providing logical support for a written argument: examples and precedents, testimony and authority, and causes and effects.

1

Providing examples and precedents

Just as a picture can sometimes be worth a thousand words, so can a well-conceived **example** be extremely valuable in arguing a point. No one in recent years has used this means of logical support to greater effect than President Ronald Reagan, who often employed a homespun example in the form of stories from his childhood or even from one of his movies to drive home a point. This paragraph, in fact, has used Reagan as an example in making *its* point: that examples are one of the staples of everyday argument.

Examples are used most often to support generalizations or to bring abstractions to life. For instance, a *Newsweek* review of the movie *Star Trek IV* makes the general statement that the movie contains "nutty throwaway lines that take a minute to sink in" and then illustrates the generalization with this example:

> When the crew, flying the Klingon warship they inherited . . . , land in Golden Gate Park, they fan out to different corners of the city. . . . Kirk's parting command, spoken like a PTA mother at the county fair: "Everybody remember where we parked."

The generalization would mean little without the example.

Examples can also help us understand abstractions. "Famine," for instance, may be difficult for us to think about in the abstract, but a graphic description of a drought-stricken community, its riverbed cracked and dry, its people listless, emaciated, and with stomachs bloated by hunger, speaks directly to our understanding.

Precedents are particular kinds of examples taken from the past. The most common use of precedent occurs in law, where an attorney may argue a case by citing the precedent of past decisions. A judge may be asked to rule that a defendant was negligent, for example, because the Supreme Court upheld a ruling of negligence in an almost identical case ten years earlier.

Precedent appears in everyday arguments as well. If you urge your best friend to work your shift because the last time she needed some time off, you worked her shift, you are arguing on the basis of precedent. Or if as part of a proposal for increased lighting in the library garage, you point out that the university has increased lighting in four similar garages in the past year, you are again arguing on the basis of precedent.

In research writing, you usually must list your sources for any examples or precedents not based on your own knowledge (see 42d). The following questions can help you check any use of example and precedent:

- How representative are the examples?
- Are they sufficient in strength or number to lead to a generalization?
- In what ways do they support your point?
- How closely does the precedent relate to the point you're trying to make? Are the situations really similar?
- How timely is the precedent? What would have been applicable in 1520 is not necessarily applicable today.

2

Citing authority and testimony

Another way to support an argument logically is to cite an **authority**. As young children, we were easily swayed by authority; it was right to do something simply because our parents (the authorities) said so. In recent years, the use of authority has figured prominently in the antismoking movement. Many Americans will remember, for instance, the dramatic impact of the U.S. surgeon general's 1963 announcement that smoking is hazardous to health. At the time, many people quit smoking, largely convinced by the authority of the person offering the evidence. Authority is currently being used in a similar way by tobacco companies to argue against evidence of the dangers of secondhand smoke.

But as with other strategies for building support for an argumentative claim, citing authorities demands careful consideration. You might consider the following questions to be sure you are using authorities effectively:

- Is the authority timely? (The argument that the United States should pursue a policy just because it was supported by Thomas Jefferson will probably fail because Jefferson's time was so radically different from ours.)
- Is the authority qualified to judge the topic at hand? (To cite a biologist in an essay on linguistics is not likely to strengthen your argument.)
- Is the authority likely to be known and respected by readers? (To cite an unfamiliar authority without some identification will lessen the impact of the evidence.)

Authorities are commonly cited in research writing (see Part 8), which often relies on the findings of other people. In addition, you may cite authorities when answering essay examination questions (see Chapter 49) or in an assignment that asks you to review the literature of any field (see Chapter 46).

Testimony—the evidence an authority presents in support of a claim— is a feature of much contemporary argument. Most familiar are the testimonials found in advertisements—a television personality promoting dog food or a star athlete speaking for cereal. In fact, we are so inundated with the use of testimonials in television advertising that we may be inclined to think of them only in terms of *misuse*. But if testimony is timely, accurate, representative, and provided by a respected authority, then it, like authority itself, can add powerful support to an argument. In an essay for a literature class, for example, you might argue that a new edition of a literary work will open up many new areas of interpretation. You could strengthen this argument by adding a quotation from the author's biographer, noting that the new edition carries out the author's intentions much more closely than the previous edition did.

In research writing, you should list your sources for authority and testimony not based on your own knowledge (see 43d).

ON VARIETIES OF ENGLISH
Bringing In Other Voices

Quoting authorities presents an opportunity to bring in other voices in support of your own. Sometimes this will prompt you to use language other than standard academic English, and in ways that support your own authority. For instance, if you're writing about political relations between Mexico and the United States, you might quote a prominent member of a Mexican American community organization; quoting that person's *own words*—which may be in a regional variety of English—can carry extra power, calling up a voice from a pertinent community.

3

Establishing causes and effects

Showing that one event is the cause—or the effect—of another can sometimes help support an argument. To take an everyday example, suppose you are trying to explain, in a petition to change your grade in a course, why you were unable to take the final examination. In such a case, you would probably try to trace the **causes** of your failure to appear—the death of your grandmother followed by the theft of your car, perhaps—so that the committee reading the petition would change your grade. In identifying the causes of a situation, you are implicitly arguing that the **effect**—your not taking the examination—should be considered anew.

Tracing causes often lays the groundwork for an argument, particularly if the effect of the causes is one we would like to change. Recent figures from the U.S. Department of Education, for example, indicate that the number of high school dropouts is rising. If we can identify and understand the causes of this increase—for example, a decline in reading skills—we may be able to make an argument for policies aimed at reversing the trend by affecting the causes in some way—such as hiring more teachers to provide reading instruction.

In college writing, you may often be asked to show causes and effects. In an environmental science class, for example, a student may argue that a national law regulating smokestack emissions from utility plants is needed because (1) acid rain on the East Coast originates from emissions at utility plants in the Midwest, (2) acid rain kills trees and other vegetation, (3) utility lobbyists have prevented midwestern states from passing strict laws controlling emissions from such plants, and (4) in the absence of such laws, acid rain will destroy most eastern forests by 2020. In this case, the first point is that the emissions cause acid rain; the second, that acid rain causes destruction in eastern forests; and the third, that states have not acted to break the cause-effect relationship established by the first two points. The fourth point ties all of the previous points together to provide an overall argument from effect: unless X, then Y.

In fact, a cause-effect relationship is often extremely difficult to establish. Scientists and politicians continue to disagree, for example, over the extent to which acid rain is responsible for the so-called dieback of many eastern forests. If we can show that X definitely causes Y, though, we will have a powerful argument at our disposal. That is why, for example, so much effort has gone into establishing a definite link between smoking and cancer and between certain dietary habits and heart disease: proving the causal link will argue most forcefully that we should alter our behavior in certain clear-cut ways.

4

Using inductive and deductive reasoning

Traditionally, logical arguments are classified as using either inductive or deductive reasoning, both of which almost always work together. **Inductive reasoning**, most simply, is the process of making a generalization based on a number of specific instances. If you find you are ill on ten occasions after eating seafood, for example, you will likely draw the inductive generalization that seafood makes you ill. It may not be an absolute certainty that the seafood was the culprit, but the *probability* lies in that direction.

We all use such inductive reasoning for simple everyday discussions, but induction can be quite complex, as demonstrated by the medical response to the sudden outbreak of an apparently new illness in the mid-1970s. This illness, later named Legionnaires' disease, resulted in many deaths. Medical researchers used a painstaking and time-consuming process of inductive elimination, examining every case in great detail to determine what the patients had in common, before they were able to generalize accurately about the cause of the disease.

Deductive reasoning, on the other hand, reaches a conclusion by assuming a general principle (known as a **major premise**) and then applying that principle to a specific case (the **minor premise**). In practice, this general principle is usually derived from induction. The inductive generalization "Seafood makes me ill," for instance, could serve as the major premise for the deductive argument "Since all seafood makes me ill, the plate of it just put before me is certain to make me ill."

The fictional detective Sherlock Holmes is famous for using deductive reasoning to solve his cases. Beginning, for instance, with the major premise "Watchdogs always bark at strangers," Holmes applied that premise to the case of a stolen racehorse and reasoned that because the watchdog did not bark when the horse was stolen, the thief was not a stranger but someone the dog knew.

Deductive arguments like these have traditionally been analyzed as **syllogisms**, three-part statements containing a major premise, a minor premise, and a conclusion.

MAJOR PREMISE All people die.

MINOR PREMISE I am a person.

CONCLUSION I will die.

Syllogisms may work in cases of classic logic, but they are simply too rigid and absolute to serve in arguments about questions that have no absolute answers, and they often lack any appeal to an audience. From Aristotle came a simpler alternative, the **enthymeme**, which calls on the audience to supply the implied major premise. Consider the following example:

This bridge is carrying twice as much traffic as it was built for, so we need to build a new bridge or restrict traffic on this one.

You can analyze this enthymeme by restating it in the form of two premises and a conclusion:

MAJOR PREMISE Bridges should carry only the amount of traffic for which they were built.

MINOR PREMISE This bridge carries twice the traffic for which it was built.

CONCLUSION We need a new bridge or traffic restrictions on this one.

Note that the major premise is one the writer can count on an audience agreeing with or supplying: safety and common sense demand that bridges carry only the amount of traffic for which they are built. By thus inspiring audience participation, an enthymeme actually gets the audience to contribute to the argument.

Jennifer Gerkin's essay in 4j rests on an enthymeme whose implied major premise she assumes her readers will accept: "Prejudice is harmful to all of us." She goes on to demonstrate her own prejudice and to show how that prejudice has harmed her as well as others.

Whether it is expressed as a syllogism or an enthymeme, a deductive conclusion is only as strong as the premises on which it is based. The citizen who argues that "Ed is a crook who shouldn't be elected to public office" is arguing deductively, based on an implied major premise: "No crook should be elected to public office." In this case, most people would agree with this major premise. So the issue in this argument rests on the minor premise—that Ed is a crook. Only if that premise can be proven satisfactorily are we likely to accept the deductive conclusion that Ed shouldn't be elected.

While we may well agree with some unstated major premises (such as that no crook should be elected), at other times the unstated premise may be more problematic. The person who says, "Don't bother to ask for Jack's help with physics—he's a jock" is arguing deductively on the basis of an implied major premise: "Jocks don't know anything about physics." In this case, careful listeners would demand proof of the unstated premise. Because bigoted or prejudiced statements often rest on this kind of reasoning, writers should be particularly alert to it. (See Chapter 29.)

5

Recognizing logical fallacies

Logical fallacies are usually defined as errors in formal reasoning. In spite of the "fallacy" label, however, they are commonplace enough and, indeed, can often work very effectively to convince audiences. Some readers will detect fallacious appeals, however—and may even reject an otherwise worthy argument that relies on them. Your time will be well spent, therefore, in learning to recognize these fallacies. Common logical fallacies include begging the question, *post hoc,* non sequitur, either-or, hasty generalization, and oversimplification.

Begging the question is a kind of circular argument that treats a question as if it has already been answered.

> That TV news provides accurate and reliable information was demonstrated conclusively on last week's *60 Minutes.* [This statement says in effect that television news is accurate and reliable because TV news says so.]

The *post hoc fallacy,* from the Latin *post hoc, ergo propter hoc,* which means "after this, therefore caused by this," assumes that just because B happened *after* A, it must have been *caused* by A.

> We should not rebuild the town docks because every time we do, a big hurricane comes along and damages them. [Does the reconstruction cause hurricanes?]

A **non sequitur** (Latin for "it does not follow") attempts to tie together two or more logically unrelated ideas as if they *were* related.

> If we can send a spacecraft to Mars, then we can discover a cure for cancer. [These are both scientific goals, but do they have anything else in common? What does achieving one have to do with achieving the other?]

The **either-or fallacy** asserts that a complex situation can have only two possible outcomes, one of which is necessary or preferable.

> If we do not build the new aqueduct system this year, residents of the Tri-cities area will be forced to move because of lack of water. [What is the evidence for this claim? Do no other alternatives exist?]

A **hasty generalization** bases a conclusion on too little evidence or on bad or misunderstood evidence.

> I couldn't understand the lecture today, so I'm sure this course will be impossible. [How can the writer be so sure of this conclusion based on only *one* piece of evidence?]

Oversimplification of the relation between causes and effects is another fallacy based on careless reasoning.

> If we prohibit the sale of alcohol, we will get rid of the problem of drunkenness. [This claim oversimplifies the relation between laws and human behavior.]

EXERCISE 5.6

The following sentences contain deductive arguments based on implied major premises. Identify each of the implied premises.

1. A dream is not an accurate picture of reality because it is heavily influenced by our subjective feelings.
2. In a recent national survey, a majority of Americans said they either smoke marijuana or do not care if others do; therefore, smoking marijuana should be legalized.
3. Active euthanasia is morally acceptable when it promotes the best interests of everyone concerned and violates no one's rights.
4. Women soldiers should not serve in combat positions because doing so would expose them to a much higher risk of death.
5. Animals can't talk, so therefore they can't feel pain as humans do.

EXERCISE 5.7

The following brief article from *Newsweek* raises some provocative questions about causes and effects, and in doing so it uses example and authority. Read the article, and assess it in terms of the questions that follow.

> Mom always told you chicken noodle soup could cure a cold. But could it prevent a disabling disease like Alzheimer's? That's what researchers are asking about a new chicken soup under development by Thomas J. Lipton Co. Inc. The still-to-be-named soup is enriched with purified lecithin, a nutrient undergoing testing as an Alzheimer's treatment. In accordance with Food and Drug Administration regulations, Lipton stops short of attaching medical claims to its new product. But the company may introduce it simply as "chicken soup with lecithin" sometime next year.
>
> The soup is the brainchild of MIT Prof. Richard Wurtman and Harvard neurologist John Growden. Wurtman and Growden approached Lipton after discovering that purified lecithin could affect the chemistry of the brain. The purified lecithin, which is more concentrated than that sold in health-food stores, raises blood levels of choline, which, in turn, may aid memory.
>
> Whether the new soup could benefit the general population is still unclear. But Wurtman and Growden are studying the product's effect on memory and fatigue. Says Lipton spokesman Larry Hicks, "The market may be much larger than we now know."

1. What is the cause-effect argument?
2. Is the link between cause and effect fully established?
3. What evidence would be required to establish that link more fully?
4. Does the use of authority or testimony help establish the link? Why, or why not?
5. What example is used in the introduction—and is it effective in illustrating the point?
6. Can you identify any logical fallacies?

EXERCISE 5.8

Analyze the advertisement in Exercise 5.4 for the use of examples, narratives, and precedents; authority and testimony; causes and effects; induction and deduction; and logical fallacies.

EXERCISE 5.9

Using your working argumentative thesis from Exercise 5.2 or 5.3, write a paragraph describing the logical appeals you would use to support the thesis.

5h

Appealing to emotion

Most successful arguments appeal to our hearts as well as to our minds. Good writers, therefore, supplement appeals to logic and reason with those designed to **enlist the emotional support** of their readers. This principle was vividly demonstrated a few years ago, when we began hearing about famine in Africa. Facts and figures (logical appeals) convinced many that the famine was real and serious. What brought an outpouring of aid, however, were not the facts and figures but the arresting photographs of children, at once skeletal and bloated, dying of starvation. In this case, the emotional appeal of the photographs spoke more powerfully than did the logical statistics. Writers can gain similarly powerful effects with the careful use of stories—and with description, concrete language, and figurative language.

1

Using description

Vivid **description** provides one of the most effective means of appealing to emotions. Travel articles and advertisements draw heavily on this principle: think of all the descriptions of sunny beaches that appear in newspapers during the dreary winter months. Description can work just as effectively in your written arguments. Using strong, descriptive details can bring a moving immediacy to any argument.

The student described in 3d1 who was at work on a proposal to make the library more accessible to students in wheelchairs had amassed plenty of facts and figures, including diagrams and maps, illustrating the problem. But her first draft seemed lifeless in spite of all her information. She decided, therefore, to ask a friend who used a wheelchair to accompany her to the library—and she revised her proposal, opening it with a detailed description of that visit and its many frustrations for her friend.

2

Using concrete language

Concrete language stands at the heart of effective description and hence helps build emotional appeal. The student urging improved wheelchair access to the library, for instance, could have said simply that her friend "had trouble entering the library." Such a general statement, however, has little impact; it does not appeal to readers' emotions or allow them to imagine themselves in a similar position. The revised version, full of concrete description, does so: "Maria inched her heavy wheelchair up the narrow, steep entrance ramp, her arms straining to pull up the last twenty feet, her face pinched with the sheer effort." (See 27c.)

3

Using figurative language

Figurative language, or figures of speech, are crucial elements in painting a detailed and vivid picture. They do so by making striking comparisons between something you are writing about and something else that helps a reader to visualize, identify with, or understand it. Figures of speech include metaphors, similes, and analogies (see 27d). **Metaphors** compare two things directly: *Richard the Lion-Hearted; old age is the evening of life.* **Similes** make comparisons using *like* or *as: Richard is as brave as a lion; old age is like the evening of life.* **Analogies** are extended metaphors or similes that compare an unfamiliar concept or process to a more familiar one to help the reader understand the unfamiliar concept:

> My daddy's face is a study. Winter moves into it and presides there. His eyes become a cliff of snow threatening to avalanche; his eyebrows bend like black limbs of leafless trees. His skin takes on the pale, cheerless yellow of winter sun; for a jaw he has the edges of a snowbound field dotted with stubble; his high forehead is the frozen sweep of the Erie, hiding currents of gelid thoughts that eddy in darkness. Wolf killer turned hawk fighter, he worked night and day to keep one from the door and the other from under the windowsills. A Vulcan guarding the flames, he gives us instructions about which doors to keep closed or opened for proper distribution of heat, lays kindling by, discusses qualities of coal, and teaches us how to rake, feed, and bank the fire. And he will not unrazor his lips until spring.
>
> – TONI MORRISON, "The Bluest Eye"

As the preceding paragraph demonstrates, metaphors, similes, and analogies can make abstract or otherwise difficult concepts understandable in terms of more concrete, everyday experience. James Watson and Francis Crick, who won the Nobel Prize for their work on the structure of DNA, used a zipper metaphor to describe how two strands of molecules could separate during cell division. A student arguing for a more streamlined course-registration process may find good use for an analogy, saying that the current process makes students feel like laboratory rats in a maze. This analogy, which suggests manipulation, victims, and a clinical coldness, creates a vivid description and hence adds emotional appeal to the argument. For an analogy to work effectively, however, it must be supported by evidence. In this case, the student would have to show that the current registration process has a number of similarities to a laboratory maze, such as confused students wandering through complex bureaucratic channels and into dead ends.

4

Shaping your appeal to your audience

As with appeals to credibility and logic, appealing to emotions is effective only insofar as it moves your audience. Of course, you can't predict absolutely any audience's emotional response, but you can consider your topic and assess its probable emotional effects. A student arguing for increased lighting in campus parking garages, for instance, might consider the emotions such a discussion might raise (fear of attackers, anger at being subjected to such danger, compassion for victims of such attacks), decide which emotions would be most appropriately appealed to, and then look for descriptive and figurative language to carry out such an appeal.

In a leaflet to be distributed on campus, for example, the student might describe the scene in a dimly lighted garage as a student parks her car and then has to walk to an exit alone down shadowy corridors. Parking in the garage might be compared to venturing into a jungle with dangerous animals lurking behind every tree.

In a proposal to the university administration, on the other hand, the student might describe past attacks on students in campus parking garages and the negative publicity and criticism these provoked among students, parents, alumni, and other groups. For the administration, the student might compare the lighting in the garages to high-risk gambling, arguing that the university is taking a significant chance with the current lighting conditions and that increased lighting would lower the odds of future attacks.

Notice that shaping your appeal to specific audiences calls on you to consider very carefully the language you use. Will formal or academic standard English speak most powerfully to them? Or would it be effective to bring in other varieties of English as well? The student arguing for better lighting in campus parking garages, for instance, would probably stick to formal standard English in a proposal to the university administration but might well want to use more informal language, even slang, in a leaflet written for students.

5

Recognizing emotional fallacies

Appeals to the emotions of an audience constitute a valid and necessary part of argument. Unfair or overblown emotional appeals, however, attempt to overcome readers' good judgment. Most common among these **emotional fallacies** are bandwagon appeal, flattery, in-crowd appeal, veiled threats, and false analogies. **Bandwagon appeal** suggests that a great movement is under way, and the reader will be a fool or a traitor not to join it.

Voters are flocking to candidate X by the millions, so you'd better cast your vote the right way. [Why should you jump on this bandwagon? Where is the evidence to support this claim?]

Flattery tries to persuade readers to do something by suggesting that they are thoughtful, intelligent, or perceptive enough to agree with the writer.

We know you have the taste to recognize that an investment in an Art-Form ring will pay off in the future. [How will it pay off?]

In-crowd appeal, a special kind of flattery, invites readers to identify with an admired and select group.

Want to know a secret that more and more of Middletown's successful young professionals are finding out about? It's Mountainbrook Manor, the condominiums that combine the best of the old with the best of the new. [Who are these "successful young professionals," and will you become one by moving to Mountainbrook Manor?]

Veiled threats try to frighten readers into agreement by hinting that they will suffer adverse consequences if they don't agree.

If Public Service Electric Company does not get an immediate 15-percent rate increase, its services to you, its customers, may be seriously affected. [How serious is this possible effect? Is it legal or likely?]

False analogies make comparisons between two situations that are *not* alike in most or important respects.

If the United States gets involved in a land war in the Middle East, it will turn out just like Vietnam. [Is there any point of analogy except that they are both wars? This example was written in 1988. The Persian Gulf War of 1991 demonstrates well the weaknesses of such analogies.]

EXERCISE 5.10

Make a list of the common human emotions that might be attached to the following topics, and suggest appropriate ways to appeal to those emotions in a specific audience you choose to address.

1. banning smoking on campus
2. assisted suicide
3. nuclear-power generation
4. television evangelism
5. steroid use among athletes

EXERCISE 5.11

Jennifer Gerkin's essay in Chapter 4 argues that people shouldn't judge others on the basis of appearance. Reread the essay, underlining emotional appeals, including descriptive passages, concrete language, and figurative language.

EXERCISE 5.12

Read the following paragraph, and then write a paragraph evaluating its use of description and figurative language.

In 1973, all women in the United States became legally entitled to have abortions performed in hospitals by licensed physicians. Before they were legal, abortions were frequently performed by persons who bore more resemblance to butchers than they did to doctors. The all-too-common result was serious complications or death for the woman. Since 1989, states have been able to restrict where and when abortions are performed. Even if the 1973 Supreme Court decision is completely reversed, abortion will not end. Instead, women will again resort to illegal abortions, and there will be a return to the slaughterhouse. Since abortions are going to take place no matter what the law says, why not have them done safely and legally in hospitals instead of in basements, alleys, or dirty compartments in some killing shed? The decision to have an abortion is not an easy one to make, and I believe that a woman who makes it deserves to have her wish carried out in the very safest way possible. Critics of abortion stress the importance of the unborn child's life. At the very least, they should also take the woman's life and safety into consideration.

EXERCISE 5.13

Using a working argumentative thesis you formulated for Exercise 5.2 or 5.3, make a list of the emotional appeals most appropriate to your topic and audience. Then spend ten to fifteen minutes brainstorming, looking for descriptive and figurative language to carry out the appeals.

USING SOURCES
Finding Support for Your Argument

In constructing a written argument, it is usually necessary—and often essential—to use sources. Even if your assignment doesn't specify that you must consult outside sources, there is often no better way to find support for your argument. The key to persuading people to accept your argument is good reasons, and the most effective way of finding and establishing these reasons is with the help of appropriate sources. You cannot, after all, expect people to simply take your word for something. You need to offer evidence from others in support of your claim. Sources can be helpful for

- demonstrating knowledge
- citing authority and testimony
- providing background information
- finding opinions that differ from your own
- demonstrating fairness

5i

Organizing an argument

Once you have assembled good reasons in support of an argumentative thesis, you must organize your material in order to present the argument convincingly.

1

The classical system

While there is no ideal or universally favored organizational framework for an argumentative essay, you may find it useful to try the classical system that was often followed by ancient Greek and Roman orators. The speaker began with an *introduction,* which stated the thesis and then gave the *background* information. Next came the different *lines of argument* and then the *consideration of opposing arguments.* A *conclusion* both summed up the argument and made a final appeal to the audience. You can adapt this format to written arguments as follows:

1. *The introduction*
   gains readers' attention and interest—with a provocative question, an anecdote, a vivid image, or an arresting quotation
   establishes your qualifications to write about your topic
   establishes common ground with readers
   demonstrates fairness
   states or implies your thesis
2. *The background*
   presents any necessary background information, including pertinent personal narrative
3. *The lines of argument*
   presents good reasons (including logical and emotional appeals) in support of your thesis
   generally presents reasons in order of importance
   demonstrates ways your argument may be in readers' best interest

4. *The consideration of alternative arguments*
   examines alternative points of view
   notes both advantages and disadvantages of alternative views
   explains why one view is better than other(s)

5. *The conclusion*
   may summarize the argument
   elaborates on the implication of your thesis
   makes clear what you want readers to think or do
   makes a strong ethical or emotional appeal

2

The Toulmin system

Another useful system of argument was developed by the philosopher Stephen Toulmin. In simplified form, it can help you organize an argumentative essay as follows:

1. Present your claim (your thesis).

2. Qualify your claim if necessary.

3. Present a series of good reasons to support your claim.

4. Explain any underlying assumptions that support your reasons.

5. Provide further evidence to support your claim (facts, statistics, testimony, and so on).

6. Acknowledge and respond to possible counterarguments.

7. Draw your conclusion.

Suppose you were writing an essay about smoking. Your claim might be that smoking should be banned. You could qualify this claim by suggesting that the ban be limited to all public places. As reasons in support of your claim, you might say that smoking causes heart disease and lung cancer and that nonsmokers are increasingly endangered by others' secondhand smoke. In addition, you might offer the reason that many public institutions and places of employment have now banned smoking entirely. Your underlying assumptions, which you could offer, include the fact that people are entitled to protection from harmful actions by others. As evidence, you could cite statistics about lung and heart disease and perhaps quote the U.S. surgeon general as an authority on the subject. One counterargument you might anticipate is that smokers have rights, too; you could respond by reminding readers that you are suggesting only a public-space ban and that smokers would be free to smoke in private places. Finally, you could state your conclusion in the strongest way possible: smoking should be banned in all public places.

3

A sample argumentative essay

Asked to write an argumentative essay on an issue of interest to her and addressed to her classmates, Jennifer Georgia decided to draw on her experience in designing her own program of study. She wanted to urge other students to think hard before choosing a course of study—and to consider designing their own. She used her own experience as well as several other good reasons to back up her argument. Her purposes for argument were twofold—to explore the advantages and disadvantages of prescribed programs of study, and to convince other students to examine their own programs critically and consider possible alternatives.

The following is her essay, roughly organized according to the classical system and annotated to point out the various parts of her argument as well as her use of pertinent ethical, logical, and emotional appeals.

Major Problems

How do we decide on a course of

study?* For me it was easy. When my college

adviser asked me to choose my major, I said

"No Problem," and unhesitatingly checked

the box marked "English." After all, I

liked English in high school.

    Is this a good way to decide on a

course of study? If not, how <u>should</u> we

choose? One thing seems certain: we should

<u>not</u> be encouraged to check off a box on a

form. Instead, we ought first to think

critically about what we want to learn--

about the topics we wish to study <u>and</u> about

the career and life path they will put us

on. Then, and only then, should we choose

our course of study.

    The decision about a major or other

course of study is crucial because it de-

termines both what we study and how we come

INTRODUCTION
GETS READERS'
ATTENTION,
PRESENTS
BACKGROUND

ESTABLISHES
COMMON
GROUND

THESIS

to think about the world. The philosopher
Kenneth Burke explains that we are inevitably affected not only by our experiences,
but also by the terminologies through which
our perceptions of those experiences are
filtered. Burke calls these filters "terministic screens" and says that they affect
our perception, highlighting some aspects
of an experience while obscuring others.
Thus the terminologies (or languages) we
use influence how we see the world and how
we think about what we see.

CITES
AUTHORITY

FIGURATIVE
LANGUAGE USED
TO EXPLAIN A
POINT

Burke extends this concept of terministic screens to the various courses in a
college curriculum, which he says are
"in effect but so many different terminologies" (41). In other words, a program's
curriculum brings with it certain frames of
reference--terminologies--that affect the
way we think about the world. In addition,
of course, a curriculum filters out or de-
emphasizes various ideas or perspectives
according to a program's agendas, thus potentially limiting our perception of the
world. In pursuing particular courses of
study, then, we are not just choosing an
academic path; we are also choosing a frame
of reference from which to see and think
about the world. The engineering student
learns to see the world from an engineer's
perspective; the criminal justice student
learns to see the world from a criminolo-
gist's perspective.

OFFERS
TESTIMONY

ESTABLISHES
CAUSE-EFFECT
RELATIONSHIP

GIVES
CONCRETE
EXAMPLES

Once I declared my major, I began to
see the world through an English major's
eyes, which helped me to see certain
things--and not to see others. I found the
required courses--almost all in periods of
English and U.S. literature--stimulating,
but I was frustrated that my many other interests had no place in my program other
than as electives or extracurricular activities. As I began to recognize art, architecture, music, language, and literature as
interrelated forms of expression, I began
to feel more and more closed in by my English program. I wanted a program that af-
firmed all these disciplines as points
along a continuum of communicative acts
rather than a program that focused exclusively on "literary" communication.

TELLS ABOUT
PERTINENT
PERSONAL
EXPERIENCE

Surely I am not the first student to
feel constrained by prescribed courses.
But such constraints are often necessary,
as those favoring set requirements are
quick to point out. Set course requirements
are needed by colleges in order to allocate
funds and do other logistical planning.
They are needed in certain fields to make
sure practitioners have necessary skills--
airplane mechanics, for example, have to
work to certain specific codes to ensure
the safety of air travel. And as the
Undergraduate Studies in English at The
Ohio State University: A Handbook points
out, they can help guide students through

DEMONSTRATES
FAIRNESS,
CONSIDERS
AND NOTES
ADVANTAGES
OF ALTERNATIVE
VIEWPOINTS

CITES SOURCE
IN SUPPORT OF
ALTERNATIVE
VIEWPOINTS

undergraduate studies and toward specific
fields (3).

If accepted unquestioningly, however,
set requirements can hinder our ability to
think critically and creatively. Indeed,
they can often keep students from thinking
about their course of study at all. And
such uncritical acceptance seems especially
dangerous at a time when, according to the
anthropologist Clifford Geertz, the boundaries between disciplines are breaking down
(19). In addition, by tending to track students, set requirements often force us to
take courses we're not interested in and
keep us from others we are interested in.
So while we come to college to gain the
credentials associated with a certain program, we also come to explore our interests
and realize our potential as well as to
prepare for future jobs. Thus it is imperative to find a balance between the college's track and our own. The college experience is supposed to be a time to explore
many paths, not to follow a totally fixed
guidebook.

In fact, the process of thinking about
and choosing what we study can be an important exercise in critical thinking. In
questioning the tracks offered by our
school, we students can shape our own development and assert our individuality.

DEDUCTIVE
REASONING

FIGURATIVE
LANGUAGE

APPEALS
DIRECTLY
TO AUDIENCE

It was through this sort of questioning that I discovered a loophole in the system at Ohio State,--a program of personalized study called the Personal Study Program, or PSP. The PSP can offer a solution to the problems experienced by many undergraduates who, like me, seek greater flexibility. The PSP allows students not only to design individual programs but, more importantly, to become actively (and critically) involved in our own education. Drawing up a PSP is not an easy process, but the rewards to me by far outweigh the frustrations. The PSP has allowed me to realize my potential in a unique way, by pursuing the many connections between language study (in my case, English, French, and Italian) and speech, music, poetry, and architecture. I have established my own "terministic screens" rather than accepting screens imposed by others. The PSP isn't for everyone, of course. But the process of looking closely at a college program or major should be for everybody, if only to be aware of its limits and strengths.

Such a step is in line with the educational philosophy of Ohio State University president Dr. E. Gordon Gee, who echoes Geertz by acknowledging that many of the boundaries that currently divide the university are "artificial." As Dr. Gee said

*GIVES
PERTINENT
PERSONAL
EXAMPLE*

*ESTABLISHES
COMMON
GROUND*

*CITES
AUTHORITY*

in a recent address to the university senate, "I challenge you to think beyond collegiate boundaries. To think creatively. To
bring to the decision process the flexibility and adaptability that we bring as scientists and scholars to our intellectual
activity" (2). As Dr. Gee suggests, it is
our critical skills and ability to think
independently and creatively that will
allow us to meet the ever-changing world
around us and to adapt to the future.
Through programs like the PSP, we can assert our independence from the institutional frameworks and afford ourselves new
dimensions for critical thinking.

OFFERS
TESTIMONY

What's your major? <u>Think</u> about it. And
then--<u>you</u> decide.

CLOSES WITH
STRONG APPEAL

Note
*A special thanks to the students of
Carrie Dirmeikis's English 110 class for
their help in responding to this paper, and
to Hakan Aytac for his valuable insights.

Works Cited

Burke, Kenneth. <u>Language as Symbolic Ac-</u>
<u>tion: Essays on Life, Literature, and</u>
<u>Method.</u> Berkeley: U. of California,
1966. 44-62.

Gee, E. Gordon. "Address to the University
Senate." The Ohio State University.
Columbus. 9 Oct. 1993.

Geertz, Clifford. <u>Local Knowledge: Further</u>
<u>Essays in Interpretive Anthropology.</u>
New York: Basic, 1983.

The Ohio State Department of English. <u>Un-
    dergraduate Studies in English at The
    Ohio State University: A Handbook.</u> Co-
    lumbus: Ohio State Dept. of English,
    1993.

EXERCISE 5.14

Using the classical or Toulmin system, draft an argument in support of one of
the theses you formulated for Exercise 5.2 or 5.3.

5j

Analyzing an argument

Here are some questions based on the classical system and the Toulmin
system that can help you judge the effectiveness of an argument.

Analyzing an argument with the classical system

1. What is there to gain readers' interest? (5i)
2. How has the writer established qualifications to write about the
   topic? by showing personal experience with it? by citing authoritative sources? (5fl)
3. What in the introduction establishes common ground with readers? (5f2)
4. Is the thesis stated? If not, will readers be able to recognize it? Is
   it sufficiently focused? (5c)
5. What background information is given? Is it sufficient? (5f)
6. What good reasons are given in support of the thesis—examples?
   precedents or authorities? testimony? cause-effect relationships?
   (5g)
7. How has the writer appealed to readers' emotions? (5h)
8. Are there any fallacies? (5f4, 5g5, 5h5)
9. Is there attention to opposing points of view? Has the writer noted
   both their advantages and disadvantages? (5f3)
10. How does the essay conclude? by summarizing the argument? elabo-
    rating on its implications? making an ethical or emotional appeal?
    Has the writer made clear what readers should think or do? (5i)

> *Analyzing an argument with the Toulmin system*

1. What is the claim or thesis? (5c)
2. How is the claim qualified? (5c)
3. What good reasons support the claim? (5d)
4. What underlying assumptions support these reasons? (5f)
5. What evidence adds support to the claim? What facts, statistics, testimony, and so on? (5g2)
6. How are counterarguments acknowledged and responded to? (5f3)

EXERCISE 5.15

Using the categories in the Toulmin system described in 5i2 and the questions above, try analyzing the argument implicit in the advertisement for Working Assets in Exercise 5.4. Write out your analysis in a page or so.

THINKING CRITICALLY ABOUT ARGUMENTS

Reading with an Eye for Argument

In this brief opinion essay from *TV Guide,* Jeff Jarvis considers the Rush Limbaugh phenomenon by reviewing a television program (*Monty*) whose star is highly reminiscent of Limbaugh. What claim(s) does Jarvis make? What ethical, logical, and emotional appeals does he offer in support of his claim(s)? How convincing are these appeals?

Rush Limbaugh is the phenom that will not shrink. Rush is huge in radio, TV, and books. Rush appeared with David Letterman the same night that Jay Leno had America's other frighteningly gigantic media monster, Howard Stern—and Rush won big. William Shatner played a Rush clone in a Columbo movie—quite an honor. And now Rush is the inspiration for a sitcom, making him even more of a laughingstock than he already is.

Now hold on, Rush fans. Already I can see you filling your pens with poison and aiming them at me. Save it. I've admitted that I kind of enjoy the guy. But he *is* getting too big for his already big britches. He's relying on infantile, cheap, smug insults about liberals who are short or have speech impediments— in lieu of real arguments or actual thought. He needs a sitcom to cut him down to size.

So here comes Henry Winkler as Monty, the conservative, ego-rich host of a TV show filled with nothing but his own caustic opinions and gags (like a find-a-blind-date-for-Janet-Reno contest). He's a Rush, all right. But we get to go home with this Rush, to his wife (the smartly appealing Kate Burton), two sharp-witted sons, and one feminist, liberal, vegetarian almost-a-daughter-in-law (China Kantner). So far, the show favors scenes at home, where Monty sneers at his son for throwing away a Yale degree to become a cook. Or he learns to support his wife when she suffers an abuse he thought liberals made up: sexual harassment. Or he wars with Kantner, the female Meathead to Winkler's well-dressed Archie Bunker. Problem is, I never imagined someone like Rush having a home or a home life. What's fascinating about him is that he seems to be the kind of guy who'd eat franks 'n' beans out of a can and sleep under velvet portraits of Ronald Reagan in a bomb shelter somewhere—yet he turns out to be smart, urbane, funny. *Monty* needs such irony. What it doesn't need is another stock sitcom family.

I wish *Monty* would spend more time in its show-within-a-show, where he lists the ugly names he's called—white trash, a Neanderthal, a blowhard, a pig—so he can shrug it all off and tell America "we have to stop being so sensitive." The guy has a point, yet even his own show ignores him and quickly moves on to a stale Clinton-at-McDonald's gag. How much more fun it would be—how much more of a challenge—if *Monty* could honestly ask whether, behind all the bluster and blather of Rush and his fellow media phenoms, there may actually be something worth listening to—or at least something worth arguing about.

– JEFF JARVIS, "Monty"

Thinking Critically about Your Own Arguments

Using the guidelines in 5j, analyze the argument in something you've recently written or in the draft you wrote for Exercise 5.14. Decide what you need to do to revise your argument, and write out a brief plan for your revision.

6

Constructing Paragraphs

THE HERO OF THE REX STOUT MYSTERIES, Nero Wolfe, once solved a case by identifying the paragraph structure of a particular writer-murderer. A person's style of paragraphing, Wolfe was later to claim, serves even more reliably than fingerprints as a stamp of identity. Like Stout's character, you probably already have a characteristic way of paragraphing, one you can learn to understand and use to advantage.

Paragraphs provide an essential way for writers to guide their readers. These important elements of prose have, in fact, existed for as long as people in the Western world have been writing. Long before the age of the printing press, sections of text were set off from one another by marks in the margin. In Greek, para graphos means "mark beside," and these marks looked like this: ¶. With the invention of movable type, printers had to fit lines of type into frames. Because they could no longer use the margins easily, they began marking a paragraph by indenting its first line, as we still do today. The old name stuck, however, and so we call these units paragraphs.

*Most simply, a **paragraph** is a group of sentences or a single sentence set off as a unit. Usually the sentences in a paragraph all revolve around one main idea. When a new idea comes up, a new paragraph begins. Within this broad general guideline, however, paragraph structure can be highly flexible, allowing writers to create many different individual effects for various writing purposes.*

6a

Paragraphing for readers

Numerous studies indicate that readers come to any piece of writing with certain conventional expectations. In terms of paragraphs, many readers have the following expectations:

- Paragraphs begin and end with important guiding information.
- The opening sentence provides direction and lets readers know what the paragraph is about.
- The middle of the paragraph develops what the paragraph is about.
- The end of the paragraph may sum up the paragraph's contents, bringing the discussion of an idea to a close in anticipation of the paragraph that follows.
- The paragraph "makes sense" as a whole, its words and sentences clearly related.
- The paragraph relates in some clear way to the paragraphs around it.

EXERCISE 6.1

The following passage consists of a series of paragraphs, run together, from an essay by the scientist Lewis Thomas. Read the passage carefully, and decide how you would divide it into paragraphs. Bring your paragraphed passage to class for discussion and for comparison with your classmates' work.

My parents' house had an attic, the darkest and strangest part of the building, reachable only by placing a stepladder beneath the trapdoor, and filled with unidentifiable articles too important to be thrown out with the trash but no longer suitable to have at hand. This mysterious space was the memory of the place. After many years, all the things deposited in it became, one by one, lost to consciousness. But they were still there, we knew, safely and comfortably stored in the tissues of the house. These days most of us live in smaller, more modern houses or in apartments, and attics have vanished. Even the deep closets in which we used to pile things up for temporary forgetting are rarely designed into new homes. Everything now is out in the open, openly acknowledged and displayed, and whenever we grow tired of a memory, an old chair, a trunkful of old letters, they are carted off to the dump for burning. This has seemed a healthier way to live, except maybe for the smoke—everything out to be looked at, nothing strange hidden under the roof, nothing forgotten because of no place left in impenetrable darkness to forget. Openness is the new life-style, no undisclosed belongings, no private secrets. Candor is the rule in architecture. The house is a machine for living, and what kind of a machine would hide away its worn-out, obsolescent parts? But it is in our nature as human beings to clutter, and we hanker for places set aside, reserved for storage. We tend to accumulate and outgrow possessions at the same time, and it is an endlessly discomforting mental task to keep sorting out the ones to get rid of. We might, we think, remember them later and find a use for them, and if they are gone for good, off to the dump, this is a source of nervousness. I think it may be one of the reasons we drum our fingers so much these days.

—LEWIS THOMAS, "The Attic of the Brain"

Everyday Use

Of all the paragraphs in a piece of writing, none is more important than the first. In fact, outside of classroom assignments—in job applications, newspaper articles, and fund-raising appeals, for example—the quality of the opening paragraph often determines whether readers bother to read further. One high school student, Ted Frantz, found himself concentrating hard on his opening paragraph as he worked on an essay describing his "major academic interest" to accompany his college application. Following is the paragraph he came up with to get his readers' attention and introduce his subject.

Picture a five-year-old boy with a stack of cards in his hands, not baseball cards but presidential flash cards. He would run around asking anybody to question him about presidents; this kid knew incredible facts and could name every president in the correct order from Washington to Bush. I was this little boy, and ever since I was five, I have had a passion for studying history.

Take some time to look at some opening paragraphs in the reading you normally do: newspapers or magazines, textbooks, "junk mail." How well do such paragraphs get and hold your attention? Bring the paragraphs you find to class for discussion.

6b

Constructing unified, coherent, and well-developed paragraphs

Let us look now at the specific elements that make up a well-written paragraph—one that makes a point in a way that is easy for readers to understand and follow. Consider the following paragraph:

> I never knew anyone who'd grown up in Jackson without being afraid of Mrs. Calloway, our librarian. She ran the Library absolutely by herself, from the desk where she sat with her back to the books and facing the stairs, her dragon eye on the front door, where who knew what kind of person might come in from the public? SILENCE in big black letters was on signs tacked up everywhere. She herself spoke in her normally commanding voice; every word could be heard all over the Library above a steady seething sound coming from her electric fan; it was the only fan in the Library and stood on her desk, turned directly onto her streaming face.
> —EUDORA WELTY, *One Writer's Beginnings*

This paragraph begins with a general statement of the main idea: that everyone who grew up in Jackson feared Mrs. Calloway. All the other sentences then give specific details about why she inspired such fear. This example demonstrates the three qualities essential to most academic paragraphs: *unity, coherence,* and *development.* It focuses on one main idea (**unity**); its parts are clearly related (**coherence**); and its main idea is supported with specifics (**development**).

Making paragraphs unified: focusing on a main idea

To be readable and effective, paragraphs generally must focus on one main idea. One good way to achieve such paragraph unity is to state the main idea clearly in one sentence and relate all the other sentences in the paragraph to that idea. The sentence that presents the main idea is called the **topic sentence**. Like the thesis for an essay, the topic sentence includes a topic and some comment on that topic (3b). In the above paragraph by Eudora Welty, the topic sentence opens the paragraph. Its topic is Mrs. Calloway; its comment, that those who grew up in Jackson were afraid of her.

1

Positioning a topic sentence

Although a topic sentence often appears at the beginning of a paragraph, it may appear anywhere in the paragraph—or it may not appear at all but, rather, be implied.

Topic sentence at the beginning

If you want readers to see your point immediately, open with the topic sentence. Such a strategy can be particularly useful in essay examinations (Chapter 49), in memos (Chapter 52), or in argumentative writing (Chapter 5). The following paragraph opens with a clear topic sentence, on which subsequent sentences build.

> *Our friendship was the source of much happiness and many memories.* We danced and snapped our fingers simultaneously to the soul tunes of the Jacksons and Stevie Wonder. We sweated together in the sweltering summer sun, trying to win the championship for our softball team. I recall the taste of pepperoni and sausage pizza as we discussed the highlights of our team's victory. Once we even became attracted to the same young man, but luckily we were able to share his friendship.

The topic sentence announces the main topic of the paragraph (a friendship) and comments on it (as the source of happiness and memories). The next four sentences elaborate on the topic by giving specific examples and concrete physical descriptions that show the reader how the happiness and memories were created.

Topic sentence at the end

When specific details lead up to a generalization, putting the topic sentence at the end of the paragraph makes sense. In the following paragraph about Alice Walker's "Everyday Use," the last sentence is a general statement that sums up and accounts for the specifics that have preceded it.

> During the visit, Dee takes the pictures, every one of them, including the one of the house that she used to live in and hate. She takes the churn top and dasher, both whittled out of a tree by one of Mama's uncles. She tries to take Grandma Dee's quilts. Mama and Maggie use these inherited items every day, not only appreciating their heritage but living it too. *Dee, on the other hand, wants these items only for decorative use, thus forsaking and ignoring their real heritage.*

In this instance, the concluding topic sentence brings the paragraph to its climax by explaining the significance of the things Dee takes.

Topic sentence at the beginning and end

Sometimes you will want to state a topic sentence at the beginning of the paragraph and then refer to it in a slightly different form at the end. Such an "echo" of the topic sentence adds emphasis, pointing up the importance you attach to the idea. In the following paragraph, the writer begins with a topic sentence announcing a problem.

> *Many of the difficulties we experience in relationships are caused by the unrealistic expectations we have of each other.* Think about it. Women are expected to feel comfortable doing most of the sacrificing. They are supposed to stay fine, firm, and forever twenty-two while doing double duty, in the home and in the workplace. The burden on men is no easier. They should be tall, handsome, and able to wine and dine the women. Many women go for the glitter and then expect these men to calm down once in a relationship and become faithful, sensitive, supportive, and loving. Let's face it. Both women and men have been unrealistic. *It's time we develop a new sensitivity toward each other and ask ourselves what it is we need from each other that is realistic and fair.*

The last sentence restates the topic sentence as a proposal for solving the problem. This echo of the topic sentence is especially appropriate, for the essay goes on to specify how the problem might be solved.

Topic sentence implied but not stated

Occasionally a topic will be so obvious that no topic sentence is necessary at all. Here is an example of such a paragraph, from an essay about working as an airport cargo handler.

> In winter the warehouse is cold and damp. There is no heat. The large steel doors that line the warehouse walls stay open most of the day. In the cold months, wind, rain, and snow blow across the floor. In the summer the warehouse becomes an oven. Dust and sand from the runways mix with the toxic fumes of fork lifts, leaving a dry, stale taste in your mouth. The high windows above the doors are covered with a thick, black dirt that kills the sun. The men work in shadows with the constant roar of jet engines blowing dangerously in their ears.
>
> —PATRICK FENTON, "Confessions of a Working Stiff"

Here the implied topic sentence might be stated as *Working conditions in the warehouse are uncomfortable, dreary, and hazardous to one's health.* But the writer does not have to state this information explicitly because we can gather it easily from the examples and specific details he provides. The description of *wind, rain, and snow* blowing across the floor in the winter, of *dust and sand* mixed with *toxic fumes* in an *oven* in summer, and of *thick, black dirt that kills the sun* and *the constant roar of jet engines* makes the general unpleasantness and danger of this workplace vividly clear.

Though implied topic sentences are common, especially in descriptions, in some college writing they may be viewed as weaknesses.

EXERCISE 6.2

Choose an essay you have written, and identify the topic sentence of each paragraph, noting where in the paragraph the topic sentence appears and whether any topic sentence is implied rather than stated. Experiment with one paragraph, positioning its topic sentence in at least two different places. What difference does the change make? If you have any implied topic sentences, try stating them explicitly. Does the paragraph become easier to read?

2

Relating each sentence to the main idea

Whether the main idea of a paragraph is stated in a topic sentence or is only implied, you have to make sure each sentence relates or contributes to the main idea. Look, for example, at the following paragraph, which opens an essay about African American music:

> When I was a teenager, there were two distinct streams of popular music: one was black, and the other was white. The former could only be heard way at the end of the radio dial, while white music dominated everywhere else. This separation was a fact of life, the equivalent of blacks sitting in the back of the bus and "whites only" signs below the Mason-Dixon line. Satchmo might grin for days on "The Ed Sullivan Show" and certain historians hold forth *ad nauseam* on the black contribution to American music, but the truth was that our worlds rarely twined.
> —MARCIA GILLESPIE, "They're Playing My Music, but Burying My Dreams"

The first sentence announces the topic (there are two streams of popular music: black and white). The second sentence relates the topic to the positions of black and white music on the radio dial, and the third sentence expands on this notion of musical separation by comparing it to the separate seats for blacks on buses and their exclusion from certain public places. The last sentence rephrases the topic sentence much more pointedly: though black music may be heard regularly on television and people have written extensively on the black contribution to American music, the worlds of black and white music were at one time separate. Each sentence clearly relates to the topic, and the paragraph as a whole is unified.

EXERCISE 6.3

The following paragraph lacks unity. Identify the topic sentence, and revise the paragraph by deleting any sentence unrelated to the topic.

> According to advertisers, one side of every woman's personality is sensual, knowing, experienced, worldly, unshockable, well versed in the art of love: in short, a woman in every sense of the word. The opposing side is shy, sweet, trusting, innocent, untried: a maiden immersed in her own purity. Many argue that men possess a split personality, too. This is exactly how I feel as a woman: forever pushed, pulled, jostled, teased, and finally lured into treading a fine line between blatant maturity and subtle innocence. No wonder so many women begin to feel like a Dr. Doolittle "Push-me, Pull-you," the animal with two heads, each facing in the opposite direction, each vying for its own desires, and neither budging an inch.

EXERCISE 6.4

Choose one of the following topic sentences, and spend some time exploring the topic (see 3a). Then write a paragraph that includes the topic sentence, making sure that each of the other sentences relates to it. Assume that the paragraph will be part of a letter you are writing to an acquaintance.

1. I found out quickly that college life was not quite what I had expected.
2. Being part of the "in crowd" used to be of utmost importance to me.
3. My work experience has taught me several important lessons.
4. Until recently, I never appreciated my parents fully.
5. I expect my college education to do more than assure me of a job.

EXERCISE 6.5

Choose an essay you have written recently, and examine the second, third, and fourth paragraphs. Does each have a topic sentence or strongly imply one? Do all the other sentences in the paragraph focus on its main idea? Would you now revise any of these paragraphs—and if so, how?

6d

Making paragraphs coherent: fitting details together

A paragraph has coherence if its details fit together clearly in a way that readers can easily follow. You can achieve paragraph coherence in three simple ways: by organizing ideas, by repeating key terms or phrases, and by using parallel structures.

1

Organizing ideas

If you take every fourth sentence of an essay and arrange those sentences, one after another, in paragraph form, you will *not* end up with a paragraph. Why not? Because the sentences will have only a haphazard relationship to one another. Though they may well be connected to the same topic, the lack of any organizational relationship will result in incoherence. Clear organization of ideas goes a long way toward creating coherence. The following discussion will review the most common means of organizing a paragraph—spatial order, chronological order, and logical order.

Using spatial order

Paragraphs organized in **spatial order** take a "tour," beginning at one point and moving, say, from near to far, left to right, north to south. Especially useful in descriptive paragraphs, spatial order allows a writer to direct readers' attention in an orderly way to various elements of something in physical space. A topic sentence may be unnecessary in such a paragraph because the paragraph's organization will be obvious to the reader. Sometimes, however, a topic sentence at the beginning of the paragraph helps set the scene, or it tells the reader what is going to be described. Note the movement from ceiling to walls to floor in the following paragraph:

> The professor's voice began to fade into the background as my eyes wandered around the classroom in the old administration building. The water-stained ceiling was cracked and peeling, and the splitting wooden beams played host to a variety of lead pipes and coils. My eyes followed these pipes down the walls and around corners until eventually I saw the electric outlets. I thought it strange that they were exposed, and not built in, until I realized that there probably had been no electricity when the building was built. Below the outlets the sunshine was falling in bright rays across the hardwood floor, and I noticed how smoothly the floor was worn. Time had taken its toll on this building.

Using chronological order

Paragraphs organized in **chronological order** arrange a series of events according to time, putting earliest events first, followed in sequence by later events, one at a time. Chronological order is used frequently in **narrative** paragraphs, which tell a story. They may not require a topic sentence if the main idea is obvious in the action. The following paragraph uses careful chronology to tell a story and build suspense so that we want to know what the last event will be. The phrases expressing time help build this suspense: *all of a sudden, three months, a year later,* and so on.

> The experience of Lloyd S., an Oregon businessperson, is one of the most convincing cases for taking vitamins. For his first forty years, Lloyd was healthy and robust. He owned a thriving nursery and loved to hike, fish, and camp. All of a sudden, he started feeling fatigued. A loss of appetite and weight soon followed, and in three months he was transformed from a ruddy, muscular man into a pallid, emaciated one. Lloyd had cancer of the pancreas. After he was given a prognosis of six months to live, his family and friends were devastated, but Lloyd was a fighter. When the conventional treatments of drugs and chemotherapy did not help, he turned to a holistic approach, which emphasized a change in diet and life style—and large doses of vitamins. After a series of blood tests to discover every possible nutritional deficiency, Lloyd was given concentrated vitamin and mineral supplements to ensure maximum cell efficiency and growth so that his body could attempt to heal itself. At the end of six months, Lloyd not only was alive but also showed improvement. A year later he was free of cancer and began the long battle to regain his original vitality. Coincidence? Perhaps. To Lloyd and me, however, his recovery became

a powerful demonstration of how the world's most intricate machine, the human body, performs—if only we supply it with the needed nutrients.

Chronological order is also commonly used in **explaining a process**—that is, in describing how something happens or how something is done: first one step, then the next, and then the next. You are already familiar with process as a means of organizing information. After all, every set of directions, every recipe, every user's manual presents a series of steps that makes up a process to be learned or followed. Here is an example.

> Before trying to play the flute, figure out how to put it together. The flute is divided into three parts: the mouthpiece, the main body, and the end piece. First remove the main body (the longest part) from the case, and set it down with the keys facing up and the openings away from you. Now pick up the mouthpiece (the piece with one hole), and attach it to the hole at the far left end of the main body by gently twisting it from side to side, in a manner similar to jiggling a door knob. Repeat the same process in attaching the end piece to the other end of the main body, taking care not to twist or smash the keys. The keys on the end piece should be lined up with those on the main body.

In college writing, you will probably use process paragraphs less often to tell readers how to do something than to explain how a process occurs in general—for example, how a bill becomes law or how aerosol sprays destroy the ozone layer of the atmosphere.

Using logical order

Paragraphs organized in **logical order** arrange details to reflect certain logical relationships. Explanations and examples of some of these relationships—illustration, definition, division and classification, comparison and contrast, cause and effect, problems and solutions, narration, and reiteration—are given in 6e. Two other logical patterns commonly used in paragraphs are *general to specific* and *specific to general*.

Paragraphs organized in a **general-to-specific** pattern usually open with a topic sentence presenting a general or abstract idea and are followed by a number of more specific points designed to substantiate or prove or elaborate on the generalization.

GENERAL TO SPECIFIC

> One of the most tragic manifestations of the pressure black people feel to assimilate is expressed in the internalization of racist perspectives. I was shocked and saddened when I first heard black professors at Stanford downgrade and express contempt for black students, expecting us

GENERAL
TOPIC

SPECIFICS

to do poorly, refusing to establish nurturing bonds. At every university I have attended as a student or worked at as a teacher, I have heard similar attitudes expressed with little or no understanding of factors that might prevent brilliant black students from performing to their full capability. Within universities, there are few educational and social spaces where students who wish to affirm positive ties to ethnicity—to blackness, to working-class backgrounds—can receive affirmation and support. Ideologically, the message is clear—assimilation is the way to gain acceptance and approval from those in power. —BELL HOOKS, *Talking Back*

Paragraphs can also follow a **specific-to-general** organization, first providing a series of specific examples or details and then tying them together with a general conclusion.

SPECIFIC TO GENERAL

At 8:01 A.M. on Saturday morning, the bright images hawk cereal: Fruit Loops, Frosted Flakes, Captain Crunch. At 8:11, it's toy time, as squads of delighted children demonstrate the pleasures of owning Barbie, Ken, or GI Joe. By 8:22, Coca-Cola is quenching thirsts everywhere, and at 8:31, kids declare devotion to their Nikes, ensuring that every child tuned in will want a pair. And so goes Saturday morning children's programming: one part "program" (and that exclusively cartoons) to three parts advertising. "Children's television" today is simply a euphemism for one long, hard sell, an initiation rite designed to create more and more American consumers.

SPECIFICS

GENERAL
TOPIC

EXERCISE 6.6

Choose one of the following topic sentences, or create one of your own, and try writing two different paragraphs on the topic, using a different organizational pattern for each. Then explain, in writing, why you used the organizational patterns you did and how effective and coherent each one was.

1. I remember very clearly the first time I ever experienced great satisfaction.
2. Explaining _____ to my parents was the hardest thing I've ever done.
3. People who are extremely vain about their looks often go to ridiculous lengths to keep up their appearance.
4. Describing my classes this term as demanding is an understatement.
5. Many people share one basic fear: speaking in public.

2

Repeating key words and phrases

A major means of building coherence in paragraphs is through **repetition**. Weaving in repeated references to key words and phrases not only links sentences but also alerts readers to the importance of those words or phrases in the larger piece of writing. Notice in the following example how the repetition of the key words *shop* (*shopping, shoppers, shops*), *market(s)*, *bargain(ing)*, *customers, buy, price, store,* and *item* helps hold the paragraph together:

> Over the centuries, *shopping* has changed in function as well as in style. Before the Industrial Revolution, most consumer goods were sold in open-air *markets, customers* who went into an actual *shop* were expected to *buy* something, and *shoppers* were always expected to *bargain* for the best possible *price.* In the nineteenth century, however, the development of the department *store* changed the relationship between buyers and sellers. Instead of visiting several *market* stalls or small *shops, customers* could now *buy* a variety of merchandise under the same roof; instead of feeling expected to *buy*, they were welcome just to look; and instead of *bargaining* with several merchants, they paid a fixed *price* for each *item.* In addition, they could return an *item* to the *store* and exchange it for a different one or get their money back. All of these changes helped transform *shopping* from serious requirement to psychological recreation.

EXERCISE 6.7

Read the following paragraph. Then identify the places where the author uses repetition of key words and phrases, and explain how they bring coherence to the paragraph.

> This is not to say that technology was an unadulterated plus in the '90s. The Information Superhighway was pretty much of a dud. Remember that? By the mid-'90s, just about everybody was hooked up to the vast international computer network, exchanging vast quantities of information at high speeds via modems and fiber-optic cable with everybody else. The problem, of course, was that even though the information was coming a lot faster, the vast majority of it, having originated with human beings, was still wrong. Eventually people realized that the Information Superhighway was essentially CB radio, but with more typing. By late in the decade millions of Americans had abandoned their computers and turned to the immensely popular new VirtuLib 2000, a $14,000 device that enables the user to experience, with uncanny realism, the sensation of reading a book. —DAVE BARRY, "The '90s"

3

Using parallel structures

Parallel structures—structures that are grammatically similar—provide another effective way of bringing coherence to a paragraph. They emphasize the connection between related ideas or events in different sentences. For example:

> William Faulkner's "Barn Burning" tells the story of a young boy trapped in a no-win situation. If he betrays his father, he loses his family. If he betrays justice, he becomes a fugitive. In trying to free himself from his trap, he does both.

In this paragraph, the writer skillfully uses the parallel structure *if he does x, he does y* in order to give the effect of a no-win situation. At the end of the paragraph, we are prepared for the last sentence in the parallel sequence: *In doing x, he does y.* As readers, we feel pulled along by the force of the parallel structures. (See Chapter 21 on using parallel structure.)

EXERCISE 6.8

Read the following paragraph from a famous essay by a woman who wants a "wife," and identify every use of repetition and parallel structure. In a brief paragraph of your own, explain how the writer uses these structures to build coherence in this paragraph.

I would like to go back to school so that I can become economically independent, support myself, and, if need be, support those dependent upon me. I want a wife who will work and send me to school. And while I am going to school I want a wife to take care of my children. I want a wife to keep track of the children's doctor and dentist appointments. And to keep track of mine, too. I want a wife to make sure my children eat properly and are kept clean. I want a wife who will wash the children's clothes and keep them mended. I want a wife who is a good nurturant attendant to my children, who arranges for their schooling, makes sure that they have an adequate social life with their peers, takes them to the park, the zoo, etc. I want a wife who takes care of the children when they are sick, a wife who arranges to be around when the children need special care, because, of course, I cannot miss classes at school. My wife must arrange to lose time at work and not lose the job. It may mean a small cut in my wife's income from time to time, but I guess I can tolerate that. Needless to say, my wife will arrange and pay for the care of the children while my wife is working.

–JUDY BRADY, "I Want a Wife"

4

Using pronouns

Writers also achieve coherence in a paragraph through the use of pronouns. Because pronouns usually refer back to nouns or other pronouns, they act as natural coherence devices, leading readers from sentence to sentence (see Chapter 13). The following paragraph, from an essay on old age, uses pronouns effectively in linking sentences to one another. Note how much slower and more awkward the paragraph would be if each pronoun were replaced with the noun it stands for. Also note that the writer uses the name when he first introduces each new artist—and then uses pronouns thereafter to refer to that person. (Italics added for emphasis.)

For such [old] persons, every new infirmity is an enemy to be outwitted, an obstacle to be overcome by force of will. *They* enjoy each little victory over *themselves,* and sometimes *they* win a major success. Renoir was one of *them. He* continued painting, and magnificently, for years after *he* was crippled by arthritis; the brush had to be strapped to *his* arm. "You don't need your hand to paint," *he* said. Goya was another of the unvanquished. At 72 *he* retired as an official painter of the Spanish court and decided to work only for *himself. His* later years were those of the famous "black paintings" in which *he* let *his* imagination run (and also of the lithographs, then a new technique). At 78 *he* escaped a reign of terror in Spain by fleeing to Bordeaux. *He* was deaf and *his* eyes were failing; in order to work *he* had to wear several pairs of spectacles, one over another, and then use a magnifying glass; but *he* was producing splendid work in a totally new style. At 80 *he* drew an ancient man propped on two sticks, with a mass of white hair and beard hiding *his* face and with the inscription "*I* am still learning."

–MALCOLM COWLEY, *The View from 80*

EXERCISE 6.9

Choose something you've written recently, and analyze three of its paragraphs. How do the pronouns bring coherence to the paragraphs? Is it clear what noun or pronoun each of the pronouns refers back to? How could you use different or additional pronouns to improve the coherence of these paragraphs?

5

Using transitional devices

Transitions are words and phrases that help bring coherence to a paragraph by signaling relationships between and among sentences. In acting as signposts, transitions such as *after all, for example, indeed, so,* and *thus* help readers follow the progression of one idea to the next within a paragraph. *Finally* indicates that a last point is at hand; *likewise,* that a similar point is about to be made; and so on. To get an idea of how important transitions are in directing readers, try reading the following paragraph, from which all transitional devices have been removed:

A PARAGRAPH WITH NO TRANSITIONS

In "The Fly," Katherine Mansfield tries to show us the "real" personality of "the boss" beneath his exterior. The fly helps her to portray this real self. The boss goes through a range of emotions and feelings. He expresses these feelings to a small but determined fly, whom the reader realizes he unconsciously relates to his son. The author basically splits up the story into three parts, with the boss's emotions and actions changing quite measurably. With old Woodifield, with himself, and with the fly, we see the boss's manipulativeness. Our understanding of him as a hard and cruel man grows.

We can, if we work at it, figure out the relationship of these ideas to one another, for this paragraph is essentially unified by one major idea. But the lack of transitions results in an abrupt, choppy rhythm that lurches from one idea to the next, dragging the confused reader behind. See how much easier the passage is to read and understand with transitions added.

THE SAME PARAGRAPH, WITH TRANSITIONS

In "The Fly," Katherine Mansfield tries to show us the "real" personality of "the boss" beneath his exterior. The fly *in the story's title* helps her to portray this real self. *In the course of the story,* the boss goes through a range of emotions. *At the end,* he *finally* expresses these feelings to a small but determined fly, whom the reader realizes he unconsciously relates to his son. *To accomplish her goal,* the author basically splits up the story into three parts, with the boss's emotions and actions changing measurably *throughout. First* with old Woodifield, *then* with himself, and *last* with the fly, we see the boss's manipulativeness. *With each part,* our understanding of him as a hard and cruel man grows.

Note how the writer carefully leads us through the points of her paragraph. Most of the transitional devices here point to movement in time, helping us follow the chronology of the story being discussed: *in the course of the story; at the end; finally; throughout; first; then; last.*

It is important to note that transitions can only clarify connections between thoughts; they cannot create connections. As a writer, you must choose transitions that fit your meaning—you should not expect a transition to provide meaning.

Commonly used transitions

TO SIGNAL SEQUENCE

again, also, and, and then, besides, finally, first . . . second . . . third, furthermore, last, moreover, next, still, too

TO SIGNAL TIME

after a few days, after a while, afterward, as long as, as soon as, at last, at that time, before, earlier, immediately, in the meantime, in the past, lately, later, meanwhile, now, presently, simultaneously, since, so far, soon, then, thereafter, until, when

TO SIGNAL COMPARISON

again, also, in the same way, likewise, once more, similarly

TO SIGNAL CONTRAST

although, but, despite, even though, however, in contrast, in spite of, instead, nevertheless, nonetheless, on the contrary, on the one hand . . . on the other hand, regardless, still, though, yet

TO SIGNAL EXAMPLES

after all, even, for example, for instance, indeed, in fact, of course, specifically, such as, the following example, to illustrate

TO SIGNAL CAUSE AND EFFECT

accordingly, as a result, because, consequently, for this purpose, hence, so, then, therefore, thereupon, thus, to this end

TO SIGNAL PLACE

above, adjacent to, below, beyond, closer to, elsewhere, far, farther on, here, near, nearby, opposite to, there, to the left, to the right

TO SIGNAL CONCESSION

although it is true that, granted that, I admit that, it may appear that, naturally, of course

TO SIGNAL SUMMARY, REPETITION, OR CONCLUSION

as a result, as has been noted, as I have said, as we have seen, as mentioned earlier, in any event, in conclusion, in other words, in short, on the whole, therefore, to summarize

For a discussion of transitional devices to link paragraphs, see 6g.

> ▶ *FOR MULTILINGUAL WRITERS*
> *Distinguishing among Transitions*
>
> Distinguishing among some very similar common transition words can be difficult for multilingual writers. The difference between *however* and *nevertheless*, for example, is a subtle one: while each introduces statements that contrast with what comes before it, *nevertheless* emphasizes the contrast whereas *however* tones it down. To help make such fine distinctions, check the usage of transitions in English dictionaries such as *The American Heritage Dictionary of the English Language* or *The Oxford Advanced Learner's Dictionary*, which provide usage notes for easily confused words.

EXERCISE 6.10

Read the following paragraph, and identify all transitional devices. Then read the paragraph with these words or phrases left out, and briefly describe, in writing, the difference the transitional devices make.

The popularity of the various regional styles of American costume, like that of the various national styles, is also related to economic and political factors. Some years ago modes often originated in the Far West and the word "California" on a garment was thought to be an allurement. Today, with power and population growth shifting to the Southwestern oil-producing states, Wild West styles—particularly those of Texas—are in vogue. This fashion, of course, is not new. For many years men who have never been nearer to a cow than the local steakhouse have worn Western costume to signify that they are independent, tough and reliable. In a story by Flannery O'Connor, for instance, the sinister traveling salesman is described as wearing "a broad-brimmed stiff gray hat of the kind used by businessmen who would like to look like cowboys"—but, it is implied, seldom succeed in doing so.

–ALISON LURIE, *The Language of Clothes*

EXERCISE 6.11

The following sentences are shown out of their original order. Look for pronouns, transitional words and phrases, and other clues to coherence. Then rearrange the sentences so that the paragraph is once again coherent.

(1) The sun came out hot and bright, endlessly, day after day. (2) They harvested half the corn, and ground the other half, stalks and all, and fed it to the cattle as fodder. (3) And in the next year the drought hit. (4) They burned it in the furnace for fuel that winter. (5) My mother and father trudged from the well to the chickens, the well to the calf pasture, the well to the barn, and from the well to the garden. (6) The crops shriveled and died. (7) With the price at four cents a bushel for the harvested crop, they couldn't afford to haul it into town. –DONNA SMITH-YACKEL, "My Mother Never Worked"

EXERCISE 6.12

Identify the devices—repetition of key words or phrases, parallel structures, pronouns, transitional expressions—that make the following paragraph coherent.

I must make two honest confessions to you, my Christian and Jewish brothers. First, I must confess that over the past few years I have been gravely disappointed with the white moderate. I have almost reached the regrettable conclusion that the Negro's great stumbling block on his stride toward freedom is not the White Citizen's Counciler or the Ku Klux Klanner, but the white moderate, who is more devoted to "order" than to justice; who prefers a negative peace which is the absence of tension to a positive peace which is the presence of justice; who constantly says, "I agree with you in the goal you seek, but I cannot agree with your methods of direct action"; who paternalistically believes he can set the timetable for another man's freedom; who lives by a mythical concept of time and who constantly advises the Negro to wait for a "more convenient season." Shallow understanding from people of good will is more frustrating than absolute misunderstanding from people of ill will. Lukewarm acceptance is much more bewildering than outright rejection.
—Martin Luther King, Jr., "Letter from Birmingham Jail"

6e

Developing paragraphs fully: providing details

In addition to being unified and coherent, a paragraph must hold readers' interest and explore its topic fully, using whatever details, evidence, and examples are necessary. Without such **development**, a paragraph may seem lifeless and abstract.

Most good writing does two things: it presents generalized ideas and explanations, and it backs up these generalities with specifics. This balance, the shifting between general and specific, is especially important at the paragraph level. If a paragraph contains nothing but specific details, with no explanation of how they should be viewed as a whole, readers may have trouble following the writer's meaning. If, on the other hand, a paragraph contains only abstract ideas and general statements, readers will soon become bored or will fail to be convinced. General statements or conclusions thus rest on specific, concrete pieces of knowledge and sensory details. Well-developed paragraphs include examples and reasons that demonstrate such knowledge and details. Consider the following poorly developed paragraph:

A POORLY DEVELOPED PARAGRAPH

No such thing as "human nature" compels people to behave, think, or react in certain ways. Rather, from the time of our infancy to our death, we are constantly being taught, by the society that surrounds us, the customs, norms, and mores of our distinct culture. Everything in culture is learned, not genetically transmitted.

This paragraph is boring. Although its main idea is clear and its sentences hold together, it fails to gain our interest, hold our attention, or convince us because it lacks any concrete illustrations. Now look at the paragraph revised to include needed specifics.

THE SAME PARAGRAPH, REVISED

Imagine a child in Ecuador dancing to salsa music at a warm family gathering, while a child in the United States is decorating a Christmas tree with bright, shiny red ornaments. Both of these children are taking part in their country's cultures. It is not by instinct that one child knows how to dance to salsa music, nor is it by instinct that the other child knows how to decorate the tree. No such thing as "human nature" compels people to behave, think, or react in certain ways. Rather, from the time of our infancy to our death, we are constantly being taught by the society that surrounds us, the customs, norms, and mores of our distinct culture. A majority of people feel that the evil in human beings is "human nature." However, the Tasaday, a "Stone Age" tribe discovered not long ago in the Philippines, do not even have equivalents in their language for the words *hatred, competition, acquisitiveness, aggression,* and *greed.* Such examples suggest that everything in culture is learned, not genetically transmitted.

Though both paragraphs argue the same point, only the second one comes to life. It does so by bringing in specific details *from* life. We want to read this paragraph, for it appeals to our senses (a child dancing; bright, shiny red ornaments) and our curiosity (who are the Tasaday?).

Almost every paragraph can be improved by making sure that its general ideas rest on enough specific detail. You can, of course, add too many details, pushing examples at the reader when no more are needed. For every writer who has to chop back jungles of detail, however, there are five whose greatest task is to irrigate deserts of generality.

EXERCISE 6.13

Rewrite the following undeveloped paragraphs by adding concrete supporting details, examples, and reasons.

1. *The introduction to an essay tentatively titled "A Week on $12.80"*
    Nothing is more frustrating to a college student than being dead broke. Not having money for enough food or for the rent, much less for entertainment, is not much fun. And of course debts for tuition and books keep piling up. No, being broke is not to be recommended.

2. *The introduction to a humorous essay contrasting cats and dogs*

Have you threatened your cat lately? If not, why not? Why not get a *real* pet—a dog? Dogs, after all, are better pets. Cats, on the other hand, are a menace to the environment.

1

Using logical patterns of development

The **patterns** shown in 3d for organizing essays can also serve as a means of developing paragraphs. These patterns include illustrating, defining, dividing and classifying, comparing and contrasting, exploring causes and effects, considering problems and solutions or questions and answers, narrating, and reiterating.

Illustrating

One of the most common ways of developing a paragraph is by **illustrating a point** with concrete examples or with good reasons.

A SINGLE EXAMPLE

The Indians made names for us children in their teasing way. Because our very busy mother kept my hair cut short, like my brothers', they called me Short Furred One, pointing to their hair and making the sign for short, the right hand with fingers pressed close together, held upward, back out, at the height intended. With me this was about two feet tall, the Indians laughing gently at my abashed face. I am told that I was given a pair of small moccasins that first time, to clear up my unhappiness at being picked out from the dusk behind the fire and my two unhappy shortcomings made conspicuous.   —MARI SANDOZ, "The Go-Along Ones"

SEVERAL REASONS

But I did not want to shoot the elephant. I watched him beating his bunch of grass against his knees, with the preoccupied grandmotherly air that elephants have. It seemed to me that it would be murder to shoot him. At that age I was not squeamish about killing animals, but I had never shot an elephant and never wanted to. (Somehow it always seems worse to kill a large animal.) Besides, there was the beast's owner to be considered. Alive, the elephant was worth at least a hundred pounds; dead, he would only be worth the value of his tusks, five pounds, possibly. But I had got to act quickly. I turned to some experienced-looking Burmans who had been there when we arrived, and asked them how the elephant had been behaving. They all said the same thing: he took no notice of you if you left him alone, but he might charge if you went too close to him.
                              —GEORGE ORWELL, "Shooting an Elephant"

Defining

You will often have occasion to develop an entire paragraph by **defining** a word or concept. Some college courses, particularly ones that deal with difficult abstractions, require writing that calls for this strategy. A philosophy exam, for instance, might require you to define concepts such as *truth* or *validity*. Often, however, you will find it necessary to combine definition with other methods of development. You may need to show examples or draw comparisons or divide a term you are defining into two parts. In the following paragraph, Tom Wolfe defines *pornoviolence,* a word he has coined, by contrasting it first with "accumulated slayings and bone crushings" and then with violence seen from the point of view of "the hero."

It is not the accumulated slayings and bone crushings that make [this TV show into] pornoviolence, however. What makes pornoviolence is that in almost every case the camera angle, therefore the viewer, is with the gun, the fist, the rock. The pornography of violence has no point of view in the old sense that novels do. You do not live the action through the hero's eyes. You live with the aggressor, whoever he may be. One moment you are the hero. The next you are the villain. No matter whose side you may be on consciously, you are in fact with the muscle, and it is you who disintegrate all comers, villains, lawmen, women, anybody. On the rare occasions in which the gun is emptied into the camera—i.e., into your face—the effect is so startling that the pornography of violence all but loses its fantasy charm. There are not nearly so many masochists as sadists among those little devils whispering into one's ears.

–TOM WOLFE, "Pornoviolence"

Dividing and classifying

Dividing breaks a single item into parts. **Classifying,** which is actually a form of dividing, groups many separate items according to their similarities. You could, for instance, develop a paragraph evaluating a history course by dividing the course into several segments—textbooks, lectures, assignments—and examining each one in turn. Or you could develop a paragraph giving an overview of history courses at your college by classifying, or grouping, the courses in a number of ways—by the time periods or geographic areas covered, by the kinds of assignments demanded, by the number of students enrolled, or by some other criterion.

DIVIDING

We all listen to music according to our separate capacities. But, for the sake of analysis, the whole listening process may become clearer if we break it up into its component parts, so to speak. In a certain sense we all listen to music on three separate planes. For lack of a better terminology, one might name these: (1) the sensuous plane, (2) the expressive plane, (3) the sheerly musical plane. The only advantage to be gained from mechanically splitting up the listening process into these hypothetical planes is the clearer view to be had of the way in which we listen.

–AARON COPLAND, *What to Listen for in Music*

CLASSIFYING

Two types of people are seduced by fad diets. Those who have always been overweight turn to them out of despair; they have tried everything, and yet nothing seems to work. The second group to succumb appear perfectly healthy but are baited by slogans such as "look good, feel good." These slogans prompt self-questioning and insecurity—do I really look good and feel good?—and as a direct result, many healthy people fall prey to fad diets. With both types of people, however, the problems surrounding such diets are numerous and dangerous. In fact, these diets provide neither intelligent nor effective answers to weight control.

Comparing and contrasting

You can develop some paragraphs easily and effectively by comparing and contrasting various aspects of the topic or by comparing and contrasting the topic with something else. **Comparing** things highlights their similarities; **contrasting** points to their differences. Whether used alone or together, comparing and contrasting both act to focus the topic at hand more clearly— we can better understand an unknown by comparing it to something we know well.

You can structure comparison-contrast paragraphs in two basic ways. One way is to present all the information about one item and then all the information about the other item (the **block method**). The other possibility is to switch back and forth between the two items, focusing on particular characteristics of each in turn (**alternating method**).

BLOCK METHOD

You could tell the veterans from the rookies by the way they were dressed. The knowledgeable ones had their heads covered by kerchiefs, so that if they were hired, tobacco dust wouldn't get in their hair; they had on clean dresses that by now were faded and shapeless, so that if they were hired they wouldn't get tobacco dust and grime on their best clothes. Those who were trying for the first time had their hair freshly done and wore attractive dresses; they wanted to make a good impression. But the dresses couldn't be seen at the distance that many were standing from the employment office, and they were crumpled in the crush.

–MARY MEBANE, "Summer Job"

ALTERNATING METHOD

Malcolm X emphasized the use of violence in his movement and employed the biblical principle of "an eye for an eye and a tooth for a tooth." King, on the other hand, felt that blacks should use nonviolent civil disobedience and employed the theme "turning the other cheek," which Malcolm X rejected as "beggarly" and "feeble." The philosophy of Malcolm X was one of revenge, and often it broke the unity of black Americans. More radical blacks supported him, while more conservative ones supported King. King thought that blacks should transcend their humanity. In contrast, Malcolm X thought they should embrace it and reserve their love for one another, regarding whites as "devils" and the "enemy." King's politics were those of a rainbow, but Malcolm X's rainbow was insistently one color—black. The distance between Martin Luther King Jr.'s thinking and Malcolm X's was the distance between growing up in the seminary and growing up on the streets, between the American dream and the American reality.

EXERCISE 6.14

Outline the preceding paragraph on Martin Luther King, Jr., and Malcolm X, noting its alternating pattern. Then rewrite the paragraph using block organization: the first part of the paragraph devoted to King, the second to Malcolm X. Finally, write a brief paragraph analyzing the two paragraphs, explaining which seems more coherent and easier to follow and why.

Exploring causes and effects

Certain topics will require you to consider the process of **cause and effect**, and you can often develop paragraphs by detailing the causes of something or the effects that something brings about. A question on geology, for instance, may lead you to write a paragraph describing the major causes of soil erosion in the Midwest—or the effects of such erosion. The following paragraph discusses the effects of television on the American family:

Television's contribution to family life has been an equivocal one. For while it has, indeed, kept the members of the family from dispersing, it has not served to bring them *together*. By its domination of the time families spend together, it destroys the special quality that distinguishes one family from another, a quality that depends to a great extent on what a family *does*, what special rituals, games, recurrent jokes, familiar songs, and shared activities it accumulates.

–MARIE WINN, *The Plug-in Drug: Television, Children, and the Family*

Considering problems and solutions or questions and answers

Paragraphs developed in the **problem-solution pattern** open with a statement of a problem, usually the topic sentence, and then offer a solution in the sentences that follow, as in this paragraph.

RVing Women's rapid growth created a dilemma for its founding mothers. They could either quit traveling and rent an office, or get a bigger RV. So they traded in the Class C for a 34-foot fifth wheel (a trailer that is hitched to the bed of a pickup truck). Now, Lovern and Zoe have an office equipped with two computers, two printers, and a copy machine in their rig, where they handle the mail and newsletter comfortably. They also publish a directory and maintain a Phonelink service so members can find each other on the road, organize caravans, and plan excursions and outings. In addition, with help from members, they have organized eight gatherings around the country, with 16 more planned for the rest of 1992. It's beginning to look as if Zoe and Lovern's new pastime is turning into their second careers.   —MARILYN MURPHY, "Roam, Sweet Home"

Similar to the problem-solution pattern is the **question-and-answer pattern** of development, which does just what its name suggests: the first sentence poses a question, and the rest of the paragraph provides the answer. Beginning with a question provides a means of getting—and focusing—readers' attention.

Narrating

Narrating allows writers to provide personal or historical accounts in order to develop ideas. Narrative paragraphs are often arranged chronologically, sometimes with such variations on chronological order as flashbacks and flash-forwards. They may lead to a **climax**, which provides the point of the story being told. Here is one student's narrative paragraph that tells a personal story in order to support a point about the dangers of racing bicycles with flimsy alloy frames. This paragraph builds to a climax, saving the most extreme point *(He couldn't even walk)* for last. It also uses **description**, adding specific, concrete details to help the reader "see" the story: *catapulted onto Vermont pavement at fifty miles an hour,* for instance, or *My Italian racing bike was pretzled.*

People who have been exposed to the risk of dangerously designed bicycle frames have paid too high a price. I saw this danger myself in the 1984 Putney Race. A Stowe-Shimano graphite frame failed, and the rider was catapulted onto Vermont pavement at fifty miles per hour. The pack of riders behind him was so dense that most other racers crashed into a tangled, sliding heap. The aftermath: four hospitalizations. I got off with some stitches, a bad road rash, and severely pulled tendons. My Italian racing bike was pretzled, and my racing was over for that summer. Others were not so lucky. An Olympic hopeful, Brian Stone of the Northstar team, woke up in a hospital bed to find that his cycling was over—and not just for that summer. His kneecap had been surgically removed. He couldn't even walk.

USING DIALOGUE

Narrative paragraphs sometimes include dialogue, to represent actual speech from the event. The dialogue in the following paragraph, for example, allows readers to hear what was said rather than hearing *about* it.

When my siblings and I were children, we vowed that we would not yell at our kids or say mean things the way Mama and Daddy did. Yet some of us have, unwittingly, broken that vow. Visiting one of my sisters and her family for the first time, I was shocked at the harsh, negative manner she used when speaking to her children. It was so much like our childhood, only there was one difference: Her children used the same nasty tone of voice when speaking to each other. When I gently called her on it and voiced my concern, she expressed surprise. Working all day and coming home to more work, she had not really noticed how she and the kids were talking to one another. I suggested that we do role playing with the kids after dinner—talking the way they talk to one another, then showing how it could be done differently. Rather than saying, "Sit your ass down. I ain't gon tell you no more," we practiced saying politely but firmly, "Would you please stop doing that and sit down?" At first the kids made fun of me and my stories about "noise pollution" and how the way we talk to one another can hurt our hearts and ears, but we could all see and feel the difference. Critical affirmation emerges only when we are willing to risk constructive confrontation and challenge.

—BELL HOOKS, *Sisters of the Yam*

USING EMBEDDED NARRATIVE

One form of narration that is characteristic of much spoken discourse **embeds a narrative**, often in the middle of a paragraph, to elaborate on a point or relate a personal experience that supports the point. In the following example, the writer embeds a narrative to explain how he got the idea for the essay.

For the term essay in Ethnic Art, we were free to write on any relevant subject. Openness, however, can bring its own headaches. With so much to choose from, a guy can feel overwhelmed. Or so I thought— until I suddenly said, "Braids and dreads: that's it!" These are the words that popped into my head as I was driving to school recently, just when I was worrying about a subject for my art paper. I was inspired, I suppose, by friends, people around me, and perhaps the rap group Kriss Kross—

all people who wear braided hair. My first thought was to write only about braids, but then I thought about people who wear their hair in a particular style of braids known as dreadlocks, like Bob Marley. As my brain kept churning, I asked myself, "What are the differences between the two hairstyles? What do these styles mean? Why are they 'in' right now?" In short, I was on my way to an exploration of what I claim is one form of ethnic art.

Reiterating

Reiterating, often used in oral as well as written discourse, is an organizational pattern you may recognize from political discourse or some styles of preaching. In this pattern, the writer states the main point of a paragraph and then reiterates it in a number of different ways, hammering home the point and often building in intensity as well. This strategy found particular power in a number of works by Martin Luther King, Jr. In the following example, King reiterates the topic of the paragraph (we are on the move) five different ways, repeating the idea like a drumbeat throughout the paragraph, building to the climactic move *to the land of freedom.*

> We are on the move now. The burning of our churches will not deter us. We are on the move now. The bombing of our homes will not dissuade us. We are on the move now. The beating and killing of our clergymen and young people will not divert us. We are on the move now. The arrest and release of known murderers will not discourage us. We are on the move now. Like an idea whose time has come, not even the marching of mighty armies can halt us. We are moving to the land of freedom.   —MARTIN LUTHER KING, JR., "Our God Is Marching On"

Combining patterns

Many paragraphs combine methods of development. In the following paragraph, the writer divides a general topic (the accounting systems used by American companies) into two subtopics (the system used to summarize a company's overall financial state and the one used to measure internal transactions) and then develops the second subtopic through illustration (the assessment of costs for a delivery truck shared by two departments) and cause and effect (the system produces some disadvantages).

> Most American companies have basically two accounting systems. One system summarizes the overall financial state to inform stockholders, bankers, and other outsiders. That system is not of interest here. The other system, called the managerial or cost accounting system, exists for an entirely different reason. It measures in detail all of the particulars of transactions between departments, divisions, and key individuals in the organization, for the purpose of untangling the interdependencies between

people. When, for example, two departments share one truck for deliveries, the cost accounting system charges each department for part of the cost of maintaining the truck and driver, so that at the end of the year, the performance of each department can be individually assessed, and the better department's manager can receive a larger raise. Of course, all of this information processing costs money, and furthermore may lead to arguments between the departments over whether the costs charged to each are fair.

–WILLIAM OUCHI, "Japanese and American Workers: Two Casts of Mind"

EXERCISE 6.15

Identify the specific method of development used in each of the following paragraphs, and explain why you think each paragraph is or is not effectively developed using that method.

1.   Other differences I saw between Florida and Germany were the scenery and the culture. Florida's scenery consisted of one-story houses and green lawns. Palm trees and occasional garbage could be seen along the road. In Germany, houses were weirdly shaped with small lawns, if any. Buildings were very close to the road, and very little garbage could be found on the streets. Driving in Germany could be hazardous as compared with driving in Florida, because in Germany there are no speed limits. Cultural differences, such as the time of day you eat and the food you eat, were apparent between Germany and Florida. Communications were obviously different, with the German language being spoken in Germany.

2.   According to Hollywood, the Indian was always the liar, the thief, the cold-blooded, ruthless killer with no compassion. For example, in many movies a wild band of Indians surround a helpless family and, for absolutely no reason at all, slaughter the whole family. The Indians depicted by Hollywood also make sneak attacks on a sleeping town, killing the townspeople and pillaging every inch of the town. In other films, the Indians rustle cattle and horses from farmers and, of course, slay the farmers. This picture of the "Old West" is one of the greatest fallacies of all time.

EXERCISE 6.16

Choose two of the following topics or two others that interest you, and brainstorm or freewrite about each one for ten minutes (see 3a1 and 3a2). Then use the information you have produced to determine what method(s) of development would be most appropriate for each topic.

1. The pleasure a hobby has given you
2. Ice Cube's image and Janet Jackson's image

3. An average Saturday morning
4. Why Monopoly is an appropriate metaphor for U.S. society
5. The best course you've ever taken

EXERCISE 6.17

Refer to the argument you drafted for Exercise 5.14, and study the ways you developed each paragraph. For one of the paragraphs, write a brief evaluation of its development. How would you expand or otherwise improve the development?

2

Determining paragraph length

While the paragraph has existed as a unit of writing for a long, long time, it has changed over the years. If you look at Edward Gibbon's *Decline and Fall of the Roman Empire* (published in the late eighteenth century), for instance, you will see paragraphs longer than most written today. In general, both paragraphs and sentences have gotten shorter over the last two hundred years. Newspapers and magazines, with their narrow columns, are partially responsible for this shift in paragraph length, for they have accustomed readers to short lines and paragraphs.

Though writers must keep their readers' expectations in mind, paragraph length must be determined primarily by content and purpose. Paragraphs should develop an idea, create any desired effects (such as suspense or humor), and advance the piece of writing. Fulfilling these aims will sometimes call for short paragraphs, sometimes for long ones. For example, in an argumentative essay, you may put all your lines of argument or all your evidence into one long paragraph to create the impression of a solid, overwhelmingly convincing thesis. In a narrative about an exciting event, on the other hand, you may use a series of short paragraphs to create suspense, to keep the reader rushing to each new paragraph to find out what happened next.

Remember that a new paragraph signals a pause in thought. Just as timing can make a crucial difference in telling a joke or a dramatic pause can make such a difference in telling a piece of news or gossip, so the pause signaled by a paragraph can lead readers to anticipate what is to follow or give them a moment to digest mentally the material presented in the previous paragraph.

Reasons to start a new paragraph

- to turn to a new idea
- to emphasize something (such as a point or an example)
- to change speakers (in dialogue)
- to lead readers to pause
- to break up lengthy text (often to take up a subtopic)
- to start the conclusion

EXERCISE 6.18

Go through some of your favorite books, looking for two paragraphs—a very long one and a very short one—that impress you as particularly effective. What main idea does each develop? What effects does each create? How does each advance the piece of writing it is a part of?

EXERCISE 6.19

Examine the paragraph breaks in something you have written recently. Explain briefly in writing why you decided on each of the breaks. Would you change any of them now? If so, how and why?

6f

Composing special-purpose paragraphs

Paragraphs serving specialized functions include opening paragraphs, concluding paragraphs, transitional paragraphs, and dialogue paragraphs.

1

Opening paragraphs

Even a good piece of writing may remain unread if it has a weak opening paragraph. In addition to announcing your topic (usually in a thesis statement), therefore, an introductory paragraph must engage readers' interest and focus their attention on what is to follow. At their best, introductory paragraphs serve as hors d'oeuvres, whetting the appetite for the following courses, or as the title sequences in a film, carefully setting the scene. Writers often leave the final drafting of the introduction until last because the focus of the piece may change during the process of writing.

One common kind of opening paragraph follows a general-to-specific pattern, ending with the thesis. In such an introduction, the writer opens with a general statement and then gets more and more specific, concluding with the most specific sentence in the paragraph—the thesis. The following paragraph illustrates such an opening:

> The United States has seen many changes in its economy during the last hundred years. Among these changes is the organization of workers. Unions were formed in the late nineteenth and early twentieth centuries to battle against long workdays and bad working conditions. It was not uncommon then for a worker to be required to work twelve or more hours a day, six days a week, in hazardous and often deadly conditions. The workers organized against their employers and won their battles. Today it is very uncommon to find such oppressive conditions in the workplace. Why, then, do unions still exist? When we examine many of the labor battles of recent years, we find that unions exist mostly as bargaining units through which workers can gain higher wages—at any cost.

GENERAL
STATEMENT

MOVE
TO
SPECIFICITY

THESIS

In this paragraph, the opening sentence introduces a general subject, changes in the U.S. economy; subsequent sentences focus more specifically on unionization; and the last sentence presents the thesis, which the rest of the essay will develop. Other ways of opening an essay include quotations, anecdotes, questions, and opinions.

Opening with a quotation

> There is a bumper sticker that reads, "Too bad ignorance isn't painful." I like that. But ignorance is. We just seldom attribute the pain to it or even recognize it when we see it. Take the postcard on my corkboard. It shows a young man in a very hip jacket smoking a cigarette. In the background is a high school with the American flag waving. The caption says, "Too cool for school. Yet too stupid for the real world." Out of the mouth of the young man is a bubble enclosing the words "Maybe I'll start a band." There could be a postcard showing a jock in a uniform saying, "I don't need school. I'm going to the NFL or NBA." Or one showing a young man or woman studying and a group of young people saying, "So you want to be white." Or something equally demeaning. We need to quit it.
>
> —Nikki Giovanni, "Racism 101"

Opening with an anecdote

I first met Angela Carter at a dinner in honor of the Chilean writer José Donoso at the home of Liz Calder, who then published all of us. My first novel was soon to be published; it was the time of Angela's darkest novel, "The Passion of New Eve." And I was a great fan. Mr. Donoso arrived looking like a Hispanic Buffalo Bill, complete with silver goatee, fringed jacket and cowboy boots, and proceeded, as I saw it, to patronize Angela terribly. His apparent ignorance of her work provoked me into a long expostulation in which I informed him that the woman he was talking to was the most brilliant writer in England. Angela liked that. By the end of the evening, we liked each other, too. That was almost 18 years ago. She was the first great writer I ever met, and she was one of the best, most loyal, most truth-telling, most inspiring friends anyone could ever have. I cannot bear it that she is dead.   –SALMAN RUSHDIE, "Angela Carter"

Opening with a question

Why are Americans terrified of using nuclear power as a source of energy? People are misinformed, or not informed at all, about its benefits and safety. If Americans would take the time to learn about what nuclear power offers, their apprehension and fear might be transformed into hope.

Opening with an opinion

Men need a men's movement about as much as women need chest hair. A brotherhood organized to counter feminists could be timely because—let's be honest—women are no more naturally inclined to equality and fairness than men are. They want power and dominion just as much as any group looking out for its own interests. Organizing to protect the welfare of males might make sense. Unfortunately, the current men's movement does not.   –JOHN RUSZKIEWICZ, *The Presence of Others*

EXERCISE 6.20

Refer once more to the argument you drafted for Exercise 5.14. Examine your introduction carefully, trying to identify the strategy you used. Then choose a different strategy from among those discussed above, and write an alternative introduction. Finally, write a paragraph evaluating which introduction is most effective, and why.

2

Concluding paragraphs

A good conclusion wraps up a piece of writing in a meaningful and memorable way. If a strong opening paragraph whets the appetite of readers or arouses their curiosity, a strong concluding paragraph satisfies them, allowing them to feel that the job the writer set out to do has indeed been completed, that their expectations have been met. A strong conclusion reminds readers of the thesis of the essay and leaves them feeling that they know a good deal more than they did when they began. The concluding paragraph provides the last opportunity for you to impress your message on your readers' minds and create desired effects. As such, it is well worth your time and effort.

One of the most common strategies for concluding uses the specific-to-general pattern, often beginning with a restatement of the thesis (but not a word-for-word repetition of it) and moving to several more general statements. The following paragraph moves in such a way, opening with a final point of contrast, specifying it in several sentences, and then ending with a much more general statement:

> Lastly, and perhaps greatest of all, there was the ability, at the end, to turn quickly from war to peace once the fighting was over. Out of the way these two men behaved at Appomattox came the possibility of a peace of reconciliation. It was a possibility not wholly realized, in the years to come, but which did, in the end, help the two sections to become one nation again . . . after a war whose bitterness might have seemed to make such a reunion wholly impossible. No part of either man's life became him more than the part he played in this brief meeting in the McLean house at Appomattox. Their behavior there put all succeeding generations of Americans in their debt. Two great Americans, Grant and Lee—very different, yet under everything very much alike. Their encounter at Appomattox was one of the great moments of American history.
> –BRUCE CATTON, "Grant and Lee: A Study in Contrasts"

Other effective strategies for concluding include questions, quotations, vivid images, calls for action, and warnings.

Concluding with a question

> All so-called "permanent" antifreeze is basically the same. It is made from a liquid known as ethylene glycol, which has two amazing properties: It has a lower freezing point than water, and a higher boiling point than water. It does not break down (lose its properties), nor will it boil away. And every permanent antifreeze starts with it as a base. Also, just about every antifreeze has now got antileak ingredients, as well as antirust and anticorrosion ingredients. Now, let's suppose that, in formulating the product, one of the companies comes up with a solution that is pink in color, as opposed to all the others, which are blue. Presto—an exclusivity claim. "Nothing else looks like it, nothing else performs like it." Or how about, "Look at ours, and look at anyone else's. You can see the difference our exclusive formula makes." Granted, I'm exaggerating. But did I prove a point?   –PAUL STEVENS, "Weasel Words: God's Little Helpers"

Concluding with a quotation

Despite the celebrity that accrued to her and the air of awesomeness with which she was surrounded in her later years, Miss Keller retained an unaffected personality, certain that her optimistic attitude toward life was justified. "I believe that all through these dark and silent years God has been using my life for a purpose I do not know," she said. "But one day I shall understand and then I will be satisfied."

–ALDEN WHITMAN, "Helen Keller: June 27, 1880–June 1, 1968"

Concluding with a vivid image

It is, in any case, finally you that I end up having to trust not to laugh, not to snicker. Even as you regard me in these lines, I try to imagine your face as you read. You who read "Aria," especially those of you with your theme-divining yellow felt pen poised in your hand, you for whom this essay is yet another "assignment," please do not forget that it is my life I am handing you in these pages—memories that are as personal for me as family photographs in an old cigar box.

–RICHARD RODRIGUEZ, from a postscript to "Aria"

Concluding with a call for action

It is now almost 40 years since the invention of nuclear weapons. We have not yet experienced a global thermonuclear war—although on more than one occasion we have come tremulously close. I do not think our luck can hold forever. Men and machines are fallible, as recent events remind us. Fools and madmen do exist, and sometimes rise to power. Concentrating always on the near future, we have ignored the long-term consequences of our actions. We have placed our civilization and our species in jeopardy.

Fortunately, it is not yet too late. We can safeguard the planetary civilization and the human family if we so choose. There is no more important or more urgent issue.

–CARL SAGAN, "The Nuclear Winter"

Concluding with a warning

Because propaganda is so effective, it is important to track it down and understand how it is used. We may eventually agree with what the propagandist says because all propaganda isn't necessarily bad; some advertising, for instance, urges us not to drive drunk, to have regular dental checkups, to contribute to the United Way. Even so, we must be aware that propaganda is being used. Otherwise, we will have consented to handing over our independence, our decision-making ability, and our brains.

–ANN McCLINTOCK, "Propaganda Techniques in Today's Advertising"

EXERCISE 6.21

Choose an essay you have recently written, and examine the conclusion carefully, trying to identify what strategy you have used. Then choose a different strategy from among those discussed above, and write a new conclusion, striving for the maximum effect on readers. Finally, describe and evaluate the techniques you used in your revision.

3

Transitional paragraphs

On some occasions, you may need to call your readers' attention very powerfully to a major transition between ideas. To do so, consider using an entire short paragraph to signal that transition, as in the following example from an essay on "television addiction." The opening paragraphs of the essay characterize addiction in general, concluding with the paragraph about its destructive elements. The one-sentence paragraph that follows arrests our attention, announcing that these general characteristics will now be related to television viewing.

> Finally a serious addiction is distinguished from a harmless pursuit of pleasure by its distinctly destructive elements. A heroin addict, for instance, leads a damaged life: his increasing need for heroin in increasing doses prevents him from working, from maintaining relationships, from developing in human ways. Similarly an alcoholic's life is narrowed and dehumanized by his dependence on alcohol.
>
> Let us consider television viewing in the light of the conditions that define serious addictions.
>
> —MARIE WINN, *The Plug-in Drug: Television, Children, and the Family*

4

Paragraphs to signal dialogue

Paragraphs of dialogue can bring added life to almost any sort of writing. The traditional way to set up dialogue in written form is simple: start a new paragraph each time the speaker changes, no matter how short each bit of conversation is. Here is an example.

> Whenever I brought a book to the job, I wrapped it in newspaper—a habit that was to persist for years in other cities and under other circumstances. But some of the white men pried into my packages when I was absent and they questioned me.

"Boy, what are you reading those books for?"
"Oh, I don't know, sir."
"That's deep stuff you're reading, boy."
"I'm just killing time, sir."
"You'll addle your brains if you don't watch out."
                                    —RICHARD WRIGHT, *Black Boy*

EXERCISE 6.22

Go through some of your favorite books, articles, or essays to find an opening or concluding paragraph that you find particularly effective. Try to analyze what makes the paragraph so effective. Then, choosing a topic of great interest to you, try to write an opening or concluding paragraph that matches the paragraph you admire—the structure of its sentences, the pattern of its development, its use of particular devices such as quotations, questions, and so on. Then compare the two paragraphs, and consider how effective your own is.

6g

Linking paragraphs

The same methods that can be used to link sentences and create coherent paragraphs can be used to link paragraphs themselves together so that a whole piece of writing flows smoothly and coherently. Some reference to the previous paragraph, either explicitly stated or merely implied, should occur in each paragraph after the introduction. As in linking sentences, you can create this reference by repeating or paraphrasing key words and terms and by using parallel structures, pronouns, and transitional expressions.

Repeating key words

In fact, human offspring remain *dependent on their parents* longer than the young of any other species.
    Children are *dependent on their parents* or other adults not only for their physical survival but also for their initiation into the uniquely human knowledge that is collectively called culture. . . .

Using parallel structure

Kennedy made an effort to assure non-Catholics that he would respect the separation of church and state, and most of them did not seem to hold his religion against him in deciding how to vote. Since his election, *the church to which a candidate belongs* has become less important in presidential politics.

The region from which a candidate comes remains an important factor. . . .

Using pronouns

Singer's tale is of a pathetic Polish Jew, Gimpel, who because of *his* strong faith believes everything *he* is told. At the beginning of the tale, we learn that Gimpel has had a gruesomely cruel life. *He* is an orphan, and all *his* life *he* has been teased and tormented for believing everything *he* hears.

Even the most ridiculous and far-fetched tales take *him* in. For example, when *he* is told that the messiah has come and *his* parents have risen from the dead, *he* goes out to search for *them*! In *his* seemingly foolish search, *he* is berated by the townsfolk.

Using transitional expressions

While the Indian, in the character of Tonto, was more positively portrayed in *The Lone Ranger,* such a portrayal was more the exception than the norm.

Moreover, despite this brief glimpse of an Indian as an ever loyal sidekick, Tonto was never accorded the same stature as the man with the white horse and silver bullets. . . .

Editing the paragraphs in your writing

1. What is the topic sentence of each paragraph? Is it stated or implied? If stated, where in the paragraph does it fall? Should it come at some other point? Would any paragraph be improved by deleting or adding a topic sentence? (6c1)

2. Which sentences, if any, do not relate in some way to the topic sentence? Is there any way to justify their inclusion? (6c2)

3. What is the most general sentence in each paragraph? If it is not the topic sentence, should it remain or be omitted? (6c2, 6d1)

4. Is each paragraph organized in a way that is easy for readers to follow? By what means are sentences linked? Do any more links need to be added? Do any of the transitional expressions try to create links between ideas that do not really exist? (6d)

5. How completely does each paragraph develop its topic sentence? What methods of development are used? Are they effective? What other methods might be used? Does the paragraph need more material? (6e)   (*Continued*)

6. Does the first sentence in each paragraph let readers know what the paragraph is about? Does the last sentence in some way conclude that paragraph's discussion? If not, does it need to?

7. How long is each paragraph? Are paragraphs varied in length? Does any paragraph seem too long or too short? Is there any point that might be given strong emphasis by a one-sentence paragraph? (6e2 and 6f3)

8. By what means are the paragraphs linked? Do any more links need to be added? Do any of the transitional expressions try to create links between ideas that do not really exist? (6g)

9. How does the introductory paragraph catch readers' interest? How exactly does it open—with a quotation? an anecdote? a question? a strong statement? How else might it open? (6f1)

10. How does the last paragraph draw the essay to a conclusion? What lasting impression will it leave with readers? How exactly does it close—with a question? a quotation? a vivid image? a warning or a call for action? How else might it conclude? (6f2)

EXERCISE 6.23

Look at the essay you drafted for Exercise 3.7 or the argument you drafted for Exercise 5.14, and identify the ways your paragraphs are linked together. Identify each use of repetition, parallel structures, pronouns, and transitional expressions, and then evaluate how effectively you have joined the paragraphs.

EXERCISE 6.24 Revising Paragraphs

The following long paragraph is from an essay in which a student attempted to assess the "American dream" after reading an essay by Joan Didion, "Some Dreamers of the Golden Dream." Read the paragraph, and decide whether or not it should be broken up into two or more paragraphs and where any new paragraphs should begin. Then explain your reasons for any changes you make and the effects that are created by any new paragraphing.

When I think of the "American dream," I visualize a white-and-blue two-story Colonial house, complete with a two-car garage, white picket fence, happily married husband and wife, two children (one boy, one girl), a dog, and family vacations across the state in the Ford station wagon. I'm not really sure where I received my information on this subject; I have just learned through the years that this is the type of life I should strive for and look forward to. The traditional

"American dream" is apparently changing, though. The white-and-blue two-story house is now a three-story mansion embedded in the cliffs of Malibu overlooking the Pacific Ocean; the happily married husband and wife have usually known the same happiness in three prior marriages; the family vacations are now two weeks in Hawaii with the Mercedes station wagon waiting for them in the Los Angeles Airport parking lot. This new and extreme version of the fairy tale is rapidly becoming everyone's new goal, according to Joan Didion's essay "Some Dreamers of the Golden Dream." Didion speaks of southern California and states that people have derived their new ideal from newspapers and movies, not from reality. I find this statement very true to life, for most people do receive the majority of their ideas about how they should live from newspapers and movies. Therefore, if the movies present an image of gorgeous beach-side mansions and expensive imported cars, then that is exactly what most people will strive for. This type of life style may not be right for every individual, though, and many people realize this too late. They spend their lives working and striving to become successful in society's eyes. Then, once they have reached their goal, they realize they are not truly happy, for they gained wealth and status for all the wrong reasons.

THINKING CRITICALLY ABOUT PARAGRAPHS

Reading with an Eye for Paragraphs

Read something by a writer you admire. Find one or two paragraphs that impress you in some way, and analyze them, using the guidelines at the end of 6g. Try to decide what makes them effective paragraphs.

Thinking about Your Own Use of Paragraphs

Examine two or three paragraphs you have written, using the guidelines at the end of 6g to evaluate the unity, coherence, and development of each one. Identify the topic of each paragraph, the topic sentence (if one is explicitly stated), any methods of development, and any means used to create coherence. Decide whether or not each paragraph successfully guides your readers, and explain your reasons. Then choose one paragraph, and revise it.

Part Two

Sentences: Making Grammatical Choices

〈〉

7. Constructing Grammatical Sentences   *156*

8. Understanding Pronoun Case   *193*

9. Using Verbs   *206*

10. Maintaining Subject-Verb Agreement   *232*

11. Maintaining Pronoun-Antecedent
Agreement   *243*

12. Using Adjectives and Adverbs   *249*

7

Constructing Grammatical Sentences

OUTSIDE OF SCHOOL, *you may not have thought very much about grammar, the main subject of this chapter. Indeed, you may agree in principle with the fifteenth-century Holy Roman emperor Sigismund, who answered a question about his Latin grammar by saying, "I am the Roman emperor and am above grammar."*

In one sense, all native speakers of a language are, like Sigismund, "above" grammar. All speakers, that is, learn the grammar of their language naturally as they learn to speak. This intuitive knowledge of grammar leads us to say, "The bright red cardinal surprised me," rather than "Cardinal bright the surprised me red"—without even thinking about it. This ability to arrange words into meaningful patterns comes, in fact, very early to each of us and accounts for the fact that young children often produce sophisticated sentences seemingly out of the blue, without having to study or "learn" a system by which to produce them.

But in another sense, none of us, including an emperor, is above grammar. As the sentence about the cardinal suggests, we are bound by certain patterns or "rules" in producing sentences. And breaking those "rules" moves a speaker from sense to nonsense, from being easily understood to being completely mis-understood.

If we learn the basic grammar of language as we learn to speak, then why bother to study it? In the first place, though all speakers know the basic grammatical "rules," these rules can generate a very broad range of sentences, some of which will be much more artful and effective than others. As someone who uses written language, you want not simply to write but to write skillfully and effectively, and understanding grammatical structures can help you do so.

Furthermore, within the basic "rules" of English grammar, wide latitude exists. Not everyone, for instance, grows up speaking with precisely the same set of grammatical rules. Knowledge of the differences can help you produce sentences that are not only grammatical but appropriate to a particular situation. The "rules" that allow a speaker to say "My sister, she work at ABC" in one situation, for example, are not quite the same as those that lead him or her to say, "My sister works at ABC," in another. If you understand grammar, you will not only understand both statements but also know when and why to use one and when the other. Finally, because language is so closely related to thought, studying our language patterns, our grammar, can give us insight into our own ways of thinking. If in some important sense we are what we say (and write), then examining the principles through which we express our meanings can help us understand ourselves as well as others.

This chapter takes a look at the basic units of grammar—those elements that allow us to produce meaningful sentences.

EXERCISE 7.1

Think of a writer whose work you enjoy, and read something by him or her. Write down some sentences you find pleasing, and try to determine what makes them memorable: the pacing and rhythm? the pictures they bring to mind? Reading them aloud is one good way to focus your attention on their rhythm and structure. Then try writing some sentences of your own, imitating the structure of the professional writer's sentences as best you can.

Everyday Use

Perhaps more than any other subject we'll ever study, grammar comes to us almost automatically, without our thinking about it or even being aware of it. Listen in, for instance, on this conversation between two six-year-olds:

Charlotte: My new bike that Grandma got me has a red basket and a loud horn, and I love it.

Anna: Can I ride it?

Charlotte: Sure, as soon as I take a turn.

This simple conversation features sophisticated grammar—subordination of one clause to another, a compound object, a series of adjectives—all used effortlessly. Listen in on a conversation, and transcribe a few sentences as we've done here. Then, using this chapter, see what grammatical structures the conversation contains.

7a

Understanding the basic grammar of sentences

A **sentence** is a grammatically complete group of words that expresses a thought. To be grammatically complete, a group of words must contain two major structural components—a subject and a predicate. The **subject** identifies what the sentence is about, and the **predicate** says or asks something about the subject or tells the subject to do something.

SUBJECT	PREDICATE
We	shall overcome.
I	have a dream.
California	is a state of mind.
You	can't touch this.
The rain in Spain	stays mainly in the plain.
Puff, the magic dragon,	lived by the sea.

Some brief sentences have one-word subjects and predicates (for example, *Time passes*) or even a one-word predicate with an implied, or "understood," subject (for example, *Stop!*). Most sentences, however, contain additional words that expand the basic subject and predicate. In the example above, for instance, the subject might have been simply *Puff;* the words *the magic dragon* say more about the subject. Similarly, the predicate of that sentence could grammatically be *lived;* the words *by the sea* expand the predicate by telling us where Puff lived.

EXERCISE 7.2

The following sentences are taken from "A Hanging," an essay by George Orwell. Identify the subject and predicate in each sentence, underlining the subject once and the predicate twice. Example:

> *One prisoner had been brought out of his cell.*

1. We set out for the gallows.
2. He was an army doctor, with a gray toothbrush moustache and a gruff voice.
3. The rest of us, magistrates and the like, followed behind.
4. The dog answered the sound with a whine.
5. The hangman, a gray-haired convict in the white uniform of the prison, was waiting beside his machine.

7b

Recognizing the parts of speech

If the basic sentence parts are subjects and predicates, the central elements of subjects and predicates are nouns and verbs. For example:

```
┌──── SUBJECT ────┐ ┌──── PREDICATE ────┐
              NOUN   VERB
```
A solitary figure waited on the platform.

Nouns and verbs are two of the eight **parts of speech,** one set of grammatical categories into which words may be classified. The other six parts of speech are pronouns, adjectives, adverbs, prepositions, conjunctions, and interjections. Many English words can function as more than one part of speech. Take the word *book,* for instance: when you *book a plane flight,* it is a verb; when you *take a good book to the beach,* it is a noun; and when you *have book knowledge,* it is an adjective.

The system of categorizing words by part of speech comes to English from Latin. The differences between Latin and English are many, of course, and the parts-of-speech system is not as precise for English as it is for Latin. Many grammarians argue that students of English grammar should focus less on the parts of speech and more on the parts of a sentence. Even so, the parts of speech remain an important part of our grammatical vocabulary, and all dictionaries use them to label their entries. In this chapter, we will see how the various parts of speech are used in sentences.

1

Recognizing verbs

The word *verb* comes from the Latin *verbum,* which simply means "word." As their derivation suggests, **verbs** are among the most important words, for they move the meaning of sentences along by showing action (*glance, jump*), occurrence (*become, happen*), or a state of being (*be, live*). Verbs change form to show *time, person, number, voice,* and *mood.*

TIME	we *work,* we *worked*
PERSON	I *work,* she *works*
NUMBER	one person *works,* two people *work*
VOICE	she *asks,* she is *asked*
MOOD	we *see,* if we *saw*

Auxiliary verbs (also called **helping verbs**) combine with other verbs (often called **main verbs**) to create *verb phrases*. Auxiliaries include the forms of *be, do,* and *have,* which are also used as main verbs, and the words *can, could, may, might, must, shall, should, will,* and *would.*

You *must get* some sleep tonight!

I *could have danced* all night.

She *would prefer* to take Italian rather than Spanish.

See Chapter 9 for a complete discussion of verbs and 10a for more on how verbs change form to show person and number.

EXERCISE 7.3

Underline each verb or verb phrase in the following sentences. Example:

Terence should sing well in Sunday's performance.

1. My future does look bright.
2. The faucet had been leaking all day.
3. Within the next few weeks, we will receive the test results.
4. One person can collect sap, a second might run the evaporator, and a third should finish the syrup.
5. A job at an animal hospital would be great.
6. At a glittering ceremony, they announced the winner.
7. The gray whale has made a comeback and is beginning to flourish because of the intense efforts by preservationists.
8. The conference will include papers from China, Brazil, and Japan.
9. We had been working ten-hour days.
10. Applicants must submit all required paperwork.

2

Recognizing nouns

The word *noun* comes from the Latin *nomen,* which means "name." That is what **nouns** do: they name things. Nouns can name persons (*aviator, child*), places (*lake, library*), things (*truck, suitcase*), or concepts (*happiness, balance*). **Proper nouns** name specific persons, places, things, or concepts: *Bill, Iowa, Supreme Court, Buddhism.* Proper nouns are capitalized (36b). **Collective nouns** name groups: *team, flock, jury* (10d).

Most nouns can be changed from **singular** (one) to **plural** (more than one) by adding *-s* or *-es: horse, horses; kiss, kisses.* Some nouns, however, have irregular plural forms: *woman, women; alumnus, alumni; mouse, mice; deer, deer* (24e). **Mass nouns** cannot be made plural because they name something that cannot easily be counted: *dust, peace, prosperity.*

Nouns can also take a possessive form to show ownership. A writer usually forms the possessive by adding an apostrophe plus *-s* to a singular noun or just an apostrophe to a plural noun: *the horse's owner, the boys' department* (33a).

Nouns are often preceded by the **articles** *a, an,* or *the: a rocket, an astronaut, the launch.* Articles are also known as **noun markers** or **determiners.** (See Chapter 55 for a complete discussion of articles.)

EXERCISE 7.4

Identify the nouns, including possessive forms, and the articles in each of the following sentences. Underline the nouns once and the articles twice. Example:

> *The Puritans' hopes were dashed when Charles II regained his father's throne.*

1. Nightlife begins in Georgetown even before the sun goes down.
2. Although plagiarism is dishonest and illegal, it does occur.
3. Thanksgiving is a grim season for turkeys.
4. Henderson's story is a tale of theft and violation.
5. In the front row sat two people, a man with slightly graying hair and a young woman in jeans.

▶ *FOR MULTILINGUAL WRITERS*
  Count and Noncount Nouns

  Is the hill covered with grass or grasses? See 55a for a discussion of count and noncount nouns.

3

Recognizing pronouns

Pronouns function as nouns in sentences and often take the place of specific nouns, serving as short forms so that we do not have to repeat a noun that has already been mentioned. A specific noun that a pronoun replaces or refers to is called the **antecedent** of the pronoun. (See Chapters 11 and 13.) In the following example, the antecedent of *she* is *Caitlin:*

> *Caitlin refused the invitation even though she wanted to go.*

You are already familiar with pronouns; we could scarcely speak or write without them. (The preceding sentence, for instance, includes the pronouns *you, we,* and *them.*) Look now at all the categories of pronouns: personal, reflexive, intensive, indefinite, demonstrative, interrogative, relative, and reciprocal.

Personal pronouns refer to specific persons or things. Each has several different forms (for example, *I, me, my, mine*) that are used according to how it functions in a sentence. (See Chapter 8.)

> I, you, he, she, it, we, they
> After the scouts made camp, *they* ran along the beach.

Reflexive pronouns refer to the subject of the sentence or clause in which they appear. They end in *-self* or *-selves.*

> myself, yourself, himself, herself, itself, oneself, ourselves, yourselves, themselves
> The seals sunned *themselves* on the warm rocks.

Intensive pronouns have the same form as reflexive pronouns. They are used to emphasize their antecedents.

> He decided to paint the apartment *himself.*

Indefinite pronouns do not refer to specific nouns, although they may refer to identifiable persons or things. They express the idea of a quantity—"all," "some," "any," or "none"—or an unspecified person or thing—"somebody," "any book." Indefinite pronouns are one of the largest categories of pronouns; the following is a partial list:

> all, anybody, both, each, everything, few, most, none, one, some
> *Somebody* screamed when the lights went out.
> We gave them *everything* we had.

Demonstrative pronouns identify or point to specific nouns.

> this, that, these, those
> *These* are Peter's books.

Interrogative pronouns are used to ask questions.

> who, which, what
> *Who* can help to set up the chairs for the meeting?

Relative pronouns introduce dependent clauses and "relate" the dependent clause to the rest of the sentence (7c4).

gram

who, which, that, what, whoever, whichever, whatever

Margaret owns the car *that* is parked by the corner.

The interrogative pronoun *who* and the relative pronouns *who* and *whoever* have different forms depending on how they are used in a sentence. (See Chapter 8.)

Reciprocal pronouns refer to the individual parts of a plural antecedent.

each other, one another

The business failed because the partners distrusted *each other*.

EXERCISE 7.5

Identify the pronouns and any antecedents in each of the following sentences, underlining the pronouns once and any antecedents twice. Example:

As identical <u><u>twins</u></u>, <u>they</u> really do understand <u>each other.</u>

1. She thanked everyone for helping.
2. The crowd that greeted the pope was the largest one I have ever seen.
3. Who knows better than Mark himself what he should do?
4. They have only themselves to blame.
5. People who are extremely fastidious often annoy those who are not.

4

Recognizing adjectives

Adjectives modify (limit the meaning of) nouns and pronouns, usually by describing, identifying, or quantifying those words.

The *red* Corvette ran off the road. [describes]

It was *defective*. [describes]

That Corvette needs to be repaired. [identifies]

We saw *several* Corvettes race by. [quantifies]

Most adjectives, like *red* in the example above, are used to describe. In addition to their basic forms, most descriptive adjectives have other forms that are used to make comparisons: *small, smaller, smallest; foolish, more foolish, most foolish, less foolish, least foolish.*

This year's attendance was *smaller* than last year's.

This year's attendance was the *smallest* in ten years.

Many of the pronouns in 7b3 can function as adjectives when they are followed by a noun.

> *That* is a dangerous intersection. [pronoun]
>
> *That* intersection is dangerous. [adjective]

Pronouns that can be used as adjectives include personal (*her* idea), interrogative (*which* model should we buy?), relative (the car *that* we want is red), demonstrative (*this* book), and indefinite (*every* item) pronouns. Other kinds of adjectives that identify or quantify are articles (*a, an, the*) and numbers (*three, sixty-fifth, five hundred*).

Proper adjectives are adjectives formed from or related to proper nouns (*Egyptian, Emersonian*). Proper adjectives are capitalized (36b).

Chapter 12 provides a complete discussion of adjectives.

5

Recognizing adverbs

Adverbs modify verbs, adjectives, other adverbs, or entire clauses. Many adverbs have an *-ly* ending, though some do not (*always, never, very, well*), and some words that end in *-ly* are not adverbs but adjectives (*friendly, lovely*). One of the most common adverbs is *not*.

> Giles and Rebecca *recently* visited Atlanta. [modifies the verb *visited*]
>
> They had an *unexpectedly* exciting trip. [modifies the adjective *exciting*]
>
> They *very* soon discovered the French Quarter. [modifies the adverb *soon*]
>
> *Frankly,* they would have liked to stay another month. [modifies the independent clause that makes up the rest of the sentence]

Adverbs often answer the questions *when? where? why? how? to what extent?* In the first example above, for instance, *recently* answers the question *when?* In the third sentence, *very* answers the question *to what extent?*

Many adverbs, like many adjectives, have different forms that are used in making comparisons: *forcefully, more forcefully, most forcefully, less forcefully, least forcefully.*

> The senator spoke *more forcefully* than her opponent.
>
> Of all the candidates, she speaks the *most forcefully.*

Conjunctive adverbs modify an entire clause and express the connection in meaning between that clause and the preceding clause (or sentence). Examples of conjunctive adverbs include *however, furthermore, therefore,* and *likewise* (7b7).

The most movable of all parts of speech, adverbs can often be placed in different positions in a sentence without changing or disrupting the meaning of the sentence. Notice in the following examples how placement creates only slight differences in emphasis:

Reluctantly, Eduardo gave up the trophy.

Eduardo *reluctantly* gave up the trophy.

Eduardo gave up the trophy *reluctantly.*

Chapter 12 provides a complete discussion of adverbs.

EXERCISE 7.6

Identify the adjectives and adverbs in each of the following sentences, underlining the adjectives once and the adverbs twice. Remember that articles and some pronouns are used as adjectives. Example:

<u><u>Inadvertently,</u></u> <u>the</u> <u>two</u> agents misquoted <u>their</u> <u>major</u> client.

1. Because time had grown perilously short, I quickly prepared the final draft.
2. Hilariously, the sly villain revealed himself at the end of the first act.
3. The somewhat shy author spoke reluctantly to six exuberant admirers.
4. I unhappily returned the sleek, new car to its owner.
5. The youngest dancer in the troupe performed a brilliant solo.
6. The most instructive of the books is, unfortunately, the longest.
7. Never before has one politician accomplished so much.
8. Late in the day, the temperature dropped precipitously.
9. Imminent starvation threatens many populations constantly.
10. Politicians must seriously consider how well their lives will withstand intense public scrutiny.

EXERCISE 7.7

Expand each of the following sentences by adding appropriate adjectives and adverbs. Delete *the* if need be. Example:

The veterinarians examined the patient.

Then *the* three *veterinarians* thoroughly *examined the* nervous *patient.*

1. A corporation can fire workers.
2. The heroine marries the prince.
3. In the painting, a road curves between hills.
4. Candles gleamed on the tabletop.
5. Feminists have staged demonstrations against the movie.

6

Recognizing prepositions

Prepositions are important structural words that express relationships—in space, time, or other senses—between nouns or pronouns and other words in a sentence.

We did not want to leave *during* the game.

The contestants waited nervously *for* the announcement.

Drive *across* the bridge, go *down* the avenue *past* three stoplights, and then turn left *before* the Gulf station.

Some common prepositions

about	at	down	near	since
above	before	during	of	through
across	behind	except	off	toward
after	below	for	on	under
against	beneath	from	onto	until
along	beside	in	out	up
among	between	inside	over	upon
around	beyond	into	past	with
as	by	like	regarding	without

SOME COMPOUND PREPOSITIONS

according to	except for	instead of
as well as	in addition to	next to
because of	in front of	out of
by way of	in place of	with regard to
due to	in spite of	

If you are in doubt about which preposition to use, consult your dictionary. Frederich Wood's *English Prepositional Idioms* is a dictionary devoted to prepositions.

A **prepositional phrase** is made up of a preposition together with the noun or pronoun it connects to the rest of the sentence (7c3).

EXERCISE 7.8

Identify and underline the prepositions. Example:

<u>In</u> the dim interior <u>of</u> the hut crouched an old man.

1. A gust of wind blew through the window, upsetting the vase on the table.
2. He ran swiftly through the brush, across the beach, and into the sea.
3. A few minutes past noon, the police arrived at the scene.
4. During our trip down the river, a rivalry developed between us.
5. The book, by Anne Morrow Lindbergh, describes the flight the Lindberghs made to the Orient by way of the Great Circle route.

7

Recognizing conjunctions

Conjunctions connect words or groups of words to each other. There are four kinds of conjunctions: coordinating conjunctions, correlative conjunctions, subordinating conjunctions, and conjunctive adverbs.

Coordinating conjunctions

Coordinating conjunctions join equivalent structures—two or more nouns, pronouns, verbs, adjectives, adverbs, prepositions, conjunctions, phrases, or clauses (20a).

COORDINATING CONJUNCTIONS			
and	or	nor	so
but	yet	for	

T. S. Eliot wrote poems *and* plays.

A strong *but* warm breeze blew across the desert.

Please print *or* type the information on the application form.

Her arguments were easy to ridicule *yet* hard to refute.

Nor, for, and *so* can connect independent clauses only.

He did not have much money, *nor* did he know how to get any.

The student glanced anxiously at the clock, *for* only twenty minutes remained in the exam period.

Ellen worked two shifts on Thursday, *so* she was tired that night.

Correlative conjunctions

Correlative conjunctions join equal elements, and they come in pairs.

CORRELATIVE CONJUNCTIONS	
both . . . and	neither . . . nor
either . . . or	not only . . . but also
just as . . . so	whether . . . or

Both W. H. Auden *and* William Carlos Williams wrote poems about Brueghel's *Fall of Icarus*.

Jeff *not only* sent a card *but also* visited me in the hospital.

Subordinating conjunctions

Subordinating conjunctions introduce adverb clauses and signal the relationship between the adverb clause and another clause, usually an independent clause. For instance, in the following sentence the subordinating conjunction *while* signals a time relationship, letting us know that the two events in the sentence happened simultaneously.

Sweat ran down my face *while* I frantically searched for my child.

SOME COMMON SUBORDINATING CONJUNCTIONS		
after	if	though
although	in order that	unless
as	once	until
as if	since	when
because	so that	where
before	than	while
even though	that	

Unless sales improve dramatically, the company will soon be bankrupt.

My grandmother began traveling *after* she sold her house.

Conjunctive adverbs

Conjunctive adverbs connect independent clauses. As their name suggests, conjunctive adverbs can be considered both adverbs and conjunctions because they modify the second clause in addition to connecting it to the preceding clause. Like many other adverbs yet unlike other conjunctions, they can be moved to different positions in a clause. For example:

The cider tasted bitter; *however,* each of us drank a tall glass of it.

The cider tasted bitter; each of us, *however,* drank a tall glass of it.

The cider tasted bitter. Each of us drank a tall glass of it, *however.*

SOME CONJUNCTIVE ADVERBS		
also	indeed	now
anyway	instead	otherwise
besides	likewise	similarly
certainly	meanwhile	still
finally	moreover	then
furthermore	namely	therefore
however	nevertheless	thus
incidentally	next	undoubtedly

Independent clauses connected by a conjunctive adverb must be separated by a semicolon or a period, not just a comma (15c).

> Some of these problems could occur at any company; *however,* many could happen only here.

EXERCISE 7.9

Underline the coordinating, correlative, and subordinating conjunctions as well as the conjunctive adverbs in each of the following sentences. Example:

> We used sleeping bags *even though* the cabin had sheets *and* blankets.

1. When we arrived at the pond, we saw many children playing there.
2. Pokey is an outside cat; nevertheless, she greets me at the front door each night as I arrive home.
3. The colt walked calmly, for he seemed to know he would win the race.
4. The shops along the waterfront were open, but business was slow.
5. The Environmental Protection Agency was once forced to buy an entire town because dioxins had rendered it uninhabitable.
6. The story was not only long but also dull.
7. I did not know whether to laugh or cry after I realized my mistake.
8. Exhausted men and women worked the pumps until their arms ached.
9. Although I live in a big city, my neighborhood has enough trees and raccoons to make me feel as if I live in the suburbs.
10. Neither Henry nor Rachel could understand the story; therefore, they did not recommend it.

8

Recognizing interjections

Interjections express surprise or emotion: *oh, ouch, ah, hey.* Interjections often stand alone, as fragments. Even when they are included in a sentence, they are not related grammatically to the rest of the sentence. They are used mostly in speaking; in writing, they are used mostly in dialogue.

"Yes! All right!" The fans screamed, jumping to their feet.

The problem suggested, *alas,* no easy solution.

7c

Recognizing the parts of a sentence

The parts-of-speech system helps us understand the way words can be used. In addition, we need to look at the parts of the sentence, for every sentence has a grammatical pattern or structure in which words function. Look at the word *book.* In 7b, we saw that *book* can function as various parts of speech—as a noun, an adjective, and a verb.

NOUN
A book is always a welcome gift.

ADJECTIVE
Henry has more book knowledge than wisdom.

VERB
How can I book a flight to Fort Worth?

Notice that *book* has exactly the same form for each part of speech. It would be impossible to recognize its meaning without the context of a particular sentence. In fact, even within a sentence, a word that can be categorized as a certain part of speech can function in more than one way.

SUBJECT
This book describes the ecology of the Everglades.

DIRECT OBJECT
I need a book about the ecology of the Everglades.

Book is a noun in both of these sentences, yet in the first it serves as the subject of the verb *describes,* while in the second it serves as the direct object of the verb *need.* Knowing a word's part of speech tells only part of the story; we have to recognize the part it plays in the pattern or structure of a particular sentence.

 *Basic sentence patterns*

> **1. SUBJECT/VERB**
>
>   S   V
> Babies cry.
>
> **2. SUBJECT/VERB/SUBJECT COMPLEMENT**
>
>   S   V   SC
> Babies seem fragile.
>
> **3. SUBJECT/VERB/DIRECT OBJECT**
>
>   S   V   DO
> Babies drink milk.
>
> **4. SUBJECT/VERB/INDIRECT OBJECT/DIRECT OBJECT**
>
>   S   V   IO   DO
> Babies give grandparents pleasure.
>
> **5. SUBJECT/VERB/DIRECT OBJECT/OBJECT COMPLEMENT**
>
>   S   V   DO   OC
> Babies make parents proud.

This section examines the essential parts of a sentence—subjects, predicates, objects, complements, phrases, and clauses—and provides practice in using them to construct sentences of various kinds.

1

Recognizing subjects

As described in 7a, almost every sentence has a stated subject, which identifies whom or what the sentence is about. The **simple subject** consists of one or more nouns or pronouns; the **complete subject** consists of the simple subject with all its modifiers. Depending on the number and kinds of modifiers, subjects can be as plain as one word or far more complex. The following examples show the complete subjects in italics, with the simple subjects labeled *ss*:

    ss
Baseball is a summer game.

        ss
Sailing over the fence, the ball crashed through Mr. Wilson's window.

    ss
Stadiums with real grass are hard to find these days.

    ss
Those who sit in the bleachers have the most fun.

A **compound subject** contains two or more simple subjects joined with a coordinating conjunction (*and, but, or*) or a correlative conjunction (*both . . . and, either . . . or, neither . . . nor, not only . . . but also*).

> *Baseball and softball* developed from cricket.
> *Both baseball and softball* developed from cricket.

The simple subject usually comes before the predicate, or verb, but not always. Sometimes writers reverse this order for effect.

> Up to the plate stepped *Casey*.
> Great was the *anticipation* among Mudville fans.

In **imperative sentences**, which express requests or commands, the subject *you* is almost always implied but not stated.

> (*You*) Keep your eye on the ball.

In questions and certain other constructions, the subject usually appears between the auxiliary verb and the main verb.

> Did *Casey* save the game?
> Never have *I* known greater disappointment.

In sentences beginning with *there* or *here* followed by a form of the verb *be* (*is, are, was, were, have been, will be,* and so on), the subject always follows the verb. *There* and *here* are never the subject.

> Here is the sad *ending* of the poem.
> There was no *joy* in Mudville.

EXERCISE 7.10

Identify the complete subject and the simple subject in each sentence. Underline the complete subject once and the simple subject twice. Example:

> The tall, powerful woman defiantly blocked the doorway.

1. The stories of Graham Greene probe the human psyche.
2. Has the new elevator been installed?
3. Here are some representative photographs.
4. The long, low, intricately carved table belonged to my aunt.
5. Some women worried about osteoporosis take calcium supplements.

2

Recognizing predicates

In addition to a subject, every sentence has a predicate, which asserts or asks something about the subject or tells the subject to do something (7a). The "hinge," or key word, of most predicates is a verb. As we saw in 7b1, a verb can include auxiliary verbs (as in this sentence, where *can* is an auxiliary and *include* is the main verb). The **simple predicate** of a sentence is the main verb and any auxiliaries; the **complete predicate** includes the simple predicate and any modifiers of the verb and any objects or complements and their modifiers. In the following examples, the complete predicates are italicized, and the simple predicates are labeled *sp*:

┌ SP ┐
My roommate *seems wonderful.*

┌ SP ┐
She *offered me the use of her word processor.*

┌───── SP ─────┐
Both of us *are planning to major in history.*

A **compound predicate** contains two or more verbs that have the same subject, usually joined by a coordinating or a correlative conjunction.

> Charles *shut the book, put it back on the shelf, and sighed.*
> The Amish *neither drive cars nor use electricity.*

On the basis of how they function in predicates, verbs can be divided into three categories: linking, transitive, and intransitive.

Linking verbs

A **linking verb** links, or joins, a subject with a **subject complement**, a word or word group that identifies or describes the subject. If it identifies the subject, the complement is a noun or pronoun (and is sometimes called a **predicate noun**). If it describes the subject, the complement is an adjective (and is sometimes called a **predicate adjective**). In the following examples, *a single mother* is a predicate noun, and *exhausted* is a predicate adjective:

┌── S ──┐ V ┌──── SC ────┐
Christine is a single mother.

S V SC
She is exhausted.

The forms of *be,* when used as main verbs rather than as auxiliary verbs, are linking verbs (like *are* in this sentence). Other verbs, such as *appear, become, feel, grow, look, make, seem, smell,* and *sound,* can also function as linking verbs, depending on the sense of the sentence.

┌─────── S ───────┐ ┌── V ──┐ ┌── SC ──┐
The abandoned farmhouse had become dilapidated.

S V ┌──── SC ────┐
It looked ready to fall down.

Transitive and intransitive verbs

If a verb is not a linking verb, it is either transitive or intransitive. A **transitive verb** expresses action that is directed toward a noun or pronoun, called the **direct object** of the verb.

S ┌── V ──┐ ┌── DO ──┐
I will analyze three poems

A direct object identifies what or who receives the action of the verb. In the preceding example, the subject and verb do not express a complete thought. The direct object completes the thought, saying *what* I will analyze.

A direct object may be followed by an **object complement,** a word or word group that describes or identifies it. Object complements may be adjectives, as in the first example below, or nouns, as in the second example.

S ┌── V ──┐ ┌────── DO ──────┐ ┌── OC ──┐
I consider Marianne Moore's poetry exquisite.

┌─────── S ───────┐ ┌ V ┐ ┌ DO ┐ ┌── OC ──┐
Her poems and personality made Moore a celebrity.

A transitive verb may also be followed by an **indirect object,** which tells to whom or what or for whom or what the verb's action is done. You might say the indirect object is the recipient of the direct object.

┌─────── S ───────┐ ┌V┐┌IO┐ ┌──── DO ────┐
Moore's poems about the Dodgers give me considerable pleasure.

┌─ S ─┐ ┌ V ┐ ┌──── IO ────┐ ┌── DO ──┐
Brooklyn owes Marianne Moore something.

An **intransitive verb** expresses action that is not directed toward an object. Therefore, an intransitive verb does not have a direct object.

┌── S ──┐ ┌── V ──┐
The Red Sox persevered.

┌── S ──┐ ┌ V ┐
Their fans watched helplessly.

The action of the verb *persevered* has no object (it makes no sense to ask, *persevered what?* or *persevered whom?*), and the action of the verb *watched* is directed toward an object that is implied but not expressed.

Some verbs that express action can be only transitive or only intransitive, but most can be used both ways, with or without a direct object.

```
         ┌────────── S ──────────┐  ┌─ V ─┐ ┌─ DO ─┐
```
A maid wearing a uniform opened the door. [transitive]
```
┌─ S ─┐ ┌─ V ─┐
```
The door opened silently. [intransitive]

EXERCISE 7.11

Underline the predicate in the following sentences. Then label each verb as linking, transitive, or intransitive. Finally, label all subject and object complements and all direct and indirect objects. Example:

```
          ┌── TV ──┐ ┌─ DO ─┐ ┌── OC ──┐
```
We considered city life unbearable.

1. California is dry in the summer.
2. The U.S. Constitution made us a nation.
3. A round of applause seemed appropriate.
4. Rock and roll will never die.
5. Advertisers promise consumers the world.

3

Recognizing and using phrases

A **phrase** is a group of words that lacks either a subject or a predicate or both. Phrases function in useful ways to add information to a sentence or shape it effectively. Look at the following sentence:

The new law will restrict smoking *in most public places.*

The basic subject of this sentence is a noun phrase, *the new law;* the basic predicate is a verb phrase, *will restrict smoking.* Additional information is provided by the prepositional phrase, *in most public places.* The prepositional phrase functions here as an adverb, telling *where* smoking will be restricted.

This section will discuss the various kinds of phrases: noun, verb, prepositional, verbal, absolute, and appositive.

Noun phrases

Made up of a noun and all its modifiers, a **noun phrase** can function in a sentence as a subject, object, or complement.

┌──────── SUBJECT ────────┐
Delicious, gooey peanut butter is surprisingly healthful.

┌─ OBJECT ─┐
Dieters prefer *green salad.*

┌─ COMPLEMENT ─┐
A tuna sandwich is *a popular lunch.*

Verb phrases

A main verb and its auxiliary verbs make up a **verb phrase**, which functions in a sentence in only one way: as a predicate.

Frank *had been depressed* for some time.

His problem *might have been caused* by tension between his parents.

Prepositional phrases

A **prepositional phrase** includes a preposition, a noun or pronoun (called the **object of the preposition**), and any modifiers of the object. Prepositional phrases function as either adjectives or adverbs.

ADJECTIVE   Our house *in Maine* was a cabin.

ADVERB   *From Cadillac Mountain,* you can see the northern lights.

EXERCISE 7.12

Following are some sentences written by the sports columnist Red Smith. Identify and underline all the prepositional phrases. Then choose two of the sentences, and write sentences that imitate their structures. Examples:

He glanced <u>about the room</u> <u>with a cocky, crooked grin.</u>

The cat stalked <u>around the yard</u> <u>in her quiet, arrogant way.</u>

1. In those days the Yankees always won the pennant.
2. Fear wasn't in his vocabulary and pain had no meaning.
3. Coaching in Columbus is not quite like coaching in New Haven.

4. He stepped out of the dugout and faced the multitude, two fists and one cap uplifted.

5. The old champ looked fit, square of shoulder and springy of tread, his skin clear, his eyes bright behind the glittering glasses.

EXERCISE 7.13

Combine each of the following pairs of sentences into one sentence by making the second sentence into one or more prepositional phrases. Example:

> *over*
> The Greeks won a tremendous victory. ~~They were fighting~~ the Persians.

1. Socrates was condemned. His fellow citizens made up the jury that condemned him.

2. Socrates faced death. He had no fear.

3. The playwright Aristophanes wrote a comedy. Its subject was Socrates.

4. Everyone thought Socrates was crazy. Only a few followers disagreed.

5. Today Socrates is honored. He founded Western philosophy.

Verbal phrases

Verbals are verb forms that do not function as verbs. Instead, they function as nouns, adjectives, or adverbs. There are three kinds of verbals: participles, gerunds, and infinitives.

The **participle** functions as an adjective. The **present participle** is the -ing form of a verb: *dreaming, being, seeing.* The **past participle** of most verbs ends in -ed: *dreamed, watched.* But some verbs have an irregular past participle: *been, seen, hidden, gone, set* (9b).

A kiss awakened the *dreaming* princess.

The cryptographers deciphered the *hidden* meaning in the message.

The **gerund** has the same form as the present participle but functions as a noun.

SUBJECT	*Writing* takes practice.
OBJECT	The organization promotes *recycling.*

The **infinitive** is the *to* form of a verb: *to dream, to be, to see.* An infinitive can function as a noun, adjective, or adverb.

NOUN	She wanted *to write.*
ADJECTIVE	They had no more time *to waste.*
ADVERB	The corporation was ready *to expand.*

A verbal can never stand alone as the verb of a sentence because it is a **nonfinite**, or "unfinished," **verb**. Take the present participle *barking,* for instance. *The terrier barking* is not a sentence; to make it a sentence, you need to add one or more auxiliary verbs: *The terrier is barking* or *The terrier had been barking.* The verb phrases *is barking* and *had been barking* are **finite verbs**: they do not need any other auxiliary to function as verbs.

Verbal phrases are made up of a verbal and any modifiers, objects, or complements. Let us turn now to examine the forms and functions of the various kinds of verbal phrases.

PARTICIPIAL PHRASES

Participial phrases consist of a present participle or a past participle and any modifiers, objects, or complements. Participial phrases always function as adjectives.

Irritated by the delay, Louise complained.

A dog *howling at the moon* kept me awake.

Notice that many participial phrases may appear in different places in a sentence, as long as it is clear which word they modify. (See Chapter 17.) Decisions about where to place participial phrases must usually be made within the larger context of a piece of writing. The choice often depends on the rhythm or emphasis the writer wants to achieve.

Fearing that I would be left alone, I quickly followed the group.

I quickly followed the group, *fearing that I would be left alone.*

GERUND PHRASES

Gerund phrases consist of a gerund and any modifiers, objects, or complements: *hoping for a victory, critical thinking.* Gerund phrases function as nouns—as a subject, a subject complement, a direct object, an indirect object, or an object of a preposition.

Opening their eyes to the problem was not easy.

His downfall was *relying too much on his computer.*

They suddenly heard *a loud wailing from the sandbox.*

```
      ┌────── IO ──────┐
```
The critics gave *Pavarotti's singing* their enthusiastic approval.
```
      ┌─ OBJ OF PREP ─┐
```
In addition to *being confused,* she was alone.

INFINITIVE PHRASES

Infinitive phrases consist of an infinitive and any modifiers, objects, or complements: *to be happy, to go to a movie tonight.* They can function as nouns, adjectives, or adverbs.

```
      ┌────── NOUN/SC ──────┐
```
My goal is *to be a biology teacher.*
```
                    ┌────── ADJECTIVE ──────┐
```
A party would be a good way *to end the semester.*
```
┌────── ADVERB ──────┐
```
To perfect a draft, always proofread carefully.

Notice that infinitive phrases used as adverbs, as in the last example above, may appear in different places in a sentence as long as it is clear which word they modify. (See Chapter 17.) For example, *To perfect a draft* could be moved to the end of its sentence. As with participial phrases, placement should depend on the effect of the phrase in the larger context.

EXERCISE 7.14

Identify each participial phrase, gerund phrase, and infinitive phrase, and specify its part of speech in the sentence. Example:

```
┌────── PARTICIPIAL-ADJ ──────┐
```
Pacing the hall with impatience, I wished my friends would arrive.

1. Buying his first Corvette was the happiest moment in Brendan's life.
2. After four years of careful saving, he got his car.
3. Our plan was to renovate the house and then to sell it.
4. Raised in Idaho, I spent plenty of time exploring nature.
5. Sitting by the window and listening to the wind blowing through the trees, I feel happy and lucky to be alive.

Absolute phrases

An **absolute phrase** usually consists of a noun or pronoun and a participle. It modifies an entire sentence rather than a particular word.

Absolutes may appear almost anywhere in a sentence and are usually set off from the rest of the sentence with commas (30a).

> I stood on the deck, *the wind whipping my hair.*
> *My fears laid to rest,* I climbed into the plane for my first solo flight.

When the participle is *being,* it is often omitted.

> The ambassador, *her head (being) high,* walked out of the room.

Appositive phrases

A noun phrase that renames the noun or pronoun that immediately precedes it is called an **appositive phrase.**

> The report, *a hefty three-volume work,* included 150 recommendations.
> We had a single desire, *to change the administration's policies.*
> Keith Gilyard, *the celebrated writer,* will appear on campus tonight.

EXERCISE 7.15

Read the following sentences, and identify and label all of the prepositional, verbal, absolute, and appositive phrases. Notice that one kind of phrase may appear within another kind. Example:

```
          ┌─────── ABSOLUTE ───────┐              ┌── PREP ──┐
His voice breaking with emotion,  Ed thanked us for the award.
          └── PREP ──┘
```

1. Approaching the rope, I suddenly fell into the icy pond.
2. To listen to k. d. lang is sheer delight.
3. The figure outlined against the sky seemed unable to move.
4. Floating on my back, I ignored my practice requirements.
5. Jane stood still, her fingers clutching the fence.
6. Bobby, a sensitive child, was filled with a mixture of awe and excitement.
7. Shocked into silence, they kept their gaze fixed on the odd creature.
8. Basking in the sunlight, I was lost in reminiscence of birch trees.
9. Ana, the leader of the group, was reluctant to relinquish any authority.
10. His favorite form of recreation was taking a nap.

Using phrases to shape and expand sentences

Phrases are valuable tools for shaping or expanding sentences. They bring in additional information, and they can help you emphasize certain parts of a sentence and de-emphasize others. In this way, they help distinguish the main idea from the extra details. Look, for instance, at the following sentence:

> Jupiter crashed through the tomato vines with the remains of a felt hat in his mouth.　　　–JOHN CHEEVER, "The Country Husband"

Cheever might have expressed the ideas in this sentence in many other ways. For instance:

> Jupiter crashed through the tomato vines. He had the remains of a felt hat in his mouth.

> Crashing through the tomato vines, Jupiter held the remains of a felt hat in his mouth.

In the first possibility, turning some of the prepositional phrases into a second sentence separates the statement into two parts and thus weakens or at least changes the impact it has on readers—perhaps because we see the crash and the torn hat at a greater chronological distance from each other. In the second possibility, turning the verb of the original sentence into a participle puts greater emphasis on what was in the dog's mouth than on his crash through the vines and thus describes a slightly different scene.

The following are examples of how some student writers used various kinds of phrases to shape and expand particular sentences:

NOUN PHRASE

That car will never win the race.

That battered, valveless, bent-up bone-shaker will never win the race.

PARTICIPIAL PHRASE

The expressway looked like a long parking lot. It was jammed with traffic that was crawling into the city.

Jammed with traffic crawling into the city, the expressway looked like a long parking lot.

ABSOLUTE PHRASE

The dictator's long period of rule was over, and he stepped into his limousine.

His long period of rule over, the dictator stepped into his limousine.

Positioning phrases

As noted earlier, many phrases can be placed either at the beginning, in the middle, or at the end of a sentence. For example:

Calling on every ounce of energy, Jo sprinted toward the finish line.

Jo, *calling on every ounce of energy,* sprinted toward the finish line.

Jo sprinted toward the finish line, *calling on every ounce of energy.*

The phrase in these examples is a participial phrase that modifies *Jo.* While changing its placement does not alter the basic meaning of the sentence, it affects rhythm and emphasis, most notably in the third example, where it changes the important concluding words of the sentence.

Prepositional, infinitive, and absolute phrases can also occupy more than one sentence position. There are no absolute guidelines for placement, but three tips may help: (1) be sure the phrase clearly modifies any word it should modify (see Chapter 17); (2) read the sentence in the context of the surrounding sentences to see which placement seems most effective to you (see 22b); and (3) decide what you want to emphasize (or not emphasize), and place phrases accordingly. Putting phrases at the beginning or end of a sentence gives more emphasis than does putting them in the middle.

EXERCISE 7.16

Use prepositional, participial, infinitive, gerund, absolute, or appositive phrases to expand each of the following sentences. Example:

The apples dropped from the limb.

In response to my vigorous shake, *the apples dropped from the limb.*

1. Nancy jogged down Willow Street.
2. She looked healthy when he saw her the second time.
3. Tomas had lost almost all of his hair.
4. The Sunday afternoon dragged.
5. Teresa looked at her mother.
6. The candidates shook hands with the voters.
7. We were uncertain what to do.
8. Ben often thought regretfully about the past.
9. The letter lay on the desk.
10. They lived in a trailer.

EXERCISE 7.17

Use a participial, infinitive, gerund, absolute, or appositive phrase to combine each of the following pairs of sentences into one sentence. Example:

His constant complaining
~~He complained constantly. This habit~~ irritated his co-workers.

1. David Klein performed a monologue. He is an actor and comedian.
2. We waited to go through customs. Our passports were in our hands.
3. She bought a new camera. This purchase lifted her spirits.
4. Michael had his ear pierced. He did this because it annoyed his parents.
5. The protesters were carrying their banners. They headed down the street.

4

Recognizing and using clauses

A **clause** is a group of words containing a subject and a predicate. There are two kinds of clauses: independent and dependent. **Independent clauses** (also known as **main clauses**) can stand alone as complete sentences.

The window is open.

The batter swung at the ball.

Pairs of independent clauses may be joined with a coordinating conjunction and a comma (7b7).

The window is open, *so* we'd better be quiet.

The batter swung at the ball, *and* the umpire called her out.

Like independent clauses, **dependent clauses** (also known as **subordinate clauses**) contain a subject and a predicate. They cannot stand alone as complete sentences, however, for they begin with a subordinating word—a subordinating conjunction (7b7) or a relative pronoun (7b3). The subordinating word connects the dependent clause to an independent clause. Each of the following sentences, for instance, consists of one brief independent clause:

The window is open.

The room feels cool.

You might combine these two independent clauses with a comma and a coordinating conjunction: *The window is open, and the room feels cool.* You could also combine the two clauses by turning one into a dependent clause.

Because the window is open, the room feels cool.

In this combination, the subordinating conjunction *because* transforms the independent clause *the window is open* into a dependent clause. In doing so, it indicates a causal relationship between the two clauses.

Dependent clauses function as nouns, adjectives, or adverbs.

Noun clauses

Noun clauses can function as subjects, direct objects, subject complements, or objects of prepositions. Thus they are always contained within another clause rather than being simply attached to it, as adjective and adverb clauses are. They usually begin with a relative pronoun (*that, which, what, who, whom, whose, whatever, whoever, whomever, whichever*) or with *when, where, whether, why,* or *how.*

        ─────── S ───────

That he had a college degree was important to her.

        ─────── DO ───────

She asked where he went to college.

        ─────── SC ───────

The real question was why she wanted to know.

        ─────── OBJ OF PREP ───────

She was looking for whatever information was available.

Notice that in each of these sentences the noun clause is an integral part of the independent clause that makes up the sentence; for example, in the second sentence the independent clause is not just *She asked* but *She asked where he went to college.*

Adjective clauses

Adjective clauses modify nouns and pronouns in another clause. Usually they immediately follow the words they modify. Most adjective clauses begin with the relative pronouns *who, whom, whose, that,* or *which.* Some begin with *when, where,* or *why.*

The surgery, *which took three hours,* was a complete success.

It was performed by the surgeon *who had developed* the procedure.

The hospital was the one *where I was born.*

Sometimes the relative pronoun introducing an adjective clause may be omitted, as in the following example.

That is one book [that] I intend to read.

Adverb clauses

Adverb clauses modify verbs, adjectives, or other adverbs. They begin with a subordinating conjunction (7b7). Like adverbs, they usually tell when, where, why, how, or to what extent.

We hiked *where there were few other hikers.*

My backpack felt heavier *than it ever had.*

I climbed as swiftly *as I could under the weight of my backpack.*

Like adverbs, adverb clauses can usually be placed in different positions in a sentence without affecting the meaning.

If you look up from the valley, you will see Half Dome.

You will see Half Dome *if you look up from the valley.*

EXERCISE 7.18

Identify the independent and dependent clauses and any subordinating conjunctions and relative pronouns in each of the following sentences. Example:

┌────── DEPENDENT CLAUSE ──────┐ ┌────── INDEPENDENT CLAUSE ──────┐
If I were going on a really long hike,   I would carry a lightweight stove.
[*If* is a subordinating conjunction.]

1. The driver who won the race was driving a tan Pontiac.
2. As a potential customer entered the store, Tony nervously attempted to retreat to the safety of the back room.
3. The names they called my grandmother still haunt me.
4. When she was deemed old enough to understand, she was told the truth, and she finally knew why her father had left home.
5. Though most of my grandfather's farm was wooded, there were also great expanses of green lawns with quiet, trickling streams.
6. I decided to bake a chocolate-cream pie, which was Lynn's favorite.
7. If Keats had lived longer, he might have written even greater poems, but his early death is perhaps part of his appeal.
8. The trip was longer than I had remembered.
9. After she finished the painting, Linda cleaned the brushes.
10. I could see that he was very tired, but I had to ask him a few questions.

Using clauses to shape and expand sentences

Like phrases, clauses are an important means of shaping sentences in particular ways or of making sentences more varied or more interesting. For example, look at the following sentences, each of which consists of one independent clause expressing one idea:

Tei's parents disliked Ken. She was determined to marry him.

See how clauses can be used to combine these ideas in one sentence.

1. Although her parents disliked Ken, Tei was determined to marry him.
2. Tei's parents disliked Ken, whom she was determined to marry.
3. Tei's parents disliked Ken, but she was determined to marry him.

In sentence 1, putting the information about the parents' dislike of Ken into a dependent adverb clause gives less emphasis to that idea and more emphasis to the idea expressed in the subject and predicate—Tei's determination to marry him. In sentence 2, on the other hand, the idea of Tei's determination is de-emphasized by being placed in a dependent adjective clause. Finally, in sentence 3, the two ideas are given equal emphasis by being expressed in two independent clauses connected by the coordinating conjunction *but*.

As you write sentences, and especially when you are revising a draft, pay attention to how you can use clauses to add details or emphasis to your ideas. (See Chapters 19–23.) The following are examples of how some student writers used various kinds of clauses to shape and expand particular sentences:

NOUN CLAUSE

Charles later learned the truth.
Charles later learned *what Vinnie had known for years.*

ADJECTIVE CLAUSE

Everything was swept away.
Everything *that he valued most in life* was swept away.

My childhood seemed entirely happy. I grew up on a large farm.
My childhood, *which was spent on a large farm,* seemed entirely happy.

ADVERB CLAUSE

Some people opposed the war, but they supported the troops.
Although some people opposed the war, they supported the troops.

Positioning clauses

Most adverb clauses can be placed at the beginning, in the middle, or at the end of a sentence.

If nothing goes wrong, the furniture will be delivered tomorrow.

The furniture, *if nothing goes wrong,* will be delivered tomorrow.

The furniture will be delivered tomorrow *if nothing goes wrong.*

Changing the position of the adverb clause *if nothing goes wrong* does not affect the basic meaning of the sentence, but it affects the rhythm and the emphasis by highlighting or downplaying the possibility that something could go wrong (17a and 22b).

EXERCISE 7.19

Expand each sentence below by adding at least one dependent clause to it. Be prepared to explain how your addition improves the sentence. Example:

> *The books tumbled from the shelves.*
>
> As the earth continued to shake, *the books tumbled from the shelves.*

1. The last guests left.
2. The German government dismantled the Berlin Wall.
3. The new computer made a strange noise.
4. Rob always borrowed money from friends.
5. The streets were ringing with loud music.
6. We stood outside for an hour.
7. The history seminar begins tomorrow.
8. Erin won the translation contest.
9. A river flowed through the forest.
10. A man was killed in that mill in 1867.

EXERCISE 7.20

The following are some sentences from the letters of E. B. White. Read each one carefully, focusing on the phrases and clauses. Underline any dependent clauses once and any phrases twice. Finally, choose two sentences, and use them as a model for sentences of your own, imitating White's structure phrase for phrase and clause for clause. Example:

I was born in 1899 and expect to live forever, searching for beauty and raising hell in general.

Sarah was hired in May and plans to work all summer, living at home and saving money for law school.

1. You can see at a glance that Professor Strunk omitted needless words.
2. Either Macmillan takes Strunk and me in our bare skins, or I want out.
3. I regard the word *hopefully* as beyond recall.
4. Life in a zoo is just the ticket for some animals and birds.
5. I recall the pleasures and satisfactions of encountering a Perelman piece in a magazine.
6. The way to read Thoreau is to enjoy him—his enthusiasms, his acute perception.
7. When I start a book, I never know what my characters are going to do, and I accept no responsibility for their eccentric behavior.
8. No sensible writer sets out deliberately to develop a style, but all writers do have distinguishing qualities, and they become very evident when you read the words.
9. When I wrote "Death of a Pig," I was simply rendering an account of what actually happened on my place—to my pig, who died, and to me, who tended him in his last hours.
10. A good many of Charlotte's descendants still live in the barn, and when the warm days of spring arrive there will be lots of tiny spiders emerging into the world.

7d

Classifying sentences

Like words, sentences can be classified in several different ways: grammatically, functionally, or rhetorically. Grammatical classification groups sentences according to how many and what types of clauses they contain. Functional classification groups them according to whether they make a statement, ask a question, issue a command, or express an exclamation. Rhetorical classification groups them according to where in the sentence the main idea is located. These methods of classification can help you analyze and assess your sentences as you write and revise.

1

Classifying sentences grammatically

Grammatically, sentences may be classified as *simple, compound, complex,* and *compound-complex.* You have already seen these types in 7c4.

Simple sentences

A **simple sentence** consists of one independent clause and no dependent clause. The subject or the predicate, or both, may be compound.

The trailer is surrounded by a wooden deck.

Both my roommate and I had left our keys in the room.

At the country club, the head pro and his assistant give lessons, run the golf shop, and try to keep the members content.

Compound sentences

A **compound sentence** consists of two or more independent clauses and no dependent clause. The clauses may be joined by a comma and a coordinating conjunction, or by a semicolon. (See Chapters 15, 20, 30, and 31.)

Occasionally a car goes up the dirt trail, and dust flies everywhere.

Alberto is obsessed with soccer; he eats, breathes, and lives the game.

Complex sentences

A **complex sentence** consists of one independent clause and at least one dependent clause.

┌──── DEPENDENT CLAUSE ────┐
Many people believe that anyone can earn a living.

┌──── DEPENDENT CLAUSE ────┐
Those who do not like to get dirty should not go camping.

┌──── DEPENDENT CLAUSE ────┐
As I awaited my interview, I sat with other nervous candidates.

Compound-complex sentences

A **compound-complex sentence** consists of two or more independent clauses and at least one dependent clause.

┌── IND CLAUSE ──┐ ┌──── DEP CLAUSE ────┐ ┌──── IND CLAUSE ────┐
I complimented Joe when he finished the job, and he seemed pleased.

```
┌──────────── IND CLAUSE ────────────┐  ┌──────────── IND CLAUSE ────────────┐
```
Sister Lucy tried her best to help Martin, but he was an undisciplined boy
```
┌──────────── DEP CLAUSE ────────────┐
```
who drove many teachers to despair.

2

Classifying sentences functionally

In terms of function, sentences can be classified as **declarative** (making a statement), **interrogative** (asking a question), **imperative** (giving a command), or **exclamatory** (expressing strong feeling).

DECLARATIVE	Kira plays oboe for the Cleveland Orchestra.
INTERROGATIVE	How long has she been with them?
IMPERATIVE	Get me a ticket for her next performance.
EXCLAMATORY	What a talented musician she is!

3

Classifying sentences rhetorically

In addition to being classified functionally and grammatically, some sentences can be classified rhetorically, as either cumulative or periodic sentences. Such a classification is important because the two patterns create very different rhythms and emphases. (See 22c3.)

EXERCISE 7.21

Classify each of the following sentences as simple, compound, complex, or compound-complex. In addition, note any sentences that could be classified as declarative, imperative, interrogative, or exclamatory.

1. Solve your problems yourself.
2. The screen door creaked and banged when she ran into the house.
3. Should he admit his mistake, or should he keep quiet and hope to avoid discovery?
4. People go on safari to watch wild animals in their natural habitat.
5. When I first arrived at college, I became confused about where I fit in and who my role models should be.
6. Keeping in mind the terrain, the weather, and the length of the hike, decide what you need to take.
7. Dreams are necessary, but they can be frustrating unless you have the means to attain them.

8. Retail sales declined as consumers cut back on discretionary spending, and many small businesses failed.

>> *Editing the sentences in your own writing*

A good way to examine your own sentences is by studying two or three examples of your own writing. Classifying each sentence—grammatically, as simple, compound, complex, or compound-complex (7d1); functionally, as declarative, interrogative, imperative, or exclamatory (7d2); rhetorically, as cumulative or periodic (7d3). Perhaps keep a tally of how many of each type of sentence you write, and then look for patterns.

1. Are your sentences varied, or do you rely heavily on one or two sentence patterns?

2. If you write mainly simple sentences, see if combining some to make compound or complex sentences makes your writing flow more smoothly.

3. If you have many compound sentences, see if revising some as complex sentences makes your writing easier to read.

4. If your sentences are all declarative, see if there's one you'd like to emphasize, and try rephrasing it as a question or exclamation.

5. If you find several short sentences in a row, try combining them into one cumulative sentence.

EXERCISE 7.22 Revising to Vary Sentence Construction

The following paragraph is adapted from a speech once given by Adlai Stevenson. The sentences have been simplified greatly. Try revising the paragraph by using phrases and clauses to combine some of the sentences. You might find it necessary to add or drop words. There is no one correct way to revise the paragraph; the object is to practice using the various structures presented in this chapter.

America is much more than an economic fact. It is much more than a geographical fact. It is a political fact. It is a moral fact. It is the first community in which men set out in principle to institutionalize freedom. It is the first community in which men set out to institutionalize responsible government. It is the first community in which they set out to institutionalize human equality. And we love it for this audacity! Jefferson and Lincoln saw in this vision "the last, best hope of man." How easy it is, contemplating this vision, to see in it "the last, best hope of man." To be a nation founded on an ideal in one sense makes our love of country a vital force. It is a more vital force than any instinctive pieties of blood. It is a more vital force than any instinctive pieties of soil.

THINKING CRITICALLY ABOUT SENTENCES

Reading with an Eye for Sentences

The following sentences come from the openings of well-known works. Read each sentence carefully, and identify the independent and dependent clauses. Then choose one sentence, and write a sentence of your own that imitates its structure clause for clause and phrase for phrase. Example:

> She is an open and trusting child, unprepared for and unaccustomed to the ambushes of family life, and perhaps it is just as well that I can offer her little of that life.   —JOAN DIDION, "On Going Home"

> Short Beach was a year-round yet transient community, used to but indifferent toward the few renters of summer cottages, so perhaps it was odd that we found it the most welcoming place on earth.

1. Most people who bother with the matter at all would admit that the English language is in a bad way, but it is generally assumed that we cannot by conscious action do anything about it.
   —GEORGE ORWELL, "Politics and the English Language"

2. We observe today not a victory of party but a celebration of freedom, symbolizing an end as well as a beginning, signifying renewal as well as change.   —JOHN F. KENNEDY, Inaugural Address

3. Once in a long while, four times so far for me, my mother brings out the metal tube that holds her medical diploma.
   —MAXINE HONG KINGSTON, "Photographs of My Parents"

4. Moths that fly by day are not properly to be called moths; they do not excite that pleasant sense of dark autumn nights and ivy blossom which the commonest yellow underwing asleep in the shadow of the curtain never fails to rouse in us.   —VIRGINIA WOOLF, "The Death of the Moth"

5. When Ulysses S. Grant and Robert E. Lee met in the parlor of a modest house at Appomattox Court House, Virginia, on April 9, 1865, to work out the terms for the surrender of Lee's Army of Northern Virginia, a great chapter in American life came to a close, and a great new chapter began.
   —BRUCE CATTON, "Grant and Lee: A Study in Contrasts"

Thinking about Your Own Sentences

Look at one or two paragraphs of something you have written recently, and classify the sentences, using the guidelines for editing sentences on p. 191. Does your classification reveal that you vary the types of sentences you use, or do you tend to write primarily one type of sentence? If you find that you depend primarily on one type, revise to include other types—for example, if you write mainly simple sentences, try combining some of them to make compound or complex sentences. If you keep a writing log, you might record this work there along with any observations you have about sentence variation.

8

Understanding Pronoun Case

*T*HE GRAMMATICAL TERM CASE *may be unfamiliar to you (since it comes, like many such terms, from Latin), but the concept it represents is one you will recognize immediately. Take a look, for example, at the italicized pronouns in the following excerpt:*

> I want a wife who will care for *me* when I am sick and sympathize with *my* pain. . . . I want a wife who will keep *my* clothes clean, ironed, mended, replaced when need be, and who will see to it that *my* personal things are kept in their proper place.   — JUDY BRADY, "I Want a Wife"

Most of us know intuitively when to use I, *when to use* me, *and when to use* my. *Our choices reflect differences in case, the form a pronoun takes to indicate its function in a sentence. The italicized words in the excerpt show the singular first-person pronoun in three different cases: the subjective case (*I*), the objective case (*me*), and the possessive case (*my*). As this example demonstrates, pronouns functioning as subjects are in the subjective case; those functioning as objects are in the objective case; and those functioning as possessives are in the possessive case.*

SUBJECTIVE PRONOUNS

I/we	you	he/she/it	they	who/ whoever

OBJECTIVE PRONOUNS

me/us	you	him/her/it	them	whom/ whomever

POSSESSIVE PRONOUNS

my/our	your	his/hers/its	their	whose
mine/ours	yours	his/hers/its	theirs	

Everyday Use

During the 1991 NCAA tournament, two members of a winning team were being interviewed on CBS. The reporter asked whether the players had "felt a win coming on." One of them responded this way: "Marcus and me—or Marcus and I, I should say—we definitely knew we could win. All we had to do was play our own game." This player certainly would have been understood by the TV audience had he stuck with "Marcus and me," but he corrected himself because he realized that *I*, rather than *me*, should be used as a subject.

The player's near misuse of pronoun case is a common one, especially in casual conversation. Make a point of listening for pronoun case—perhaps in conversation, or in TV interviews—and then look for examples in printed conversations or interviews. Do you find that pronoun case is used differently in talk than in print? If so, how?

8a

Using the subjective case

A pronoun should be in the **subjective case** when it is a subject of a clause, a subject complement, or an appositive renaming a subject or subject complement (7b2 and 3 and 7c).

SUBJECT OF AN INDEPENDENT CLAUSE

They could either fight or face certain death with the lions.

We felt that Betty was enthusiastic and wanted to learn the material.

My brother and *I* adored our grandparents.

Who wrote "Araby"?

You must be kidding.

SUBJECT OF A DEPENDENT CLAUSE

Before *they* could get to the front, the war ended.

Roberto told the story to Carla, *who* told all her friends.

Give credit to the ones *who* did the work.

Our group appealed to *whoever* was willing to listen.

SUBJECT COMPLEMENT

Even though pronouns used as subject complements should, grammatically, be in the subjective case, Americans often use the objective case, especially in conversation: *Who's there? It's me.* To many speakers of English, *it's me* sounds preferable to *it's I.* Nevertheless, you should use the subjective case for all formal writing.

The first person to see Monty after the awards was *she.*
The main supporters of recycling were Jean and *I.*
It is *he* who brings life and spirit to the class.
If I were *she,* I would worry about other things.

If you find the subjective case for a subject complement stilted or awkward, try rewriting the sentence using the pronoun as the subject.

She was the first person to see Monty after the awards.

APPOSITIVE RENAMING A SUBJECT

Three students—Peter, Richard, and *she*—worked on the report.

APPOSITIVE RENAMING A SUBJECT COMPLEMENT

The finalists were two dark horses, Michael and *I.*

8b

Using the objective case

A pronoun should be in the **objective case** when it functions as a direct or indirect object (of a verb or verbal), a subject of an infinitive, an object of a preposition, or an appositive renaming an object (7b3 and 7c3).

OBJECT OF A VERB

The professor surprised *us* with a quiz. [direct object of *surprised*]
The grateful owner gave *him* a reward. [indirect object of *gave*]
Presidents usually rely on advisors *whom* they have known for years. [direct object of *have known*]

OBJECT OF A VERBAL

The Parisians were wonderful about helping *me,* and I ended the year speaking fluent French. [direct object of gerund]

Wishing *her* luck, the coach stepped back to watch the performance. [indirect object of participle]

Leonard offered to show *him* around town. [direct object of infinitive]

SUBJECT OF AN INFINITIVE

The objective case is also used in sentences like the following, where the pronoun is preceded by a verb and followed by an infinitive. Though the pronoun in such constructions is called the subject of the infinitive, it is in the objective case because it is the object of the sentence's verb.

Writing helps *me* to know myself better.

The student campaigners convinced his wife and *him* to vote in favor of the school bond.

The trip led *us* to appreciate how much California owes to Mexico.

OBJECT OF A PREPOSITION

Several of my friends went with *me*.

Alice planned a surprise party for *them*.

APPOSITIVE RENAMING AN OBJECT

We selected two managers, Joan and *her*, to attend the seminar.

8c

Using the possessive case

A pronoun should be in the **possessive case** when it shows possession or ownership. Notice that there are two forms of possessive pronouns: adjective forms, which are used before nouns or gerunds (*my, your, his, her, its, our, their, whose*), and noun forms, which take the place of a noun (*mine, yours, his, hers, its, ours, theirs, whose*).

ADJECTIVE FORMS

Many of Hitchcock's movies put viewers on the edge of *their* seats.

Whose life is it, anyway?

The sound of *his* hammering echoed through the corridor.

NOUN FORMS

The responsibility is *hers*.

"It's *mine!*" declared the child, clutching the golf club.

Whose is this blue backpack?

Using possessive pronouns before gerunds

A pronoun that appears before a gerund should be in the possessive case (*my/our, your, his/her/its, their*). **Gerunds** are *-ing* forms of verbs that function as nouns (*writing, sailing*). (See 7c3.)

I remember *his* singing.

What can be tricky is distinguishing gerunds from present participles, for both are *-ing* forms of verbs. **Present participles**, however, function as adjectives and modify the pronouns, which are in the objective case (*me/us, you, him/her/it, them*).

I remember *him* singing.

Notice the difference in meaning in the two examples about the singer. In the first, the memory is of *singing*, which is a gerund, modified by the possessive pronoun *his*. In the second, the memory is of *him*, which is a direct object of *remember* and thus is in the objective case; *singing* is a present participle modifying *him*.

EXERCISE 8.1

The following passage comes from "University Days," James Thurber's classic, though highly insensitive, essay about his years as a student at Ohio State University. Most of its pronouns have been removed. Put a correct pronoun in each blank, labeling each one as subjective, objective, or possessive case.

Another course that I didn't like, but somehow managed to pass, was economics. _____ went to that class straight from the botany class, which didn't help _____ to understand either subject. _____ used to get them mixed up. But not as mixed up as another student in _____ economics class who came there direct from a physics laboratory. _____ was a tackle on the football team, named Bolenciecwcz. At that time Ohio State University had one of the best football teams in the country, and Bolenciecwcz was one of _____ outstanding stars. In order to be eligible to play it was necessary for _____ to keep up in _____ studies, a very difficult matter, for while _____ was not dumber than an ox _____ was not any smarter. Most of _____ professors were lenient and helped _____ along. None gave _____ more hints in answering questions or asked _____ simpler ones than the economics professor, a thin, timid man named Bassum. One day when _____ were on the subject of transportation and distribution, it came Bolenciecwcz's turn to answer a question. "Name one means of transportation," the professor said to _____. No light came into the big tackle's eyes. "Just any means of transportation," said the professor. Bolenciecwcz sat staring at _____. "That is," pursued the professor, "any medium, agency, or method of going from one place to another." Bolenciecwcz had the look of a man _____ is being led into a trap. "You may choose among steam, horse-drawn, or electrically propelled vehicles," said the instructor. "I might suggest the one which _____ commonly take in making long journeys across land." There was a profound silence in which everybody stirred uneasily, including Bolenciecwcz and Mr. Bassum. Mr. Bassum abruptly broke this silence in an amazing manner. "Choo-choo-choo," _____ said, in a low voice, and turned instantly scarlet. _____ glanced appealingly around the room. All of _____, of course, shared Mr. Bassum's desire that Bolenciecwcz should stay abreast of the class in economics, for the Illinois game, one of the hardest and most important of the season, was only a week off. "Toot, toot, too-tooooooot!" some student with a deep voice moaned, and _____ all looked encouragingly at Bolenciecwcz. Somebody else gave a fine imitation of a locomotive letting off steam. Mr. Bassum himself rounded off the little show. "Ding, dong, ding, dong," _____ said, hopefully. Bolenciecwcz was staring at the floor now, trying to think, _____ great brow furrowed, _____ huge hands rubbing to-gether, _____ face red.   – JAMES THURBER, "University Days"

Now write a paragraph or two about your own least—or most—favorite class. When you are finished, underline all the personal pronouns you used, and label each one for case.

EXERCISE 8.2

Insert a correct possessive pronoun in the blank in each sentence. Example:

> <u>My</u> eyes ached after studying for ten hours.

1. Your parents must be pleased about _____ going back to college.
2. Ken's dinner arrived quickly, but Rose waited an hour for _____.
3. We agreed to pool _____ knowledge.
4. Even many supporters of Lincoln opposed _____ freeing the slaves.
5. _____ responsibility should it be to teach moral values?

8d

Using *who, whoever, whom,* and *whomever*

A common problem with pronoun case is deciding whether to use *who* or *whom*. In speech and even in some informal writing, *whom* has become a rarely used word. Even when traditional grammar requires *whom*, many Americans use *who* instead. Nevertheless, in formal written English, which includes most college writing, the case of the pronoun should reflect its grammatical function. *Who* and *whoever* are the subjective case forms and should be used when the pronoun is a subject or subject complement. *Whom* and *whomever* are the objective case forms and should be used when the pronoun is a direct or indirect object or the object of a preposition.

Most writers find that two particular situations can lead to confusion with *who* and *whom:* when they begin a question and when they introduce a dependent clause. In a dependent clause, you may also have to choose between *whoever* and *whomever* (7c4).

1

Beginning a question with *who* or *whom*

You can determine whether to use *who* or *whom* at the beginning of a question by answering the question using a personal pronoun. If the answer is in the subjective case, use *who;* if it is in the objective case, use *whom.*

> *Who* wrote the story?
> [*She* wrote the story. *She* is subjective; thus *who* is correct.]
>
> *Whom* did you visit?
> [I visited *them. Them* is objective; thus *whom* is correct.]

If the *who/whom* clause is interrupted by another expression (such as *did you say* or *does she think*), answering the question using a personal pronoun will still tell you the right case to use.

> *Who* do you think wrote the story?
> [I think *she* wrote the story. *She* is subjective; thus *who* is correct.]

2

Beginning a dependent clause with *who, whoever, whom,* or *whomever*

Pronoun case in a dependent clause is determined by its function in the clause, no matter how that clause functions in the sentence. If the pronoun acts as a subject or subject complement in the clause, use *who* or *whoever.* If the pronoun acts as an object, use *whom* or *whomever* (7c4).

> The new president was not *whom* she had expected. [*Whom* is the object of the verb *had expected* in the clause *whom she had expected.* Though the clause as a whole is the complement of the verb *was,* the pronoun should be in the objective case.]

The center is open to *whoever* wants to use it. [*Whoever* is the subject of the clause *whoever wants to use it*. Though the clause as a whole is the object of the preposition *to*, the pronoun should be in the subjective case.]

Richard feels like a knight *who* is headed for great adventure. [*Who* is the subject of the clause *who is headed for great adventure*.]

Whomever the party suspected of disloyalty was executed. [*Whomever* is the object of *suspected* in the clause *Whomever the party suspected of disloyalty*. Though the clause as a whole is the subject of the sentence, the pronoun should be in the objective case.]

If you are not sure which case to use, try separating the dependent clause from the rest of the sentence and looking at it in isolation. Rewrite the clause as a new sentence with a personal pronoun instead of *who(ever)* or *whom(ever)*. If the pronoun is in the subjective case, use *who* or *whoever*; if it is in the objective case, use *whom* or *whomever*.

Anyone can hypnotize a person (*who/whom*) wants to be hypnotized. [Isolate the clause *who/whom wants to be hypnotized*. Substituting a personal pronoun gives you *he wants to be hypnotized*. *He* is subjective case; thus, *Anyone can hypnotize a person* **who** *wants to be hypnotized*.]

The minister grimaced at (*whoever/whomever*) made any noise. [Isolate the clause *whoever/whomever made any noise*. Substituting a personal pronoun gives you *they made any noise*. *They* is subjective case; therefore, *The minister grimaced at* **whoever** *made any noise*.]

The minister smiled at (*whoever/whomever*) she greeted. [Isolate the clause *she greeted whoever/whomever*. Substituting a personal pronoun gives you *she greeted them*. *Them* is objective case; therefore, *The minister smiled at* **whomever** *she greeted*.]

If the dependent clause is interrupted by an expression such as *he thinks* or *she says*, delete the expression when you isolate the clause.

The minister grimaced at (*whoever/whomever*) she thought made any noise. [Isolate the clause *whoever/whomever made any noise*, deleting the interrupting expression *she thought*. Substituting a personal pronoun gives you *they made any noise*. *They* is subjective case; therefore, *The minister grimaced at* **whoever** *she thought made any noise*.]

EXERCISE 8.3

Insert *who*, *whoever*, *whom*, or *whomever* appropriately in the blank in each of the following sentences. Example:

She is someone who will go far.

1. _____ shall I say is calling?
2. _____ the voters choose faces an almost impossible challenge.
3. The manager promised to reward _____ sold the most cars.
4. Professor Quiñones asked _____ we wanted to collaborate with.
5. _____ will the new tax law benefit most?

8e

Using case in compound structures

Most problems with the case of personal pronouns occur when the pronoun is part of a compound subject, complement, or object. Each part of a compound structure should be in the same case as it would if used alone. That is, pronouns in compound subjects and compound subject complements should be in the subjective case; pronouns in compound objects should be in the objective case.

SUBJECTS

Mrs. Wentzel and *I* simply could not exist in the same classroom.
When *Zelda* and *he* were first married, they lived in New York.

SUBJECT COMPLEMENTS

The winners of the competition were *Renata* and *he*.
The next two speakers will be *Philip* and *she*.

OBJECTS OF VERBS

The boss invited *her* and *her family* to dinner. [direct object]
They offered *Gail* and *her* a summer internship. [indirect object]

OBJECTS OF PREPOSITIONS

This morning saw yet another conflict between *my sister* and *me*.
My aunt put me in the room once shared by *my uncle* and *her*.

To decide whether to use the subjective or the objective case in a compound structure, make each part of the compound into a separate sentence.

Come to the park with Bob and (*I/me*). [Separating the compound structure gives you *come to the park with Bob* and *come to the park with me*; thus, *Come to the park with Bob and me.*]

8f

Using case in appositives

Pronoun case in an appositive is determined by the word that the appositive renames. If the word functions as a subject or subject complement, the pronoun should be in the subjective case; if it functions as an object, the pronoun should be in the objective case.

> All three panelists—Arlene, Tony, and *I*—were stumped by the question. [*Panelists* is the subject of the sentence, so the pronoun in the appositive *Arlene, Tony, and I* should be in the subjective case.]

> The poker game that night produced three big winners, my grandmother, Aunt Rose, and *me*. [*Winners* is the direct object of the verb *produced*, so the pronoun in the appositive *my grandmother, Aunt Rose, and me* should be in the objective case.]

8g

Using case in elliptical constructions

Elliptical constructions are those in which some words are left out but understood. In comparisons with *than* or *as*, we often leave words unsaid: *I see Elizabeth more often than* [*I see*] *her sister.* When sentences with such constructions end in a pronoun, the pronoun should be in the case it would be in if the construction were complete.

> His brother has always been more athletic than *he* [is].

In some constructions like this, the case of the pronoun depends on the meaning intended.

ELLIPTICAL	Willie likes Lily more than *she*.
COMPLETE	Willie likes Lily more than *she* [likes Lily].
ELLIPTICAL	Willie likes Lily more than *her*.
COMPLETE	Willie likes Lily more than [he likes] *her*.

As these examples demonstrate, use the subjective case if the pronoun is actually the subject of an omitted verb; use the objective case if it is an object of an omitted verb.

8h

Using *we* and *us* before a noun

When the first-person plural pronoun is used before a noun, the case of the pronoun depends on the way the noun functions in the sentence. If the noun functions as a subject or subject complement, the pronoun should be in the subjective case (*we*). If the noun functions as an object, the pronoun should be in the objective case (*us*).

We fans never give up hope. [*Fans* is the subject.]

The Orioles depend on *us* fans. [*Fans* is the object of a preposition.]

If you are unsure about which case to use, recasting the sentence without the noun will give you the answer. Use whichever pronoun would be correct if the noun were omitted: *We never give up hope. The Orioles depend on us.*

EXERCISE 8.4

Choose the appropriate pronoun from the pair in parentheses in each of the following sentences. Example:

The possibility of (their/them) succeeding never occurred to me.

1. The relationship between (*they/them*) and their brother was often strained.
2. When I was in high school, I had one teacher (*who/whom*) I truly admired.
3. At the time, I had three friends who were indeed stronger, better looking, and more popular than (*I/me*).
4. The only candidates left in the race were (*he/him*) and Clinton.
5. Maria became more and more interested in (*his/him*) assisting her with planning her presentation.
6. When Jessica and (*she/her*) first met, they despised each other.
7. The two violinists, Sergei and (*he/him*), played as though they had a single musical mind.
8. Soap operas appeal to (*whoever/whomever*) is interested in intrigue, suspense, joy, pain, grief, romance, fidelity, sex, and violence.
9. Tomorrow (*we/us*) raw recruits will have our first on-the-job test.
10. The only experts (*who/whom*) they can recommend are the two magicians who trained them.

EXERCISE 8.5

Edit each of the following sentences to correct errors in pronoun case. (Not all sentences contain errors.) Example:

> *she*
> *Of the group, only ~~her~~ and I finished the race.*

1. The readers, her and me, agreed that the story was very suspenseful.
2. Just between you and I, this course is a disaster!
3. The people who Jay worked with were very cold and unsociable.
4. Who would have thought that twenty years later he would be king?
5. Roderigo becomes involved in the plot without him knowing it.
6. Only him, a few cabinet members, and several military leaders were aware of the steady advance Japan was making toward Pearl Harbor.
7. All of the job candidates were far more experienced than I.
8. As out-of-towners, my buddy and me did not know too many people.
9. I never got to play that role in front of an audience, but I am one of the few performers who really did break a leg.
10. Connor always lent money to whomever asked him for it.

≫ *Editing case*

1. Are all pronouns after forms of the verb *be* in the subjective case? *It's me* is common in spoken English, but in writing it should be *It is I*. (8a)

2. To check for correct use of *who* and *whom* (and *whoever* and *whomever*), especially at the beginning of a question or dependent clause, try substituting *he* or *him*. If *he* is correct, use *who* (or *whoever*); if *him*, use *whom* or *whomever*. (8d)

3. In compound structures, make sure any pronouns are in the same case they would be in if used alone. (*She and Jake were living in Spain.*) (8e)

4. When a pronoun follows *than* or *as*, complete the sentence mentally. If the pronoun is the subject of an unstated verb, it should be in the subjective case (*I like her better than he* [*likes her*].) If the pronoun is the object of an unstated verb, put it in the objective case (*I like her better than* [*I like*] *him.*) (8g)

5. Circle all the pronouns to see if you rely too heavily on any one pronoun or case. Check especially for overuse of *I*.

THINKING CRITICALLY ABOUT PRONOUN CASE

Reading with Attention to Pronoun Case

The poet e. e. cummings often broke the standard rules of grammar and word order to create particular effects in his poetry. Read the following poem, and note the function of each pronoun. Then rearrange the words of the poem so that they follow as closely as possible the normal order they would take in an ordinary sentence. How does pronoun case give you a clue to this arrangement?

Me up at does

out of the floor
quietly Stare

a poisoned mouse

still who alive

is asking What
have i done that

You wouldn't have   – e. e. cummings

Thinking about Your Own Use of Pronoun Case

Research shows that one of the most overused words in any language is the word for *I*. Whenever you write anything that includes your own opinions, you probably rely to some degree on first-person pronouns, singular and plural. Read over the paragraph(s) you wrote in Exercise 8.1 with attention to your use of pronouns. Do you find any patterns? If you find that you rely heavily on any one case— that half your sentences begin with *I*, for example—decide whether your writing seems at all monotonous as a result. If so, try revising, paying attention to pronoun case. See, in other words, whether revising some sentences to change *I* to *me* (or vice versa) brings greater variety to your writing. If you keep a writing log, you might enter your work in it, noting what you have learned about your use of pronoun case.

9

Using Verbs

WHEN USED SKILLFULLY, *verbs can be the heartbeat of prose, moving it along, enlivening it, carrying its action. Verbs are extremely flexible and can change form to mark grammatical agreement with the subject or to indicate* tense, voice, *or* mood.

CHANGE IN TENSE	The runner *skims* around the track. [present tense]
	The runner *skimmed* around the track. [past tense]
CHANGE IN VOICE	She *savors* every step. [active voice]
	Every step *is savored*. [passive voice]
CHANGE IN MOOD	She *is* completely content. [indicative]
	If she *were* not content, she would not be smiling. [subjunctive]

This chapter explores in detail the way verbs work, with attention to form, tense, voice, and mood. (Chapter 10 explores subject-verb agreement, and Chapter 56 provides further details about verbs for multilingual writers.)

VERB FORMS

Except for *be*, all English verbs have five possible forms.

BASE FORM	PAST TENSE	PAST PARTICIPLE	PRESENT PARTICIPLE	-S FORM
talk	talked	talked	talking	talks
adore	adored	adored	adoring	adores
jog	jogged	jogged	jogging	jogs

Everyday Use

Restaurant menus are often a good source of verbs in action. One famous place in Boston offers, for instance, to bake, broil, pan-fry, deep-fry, poach, sauté, fricassee, or scallop any of the fish entrees on its menu. To someone ordering—or cooking—at this restaurant, the important distinctions lie entirely in the verbs.

Choose some kind of text you read regularly—the sports section, perhaps, or a cookbook, or a piece of your own writing—and have a look at the verbs. Note down some interesting examples.

The **base form** is the one listed in the dictionary. For all verbs except *be,* it is the form used to indicate action that takes place in the present when the subject is a plural noun or the pronoun *I, you, we,* or *they.*

> During the ritual, the women *go* into trances.
>
> The men *take* knives and *point* them at their chests.

The **past tense** is used to indicate action that took place entirely in the past. For most verbs, it is formed by adding *-ed* or *-d* to the base form. Some verbs, however, have irregular past-tense forms (9b). *Be* has two past-tense forms, *was* and *were.*

> The Globe *served* as the playhouse for many of Shakespeare's works.
>
> In 1613, it *caught* fire and *burned* to the ground.
>
> We *were* in England last year.

The **past participle** is used to form perfect tenses (9d–f), passive voice (pp. 224–226), and adjectives. It usually has the same form as the past tense, though some verbs have irregular past participles (9b). The past participle cannot function alone as a predicate but must be used with the auxiliary verbs *have* or *be.*

> She *had accomplished* the impossible. [past perfect]
>
> No one *was injured* in the explosion. [passive voice]
>
> *Standardized* tests usually require *sharpened* pencils. [adjective]

The **present participle** is constructed by adding *-ing* to the base form. Like the past participle, it cannot function alone as a predicate but must be used with auxiliary verbs to indicate continuing action. The present participle can also function as an adjective or as a noun (a gerund). (See 7c3.)

Many students *are competing* in the race. [continuing action]

He tried to comfort the *crying* child. [adjective]

Climbing the mountain took all afternoon. [noun (gerund)]

Except with *be* and *have,* the **-s form** consists of the base form plus *-s* or *-es.* This form indicates the present tense for third-person singular subjects. All singular nouns, *he, she,* and *it,* and many indefinite pronouns (such as *everyone* or *someone*) are third-person singular.

The dog *snaps* at people who try to pet it.

She usually *takes* the shortcut across campus.

No one *believes* his story.

Note that the *-s* form occurs *only* in the third-person singular of the present tense.

	SINGULAR	PLURAL
FIRST PERSON	I wish	we wish
SECOND PERSON	you wish	you wish
THIRD PERSON	he/she/it wishes	they wish
	Joe wishes	children wish
	someone wishes	many wish

The third-person singular forms of *be* and *have* are *is* and *has.*

The second stage of the ritual *is* the so-called liminal stage.

A whale *has* lungs instead of gills.

⟫ *Editing -s and -es endings*

If you tend to leave off the *-s* and *-es* verb endings in academic and professional writing, you should check for them systematically.

1. Underline every verb, and then circle all verbs in the present tense.
2. Find the subject of every verb you circle.
3. If the subject is a singular noun; *he, she,* or *it;* or an indefinite pronoun that is singular in meaning, be sure the verb ends in *-s* or *-es.* If it is not third-person singular, the verb should not have an *-s* or *-es* ending.
4. Be careful when you see auxiliary verbs such as *can* or *may* (9a). Auxiliaries that *sound* like the present tense (*She can help*) are used with the base form, never with the *-s* or *-es* form.

Forms of be

Be has three forms in the present tense (*am, is, are*) and two in the past tense (*was, were*).

Present tense

	SINGULAR	PLURAL
FIRST PERSON	I *am*	we *are*
SECOND PERSON	you *are*	you *are*
THIRD PERSON	he/she/it *is*	they *are*
	Jane *is*	children *are*
	somebody *is*	some *are*

Past tense

	SINGULAR	PLURAL
FIRST PERSON	I *was*	we *were*
SECOND PERSON	you *were*	you *were*
THIRD PERSON	he/she/it *was*	they *were*
	Jane *was*	children *were*
	somebody *was*	some *were*

ON VARIETIES OF ENGLISH
Uses of be

My sister at work. She be there every day 'til five.

These sentences illustrate two common uses of the verb *be.* The first shows the absence of *be* where contracted forms of *is* or *are* may occur in standard academic English; the same sentence in standard academic English would read "My sister's at work." or "My sister's at work now." The second shows the use of "habitual *be,*" indicating that something is always, usually, or habitually the case. The same sentence in standard academic English would read "She's there every day until five."

These uses of *be* are common in the discourse of many African American speakers and some southern white speakers. You will see them frequently in African American and southern literature, especially in dialogue, for they are common patterns in spoken language. You may well have occasion to quote dialogue featuring these patterns in your own academic writing; doing so can be a good way of evoking particular regions or communities.

In general, however, most academic writing calls for standard academic English. See Chapter 28 on using varieties of English appropriately.

EXERCISE 9.1

Write a paragraph about a past event in your life—a visit, a job, anything you wish to write about. Then look at the verbs. How many different verbs do you use? How many different verb tenses? Which verbs might you like to replace?

Using auxiliary verbs

Sometimes called helping verbs, **auxiliary verbs** are used with a base form, present participle, or past participle to create verb phrases. The base form or participle in a verb phrase is called the **main verb.** The most common auxiliaries are forms of *have, be,* and *do,* which are used to indicate completed, continuing, or future action, the passive voice, emphasis, questions, and negative statements.

> We *did consider* all viewpoints. [completed action]
>
> The college *is building* a new dormitory. [continuing action]
>
> They *will explain* the procedure. [future action]
>
> We *were warned.* [passive voice]
>
> I *do respect* this viewpoint. [emphasis]
>
> *Do* you *know* the answer? [question]
>
> He *does* not *like* wearing a tie. [negative statement]

Modal auxiliaries—*can, could, might, may, must, ought to, should, would*— show possibility, necessity, obligation, and so on.

> You *can see* three states from the top of the mountain. [possibility]
>
> I *must try* harder to go to bed early. [necessity]
>
> She *should visit* her parents more often. [obligation]

▶ *FOR MULTILINGUAL WRITERS*
Using Modal Auxiliaries

Why do we not say "Alice can to read Latin"? For discussion of *can* and other modal auxiliaries, see 56e.

EXERCISE 9.2

Edit the following sentences so that all verb forms are appropriate for standard academic English. (Some of the sentences do not require any change.) Example:

> *seems* *make*
> Although Joe ~~seem~~ in control, his actions ~~making~~ me wonder.

1. When the dance begin, a man in costume appears.
2. The man have long fingernails and a mask.
3. All of the people in the village participate in the ceremony.
4. The doctor works two nights a week at a clinic.
5. A hot shower always relax me.
6. The thought of nuclear war be terrifying to most people.
7. New mothers often be suffering from depression.
8. He don't know whether to try again or to give up.
9. The deposit refunded if the customer don't buy the equipment.
10. Mayor Burns running for reelection this fall.

9b

Using regular and irregular verbs

A verb is **regular** when its past tense and past participle are formed by adding -ed or -d to the base form.

BASE FORM	PAST TENSE	PAST PARTICIPLE
love	loved	loved
honor	honored	honored
obey	obeyed	obeyed

≫ *Editing* -ed *or* -d *endings*

Speakers who skip over the -ed or -d endings in conversation may forget to include them in writing. If you tend to drop these endings, make a point of systematically checking for them when proofreading. Underline all the verbs, and then underline a second time any that are past tense or past participles. Check each of these for an -ed or -d ending. Unless the verb is irregular (see list following), it should end in -ed or -d.

Irregular verbs

A verb is **irregular** when it does not follow the *-ed* or *-d* pattern. The past tense and past participle of irregular verbs are most often formed by changing an internal vowel: *begin, began, begun.* In some such verbs, *-en* or *-n* is also added to the past participle: *break, broke, broken.* Other verbs change more radically: *go, went, gone.* Still others do not change at all: *hurt, hurt, hurt.* If you are unsure of the correct verb form, consult your dictionary, which lists any irregular forms under the entry for the base form.

≫ *Some common irregular verbs*

BASE FORM	PAST TENSE	PAST PARTICIPLE
arise	arose	arisen
be	was/were	been
bear	bore	borne, born
beat	beat	beaten
become	became	become
begin	began	begun
bite	bit	bitten, bit
blow	blew	blown
break	broke	broken
bring	brought	brought
broadcast	broadcast	broadcast
build	built	built
burn	burned, burnt	burned, burnt
burst	burst	burst
buy	bought	bought
catch	caught	caught
choose	chose	chosen
come	came	come
cost	cost	cost
cut	cut	cut
dig	dug	dug
dive	dived, dove	dived
do	did	done
draw	drew	drawn
dream	dreamed, dreamt	dreamed, dreamt
drink	drank	drunk
drive	drove	driven
eat	ate	eaten
fall	fell	fallen
feel	felt	felt

(Continued)

BASE FORM	PAST TENSE	PAST PARTICIPLE
fight	fought	fought
find	found	found
fly	flew	flown
forget	forgot	forgotten, forgot
freeze	froze	frozen
get	got	gotten, got
give	gave	given
go	went	gone
grow	grew	grown
hang (suspend)[1]	hung	hung
have	had	had
hear	heard	heard
hide	hid	hidden
hit	hit	hit
keep	kept	kept
know	knew	known
lay	laid	laid
lead	led	led
leave	left	left
lend	lent	lent
let	let	let
lie (recline)[2]	lay	lain
lose	lost	lost
make	made	made
mean	meant	meant
meet	met	met
pay	paid	paid
prove	proved	proved, proven
put	put	put
read	read	read
ride	rode	ridden
ring	rang	rung
rise	rose	risen
run	ran	run
say	said	said
see	saw	seen
send	sent	sent
set	set	set
shake	shook	shaken

(*Continued*)

[1]*Hang* meaning "execute by hanging" is regular: *hang, hanged, hanged.*
[2]*Lie* meaning "tell a falsehood" is regular: *lie, lied, lied.*

BASE FORM	PAST TENSE	PAST PARTICIPLE
shoot	shot	shot
show	showed	showed, shown
shrink	shrank	shrunk
sing	sang	sung
sink	sank	sunk
sit	sat	sat
sleep	slept	slept
speak	spoke	spoken
spend	spent	spent
spread	spread	spread
spring	sprang, sprung	sprung
stand	stood	stood
steal	stole	stolen
strike	struck	struck, stricken
swim	swam	swum
swing	swung	swung
take	took	taken
teach	taught	taught
tear	tore	torn
tell	told	told
think	thought	thought
throw	threw	thrown
wake	woke, waked	waked, woken
wear	wore	worn
win	won	won
wind	wound	wound
write	wrote	written

EXERCISE 9.3

Complete each of the following sentences by filling in each blank with the past tense or past participle of the verb listed in parentheses. Example:

> They had already __eaten__ (eat) the beef; later they __ate__ (eat) the ham.

1. Clearly this short story would not have _____ (be) so effective if it had been _____ (write) in the third person.

2. After she had _____ (make) her decision, she _____ (find) that the constant anxiety was no longer a factor in her daily life.

3. The process of hazing _____ (begin) soon after fraternities were formed.

4. Hearns _____ (lose) control of the fight, and Nolan _____ (take) advantage of this loss.

5. When Maria Callas _____ (make) her debut at the Metropolitan Opera, some people _____ (know) that music history was being made.

6. Katherine Dunn, an unorthodox novelist who _____ (choose) thorny subjects, has now _____ (become) a cause for some dedicated readers.

7. Reluctantly Marisol _____ (shake) her head in disagreement; she had _____ (bring) with her the necessary evidence to disprove John's claim.

8. Roberto had _____ (fling) his hat into the ring and had assembled the best advisors he had _____ (be) able to find.

9. When Charles admitted that he had _____ (break) into the apartment, he said that he had _____ (lose) his keys.

10. I discovered that I had _____ (fall) into a rut; for several months I had neither _____ (break) my routines nor _____ (do) anything new.

EXERCISE 9.4

Where necessary, edit the following sentences to eliminate any inappropriate verb forms. Example:

    began
She ~~begin~~ *the examination on time.*

1. Socrates drank the hemlock calmly and died a few hours later.

2. The band had sang its last song before the fight begun.

3. When the battle was over, the rebels had been beat badly.

4. By the mid-1970s, New York had almost went bankrupt.

5. The lake freezed early this year.

9c

Using *lie* and *lay, sit* and *set, rise* and *raise*

Three pairs of verbs—*lie* and *lay, sit* and *set,* and *rise* and *raise*—cause problems for many writers because both verbs in each pair have similar-sounding forms and somewhat related meanings. In each pair, one of the verbs is **transitive,** meaning that it takes a direct object; the other is **intransitive,** meaning that it does not take an object. The best way to avoid confusing the two is to memorize their forms and meanings—or to use synonyms. All these verbs except *raise* are irregular.

BASE FORM	PAST TENSE	PAST PARTICIPLE	PRESENT PARTICIPLE	-S FORM
lie	lay	lain	lying	lies
lay	laid	laid	laying	lays
sit	sat	sat	sitting	sits
set	set	set	setting	sets
rise	rose	risen	rising	rises
raise	raised	raised	raising	raises

Lie is intransitive and means "recline" or "be situated." *Lay* is transitive and means "put" or "place." This pair is especially confusing because *lay* is also the past-tense form of *lie*.

INTRANSITIVE	He *lay* on the floor unable to move.
TRANSITIVE	I *laid* the package on the counter.

Sit is intransitive and means "be seated." *Set* usually is transitive and means "put" or "place."

INTRANSITIVE	She *sat* in the rocking chair, daydreaming.
TRANSITIVE	She *set* the vase on the table.

Rise is intransitive and means "get up" or "go up." *Raise* is transitive and means "lift" or "cause to go up."

INTRANSITIVE	He *rose* from the bed and left the room.
TRANSITIVE	He *raised* himself to a sitting position.
INTRANSITIVE	The price of coffee is *rising*.
TRANSITIVE	The store is *raising* the price of coffee.

EXERCISE 9.5

Choose the appropriate verb form in each of the following sentences.

1. Sometimes she just (*lies/lays*) and stares at the ceiling.
2. I (*lay/laid*) my books down just as the telephone rang.
3. The doctor asked the patient to (*lie/lay*) on his side for an injection.
4. He used whatever was (*lying/laying*) around the house.
5. Doctors urge us to (*sit/set*) aside fad diets once and for all.

6. I (*sat/set*) back, closed my eyes, and began to meditate.

7. (*Sitting/Setting*) in the sun too long can lead to skin cancer.

8. The Federal Reserve Bank is planning to (*rise/raise*) interest rates.

9. When the temperature (*rises/raises*), the humidity usually declines.

10. We (*rose/raised*) every morning at six and went jogging.

VERB TENSES

Tenses show when the action expressed by the verb takes place. We characteristically think of time in terms of present, past, and future; and the three *simple tenses* are the present tense, the past tense, and the future tense.

PRESENT TENSE	I jump
PAST TENSE	I jumped
FUTURE TENSE	I will jump

More complex aspects of time, such as ongoing or completed actions or conditions, are expressed through *progressive, perfect,* and *perfect progressive forms* of the simple tenses. Although such terminology sounds complicated in the abstract, you regularly use all these forms. Here are all the tense forms of one verb, *ask*.

SIMPLE PRESENT	she *asks*
SIMPLE PAST	she *asked*
SIMPLE FUTURE	she *will ask*
PRESENT PERFECT	she *has asked*
PAST PERFECT	she *had asked*
FUTURE PERFECT	she *will have asked*
PRESENT PROGRESSIVE	she *is asking*
PAST PROGRESSIVE	she *was asking*
FUTURE PROGRESSIVE	she *will be asking*
PRESENT PERFECT PROGRESSIVE	she *has been asking*
PROGRESSIVE PAST PERFECT	she *had been asking*
FUTURE PERFECT PROGRESSIVE	she *will have been asking*

The simple tenses locate an action only within the three basic time frames of present, past, and future. The perfect form of each tense expresses the idea of a *completed* action in the present, past, or future; and the progressive form expresses the idea of a *continuing* action. Finally, the perfect progressive form expresses the idea of an action that *continues up to some point* in the present, past, or future.

9d

Using the present tense forms

The **simple present** indicates actions occurring at the time of speaking, as well as those occurring habitually and those considered to be general truths or scientific facts. In addition, with appropriate time expressions, the simple present can be used to indicate a scheduled future event.

> They *are* very angry about the decision.
>
> I *eat* breakfast every day at 8:00 A.M.
>
> Love *conquers* all.
>
> Water *freezes* at zero degrees Celsius.
>
> Residents of Greenland *endure* bitter cold for most of the year.
>
> Classes *begin* next week.

The simple present is also used in discussing literary and artistic works created in the past that exist in our experience. For example, a literary character such as Ishmael in *Moby-Dick,* created by Herman Melville over a century ago, exists in our present time as well.

> Ishmael slowly *comes* to realize all that *is* at stake in the search for the white whale.

The **present progressive** indicates actions that are ongoing or continuous in the present.

> Yolanda *is applying* for a scholarship.

The present progressive is typically used to describe an action that is happening at the moment of speaking, in contrast to the simple present, which more often indicates habitual actions.

PRESENT PROGRESSIVE	You *are driving* too fast.
SIMPLE PRESENT	I always *drive* carefully.

With an appropriate expression of time, the present progressive can also be used to indicate a scheduled event in the future.

> We *are having* friends over for dinner tomorrow night.

The **present perfect** indicates actions begun in the past and either completed at some unspecified time in the past or continuing into the present.

> Uncontrolled logging *has destroyed* many tropical forests.
> Anti-abortion activists *have tried* to reverse the decision.

The **present perfect progressive** indicates an ongoing action begun in the past and continuing into the present.

> The two sides *have been trying* to settle the case out of court.

9e

Using the past tense forms

The **simple past** indicates actions that occurred at a specific time and do not extend into the present.

> She *felt* better as soon as her exams were over.
> Germany *invaded* Poland on September 1, 1939.

The **past progressive** indicates continuing actions in the past, often with specified limits.

> Lenin *was living* in exile in Zurich when the czar was overthrown.
> In the 1980s, many of the baby boomers *were becoming* parents.

The **past perfect** indicates actions that were completed by a specific time in the past or before some other past action occurred.

> By the fourth century, Christianity *had become* the state religion.
> Homesteaders found that speculators *had* already *taken* the best land.

The **past perfect progressive** indicates continuing actions in the past that began before a specific time or before some other past action began.

> I *had been living* beyond my means for years before I went bankrupt.
> Carter *had been planning* a naval career until his father died.

9f

Using the future tense forms

The **simple future** indicates actions that have yet to begin.

The exhibition *will come* to Washington in September.

I *shall graduate* the year after next.

The **future progressive** indicates continuing actions in the future.

The loans *will be coming* due in the next two years.

A team of international observers *will be monitoring* the elections.

The **future perfect** indicates actions that will be completed by or before some specified time in the future.

If no one shows up, all our work *will have been* futile.

In ten years, the original investment *will have doubled*.

The **future perfect progressive** indicates continuing actions that will be completed by some specified time in the future.

By the time the session ends, the negotiators *will have been working* for ten hours without a break.

In May, I *will have been living* in Tucson for five years.

≫ *Editing verb tenses*

Errors in verb tenses take several forms. Some are errors in verb form: writing *seen* for *saw*, for example, which is an instance of confusing the standard participle and past tense forms. Others are errors in tense: using the simple past (*Uncle Charlie arrived*) when meaning requires the present perfect (*Uncle Charlie has arrived*). Still others result from using an inappropriate variety of English (*she nervous*) in situations calling for standard academic English (*she's nervous*).

If you have trouble with verb tenses, the best thing you can do is to keep a log of your errors and then look for patterns in them. Once you can identify specific problems, you can make a point of routinely checking for them as you proofread.

EXERCISE 9.6

Complete each of the following sentences by filling in the blank with an appropriate form of the verb listed in parentheses. Since more than one form will sometimes be possible, be prepared to explain the reasons for your choices.

1. In spite of the poor turnout for today's referendum, local officials _____ (expect) the bond issue to pass.

2. Ever since the first nuclear power plants were built, opponents _____ (predict) disaster.

3. Thousands of Irish peasants _____ (emigrate) to America after the potato famine of the 1840s.

4. The newspaper _____ (arrive) late every day this week.

5. The committee _____ (meet) again next week.

6. President Kennedy was shot while he _____ (ride) in a limousine.

7. By eleven o'clock this morning, stock prices _____ (fall) fifteen points.

8. By the time a child born today enters first grade, he or she _____ (watch) thousands of television commercials.

9. In "The Road Not Taken," the poet _____ (come) to a fork in the road.

10. The supply of a product _____ (rise) when the demand is great.

EXERCISE 9.7

Read the following passage from a conversation with Maya Angelou, and identify the tenses of each italicized verb. Then, write a paragraph or two describing your own morning routine, and identify the tenses of the verbs you use.

I *wake* usually about six and *get* immediately out of bed. Then I *begin* to wonder why. . . . I *make* very strong coffee and *sit* in the sunroom with the newspaper, the *Winston-Salem Journal*, the only paper in town.

I *love* to read the letters to the editor. I *like* to see what *angers* people: only one in a hundred says "I *love* what you're doing"; the other ninety-nine *say* they *hate* the paper or this *is* nonsense or that *is* absolutely wrong. I *feel* as if I've just *met* eight people, little human vignettes. . . .

At about 8:30 I *start* looking at the house because the housekeeper *arrives* at nine and I'm still too well brought-up to *offer* Mrs. Cunningham a house in too much disarray so I *straighten* up before she comes in. She *has been* my housekeeper for six years now—my sister *has suggested* that in another life she *was* a staff-sergeant. I *give* to her and she *gives* to me and we *live* together with a lot of laughter. My secretary, Mrs. Garris, also *comes* at nine and that's when real life *begins*. Mrs. Garris *is* a lovely Southern black lady with efficiency and grace vying for dominance in her spirit. She *says*, "Ms. Angelou, you've *got* to sign this, send that, agree to that, deny this . . ." and I *say*, "Mrs. Garris, I *will talk* to you in an hour."

Using verb tenses in sequences

Because tense is crucial to our understanding of when actions occur and because time relationships can be very complex, careful and accurate use of tenses is important to clear writing. Even the simplest narrative describes actions that take place at different times; using particular tenses for particular actions allows readers to follow such time changes readily.

The relationship between the tense of the verb in the independent clause of a sentence and the tense of a verb in a dependent clause or a verbal is called the **sequence of tenses**. In general, the verb in a dependent clause may be in any tense form required for your meaning. The only limitation is that the relationship between the forms in the independent and dependent clauses makes sense. For example, all of the following make sense and are acceptable grammatically:

He *lent* her the money because he *is* a generous man. [past, present]

He *lent* her the money because he *loved* her. [past, past]

He *lent* her the money because she *will invest* it wisely. [past, future]

Even though in general you can use almost any sequence of tenses, in a particular sentence the tense of the verb in the dependent clause may be limited by the meaning. For example, it makes no sense to say, *He lent her the money because he will love her,* or *He lent her the money because she had invested it wisely.*

1

Verb sequence with infinitives

An infinitive is *to* plus the base form (*to go, to be*). Use the **present infinitive** to indicate actions occurring at the same time as or later than the action of the predicate verb.

I *wanted to swim* in the ocean last summer. [The wanting and the swimming occurred at the same time in the past.]

I *expect to swim* in the ocean next summer. [The expecting is present; the swimming is in the future.]

Use the **perfect infinitive** (*to have* plus the past participle) to indicate actions occurring before the action of the predicate verb.

> She *seems to have become* a recluse. [The condition of becoming a recluse took place before the "seeming."]

> He *was reported to have left* his fortune to his cat. [The leaving of the fortune took place before the reporting.]

2

Verb sequence with participles

Use the **present participle** (base form plus *-ing*) to indicate actions occurring at the same time as that of the predicate verb.

> *Seeking* to relieve unemployment, Roosevelt *established* several public works programs. [Both the seeking and the establishment of the programs occurred simultaneously in the past.]

Use the **past participle** or the **present perfect participle** (*having* plus the past participle) to indicate action occurring before that of the predicate verb.

> *Flown* to the front, the troops *joined* their hard-pressed comrades. [The flying occurred before the joining.]

> *Having crushed* all opposition at home, he *launched* a war of conquest. [He launched the war after he crushed the opposition.]

3

Verb sequence and habitual actions

One common error in verb usage occurs when indicating repeated or habitual actions. In conversation, we all hear people use *will* or *would* to describe habitual actions; in writing, however, you should stick to the present and past tenses.

UNEDITED	When I have a deadline, I *will work* all night.
EDITED	When I have a deadline, I *work* all night.
UNEDITED	While we sat on the porch, the children *would play*.
EDITED	While we sat on the porch, the children *played*.

EXERCISE 9.8

Edit each of the following sentences to create the appropriate sequence of tenses from the verb in the predicate to the participle or infinitive. Example:

> *have sent*
> He needs to ~~send~~ in his application before today.

1. When he was twenty-one, he wanted to have become a millionaire by the age of thirty.
2. Leaving England in December, the settlers arrived in Virginia in May.
3. They hoped to plant their garden by now.
4. Cutting off all contact with family, he did not know whom to ask for help.
5. Having sung in the shower, he did not hear the doorbell.

VOICE

Voice is the feature of transitive verbs that tells whether the subject is acting (*he questions us*) or being acted upon (*he is questioned*). When the subject is acting, the verb is in the **active voice**; when the subject is being acted upon, the verb is in the **passive voice**. The passive voice is formed, as in this sentence, by using the appropriate form of the auxiliary verb *be* followed by the past participle of the main verb.

	ACTIVE VOICE	PASSIVE VOICE
PRESENT	He *questions* us.	He *is questioned.*
PAST	He *questioned* us.	He *was questioned.*
FUTURE	He *will question* us.	He *will be questioned.*
PRESENT PERFECT	He *has questioned* us.	He *has been questioned.*
PAST PERFECT	He *had questioned* us.	He *had been questioned.*
FUTURE PERFECT	He *will have questioned* us.	He *will have been questioned.*

Most contemporary writers use the active voice as much as possible because it makes prose more *active,* more lively. To say that *the mail was opened* (passive voice) does not give the sense of action or immediacy that *Lorraine opened the mail* (active voice) does. In the passive construction, the mail is just there—being opened by no one or nothing in particular. Even adding *by Lorraine* does not do much to enliven the passive version. When passive-voice verbs pile up in a passage, that passage will generally be hard to understand and remember.

The most problematic use of the passive voice occurs when writers seek to avoid taking responsibility for what they have written. A university president who announces that "it is recommended that fees be raised substantially" skirts a number of pressing questions: recommended by whom? raised by whom?

In spite of such questionable uses, however, the passive voice can work to good advantage in some situations. Reporters often use the passive voice to protect the confidentiality of their sources, as in the familiar phrase *it is reported that,* or when the performer of an action is unknown or less important than the recipient. When Tom Wicker submitted his article on the assassination of President Kennedy to the *New York Times,* he began this way:

> DALLAS, Nov. 22—President John Fitzgerald Kennedy was shot and killed by an assassin today.
> He died of a wound in the brain caused by a rifle bullet that was fired at him as he was riding through downtown Dallas in a motorcade.
> Vice President Lyndon Baines Johnson, who was riding in the third car behind Mr. Kennedy's, was sworn in as the 36th President of the United States 99 minutes after Mr. Kennedy's death.
> —TOM WICKER, *New York Times*

Wicker's article uses the passive voice with good reason: he wants the focus of the sentences on Kennedy, not on who killed him, and on Johnson, not on who swore him in.

Writers, then, must decide for themselves when the passive voice is appropriate and when it is not. If you find that you use the passive a great deal, practice shifting your sentences to the active voice. To do so, convert the subject of the verb into a direct or indirect object, and make the performer of the action into the subject (14c and 23b).

PASSIVE	The test administrator *was told* to give students an electric shock each time a wrong answer *was given.*
ACTIVE	Researchers *told* the test administrator to give the students an electric shock each time they *gave* a wrong answer.
PASSIVE	I *was awakened* promptly at seven by the alarm clock.
ACTIVE	The alarm clock *awakened* me promptly at seven.

ON VARIETIES OF ENGLISH
Passive Voice in Scientific Writing

Much technical and scientific writing uses the passive voice effectively to highlight the object or phenomenon being studied rather than the person or persons doing the studying. Look at the following example, from an essay describing brain surgery:

> A curved incision was made behind the hairline so it would be concealed when the hair grew back. It extended almost from ear to ear. Plastic clips were applied to the cut edges of the scalp to arrest bleeding. The scalp

was folded back to the level of the eyebrows. Incisions were made in the muscle of the right temple, and three sets of holes were drilled near the temple and the top of the head because the tumor had to be approached from directly in front. The drill, powered by nitrogen, was replaced with a fluted steel blade, and the holes were connected. The incised piece of skull was pried loose and held out of the way by a large sponge.

–Roy C. Selby, Jr., "A Delicate Operation"

EXERCISE 9.9

Convert each sentence from active to passive voice or from passive to active, and note the differences in emphasis these changes make. Example:

Machiavelli advises the prince to gain the friendship of the people.

The prince is advised by Machiavelli to gain the friendship of the people.

1. Huge pine trees were uprooted by the storm.
2. Marianne avoided such things as elevators, subways, and closets.
3. For months, the baby kangaroo is protected, fed, and taught how to survive by its mother.
4. The lawns and rooftops were covered with the first snow of winter.
5. Flannery O'Connor employs the images of both a boxcar and a swinging bridge to show the inconsistencies between Mrs. Turpin's classification of people and God's classification of people.

EXERCISE 9.10

Look at several essays you have written recently or pieces of writing by others that you particularly like, and find examples of both the active voice and the passive voice. Convert each of the examples to the other voice, and note the difference in emphasis and rhythm the changes make.

MOOD

The **mood** of a verb indicates the attitude of the writer toward what he or she is saying or writing. Different moods are used to express a fact, opinion, or inquiry (indicative mood); a command or request (imperative mood); or a wish, requirement, or condition contrary to fact (subjunctive mood). Compare, for example, the three sentences that follow:

INDICATIVE	I *did* the right thing.
IMPERATIVE	*Do* the right thing.
SUBJUNCTIVE	If I *were to do* the right thing, I would be content.

Most frequently used is the **indicative mood**, the one for stating facts or opinions or for asking questions.

The Frisbees *soar* through the air.

People *should recycle* their garbage.

Where *are* you *going?*

The **imperative mood** is used for giving commands and instructions or making requests. It is the base form of the verb. Sentences with the imperative mood in the main clause almost always omit the subject (*you*). In these cases, the subject is said to be understood.

Take the appropriate wrench, and *loosen* the plug counterclockwise.

Sit down at once!

Help!

The **subjunctive mood** expresses wishes, conditions that are contrary to fact, requests, or demands. It is used primarily in dependent clauses beginning with *that* or *if.*

If I *were* in charge, things would be different.

9h

Using the subjunctive

The present tense of the subjunctive uses the base form.

PRESENT

It is important that children *be* psychologically ready for a new sibling.

The only requirement is that the relationship between forms in the two clauses *make* sense.

The past tense of the subjunctive is the same as the past indicative except in the verb *be,* which uses *were* for all subjects.

PAST

He spent money as if he *had* infinite credit.

If the store *were* better located, it would attract more customers.

Because the subjunctive can create a rather formal tone, many people today tend to substitute the indicative in informal conversation.

> **INFORMAL**   If I *was* a better typist, I would type my own papers.
>
> **FORMAL**   If I *were* a better typist, I would type my own papers.

Nevertheless, formal writing still requires the use of the subjunctive in the following kinds of dependent clauses.

1

Dependent clauses expressing a wish

I wish I *were* with you right now.

He wished that his mother *were* still living nearby.

2

Dependent clauses beginning with *if* and expressing a condition that does not exist

> If the federal government *were* to ban the sale of tobacco, tobacco companies and distributors would suffer a great loss.
>
> If no one *were allowed* to ignore the rules, language would stagnate.

One common error is to use the conditional in both clauses. Notice the proper verb sequence: use the subjunctive in the *if* clause and the conditional (*would*) in the main clause.

> **UNEDITED**   If I *would have played* harder, I would have won.
>
> **EDITED**   If I *had played* harder, I would have won.

3

Dependent clauses beginning with *as if* and *as though*

> He cautiously started down the trail as if he *were walking* on thin ice.
>
> During the 1920s, Americans speculated in Florida real estate as though it *were* a risk-free investment.

4

Dependent clauses beginning with *that* and expressing a demand, request, requirement, or suggestion

> It is requested that each member *contribute* ten dollars.
>
> The job demands that the employee *be* in good physical condition.

▶ *FOR MULTILINGUAL WRITERS*
Writing Conditional Sentences

"If you practiced writing every day, it would eventually seem much easier to you." For discussion of this and other conditional sentences, see 58f.

EXERCISE 9.11

Revise any of the following sentences that do not use the appropriate subjunctive verb forms required in formal writing. Example:

> *were*
> I saw how carefully he moved, as if he ~~was~~ caring for an infant.

1. Her stepsisters treated Cinderella as though she was a servant.

2. Hamlet wishes he was not responsible for avenging his murdered father.

3. Freud recommended that an analyst use dreams as a means of studying the human personality.

4. If more money was available, we would be able to offer more scholarships.

5. It is necessary that the manager knows how to do any job in the store.

EXERCISE 9.12

The poem below is a famous example of nonsense verse, one that plays games with words—and freely *invents* words. Read the poem out loud, and then underline all the verbs, whether actual English words (like *bite*) or made-up ones (like *outgrabe*). How do you know which made-up words are verbs?

> 'Twas brillig, and the slithy toves
>   Did gyre and gimble in the wabe;
> All mimsy were the borogoves,
>   And the mome raths outgrabe.
> "Beware the Jabberwock, my son!
>   The jaws that bite, the claws that catch!
> Beware the Jubjub bird, and shun
>   The frumious Bandersnatch!"
>
> He took his vorpal sword in hand:
>   Long time the manxome foe he sought—
> So rested he by the Tumtum tree,
>   And stood awhile in thought.
>
> And as in uffish thought he stood,
>   The Jabberwock, with eyes of flame,
> Came whiffling through the tulgey wood,
>   And burbled as it came!

One, two! One, two! And through and through
    The vorpal blade went snicker-snack!
He left it dead, and with its head
    He went galumphing back.

"And hast thou slain the Jabberwock?
    Come to my arms, my beamish boy!
O frabjous day! Callooh! Callay!"
    He chortled in his joy.

'Twas brillig, and the slithy toves
    Did gyre and gimble in the wabe;
And mimsy were the borogoves,
    And the mome raths outgrabe.
        –LEWIS CARROLL, "Jabberwocky"

≫ *Editing the verbs in your own writing*

1. Circle all forms of *be, do,* and *have*. Decide in each case if you can substitute a stronger, more specific verb.

2. Check all uses of the passive voice for appropriateness (pp. 224–26).

3. Double-check forms of *lie* and *lay, sit* and *set, rise* and *raise*. Decide whether you need a transitive or intransitive verb, and see that you use the correct one. Then see that the word you use has your intended meaning (9c).

4. If you have trouble with verb endings, check for them using the guidelines on p. 208 for *-s/-es* and p. 211 for *-ed/-d.*

5. If you have problems with verb tenses, use the guidelines in 9f to check over your verbs.

6. Check all verbs that introduce sources (quotations, paraphrases, and summaries). Do you rely on the most general verbs (*say, write, ask,* for instance)? If so, try replacing these with more vivid, specific verbs (*claim, insist, wonder,* for instance). See 43d1 for a list of verbs to use for incorporating source materials.

USING SOURCES
Choosing Verbs to Integrate Sources

    When you paraphrase, quote, or summarize other sources, you should choose your "signal" verbs carefully. Though you can almost always use the most general verb, *say* or *write* (as *Mary Gordon writes*), you can usually find other verbs that convey your source's stance more precisely (such as, *Gordon comments, counters, suggests*). Is your source commenting on something, disagreeing with someone, making a suggestion? See 43d1 for a list of verbs for incorporating source materials into your own writing.

THINKING CRITICALLY ABOUT VERBS

Reading with an Eye for Verbs

Some years ago a newspaper in San Francisco ran the headline "Giants Crush Cardinals, 3–1," provoking the following friendly advice from John Updike about the art of baseball-headline verbs:

> The correct verb, San Francisco, is *whip*. Notice the vigor, force, and scorn obtained. . . . [These examples] may prove helpful: 3–1—*whip*, 3–2—*shade*, 2–1—*edge*. 4–1 gets the coveted verb *vanquish*. Rule: Any three-run margin, *provided the winning total does not exceed ten*, may be described as a vanquishing.

Double-digit scores, Updike continues, merit such verbs as *annihilate, obliterate,* and *humiliate*. (Thus, "A's Annihilate O's, 13–2.") And if the home team is on the short end of the score, *shade* should become *squeak by*. Finally, Updike advises, use of *bow* (A's bow to O's) can allow the home team, while losing, "to be given the active position in the sentence and an appearance of graciousness as well."

Take the time to study a newspaper with an eye for its verbs. Copy down several examples of strong verbs as well as a few examples of weak or overused verbs. For the weak ones, try to come up with better choices.

Thinking about Your Own Use of Verbs

Three of the most overused verbs in the English language are *be, do,* and *have*. Writing that relies too heavily on these verbs almost always bores readers. Look now at the description you wrote for Exercise 9.1 or at anything else you've written recently to see if you rely too heavily on these verbs. Revise accordingly.

10

Maintaining Subject-Verb Agreement

*I*N ORDINARY LANGUAGE, *agreement refers to an accord or a correspondence between ideas or actions: you reach an* agreement *with your boss about salary; the United States and North Korea negotiate an* agreement *about nuclear arms. This ordinary meaning of* agreement *covers its grammatical use as well. When subjects and verbs match each other in person and in number, we say that they "agree." This chapter takes a close look at the conventions governing such agreement.*

A verb must agree with its subject in number (singular or plural) and in person (first, second, or third).

Toni Morrison comes from Lorain, Ohio. [third-person singular]

We very much *want* to read her work. [first-person plural]

Black *women* from the North *appear* in her novels. [third-person plural]

In practice, only a very few subject-verb constructions cause confusion, so we will look at those constructions in detail.

10a

Making verbs agree with third-person singular subjects

English once used a complex system of verb endings to reflect the person, number, and gender of each subject. Over the centuries, however, most such endings have disappeared from use. Today the main kinds of subjects requiring a special verb form are third-person singular subjects: singular nouns and third-person singular pronouns. To make a present tense verb agree with a third-person singular subject, we normally add *-s* or *-es* to the base form.

> A vegetarian diet *lowers* the risk of heart disease.
>
> She *misses* her friends from high school.

The only two verbs that do not follow this *-s* or *-es* pattern for third-person singular subjects in the present tense are *have* and *be*. *Have* changes to *has*; *be* has different forms for both the first and third persons and for both the present and past tense (9b).

Notice that although an *-s* or *-es* ending indicates a plural noun, the same kind of ending indicates a "singular" verb form. If the subject is a *plural* noun, the verb form does *not* take the *-s* or *-es*.

> A car *needs* regular maintenance.
>
> Cars *need* regular maintenance.

ON VARIETIES OF ENGLISH
-s and -es endings

> She go to work seven days a week.
>
> He don't take it to heart.

The above two sentences are typical of some varieties of African American English as well as in some nonstandard white English, in which third-person singular verbs are not marked by *-s* or *-es*. (The verb forms used in standard academic English, by contrast, are *she goes* and *he doesn't*.) You will often see verb forms such as those in the sentences above in African American literature, especially in dialogue, and you may well quote passages written in this and other varieties of English in your own academic writing. Doing so allows you as a writer to add other people's words to your own. In most of your academic writing, however, take care to add *-s* or *-es* to third-person singular verb forms.

10b

Making the subject and verb agree when separated by other words

When the simple subject is separated from the verb by other structures, such as a prepositional phrase, make the verb agree with the subject and not with another noun that is closer to the verb.

Everyday Use

Subjects and verbs are at work in almost every statement you make, and you make them "agree" effortlessly most of the time. Look, for instance, at three sentences taken from a recent broadcast of a baseball game. The subjects and verbs are italicized.

> *Guzman powers* another blistering curve ball over the plate.
>
> *The Yanks move* on to Milwaukee tomorrow.
>
> *The duel* of the no-hitters *continues* into the eighth.

Take time to listen to someone reporting an event—a play-by-play announcer, perhaps, or an on-the-scene reporter. Note down some of the subject-verb combinations. Do you find any that don't sound right, that might not "agree"?

> S   V
> A *vase* of flowers *makes* a room attractive.

> S   V
> Many *books* on the best-seller list *have* little literary value.

Many writers forget to maintain agreement when a plural noun falls between a singular subject and the verb, as in the first example above, or when a singular noun falls between a plural subject and the verb, as in the second example. In the first sentence, notice that the simple subject is *vase,* not *flowers,* which is the object of the preposition *of.* In the second sentence, the simple subject is *books,* not *list,* which is the object of the preposition *on.*

Also be careful when a simple subject is followed by a phrase beginning with *as well as, along with, together with, in addition to,* or other prepositions. Make the verb agree with the simple subject, not with a noun in the intervening phrase.

> S   V
> The *president*, along with many senators, *opposes* the bill.

> S   V
> A *passenger*, as well as the driver, *was injured* in the accident.

Some writers think it awkward to use a singular verb form when the complete subject, including the intervening phrase, expresses a plural idea. If sentences like the ones above strike you as awkward, try making the subject plural and using a plural verb form (10c). Consider these possible revisions for the sentences above.

The president and many senators *oppose* the bill.

Both the driver and a passenger *were injured* in the accident.

If you know that you have problems with subject-verb agreement when the simple subject and the verb are separated by other words, identify the simple subject and the verb and then mentally delete any intervening words to make sure that the subject and verb agree in number and person.

EXERCISE 10.1

Visiting relatives is/are treacherous. Either of these verbs makes a grammatically acceptable sentence, "agreeing" with a subject, yet they result in two very different statements. Complete the sentence by choosing one of the verbs, and write out a brief statement of the two possible meanings. Then write a paragraph or two about visiting relatives. Finally, study your passage for its use of subjects and verbs. Do you have any questions about subject-verb agreement?

EXERCISE 10.2

Underline the appropriate verb form in each of the following sentences. Example:

The benefits of family planning (is/<u>are</u>) *not apparent to many peasants.*

1. Starving children and world peace (*is/are*) two of my concerns.
2. Dershowitz, together with his aide, (*presents/present*) a cogent argument.
3. Walls of glass (*characterizes/characterize*) much modern architecture.
4. The system of sororities and fraternities (*supplies/supply*) much of the social life on some college campuses.
5. The buck (*stops/stop*) here.
6. The soldiers, along with their commanding officer, (*was/were*) cited for bravery beyond the call of duty.
7. In many species, the male, as well as the female, (*cares/care*) for the off-spring.
8. He (*holds/hold*) a controlling interest in the company.
9. The author of those stories (*writes/write*) beautifully.
10. Current research on AIDS, in spite of the best efforts of hundreds of scientists, (*leaves/leave*) serious questions unanswered.

10c

Making verbs agree with compound subjects

Two or more subjects joined by *and* generally require a plural verb form.

Tony and his friends *commute* every day from Louisville.
A backpack, a canteen, and a rifle *were issued* to each recruit.

When subjects joined by *and* are considered a single unit or refer to a single person or thing, they take a singular verb form.

Drinking and driving *remains* a major cause of highway fatalities.
Fried ham and grits *is* Duane's idea of a great breakfast.
His closest friend and political ally *was* his brother.

If the word *each* or *every* precedes singular subjects joined by *and,* the verb form is singular.

Each boy and girl *chooses* one gift to take home.
Every city, town, and village *has* a Main Street.

For compound subjects whose parts are joined by *or* or *nor,* the verb agrees in number and person with the part closest to the verb.

Laws, rules, or convention *governs* most of our everyday decisions.

Neither my roommate nor my parents *plan* to vote.

Neither Maria nor you *were* among the finalists.

Either you or I *am* wrong.

To avoid awkwardness with compound subjects made up of both singular and plural parts, place a plural part closest to the verb.

| AWKWARD | Either the witnesses or the defendant *is* lying. |
| REVISED | Either the defendant or the witnesses *are* lying. |

10d

Making verbs agree with collective-noun subjects

Collective nouns, such as *family, team, audience, group, jury, crowd, band, class, flock,* and *committee,* are singular in form but refer to a group of individual persons or things. When used as subjects, collective nouns can take either singular or plural verb forms, depending on the context. When they refer to a group as a single unit, they take a singular verb form.

> The team wearing red and black *controls* the ball.
>
> Waving banners frenetically, the crowd *screams* its support.

When they refer to the individual members of a collective, however, they take a plural verb form.

> The family of ducklings *scatter* when the cat approaches.
>
> The committee *have* not agreed on many points.

The meaning of a sentence as a whole is your guide to whether the collective noun refers to a unit or to the separate parts of a unit.

> After deliberating, the jury *reports* its verdict. [as a single unit]
>
> The jury still *disagree* on a number of counts. [as separate individuals]

10e

Making verbs agree with indefinite-pronoun subjects

Indefinite pronouns are those that do not refer to specific persons or things. Most take singular verb forms.

≫ *Common indefinite pronouns*

another	each	much	one
any	either	neither	other
anybody	everybody	nobody	somebody
anyone	everyone	no one	someone
anything	everything	nothing	something

> Of the two jobs, neither *holds* much appeal.
>
> Each of the plays *depicts* a hero undone by a tragic flaw.

Both, few, many, others, and *several* take plural verb forms.

> Though many *apply,* few *are* chosen.

Several indefinite pronouns—*all, any, enough, more, most, none, some*—can be singular or plural, depending on the noun they refer to.

SINGULAR   All of the cake *was* eaten.

PLURAL   All of the candidates *promise* to improve the schools.

(See 11c for a discussion of indefinite pronoun–antecedent agreement.)

10f

Making verbs agree with relative-pronoun subjects

When the relative pronouns, *who, which,* or *that* act as the subject of a dependent clause, the verb in the clause should agree in number with the antecedent of the pronoun.

> Fear is an ingredient that *goes* into creating stereotypes. [*That* refers to *ingredient;* hence, the singular verb form *goes.*]

> Guilt, jealousy, and fear are ingredients that *go* into creating stereotypes. [*That* refers to *ingredients;* hence, the plural verb form *go.*]

When the phrase *one of the* precedes the relative pronoun, you have to be especially careful to determine whether the pronoun refers to the word *one* or to another word. Look at the following sentence:

Alex is one of the *employees* who always *work* overtime.

In this sentence, a number of employees always work overtime, and Alex is among them. Thus *who* refers to *employees,* and the verb form is plural. Now look at the following sentence:

Alex is the only *one* of the employees who always *works* overtime.

In this sentence, only one employee always works overtime, and that employee is Alex. Thus *one,* and not *employees,* is the antecedent of *who,* and the verb form is singular.

10g

Making linking verbs agree with their subjects, not with their complements

A linking verb should agree with its subject, which precedes it, not with the subject complement, which follows it (7c2).

> The signings of three key treaties *are* the topic of my talk. [The subject is *signings.*]

> Nero Wolfe's passion *was* orchids. [The subject is *passion.*]

10h

Making verbs agree with subjects that are plural in form but singular in meaning

Some nouns that seem to be plural in form (such as *mathematics* and *measles*) are singular in meaning and take singular verb forms.

Mathematics *is* not always an exact science.

Measles still *strikes* many Americans.

Other nouns of this kind (such as *statistics* and *politics*) may be either singular or plural. In the first sentence below, *statistics* refers to a single course of study; hence, it takes a singular verb form. In the second sentence, *statistics* refers to a number of figures; hence, it takes a plural verb form.

Statistics *is* a course I really dread.

The statistics in that study *are* highly questionable.

Data, the plural form of the word *datum,* is often used informally as if it were singular, but it is grammatically plural and should, in college and other formal writing, be used with a plural verb.

INFORMAL	The data *is* all in.
FORMAL	The data *are* all in.

10i

Making verbs agree with subjects that follow them

In English, verbs usually follow subjects. When this order is reversed, it is easy to become confused. Make the verb agree with the subject, not with a noun that happens to precede it.

Beside the barn *stand* silos filled with grain. [The subject is *silos.*]

Another common inversion of subject-verb order occurs in sentences beginning with *there is* or *there are* (or *there was* or *there were*). *There* serves only as an introductory word, or expletive (23a1); the subject follows the verb.

There *are* five basic positions in classical ballet. [The subject is *positions.*]

10j

Making verbs agree with titles and words used as words

When the subject is the title of a book, film, or other work of art, the verb form is singular even if the title is plural in form.

> *One Writer's Beginnings describes* Eudora Welty's childhood.

Similarly, a word referred to as a word requires a singular verb form even if the word itself is plural.

> *Steroids is* a little word that packs a big punch in the world of sports.

⟫ *Editing for subject-verb agreement*

> Underline each finite verb. Then identify the subject that corresponds to the verb. Put the two together to see if they agree. For example, the sentence *The players on our side is sure to win* can be stripped down to a simple subject-verb *players is.* Bringing together the subject and verb in this way helps some writers to recognize agreement problems; here the verb should be *are: players are.* Check especially the following kinds of subjects.
>
> 1. *Compound subjects.* Those joined by *and* usually take a plural verb. With those joined by *or* or *nor,* however, the verb agrees with the part of the subject closest to the verb. (10c)
>
> 2. *Collective-noun subjects.* These take a singular verb when they refer to a group as a single unit, a plural verb when they refer to individual members of a group. (10d)
>
> 3. *Indefinite-pronoun subjects.* Most take a singular verb; *both, few, many, others,* and *several* take a plural verb. (10e)

EXERCISE 10.3

Revise any of the following sentences as necessary to establish subject-verb agreement. (Some of the sentences do not require any change.) Example:

> *darts*
> Into the shadows ~~dart~~ the frightened raccoon.

1. Every check and money order cost fifty cents.
2. Talking and getting up from my seat was my crime.

3. If rhythm and blues is your kind of music, try Mary Lou's.

4. His merry disposition and his recognized success in business make him popular in the community.

5. *The vapors* were a Victorian term for hypochondria.

6. Neither the lighting nor the frame display the painting well.

7. In the foreground is two women playing musical instruments.

8. Most of the voters support a reduction in nuclear weapons.

9. Each of the entrants rehearse for a minimum of three hours daily.

10. Neither her manner nor her tantrums intimidates the staff.

11. The audience always respond to Pavarotti.

12. My grandmother is the only one of my relatives who still goes to church.

13. *Our Tapes* were one of Fitzgerald's earlier titles for *Tender Is the Night*.

14. Sweden was one of the few European countries that was neutral in 1943.

15. Politics have been defined as the art of the possible.

EXERCISE 10.4

Underline the appropriate verbs in parentheses in the following passage about the Iks, a tribe in Uganda.

The solitary Ik, isolated in the ruins of an exploded culture, (*has/have*) built a new defense for himself. If you (*lives/live*) in an unworkable society, you can make up one of your own, and this (*is/are*) what the Iks (*has/have*) done. Each Ik (*has/have*) become a one-man tribe on its own, a constituency.

Now everything (*falls/fall*) into place. This is why they do (*seems/seem*), after all, vaguely familiar to all of us. We've seen them before. This is precisely the way groups of one size or another, ranging from committee to nations, (*behaves/behave*). It is, of course, this aspect of humanity that (*has/have*) lagged behind the rest of evolution, and this is why the Ik (*seems/seem*) so primitive. In his absolute selfishness, his incapacity to give anything away, no matter what, he (*is/are*) a successful committee. —Lewis Thomas, "The Iks"

THINKING CRITICALLY ABOUT SUBJECT-VERB AGREEMENT

Reading with an Eye for Subject-Verb Agreement

The following passage, from a 1990 essay questioning suggestions that our society is returning to more traditional values, especially marriage, includes several instances of complicated subject-verb agreement. Read the passage, paying close attention to the subjects and verbs and noting the rules governing subject-verb agreement in each case.

> For me, none of [these assumptions about marriage] add up. Between the public statistic and the private reality lies a sea of contradiction in which these pronouncements drown. Marriage seems to me more conflict-ridden than ever, and the divorce rate—with or without new babies in the house—remains constant. The fabric of men-and-women-as-they-once-were is so thin in places no amount of patching can weave that cloth together again. The longing for connection may be strong, but even stronger is the growing perception that only people who are real to themselves can connect. Two shall be as one is over, no matter how lonely we get.
>
> —VIVIAN GORNICK, "Who Says We Haven't Made a Revolution?"

Thinking about Your Own Use of Subject-Verb Agreement

Return to the passage you wrote for Exercise 10.1. Using the information in this chapter, especially the guidelines in 10j, examine each subject and its verb. Have you maintained subject-verb agreement throughout? Revise to correct any errors you find, and then look for any patterns in your writing. If you find any, make a note to yourself (in a writing log, if you keep one) of things to look for routinely as you revise your writing.

11

Maintaining Pronoun-Antecedent Agreement

*P*RONOUNS *"ARE TRICKY RATHER THAN DIFFICULT," says* H. W. Fowler *in* A Dictionary of Modern English Usage. *The "trickiness" Fowler notes comes primarily from the fact that pronouns always stand in for another word, a noun or some other pronoun, called the* antecedent. *Making sure that the pronoun and its antecedent match up, or "agree," is a task every writer faces.*

Like a verb with its subject, a pronoun must agree with its antecedent in person and number. In addition, a third-person singular pronoun must agree with its antecedent in gender—*masculine, feminine, or neuter. Study two examples from Maya Angelou:*

> The English teacher spoke with deliberation, as if *she* were testing the taste of the words. [third-person singular, feminine]

> I would never again work to make people smile inanely and would take on the responsibility of making *them* think. [third-person plural]

EXERCISE 11.1

Take a moment to think of some memorable object from your life—a special toy, perhaps, or a now dog-eared favorite book—anything you remember well. Picture it as clearly as you can, and then write a paragraph or two describing it: what it looks like, how you use or used it, how you feel about it or remember it. Then look over your description, identifying every pronoun. Can you find clear antecedents for each one?

11a

Making pronouns agree with compound antecedents

A compound antecedent whose parts are joined by *and* requires a plural pronoun.

> My parents and I tried to resolve *our* disagreement.

> Keith, Jane, and Beth wrote a critical review, and nobody challenged *them*.

When a compound antecedent is preceded by *each* or *every*, however, it takes a singular pronoun.

> Every plant and animal has *its* own ecological niche.

A compound antecedent that refers to a single person or thing also takes a singular pronoun.

> The producer and director invested all of *her* savings in the film.

With a compound antecedent whose parts are joined by *or* or *nor*, the pronoun agrees with the nearest antecedent. This kind of sentence, however, can be awkward and may need to be revised if the parts of the antecedent are of different genders or persons.

Everyday Use

Take the Interstate until you come to Exit 3 and then 313. Go past it, and take the next exit, which will be Broadway.

The above directions, intended to lead an out-of-towner to her friend's house, provide a good example of the importance of maintaining pronoun-antecedent agreement. The little word *it* in this example is very important. Does *it* mean Exit 3, or does *it* mean 313—or are they perhaps the same thing? If the visitor doesn't already know, or if the exit *and* 313 aren't both clearly marked, she could have difficulty finding her way.

Make a point of looking—or listening—for pronouns in some everyday situation. Directions, perhaps for using an appliance or finding a destination, are a good place to look. It might be interesting to compare written and spoken directions, to see whether pronouns are used differently. Are writers more careful than speakers?

AWKWARD	For us to win the meet, you or Charlyce must win *her* next dive.
REVISED	For us to win the meet, you must win *your* next dive, or Charlyce must win *hers*.

With compound antecedents containing both singular and plural parts, the sentence may sound awkward unless a plural part comes last.

AWKWARD	Neither the radio stations nor the newspaper would reveal *its* sources.
REVISED	Neither the newspaper nor the radio stations would reveal *their* sources.

11b

Making pronouns agree with collective-noun antecedents

When a collective-noun antecedent (*herd, team, audience*) refers to a single unit, it requires a singular pronoun.

The audience fixed *its* attention on center stage.

Finally, our team scored *its* first victory.

When such an antecedent refers to the individual parts of the unit, however, it requires a plural pronoun.

The crew divided the loot among *themselves*.

The director chose this cast because *they* had experience in the roles.

Remember that collective nouns referring to single units require not only singular pronouns but also singular verb forms. Collective nouns referring to separate individuals in a unit, on the other hand, require plural pronouns and plural verb forms.

Each generation *has its* own slang. [*generation* as single unit]

That generation *have* sold *their* souls for money. [*generation* as separate individuals]

11c

Making pronouns agree with indefinite-pronoun antecedents

A pronoun whose antecedent is an indefinite pronoun should agree with it in number. Indefinite pronouns may be always singular (as with *one*) or plural (as with *many*), or their number may depend on their context (10e).

One of the ballerinas lost *her* balance. [singular]
Many in the audience jumped to *their* feet. [plural]
Some of the furniture was showing *its* age. [singular meaning for *some*]
Some of the farmers abandoned *their* land. [plural meaning for *some*]

11d

Checking for sexist pronouns

One somewhat complicated problem in pronoun-antecedent agreement involves a pronoun referring to a singular antecedent that may be either male or female. Look at the following passage:

The Country Club pool was small. One diving board, no spinning top. But its size only seemed to me to be a measure of its exclusiveness. *Whoever* had laid out plans for the Country Club was an entrepreneur with an eye for the one beautiful, rolling and wooded piece of land outside Ames. *He* must have known immediately that such an acreage had to be saved; *he* had a true aristocrat's instinct and converted it into a private preserve.
– Susan Allen Toth, "Swimming Pools"

Notice that although the author apparently does not know who laid out the plans for the Country Club, she uses the pronoun *he* to refer to this person. In traditional English grammar, writers used masculine pronouns, known as the generic *he*, in such cases. In recent decades, however, many people have pointed out that such wording ignores or even excludes females—and thus should be avoided. There are several ways of doing so.

⪢ *Ways of avoiding the generic use of* he, his, *or* him

Look at the following sentence:
Every citizen should know *his* rights under the law.

Now consider three ways to express the same idea without *his.*

1. Revising to make the antecedent plural
   All citizens should know their *rights under the law.*
2. Revising the sentence altogether
   Everyone should have some knowledge of basic legal rights.
3. Using both masculine and feminine pronouns
   Every citizen should know his or her *rights under the law.*

The last option, using both masculine and feminine pronouns, can be awkward, especially when repeated several times in a passage. Be careful not to overuse this option.

When an antecedent is an indefinite pronoun, such as *anybody* or *each,* you can avoid the generic *he* by using a plural pronoun. For example:

Everybody had *their* own theory about Nancy's resignation.

You will probably hear, and perhaps use, such sentences in conversation, but be careful about using them in writing. Although this usage—*everybody* with the plural pronoun *their*—is now gaining acceptance, many readers will consider it excessively informal or even incorrect. *Everybody* is grammatically singular and hence calls for a singular pronoun. See 10e for a list of indefinite pronouns and 29a for more discussion of ways to avoid sexist language.

≫ *Editing for pronoun-antecedent agreement*

Circle all pronouns, and then identify the antecedent of each one. Check to see that the pronoun agrees in person and number with its antecedent; if it does not, revise the pronoun accordingly. Look especially carefully at any compound antecedents (11a), indefinite-pronoun antecedents (10e and 11c), and collective-noun antecedents (11b) to see that the pronouns agree in both person and number.

EXERCISE 11.2

Revise the following sentences as needed to create pronoun-antecedent agreement and to eliminate the generic *he* and any awkward pronoun references. Some can be revised in more than one way, and some do not require any change. Example:

Every graduate submitted his diploma card.
Every graduate submitted his *or* her *diploma card.*
All graduates submitted their *diploma cards.*

1. With tuition on the rise, a student has to save money wherever they can.

2. Not everyone gets along with his roommate, but the two can usually manage to tolerate each other temporarily.

3. Congress usually resists presidential attempts to encroach on what they consider their authority.

4. Either Tom or Teresa will always share their opinion.

5. If his own knowledge is all the reader has to go by, how can he identify one source as more reliable than another?

6. Every house and apartment has their advantages and their drawbacks.

7. Neither the scouts nor their leader knew their way out of the forest.

8. Our team no longer wears red and white.

9. To create a positive impression, a candidate attempts to flood the media with favorable publicity about themselves.

10. I often turn on the fan and the light and neglect to turn it off.

THINKING CRITICALLY ABOUT PRONOUN AGREEMENT

Reading with Attention to Pronouns

Following is a paragraph from *Democracy in America,* Alexis de Tocqueville's classic critique of American institutions and culture, which was first published in 1835. Read the paragraph with an eye for pronouns. Does the use of the masculine pronoun to refer to both men and women seem odd to you? Revise the paragraph to eliminate this generic use of masculine pronouns.

> After the birth of a human being, his early years are obscurely spent in the toils or pleasures of childhood. As he grows up, the world receives him, when his manhood begins, and he enters into contact with his fellows. He is then studied for the first time, and it is imagined that the germ of the vices and the virtues of his maturer years is then formed. This, if I am not mistaken, is a great error. We must begin higher up; we must watch the infant in his mother's arms; we must see the first images which the external world casts upon the dark mirror of his mind, the first occurrences which he witnesses; we must hear the first words which awaken the sleeping powers of thought, and stand by his earliest efforts,—if we would understand the prejudices, the habits, and the passions which will rule his life. The entire man is, so to speak, to be seen in the cradle of the child.　　—ALEXIS DE TOCQUEVILLE, *Democracy in America*

Thinking about Your Own Use of Pronouns

In a paragraph or two, describe some "typical" person—a typical student at your school, a typical citizen in your hometown, a typical new parent, whatever. You might begin with the sentence "The typical _____ is . . ." Then analyze your description for agreement between pronouns and their antecedents.

12

Using Adjectives
and Adverbs

AS WORDS THAT DESCRIBE OTHER WORDS, *adjectives and adverbs add liveliness and color to the flat gray surface of writing, helping writers* show *rather than just* tell. *Adjectives and adverbs allow us to show readers what we want them to see—to help them visualize objects, scenes, or even abstractions. See how much Dorothy West relies on adjectives and adverbs in the following description.*

> With a *long blackened fireplace* stick Mama *carefully* tilted the lid of the *three-legged* skillet to see if her cornbread was *done*. . . . *Gently* she let the lid drop. . . .   — DOROTHY WEST, *The Living Is Easy*

West could have said simply, "Mama checked to see if her cornbread was done." But we would not be able to picture the scene as we do in the passage above. Adjectives such as blackened *and* three-legged *and adverbs such as* carefully *and* gently *create a vivid image of Mama and evoke a definite impression of West's own attitude about her subject.*

But if adjectives and adverbs can create many dramatic effects, they can also betray a writer who uses them inappropriately. Like any other part of speech, they must follow certain rules and conventions. This chapter discusses some of these rules and conventions and common problems that writers have with adjectives and adverbs.

12a

Distinguishing adjectives from adverbs

Although adjectives and adverbs both modify other words, each modifies different parts of speech. **Adjectives** modify nouns and pronouns, answering the questions *which? how many?* or *what kind?* Many adjectives are formed by adding the suffixes *-able, -ful, -ish, -less,* or *-y* to nouns and verbs.

Helpless customers wrote *angry* letters to *the* company.

His one comfortable chair is covered in *a colorful Spanish* fabric.

Participles and infinitives can also function as adjectives (7c3).

The *perplexed* clerk looked at me with a *questioning* expression.

I could not decide which cap *to buy.*

Although adjectives usually precede the words they modify, they sometimes follow instead. An adjective can also appear after a linking verb as a subject complement modifying the subject (7c2 and 12b).

Butler found the Victorian family *stifling.*

Tennis is *difficult* for him.

Adverbs modify verbs, adjectives, and other adverbs; they answer the questions *how? when? where?* or *to what extent?* Many adverbs are formed by adding *-ly* to adjectives.

The children ran *outdoors.* [modifies the verb *ran*]

He was *not* content to wait. [modifies the adjective *content*]

The shack leaned *slightly* backward. [modifies the adverb *backward*]

Adverbs can also modify an entire clause.

Fortunately, the rain had ended before the wedding.

Infinitives can function as adverbs (7c3).

Everyday Use

Adjectives often carry indispensable shades of meaning. In basketball, for example, there's an important difference between a *slam dunk* and an *alley-oop dunk,* a *flagrant foul* and a *technical foul,* a *layup* and a *reverse layup.* Consider as well the distinction between *talk* and *trash talk,* or *color commentary* and *play-by-play commentary.* In each case, the difference is in the adjectives. Look in the newspaper for examples of adjectives that carry significant meaning in a sport or other activity that you know well. Of the adjectives you find, which ones add vividness to the writing, and which ones add essential information?

The news was almost too good *to believe.* [modifies the adjective *good*]

While adjectives are closely tied to the words they modify, adverbs that modify verbs or clauses can often occur in various places.

Olajuwon *easily* grabbed the rebound.

Olajuwon grabbed the rebound *easily.*

Easily, Olajuwon grabbed the rebound.

Since adjectives and adverbs both act as modifiers, often have similar forms, and in some cases can occupy the same positions in sentences, sometimes the only way of identifying a word as one or the other is to identify its function in the sentence. Remember: adjectives modify nouns and pronouns; adverbs modify verbs, adjectives, and other adverbs.

▶ *FOR MULTILINGUAL WRITERS*
  Determining Adjective Sequence

  Do you say "these beautiful old-fashioned kitchen tiles" or "these old-fashioned beautiful kitchen tiles"? See 55e for guidelines on adjective sequence in English sentences.

EXERCISE 12.1

Read the following passage, noting the adjectives and adverbs (all italicized).

In our *hellbent* earnestness to romanticize the cowboy we've *ironically* disesteemed his *true* character. . . . Instead of the *macho, trigger-happy* man our culture has *perversely* wanted him to be, the cowboy is *more apt* to be *convivial, quirky,* and *softhearted.* . . . – GRETEL EHRLICH, "About Men"

Think of a group you might like to write a thumbnail sketch of, as Ehrlich does in her passage about cowboys. Then try writing one or two sentences that characterize this group. Check over your sketch, noting the words that do the most to paint a picture of your subject. Using this chapter as a guide, see how many of them are adjectives and adverbs.

EXERCISE 12.2

Read the following paragraph with an eye for the adjectives and adverbs. Identify each one, and determine which word each modifies.

The peacock does most of his serious strutting in the spring and summer when he has a full tail to do it with. Usually he begins shortly after breakfast, struts for several hours, desists in the heat of the day, and begins again in the late afternoon. Each cock has a favorite station where he performs every day in the hope of attracting some passing hen; but if I have found anyone indifferent to the peacock's display, besides the telephone lineman, it is the peahen. She seldom casts an eye at it. The cock, his tail raised in a shimmering arch around him, will turn this way and that, and with his clay-colored wing feathers touching the ground, will dance forward and backward, his neck curved, his beak parted, his eyes glittering. Meanwhile the hen goes about her business, diligently searching the ground as if any bug in the grass were of more importance than the unfurled map of the universe which floats nearby.

– FLANNERY O'CONNOR, "The King of the Birds"

12b

Using adjectives after linking verbs

Use adjectives, not the corresponding -ly adverbs, after linking verbs. The most frequently used linking verbs are forms of *be*, but they also include sensory verbs—such as *look, appear, seem, sound, feel, smell,* and *taste*—and verbs of becoming such as *become, grow, prove,* and *turn* (7c2). When they function as linking verbs, they are always followed by adjectives (or nouns). Most of these verbs, however, can also be used to express action. When they express action, they can be followed by adverbs.

> Otis Thorpe looked *angry*. [linking verb with adjective]
>
> He looked *angrily* at the referee. [action verb with adverb]

12c

Using adverbs to modify verbs, adjectives, and adverbs

Use adverbs, not adjectives, to modify verbs, adjectives, and other adverbs.

> NOT   Jackie always dressed *elegant*.
>
> BUT   Jackie always dressed *elegantly*.

Good *and* well, bad *and* badly

The modifiers *good, well, bad,* and *badly* cause problems for many writers because the distinctions between *good* and *well* and between *bad* and *badly* are often not observed in conversation and because *well* can function as either an adjective or an adverb.

Good and *bad* are adjectives, and both can be used after a linking verb.

The weather looks *good* today.

I feel *bad* for the Chicago fans.

Do not use *good* or *bad* to modify a verb, an adjective, or an adverb; use *well* or *badly* instead.

NOT   He plays the trumpet *good* and the trombone not *bad.*

BUT   He plays the trumpet *well* and the trombone not *badly.*

Badly is an adverb and can be used to modify a verb, an adjective, or another adverb. Do not use it after a linking verb; use *bad* instead.

In her first recital, the soprano sang *badly.*

NOT   The clams tasted *badly.*

BUT   The clams tasted *bad.*

Well can be either an adjective (meaning "in good health") or an adverb.

ADJECTIVE   After a week of rest, Julio felt *well* again.

ADVERB   She plays *well* enough to make the team.

Real *and* really

Be careful also to observe the distinction between *real* and *really.* In conversation, the adjective *real* is often used in place of the adverb *really,* but in college writing, use the adverb form. And take care not to overuse *really.*

INFORMAL   The audience was *real* disappointed by the show.

FORMAL   The audience was *really* disappointed by the show.

ON VARIETIES OF ENGLISH
Right Smart, Way Past Cool

Most regions have certain characteristic adverbs. Some of the most colorful regional adverbs are intensifiers, words for saying *very* or *really.* In parts of the South, for example, and particularly in Appalachia, you are likely to come across the following adverbs:

He paid a *right* smart price for that car.

She was *plumb* tuckered out.

In each case, the adverb acts to intensify the meaning: *He paid a very considerable price. She was completely exhausted.* Consider two other examples, the first overheard in New York City, the second in Oakland, California:

It seems like *way* long ago that we were on vacation.

They looked *way past* cool in their new sneakers.

As with all language, adverb use is governed by appropriateness. Using a regional variety of English is appropriate in that region, and to evoke that region—in writing about a family member who lives in Minnesota, for example, you might well quote her, thus bringing some Midwestern expressions into your writing. For most academic writing, however, you should use standard academic English; see Chapter 28 for guidelines on using different varieties of language.

EXERCISE 12.3

Revise each of the following sentences to maintain correct adverb and adjective use. Then identify each adjective or adverb that you have revised, and point out the word each modifies.

> *superbly*
> The attorney delivered a ~~superb~~ conceived summation.

1. Honest lawyers are not complete obsessed with status or money.
2. First he acts negative to her, and then in the next episode he proposes marriage!
3. Hypochondriacs call a doctor whenever they feel badly.
4. Christmas Day was real cold, and it was raining heavy.
5. The executive spoke forceful about the new union regulations.
6. Regrettably, the youngster was hurt bad in the accident.
7. The skater performed good despite the intense competition.
8. The instructor felt well about her presentation.
9. On the new stereo, many of the CDs, records, and tapes sounded differently.
10. They brought up their children very strict.

12d

Using comparatives and superlatives

In addition to their simple, or positive, form, many adjectives and adverbs have two other forms, the **comparative** and **superlative**, that are used for making comparisons.

POSITIVE	COMPARATIVE	SUPERLATIVE
large	larger	largest
early	earlier	earliest
careful	more careful	most careful
happily	more happily	most happily

Canada is *larger* than the United States.

My son needs to be *more careful* with his money.

They are the *most happily* married couple I know.

As these examples suggest, the comparative and superlative of most short (one-syllable and some two-syllable) adjectives are usually formed by adding the endings *-er* and *-est*. *More* and *most* are also used with short adjectives, however, and can sometimes create a more formal tone. The only way to form the comparative and superlative of longer adjectives—three syllables or more—and of most adverbs is with *more* and *most*. If you are not sure whether an adjective or adverb has *-er* and *-est* forms, consult the dictionary entry for the simple form, where any *-er* and *-est* forms are usually listed.

1

Recognizing irregular forms

Some adjectives and adverbs have irregular comparative and superlative forms. Here is a list of them.

POSITIVE	COMPARATIVE	SUPERLATIVE
Adjectives		
good	better	best
well	better	best
bad	worse	worst
ill	worse	worst
little (quantity)	less	least
many	more	most
some	more	most
much	more	most

POSITIVE	COMPARATIVE	SUPERLATIVE
Adverbs		
well	better	best
ill	worse	worst
badly	worse	worst

2

Distinguishing between comparatives and superlatives

The comparative is used to compare two things, the superlative to compare three or more.

Rome is a much *older* city than New York.

Damascus is one of the *oldest* cities in the world.

In conversation, you will often hear the superlative form used even when only two things are being compared: *Of the two paintings, the one by Klee is the most interesting.* In college writing, however, use the comparative: *Of the two paintings, the one by Klee is the more interesting.*

3

Checking for double comparatives and superlatives

Double comparatives and superlatives unnecessarily use both the *-er* or *-est* ending and *more* or *most.* Occasionally, they can act to build a special emphasis, as in the title of Spike Lee's movie *Mo' Better Blues.* In college writing, however, make sure not to use *more* or *most* before adjectives or adverbs ending in *-er* or *-est.*

INCORRECT	Paris is the *most loveliest* city in the world.
REVISED	Paris is the *loveliest* city in the world

INCORRECT	Rome lasted *more longer* than Carthage.
REVISED	Rome lasted *longer* than Carthage.
OR	Rome lasted *much longer* than Carthage.

4

Checking for incomplete comparisons

In speaking, we sometimes use incomplete comparisons—ones that specify only one of the things being compared—because the context makes the rest of the comparison clear. If, after comparing an essay of yours with a classmate's, you say "Yours is better," the context makes it clear that you mean "Yours is better *than mine*." In writing, that context may not exist. So take time when editing to check for incomplete comparisons—and to complete them if they are unclear.

INCOMPLETE	The patients taking the drug appeared *healthier*.
COMPLETE	The patients taking the drug appeared *healthier than those receiving a placebo*.
INCOMPLETE	I consider Mozart *the greatest*.
COMPLETE	I consider Mozart *the greatest of all composers*.

EXERCISE 12.4

Choose three of the following numbered words, and for each one write a brief passage that uses its simple, comparative, and superlative forms. Example:

frisky   *friskier*   *friskiest*

George adopted a small, *frisky* puppy named Brutus. Quickly, Brutus became even *friskier,* chasing neighbors and jumping on children. He was at his *friskiest* the day Aunt Victoria came to visit.

1. loudly
2. well (adverb)
3. wholesome
4. some
5. little
6. rare
7. good
8. thirsty
9. heavily
10. sarcastically

12e

Using nouns as modifiers

Sometimes a noun can function as an adjective by modifying another noun, as in the following examples:

| chicken soup | control center | day care |
| money supply | space station | law school |

In familiar terms such as those above, we have no trouble understanding the meaning. In fact, a phrase like *chicken soup* is the most succinct way of expressing the idea of soup made from chicken. If noun modifiers pile up, however, they can obscure meaning and should thus be revised.

AWKWARD	The cold war–era Rosenberg espionage trial and execution continues to arouse controversy.
REVISED	The Rosenbergs' trial and execution for espionage during the cold war era continues to arouse controversy.

Here the string of nouns is broken up by turning *Rosenberg* into a possessive and *espionage* and *era* into objects of prepositions.

EXERCISE 12.5

Revise each of the following sentences to use modifiers correctly, clearly, and effectively. Many of the sentences can be revised in more than one way. Example:

> *He is sponsoring a housing project finance plan approval bill.*
> *He is sponsoring a bill to approve a financial plan for the housing project.*

1. In the Macbeths' marriage, Lady Macbeth is presented as the most ambitious of the two.
2. The article argued that walking is more healthier than jogging.
3. St. Francis made Assisi one of the famousest towns in Italy.
4. Most of the elderly are women because women tend to live longer.
5. Minneapolis is the largest of the Twin Cities.
6. A University of Arizona Lunar and Planetary Laboratory research scientist agrees that mining asteroids may well prove economically important.
7. My graduation day will be the most happiest day of my life.
8. The student cafeteria is operated by a college food service system chain.
9. Japanese cars captured much of the American market because American consumers found they were more reliable.
10. I think *Oedipus Rex* is a successfuler play than *The Sandbox*.

⫸ *Editing adjectives and adverbs*

1. Identify all the adjectives and adverbs, and scrutinize each one carefully to see whether it's the best word possible. Considering one or two synonyms for each one might help you to decide.
2. Is each adjective and adverb really necessary? See if a more specific noun would do away with the need for an adjective (*mansion* rather than *enormous house*, for instance); do the same with verbs and adverbs.

3. Look for places where you might make your writing more vivid or specific by adding an adjective or adverb.

4. Be sure that adjectives modify nouns or pronouns and that adverbs modify verbs, adjectives, or other adverbs. (12a)

5. Check for proper use of *good* and *well, bad* and *badly, real* and *really.* Be sure you don't overuse *really.* (12c)

6. Check all comparisons to see that they're complete. (12d4)

7. Be sure cumulative adjectives are in the right order. (55e)

USING SOURCES
Quoting Passages with Effective Adjectives

To quote, summarize, or paraphrase? Sometimes it can be difficult to decide how exactly to incorporate materials from outside sources in your own writing. Adjectives can help you decide: if your source uses adjectives that are especially vivid or apt—ones you would *not* wish to replace—you should consider quoting the passage directly.

THINKING CRITICALLY ABOUT ADJECTIVES AND ADVERBS

Reading with an Eye for Adjectives and Adverbs

Gwendolyn Brooks "describes the 'graceful life' as one where people glide over floors in softly glowing rooms, smile correctly over trays of silver, cinnamon, and cream, and retire in quiet elegance."

– MARY HELEN WASHINGTON, "Taming All That Anger Down"

Identify the adjectives and adverbs in the above passage, and comment on what they add to the writing. What would be lost if they were removed? What can you conclude about using adjectives and adverbs in your own writing?

Thinking about Your Own Use of Adjectives and Adverbs

Think of something you can observe or examine closely, and take a few minutes to study it. In a paragraph or two, describe your subject for someone who has never seen it. Using the guidelines above, check your use of adjectives and adverbs and revise your paragraphs. How would you characterize your use of adjectives and adverbs—do you overuse them? Put these thoughts in your writing log if you keep one.

Part Three

Sentences: Making Conventional Choices

<>

13. Maintaining Clear Pronoun Reference   *262*

14. Recognizing Shifts   *271*

15. Identifying Comma Splices and Fused Sentences   *281*

16. Recognizing Sentence Fragments   *290*

17. Placing Modifiers Appropriately   *297*

18. Maintaining Consistent and Complete Grammatical Structures   *307*

13

Maintaining Clear Pronoun Reference

CLEAR PRONOUN REFERENCE OILS THE WHEELS OF GOOD PROSE, helping avoid unnecessary repetition and moving a passage along easily. One of your key responsibilities to your readers is making sure that any pronouns refer clearly to their antecedents. See, for example, the effect pronouns have in the following paragraph:

> *He* was crude, certainly, my Uncle Jake; *he* was coarse, of course; gross, it goes without saying; uncouth, beyond question. But was *he* vulgar? I don't think *he* was. For one thing, *he* was good-hearted, and it somehow seems wrong to call anyone vulgar who is good-hearted. But more to the point, I don't think that if you had accused *him* of being vulgar, *he* would have known what the devil you were talking about. To be vulgar requires at least a modicum of pretension, and this Uncle Jake sorely lacked.
>
> –JOSEPH EPSTEIN, "What Is Vulgar?"

If you read the paragraph again, repeating Uncle Jake *in place of every* he *and* him, *you can see how useful these pronouns can be. Now look what happens if another uncle is added to the story:*

> *He* was crude, certainly, my Uncle Jake, and my Uncle Alfred was sloppy; *he* was coarse, of course. . . .

In this instance, the reference for the first he *is clear, because it is followed by* Uncle Jake. *But what about the second* he—*does it refer to Uncle Jake or to Uncle Alfred?*

This chapter will alert you to ways of avoiding such problems in your own writing by maintaining clear pronoun reference. Doing so is a fairly simple matter—of identifying each pronoun, finding the word or phrase it substitutes for, and making sure the pronoun cannot mistakenly refer to any other word as well.

EXERCISE 13.1

Turn back to the passage about Uncle Jake. Think of two uncles (or two aunts or two other relatives) you might describe, and do so in a brief paragraph. Look then at your passage to see how you've used pronouns.

13a

Matching pronouns to their appropriate antecedents

If more than one possible antecedent for a personal pronoun appears in a sentence or passage, the pronoun should refer clearly and unambiguously to only *one* of them. Notice, in the following passage, how Eudora Welty uses pronouns carefully to help readers tell which of two male characters, Sonny and Bowman, she is referring to. The passage describes Sonny frisking Bowman for a concealed gun.

> Sonny came over and put *his* hands on *him*. Bowman felt *them* pass (*they* were professional too) across *his* chest, over *his* hips. He could feel Sonny's eyes upon *him* in the dark.
> —EUDORA WELTY, "Death of a Traveling Salesman"

In the following sentences, however, from an essay about the same story, the pronoun does not refer clearly to only one antecedent:

AMBIGUOUS	The meeting between Bowman and Sonny makes *him* compare *his* own unsatisfying domestic life with one that is emotionally secure.
CLEAR	The meeting between Bowman and Sonny makes *Bowman* compare his own unsatisfying domestic life with one that is emotionally secure.
CLEAR	Meeting Sonny makes *Bowman* compare *his* own unsatisfying domestic life with one that is emotionally secure.
CLEAR	After meeting Sonny, whose domestic life is emotionally secure, *Bowman* finds his own domestic life unsatisfying.

In the ambiguous sentence, readers cannot determine whether Bowman or Sonny is the antecedent of *him* and *his*. All three revisions make the reference clear. The first does so by replacing a pronoun (*him*) with a noun (*Bowman*), but it requires repeating the noun. The second eliminates one pronoun, and the third recasts the sentence altogether.

Everyday Use

Those little words that are pronouns can carry a lot of weight in conversation. Speakers of English rely constantly on clear pronoun choices to help communicate effectively in a wide range of situations: explaining to a service person what it is your computer will *not* do; describing to an insurance agent precisely the kinds of coverage you need; telling a mechanic about the strange noise your car is making. A driver we know recently faced his challenge:

Mechanic:	*So what's the problem?*
Driver:	*On rainy days, it really acts weird.*
Mechanic:	*It won't start on rainy days?*
Driver:	*Sometimes it won't start. But there are other problems too. All those little lights on the dashboard light up at once. That white needle goes all the way over, and the little gauge there jiggles around nervously.*
Mechanic:	*Hmmm. Does it crank?*
Driver:	*The little gauge?*
Mechanic:	*The car. The engine.*

This conversation shows pronoun reference in use. The one breakdown in communication occurs because the driver assumes that the mechanic's question—"Does it crank?"—refers to the last thing the driver mentioned—"the little gauge." The mechanic, however, is using *it* to refer to *the car*, not the gauge. Can you think of times when unclear pronoun reference has made for confusion?

If you are reporting what someone said to someone else, check carefully for ambiguous pronoun reference. Reporting someone's words directly, in quotation marks, is one sure way to eliminate ambiguity.

AMBIGUOUS	Kerry told Ellen she should be ready soon.
CLEAR	Kerry told Ellen to be ready soon.
CLEAR	Kerry told Ellen, "I should be ready soon."
CLEAR	Kerry told Ellen, "You should be ready soon."

13b

Keeping pronouns and antecedents close together

If a pronoun is too far from its antecedent, readers will have trouble making the connection between the two.

CONFUSING	The right-to-life coalition believes that a *zygote*, an egg at the moment of fertilization, is as deserving of protection as is the born human being and thus that abortion is as much murder as is the killing of a child. The coalition's focus is on what *it* will become as much as on what *it* is now.
CLEAR	The right-to-life coalition believes that a *zygote*, an egg at the moment of fertilization, is as deserving of protection as is the born human being and thus that abortion is as much murder as is the killing of a child. The coalition's focus is on what *the zygote* will become as much as on what *it* is now.

EXERCISE 13.2

Revise each of the following items to clarify pronoun reference. All the items can be revised in more than one way. If a pronoun refers ambiguously to more than one possible antecedent, revise the sentence in at least two different ways, reflecting each possible meaning. Example:

After Jane left, Miranda found her keys.

Miranda found Jane's keys after Jane left.

Miranda found her own keys after Jane left.

1. Anna smiled at her mother as she opened the birthday package.
2. Lear divides his kingdom between the two older daughters, Goneril and Regan, whose extravagant professions of love are more flattering than the simple affection of the youngest daughter, Cordelia. The consequences of this error in judgment soon become apparent, as they prove neither grateful nor kind to him.
3. The tragedy of child abuse is that even after the children of abusive parents grow up, they often continue the sad tradition of cruelty.
4. New England helped shape many aspects of American culture, including education, religion, and government. As New Englanders moved west, they carried its institutions with them.
5. Ira told Ed he needed a vacation.
6. Bill broke the news of his promotion to Ed.
7. After Ed hired Paul, he felt relieved.
8. When drug therapy is combined with psychotherapy, the patients relate better to their therapists, are less vulnerable to what disturbs them, and are more responsive to them.
9. Not long after the company set up the subsidiary, it went bankrupt.
10. Quint trusted Smith because she had worked for her before.

13c

Recognizing troublesome pronoun reference

Matching a pronoun to one specific antecedent and keeping pronouns and antecedents close together will take you a long way toward establishing clear pronoun reference. A few pronouns, however, cause particular problems for writers. The sections that follow provide practice in checking to see that these pronouns are used clearly and properly.

1

Checking for vague and ambiguous *it*, *this*, *that*, and *which*

Writers are often tempted to use *it*, *this*, *that*, or *which* as a kind of shortcut, a quick and easy way of referring to something mentioned earlier. But such shortcuts can often cause confusion. Make sure that these pronouns refer clearly to a specific antecedent.

VAGUE	When they realized the bill would be defeated, they tried to postpone the vote. However, *it* failed. [What does *it* refer to—the bill, the attempt to postpone a vote on it, or perhaps both?]
CLEAR	When they realized the bill would be defeated, they tried to postpone the vote. However, *the attempt* failed.
VAGUE	Today has been wonderful: I've finished my last paper, gotten an A on my art final, and registered for graduation. Because of *this*, I plan to celebrate. [Does *this* refer only to the graduation? Or are all the events reason for the celebration?]
CLEAR	Today has been wonderful: I've finished my last paper, gotten an A on my art final, and registered for graduation. Because of *these feats*, I plan to celebrate.
AMBIGUOUS	She read a review of the book, *which* confused her. [What does *which* refer to: the review or the book?]
CLEAR	She read a review of the book, *a work* that confused her.
CLEAR	She read a review of the book; *the review* confused her.

If *that* or *which* opens a clause that refers to a specific noun, put *that* or *which* directly after the noun, if possible.

AMBIGUOUS	We worked all night on the float for the Rose Parade *that* our club was going to sponsor. [Does *that* refer to the float or the Rose Parade?]

CLEAR   We worked all night on the float *that* our club was going to sponsor for the Rose Parade.

2

Checking for appropriate use of *who, which,* and *that*

Be careful to use the relative pronouns *who, which,* and *that* appropriately. *Who* refers primarily to people or to animals with names. *Which* refers to animals or to things, and *that* refers to animals, things, and occasionally anonymous or collective groups of people. (See the Glossary of Usage for more on *that* and *which*.)

Stephen Jay Gould, *who* has won many awards for his writing about science, teaches at Harvard.

The whale, *which* has only one baby a year, is subject to extinction because it reproduces so slowly.

Laboratories *that* harm animals have become controversial.

3

Checking for indefinite use of *you* and *they*

In conversation, we frequently use *you* and *they* in an indefinite sense, as in such expressions as *you never know* and *on television, they said*. In college and professional writing, however, such constructions are inappropriately informal. Be careful to use *you* only to mean "you, the reader," and *they* only to refer to a clear antecedent.

INAPPROPRIATE   Commercials try to make *you* buy without thinking.

REVISED   Commercials try to make *people* buy without thinking.

INAPPROPRIATE   In France, *they* allow dogs in most restaurants.

REVISED   Most restaurants in France allow dogs.

4

Checking for adjectives or possessives used as antecedents

Pronouns should not refer to adjectives or possessives as antecedents. Though an adjective or possessive may clearly imply a noun antecedent, it does not serve as a clear antecedent.

INAPPROPRIATE   In Welty's story, *she* characterizes Bowman as a man unaware of his own isolation.

REVISED   In her story, Welty characterizes Bowman as a man unaware of his own isolation.

REVISED   In Welty's story, Bowman is characterized as a man unaware of his own isolation.

▶ *FOR MULTILINGUAL WRITERS:*
Using Pronoun Subjects

In some languages—Spanish and Russian, for instance—personal pronoun subjects are largely unnecessary because the verb ending shows person and number. In other languages, such as Arabic, personal pronouns are added to the verbs as suffixes or prefixes. Native speakers of these languages sometimes tend to "overcorrect" in English by doubling the subject, as in *Jaime he lives next door.* Such a double subject is inappropriate in English. Therefore, if you are using a pronoun as a subject, make sure that you have not used a proper noun subject as well: *He lives next door to us.*

≫ *Editing for clear pronoun reference*

1. Find all the pronouns in your draft, and then identify the specific noun that is the antecedent of each one.
2. If you cannot find a noun antecedent, replace the pronoun with a noun, or supply an antecedent to which the pronoun clearly refers.
3. Next look to see if the pronoun could be misunderstood to refer to a noun other than its antecedent. If so, replace the pronoun with the appropriate noun, or revise the sentence so that the pronoun can refer to only one possible antecedent.
4. Finally, look at any pronoun that seems far from its antecedent. If a reader might have trouble relating the pronoun to its antecedent, replace the pronoun with the appropriate noun.

EXERCISE 13.3

Revise the following sentences to establish clear and appropriate pronoun reference. Most of the sentences can be revised in more than one way. Example:

~~It~~ is a pleasure ^T to attend professor Lang's lectures.

1. On the turnpike, they charge very high prices for gasoline.
2. In Texas, you often hear about the influence of big oil corporations.
3. They said on the radio that somebody had won the lottery.

4. A friend of mine recently had a conversation with a veteran that changed his view of the Persian Gulf War.

5. She dropped off a friend which had gone to the party with her.

6. Not only was the parcel damaged, but they said I owed postage.

7. I always carry an umbrella because you never know when it might rain.

8. Company policy prohibited smoking, which many employees resented.

9. Didion's essay "Goodbye to All That" describes how she left New York.

10. In Tom Jobim's lyrics, he often describes the beaches of Rio.

EXERCISE 13.4   Revising to Clarify Pronoun Reference

Revise to establish a clear antecedent for every pronoun that needs one.

In Paul Fussell's essay "My War," he writes about his experience in combat during World War II, which he says still haunts his life. Fussell confesses that he joined the infantry ROTC in 1939 as a way of getting out of gym class, where he would have been forced to expose his "fat and flabby" body to the ridicule of his classmates. However, it proved to be a serious miscalculation. After the United States entered the war in 1941, other male college students were able to join officer training programs in specialized fields that kept them out of combat. If you were already in an ROTC unit associated with the infantry, though, you were trapped in it. That was how Fussell came to be shipped to France as a rifle-platoon leader in 1944. Almost immediately they sent him to the front, where he soon developed pneumonia because of insufficient winter clothing. He spent a month in hospitals; because he did not want to worry his parents, however, he told them it was just the flu. When he returned to the front, he was wounded by a shell that killed his sergeant, which had been with him since basic training.

THINKING CRITICALLY ABOUT PRONOUN REFERENCE

Reading with Attention to Pronoun Reference

The following poem depends on its title to supply the antecedent for the pronouns that follow and that knit the poem together. Read the poem out loud, and then provide its one-word title. How did you know what the title should be? Then try writing a poem of your own (perhaps three or four verses) like this one, using pronouns and other words to give "clues" to your title.

His art is eccentricity, his aim
How not to hit the mark he seems to aim at,

His passion how to avoid the obvious,
His technique how to vary the avoidance.

The others throw to be comprehended. He
Throws to be a moment misunderstood.

Yet not too much. Not too errant, arrant, wild,
But every seeming aberration willed.

Not to, yet still, still to communicate
Making the batter understand too late.

—ROBERT FRANCIS

Thinking about Your Own Use of Pronoun Reference

Turn to something you've written, and analyze your use of pronouns. Do any pronouns not refer clearly and directly to the correct antecedent? Could any antecedents be ambiguous? Using the guidelines on p. 268, revise as necessary. Note any patterns in your use of pronouns—in a writing log, if you keep one.

14

Recognizing Shifts

A SHIFT IN WRITING is, most simply, an abrupt change of some sort that results in inconsistency. Consider, for example, the very famous opening lines of The Adventures of Huckleberry Finn:

> You don't know about me without you have read a book by the name of *The Adventures of Tom Sawyer;* but that ain't no matter. That book was made by Mr. Mark Twain, and he told the truth, mainly. There was things which he stretched, but mainly he told the truth.

Now replace the last sentence with this one: In a few instances Mr. Twain may have exaggerated slightly; however, for the most part, he showed proper respect for factuality. *As readers, we would be jolted and no doubt confused by such a shift in tone, from exaggerated informality to almost straitlaced formality.*

Such a shift, because it is so blatant, is hard to miss. This chapter will help you recognize shifts that are a bit more subtle and will offer strategies for revising to eliminate them. These include shifts in the tense, mood, and voice of verbs; in the person and number of pronouns; from direct to indirect discourse; and in tone and diction. If you have had such shifts pointed out in your writing, checking for them should become a regular part of your writing process.

EXERCISE 14.1

Look at the passage from *Huckleberry Finn* above. Now imagine a very different Huck Finn, one in a suit, bow tie, and starched shirt, introducing the story to, say, Queen Victoria. How might a formal and serious Huck write the passage? Write such a passage, and then look at those done by two or three classmates. Compare notes on how you each accomplished the shift in tone.

14a

Recognizing shifts in tense

If the verbs in a sentence or passage refer to actions occurring at different times, they may require different tenses: *Mac started the kennel because he had always loved dogs.* Be careful, however, not to change tenses unnecessarily or in a way that does not make sense. Look at this sentence: *Clarissa yowled until her owner looks up.* The shift in tenses from past to present confuses readers, who are left to guess which tense is correct.

INCONSISTENT	A few countries *produce* almost all of the world's illegal drugs, but addiction *affected* many more countries.
REVISED	A few countries *produce* almost all of the world's illegal drugs, but addiction *affects* many more countries.
INCONSISTENT	Some people never really *settle* into a profession. Such people *found* jobs only when they *needed* food or shelter.
REVISED	Some people never really *settle* into a profession. Such people *find* jobs only when they *need* food or shelter.

(See Chapter 9 for a complete discussion of verb tense.)

≫ *Editing unnecessary shifts in tense*

Because we deliberately—and necessarily—shift back and forth among tenses all the time, spotting those tense shifts that are not logically consistent can be difficult. If you have problems with tense shifts, the following strategies might help:

1. Circle all the verbs in your draft.
2. Look at the verbs in sequence, and check that any shift from one tense to another is logically consistent. Check for consistency both within a sentence and between sentences. You might even find it helpful to make a time line charting the various tenses used.
3. If you find any illogical shifts in tense, revise to eliminate them.

EXERCISE 14.2

Revise any of the following sentences in which you find unnecessary shifts in verb tense. Most of the sentences can be revised in more than one way. Example:

does
The newspaper covers campus events, but it ~~did~~ not appeal to students.

1. The day is hot, stifling, and typical of July, a day when no one willingly ventured out onto the burning asphalt.
2. Then, suddenly, the big day arrives. The children were still a bit sleepy, for their anticipation had kept them awake.
3. The importance of music to society is evident throughout the entire magazine. A good example was the first advertisement.
4. A cloud of snow powder rose as skis and poles fly in every direction.
5. The fitness mania of the 1970s gave way to the greed of the 1980s, which in turn gives way to the occupational insecurity of the 1990s.

14b

Recognizing shifts in mood

Be careful not to shift from one mood to another without reason. The mood of a verb can be indicative (He _closes_ the door), imperative (_Close the door_), or subjunctive (If the door _were closed_, . . .). (See pp. 226–27.)

INCONSISTENT	_Keep_ your eye on the ball, and you _should bend_ your knees. [shift from imperative to indicative]
REVISED	_Keep_ your eye on the ball, and _bend_ your knees.
INCONSISTENT	I asked that Rhonda _tutor_ the Laotian children in English and that she _teaches_ them some American games as well. [shift from subjunctive to indicative]
REVISED	I asked that Rhonda _tutor_ the Laotian children in English and that she _teach_ them some American games as well.

Everyday Use

Dramatic or even outrageous shifts are a staple of comedians and humor writers. Here is columnist Dave Barry: "I would have to say that the greatest single achievement of the American medical establishment is nasal spray." Part of Barry's humor comes from his tendency to shift tone, from the serious (the American medical establishment) to the banal (nasal spray). If you have a favorite comedian or comic strip, look for such shifts in tone. What role do they play in making you laugh?

EXERCISE 14.3

Revise the following sentences to eliminate any unnecessary shifts in mood. Example:

> Walk over to the field house, and then ~~you should~~ get in line.

1. Place a test strip on the subject area; you should expose the test strip to light and develop it for two and a half minutes.
2. I think it is better that Grandfather die painlessly, bravely, and with dignity than that he continues to live in terrible physical pain.
3. Whether women be homemakers or are executives, they deserve respect.
4. The coroner asked that we be quiet and that we should be attentive.
5. Say no to drugs, and you should consider alcohol a drug, too!

14c

Recognizing shifts in voice

Do not shift unnecessarily between the active voice (*She sold the furniture*) and the passive voice (*The furniture was sold*). Sometimes a shift in voice is perfectly justified. In the sentence *I am known for being unpredictable and adventurous, but I consider myself a practical person*, the shift from passive (*am known*) to active (*consider*) allows the writer to keep the emphasis on the subject *I*. Making both verbs active (*People know me as an unpredictable and adventurous person, but I consider myself a practical person*) changes the focus of the sentence. Often, however, shifts in voice merely confuse readers. (See Chapter 9, pp. 224–26.)

INCONSISTENT	Although she confessed to the crime, her accomplice was not identified by her.
REVISED	Although she confessed to the crime, she did not identify her accomplice.
INCONSISTENT	Four youngsters approached him, and he was asked to buy a raffle ticket.
REVISED	Four youngsters approached him and asked him to buy a raffle ticket.

EXERCISE 14.4

Revise each of the following sentences that contains an unnecessary shift in voice. One of the sentences does not require any change. Example:

she prefers jazz.
Although she enjoys rock music, ~~jazz is preferred by her.~~

1. My grandmother was wise, but her wisdom was usually ignored by the family.
2. Once these shells housed creatures; now they are crushed by the waves.
3. When someone says "roommate" to a high school senior bound for college, thoughts of no privacy and potential fights are conjured up.
4. The first thing that is seen as we start down the slope is a green banner.
5. The physician moves the knee around to observe the connections of the cartilage and ligaments, and a fluid is injected into the joint.

14d

Recognizing shifts in person and number

Do not shift unnecessarily between first person (*I, we*), second person (*you*), and third person (*he, she, it, one,* or *they*) or between singular and plural. Such shifts in person and number create confusion.

INCONSISTENT	*One* can do well in college if *you* budget *your* time carefully.
REVISED	*One* can do well in college if *one* budgets time carefully.
REVISED	*You* can do well in college if *you* budget *your* time carefully.
INCONSISTENT	*Nurses* are paid much less than doctors, even though *a nurse* has the primary responsibility for daily patient care.
REVISED	*Nurses* are paid much less than doctors, even though *nurses* have the primary responsibility for daily patient care.

Many shifts in number are actually problems with pronoun-antecedent agreement (see Chapter 11).

INCONSISTENT	I have difficulty seeing another *person's* position, especially if *their* opinion contradicts mine.
REVISED	I have difficulty seeing other *people's* positions, especially if *their* opinions contradict mine.
REVISED	I have difficulty seeing another *person's* position, especially if *his* or *her* opinion contradicts mine.

≫ *Editing unnecessary pronoun shifts*

1. Circle all the pronouns in your draft.
2. Draw a line from pronoun to pronoun looking for shifts, especially among *I, you,* and *one.*
3. If any of the shifts are illogical, revise to eliminate them.

EXERCISE 14.5

Revise each of the following sentences to eliminate any unnecessary shifts in person or number. Some sentences can be revised in more than one way. Example:

> *When a person goes to college, you face many new situations.*
>
> *When a person goes to college, he or she faces many new situations.*
>
> *When people go to college, they face many new situations.*

1. Suddenly we heard an explosion of wings off to our right, and you could see a hundred or more ducks lifting off from the water.
2. Workers with computer skills were in great demand, and a programmer could almost name their salary.
3. I liked the sense of individualism, the crowd yelling for you, and the feeling that I was in command.
4. Every new employee must undergo one week of observation; they must check with their supervisor for permission to leave.
5. To perform well in a leadership position, a person needs to feel that they are respected by others.

14e

Recognizing shifts between direct and indirect discourse

When you quote someone's exact words, setting them off in quotation marks, you are using **direct discourse.** When, on the other hand, you report what someone says without repeating the exact words, you are using **indirect discourse.**

DIRECT   Ambrose Bierce defined *love* as "a temporary insanity curable by marriage."

| INDIRECT | Ambrose Bierce said that love is a momentary madness that can be taken care of by marriage. |

Shifting between direct and indirect discourse in the same sentence can cause problems, especially with questions.

INCONSISTENT	Bob asked what could he do to help?
DIRECT	Bob asked, "What can I do to help?"
INDIRECT	Bob asked what he could do to help.

USING SOURCES
Shifting between Direct and Indirect Discourse

When weaving a source's words into your own prose, be careful not to shift awkwardly, or ungrammatically, from direct to indirect discourse (or the reverse). For instance:

INCONSISTENT	Chief Seattle *said* that one nation *followed* another "like the waves of the sea," and therefore "regret *is* useless." [Shifting from indirect to direct discourse results in inconsistent verb sequence.]
DIRECT	Chief Seattle said that "nation follows nation, like the waves of the sea" and that therefore "regret is useless."
INDIRECT	Chief Seattle said that nations come and go, like everything in nature, and that therefore feeling sad is useless.

In general, you should use direct discourse for words that are memorable or otherwise important and indirect discourse when the exact words are less important than their content. In the previous example, direct quotation is probably more appropriate, for Chief Seattle's words are poetic and memorable. In some contexts, however, a writer might want to paraphrase his words, as in the indirect example—for instance, if Chief Seattle is already quoted in many other places in the same work.

EXERCISE 14.6

Revise each of the following sentences to eliminate the shifts between direct and indirect discourse by putting the direct discourse into indirect form. Example:

Steven Pinker stated that his book is meant for people who use language.

1. Loren Eiseley feels an urge to join the birds in their soundless flight, but in the end he knows that he cannot, and "I was, after all, only a man."

2. According to the article, the ozone layer is rapidly dwindling, and "we are endangering the lives of future generations."

3. The instructor told us, "Please read the next two stories before the next class" and that she might give us a quiz on them.

4. Oscar Wilde wrote that books cannot be divided into moral and immoral categories, and "books are either well-written or badly written."

5. Richard Rodriguez acknowledged that intimacy was not created by a language; "it is created by intimates."

14f

Recognizing shifts in tone and diction

Tone in writing refers to the way the writer's attitude toward the topic and/or audience comes across to the audience. (See 4g4.) Tone is closely related to **diction**, or word choice—not only the choice of individual words but the overall level of formality, technicality, or other effects created by the individual words. Within a sentence, a paragraph, or an entire piece of writing, be careful not to change your tone or level of diction unless you have a reason for doing so.

Tone

When they are used for emphasis or humor, shifts in tone can be effective. Mark Twain was a master of such shifts. In the following passage, he presents a mock graduation address, beginning with a serious tone and then shifting at the beginning of the second paragraph to characteristic humor.

> Being told I would be expected to talk here, I inquired what sort of a talk I ought to make. They said it should be something suitable to youth—something didactic, instructive, or something in the nature of good advice. Very well. I have a few things in my mind which I have often longed to say for the instruction of the young; for it is in one's tender early years that such things will best take root and be most enduring and most valuable. First, then, I will say to you, my young friends—and I say it beseechingly, urgingly—
> Always obey your parents, when they are present. This is the best policy in the long run, because if you don't they will make you. Most parents think they know better than you do, and you can generally make more by humoring that superstition than you can by acting on your own better judgment. —MARK TWAIN, "Advice to Youth"

Unintended shifts in tone, on the other hand, confuse readers and leave them wondering what the writer's real attitude is. In the following passage, the tone shifts in the last sentence.

INCONSISTENT

The question of child care forces a society to make profound decisions about its economic values. Can most families with children actually live adequately on only one salary? If some conservatives had their way, June Cleaver would still be stuck in the kitchen baking cookies for Wally and the Beaver and waiting for Ward to bring home the bacon, except that with only one income, the Cleaver family would be lucky to afford hot dogs.

The first two sentences set a serious, formal tone, discussing child care in fairly general, abstract terms, but in the third sentence the writer shifts suddenly to a sarcastic attack based on references to television characters of an earlier era. Readers cannot tell whether the writer is presenting a serious analysis of the child care issue or a passionate argument about a hotly debated topic. See how the passage was revised to make the tone consistent.

REVISED

The question of child care forces a society to make profound decisions about its economic values. Can most families with young children actually live adequately on only one salary? Some conservatives believe that women with young children should not work outside the home, but many are forced to do so for financial reasons.

Diction

Like shifts in tone, inappropriate shifts in level of diction can confuse readers. In general, diction may be classified as technical (*Araucaria araucana* instead of *monkey puzzle tree*), informal or colloquial (*Give me a ring if there's anything I can do*), formal (*Please inform me if I can be of further assistance*), or slang (*He used to be a real jock, but now he's a couch potato*). In the following sentences, the diction shifts from formal to highly informal, giving an odd, disjointed feeling to the passage.

INCONSISTENT

Since taking office, Prime Minister Cresson has been bombarded with *really gross* news, including *tons of* strikes, record unemployment, several scandals, and even *bitching* from colleagues in her own party.

REVISED

Since taking office, Prime Minister Cresson has been bombarded with unrelenting bad news, including a wave of strikes, record unemployment, several scandals, and even sniping from colleagues in her own party.

THINKING CRITICALLY ABOUT SHIFTS

Reading with an Eye for Shifts

The following paragraph includes several *necessary* shifts in person and number. Read the paragraph carefully, marking off all such shifts. Notice how careful the author must be as he shifts back and forth among pronouns.

It has been one of the great errors of our time to think that by thinking about thinking, and then talking about it, we could possibly straighten out and tidy up our minds. There is no delusion more damaging than to get the idea in your head that you understand the functioning of your own brain. Once you acquire such a notion, you run the danger of moving in to take charge, guiding your thoughts, shepherding your mind from place to place, *controlling* it, making lists of regulations. The human mind is not meant to be governed, certainly not by any book of rules yet written; it is supposed to run itself, and we are obliged to follow it along, trying to keep up with it as best we can. It is all very well to be aware of your awareness, even proud of it, but never try to operate it. You are not up to the job. —LEWIS THOMAS, "The Attic of the Brain"

Thinking about Any Shifts in Your Own Writing

Find an article about a well-known person you admire. Then write a paragraph or two about him or her, making a point of using both direct and indirect discourse. Using the information in 14e, check your writing for any inappropriate shifts between direct and indirect discourse, and revise as necessary.

15

Identifying Comma Splices and Fused Sentences

*T*HE TERMS COMMA SPLICE *AND* FUSED SENTENCE *grow out of metaphors based on the words* splice *and* fuse. *In grammatical terms, a **comma splice** occurs when two independent clauses are joined with only a comma; a **fused sentence** occurs when two independent clauses are joined with no punctuation or connecting word between them.*

SPLICE	It was already spring, the tulips were in bloom.
FUSED	It was already spring the tulips were in bloom.

Comma splices and fused sentences appear frequently in literary and journalistic writing, for, like many other structures we commonly identify as "errors," each can be used to powerful effect. In the following passage, see how comma splices create momentum and build to a climax.

> Golden eagles sit in every tree and watch us watch them watch us, although there are bird experts who will tell you in all seriousness that there are NO golden eagles here. Bald eagles are common, ospreys abound, we have herons and mergansers and kingfishers, we have logging with percherons and belgians, we have park land and nature trails, we have enough oddballs, weirdos, and loons to satisfy anybody. —ANNE CAMERON

In the second sentence, six independent clauses are spliced together with commas. The effect is a rush of details, from the rather oddball birds to the oddball people and finally to the loons, *a word that can apply to either birds or people.*

In your college writing, you will seldom if ever wish to focus attention on sentences in this particular way. In fact, doing so will almost always be identified not as a means of creating emphasis or special effect but as an error. This chapter aims to help you learn to recognize comma splices and fused sentences in your own writing and provides five methods of revising to eliminate them.

Everyday Use

While we certainly pause as we speak in order to mark off our thoughts or to add emphasis, we do not "speak" punctuation. In fact, excited conversation may contain many comma splices, which then appear in dialogue to represent the rhythms of speech. For example:

> "What about Tom?"
> "We can tell your father and Billy that Tom's mother called, he was sick, his grandmother died, anything, just so we don't have to bring him with us."
> —THOMAS ROCKWELL, *How to Eat Fried Worms*

The comma splices in this dialogue are effective because they convey the speech patterns of two ten-year-old boys; they would not, however, be appropriate (or effective) in most college writing. Try revising the above dialogue to make it sound more formal. You may see some ways—and reasons—to keep comma splices out of your own writing.

EXERCISE 15.1

If you listen carefully, you may well "hear" comma splices and fused sentences in conversations around you. Try to transcribe a few minutes of conversation among a few friends. Look for comma splices or fused sentences, using the guidelines that follow.

>> *Checking for comma splices and fused sentences*

1. Underline every independent clause in your draft. (7c4)
2. Look for places where independent clauses fall one after another, and look at what comes between them. If you find no punctuation, you have identified a fused sentence.
3. If you find only a comma between independent clauses and no conjunction (*and, but, or, for, so,* or *yet*), you have identified a comma splice.
4. See if any clauses are linked by conjunctive adverbs—words like *however, then,* or *therefore* (see 7b7 for a list)—and then make sure

that a semicolon precedes the conjunctive adverb. If it does not, you have a comma splice.

5. Revise any fused sentences or comma splices using one of the five methods listed below.

Five methods of eliminating comma splices and fused sentences

- Separating clauses into two sentences (15a)
- Linking clauses with a comma and a coordinating conjunction (15b)
- Linking clauses with a semicolon (15c)
- Recasting two clauses as *one* independent clause (15d)
- Recasting one independent clause as a dependent clause (15e)

As a writer, you must decide which method to use in revising—or avoiding— comma splices and fused sentences. The choice requires looking at the sentences before and after the ones you are revising to determine how a particular method will affect the rhythm of the passage, and it may also require reading the passage aloud to see how the revision sounds.

▶

FOR MULTILINGUAL WRITERS
Judging Sentence Length

If you speak a language that tends to value very long sentences, you may string together sentences in English in a way that results in comma-splice errors. If this represents a problem area for you, you can benefit by paying especially close attention to the checking guidelines above. Note that in standard academic and professional English, a sentence should contain only one main clause, *unless* the clauses are joined by a comma and a coordinating conjunction or by a semicolon.

15a

Separating clauses into two sentences

The simplest way to revise comma splices or fused sentences is to separate them into two sentences.

COMMA SPLICE   Emma encourages Harriet to reject a proposal from a young farmer and to expect one from Mr. Elton, her interference soon leads to embarrassment.

| FUSED SENTENCE | Emma encourages Harriet to reject a proposal from a young farmer and to expect one from Mr. Elton her interference soon leads to embarrassment. |
| REVISED | Emma encourages Harriet to reject a proposal from a young farmer and to expect one from Mr. Elton. Her interference soon leads to embarrassment. |

Although this method may be the simplest, it is not always the most appropriate. In the preceding example, choosing to divide the two independent clauses into two separate sentences makes good sentence sense. The combined sentences contain twenty-four words, and dividing them into two sentences of eighteen and six words adds emphasis to the last six words, which are now in a sentence of their own. If the two spliced or fused clauses are very short, however, dividing them into two separate sentences may not succeed so well.

COMMA SPLICE	Emma gives Harriet advice about marriage proposals, she soon regrets having done so.
FUSED SENTENCE	Emma gives Harriet advice about marriage proposals she soon regrets having done so.
REVISED	Emma gives Harriet advice about marriage proposals. She soon regrets having done so.

Here the two short sentences in a row, both opening with the subject, sound abrupt and overly terse, and some other method of revision would probably be preferable. (See Chapter 22.)

15b

Linking clauses with a comma and a coordinating conjunction

For comma splices and fused sentences in which the two clauses are fairly closely related and equally important, another alternative for revision is to use a comma and a coordinating conjunction: *and, but, or, nor, for, so,* or *yet.* Using a coordinating conjunction helps indicate what kind of link exists between the ideas in the two clauses. For instance, *but* and *yet* signal opposition or contrast (*I am strong, but she is stronger*); *for* and *so* signal cause-effect relationships (*The cabin was bitterly cold, so we built a fire*).

| COMMA SPLICE | I should pay my tuition, I need a new car. |
| FUSED SENTENCE | I should pay my tuition I need a new car. |

> REVISED   I should pay my tuition, *but* I need a new car.

In the preceding example, the two clauses represent contrasting alternatives, so *but* is an appropriate conjunction to link them. (See 20a for more on using coordinating conjunctions to write more varied and interesting sentences.)

15c

Linking clauses with a semicolon

If the ideas in the two independent clauses in a comma splice or fused sentence are closely related and you want to give them equal emphasis, link them with a semicolon.

COMMA SPLICE	This photograph is not at all realistic, it even uses dream-like images to convey its message.
FUSED SENTENCE	This photograph is not at all realistic it even uses dream-like images to convey its message.
REVISED	This photograph is not at all realistic; it even uses dream-like images to convey its message.

Here the second independent clause elaborates on the statement in the first independent clause, offering evidence that the photograph is not at all realistic. Because the two independent clauses are closely related and of equal importance, linking them with a semicolon makes sense.

Punctuating clauses linked with a conjunctive adverb or a transitional phrase

Be careful when linking clauses with conjunctive adverbs (words like *however, thus, also;* see 7b7) or transitional phrases (*in fact, in contrast, in addition;* see 6d5). Such words and phrases must be used with a semicolon, a period, or a coordinating conjunction.

COMMA SPLICE	Most Third World countries have very high birthrates, therefore most of their citizens are young.
FUSED SENTENCE	Most Third World countries have very high birthrates therefore most of their citizens are young.
REVISED	Most Third World countries have very high birthrates; therefore, most of their citizens are young.
REVISED	Most Third World countries have very high birthrates. Therefore, most of their citizens are young.

REVISED	Most Third World countries have very high birthrates; most of their citizens, therefore, are young.
REVISED	Most Third World countries have very high birthrates, and therefore most of their citizens are young.

As you can see, any of the three methods discussed thus far can be used to revise a comma splice or fused sentence that uses a conjunctive adverb or transitional phrase inappropriately. The context of the passage can help you decide which method to choose. Notice that conjunctive adverbs and transitional phrases can appear in various positions in the clause. These words and expressions are usually set off from the rest of the clause by commas (see 30a and e).

15d

Recasting two clauses as one independent clause

Sometimes two independent clauses that are spliced or fused together can be reduced to a single independent clause.

COMMA SPLICE	Many people complain that a large part of their mail is advertisements, most of the rest is bills.
FUSED SENTENCE	Many people complain that a large part of their mail is advertisements most of the rest is bills.
REVISED	Many people complain that most of their mail is advertisements and bills.

The revision combines the phrases *a large part of their mail* and *most of the rest* into the phrase *most of their mail* and connects the words *advertisements* and *bills* with the conjunction *and*. These changes reduce the two independent clauses to a single clause that is more direct and succinct. (See 19b for more ways to avoid needless repetition.)

15e

Recasting one independent clause as a dependent clause

Another option for revising two spliced or fused independent clauses is to convert one of them to a dependent clause. This method is most appropriate when the meaning or effect of one clause is dependent on the other or when one is less important than the other.

COMMA SPLICE	Zora Neale Hurston is regarded as one of America's major novelists, she died in obscurity.
FUSED SENTENCE	Zora Neale Hurston is regarded as one of America's major novelists she died in obscurity.
REVISED	*Although* Zora Neale Hurston is regarded as one of America's major novelists, she died in obscurity.

In the preceding example, the first clause stands in contrast to the second one: in contrast to Hurston's importance today (she is held in high esteem) are the circumstances of her death (obscurity). In the revision, the writer chose to emphasize the second clause and to make the first one into a dependent clause by adding the subordinating conjunction *although*. (For a list of subordinating conjunctions, see 7b7.)

COMMA SPLICE	The arts and crafts movement called for handmade objects, it reacted against mass production.
FUSED SENTENCE	The arts and crafts movement called for handmade objects it reacted against mass production.
REVISED	The arts and crafts movement, *which reacted against mass production,* called for handmade objects.

In this example, both clauses discuss related aspects of the arts and crafts movement. In the revision, the writer chose to emphasize the first clause, the one describing what the movement advocated, and to make the second clause, the one describing what it reacted against, into a dependent clause by adding the relative pronoun *which*. (For a list of relative pronouns, see 7b3.)

Notice that dependent clauses must often be set off from the rest of the sentence with commas. (See Chapter 30. See also 22a2 and 22b3, about using dependent clauses to write varied and effective sentences.)

EXERCISE 15.2

Revise to correct the comma splice or fused sentence using *two* of the methods in this chapter. Use each of the methods at least once. Example:

> I had misgivings about the marriage, I did not attend the ceremony.
>
> I had misgivings about the marriage, so I did not attend the ceremony.
>
> Because I had misgivings about the marriage, I did not attend the ceremony.

1. I was sitting on a log bridge, the sun sank low in the sky.
2. Reporters today have no choice they must use computers.

3. I completed the test, I was uncertain about the last essay question.

4. My mother taught me to read my grandmother taught me to *love* to read.

5. *David Copperfield* was written as a serial it is ideal for television.

6. Lincoln called for troops to fight the Confederacy, four more Southern states seceded as a result.

7. The California condor is almost extinct scientists are trying to save it.

8. E. B. White died in 1985 his work continues to inspire readers.

9. Václav Havel was once imprisoned as a dissident, still, he eventually became president of Czechoslovakia.

10. The music lifted her spirits she stopped sighing and began to sing.

EXERCISE 15.3

Revise the following paragraph, eliminating all comma splices by using a period or a semicolon. Then revise the paragraph again, this time using any of the other methods in this chapter. Comment on the two revisions. What differences in rhythm do you detect? Which version do you prefer, and why?

My sister Mary decided to paint her house last summer, thus, she had to buy some paint. She wanted inexpensive paint, at the same time, it had to go on easily and cover well, that combination was unrealistic to start with. She had never done exterior painting before, in fact she did not even own a ladder. She was a complete beginner, on the other hand, she was a hard worker and was willing to learn. She got her husband, Dan, to take a week off from work, likewise she let her two teenage sons take three days off from school to help. Mary went out and bought the "dark green" paint for $6.99 a gallon, it must have been mostly water, in fact, you could almost see through it. Mary and Dan and the boys put one coat of this paint on the house, as a result, their white house turned a streaky light green. Dan and the boys rebelled, declaring they would not work anymore with such cheap paint. Mary was forced to buy all new paint, even so, the house did not really get painted until September.

EXERCISE 15.4   Revising for Comma Splices and Fused Sentences

Revise the following paragraph, eliminating the comma splices and fused sentences using any of the methods discussed in this chapter. Then revise the paragraph again, this time eliminating each comma splice and fused sentence by a *different* method. Decide which paragraph is more effective, and why. Finally, compare the revision you prefer with the revisions of several other students, and discuss the ways in which the versions differ in meaning.

Gardening can be very satisfying, it is also hard work people who just see the pretty flowers may not realize this. My mother spends long hours every spring tilling the soil, she moves many wheelbarrow-loads of disgusting cow manure and chicken droppings, in fact, the whole early part of gardening is nauseating. The whole garden area has to be rototilled every year, this process is not much like the ad showing people walking quietly behind the rototiller, on the contrary, my father has to fight that machine every inch of the way, sweating so much he looks like Hulk Hogan after a hard bout. Then the planting all must be done by hand, my back aches, my hands get raw, my skin gets sunburned. I get filthy whenever I go near that garden my mother always asks me to help, though. When harvest time comes the effort is *almost* worth it, however, there are always extra zucchinis I give away at school everybody else is trying to give away zucchinis, too. We also have tomatoes, lettuce, there is always more than we need and we feel bad wasting it wouldn't you like this nice bag of cucumbers?

THINKING CRITICALLY ABOUT COMMA SPLICES AND FUSED SENTENCES

Reading with an Eye for Special Effects

E. M. Forster is known as a careful and correct stylist, yet he often deviates from the "correct" to create special effects. Look, for example, at the way he uses a comma splice in the following passage:

One of the evils of money is that it tempts us to look at it rather than at the things that it buys. They are dimmed because of the metal and the paper through which we receive them. That is the fundamental deceitfulness of riches, which kept worrying Christ. That is the treachery of the purse, the wallet and the bank-balance, even from the capitalist point of view. They were invented as a convenience to the flesh, they have become a chain for the spirit.

                                        –E. M. FORSTER, "The Last Parade"

Forster uses a comma splice in the last sentence to emphasize parallel ideas; any conjunction, even *and*, would change the causal relationship he wishes to show. The effect is to stop us in our tracks—because the grammar is unexpected, it attracts just the attention that Forster wants for his statement.

Look through some stories or essays to find some comma splices and fused sentences. Copy down one or two and enough of the surrounding text to show context, and comment in writing on the effect they create.

Thinking about Any Comma Splices and Fused Sentences in Your Own Writing

Go through some essays you have written, checking for comma splices and fused sentences. Revise any you find, using one of the methods in this chapter. Comment on your chosen methods—in your writing log, if you are keeping one.

16

Recognizing Sentence Fragments

SENTENCE FRAGMENTS are groups of words punctuated as sentences but lacking some element grammatically necessary to a sentence, usually either a subject or a finite verb. We see them sometimes in literary works used to add dramatic emphasis, to speed up rhythm, or to create realistic dialogue. For example:

> The history of England is the history of the male line, not of the female. Of our fathers we know always some fact, some distinction. They were soldiers or they were sailors; they filled that office or they made that law. But of our mothers, our grandmothers, our great-grandmothers, what remains? *Nothing but a tradition.* One was beautiful; one was red-haired; one was kissed by a Queen. We know nothing of them except their names and the dates of their marriages and the number of children they bore.
>
> —VIRGINIA WOOLF, "Women and Literature"

Nothing but a tradition. This fragment brings drama to Woolf's statement, arresting readers' attention in a way that a complete sentence would not, giving added emphasis to the word nothing and thus to Woolf's point.

Sentence fragments can pose potential problems for you as a student writer, however, for although you will read them in literature, hear them in conversation, and see them everywhere in advertising, they are usually considered "errors" in most academic prose. This chapter will provide you with practice at recognizing and revising them.

EXERCISE 16.1

Look at the Toyota advertisement in the box on p. 292. Go through it, identifying every sentence fragment. Then rewrite the advertisement, making all sentences complete. Finally, compare your version with the original and your classmates' versions. Which do you find most effective, and why?

Checking for sentence fragments

If you have a tendency to write fragments, you should check for them in all your writing. A group of words must meet the following three criteria to be a complete sentence. If it does not meet all three, it is a fragment and must be revised.

1. It must have a subject. (7c1)
2. It must have a finite verb, not just a verbal phrase. (7c3)
3. Unless it is a question, it must have at least one clause that does *not* begin with a subordinating word. These are some common subordinating words.

although	if	when
as	since	where
because	that	whether
before	though	who
how	unless	why

(For other subordinating words, see 7b3 for a list of relative pronouns and 7b7 for a list of subordinating conjunctions.)

Two methods of eliminating fragments

In general, a fragment can be revised by combining it with an independent clause or by turning it into an independent clause.

FRAGMENT	The beaver dam holding back the shallow pond.
REVISED	I saw the beaver dam holding back the shallow pond. [combined with independent clause *I saw*]
REVISED	The beaver dam was holding back the shallow pond. [turned into independent clause by adding *was* to the participle *holding*, making verb finite]
FRAGMENT	Barely seven inches long, with nothing but a barrel, a handle, and a trigger.
REVISED	He was holding a gun barely seven inches long, with nothing but a barrel, a handle, and a trigger.
REVISED	It was barely seven inches long, with nothing but a barrel, a handle, and a trigger.

> *Everyday Use*
>
> If you pay close attention to advertisements, you will find sentence fragments in frequent, everyday use. Look, for instance, at an excerpt from a recent Toyota advertisement.
>
> *Our Lifetime Guarantee may come as a shock.*
>
> *Or a strut. Or a muffler. Because once you pay to replace them, Toyota's Lifetime Guarantee covers parts and labor on any dealer-installed muffler, shock, or strut for as long as you own your Toyota! So if anything should ever go wrong, your Toyota dealer will fix it. Absolutely free.*
>
> Browse through the advertisements in a few magazines, or look at billboards and other signs, noting the use of fragments. Why do you think they are so often used in advertising? What effects do they create?

16a

Revising phrase fragments

Phrases, groups of words lacking either a subject, a finite verb, or both, appear frequently as fragments. Most common are verbal phrases, prepositional phrases, noun phrases, and appositive phrases.

Verbal-phrase fragments

A verbal phrase includes a gerund, an infinitive, a present participle or a past participle, and any objects or modifiers (7c3). Verbal-phrase fragments lack a finite verb and often a subject. To revise, combine them with an independent clause, or make them a separate sentence.

FRAGMENT	Vivian stayed out of school for three months after Laurel was born. *To recuperate and to take care of her.*
REVISED	Vivian stayed out of school for three months after Laurel was born to recuperate and to take care of her. [combined with independent clause]
REVISED	Vivian stayed out of school for three months after Laurel was born. She did so to recuperate and to take care of her. [turned into complete sentence]

Prepositional-phrase fragments

A prepositional phrase consists of a preposition, its object, and any modifiers of the object (see 7c3). Prepositional-phrase fragments contain neither subjects nor finite verbs. Usually you can best revise them by simply joining them to the independent clause containing the word they modify.

FRAGMENT	Several civic groups are sponsoring public debates. *With discussions afterward.*
REVISED	Several civic groups are sponsoring public debates with discussions afterward.

Noun-phrase fragments

A noun phrase consists of a noun together with any adjectives, phrases, or clauses that modify it (see 7c3). Noun-phrase fragments contain a subject but no finite verb, and they frequently appear before fragments containing a verb but no subject. You can best revise such fragments by combining them into one sentence containing both a subject *and* a verb.

FRAGMENTS	*His editorial making a plea for better facilities for severely handicapped children. Pointed out that these facilities are always located in poor areas.*
REVISED	In his editorial making a plea for better facilities for severely handicapped children, he pointed out that these facilities are always located in poor areas.
REVISED	His editorial making a plea for better facilities for severely handicapped children pointed out that these facilities are always located in poor areas.

Appositive-phrase fragments

An appositive phrase is a noun phrase that renames or describes another noun (see 7c3). You can revise appositive-phrase fragments by joining them to the independent clause containing the noun to which the appositive phrase refers.

FRAGMENT	One of our nation's most cherished dreams may be in danger. *The dream of a good education for every child.*
REVISED	One of our nation's most cherished dreams, the dream of a good education for every child, may be in danger.
REVISED	One of our nation's most cherished dreams may be in danger: the dream of a good education for every child. [In this revision, the use of the colon creates greater emphasis.]

16b

Revising compound-predicate fragments

A compound predicate consists of two or more verbs, along with their modifiers and objects, that have the same subject (see 7c2). Compound-predicate fragments occur when one part of this predicate is punctuated as a separate sentence although it lacks a subject. These fragments usually begin with a conjunction. You can revise them by attaching them to the independent clause that contains the rest of the predicate.

> FRAGMENT   They sold their house. *And moved into an apartment.*
>
> REVISED   They sold their house and moved into an apartment.

EXERCISE 16.2

Revise each of the following items to eliminate any sentence fragments, either by combining fragments with independent clauses or by rewriting them as separate sentences. Example:

> *Zoe looked close to tears. Standing with her head bowed.*
>
> *Standing with her head bowed, Zoe looked close to tears.*
>
> *Zoe looked close to tears. She was standing with her head bowed.*

1. Small, long-veined, fuzzy green leaves. Add to the appeal of this newly developed variety of carrot.

2. Living with gusto. That is what many Americans yearn for.

3. The region has dry, sandy soil. Blown into strange formations by the ever-present wind.

4. The climbers had two choices. To go over a four-hundred-foot cliff or to turn back. They decided to make the attempt.

5. Connie picked up the cat and started playing with it. It scratched her neck. With its sharp little claws.

6. Bush promoted one tax change. A reduction in the capital gains tax.

7. Trying to carry a portfolio, art box, illustration boards, and drawing pads. I must have looked ridiculous.

8. Organized crime has been able to attract graduates just as big business has. With good pay and the best equipment money can buy.

9. Joan Didion has investigated politics. And explored human emotions.

10. Wollstonecraft believed in universal public education. Also, in education that forms the heart and strengthens the body.

16c

Revising dependent-clause fragments

Unlike phrases, dependent clauses contain both a subject and a finite verb. Because they *depend* on an independent clause to complete their meaning, however, they cannot stand alone as grammatically complete sentences (see 7c4). Such clauses usually begin with a subordinating conjunction—such as *after, even though, if, whereas* (see 7b7)—or a relative pronoun—such as *who, which, that* (see 7b3). You can usually revise dependent-clause fragments either by combining the dependent clause with the independent clause that precedes or follows it or by deleting the subordinating word to create an independent clause.

FRAGMENT	*If a woman chooses a less demanding career track.* She sacrifices some earning potential.
REVISED	If a woman chooses a less demanding career track, she sacrifices some earning potential.
FRAGMENT	Eudora Welty grew up in Mississippi. *Whereas Alice Walker spent her childhood in Georgia.*
REVISED	Eudora Welty grew up in Mississippi, whereas Alice Walker spent her childhood in Georgia.
FRAGMENT	Injuries in automobile accidents occur in two ways. *When an occupant is hurt by something inside the car or when an occupant is thrown from the car.*
REVISED	Injuries in automobile accidents occur in two ways: when an occupant is hurt by something inside the car or when an occupant is thrown from the car.
REVISED	Injuries in automobile accidents occur in two ways. An occupant is hurt by something inside the car, or an occupant is thrown from the car.

EXERCISE 16.3

Identify all the sentence fragments in the following items, and explain why each is grammatically incomplete. Then revise each one in at least two ways. Example:

Controlling my temper. That has been one of my goals this year.

Controlling my temper has been one of my goals this year.

One of my goals this year has been controlling my temper.

1. When Rick was in the fifth grade. His parents often left him with his sister.
2. The protagonist comes to a decision. To leave his family.
3. Fear, one of the basic emotions people have experienced throughout time.
4. We were thankful for a hot shower. After a week in the wilderness.
5. I plan to buy a computer. Which will help me organize my finances.
6. Forster stopped writing novels after *A Passage to India*. One of the greatest novels of the twentieth century.
7. Sylvia Plath achieved new status. Because of *Ariel*, her final poems.
8. I loved *Beloved*. And knew Toni Morrison deserved the Nobel Prize.
9. The president appointed five members. Who drew up a set of bylaws.
10. One might say that rebellion is normal. Because the younger generation often rejects the ways of its elders.

THINKING CRITICALLY ABOUT FRAGMENTS

Reading with an Eye for Fragments

Identify the fragments in the passage below. What effect does the writer achieve by using fragments rather than complete sentences?

> On Sundays, for religion, we went up on the hill. Skipping along the hexagon-shaped tile in Colonial Park. Darting up the steps to Edgecomb Avenue. Stopping in the candy store on St. Nicholas to load up. Leaning forward for leverage to finish the climb up to the church. I was always impressed by this particular house of the Lord.   —KEITH GILYARD, *Voices of the Self*

Thinking about Any Fragments in Your Own Writing

Read through some essays you have written. Using the guidelines on p. 291, see if you find any sentence fragments. If you find any, can you recognize any patterns? Do you write fragments when you're attempting to add emphasis? Are they all dependent clauses? phrases? Note any patterns you discover (in your writing log, if you keep one), and make a point of checking your writing for them routinely. Finally, revise any fragments to form complete sentences.

17

Placing Modifiers Appropriately

MODIFIERS—*adjectives, adverbs, and the various kinds of phrases and clauses used as adjectives and adverbs—enrich writing by making it more concrete, vivid, and memorable. As a writer, you want to take full advantage of them. Look, for example, at the following sentence:*

> She wore the kind of clothes he liked, simple, unadorned and yet completely feminine, white gloves on Sundays, small black leather pocketbooks, carefully polished shoes, pretty small hats, a feather the only gay note on her best felt hat, and the seams in her stockings always straight.
> —ANN PETRY, *The Narrows*

This sentence could have stopped after the first clause. "She wore the kind of clothes he liked." Everything that follows is built on modifiers; they bring the sentence to life and help readers picture the clothes she wore.

To be effective, modifiers must be carefully placed and must refer clearly and unambiguously to some word or words in the sentence. In the above sentence, for example, completely *modifies* feminine; *if it were placed elsewhere in the sentence, we would have a different statement: "completely unadorned and yet feminine," perhaps. And look at the difference if* only *were placed somewhere else: white gloves "only on Sundays," for instance—or even "only white gloves on Sundays"!*

We often see modifiers used ineffectively, however, even in the work of professional writers, for modifiers are among the most difficult things to spot when editing. This chapter will examine three types of problem modifiers— misplaced, disruptive, and dangling—and ways of revising them.

EXERCISE 17.1

Maya Angelou relies heavily on modifiers in the following description of herself at an awkward age:

I was too tall and raw-skinny. My large extroverted teeth protruded in an excitement to be seen, and I, attempting to thwart their success, rarely smiled. Although I lathered Dixie Peach in my hair, the thick black mass crinkled and kinked and resisted the smothering pomade to burst free around my head like a cloud of angry bees.
— MAYA ANGELOU, *Singin' and Swingin' and Gettin' Merry Like Christmas*

Think for a few minutes about some of the awkward stages you remember going through. Brainstorm a bit by completing these thoughts: "I was too . . ." or "What I remember most about being fifteen was . . ." Spend ten minutes or so writing a brief description about yourself then. Underline all the words you recognize as modifiers, then revise your passage by eliminating them all. Compare the two versions, and think about what modifiers add to your writing.

17a

Revising misplaced modifiers

Misplaced modifiers are words, phrases, and clauses that cause ambiguity or confusion because they are not placed as close to the words they modify as they might be or because they could modify the words either before or after them.

1

Misplaced words and phrases

In the sentence *Softly I could hear the tumbleweeds rustling in the wind*, the adverb *softly* seems to modify *could hear*. Yet the writer obviously meant it to modify *rustling* (because one cannot hear "softly"). Such confusion can be avoided by placing a modifier close to the word or words to which it actually refers.

I could hear the tumbleweeds *softly* rustling in the wind.

I could hear the tumbleweeds rustling *softly* in the wind.

Be especially careful with the placement of **limiting modifiers** like *almost, even, hardly, just, merely, nearly, only, scarcely,* and *simply.* In general, these modifiers should be placed right before the words they modify. Putting such words in other positions may produce not just ambiguity but a completely different meaning. See the following, for example:

AMBIGUOUS   The court only hears civil cases on Tuesdays.

CLEAR	The court hears *only* civil cases on Tuesdays.
CLEAR	The court hears civil cases *only* on Tuesdays.

In the first sentence, placing *only* before the verb makes the meaning ambiguous. Does the writer mean that civil cases are the only cases heard on Tuesdays or that those are the only days when civil cases are heard? The other sentences each express one of these meanings clearly.

Phrases also should ordinarily be placed close to the words they modify. The most common type of phrase modifier, the prepositional phrase, usually appears right after the word it modifies. In the following sentences, note how misplaced prepositional phrases cause confusion:

MISPLACED	The runners stood ignoring the crowd in their lanes. [This sentence implies that the crowd was in the lanes.]
REVISED	The runners *stood in their lanes*, ignoring the crowd.
MISPLACED	She teaches a seminar this term on voodoo at Skyline College. [Surely the voodoo was not at the college.]
REVISED	She teaches *a seminar on voodoo* this term at Skyline College.

Participial phrases usually appear right before or after the words they modify. See how misplacing these phrases can lead to confusion.

MISPLACED	I pointed out the moose head to my guests mounted on the wall. [This sentence implies that the guests were mounted on the wall.]
REVISED	I pointed out to my guests the *moose head mounted on the wall*.
MISPLACED	Billowing from every window, we saw clouds of smoke. [People cannot billow from windows.]
REVISED	We saw *clouds of smoke billowing from every window*.

Everyday Use

You will find modifiers in abundance at any store, urging you to choose the *latest* swimsuits, *designer beach* towels, *Coppertone* lotion, and *sand* toys. In fact, you will find modifiers at work in many public places. Consider, for instance, the modifiers from a sign at a public beach: *strong* surf, *hidden* currents, *dangerous* waves, *no* lifeguard. Jot down some of the modifiers you see around you, and then bring them to class for discussion. What is the primary function of these modifiers—to provide information? to make a product sound more appealing? something else?

2

Misplaced clauses

Although you have more flexibility in the placement of dependent clauses than you have in the placement of modifying words and phrases, you should still try whenever possible to place them close to whatever word or phrase you wish them to modify. If you do not, unintended meanings can result.

MISPLACED	The trees trimmed in the shapes of animals that line the walks delight visitors. [Do animals line the walks?]
REVISED	The *trees that line the walks* are trimmed in the shapes of animals and delight visitors.
MISPLACED	Nixon told reporters that he planned to get out of politics after he lost the 1962 gubernatorial race. [The sentence implies that Nixon planned to lose the race.]
REVISED	*After he lost the 1962 gubernatorial race*, Nixon told reporters that he planned to get out of politics.

EXERCISE 17.2

Revise each of the following sentences by moving any misplaced modifiers so that they clearly modify the words they are intended to. Example:

Politicians are supported by the people when they propose sensible plans.

1. The tenor captivated the entire audience singing with verve.
2. The city almost spent two million dollars on the new stadium.
3. On the day in question, the patient was not normally able to breathe.
4. The clothes were full of holes that I was giving away.
5. Elderly people and students live in the neighborhood surrounding the university, which is full of identical tract houses.
6. Doctors recommend a new test for cancer, which is painless.
7. I went through the process of taxiing and taking off in my mind.
8. I knew that the investment would pay off in a dramatic way before I decided to buy the stock.
9. The bank offered flood insurance to the homeowners underwritten by the federal government.
10. Revolving out of control, the maintenance worker shut down the turbine.

3

Squinting modifiers

If a modifier can refer to *either* the word(s) before it *or* the word(s) after it, it is called a **squinting modifier**. For example:

SQUINTING Students who practice writing *often* will benefit.

The modifier *often* might describe either *practice* or *will benefit*. That is, the sentence might have either of the following meanings:

REVISED Students who *often practice* writing will benefit.

REVISED Students who practice writing *will often* benefit.

If a sentence could be read more than one way because of your placement of a modifier, put the modifier where it clearly relates to only a single term.

EXERCISE 17.3

Revise each of the following sentences in at least two ways. Move the squinting modifier so that it unambiguously modifies either the word(s) before it or the word(s) after it. Example:

The course we hoped would engross us completely bored us.

The course we hoped would completely engross us bored us.

The course we hoped would engross us bored us completely.

1. He remembered vividly enjoying the sound of Mrs. McIntosh's singing.
2. The mayor promised after her reelection she would not raise taxes.
3. The collector who owned the painting originally planned to leave it to a museum.
4. Doctors can now restore limbs that have been severed partially to a functioning condition.
5. The speaker said when he finished he would answer questions.

17b

Revising disruptive modifiers

Whereas misplaced modifiers confuse readers by appearing to modify the wrong word(s), **disruptive modifiers** interrupt the connections between parts of a grammatical structure or a sentence, making it hard for readers to follow the progress of the thought. Be careful not to place modifiers in such a way that they disrupt the normal grammatical flow of a sentence.

1

Modifiers splitting an infinitive

In general, do not split an infinitive by placing a modifier between the *to* and the verb. Doing so makes it hard for readers to recognize that the two go together.

| DISRUPTIVE | Hitler expected the British to fairly quickly surrender. |
| REVISED | Hitler expected the British *to surrender* fairly quickly. |

In some cases, however, a modifier sounds awkward in any other position. To avoid a split infinitive in such cases, it may be best to reword the sentence to eliminate the infinitive altogether.

| SPLIT | I hope *to* almost *equal* my last year's income. |
| REWRITTEN | I hope that I will earn almost as much as I did last year. |

2

Modifiers between the parts of a verb phrase

A verb phrase consists of a main verb together with one or more auxiliary verbs: *had studied, will be moving* (see 7c3). Modifiers consisting of one or even two or three adverbs can often appear between parts of a verb phrase without causing awkwardness: *He had very seldom actually fired a gun in the line of duty*. In general, however, do not interrupt a verb phrase with modifiers that are phrases or clauses.

DISRUPTIVE	Vegetables will, if they are cooked too long, lose most of their nutritional value.
REVISED	Vegetables *will lose* most of their nutritional value if they are cooked too long.
REVISED	If they are cooked too long, vegetables *will lose* most of their nutritional value.

3

Modifiers between a subject and a verb

Adjective phrases and clauses often appear between a subject and verb: *The books that the librarians had decided were no longer useful were discarded*. In general, however, do not use an adverb clause or phrase in this position; it disrupts the natural progression from subject to verb that readers expect.

DISRUPTIVE	The books, because the librarians had decided they were no longer useful, were discarded.
REVISED	The *books were discarded* because the librarians had decided they were no longer useful.

4

Modifiers between a verb and an object or a subject complement

In general, do not place an adverb phrase or clause between a verb and a direct object or subject complement, because readers expect the object or complement to follow directly after the verb.

DISRUPTIVE	He bought with his first paycheck a secondhand car.
REVISED	He *bought a secondhand car* with his first paycheck.
REVISED	With his first paycheck, he *bought a secondhand car.*

EXERCISE 17.4

Revise each of the following sentences by moving the disruptive modifier so that the sentence reads smoothly. Example:

> a
> *Aggressive individuals turned* |*during the 1980s*,|*to the real estate market.*

1. Eastern North America was, when Europeans arrived, covered in forest.
2. The exhibit, because of extensive publicity, attracted large audiences.
3. The architect wanted to eventually design public buildings.
4. Bookstores sold, in the first week after publication, fifty thousand copies.
5. The stock exchange became, because of the sudden trading, a chaotic circus.

17c

Revising dangling modifiers

Dangling modifiers are words (usually adverbs), phrases (prepositional or participial), and elliptical clauses (clauses from which a word or words have been left out) that modify nothing in particular in the rest of a sentence. They often seem to modify something that is suggested or implied but not actually present in the sentence. Such modifiers are called dangling because they hang loosely from the rest of the sentence, attached to no specific element. They frequently appear at the beginnings or ends of sentences. The following sentence appeared in a recent magazine article. Can you spot the dangling modifier? *Driving nonstop, Salishan Lodge is located two hours from Portland.*

To revise dangling modifiers, you can change the subject of the main clause so that the modifier clearly refers to it, or you can change the dangling modifier itself into a phrase or a nonelliptical clause that clearly modifies an existing part of the sentence. You could revise the sentence above to read, *Driving nonstop from Portland, you can reach Salishan Lodge in two hours.* Or, *If you drive nonstop from Portland, you can reach Salishan Lodge in two hours.*

1

Dangling words and phrases

DANGLING	Reluctantly, the hound was given away to a neighbor. [Was the dog reluctant, or was someone else who's not mentioned?]
REVISED	Reluctantly, *the family* gave away the hound to a neighbor.
DANGLING	As a young boy, his grandmother told stories of her years as a country schoolteacher. [His grandmother was never a young boy.]
REVISED	*As a young boy, he* heard his grandmother tell stories of her years as a country schoolteacher.
REVISED	*When he was a young boy*, his grandmother told stories of her years as a country schoolteacher.
DANGLING	Thumbing through the magazine, my eyes automatically noticed the perfume ads. [Eyes cannot thumb through magazines.]
REVISED	*In thumbing through the magazine,* I automatically noticed the perfume ads.
REVISED	My eyes automatically noticed the perfume ads *as I was thumbing through the magazine.*

EXERCISE 17.5

Revise each of the following sentences to correct the dangling phrases. Example:

a viewer gets

Watching television news, ̯an impression is given of constant disaster.

1. High ratings are pursued by emphasizing fires and murders.
2. Interviewing grieving relatives, no consideration is shown for their privacy.

3. To provide comic relief, heat waves and blizzards are attributed to the weather forecaster.

4. Chosen for their looks, the newscasters' journalistic credentials are often weak.

5. As a visual medium, complex issues are hard to present in a televised format.

2

Dangling elliptical clauses

DANGLING	A rabbit's teeth are never used for defense even when cornered. [Is it the teeth that are cornered?]
REVISED	*Even when cornered, a rabbit* never uses its teeth for defense.
REVISED	A rabbit's teeth are never used for defense, *even when the animal is cornered.*
DANGLING	Although a reserved and private man, everyone who met him seemed to like him. [The elliptical clause cannot refer to *everyone*.]
REVISED	*Although he was a reserved and private man*, everyone who met him seemed to like him.
REVISED	*Although a reserved and private man*, he seemed to be liked by everyone who met him.

EXERCISE 17.6

Revise each of the following sentences to correct any dangling elliptical clauses. Example:

While cycling through southern France, the Roman ruins impressed me.

I was impressed by
∧

1. However unhappy, my part-time job is something I have to put up with.

2. While attending a performance at Ford's Theater, Booth shot Lincoln.

3. A waiter's job can become very stressful when faced with a busy restaurant full of hungry people.

4. Dreams are somewhat like a jigsaw puzzle; if put together in the correct order, organization and coherence become obvious.

5. No matter how costly, my family insists on a college education.

⋙ *Editing misplaced or dangling modifiers*

1. Identify all the modifying words, phrases, and clauses in each sentence, and draw an arrow from each modifier to the word it modifies.

2. If a modifier is far from what it modifies, try to move the two closer together.

3. Then check to see if any modifier could be misunderstood to refer to a word other than the one it is intended to modify. If so, move the modifier so that it refers clearly to only the intended word.

4. If you cannot find a word to which the modifier refers, revise the sentence to supply such a word, or revise the modifier itself so that it clearly refers to a word already in the sentence.

THINKING CRITICALLY ABOUT MODIFIERS

Reading with an Eye for Modifiers

E. B. White was a master of precise wording, choosing—and positioning—his words with great care. Read the following sentences by White, paying attention to the limiting modifiers italicized in each one. Identify which word or words each one modifies. Then try moving the modifier to some other spot in the sentence, and consider how the meaning of the sentence changes as a result.

1. When we got back for a swim before lunch, the lake was exactly where we had left it, the same number of inches from the dock, and there was *only* the mere suggestion of a breeze.   –"Once More to the Lake"

2. Most of the time she *simply* rode in a standing position, well aft on the beast, her hands hanging easily at her sides, her head erect, her straw-colored ponytail lightly brushing her shoulders, the blood of exertion showing faintly through the tan of her skin.   –"The Ring of Time"

3. *Even* our new shoes seemed to be working out all right and weren't hurting much.   –"Twins"

4. It was, among other things, the sort of railroad you would occasionally ride *just* for the hell of it, a higher existence into which you would escape unconsciously and without hesitation.   –"Progress and Change"

Thinking about Your Own Use of Modifiers

Look at two pages of a draft (or refer to the description you did in Exercise 17.1), examining them for clear and effective modifiers. Can you identify any misplaced, disruptive, or dangling modifiers? Using the guidelines in this chapter, revise as need be. Then look for patterns—in the kinds of modifiers you use and in any problems you have placing them. Make a note of what you find.

18

Maintaining Consistent and Complete Grammatical Structures

ABOUT TWENTY YEARS AGO, a writing instructor who had studied thousands of student essays came to a simple but profound conclusion about many of the sentences in the essays. Though at first glance the sentences seemed incoherent or nonsensical, they actually fell into certain patterns. They could be better characterized, the instructor decided, either as (1) unsuccessful attempts to combine sentence structures that did not fit together grammatically or sensibly or as (2) sentences missing some element necessary to complete meaning. In fact, many writers who produce garbled sentences do so in an attempt to use complex and sophisticated structures. What look like "errors," then, may be steppingstones on a writer's way to greater stylistic maturity. This chapter will provide practice in recognizing such mixed or incomplete structures and, more important, in revising or building on them.

18a

Making grammatical patterns consistent

In writing, inconsistent structures can pose problems for both writers and readers. One such inconsistency, a **mixed structure**, results from beginning a sentence with one grammatical pattern and then switching to another one. The following sentence, for instance, starts out one way and ends another:

> **MIXED** The fact that I get up at 5:00 A.M., which explains why I'm always tired in the evening.

The sentence starts out with a subject (*fact*) followed by a dependent clause (*that I get up at 5:00 A.M.*). This structure should lead to a predicate to complete the independent clause begun by *The fact*, but instead the writer shifts to another dependent clause (*which explains why I'm always tired in the evening*). Thus the independent clause is never completed, and what results is a fragment. This fragment could be revised into a complete sentence in at least two ways.

REVISED	The fact that I get up at 5:00 A.M. explains why I'm always tired in the evening. [Deleting *which* changes the second dependent clause into a predicate.]
REVISED	I get up at 5:00 A.M., which explains why I'm always so tired in the evening. [Deleting *The fact that* makes the first dependent clause into an independent clause.]

EXERCISE 18.1

Assume you have been asked to edit the following notice (discovered in a New York grocery store). Look for at least two ways to make the sentences consistent.

For all workers who do not work on Wednesday will not receive their checks on Wednesday. Thursday is payday, and when you will receive your check. Thank you for your cooperation. —MANAGEMENT

Although most listeners would have little difficulty in following a speaker's intended meaning, failure to maintain consistent grammatical patterns often leads to confusion, especially in writing. If you have ever had mixed sentences pointed out in your writing, proofread carefully for them. Look especially at the relationships between subject and predicate and between clauses. Here are some other examples of mixed sentences.

MIXED	Because hope was the only thing left when Pandora finally closed up the mythical box explains why we never lose hope no matter how bad life gets. [The adverb clause beginning with *Because* is followed not by an independent clause but by a predicate (beginning with *explains*), which lacks a subject.]
REVISED	Because hope was the only thing left when Pandora finally closed up the mythical box, we never lose hope no matter how bad life gets. [Deleting *explains why* changes the original predicate into an independent clause to which the adverb clause can be attached.]
MIXED	Some of the things that went on this year, I don't know how any other team survived. [This sentence begins with a subject, *some of the things that went on this year*, leading the reader to expect a predicate to complete the thought. Instead, it is followed by another subject.]

REVISED   In light of some of the things that went on this year, I
               don't know how any other team survived. [Adding *in
               light of* subordinates the first part of the sentence so that
               there's now one clear subject and predicate and thus one
               complete thought.]

REVISED   Some of the things that went on this year make me
               wonder how any other team survived. [Changing *I don't
               know* to *make me wonder* eliminates one subject.]

18b

Matching subjects and predicates

Another kind of mixed sentence occurs when a subject and predicate
(7c1 and 7c2) do not fit together grammatically or simply do not make sense
together. Such a mismatch, called **faulty predication**, often appears in a
sentence where a subject complement and its subject do not make sense
together. Many cases of faulty predication result from using forms of *be*
when another verb would be stronger.

FAULTY   A characteristic that I admire is a person who is generous.

This sentence says that a person is a kind of characteristic. To make its
subject and predicate consistent, you could change either the subject or the
complement to make them both refer to either persons or characteristics,
or you could rewrite the sentence to change the verb.

Everyday Use

If you listen carefully to the conversations around you, you will hear
inconsistent and incomplete grammatical structures, particularly in
lively or heated discussion. For instance:

*"The Bulls are . . . They must be the best team in . . . not in the
league even . . . in the country."*
*"Wait till the Lakers take them. Because you know the Magic Men,
they make magic happen, in a SWEEP."*

In the flow of informal conversation, such structures pose few problems for speakers and listeners. To verify this statement, listen
carefully for inconsistent and incomplete structures in conversations, and think for a moment about what helps you understand
them with ease.

REVISED   A *characteristic* that I admire is *generosity.*

REVISED   A *kind of person* that I admire is *one who is generous.*

REVISED   I *admire* a person who is generous.

The verb *be* also leads to faulty predication when it is used before an adverb clause opening with *when* or *where.*

FAULTY   A stereotype is when someone characterizes a group unfairly.

Although you will often hear constructions like this in conversation, an adverb clause used as a subject complement in academic or other formal writing is considered weak. To revise the sentence above, you can change the complement to a noun that will grammatically match the subject *stereotype*, or you can rewrite the sentence to change the verb.

REVISED   A *stereotype* is an unfair *characterization* of a group.

REVISED   A *stereotype characterizes* a group unfairly.

REVISED   *When someone characterizes a group unfairly,* he or she *creates* a stereotype.

Using *the reason (that)* . . . *is because* causes inconsistency between the subject and the subject complement. It is another form of faulty predication.

FAULTY   The reason I like to play soccer is because it provides aerobic exercise.

REVISED   I like to play soccer *because* it provides aerobic exercise. [Deleting *the reason (that)* leaves an independent clause to which the *because* clause can be attached.]

REVISED   *The reason* I like to play soccer *is that* it provides aerobic exercise. [Changing *because* to *that* makes the adverb clause into a noun clause that can function as a subject complement. In other words, *that it provides aerobic exercise* renames *reason*, as a subject complement should.]

Faulty predication also occurs with verbs other than *be.* For example:

FAULTY   The rules of the corporation expect employees to be properly dressed. [*Rules* cannot expect anything.]

REVISED   As its rules state, the corporation expects employees to be properly dressed.

REVISED   The rules of the corporation require that employees be properly dressed.

FAULTY	The success of *Playboy* was widely imitated by other men's magazines. [*Success* cannot be imitated.]
REVISED	*Playboy* was widely imitated by other men's magazines.
REVISED	The success of *Playboy* led other men's magazines to imitate it.

EXERCISE 18.2

Revise each of the following sentences in two ways to make its structures consistent in grammar and meaning. Example:

The fact that our room was cold we put a heater between our beds.

Because our room was cold, we put a heater between our beds.

The fact that our room was cold led us to put a heater between our beds.

1. My interest in a political career would satisfy my desire for public service.
2. To determine your rank, your supervisor should be consulted.
3. The reason air-pollution standards should not be relaxed is because many people would suffer.
4. By not prosecuting white-collar crime as vigorously as violent crime encourages white-collar criminals to think they can ignore the law.
5. Herman Melville's stature is unchallenged, including not only *Moby-Dick* but also many legendary short stories.
6. A confluence is where two rivers join to form one.
7. Hawthorne's short stories are experiences drawn from his own life.
8. When Oedipus suddenly realizes he has killed his father and married his mother causes a "shock of recognition."
9. One controversial element of the curriculum has been colleges with a required course in Western culture.
10. The European discovery of Australia became a penal colony for Britain.

18c

Using elliptical structures carefully

Sometimes writers can avoid repetition and gain emphasis by using **elliptical structures**, in which they omit certain words or phrases in compound structures, as the following sentences by Eudora Welty demonstrate. Omitted words are in brackets.

That bell belonged to the figure of Miss Duling as though it grew directly out of her right arm, as wings grew out of an angel or a tail [grew] out of the devil.

Her gaze was in general sweeping, then suddenly at the point of concentration [it was] upon you.

These sentences are clear and effective because the omitted words match those in the other part. In the following sentence, however, the omitted verb does not match the one that occurs in the first part, and so the sentence is incomplete and must be revised to include both verbs.

INCOMPLETE   His skills are weak, and his performance only average.

REVISED   His skills *are* weak, and his performance *is* only average.

18d

Checking for missing words

In the rush of composing, when the brain almost always runs ahead of the hand, writers sometimes accidentally leave out words, especially short ones like articles, pronouns, and prepositions. The best way to catch such inadvertent omissions is to proofread carefully, reading each sentence slowly—and aloud. If at all possible, read to someone else. If a word or phrase is missing, one of you should hear its omission.

INCOMPLETE   The professor's heavy German accent made difficult for the class understand her lectures.

REVISED   The professor's heavy German accent made *it* difficult for the class *to* understand her lectures.

Especially in speaking, we often omit *that* before a noun clause: *Yesterday, I realized* [*that*] *I was hopelessly behind in my work.* In this instance, the omission does not obscure meaning. If any possible confusion could arise, however, be sure to include the *that* in writing.

UNCLEAR   I noticed many motorcycles from the 1940s had become classics. [Readers at first assume *many motorcycles* is the object of *noticed* rather than the subject of the subordinate clause.]

REVISED   I noticed *that* many motorcycles from the 1940s had become classics.

18e

Making comparisons complete, consistent, and clear

As you revise your writing, check comparative structures closely, remembering that when you compare two or more things, the comparison must be *complete, logically consistent*, and *clear*. (See 12d for more on comparative and superlative forms.)

Complete comparisons

INCOMPLETE	I was embarrassed because my parents were so different. [Different from what?]
REVISED	I was embarrassed because my parents were so different *from those of my friends.*

Logically consistent comparisons

ILLOGICAL	Woodberry's biography is better than Fields. [This sentence compares *biography*, a book, with *Fields*, a person.]
REVISED	Woodberry's biography is better than *the one by* Fields.
REVISED	Woodberry's biography is better than *Fields's is.*

Clear comparisons

UNCLEAR	Ted always felt more affection for his brother than his sister. [Did Ted feel more affection for his brother than his sister did or more affection for his brother than he felt for his sister?]
REVISED	Ted always felt more affection for his brother than *he did for* his sister.
REVISED	Ted always felt more affection for his brother than his sister *did.*

≫ *Editing comparisons*

1. Look first for places where things are compared. Look for words like *different* or *prefer* as well as for comparative and superlative forms like *more, most, better, best, larger, oldest,* and so forth. Underline each comparison. *(Continued)*

2. Are both things being compared specifically stated? If not, revise to include the one that is missing.

3. Are the things being compared logically consistent—for example, is the setting of a film compared with the setting of another film rather than with the other film itself? If the comparison is not logical, revise to make it so.

4. Could the comparison be misunderstood in any way? If so, revise to eliminate the ambiguity.

EXERCISE 18.3

Revise each of the following sentences to eliminate any inappropriate elliptical constructions; to make comparisons complete, logically consistent, and clear; and to supply any other omitted words that are necessary for meaning. Example:

> Most of the candidates are bright, and one ⟨is⟩ brilliant.

1. My new stepmother makes my father happier.

2. Argentina and Peru were colonized by Spain, and Brazil by Portugal.

3. She argued that children are even more important for men than women.

4. Was the dictatorship in Iraq any worse than many other countries?

5. The personalities of marijuana smokers are different from nonsmokers.

EXERCISE 18.4   Revising for Consistency and Completeness

Revise this paragraph to make every sentence grammatically and logically consistent and complete.

The reason I believe the United States should have a military draft is because draft would make us better citizens. By requiring the same sacrifice from every young person would make everyone feel part a common effort. In addition, a draft is fairer. When an army is made up of volunteers come mostly from the poor and minority groups. During the Persian Gulf War, news reports showed blacks were overrepresented among the troops, largely because their economic options were more limited than young whites and the military thus more attractive as a career. I also feel that women should be subject to the draft. A quality that the military needs is soldiers who are dedicated, and women soldiers have shown that they are more dedicated to their jobs than men. The requirements of a modern army also need skills that more women possess. Equality is when both sexes have equal responsibilities as well as equal opportunity.

THINKING CRITICALLY ABOUT CONSISTENCY AND COMPLETENESS

Reading with an Eye for Inconsistent Structures

Mixed and inconsistent structures appear even in the writing of professionals. Read the following sentences carefully, identifying the problem in each and offering revisions.

The U.S. military attaché to Greece was killed today on the small street where he lived by a car bomb that blew his armor-plated car off the road as he was driving to work. —ASSOCIATED PRESS

Inert, apparently harmless gases used in refrigeration deplete the protective ozone layer; they increase the amount of deadly ultraviolet radiation from the sun that reaches the surface of the Earth, destroying vast numbers of unprotected microorganisms that lie at the base of a poorly understood food chain—at the top of which precariously teeter we. —CARL SAGAN

Thinking about Any Mixed or Incomplete Structures in Your Writing

Read over three or four paragraphs from a draft or completed essay you have written recently, checking for mixed sentences and incomplete or missing structures. Revise the paragraphs to correct any problems you find. If you find any, do you recognize any patterns? If so, make a note of them for future reference (in your writing log, if you keep one).

Part Four

Sentences: Making Stylistic Choices

―――――――― ⟨⟩ ――――――――

19. Constructing Effective Sentences *318*

20. Creating Coordinate and Subordinate
Structures *328*

21. Creating and Maintaining Parallel
Structures *340*

22. Varying Sentence Structures *349*

23. Creating Memorable Prose *362*

19

Constructing Effective Sentences

PUT MOST SIMPLY, *effective sentences have two main characteristics: they empha-size ideas clearly, and they do so as concisely as possible.*

But how do writers create such sentences? One way is by carrying out what philosopher Kenneth Burke calls "the arousal and fulfillment of desire." Substituting the more mundane expectations *for Burke's deliberately provocative* desire *illustrates what we mean: an* **effective sentence** *is one that creates or appeals to certain expectations and then either fulfills them or—as is sometimes the case—startles or amuses or alarms readers by* not *fulfilling them. Look at the following sentence:*

> I sometimes think of the reader as a cat, endlessly fastidious, capable, by turns, of mordant indifference and riveted attention, luxurious, recumbent, and ever poised. — PATRICIA HAMPL, "Memory and Imagination"

This sentence fulfills expectations by following up on the image of the reader as cat with cat imagery ("endlessly fastidious," "luxurious"). In addition, the sentence is structured so as to pull its readers along, saving its most powerful image for the end: the catlike reader, "ever poised."

The writer of the following sentence, on the other hand, surprises readers by breaking *expectations:*

> He was a tall, dark, and handsome creep.

In this sentence, the writer plays on readers' expectations with the loaded words tall, dark, *and* handsome—*only to undercut those expectations with the final* creep.

You may want to try using such an element of surprise to create effective sentences. The rest of this chapter, however, will focus on two basic devices writers use to fulfill rather than break expectations: emphasis *and* conciseness.

> *Everyday Use*
>
> You can see the importance of emphasis and conciseness in directions, particularly those on medicines. Here, for instance, are some directions found on one common prescription drug.
>
> *Take one tablet daily. Some nonprescription drugs may aggravate your condition, so read all labels carefully. If any include a warning, check with your doctor. Refill prescription only until 12/12/97.*
>
> These directions aim to state their message as emphatically (to relay important information) and concisely (to fit on a small label) as possible. Look around for other directions that do the same—on health products, traffic signs, and so on. Bring the sentences you find to class to compare with those your classmates found, and see if together you can draw any conclusions about what makes language concise and emphatic.

EXERCISE 19.1

Study Patricia Hampl's sentence on the preceding page. Then write a sentence of your own that imitates hers, beginning as she does: "I sometimes think of _____ as _____ , . . ." Decide whether or not the sentence fulfills expectations set up by the opening words. Example:

> *I sometimes think of television as a shrew, incessantly noisy, demanding attention at all times to its advertising and mindless programming, insistently shrill, forever heckling.*

Emphasizing main ideas

Effective sentences put the spotlight on main ideas, letting readers know which elements are most important. We call this spotlighting of significant words and ideas **emphasis**. Careful control of the emphasis in each sentence will make your writing easier and more enjoyable to read. This section focuses on the ways you can emphasize main ideas by putting them in closing and opening positions and by arranging them in climactic order.

1

Using closing and opening positions for emphasis

When you read a sentence, what are you most likely to remember? Other things being equal, you remember the end. This is the part of the sentence that should move the writing forward by providing new information, as it does in the following example:

To protect her skin, she took *plenty of sun-block lotion.*

A less emphatic but still important position in a sentence is the opening, which hooks up the new sentence with what has come before.

When Rosita went to the beach, she was anxious not to get a sunburn. *To protect her skin,* she took plenty of sun-block lotion.

In this example, *to protect her skin* connects the new sentence to *anxious not to get a sunburn* in the sentence before. The second sentence would lose emphasis if the key words, *plenty of sun-block lotion,* were buried in the middle, as in the following version:

To protect her skin, she took *plenty of sun-block lotion,* and she also planned to stay under a beach umbrella most of the time.

Placing relatively unimportant information in the memorable closing position of a sentence can have the effect of undercutting proper emphasis or even of giving more emphasis to the closing words than you intend. Consider the following example:

She contributed $500,000 to the campaign last month.

Revised to emphasize the contribution, the sentence reads,

Last month she contributed $500,000 to the campaign.

To emphasize the amount of the contribution even more, the sentence could be reworded this way.

Last month she gave the campaign committee $500,000.

2

Using climactic order

Presenting ideas in **climactic order** means arranging them in order of increasing importance, power, or drama: building to climax. The following sentences show climactic order at work:

Dissidents risk social rejection, forced relocation, long imprisonment, and almost certain death.

After they've finished with the pantry, the medicine cabinet, and the attic, [neat people] will throw out the red geranium (too many leaves), sell the dog (too many fleas), and send the children off to boarding school (too many scuffmarks on the hardwood floors).

        — SUZANNE BRITT, "Neat People vs. Sloppy People"

Each of the preceding examples derives much of its power from the sequencing of its details. If the first sentence concluded with "long imprisonment" rather than "almost certain death," it would not make such an emphatic statement. Similarly, the second example saves its most dramatic item for last, making its point forcefully. The following sentence fails to achieve strong emphasis because its verbs are not sequenced in order of increasing power:

   UNEMPHATIC   Soap operas assault our eyes, damage our brain cells, and offend our ears.

   REVISED   Soap operas offend our ears, assault our eyes, and damage our brain cells.

≫ *Editing for sentence emphasis*

As you revise a draft, follow these steps to make sure that each sentence emphasizes the ideas you *want* emphasized.

1. Identify the word or words you want to receive special emphasis. If those words are buried in the middle of the sentence, revise the sentence to change their position, remembering that the end and the beginning are generally most emphatic.

2. Note any sentences that include a series of three or more words, phrases, or clauses. Check to see whether the items in the series could be arranged in climactic order and, if so, whether they are. If they could be but are not, decide whether the sentence would be stronger with climactic order, and rearrange if necessary.

See how the sentence below can be revised using these steps:

For completely false "reasons," we in the Student Senate have for years been saddled with the burdens, which we're tired of, of low budgets, no real legislative power, and a depressing room to meet in.

The main point the writer wants to emphasize, that the Student Senate is tired of being saddled with poor conditions and no power, is obscured by unemphatic placement in the middle of the sentence.

(Continued)

> **REVISED FOR EMPHASIS**
>
> *We in the Student Senate are tired of having been saddled for years, for completely false "reasons," with the burdens of low budgets, no real legislative power, and a depressing room to meet in.*
>
> The items in the series at the end of the sentence do not seem to be in any particular order, even though they could be. If the meeting room is least important and the lack of power most important, the revision might read as follows:
>
> **REVISED FOR CLIMACTIC ORDER**
>
> *We in the Student Senate are tired of having been saddled for years, for completely false "reasons," with the burdens of a depressing room to meet in, low budgets, and no real legislative power.*

EXERCISE 19.2

Revise each of the following sentences to highlight what you take to be the main or most important ideas. Example:

> *Theories about dinosaurs run the gamut—simple lizards, fully adapted warmblooded creatures, hybrids of coldblooded capabilities.*

1. All medical papers, whether initial investigation, presentation of final statistics, or reports on work in progress, must undergo rigorous scrutiny.
2. Also notable is the image of chrysanthemums throughout the story.
3. Nancy Kerrigan went on to receive the silver medal in figure skating at the 1994 Winter Olympics, despite the preceding media circus.
4. The presence of the Indian in these movies always conjures up destructive stereotypes of bloodthirsty war parties, horse thieves, and drunkenness.
5. Victorian women were warned that if they smoked, they would become sterile, grow a moustache, die young, or contract tuberculosis.

19b

Being concise

In general, effective sentences are as **concise** as possible. More often than not, making a point in the fewest possible words is a hallmark of effective prose. Look at the following sentence:

Her constant and continual use of vulgar expressions with obscene meanings indicated to her pre-elementary supervisory group that she was rather
deficient in terms of her ability to interact in an efficient manner with
peers in her potential interaction group.

Why write that when you could instead write the following?

Her constant use of four-letter words told the day-care workers she might
have trouble getting along with other four-year-olds.

This example demonstrates how radical a change can be wrought by snipping
away at the underbrush of *unnecessary* words. Doing so involves several kinds
of changes: eliminating redundant words, eliminating buzzwords, replacing
wordy phrases, and simplifying grammatical structures.

1

Eliminating redundant words

Sometimes writers add words for emphasis, saying that something is
large *in size* or red *in color* or that two ingredients should be combined
together. The italicized words are **redundant**, or unnecessary for meaning,
as are the ones below.

REDUNDANT	*Compulsory* attendance at assemblies *is required.*
REVISED	Attendance at assemblies *is required.*
REDUNDANT	The auction featured *contemporary* "antiques" *made recently.*
REVISED	The auction featured *contemporary* "antiques."
REVISED	The auction featured "antiques" *made recently.*

2

Eliminating buzzwords

Buzzwords are another category of words that can usually be eliminated. These words might sound meaningful, perhaps even important, but
too often contribute no real meaning. In general, they should be deleted
or replaced.

COMMON BUZZWORDS

angle, area, aspect, case, character, element, factor, field, kind, nature,
scope, situation, type

Many modifiers are used in such an all-purpose way that they have become
buzzwords, adding no meaning to a statement.

absolutely, awesome, awfully, central, definitely, fine, great, literally, major, quite, really, very

Taken together, buzzwords can build up whole sentences that say almost nothing at all.

The scope of this thing, the importance of this field, is so absolutely vital that I get really overwhelmed at the significance of the situation.

Because buzzwords tend to make writing dull as well as wordy, use them sparingly. When you cannot simply delete them, try to think of a more specific term that says what you mean.

The housing situation can have a really significant impact on the social aspect of a student's life.

Housing can strongly influence a student's social life.

3

Replacing wordy phrases

Many wordy phrases can be reduced to a single word or two. Doing so will make your writing more concise and thus easier to read.

at the present time	now/today
at that point in time	then
in the event that	if
form a consensus of opinion	agree
exhibit a tendency to	end to

I see no reason at this point in time why we should not rely, as has often been the case in the past, on the good offices of the mayor.

We should rely now, as we have in the past, on the help of the mayor.

Sometimes writers resort to this kind of wordiness because they think it sounds more formal, more official. Such might have been the case in what has come to be a classic story about the dangers of wordiness.

A plumber wrote to the Federal Bureau of Standards that he had found hydrochloric acid did a fine job of clearing out his clogged drains.

The bureau answered: "The effectiveness and efficiency of hydrochloric acid is indisputable, but the corrosive or detrimental residue is incompatible with metallic permanence."

The plumber replied he was delighted the bureau agreed with him.

Then the bureau wrote: "We cannot and must not assume responsibility or admit to culpability in event of the production of toxic and noxious residue with hydrochloric acid and, therefore, recommend you use an alternate or secondary procedure."

Again the plumber said he was delighted the bureau agreed.

At last the bureau wrote, with admirable unity, emphasis, and concision, a reply that spoke volumes to the plumber: "Don't use hydrochloric acid. It eats the hell out of the pipes."

As this example indicates, corporate, bureaucratic, academic, and scientific writing is a major source of wordiness. Although the writer may think such language sounds impressive, it usually sounds only pompous. (See 27a3.)

4

Simplifying grammatical structures

Using the simplest grammatical structures possible will tighten and strengthen your sentences considerably. In the following example, notice how conciseness results from reducing an adjective clause to an appositive phrase, deleting a grammatically unnecessary *to be*, and reducing an adverb phrase to a one-word adverb:

WORDY	Kennedy, who was only the second Roman Catholic to be nominated for the presidency by a major party, had to handle the religion issue in a delicate manner.
REVISED	Kennedy, only the second Roman Catholic nominated for the presidency by a major party, had to handle the religion issue delicately.

In the following example, reducing an adverb clause to an elliptical form and combining two sentences produces one concise sentence:

WORDY	When she was questioned about her previous job, she seemed nervous. She also tried to change the subject.
REVISED	When questioned about her previous job, she seemed nervous and tried to change the subject.

Other ways to simplify grammatical structures include using strong verbs and nouns, avoiding expletive constructions, and using the active rather than the passive voice. These methods are discussed in Chapter 23.

>> *Editing for conciseness*

1. Look for redundant words. If you are unsure about a word, read the sentence without it; if your meaning is not affected, leave the word out.

2. Look for buzzwords—words like *aspect* or *factor* or *type*—and take them out. Does your meaning change? If so, can you replace the buzzword with a more meaningful term?

3. Look for meaningless modifiers—words like *definitely, quite,* and *very.* Unless your meaning is not clear without them, leave them out.

4. Do you use any wordy phrases? If you do, see if you can replace them with a single word—instead of *because of the fact that,* try *because*; rather than *for the purpose of,* try *for.*

5. Finally, look for grammatical structures that might be simplified: adjective clauses that could be reduced to appositive phrases, expletive constructions that could be eliminated, and consecutive sentences with the same subject or predicate that could be combined into one sentence.

EXERCISE 19.3

Make each of the following sentences clear and concise by eliminating unnecessary words and phrases. Example:

> *summarize.*
> Let me ~~fill you in on the main points of the overall picture here.~~

1. At the present time, many different forms of hazing occur, such as various forms of physical abuse and also mental abuse.

2. Many people have a tendency toward the expansion of their sentences by the superfluous addition of extra words that are not really needed for the meaning of the sentences.

3. One of the major problems that is faced at this point in time is that there is world hunger.

4. After I stopped the practice of exercising regularly, I became ten pounds heavier in weight in a relatively short amount of time.

5. There are numerous theories that have been proposed by scientists as to why dinosaurs reached the point of becoming extinct.

EXERCISE 19.4   Revising for Emphasis and Conciseness

Revise the following paragraph so that each sentence emphasizes its main idea and is as concise as possible. Combine or divide sentences if necessary.

At the present time, one of the most serious problems that faces Americans in the area of public policy is the increasing rise in the cost of health care, which has occurred over an extended period of time. One major aspect of the severe crisis in health care costs is that more and more expensive medical technology is being developed and marketed to doctors and hospitals. Even hospitals that are small in size want the latest kind of diagnostic device. The high cost of this expensive equipment is passed on to consumers, who are the patients. It is then passed on to insurance companies. Therefore, many employers are charging their employees more for health insurance because they themselves are having to pay higher and higher premiums. Others are reducing the employees' coverage to a significant extent. Meanwhile, almost 40 million Americans suffer from the condition of a lack of any health insurance. In the event that they have an illness or an injury, they must go to a hospital emergency room. In large cities, emergency rooms are being overwhelmed by people seeking treatment for everything from life-threatening gunshot wounds to broken bones.

THINKING CRITICALLY ABOUT SENTENCES

Reading with an Eye for Sentence Style

Here are two sentences from "A Sweet Devouring," Eudora Welty's essay about the pleasures of reading. Each sentence makes a powerfully emphatic statement. Read each one, and decide how Welty achieves such strong emphasis. Then read something by a favorite writer, looking for strong, emphatic sentences. Bring in one or two sentences to compare with those chosen by your classmates.

1. The pleasures of reading itself—who doesn't remember?—were like those of a Christmas cake, a sweet devouring.
2. And then I went again to the home shelves and my lucky hand reached and found Mark Twain—twenty-four volumes, not a series, and good all the way through.

Thinking about Your Own Sentences

Find two or three paragraphs you have written recently, and study them with an eye for buzzwords. Using 19b2 for guidance, eliminate meaningless words such as *aspect, factor, quite,* or *very.* Compare notes with one or two classmates to see what buzzwords, if any, you all tend to use. Finally, make a note of those you use (in your writing log, if you keep one) so that you can avoid them in the future.

20

Creating Coordinate and Subordinate Structures

CREATING EFFECTIVE SENTENCES *calls on a writer to act as a conductor, directing the arrangement and flow of verbal passages just as the conductor of an orchestra does with musical passages. Such effective orchestration very often involves creating sentences that use* coordinate *and* subordinate *structures.* **Coordinate structures** *give essentially equal importance to two or more words, phrases, or clauses, often linking them with coordinating conjunctions like* and *or* but. **Subordinate structures***, on the other hand, create different levels of significance, stressing some ideas by expressing them in independent clauses or with key nouns or verbs and subordinating others by putting them in dependent clauses, phrases, or single words.*

Learning to use different kinds of coordinate and subordinate structures will increase your sentence repertoire and allow you to write varied, interesting, and effective sentences. Look at the following sentences:

> Kit went through the new part of the library to the old part.
> He walked around for a while.
> Then he went to the periodicals section.
> He started looking at the *Times* on microfilm.

We could choose to combine these sentences in several ways.

USING COORDINATION

Kit went through the new part of the library to the old part, and he walked around for a while; then he went to the periodicals section and started looking at the *Times* on microfilm.

USING SUBORDINATION

After going through the new part of the library to the old part and walking around for a while, Kit went to the periodicals section, where he started looking at the *Times* on microfilm.

In the example that uses coordination, all four actions—going through the new part of the library to the old part, walking around, going to the periodicals section, and looking at the Times—*are given the same emphasis by being placed in three independent clauses, the last of which has a compound predicate.*

The second combination gives a different emphasis, suggesting that Kit's destination, the periodicals section, is most important. The action of his going there is expressed in an independent clause, whereas the other three actions are given less emphasis by being placed in a prepositional phrase (with compound gerund-phrase objects) and in a dependent clause.

In addition to indicating emphasis, coordination and subordination can create special, sometimes dramatic effects in writing. As a writer, you must often decide whether to use coordination, subordination, both, or neither, depending on which structure provides the emphasis and effect you want to achieve. This chapter will furnish you with some guidelines for using these structures appropriately.

Everyday Use

If you think about how you use coordination and subordination every day, you may notice a difference in your spoken and written language. In speech, people tend to prefer coordination, often using *and* and *so* as all-purpose connectors. For instance:

I'm going home now, and I'll see you later.

The relationship between these two clauses may be clear in speech, which occurs in some larger context and provides clues with voice, facial expressions, and gestures. But in writing, the relationship—and thus the meaning—might be less than perfectly clear. It could, for instance, have at least two rather different meanings.

Because I'm going home now, I'll see you later.

I'm going home now because I'll see you later.

The differences between these two sentences are expressed by subordination, and so they demonstrate well the reason subordinate structures are valued—and sometimes needed—in writing: they make logical connections explicit.

Make a point of listening to yourself talk, and see if you rely on coordinate structures (listen for words like *and*, *so*, and *but*). Jot down a few "coordinated" sentences, and then decide whether any of them would, in writing, be more appropriately phrased with subordination.

EXERCISE 20.1

The following sentence uses coordination to link two ideas. Revise the sentence to use subordination instead. What effect does this change have on the sentence's meaning? Then compare your sentence with ones done by some classmates. Did you all subordinate the same clause?

Many young children love to climb trees, but my daughter was a cautious and grown-up eleven.   – SUSAN ALLEN TOTH, "Free to Just Be"

20a

Using coordination to relate equal ideas

What can you say about the following passage?

> It was my birthday today, and I took cupcakes to school, and I wore a birthday crown, and we ate cupcakes, and we sang "Happy Birthday," and I sat in the middle, and I'm six years old.

We realize early on that the writer is a child—or someone writing from a child's point of view. Because the passage mentions cupcakes and school and a crown, we make this assumption even before we find out, in the last clause, that the writer is six years old. But the *style* of this passage, as well as its content, helps identify the writer. We get a clue from the seven short independent clauses strung together like beads with the coordinating conjunction *and*, a style typical of young writers who are learning to sequence events in a story. Note that aside from the clue "I'm six years old" at the very end of the sentence (generally an emphatic spot), we are given no grammatical signals to tell us how these clauses rank in importance. Were the cupcakes most significant to the writer? the birthday crown? We cannot tell because the coordinate structure makes all the clauses grammatical equals.

Not all coordination must sound like "Run, Spot, run," however. When used well, coordinate structures relate separate but equal elements, making clear the emphasis given to different ideas. The precise relationship is stated in the element that links the ideas, usually a coordinating conjunction (*and, but, for, nor, or, so, yet*) or a semicolon. The following sentences by N. Scott Momaday all use coordination, but note that the precise relationship between clauses differs in each sentence, as expressed in the connecting element.

> They acquired horses, *and* their ancient nomadic spirit was suddenly free of the ground.

There is perfect freedom in the mountains, *but* it belongs to the eagle and the elk, the badger and the bear.

No longer were they slaves to the simple necessity of survival; they were a lordly and dangerous society of fighters and thieves, hunters and priests of the sun.   — N. Scott Momaday, *The Way to Rainy Mountain*

Using coordination for special effect

Coordination can be used to create special effects, as in a passage by Carl Sandburg describing the reaction of the American people to Abraham Lincoln's assassination.

> Men tried to talk about it and the words failed and they came back to silence.
> To say nothing was best.
> Lincoln was dead.
> Was there anything more to say?
> Yes, they would go through the motions of grief and they would take part in a national funeral and a ceremony of humiliation and abasement and tears.
> But words were no help.
> Lincoln was dead.
>   — Carl Sandburg, *Abraham Lincoln: The War Years*

Together with the other short simple sentences, the coordinate clauses, phrases, and words in the first and fifth sentences create a powerful effect. Everything in the passage is grammatically equal, flattened out by the pain and shock of the death. In this way, the sentence structure and grammar mirror the dazed state of the populace. The short sentences and clauses are almost like sobs that illustrate the thought of the first sentence, that "the words failed."

The formal name for the conspicuous use of conjunctions is **polysyndeton**, from Greek *poly* ("many") and *syndeton* ("connectives"). An additional example:

> Satan pursues his way. And swims, or sinks, or wades, or creeps, or flies.
>   — Milton, *Paradise Lost*

Milton's use of *or* between the verbs piles up images of movement, giving the impression that Satan can use *any* kind of movement and still cannot be stopped.

> He [the writer] must teach himself that the basest of all things is to be afraid; and, teaching himself that, forget it forever, leaving no room in his workshop for anything but the old verities and truths of the heart, the

old universal truths lacking which any story is ephemeral and doomed—
love and honor and pity and pride and compassion and sacrifice.

         – WILLIAM FAULKNER, Nobel Prize Acceptance Speech

Here the repetition of *and* between lofty abstract nouns creates a solemn
rhythm, almost like the tolling of a bell.

> Are you familiar with Motel 8? It's a chain of cheesy cheap motels across
> the South—twenty dollars a night gets you peeling beaverboard walls *and*
> thin pink blankets. There's no phone in the room, *but* a TV set that's
> always tuned to the Nashville Channel, *and* an air conditioner that's always
> got a screw or three loose *and* vibrates like a 747 on takeoff. You see piles
> of emptied cigarette butts in the parking lot, *and* always cigarette burns
> on the table, *and* more cigarette burns on the carpet, *and* a poorly repaired
> hole in the wall where some redneck put his fist through it in anger at his
> pregnant sixteen-year-old wife who didn't wanna go out to the Ponderosa.

Here the use of *and* and *but* results in a catalog of colorful, if somewhat
unsavory, details. By stringing together images in this way, the author presents them in a kind of heap, which contributes to the overall impression
of the Motel 8.

⟫ *Editing for coordination*

1. Identify all uses of *and, but, for, or, nor, so, yet,* and semicolons.
2. How many coordinate structures have you identified? If you find
   only a few, consider whether any other ideas or other elements
   should be linked in some way.
3. Look on either side of each conjunction or semicolon. Do the words,
   phrases, or clauses that it links really need to be connected? Are
   they *equally important* ideas? If not, revise to eliminate the coordinate
   structure or to substitute a subordinate one.
4. Finally, is the relationship between any coordinate elements clear
   and logical? If not, try substituting a different coordinating structure.
   In sentences with semicolons, consider adding a conjunctive adverb
   (*certainly, however, therefore,* and so on—see 7b7 for a more complete list) to clarify the relationship between ideas.

Revising for more effective coordination

    See how the following passage can be analyzed and revised using the
preceding guidelines.

Watching television is a popular way to spend leisure time and makes viewers apathetic. Many people come home tired in the evening, and so they turn on the TV to relax. They may intend to watch just the news, but then a game show comes on next, and they decide to watch a little of that, or they get too comfortable to get out of the recliner, and they end up spending the whole evening hypnotized by electronic sounds and images. This pattern becomes a habit for too many Americans. These people become indifferent to their real lives. Their family members and friends come to seem less real to them than glamorous and vivid television personalities. Their daily existence seems dull, too, compared with the dramatic or hilarious events on the screen.

Watching television is a popular way to spend leisure time, but excessive viewing makes people apathetic and indifferent to their real lives. Many people who come home tired in the evening turn on the TV to relax. Although they may intend to watch just the news, they decide to watch a little of the game show that comes on next, or they get too comfortable to get out of the recliner. Consequently, they end up spending the whole evening hypnotized by electronic sounds and images. This pattern becomes a habit for too many Americans. Their family members and friends come to seem less real to them than glamorous and vivid television personalities; their daily existence seems dull compared with the dramatic or hilarious events on the screen.

In the first sentence, the relationship of the ideas connected by *and* is confusing. What does being a popular way to spend leisure time have to do with being apathetic? The revision better relates the clauses by changing *and* to *but*. It also adds information from later in the paragraph to explain "apathetic."

In the next sentence, *and* gives equal emphasis to coming home and turning on the TV. Subordinating the clause about coming home puts needed emphasis on the more important information, about the TV. The next five independent clauses are connected with coordinating conjunctions. Although their ideas are related, stringing them together creates a jerky, monotonous effect and does not make clear to the reader that some of them are much more important than others. The revision turns two of the clauses into subordinate structures and the last one, the most important, into a separate sentence beginning with a conjunctive adverb.

Finally, the last two sentences are very closely related, but the only signal of the relationship is the word *too*. The revision strengthens the connection by combining these sentences into one, with a semicolon between the clauses.

EXERCISE 20.2

Using the principles of coordination to signal equal importance or to create special emphasis, combine and revise the following twelve short sentences into several longer and more effective ones. Add or delete words as necessary.

The bull-riding arena was fairly crowded.
The crowd made no impression on me.
I had made a decision.
It was now time to prove myself.
I was scared.
I walked to the entry window.
I laid my money on the counter.
The clerk held up a Stetson hat filled with slips of paper.
I reached in.
I picked one.
The slip held the number of the bull I was to ride.
I headed toward the stock corral.

20b

Using subordination to distinguish main ideas

Subordination provides the means of distinguishing major points from minor points or bringing in supporting context or details. If, for instance, you put your main idea in an independent clause, you might then put any lesser ideas in dependent clauses, phrases, or even single words. Look at the following sentence, which shows the subordinated point in italics:

Mrs. Viola Cullinan was a plump woman *who lived in a three-bedroom house somewhere behind the post office.*
— MAYA ANGELOU, "My Name Is Margaret"

In this sentence, the dependent clause adds information about Mrs. Cullinan. While the information is important, it is grammatically subordinate to the independent clause, which carries the main idea: *Mrs. Viola Cullinan was a plump woman.*

Notice that the choice of what to subordinate rests with the writer and depends on the intended meaning. Angelou might have given the same basic information differently: *Mrs. Viola Cullinan, a plump woman, lived in a three-bedroom house somewhere behind the post office.* Subordinating the information about Mrs. Cullinan's size to that about her house would have resulted in a slightly different meaning, of course. As a writer, you must think carefully about where you want your emphasis to be and subordinate accordingly.

Besides adding information, subordination also helps establish logical relationships among facts. These relationships are often specified by subordinating conjunctions—words such as *after, because,* or *so.* (See 7b7.) Look, for example, at two more sentences by Maya Angelou, shown with the subordinate clauses italicized and the subordinating conjunctions underlined.

> I left the front door wide open <u>so</u> *all the neighbors could hear.* She usually rested her smile until late afternoon <u>when</u> *her women friends dropped in and Miss Glory, the cook, served them cold drinks on the closed-in porch.*
> – MAYA ANGELOU, "My Name Is Margaret"

Subordination can be used to combine short sentences in ways that signal logical relationships. For example:

SEPARATE SENTENCES

The children opened the cage.

The parrot flew out of the window.

I had forgotten to close it.

COMBINED SENTENCE

When the children opened the cage, the parrot flew out of the window, *which* I had forgotten to close.

Depending on what grammatical structures you use to subordinate, you can call attention to a less important element of a sentence in various ways, as the following series demonstrates.

> The parks report was persuasively written. It contained five typed pages. [no subordination]
>
> The parks report, *which contained five typed pages,* was persuasively written. [clause]
>
> The parks report, *containing five typed pages,* was persuasively written. [participial phrase]
>
> The *five-page* parks report was persuasively written. [adjective]
>
> The parks report, *five typed pages,* was persuasively written. [appositive]

EXERCISE 20.3

Combine each of the following sets of sentences into one sentence that uses subordination to signal the relationships among ideas. Example:

I was looking over my books.
I noticed that Burr was missing.
This book is a favorite of my roommate's.

While I was looking over my books, I noticed that Burr, one of my roommate's favorite books, was missing.

1. I walked into the shelter.
   Men, women, and children were slumped against the wall.
   Shopping carts containing families' belongings lay on their sides.

2. Barbra Streisand announced her first concert tour in years.
   Ticket sales were advertised.
   Fans lined up as many as forty-eight hours in advance.

3. We had dug a seventy-foot ditch.
   My boss would pour gravel into the ditch.
   I would level the gravel with a shovel.

4. *Working* was written by Studs Terkel.
   It is an important book.
   It examines the situation of the American worker.

5. The scenery there is beautiful.
   The mountains have caps of snow.
   The lakes are deep and full of fish.
   The pastures are green.
   It is an ideal spot to spend spring break.

Using subordination for special effect

Carefully used subordination can create powerful effects. Some particularly fine examples come from Martin Luther King, Jr. In the following passage, he piles up dependent clauses to gain emphasis for his main statement, given in the independent clause. This emphasis is heightened by the repetition of the subordinating conjunction *when* to suggest forcefully "why we find it difficult to wait."

Perhaps it is easy for those who have never felt the stinging darts of segregation to say, "Wait." But *when* you have seen vicious mobs lynch your mothers and fathers at will and drown your sisters and brothers at whim; *when* you have seen hate-filled policemen curse, kick, and even kill your black brothers and sisters; . . . *when* you have to concoct an answer for a five-year-old son who is asking: "Daddy, why do white people treat colored people so mean?"; *when* you take a cross-country drive and find it necessary to sleep night after night in the uncomfortable corners of your automobile because no motel will accept you; . . . *when* your first name

becomes "nigger," your middle name becomes "boy" (however old you are) and your last name becomes "John," and your wife and mother are never given the respected title "Mrs."; . . . *when* you are forever fighting a degenerating sense of "nobodiness"—then you will understand why we find it difficult to wait.
— MARTIN LUTHER KING, JR., "Letter from Birmingham Jail"

Look now at a student example that uses subordination:

> *Though* dogs are messy and hard to train, *though* they chew up my shoes and give me the blues, *though* they howl like wolves but jump at their own shadows, *though* they eat me out of house and home—still, I love them all.

A dependent clause can also be used to create an ironic effect, if it somehow undercuts the independent clause. Probably no American writer was better at using this technique than Mark Twain. In a tongue-in-cheek commencement address, Twain once opened a paragraph with this sentence (which you can see in context in 14f as an example of a shift in tone).

> Always obey your parents, *when they are present.*
> — MARK TWAIN, "Advice to Youth"

In undercutting the parental authority asserted in the independent clause, this dependent clause creates irony—and makes us laugh. Now look at a student writer's use of the same technique:

> Never eat fattening foods—*unless you are hungry.*

Like coordination, however, subordination can be used excessively. When too many subordinating structures, usually dependent clauses, are strung together, readers have trouble keeping track of the main idea expressed in the independent clause. Look, for example, at the following:

TOO MUCH SUBORDINATION

> Philip II sent the Spanish Armada to conquer England, which was ruled by Elizabeth, who had executed Mary because she was plotting to overthrow Elizabeth, who was a Protestant, whereas Mary and Philip were Roman Catholics.

The long string of subordinate clauses in this sentence makes the relationship of the ideas hard to follow. It also makes the idea in the independent clause at the beginning hard for readers to remember. See how changing one of the dependent clauses to the independent clause in a new sentence and reducing two others to appositive phrases makes the relationship of ideas clearer.

REVISED

Philip II sent the Spanish Armada to conquer England, which was ruled by Elizabeth, a Protestant. She had executed Mary, a Roman Catholic like Philip, because Mary was plotting to overthrow her.

Editing your use of subordination

1. Underline the main ideas in each paragraph, perhaps underlining major ideas twice, lesser ones once.

2. If the most important ideas are not in independent clauses, try revising so that they are.

3. Try subordinating the less important ideas by putting them in dependent clauses or phrases.

4. Do any sentences contain more than three dependent clauses strung together? If so, does the main idea of the sentence get lost?

5. Examine any subordinating conjunctions you use—words like *although, if,* and *unless* (see 7b7)—to see that they express the correct relationship between clauses.

Revising for more effective subordination

Study the following passage about Edgar Allan Poe's "William Wilson," a strange tale about a young man who meets his double.

> In the years at the academy, the two William Wilsons shared a bizarre relationship. The second Wilson established himself as equal to the first. He was equal both in the classroom and on the playground. The first Wilson was used to feeling superior to his schoolmates, so he was quite disturbed at the thought of having an equal. He was especially disturbed that this equal had the same name and birthdate.

This passage depends heavily on simple sentences and simple coordination. Underlining the most important ideas indicates what might be subordinated to them, and the revision changes three of the less important ideas into a pair of prepositional phrases, an adjective clause, and an appositive phrase (all shown in italics).

> In the years at the academy, the two William Wilsons shared a bizarre relationship. The second Wilson established himself as equal to the first, *both in the classroom and on the playground.* The first Wilson, *who was used to feeling superior to his schoolmates,* was quite disturbed at the thought of having an equal, *especially one with the same name and birthdate.*

EXERCISE 20.4

Revise the following paragraph, using coordination and subordination where appropriate to clarify the relationships between ideas.

> I stayed with my friend Louise. She owns a huge, mangy wolf. It is actually a seven-eighths wolf cross. The poor creature is allergic to everything. It looks like a shabby, moth-eaten exhibit of a stuffed wolf in a third-rate museum. Louise and Bill feed it rice and raw potatoes. It slavers all over everything. It never goes out of the house. It sleeps on the beds. They are covered with animal hair. It makes no sounds. It just looks at you with those sunken, wild eyes. It is not dangerous or ferocious. It is just completely miserable. This animal should never have been born. It's trying to tell you that with every twitch.

THINKING CRITICALLY ABOUT COORDINATION AND SUBORDINATION

Reading with an Eye for Coordination and Subordination

Read over the first draft of "The Smart One," in 3f, paying special attention to the coordination and subordination. Do you notice any patterns—is there some of each? more of one than the other? Analyze one paragraph, identifying the coordination and subordination. Are they used appropriately? If not, revise the paragraph following the guidelines in this chapter.

Thinking about Your Own Use of Coordination and Subordination

Analyze two paragraphs from one of your drafts. Do the independent clauses contain the main ideas? How many dependent clauses do you find? Should the ideas in the dependent clauses be subordinate to the ones in the independent clauses? Following the advice in this chapter, revise the paragraphs to use coordination and subordination effectively. What conclusions can you draw about your use of coordination and subordination? Note them down (in your writing log, if you keep one).

21

Creating and Maintaining Parallel Structures

PARALLEL GRAMMATICAL STRUCTURES form many of our most familiar phrases: sink or swim, rise and shine, shape up or ship out. *But* **parallelism,** *expressing parallel elements in the same grammatical form, goes far beyond such clichés and, in fact, characterizes some of the most elegant passages in our language. Look, for example, at how E. B. White uses parallel structures to describe the enchantment of watching a bareback circus rider practicing her act:*

> The enchantment grew *not out of anything that happened* or *was* performed *but out of something that seemed* to go round and around and around with the girl, attending her, a steady gleam in the shape of a circle—a ring *of ambition, of happiness, of youth.*
>
> – E. B. WHITE, "The Ring of Time"

Just as the young woman goes "round and around and around," balanced easily on her horse, so the sentence circles rhythmically too, balanced by a series of parallel phrases and clauses. Read the sentence aloud, and you will hear the effect of those parallel structures rocking gently back and forth as does the horse in the ring. This chapter will help you use parallelism to create pleasing rhythmic effects in your own writing.

21a

Using parallel structures in a series

All items in a series should be in parallel form—all nouns, all prepositional phrases, all adverb clauses, and so on. Such parallelism makes a series both graceful and easy to follow.

The quarter horse *skipped, pranced,* and absolutely *sashayed* onto the track. [verbs]

Three subjects guaranteed to cause a fight are *politics, religion,* and *money.* [nouns]

The car rolled *down the hill, over the lawn,* and *into the swimming pool.* [prepositional phrases]

As more and more antismoking laws are passed, we see legions of potential nonsmokers *munching Nicorette, gnawing peppermints, chewing pencils, knitting sweaters,* or *practicing self-hypnotism.* [participial phrases]

Pushing a pen or pencil, pounding a typewriter, or *punching a word processor* just does not appeal to me. [gerund phrases]

When parallel elements are *not* presented in parallel grammatical form, the result can be awkward and even difficult to follow.

NONPARALLEL   The duties of the job included baby-sitting, house-cleaning, and the preparation of the meals.

PARALLEL   The duties of the job included *baby-sitting, house-cleaning,* and *preparing the meals.*

Lists

Items in a list should also be parallel in structure. Notice the lack of parallelism in the following list:

1. Coffee *to be made* only by library staff.
2. Coffee service *to be closed* at 4:00 P.M.
3. Doughnuts *to be kept* in cabinet.
4. No faculty members *should handle* coffee materials.

The fourth item on the list is not parallel with the others because it is a full sentence, not a phrase. Rewritten to maintain parallelism, this item could read: *Coffee materials <u>not to be handled</u> by faculty members.*

A formal outline should also be parallel in form. (See 3e.)

EXERCISE 21.1

Using two of the example sentences in 21a as models, write two sentences of your own that include a series of parallel phrases.

Everyday Use

If you are in the habit of reading bumper stickers, you have probably seen parallelism at work in everyday language. Here are a couple of bumper-sticker messages we've seen recently.

Children on board; parents on Valium.
Save the trees—ax the loggers.

Note down some examples of parallel structures you see—on bumper stickers, T-shirts, wherever. Why do you think messages of this sort are often written in parallel form? A good way to explore this question might be by revising one of the parallel structures you find to make it *not* parallel. Does one version better catch your attention and stick in your mind?

21b

Using parallel structures with pairs

One effective use of parallel structures occurs in the pairing of two ideas. The more nearly parallel the two structures are, the stronger the connection between the ideas will be. Parallel structures are especially appropriate when two ideas are being compared or contrasted.

> History became popular, and historians became alarmed.
> — WILL DURANT

> We die. That may be the meaning of life. But we *do* language. That may be the measure of our lives. — TONI MORRISON

When two clauses in a sentence express compared or contrasted ideas in exactly or almost exactly parallel structures, they produce a **balanced sentence**, one with two parts that "mirror" each other. Balanced sentences create an especially forceful impression.

> Mankind must put an end to war, or war will put an end to mankind.
> — JOHN F. KENNEDY

> There is much in your book that is original and valuable—but what is original is not valuable, and what is valuable is not original.
> — SAMUEL JOHNSON

With coordinating conjunctions

In general, use the same grammatical structure on both sides of any of the coordinating conjunctions—*and, but, or, nor, for, so, yet.*

We performed *whenever folks would listen* and *wherever they would pay.*

When elements connected by a coordinating conjunction are not parallel in form, the relationship of the elements can be hard to see.

NONPARALLEL	Consult a friend *in your class* or *who is good at math.*
PARALLEL	Consult a friend *who is in your class* or *who is good at math.*
PARALLEL	Consult a friend who *is in your class* or *is good at math.*

With correlative conjunctions

Use the same structure after both parts of a correlative conjunction—*either . . . or, both . . . and, neither . . . nor, not . . . but, not only . . . but also, just as . . . so, whether . . . or.*

The organization provided both *scholarships for young artists* and *grants for established ones.*

NONPARALLEL	I wanted not only *to go away to school* but also *to New England.*
PARALLEL	I wanted not only *to go away to school* but also *to live in New England.*

EXERCISE 21.2

Complete the following sentences, using parallel words or phrases in each case. Example:

> The wise politician promises the possible, effects the unavoidable, and accepts the inevitable.

1. Before we depart, we must _____, _____, and _____.
2. My favorite pastimes include _____, _____, and _____.
3. We must either _____ or _____.
4. I want not only _____ but also _____.
5. Graduates find that the job market _____, _____, and _____.

EXERCISE 21.3

Revise the following sentences to eliminate any errors in parallel structure. Example:

> *caning*
> I enjoy skiing, playing the piano, and ~~I cane~~ chairs.

1. I remember entering the stark canyon in North Dakota, searching the rubble by day, sleeping in a tent by night, and at last discovered dinosaur bones.

2. I will always remember how the girls dressed in green plaid skirts and the boys wearing green plaid ties.

3. It was a question of either reducing their staff, or they had to somehow find new customers for their baked potatoes.

4. To need a new pair of shoes and not being able to afford them is sad.

5. I'll never forget the good times we had—skiing, the swims, and especially that you taught me the basics of how to wind-surf.

6. Too many students come to college only for fun, to find a husband or wife, or in order to put off having to go to work.

7. There are two types of wallflowers: the male wallflower is known as the nerd, and the female, who is known as the skeeve.

8. Her job was to show new products, help with sales, and an opportunity to be part of advertising.

9. The Greek system not only provides the individual with a circle of friends but also it contributes to the development of leadership skills.

10. Stress can result in low self-esteem, total frustration, being unable to sleep, nervous breakdown, or eventually in suicide.

21c

Including all necessary words

In addition to making parallel elements grammatically similar, be careful to include any words—prepositions, articles, verb forms, and so on—that are necessary for clarity, grammar, or idiom.

CONFUSING	We'll move to a town in the Southwest or Mexico. [To a town in Mexico or to Mexico in general?]
CLEAR	We'll move *to a town in the Southwest* or *to Mexico.*
CLEAR	We'll move to a town *in the Southwest* or *in Mexico.*

UNGRAMMATICAL	I had never before and would never again see such a sight. [*Had . . . see* is not grammatical.]
GRAMMATICAL	I *had never before seen* and *would never again see* such a sight.

21d

Using parallel structures for emphasis and effect

Parallel structures can help a writer emphasize the most important ideas in a sentence. Look at the following sentence:

> I would like to promise her that she will grow up with a sense of her cousins and of rivers and of her great-grandmother's teacups, would like to pledge her a picnic on a river with fried chicken and her hair uncombed, would like to give her *home* for her birthday, but we live differently now and I can promise her nothing like that.
>
> – JOAN DIDION, "On Going Home"

The first two parallel phrases, *would like to promise her . . .* , *would like to pledge her . . .* , provide a series of specific concrete details and images that leads up to the general statement in the last phrase, that Didion would like to give her daughter a sense of "home." Although Didion could have stated this general point first and then gone on to illustrate it with concrete details, she achieves greater emphasis by making it the last in a series of parallel structures arranged in climactic order. (See 19a for more on emphasis.)

Besides emphasizing main ideas, parallel structures can create a number of different stylistic effects. One of these is orderliness, a sense of steady or building rhythm, as in the following sentence:

> Most police work is concerned with scared people who have been bitten by dogs, frantic people whose children have run away from home, old people who have no one to talk to, and impatient people whose first response to any situation is to "call the cops."

Note here how the repetition of the parallel phrases *scared people . . . , frantic people . . . , old people . . . , impatient people . . .* builds a rhythm, or beat, that leads us to expect more of the same.

> At work, he may have time to gulp down a cup of coffee if the dining halls are running smoothly, if all the workers show up, and if the boss is not asking questions.

This sentence creates an impression of somewhat desperate activity as it piles up the three parallel *if* clauses.

The Wild Man process involves five basic phases: Sweating, Yelling, Crying, Drum-Beating, and Ripping Your Shirt Off Even if It's Expensive.
— JOE BOB BRIGGS, "Get in Touch with Your Ancient Spear"

This sentence is made more emphatic and intense by the parallelism.

≫ Editing for parallelism

1. Look for series of three or more items in the same sentence, and make all items parallel in structure. (21a) If there is some item you'd like to emphasize, try putting it at the end of the series. (21d)

2. Now look for places where two ideas are compared, contrasted, or otherwise paired in the same sentence. Often these ideas will appear on either side of *and, but, or, nor, for, so, yet* or after each part of a correlative conjunction (*both . . . and, either . . . or, neither . . . nor, not only . . . but also, whether . . . or, just as . . . so*). Revise if necessary to make both ideas parallel. (21b)

3. Be sure that you have included all words—articles, prepositions, the *to* of the infinitive, and so on—necessary for clarity. (21c)

4. Be sure all items in lists are parallel in form.

EXERCISE 21.4

Underline the parallel structures in the following passage. Then use the passage as a model to create a passage that uses parallelism in a similar way. You might begin such a passage with "At the _____ of the room, ..."

At the back of the room, standing on a furry white rug, was the long banquet table, dressed in damask, accented by groups of thin silver candlesticks bearing white candles, and laden with lovely food: cold chicken, lobster, candied yam fruit combinations, potato salad in a great golden dish, corn sticks, a cheese fluff in spiked tomato cups, fruit cake, angel cake, sunshine cake.
— GWENDOLYN BROOKS, *Maud Martha*

USING SOURCES
Maintaining Parallelism in Headings

Parallel structures are particularly important in the headings and sub-headings of reports, research projects, and long essays. In addition to serving as guideposts for your readers, headings divide complex or lengthy material into manageable segments. In adding headings, keep in mind the following details about parallelism:

- If you have more than one level of heading and subheading, each level should be parallel in form. You might center one level, underline another, and so on. Whatever form you decide on, be sure that all the headings in each level have the same form.

- At each level, headings should also be parallel in wording—all nouns, all gerunds, all infinitive phrases, and so on.

EXERCISE 21.5   Revising for Parallelism

Revise the following paragraph to maintain parallelism and to supply all words necessary for clarity, grammar, and idiom in parallel structures.

> Growing up in a large city provides a very different experience from a suburban childhood. Suburban children undoubtedly enjoy many advantages over those who live in a city, including lawns to play ball on, trees for climbing, and often the schools are better. However, in recent years many people raised in the suburbs but who moved to large cities as young adults are deciding to bring up their own children in an urban setting. Their reasons for doing so include what they consider the cultural advantages of the city, the feeling that they will be able to spend more time with their children if they do not have to commute so far to work, and also they want to expose the children to a greater diversity of social and economic groups than most suburbs offer. Just as their own parents left the city for the space and calm of suburbia, so crowds and excitement are why today's parents are returning to it. Wherever they bring up their children, though, parents have never nor will they ever find utopia.

THINKING CRITICALLY ABOUT PARALLELISM

Reading with an Eye for Parallelism

Read the following paragraph about a bareback rider practicing her circus act, and identify all the parallel structures. Consider what effect they create on you as a reader, and try to decide why the author chose to put his ideas in such overtly parallel form. Try imitating the next-to-last sentence, the one beginning *In a week or two.*

> The richness of the scene was in its plainness, its natural condition—of horse, of ring, of girl, even to the girl's bare feet that gripped the bare back of her proud and ridiculous mount. The enchantment grew not out of anything that happened or was performed but out of something that seemed to go round

and around and around with the girl, attending her, a steady gleam in the shape of a circle—a ring of ambition, of happiness, of youth. (And the positive pleasures of equilibrium under difficulties.) In a week or two, all would be changed, all (or almost all) lost: the girl would wear makeup, the horse would wear gold, the ring would be painted, the bark would be clean for the feet of the horse, the girl's feet would be clean for the slippers that she'd wear. All, all would be lost.

– E. B. WHITE, "The Ring of Time"

Thinking about Your Own Use of Parallelism

Read carefully several paragraphs from a draft you have recently written, noting any series of words, phrases, or clauses. Using the guidelines on p. 346, determine whether they are parallel, and if not, revise them for parallelism. Then reread the paragraphs, looking for places where parallel structures would add emphasis or clarity, and revise accordingly. Can you draw any conclusions about your use of parallelism? Make a note of them (in your writing log, if you keep one).

22

Varying Sentence Structures

ROW UPON ROW OF TREES identical in size and shape may appeal at some level to our sense of orderliness, but in spite of that appeal the rows soon become boring. Constant uniformity in anything, in fact, soon gets tiresome; perhaps variety is the spice of life. Certainly that is true in sentence structures, where sameness can result in dull, listless prose.

The truth of this maxim was illustrated anew not long ago in a college classroom discussion of one student's essay. The group had worked on the essay for most of an hour, correcting errors, reorganizing paragraphs, clarifying the major points. Finally, one person said, "Okay, okay—but it's still boring." All of the others, including the author, agreed. But they were stuck. The group could not come up with any new ideas and was about ready to give up when one student exclaimed, "I've got it! Look at these sentences. They all look about the same length!"

And they were. In fact, impossible as it may sound, every sentence in the essay was between twenty-two and twenty-five words long. Once the students realized this, they could begin to work again, carving some of the sentences into very short ones and combining others to create new rhythms. The essay took on new life as its boring sameness faded away.

This chapter will examine ways to use the traditional foes of boring sentences—variety in length, in openings, and in grammatical, functional, and rhetorical patterns.

EXERCISE 22.1

Look at a piece of your writing. Count the words in each sentence to see how much your sentences vary in length. Choose one paragraph, and spend ten or fifteen minutes working to vary sentence length. Bring both versions to class.

22a

Varying sentence length

The situation described in the introduction illustrates perfectly the need for varying sentence length. Doing so not only makes prose more readable and interesting but also creates a pleasing rhythmic effect, what some students call "flow."

Deciding how and when to vary and balance sentence length is not always easy, however. How short is too short? How long is too long? Is there a "just right" length for a particular sentence or idea?

These questions are difficult to answer because the answers depend on, among other things, the writer's purpose, intended audience, and topic. A children's story, for instance, may call for mostly short sentences while an article on nuclear disarmament in the *Atlantic* may call for considerably longer ones. In other words, in different situations either very long or very short sentences can be effective.

1

Using short sentences

Very short sentences can often pack a powerful punch. Study the following famous short sentences, and see if you agree that each owes much of its power to its brevity and that more words would detract.

Nice guys finish last.	Let them eat cake.
Love conquers all.	War is hell.

The following passage from a speech illustrates how effective a series of short sentences and other short structures—including sentence fragments—can be.

> What treaty that the whites have kept has the red man broken? Not one. What treaty that the white men ever made with us have they kept? Not one. When I was a boy the Sioux owned the world; the sun rose and set on their land; they sent ten thousand men to battle. Where are the warriors today? Who slew them? Where are our lands? Who owns them?
> – SITTING BULL, *Touch the Earth*

Notice how Sitting Bull's short questions, clauses, and fragments build a rhythm that gives power to his indictment of the white world. Repeated short sentences, if used with awareness of their effect, can go far beyond "See Spot run" to create a rhythmic beat and cadenced dignity.

2

Using long sentences

In contrast to short sentences, long sentences are particularly useful for presenting a set of complex, interlocking ideas. The following paragraph shows how a series of long sentences can be used effectively in this way:

> Femininity pleases men because it makes them appear more masculine by contrast; and, in truth, conferring an extra portion of unearned gender distinction on men, an unchallenged space in which to breathe freely and feel stronger, wiser, more competent, is femininity's special gift. One could say that masculinity is often an effort to please women, but masculinity is known to please by displays of mastery and competence while femininity pleases by suggesting that these concerns, except in small matters, are beyond its intent. Whimsy, unpredictability and patterns of thinking and behavior that are dominated by emotion, such as tearful expressions of sentiment and fear, are thought to be feminine precisely because they lie outside the established route to success.
>
> – SUSAN BROWNMILLER, *Femininity*

Each of the three long sentences encapsulates the complex relationships between femininity and masculinity and between women and men that Brownmiller is seeking to explore. Short sentences would probably not work as effectively here because they could not adequately express the complexity of the ideas being presented.

Everyday Use

Very short "capsule" reviews usually contain varied sentence structures, perhaps to keep readers' attention with a snappy, fast-paced description. A *Newsweek* column included the following brief review:

Thelma & Louise *looks like an* Easy Rider *for women. A good idea. But this isn't going to have men lining up in droves or cheering for more.*

The writer of this review varies sentence length by using a three-word fragment between two longer sentences and varies openings as well, beginning one sentence not with the subject but with *but*. This variety helps make the brief synopsis easy to read and remember.

Study some "capsule" reviews in a magazine or newspaper (or on TV), noting the variety of sentences used. Bring a few examples to class to compare with those found by classmates. Can you draw any conclusions about the effect of sentence variety on readers?

3

Alternating short and long sentences

Although series of short and long sentences can both be effective in individual situations, frequent alternation in sentence length characterizes much memorable writing. After one or more long sentences that express complex ideas or images, the pith of a short sentence can be refreshing and arresting. For example:

> The fire of, I think, five machine-guns was pouring upon us, and there was a series of heavy crashes caused by the Fascists flinging bombs over their own parapet in the most idiotic manner. It was intensely dark.
>
> – GEORGE ORWELL, *Homage to Catalonia*

Similarly, a long sentence that follows several short ones can serve as a climax or summation that relaxes the tension or fulfills the expectation created by the series, giving readers a sense of completion. For example:

> But it is under siege, too. Santa Fe, so recently hardly more than a remote and rather secretive village, is chic these days. The smart, the modish, the merely rich move in. The haven is embattled. The old hands watch thoughtfully as Santa Fe, *dear* Santa Fe, slowly but inexorably changes its character—as the condominiums spring up over the foothills, as the Soak Hot-Tub Club offers its twelve hot-tub suites with individual stereo and mood lighting, as downtown land reaches $100,000 an acre— as the triviality of things, the cuteness, the sham and the opportunism, spreads like a tinsel stain across the town.
>
> – JAN MORRIS, "Capital of the Holy Faith"

Notice the difference between these two passages, one of which contains sentences of fairly uniform length and the other of which varies sentence length. For example:

UNIFORM LENGTHS

The house is a fixer-upper, of course. For the past two days, I've been fixing things. It seems like the past two decades. I've been crawling about in the basement, which is dirt-floored, trying to learn to fix copper plumbing. The people renting the house last winter froze and burst the pipes. As a result, I have to put in all new stuff, learning as I go. With five-foot headroom, it's a real joy to be playing with torch and hot solder down there. I climb around oozing soil pipes from another era. I crouch Quasimodo-like, measuring, cutting, squatting, slouching, until my back is permanently bent. I have been picking spiders out of my beard, and my clothes are indescribable.

VARIED LENGTHS

The house is a fixer-upper, of course, and so for the past two days (it seems like the past two decades), I've been fixing things, crawling about in the basement—dirt-floored, naturally—trying to learn to fix copper plumbing. What a nightmare! The people renting the house last winter froze and burst the pipes, and so I have to put in all new stuff. I'm learning as I go. With five-foot headroom, it's a real joy to be playing with torch and hot solder down there, climbing around oozing soil pipes from another era, crouching Quasimodo-like, measuring, cutting, squatting, slouching. My back is permanently bent. My beard is full of spiders. My clothes are indescribable.

In the second version, the writer uses coordination and subordination to combine the first four sentences of the first version into one long sentence that connects the main ideas of a "fixer-upper," doing the fixing, and crawling about the basement. He then adds a very short exclamatory sentence that both sums up the ideas in the first sentence and points ahead to the rest of the passage. Next he combines two closely related ideas, about burst pipes and the installation of new ones, into one sentence of medium length, changing the participial phrase *learning as I go* into a separate short sentence. The next three sentences of the original version, all dealing with the ordeal of working in the basement, are combined into one long sentence. Finally, a dependent clause and the two short clauses of a compound sentence are separated into three short, parallel sentences (see Chapter 21), which give a blunt, hammering effect to the writer's expression of his complaints.

⧸⧸⧸ *Editing to vary sentence length*

1. Count the words in each sentence, and underline the longest and shortest sentences in each paragraph.

2. If the difference between the longest and shortest sentences is fairly small—say, five words or fewer—consider revising the paragraph to create greater variety in length. Do not, however, change sentences arbitrarily. Think about the ideas you want to emphasize, and try to arrange your sentence lengths in a way that emphasizes them. Start by asking the questions in 3 and 4.

3. Do two or more short sentences in a row express closely related ideas? If so, could you make the relationship between these ideas clearer or more precise by combining them into a single longer sentence?

(Continued)

4. Is there a long sentence that contains two or three important ideas? Would these ideas be more emphatic if each was expressed in a short sentence of its own?

EXERCISE 22.2

The following paragraph can be improved by varying sentence length. Read it aloud to get a sense of how it sounds. Then revise it, creating some short emphatic sentences and combining other sentences to create more effective long sentences. Add words or change punctuation as you need to.

Before beginning to play bridge, it is necessary to have the proper materials, the correct number of people, and a knowledge of the rank of suits and cards. The necessary materials include a full deck of playing cards (minus the jokers) and a score pad, along with a pen or pencil. Bridge is played by four people grouped into two partnerships, which are usually decided by drawing cards from a shuffled deck. The two players who draw the highest cards and the two who draw the lowest are partners, and the partners sit across from each other. The person who draws the highest card during partnership is the first dealer. Starting with the person on his or her left and going clockwise, the dealer deals each person one card at a time, face down. The deal continues until all four players have thirteen cards apiece. After the deal, the players sort their cards by suit, usually alternating black and red suits. The players then arrange the cards in ranking order from the highest, the ace, to the lowest, the deuce. The five highest cards, the ace, king, queen, jack, and ten, are referred to as honors. There is one suit that has great power and outranks every other one, the trump suit, which is designated at the start of the game.

22b

Varying sentence openings

In making prose readable and interesting, beginning sentences in different ways is just as important as writing sentences of different lengths. For instance, when each sentence begins with the subject of an independent clause, a passage may seem to lurch or jerk along.

The way football and basketball are played is as interesting as the players. *Football* is a game of precision. *Each play* is diagrammed to accomplish a certain goal, and a coach designs the plays the way an engineer would design a bridge. *Basketball* is a game of availability. A *basketball game* looks like a track meet; the team that drops of exhaustion first loses. *Basketball players* are also often compared to artists. *The players' moves and slam dunks* are their masterpieces.

Varying sentence openings can prevent this jerky effect. This section will focus on three ways of varying openings—with transitional expressions; with prepositional, verbal, and absolute phrases; and with dependent clauses.

1

Using transitional expressions

See how transitions bring variety and clarity to this passage.

> In order to be alert Friday morning in New York, I planned to take the shuttle from Washington Thursday night. *On Thursday morning* it began to snow in Washington and to snow even harder in New York. *By mid-afternoon* I decided not to risk the shuttle and caught a train to New York. *Seven hours later* the train completed its three-hour trip. I arrived at Penn Station to find a city shut down by the worst blizzard since 1947.
> – LINDA ELLERBEE, *"And So It Goes"*

Here the transitional words establish chronology and help carry us smoothly through the paragraph. Many other transitional expressions can be used to vary sentence openings. See 6d5 for a detailed list.

2

Using phrases

Prepositional, verbal, and absolute phrases can also provide variety in sentence openers.

PREPOSITIONAL PHRASES

At each desk, a computer printout gives the necessary data.

From a few scraps of wood in the Middle Ages to a precisely carved, electrified instrument in the 1990s, the guitar has gone through uncounted changes.

VERBAL PHRASES

Frustrated by the delays, the drivers started honking their horns.

To qualify for flight training, one must be in good physical condition.

ABSOLUTE PHRASES

Our hopes for snow shattered, we started home.

Baton raised in a salute, the maestro readied the orchestra.

3

Using dependent clauses

Dependent clauses are another way to open a sentence.

While the boss sat on his tractor, I was down in a ditch, pounding in stakes and leveling out the bottom.
What they want is a place to call home.
Because the hills were dry, the fire spread rapidly.

> *Editing to vary sentence openings*

Underline the subject of each sentence. If most of your sentences begin with the subject, revise some of them so they open in other ways. Consider the following suggestions.

1. Look for sentences that are related to the preceding sentence in a specific chronological, spatial, or logical way that could be signaled by a transitional expression. (6d5 and 22b1)

2. Try rewording some sentences to begin with a phrase. (7c3 and 22b2)

3. If you have two related sentences, one after the other, see if it would be logical to combine them into one sentence, making the first a dependent clause. (7c4 and 22b3)

Revising to vary sentence openings

The following passage uses only subject openings; see how varying the sentence openings makes the passage easier to read:

FIRST DRAFT

Most marathon runners find that running with another person is helpful. *They* must not be afraid to pass this person, though, in order to run as well as possible. *Runners* must realize furthermore that even if they do not win the race, they achieve a victory by pushing their bodies to finish.

REVISED

Most marathon runners find that running with another person is helpful. In order to run as well as possible, though, *they* must not be afraid to pass this person. Furthermore, *runners* must realize that even if they do not win the race, they achieve victory by pushing their bodies to finish.

EXERCISE 22.3

Go back to the paragraph comparing football and basketball in 22b. Using transitional expressions, phrases, and/or dependent clauses, revise the paragraph to vary its sentence openings and thus make it smoother and more coherent.

22c

Varying sentence types

In addition to using different lengths and openings, you can help vary your sentence structures by using different *types* of sentences. Sentences can be classified in three different ways: grammatically, functionally, and rhetorically. (See 7d.)

1

Grammatical types

Grammatically, sentences fall into four categories—**simple, compound, complex**, and **compound-complex**—based on the number of independent and dependent clauses they contain. (See 7d1.) Varying your sentences among these grammatical types can go a long way toward creating readable, effective prose.

2

Functional types

Functional types of sentences can be **declarative** (making a statement), **interrogative** (asking a question), **imperative** (giving a command), and **exclamatory** (expressing strong feeling). Most sentences are declarative, but occasionally a command, a question, or an exclamation of some kind are appropriate for your purpose. (See 7d2.) Note how they are used in the following examples:

COMMAND

Coal-burning plants undoubtedly harm the environment in various ways; among others, they contribute to acid rain. *But consider the alternatives.*

QUESTION

We kept pressing on. *And why? Why would sixteen middle-aged people try to backpack thirty-seven miles?* At this point, I was not at all sure.

EXCLAMATION

Divorcés! They were everywhere! Sometimes he felt like a new member of an enormous club, the Divorcés of America, that he had never before even heard of.

3

Rhetorical types

Periodic and cumulative sentences spotlight sentence endings and beginnings and can be especially helpful in achieving sentence variety. Although not all sentences can be classified as cumulative or periodic, these types can create strong effects.

Periodic sentences

Periodic sentences postpone the main idea (usually in an independent clause) until the very end of the sentence. Effectively written periodic sentences are especially useful for creating tension or building toward a climactic or surprise ending. At their best, they keep us alert by holding information in a kind of "suspended animation" until the end. Note in each of the following examples how the writer holds back the main idea, thus using the end of the sentence to shock or inspire.

Early one morning, under the arc of a lamp, carefully, silently, in smock and leather gloves, *old Doctor Manza grafted a cat's head onto a chicken's trunk.*
— DYLAN THOMAS

Even though large tracts of Europe and many old and famous states have fallen or may fall into the grasp of the Gestapo and all the odious apparatus of Nazi rule, *we shall not flag or fail.* — WINSTON CHURCHILL

Look at the following sentence and its revision to see how periodic order can provide emphasis:

COMPLEX SENTENCE

The nations of the world have no alternative but coexistence because another world war would be unwinnable and because total destruction would certainly occur.

REVISED AS A PERIODIC SENTENCE

Because another world war would be unwinnable and because total destruction would certainly occur, the nations of the world have no alternative but coexistence.

Nothing is wrong with the first sentence, which conveys the information clearly. But to put greater emphasis on the idea in the independent clause of the sentence—"no alternative but coexistence"—the writer chose to revise using the periodic pattern.

Cumulative sentences

Cumulative sentences, which begin with an independent clause and then add details in phrases and other clauses, are the dominant rhetorical pattern today, far more common than periodic sentences. They are useful when you want to provide both immediate understanding of the main idea and a great deal of supporting detail. The writers of the following sentences use the cumulative pattern not only to add important detail but also to end with a strong word or image.

> From boyhood to manhood, *I have remembered him in a single image*—seated, asleep on the sofa, his head thrown back in a hideous corpselike grin, the evening newspaper spread out before him.
> — RICHARD RODRIGUEZ, "My Parents"

> *Powther threw small secret appraising glances at the coffee cup*, lipstick all around the edges, brown stains on the side where the coffee had dripped and spilled over, the saucer splotched with a whole series of dark brown rings.   — ANN PETRY, *The Narrows*

ON VARIETIES OF ENGLISH
Conventional Sentence Patterns in Some Fields

Some fields explicitly avoid variation in sentence structure and length. Many technical writers, and particularly those who write manuals that will be translated into numerous languages, must follow stringent rules for sentence structure and length. Technical writers working for Hewlett-Packard, for example, are required to adhere strictly to subject-verb-object order in all sentences and to keep all sentences to fifteen words at most.

EXERCISE 22.4

Revise the following sentences twice, as periodic and cumulative sentences.

1. Straggling hesitantly into the square, the survivors of the bombing carried their children, comforted the bereaved, and supported the injured.
2. I became the best salesperson in our store once I mastered the problems that I had encountered at the beginning and once I became thoroughly familiar with the stock.

≫ *Editing to vary sentence types*

1. Mark each sentence as simple, compound, complex, or compound-complex. If any one or two patterns predominate, combine, divide, and otherwise revise sentences to vary the grammatical types in your draft. (22c1)

2. Next note any sentences that are commands, questions, or exclamations. Consider whether the ideas in any declarative sentences might be emphasized effectively as commands, questions, or exclamations. (22c2)

3. Look for cumulative and periodic sentences. (22c3) Many sentences will be neither. Then look for ideas with much detail or with colorful images. Would they be best expressed as cumulative sentences? And look for ideas that could use greater emphasis—would they get such emphasis in periodic sentences?

Revising to vary sentence types

Study how the following sentences are identified and then revised:

FIRST DRAFT

The purpose of speech is most often to persuade. [simple] It is seldom to generate understanding or to stimulate thoughtful response. [simple] Speeches on television take advantage of this fact. [simple] A televised speech gives viewers the time only to receive information, to respond emotionally to it, to "feel" it. [simple, cumulative] Viewers can simply enjoy or deplore its impact. [simple] Unlike a televised speech, a written speech can be read, reread, and analyzed. [simple] The reader can thoroughly process and analyze it. [simple] For this reason, I prefer to read and study a speech, not watch and instantly swallow it. [simple] This preference is limited to speeches that may be of great importance to me. [simple]

REVISED

The purpose of speech is most often not to generate understanding or to stimulate thoughtful response; rather, its purpose is merely to persuade. [compound] A televised speech takes advantage of this merely persuasive purpose by giving viewers time only to receive information, to respond emotionally to it, to "feel" or simply enjoy or deplore it. [simple, cumulative] Unlike a televised speech, a written speech can be read and reread, thoroughly analyzed and processed. [simple, periodic] For this reason, I prefer to read and study, not watch and instantly "swallow," any speech that may be of great importance to me. [complex]

EXERCISE 22.5   Revising for Sentence Variety

The following is an introductory paragraph from an essay. Analyze the paragraph carefully, noting for each sentence its length, its kind of opening, and its grammatical and rhetorical type. Then revise the paragraph to add variety in sentence length, sentence openings, and sentence types.

> When we arrived at the accident scene, I could tell that the injuries were not minor. I walked up to the car nearest me to check the injuries of the people inside. I looked through the driver's window and saw the woman's body entangled in the steering wheel. I told dispatch, via two-way radio, to send medics "code red, lights and siren." I then went to see how the passenger in the car was. The passenger appeared to be in shock and had a broken leg. The officer walked over and checked the other vehicle. The driver of the other vehicle had received no injuries at all.

THINKING CRITICALLY ABOUT SENTENCE VARIETY

Reading with an Eye for Sentence Variety

Read something by an author you admire. Analyze two paragraphs for sentence length, opening, and type. Compare the sentence variety in these paragraphs with that in one of your paragraphs—perhaps the one you analyzed in Exercise 22.1. What similarities or differences do you recognize, and what conclusions can you draw about sentence variety?

Thinking about Sentence Variety in Your Own Writing

Choose several paragraphs of an essay you have written, and examine them very carefully for variety of sentence structure. For each sentence, note the length, the kind of opening, and the grammatical, functional, and rhetorical type. Then revise the paragraphs to achieve as wide a range of variation as possible in these characteristics. Read the original and revised versions aloud, noting the differences in rhythm and impact. For future use, note down (in your writing log, if you keep one) any thoughts you have about sentence variety.

23

Creating Memorable Prose

*H*OW MANY TIMES HAVE YOU READ SOMETHING *so striking that you wanted immediately to share it with a friend? And how many times have you remembered the exact words of something you have read or heard? All of us recognize, and can even quote, certain passages from literature or history or music—the opening of A Tale of Two Cities, perhaps, or passages from "I Have a Dream" or lyrics to a well-known tune.*

As students of writing, we would profit by taking the time to examine some of the elements that make pieces such as these so memorable. Consider, for instance, some lines from one of the most quoted speeches of our century, John F. Kennedy's Inaugural Address.

> Let every nation know, whether it wishes us well or ill, that we shall pay any price, bear any burden, meet any hardship, support any friend, oppose any foe to assure the survival and the success of liberty.
>
> In your hands, my fellow citizens, more than mine, will rest the final success or failure of our course.
>
> And so, my fellow Americans, ask not what your country can do for you; ask what you can do for your country.
>
> – JOHN F. KENNEDY, Inaugural Address

What strategies did Kennedy use to make these lines so very memorable? First would be his use of repetition: *in the first sentence, the repetition of short verb phrases, each with the word* any, *creates a powerful, hammerlike rhythm. Second might be his use of* inverted word order: *in the second sentence, saving the subject until the end of the sentence adds dramatic emphasis to his statement. Third would be his use of* antithesis, *seen in the last sentence in the two parallel clauses that accentuate the contrast of self and country. Finally, Kennedy's reliance on* strong verbs *and the* active voice *results in prose that is lively and thus memorable.*

Each of these strategies and devices can be used to good effect by all writers. This chapter will examine each one and offer practice to help you use them in your work, to make your writing not only worth reading but worth remembering.

EXERCISE 23.1

Think of something in your current reading that sticks in your mind as particularly memorable. Then find that piece, and reread it to try to identify what makes the passage so memorable. Choose one sentence you especially like, and try imitating its structure in a sentence of your own.

Everyday Use

Like the clothes we wear, the words we choose and the way we use them bring memorable qualities to our language. Nowhere are such choices more evident in daily life than in music. Every songwriter knows the importance of creating lyrics and rhythms that listeners will remember.

Rap music demands careful attention to stylistic choices, for its lyrics must be concise as well as memorable. Here's an example from Queen Latifah and Monie Love's "Ladies First."

I'm conversating to the folks who have no whatsoever clue
So listen very carefully as I break it down for you
Merrily, merrily, merrily, merrily, hyper, happy, overjoyed
Pleased with all the beats and rhymes my sister has employed
Slick and smooth, throwing down, the sound totally a yes
Let me state the position: Ladies first, yes?

Yes!

Look at the words and structures that the writer here has chosen in order to make the lyrics memorable: the active verbs ("listen"), the inversion of normal word order ("no whatsoever clue"), the powerful use of repetition ("merrily, merrily, merrily, merrily"), and especially the three "yes's" that drive home both the rhythm and the point. What do you find most memorable about this particular rap?

Think of some music and lyrics that you find particularly memorable. Listen to the song, and jot down its exact words. What has the writer done to make the lyrics memorable?

23a

Choosing strong verbs

The greatest writers in any language are those with a genius for choosing the precise words that will arrest and hold a reader's attention. In your own writing, you can help gain this attention by using precise nouns and adjectives instead of vague, catchall buzzwords. (See 19b2.) Perhaps even more important, however, you can use strong, precise verbs instead of weak, catchall verbs and instead of nouns.

1

Using strong, precise verbs

Verbs serve as the real workhorses of our language. Take a look, for instance, at the strong, precise verbs in the following passage:

> A fire engine, out for a trial spin, *roared* past Emerson's house, hot with readiness for public duty. Over the barn roofs the martens *dipped* and *chittered*. A swarthy daughter of an asparagus grower, in culottes, shirt, and bandanna, *pedalled* past on her bicycle.   – E. B. WHITE, "Walden"

Instead of the italicized verbs, White could have used more general verbs such as *drove, flew, called*, and *rode*. But the more precise verbs are stronger because they give readers vivid sensory impressions of the actions they express. In White's verbs, readers can hear the roar of the fire engine, see the martens swooping downward and hear them chirping shrilly, and feel the young woman pushing on the pedals of her bicycle.

Some of the most common verbs in English—especially *be, do*, and *have*—carry little or no sense of specific action, and many writers tend to overuse them in situations where more precise verbs would be clearer and more effective. Look at how the following sentences are strengthened by replacing them with more precise verbs:

WEAK	Constant viewing of rock videos *is* harmful to children's emotional development.
REVISED	Constant viewing of rock videos *stunts* and *distorts* children's emotional development.
WEAK	In front of the hotel, an artist would *do* your portrait on a framed sheet of glass.
REVISED	In front of the hotel, an artist would *etch* your portrait on a framed sheet of glass.
WEAK	We *had* basic training at Fort Ord.
REVISED	We *sweated* through basic training at Fort Ord.

The verb *be* is essential to writing; indeed, it appears in some of the most memorable English prose, such as the opening of the Gospel According to John.

> In the beginning was the Word, and the Word was with God, and the Word was God.

But as the three examples above illustrate, *be* can often be replaced by verbs that express action. As a general rule, if forms of *be* (*is, are, was, were, has been*, and so on) account for more than about a third of the verbs in a piece of writing, the writing may well seem static and flat.

Expletives

One potentially weak verb construction to watch out for is the **expletive**, which begins with *there* or *it* followed by a form of *be* (*there are, it is,* and so on). Expletives can offer effective ways of introducing an idea with extra emphasis, as June Jordan does in the following sentence:

> *It is* for us, the living, to ensure that We the People shall become the powerful. — JUNE JORDAN, "Inside America"

Here the *it is* slows down the opening of the sentence and sets up a rather formal rhythm that adds emphasis to the main idea. Often, however, writers do not use expletive openings to add emphasis. Instead, they merely overuse them, creating sentences that needlessly bury action in nouns, verbals, or dependent clauses. Notice how the following sentences are strengthened by deleting the expletives:

WEAK	*There are* many people who fear success because they believe they do not deserve it.
REVISED	Many people *fear* success because they believe they do not deserve it.
WEAK	*It is* necessary for presidential candidates to perform well on television.
REVISED	Presidential candidates *must perform* well on television.

2

Changing nouns to verbs

Much modern writing tends to express action by using nouns that are formed from verbs, a process called **nominalization**. Although nominalization can help make prose clearer and more concise—for example, using *abolition* instead of *the process of abolishing*—it can also produce the opposite effect, making a sentence unnecessarily wordy and hard to read. Nominalization reduces the *active* quality of a sentence, burying the action in an abstract noun and forcing the writer to use weak, generalized verbs and too many prepositional phrases. Too often, writers use nominalizations not to make a complex process easier to talk about but to make an idea *sound* more complex and abstract than it really is. Bureaucratic writing especially tends to use excessive nominalization in this way.

You can decide when to use a nominalized form and when to use the verb from which it derives by asking one question: which is most readily understandable? Look at the following sentence:

> The firm is now engaged in an assessment of its procedures for the development of new products.

This sentence scarcely impresses itself on our memories, and it sounds pretentious and stuffy as well. In contrast, note the more easily understood and forceful version.

> The firm is now assessing its procedures for developing new products.

⫸ Editing verbs and nouns

1. Underline all verbs, and look to see whether you rely too much on *be, do,* and *have.* If so, try to substitute more specific verbs. (23a1)
2. Note nouns whose meaning could be expressed by a verb. Try revising using the verb instead of the noun. (23a2)
3. Identify all expletives, and delete any that are not used to create special emphasis. (23a1)
4. Look for passive verbs, and decide whether they obscure the performer of the action or dull the sentence. If so, recast the sentence in the active voice. (23b)

Revising for verbs and nouns

Consider how the following passage can be revised using these steps:

Last February, when I made the determination to buy a house, I opened a separate checking (and savings) account in order to give attention more easily to my household expenses. (There is a credit union policy that for every checking account there must be a matching savings account: thus the dormant savings account.) This new checking account was where the deposit of the inheritance from my grandmother occurred along with any other accumulation of money from outside sources.

REVISED

Last February, when I determined to buy a house, I opened a separate checking (and savings) account to deal more easily with household expenses. (Credit union policy demands a matching savings account for every checking account; thus the dormant savings account.) Into this new checking account I deposited the inheritance from my grandmother, along with any other money I accumulated from outside sources.

EXERCISE 23.2

Revise the following paragraph to eliminate weak verbs and unnecessary nominalizations and expletives.

There has long been resistance to the proposition that the effectiveness of educational methods and teachers must be measured in terms of the results secured. Those responsible for the evaluation of teachers have put emphasis on procedures in teaching and have seldom made an examination of the products, that is, the efficiency of the teacher as indicated by what his or her pupils can do following instruction. However, we are beginning to see an increasing number of bold proposals founded on the assumption that the American public has expectations of improved results from schooling. As public support of education increases, there will be greater insistence on making judgments about a teacher in the light of his or her ability to enhance the learning of pupils.

23b

Choosing between active and passive voice

In addition to choosing strong, precise verbs, you can help make your prose memorable by alternating those verbs appropriately between active and passive voice. Look at the following paragraph:

A young man might go into military flight training believing that he was entering some sort of technical school in which he was simply going to acquire a certain set of skills. Instead, he found himself all at once enclosed in a fraternity. And in this fraternity, even though it was military, men were not rated by their outward rank as ensigns, lieutenants, commanders, or whatever. No, herein the world was divided into those who had it and those who did not. This quality, this *it*, was never named, however, nor was it talked about in any way.

— TOM WOLFE, *The Right Stuff*

In this paragraph, Wolfe introduces the indefinable quality that he has made the title of his book. Notice that in the first sentence, the focus is on someone *doing* things: going into flight training, entering a school, acquiring skills. All of the verbs are in the active voice.

In the second sentence, the verb is still active. But notice that because the subject and object are the same person, because the subject of the verb *found* also receives the action of the verb, the sentence has the *feel* of being in the passive voice, as if *was enclosed* were the verb. And in the independent clauses of the last three sentences, the focus clearly shifts to things *being done* (or not done): men not being rated, the world being divided, and a quality never being named or talked about. The persons doing these things are unimportant or unknown; in fact, like the quality itself, they are never named, and the verbs are in the passive voice. Notice, however, that Wolfe uses the active voice when he focuses on the persons "who had it and those who did not."

Try to use the active voice whenever possible. Because the passive diverts attention from the performer of an action and because it is usually wordier than the active voice, its excessive use makes for dull and difficult reading.

But as Wolfe's paragraph indicates, the passive can be used very effectively in certain situations: when the performer is unknown, unwilling to be identified, or less important than the recipient of the action. In the last sentence, for example, Wolfe could have written *No one ever named this quality, this it, however, nor did anyone talk about it in any way*. By using the passive voice, however, he focuses attention on the quality itself rather than on the persons who do not name or talk about it; in fact, by not mentioning them, he heightens the sense of a mysterious quality that cannot be defined. (See Chapter 9 for further discussion of voice.)

EXERCISE 23.3

Look at the following sentences, in which some of the verbs are active and some passive. Then rewrite each sentence in the other voice, and decide which version you prefer and why. Example:

> *I*
> ~~You are~~ hereby relieved *you* of your duties. ~~by me.~~

1. In Gower's research, it was found that pythons often dwell in trees and live near rivers.

2. They started shooting pool, and before Cathy knew it, she owed the kid ten dollars.

3. When I was eight, my father's crazy dreams uprooted our family from Florida to California.

4. For me, living in a dorm was more easily adjusted to than living in an apartment.

5. The image of American Indians has been totally distorted by Hollywood in most of its films about the West.

Creating special effects

Contemporary movies often succeed or fail on the basis of their special effects. Similarly, special effects like repetition, antithesis, and inversion can animate your prose and help make it memorable.

1

Using repetition

Carefully used, repetition of sounds, words, phrases, or other grammatical constructions serves as a powerful stylistic device. Orators in particular have long known its power. Here is a famous use of repetition, from one of Sir Winston Churchill's addresses to the British people during World War II.

> We shall not flag or fail, we shall go on to the end. We shall fight in France, we shall fight on the seas and oceans, we shall fight with growing confidence and growing strength in the air, we shall defend our island, whatever the cost may be; we shall fight on the beaches, . . . we shall fight in the fields and in the streets, . . . we shall never surrender.
> —WINSTON CHURCHILL

In this passage, the constantly hammering *we shall* accompanied by the repetition of *f* sounds (*flag, fail, fight, France, confidence, defend, fields*) has the effect of strengthening British resolve.

Though we may not be prime ministers, we can use repetition to equally good effect. Here are some examples.

> So my dream date turned into a nightmare. Where was the quiet, considerate, caring guy I thought I had met? In his place appeared this jerk. He strutted, he postured, he preened—and then he bragged, he bellowed, he practically brayed—just like the donkey he so much reminded me of.

> We need science, more and better science, not for its technology, not for leisure, not even for health or longevity, but for the hope of wisdom which our kind of culture must acquire for its survival.
> — LEWIS THOMAS "Medical Lessons from History"

Be careful, however, to use repetition only for a deliberate purpose. (See 19b.)

EXERCISE 23.4

Go through the examples in 23c1, identifying the uses of repetition. Using one example as a model, write a passage of your own that uses repetition effectively.

2

Using antithesis

Another special effect that can contribute to memorable writing is **antithesis**, the use of parallel structures to highlight contrast or opposition. Like other uses of parallelism (see Chapter 21), antithesis provides a pleasing rhythm that calls readers' attention to the contrast, often in a startling or amusing way. For example:

> Love is an ideal thing, marriage a real thing.

> The congregation didn't think much of the new preacher, and what the new preacher thought of the congregation she didn't wish to say.

> It is a sin to believe evil of others—but it is not a mistake.
> – H. L. MENCKEN

EXERCISE 23.5

Using one of the examples above, create a sentence of your own that uses antithesis. Then consider whether the antithesis makes the sentence more memorable or effective. You might begin by thinking of opposites you could build on: hope-despair, good-evil, fire-ice. Or you might begin with a topic you want to write about: success, greed, generosity, and so on.

ON VARIETIES OF ENGLISH
Multiple Negation

Most speakers of English sometimes use more than one negative at a time—saying, for instance, "I can't hardly see you." Multiple negatives, in fact, have a long history in English (and can be found in the works of Chaucer and Shakespeare, for example). It was only in the eighteenth century, in an effort to make English more "logical," that double negatives came to be seen as incorrect.

In fact, double negatives are used for emphasis in many areas of the South—to say, for example, "Can't nothing be done." Double negatives—and triple, quadruple, and more—are used as a rule by many speakers of African American English Vernacular—saying, for example, "Don't none of my people come from up North."

For all their use in regional and ethnic varieties of English (and in many other languages, including French and Russian), multiple negatives are not used in standard academic English. In your college writing, you may well have reason to quote passages that include multiple negatives, whether you're quoting Shakespeare, Toni Morrison, or your grandmother, but you should not otherwise use multiple negatives.

3

Using inverted word order

Inversion of the usual word order can make writing memorable by creating surprise or putting emphasis on a particular word or phrase. Word order in English is usually subject-verb-object/complement (if any). Inversion refers to any change in that order, such as putting the verb before the subject or the object before the subject and verb.

NORMAL Two dead birds plummeted out of the tree.

INVERTED Out of the tree plummeted two dead birds.

The inverted word order makes for a more dramatic sentence by putting the emphasis at the end, on *two dead birds*.

As with any unusual sentence pattern, inverted word order should be used sparingly, but it can indeed create special effects.

Into this grey lake plopped the thought, I know this man, don't I?
                                                        — DORIS LESSING

In a hole in the ground there lived a hobbit.   — J. R. R. TOLKIEN

Into her head flowed the whole of the poem she had found in that book.
                                                        — EUDORA WELTY

EXERCISE 23.6

After studying the examples of inversion above, look at something you have written, and find a sentence that might be more effective with inverted word order. Experiment with the word order, reading the results aloud and comparing differences in effect.

EXERCISE 23.7

Prose can be memorable for reasons quite different from those presented in this chapter. The Bulwer-Lytton Competition, known less formally as the Wretched Writing contest, challenges writers to produce an opening sentence to a novel, one that will celebrate the possibilities of "deliberate wretchedness" without hurting anyone's feelings. Here are two finalists.

1. It was the eve of the yearly whale-slaughtering festival, thought Mamook as her horny fingers relentlessly pushed the whalebone needle through the sole of the mukluk; and suddenly, unaccountably, uncontrollably, she began to blubber.

2. When the last of the afterglow faded and the air was still, Josh liked to sit in the porch swing, in the dark, and test his night vision by spitting through the banisters.

Write an opening sentence for a story. Try to make it a "wonderfully bad" sentence. And why not enter it in the contest? Just send it to the Bulwer-Lytton Competition, c/o Professor Scott Rice, San Jose State University, San Jose, CA 95192.

THINKING CRITICALLY ABOUT PROSE STYLE

Reading with an Eye for Prose Style

Chapters 19–23 have presented many elements that mark effective prose. One amusing way to practice these elements lies in a special kind of imitation. Choose a writer you admire—Virginia Woolf, Chaucer, Leslie Silko, Stephen King, Salt 'n' Pepa, whoever. Reread this writer's work, getting a feel for the rhythms, the structures, the special effects. Make a list of the elements that contribute to the distinctive style. Then choose a well-known story, and retell it in that style. Following is the opening of "The Three Little Pigs" as one student imagined Edgar Allan Poe might have done it.

It began as a mere infatuation. I admired them from afar, with a longing which only a wolf may know. Soon, these feelings turned to torment. Were I even to set eyes upon their porcine forms, the bowels of my soul raged, as if goaded by some festering poison. As the chilling winds of November howled, my gullet yearned for them. I soon feasted only upon an earnest and consuming desire for the moment of their decease.

Thinking about Your Own Prose Style

Read over something you have written, looking for memorable sentences. If few sentences catch your eye, choose some that show promise—ones with strong verbs or a pleasing rhythm, perhaps. Using this chapter for guidance, try revising one or two sentences to make them more effective and memorable. Finally, note some ways in which your writing is effective and some strategies for making it more effective. If you keep a writing log, make your notes there.

Part Five

Selecting
Effective Words

<>

24. Mastering Spelling   *374*

25. Using Dictionaries   *393*

26. Enriching Vocabulary   *402*

27. Considering Diction   *413*

28. Considering Language Variety   *432*

29. Considering Others:
Building Common Ground   *445*

24

Mastering Spelling

W<small>HEN HUMORIST DAVE BARRY</small> *quips that English spelling is "unusual" "because our language is a rich verbal tapestry woven together from the tongues of the Greeks, the Latins, the Angles, the Klaxtons, the Celtics, the 76ers, and many other ancient peoples, all of whom had severe drinking problems," he is exaggerating, of course—but not much. For English has come in contact with many other languages—German, Latin, Danish, Norse, and Norman French, to name a few—during the course of its evolution, and that contact helps make English spelling complex. For example, English includes at least twelve different ways of representing the sh sound: <u>sh</u>oe, <u>s</u>ugar, o<u>ce</u>an, i<u>ss</u>ue, na<u>ti</u>on, <u>sch</u>ist, <u>psh</u>aw, suspi<u>ci</u>on, con<u>sci</u>ous, nau<u>se</u>ous, man<u>si</u>on, and fu<u>chs</u>ia. As everyone who has ever struggled to remember—or to find—a correct spelling knows, this complexity can lead to much frustration, and in fact, some have called for "spelling liberation." President Andrew Jackson once exclaimed in exasperation, "It's a damn poor mind that can think of only one way to spell a word!"*

Despite this tradition of complaint, modern linguists have demonstrated that English spelling is much more regular than is commonly thought and that this regularity relates not only to sound-letter connections but also to our stored visual memory of related words. We know that president is not spelled "presadent," for example, because we recognize its relation to preside. The good news, then, is simply this: careful attention to your own spelling patterns and attention to some fairly straightforward guidelines of English spelling can help you master spelling.

EXERCISE 24.1

Listen in on some conversations—on the bus, in line for a movie, at a cafeteria. Jot down some of one conversation, capturing it as accurately as possible. Then look carefully at the words and their spellings. Are any of these words *not* found in a dictionary? If so, how did you decide how to spell them?

24a

Mastering the most commonly misspelled words

Eudora Welty reports that she once failed to make one hundred on a spelling test because she misspelled *uncle,* a mistake that her mother took very hard. "You couldn't spell *uncle*?" her mother said. "When you've got those five perfectly splendid uncles in West Virginia? What would *they* say to that?"

The three thousand first-year essays that were used in the research for this book revealed a fairly small number of persistently misspelled words, and Welty's mother would no doubt be glad to hear that *uncle* was not among them. A list of the fifty most common misspellings appears below. Look it over carefully, and compare it with words you have trouble spelling correctly. (See 24f for ways to establish your own spelling inventory.)

≫ *The fifty most commonly misspelled words*

1. their/there/they're	18. through	35. business/-es
2. too/to	19. until	36. dependent
3. a lot	20. where	37. every day
4. noticeable	21. successful/-ly	38. may be
5. receive/-d/-s	22. truly	39. occasion/-s
6. lose	23. argument/-s	40. occurrences
7. you're/your	24. experience/-s	41. woman
8. an/and	25. environment	42. all right
9. develop/-s	26. exercise/-s/-ing	43. apparent/-ly
10. definitely	27. necessary	44. categories
11. than/then	28. sense	45. final/-ly
12. believe/-d/-s	29. therefore	46. immediate/-ly
13. occurred	30. accept/-ed	47. roommate/-s
14. affect/-s	31. heroes	48. against
15. cannot	32. professor	49. before
16. separate	33. whether	50. beginning
17. success	34. without	

EXERCISE 24.2

Choose the correct spelling from the pair of words in the parentheses in each of the sentences below. After checking your answers, compare your misspellings with the list of fifty words most frequently misspelled. Enter the words you misspelled in your spelling log, and keep them near your typewriter or computer.

1. (*Their/There/They're*) going to put (*their/there/they're*) new stereo system over (*their/there/they're*) in the corner.

2. My little brother wants (*to/too*) go swimming (*to/too*).

3. The (*begining/beginning*) of school is (*a lot/alot*) earlier this year than last.

4. The rise in temperature isn't (*noticable/noticeable*) (*until/untill*) the humidity rises.

5. The accident (*occured/occurred*) (*before/befour*) I could step aside.

6. We couldn't (*beleive/believe*) the national champions were expected to (*loose/lose*) the playoffs.

7. In making your major life decisions, (*your/you're*) (*definately/definitely*) on (*your/you're*) own.

8. Nothing (*affects/effects*) (*success/sucess*) more (*than/then*) self-confidence or (*its/it's*) absence.

9. We (*received/recieved*) our notice (*threw/through*) the mail.

10. The group hopes to (*develop/develope*) a (*truely/truly*) (*succesful/successful*) fast-food franchise.

11. We (*can not/cannot*) easily (*separate/seperate*) fact and opinion.

12. Please tell me (*wear/where*) (*an/and*) when we should meet.

13. Our (*argumants/arguments*) (*against/aginst*) continuing to pollute the (*enviroment/environment*) fell on deaf ears.

14. Local (*busineses/businesses*) are (*dependant/dependent*) on the summer tourist trade.

15. (*Heroes/Heros*) are (*necesary/necessary*) to every culture's mythology.

16. Our first (*experiance/experience*) with aerobic (*exercise/exercize*) left us tired.

17. The (*professor/profesor*) agreed to (*accept/except*) our final research essays on Friday.

18. She qualified for three (*catagories/categories*) in the (*final/finel*) gymnastics competition.

19. The two (*roomates/roommates*) would be lost (*without/witout*) each other.

20. We intend to celebrate the (*ocasion/occasion*) (*weather/whether*) or not the (*weather/whether*) cooperates.

21. The plane to Chicago (*may be/maybe*) late; (*therefore/therfore*), we don't need to leave for the airport (*imediately/immediately*).

22. A (*woman's/women's*) place is now wherever she wants it to be.

23. Police departments report (*occurences/occurrences*) of more and more burglaries (*every day/everyday*).

24. (*Its/It's*) not (*all right/alright*) to forgo common (*since/sense*).

25. (*Aparently/Apparently*), the shipment of books never arrived.

Everyday Use

Andrew Jackson's comment on page 374 is just as true today as it was over a hundred years ago. A short drive along an interstate turned up the following examples of alternative spellings.

Kountry Kitchen

Kutz for Mutz

Phat Phil's Phine Phood

Keep an eye out for fanciful or amusing spellings. Find two or three examples, and decide what purpose the writer might have had for the misspelling (assuming it was intentional).

24b

Recognizing homonyms

Of the words most often misspelled by college students, the largest number are **homonyms**—words that sound alike but have different spellings and meanings. English has many homonyms, but a relatively small number of them—eight pairs or trios—cause student writers frequent trouble. If you tend to confuse any of these words, now is a good time to study them, looking for some twist of memory to help you remember the differences.

≫ *The most troublesome homonyms*

their (possessive form of *they*)
there (in that place)
they're (contraction of *they are*)

to (in the direction of)
too (in addition; excessive)
two (number between one and three)

weather (climatic conditions)
whether (if)

accept (to take or receive)
except (to leave out)

who's (contraction of *who is* or *who has*)
whose (possessive form of *who*)

its (possessive form of *it*)
it's (contraction of *it is* or *it has*)

your (possessive form of *you*)
you're (contraction of *you are*)

affect (an emotion; to have an influence)
effect (a result; to cause to happen)

Other homonyms and frequently confused words

advice (suggestion)
advise (to suggest [to])

allude (to refer)
elude (to avoid or escape)

allusion (reference)
illusion (false idea or appearance)

altar (sacred platform or table)
alter (to change)

are (form of *be*)
our (belonging to us)

bare (uncovered)
bear (animal; to carry or endure)

board (piece of lumber)
bored (uninterested)

brake (device for stopping)
break (to fragment)

buy (to purchase)
by (near; beside; through)

capital (principal city)
capitol (legislators' building)

cite (to refer to)
sight (seeing; something seen)
site (location)

coarse (rough or crude)
course (plan of study; path)

complement (something that completes; to make complete)
compliment (praise; to praise)

conscience (feeling of right and wrong)
conscious (mentally aware)

council (leadership group)
counsel (advice; to advise)

dairy (source of milk)
diary (journal)

desert (dry area; to abandon)
dessert (sweet course of a meal)

device (something planned or invented)
devise (to plan or invent)

die (to expire)
dye (color; to color)

elicit (to draw forth)
illicit (illegal)

eminent (distinguished)
immanent (inherent)
imminent (expected in the immediate future)

fair (just or right; light in complexion; an exposition)
fare (price of transportation; to go through an experience)

forth (forward; out into view)
fourth (between third and fifth)

gorilla (ape)
guerrilla (irregular soldier)

hear (to perceive with the ears)
here (in this place)

heard (past tense of *hear*)
herd (group of animals)

hoarse (sounding rough or harsh)
horse (animal)

know (to understand)
no (opposite of *yes*)

lead (a metal; to go before)
led (past tense of *lead*)

loose (not tight; not confined)

lose (to misplace; to fail to win)

meat (flesh used as food)

meet (to encounter)

passed (went by; received a passing grade)

past (beyond; events that have already occurred)

patience (quality of being patient)

patients (persons under medical care)

peace (absence of war)

piece (part)

personal (private or individual)

personnel (employees)

plain (simple, not fancy; flat land)

plane (airplane; tool; flat surface)

presence (condition of being)

presents (gifts; gives)

principal (most important; head of a school)

principle (fundamental truth)

rain (precipitation)

rein (strap to control a horse)

reign (period of rule; to rule)

right (correct; opposite of left)

rite (ceremony)

write (to produce words on a surface)

road (street or highway)

rode (past tense of *ride*)

scene (setting; view)

seen (past participle of *see*)

sense (feeling; intelligence)

since (from the time that; because)

stationary (unmoving)

stationery (writing paper)

than (as compared with)

then (at that time; therefore)

threw (past tense of *throw*)

thorough (complete)

through (in one side of and out the other; by means of)

waist (part of the body)

waste (to squander)

weak (feeble)

week (seven days)

wear (to put onto the body)

were (past tense of *be*)

where (in what place)

which (what; that)

witch (woman with supernatural power)

EXERCISE 24.3

Choose the appropriate word in parentheses to fill each blank.

If _____ (*your/you're*) looking for summer fun, _____ (*accept/except*) the friendly _____ (*advice/advise*) of thousands of happy adventurers: spend three _____ (*weaks/weeks*) kayaking _____ (*threw/thorough/through*) the inside passage _____ (*to/too/two*) Alaska. For ten years, Outings, Inc., has

_____ (*lead/led*) groups of novice kayakers _____ (*passed/past*) some of the most breathtaking scenery in North America. _____ (*Their/There/They're*) goal is simple: to give participants the time of _____ (*their/there/they're*) lives. As one of last year's adventurers said, "_____ (*Its/It's*) a trip I will remember vividly, one that _____ (*affected/effected*) me powerfully."

1

Recognizing homonyms with more than one form

One special group of homonyms appearing in the list of words most often misspelled by college writers is words written sometimes as one word and other times as two words. The correct spelling depends on the meaning. Note the differences illustrated here.

Of course, they did not wear *everyday* clothes *every day* of the year.

Ideally, children *always* love their parents—in *all ways.*

By the time we were *all ready* for the game to begin, the coach's patience was *already* exhausted.

We *may be* on time for the meeting, or *maybe* we won't be!

Nobody was surprised when the police officers announced that they had found *no body* at the scene of the crime.

The study of three thousand first-year essays mentioned earlier in this chapter revealed three particularly troublesome words that are often written in the wrong form. Two of them are always written as two words; *a lot* and *all right.* The third is written as one word: *cannot.* If you tend to misspell these words, take time now to commit the correct spelling to memory.

▶ *FOR MULTILINGUAL WRITERS*
Recognizing American Spellings

Spelling varies slightly among English-speaking countries. The following are some words that are spelled differently in American and British English. If you have learned British English, you will want to be aware of some spelling differences in British and American English. For example:

AMERICAN	BRITISH
center	centre
check	cheque
color	colour
criticize	criticise
judgment	judgement

24c

Linking spelling and pronunciation

Even for words that are not homonyms, pronunciation often leads spellers astray. Pronunciation can vary considerably from one region to another, and the informality of spoken English allows us to slur or blur letters or syllables. The best way to link spelling and pronunciation is to learn to pronounce words mentally as they look, every letter and syllable included (so that, for example, you hear the *b* at the end of *crumb*) and to enunciate them slowly and clearly when you are trying to spell them. Words that you have never seen in print may provide special challenges if you try to spell them *as you think they sound*. If you have heard the word *nerve-racking*, for example, but have never seen it written and do not know the word *rack*, you might easily write *nerve-wrecking*, especially since the meaning seems to fit.

1

Noting unpronounced letters or syllables

Learning to "see" words with unpronounced letters or syllables will help you spell them correctly. Here are some frequently misspelled words of this kind with their unpronounced letters or syllables italicized.

can*d*idate	foreign	pro*b*ably
condem*n*	gover*n*ment	quan*t*ity
dif*f*erent	int*e*rest	rest*au*rant
drastical*l*y	lib*r*ary	sep*a*rate (adjective)
environ*n*ment	mar*r*iage	surprise
Feb*r*uary	mus*c*le	We*d*nesday

2

Noting unstressed vowels

In English words, *a*, *i*, and *e* often sound alike in syllables that are not stressed. Hearing the word *definite*, for instance, gives us few clues as to whether the vowels in the second and third syllables should be *i*'s or *a*'s. In this case, remembering how the related word *finite* looks or sounds helps us know that the *i*'s are correct. If you are puzzled about how to spell a word with unstressed vowels, try to think of a related word that will give you a clue to the correct spelling. Then check your dictionary.

24d

Taking advantage of spelling rules

Fortunately, English spelling does follow some general rules that can be of enormous help to writers. This section focuses on those rules closely related to commonly misspelled words.

1

Remembering "*i* before *e*"

Most of you probably memorized the "*i* before *e*" rule long ago. Here is a slightly expanded version.

> *i* before *e* except after *c*
> or when pronounced "ay"
> as in *neighbor* or *weigh*
> or in *weird* exceptions like *either*
> and *species*

_I_ BEFORE _E_

ach*ie*ve	exper*ie*nce	rel*ie*ve
bel*ie*ve	f*ie*ld	th*ie*f
br*ie*f	fr*ie*nd	
ch*ie*f	p*ie*ce	

EXCEPT AFTER _C_

c*ei*ling	dec*ei*ve	perc*ei*ve
conc*ei*ve	rec*ei*ve	

OR WHEN PRONOUNCED "AY"

n*ei*ghbor	w*ei*gh	*ei*ghth

OR IN WEIRD EXCEPTIONS

either	seize	species
weird	foreign	ancient
neither	height	conscience
leisure	caffeine	science

EXERCISE 24.4

Insert either *ei* or *ie* in the blank in each of the following words.

     1. sl____gh   2. consc____nce   3. anc____nt

4. l____sure	7. ch____f	9. ach____ve
5. p____rce	8. rec____ve	10. h____ress
6. caff____ne		

2

Adding prefixes

Prefixes are verbal elements placed at the beginnings of words to add to or qualify their meaning. The prefix *re-*, for example, adds repetition to the meaning of a word: *reappear* means "appear again." (See 26c for more information about prefixes.) Prefixes do not change the spelling of the words they are added to, even when the last letter of the prefix and the first letter of the word it is added to are the same. In such cases, keep both letters.

dis- + service = disservice   over- + rate = overrate

Some prefixes require the use of hyphens. For a discussion of such usage, see 39c. If you are in doubt about whether to hyphenate a word beginning with a prefix, always check your dictionary.

3

Adding suffixes

Suffixes are verbal elements placed at the *ends* of words in order to form related words. For example, we can build on the basic word *short* to get the following words: short*age*, short*en*, short*er*, short*ly*, short*ness*. This section will provide guidance to spelling words with suffixes.

Dropping the final e

For words ending in an unpronounced *e* (*receive, lose, definite*), you must decide whether or not to drop the *e* when adding a suffix. In general, if the suffix starts with a vowel, *drop the e.*

explore + -ation = exploration   exercise + -ing = exercising
imagine + -able = imaginable   continue + -ous = continuous
future + -ism = futurism   productive + -ity = productivity

EXCEPTIONS

To distinguish homonyms or potentially confusing words

dye + -ing = dyeing (not *dying*)   singe + -ing = singeing
                                                                    (not *singing*)

To clarify pronunciation

be + -ing = being (not *bing*)   shoe + -ing = shoeing
                                                    (not *shoing*)

To keep the sound of *c* or *g* soft

notice + -able = noticeable   marriage + -able = marriageable
peace + -able = peaceable   courage + -ous = courageous

Keeping the final e

If the suffix starts with a consonant, *keep* the e.

force + -ful = forceful   state + -ly = stately
excite + -ment = excitement   same + -ness = sameness

EXCEPTIONS

argue + -ment = argument   true + -ly = truly
judge + -ment = judgment   whole + -ly = wholly
due + -ly = duly   nine + -th = ninth

EXERCISE 24.5

Combine each of the following words and suffixes, dropping the unpronounced *e* when necessary.

1. future + -ism   5. malice + -ious   9. exercise + -ing
2. whole + -ly   6. dye + -ing   10. outrage + -ous
3. argue + -ment   7. hope + -ful
4. lone + -ly   8. continue + -ous

Using -ally

Use -ally if the base word ends in *ic*.

drastic + -ally = drastically   tragic + -ally = tragically
basic + -ally = basically   frantic + -ally = frantically

Using -ly

Use -ly if the base word does not end in *ic*.

apparent + -ly = apparently   quick + -ly = quickly
certain + -ly = certainly   supposed + -ly = supposedly
conscious + -ly = consciously

EXCEPTION

public + -ly = publicly

Using -cede, -ceed, and -sede

The suffixes *-cede, -ceed,* and *-sede* are especially easy to master because almost all words ending in the sound pronounced "seed" use the spelling *-cede*. Use *-sede* with only one word: *supersede*. Use *-ceed* with only three words: *exceed, proceed, succeed*. Use *-cede* with all other words ending in the "seed" sound.

accede	intercede	recede
concede	precede	secede

Words ending in a consonant and y

You must sometimes change the y to i when you add a suffix to words ending in y. In general, if it is preceded by a consonant, change the y.

bounty + -ful = bountiful	breezy + -ness = breeziness
try + -ed = tried	busy + -ily = busily
silly + -er = sillier	

EXCEPTIONS

Keep the y before the suffix *-ing*.

dry + -ing = drying	carry + -ing = carrying
liquefy + -ing = liquefying	vary + -ing = varying

Keep the y in some one-syllable base words.

shy + -er = shyer	wry + -ness = wryness
dry + -ly = dryly	

Keep the y if the base word is a proper name.

Kennedy + -esque = Kennedyesque

Words ending in a vowel and y

If the y is preceded by a vowel, keep the y.

joy + -ous = joyous	employ + -ment = employment
play + -ful = playful	buoy + -ed = buoyed

EXCEPTIONS

day + -ly = daily	gay + -ly = gaily

EXERCISE 24.6

Combine each of the following words and suffixes, changing the final *y* to *i* when necessary.

1. lonely + -er
2. carry + -ing
3. defy + -ance
4. study + -ous
5. supply + -ed
6. duty + -ful
7. likely + -hood
8. obey + -ed
9. rainy + -est
10. coy + -ly

Doubling the final consonant

When a suffix is added to a word that ends in a consonant, the consonant is sometimes doubled. If the word ends in consonant + vowel + consonant, the suffix begins with a vowel, and the word contains only one syllable or ends in an accented syllable, double the final consonant.

stop + -ing = stopping
slap + -ed = slapped
hot + -est = hottest
run + -er = runner

begin + -ing = beginning
occur + -ence = occurrence
refer + -ing = referring

DO NOT DOUBLE THE CONSONANT

If it is preceded by more than one vowel or by another consonant

bait + -ing = baiting
sleep + -ing = sleeping

fight + -er = fighter
start + -ed = started

If the suffix begins with a consonant

ship + -ment = shipment

fit + -ness = fitness

If the word is not accented on the last syllable

benefit + -ing = benefiting

fasten + -er = fastener

If the accent shifts from the last to the first syllable when the suffix is added

infer + -ence = inference

prefer + -ence = preference

If the last letter of the word and the first letter of the suffix are the same. In this case, simply keep both letters.

mortal + -ly = mortally
room + -mate = roommate

rotten + -ness = rottenness
usual + -ly = usually

EXERCISE 24.7

Combine each of the following words and suffixes, doubling the final consonant when necessary.

1. occur + -ed
2. fast + -est
3. skip + -er
4. refer + -ence
5. commit + -ment
6. regret + -able
7. submit + -ed
8. drastic + -ally
9. benefit + -ed
10. weep + -ing

24e

Making words plural

Making singular nouns plural calls for the use of several different spelling guidelines.

Adding -s

For most words, add -s.

pencil, pencils   book, books   computer, computers

Adding -es

For words ending in s, ch, sh, x, or z, add es.

Jones, Joneses   fox, foxes   flash, flashes
bus, buses   church, churches   buzz, buzzes

For words ending in o, add -es if the o is preceded by a consonant.

potato, potatoes   hero, heroes   veto, vetoes

EXCEPTIONS

memo, memos   piano, pianos
pro, pros   solo, solos

Add -s if the o is preceded by a vowel.

rodeo, rodeos   patio, patios
zoo, zoos   curio, curios

Words ending in f *or* fe

For some words ending in *f* or *fe,* change *f* to *v* and add *-s* or *-es.*

calf, calves	life, lives	leaf, leaves
half, halves	wife, wives	hoof, hooves
self, selves	shelf, shelves	knife, knives

Words ending in y

For words ending in *y,* change *y* to *i* and add *-es* if the *y* is preceded by a consonant.

theory, theories	huckleberry, huckleberries
eighty, eighties	sky, skies

EXCEPTIONS

To form the plural of any proper name ending in *y,* just add *-s.*

Henry, Henrys

Keep the *y* and add *-s* if the *y* is preceded by a vowel.

guy, guys	attorney, attorneys
delay, delays	alloy, alloys

Irregular plurals

For irregular plurals and nouns that have the same form in the singular and plural, memorize those you do not already know.

man, men	bacterium, bacteria	deer, deer
woman, women	locus, loci	sheep, sheep
child, children	alga, algae	moose, moose
foot, feet	basis, bases	series, series
tooth, teeth	datum, data	species, species

Compound words

For compound nouns written as one word, make the last part of the compound plural.

briefcase, briefcases
mailbox, mailboxes
bookshelf, bookshelves
grandchild, grandchildren

For compound nouns written as separate words or hyphenated, make the most important part of the compound plural.

> brother-in-law, brothers-in-law
> lieutenant governor, lieutenant governors
> sergeant major, sergeants major
> leap year, leap years
> bus stop, bus stops

EXERCISE 24.8

Form the plural of each of the following words.

1. tomato	6. spoof	11. stepchild
2. hoof	7. beach	12. turkey
3. volunteer	8. yourself	13. heir apparent
4. baby	9. golf club	14. radio
5. dish	10. rose	15. phenomenon

24f

Taking a personal spelling inventory

This chapter has surveyed general spelling rules and guidelines. You now need to tailor this advice to your own spelling patterns and problems. Doing so means becoming a detective, looking for clues in as large and varied a sample of your prose as you have time to examine.

1

Identifying troublesome words and patterns

You can begin your inventory by looking through several pieces of your writing and making a list of every misspelled word. Whenever possible, identify the guideline in this chapter that deals with the misspelling. Here is the beginning of one student's inventory.

WORD	MISSPELLING	GUIDELINE
their	there	homonyms
receiving	recieving	"*i* before *e*"
hastiest	hastyest	final *y* + suffix

WORD	MISSPELLING	GUIDELINE
beginning	begining	final consonant + suffix
affect	effect	homonyms
sharing	shareing	final *e* + suffix
environment	enviroment	unpronounced letters
theories	theorys	final *y* + plural
dissatisfied	disatisfied	prefixes

2

Using a spell checker

Some good news, perhaps, is that writers now have a special tool to help with spelling: the spell checker, a program included on most word processors that helps find incorrect spellings. We say *perhaps* this is good news, however, for a reason. A comparison of spelling errors in first-year essays that were handwritten or typed with those in first-year essays that were produced on a word processor either with or without a spell checker produced these interesting results.

handwritten or typed	1.74 errors per essay
word-processed *without* spell checker	3.81 errors per essay
word-processed *with* spell checker	1.60 errors per essay

These findings make an important point about writing on a word processor: seeing your words on screen or in nice neat typescript may make it difficult to "see" your spelling errors. Indeed, keyboarding often introduces new spelling errors, and the "clean" copy can, in a way, conceal these errors. If you use a word processor without a spell checker, you probably need to proofread more carefully than ever before.

These results also tell us that spell checkers alone won't correct spelling errors. Students using spell checkers misspelled almost as many words as did students who handwrote or typed their essays. To benefit from this tool, therefore, you must understand how to use a spell checker accurately and efficiently, and you must learn to adapt the spell checker to your own needs. And you must turn it on: just as a seat belt can save your life only if you wear it, so a spell checker can improve your spelling only if you use it.

≫ *Using a spell checker*

1. Use your spell checker. Check every word it calls to your attention.
2. Keep a dictionary near your computer, and look up *any* word the spell checker highlights that you aren't absolutely sure of.

3. Remember that spell-checker dictionaries are limited; they don't recognize most proper names, foreign words, or specialized language. If your program has a "learn" option, enter into your spell-checker dictionary any words you use regularly and have trouble spelling. Add also your own spelling "demons."

4. Remember that spell checkers do not recognize homonym errors (misspelling *there* as *their*, for example). (24b) If you know that you mix up certain words, therefore, you should check for them after running your spell checker. You may be able to use the search function to identify words you need to check—every *there*, *their*, and *they're*, for instance.

5. Remember that spell checkers are not sensitive to capitalization. If you write "president clinton," the spell checker won't question it.

6. Proofread carefully, even after you have used the spell checker.

3

Building on visualization and memory cues

Before the advent of printing—and photocopying machines—people learned to train their memories extensively. You can activate your memory first by **visualizing** correct spellings or making mental pictures of how a word looks. You can also learn to use memory cues, or **mnemonic devices** (named for the Greek goddess of memory, Mnemosyne), in mastering words that tend to trip you up. Here are one student's memory cues.

WORD; MISSPELLING	CUE
a lot; alot	I wouldn't write *alittle*, would I?
government; goverment	Government should serve those it *governs*.
separate; seperate	*Separate* rates two *a's*.
definitely; definately	There are a *finite* number of ways to spell *definitely*.

EXERCISE 24.9   Revising for Spelling

Correct each misspelling in the passage below. Whenever possible, classify the misspelling according to one of the guidelines in this chapter. Then draw up three or four spelling tips you could give this particular student.

For me, the ideel ocupation is an arangement in which I would play with a band for six months and tour the other six months of the year. I wouldn't want to teach music because I would probly have to teach in a school where many students are forced by there parents to take music. When children are forced to do something, its likly that they won't enjoy it. If I were able to both tour an teach, however, I would be happy.

I'm realy glad that I've gotten involved in music; it looks as if I'm destined to be a profesional musician. Surly I don't know what else I could do; I dout I'd be a good administrater or bussiness executive or lawyer. And the idea of being a doctor or denist and probing around people's bodys or looking at teeth that have huge, roting cavities isn't appealing to me. The more I think about it, the happyer I am with my music. I definately plan to pursue that career.

THINKING CRITICALLY ABOUT YOUR OWN SPELLING

If you are keeping a writing log, devote a section of it to a personal spelling inventory. Choose a sample of your recent writing, and identify every misspelling. If you have any drafts in a word processor, use a spell checker. Then, following the format presented in 24f1, enter the word, your misspelling, and the guideline or pattern that relates to it. For persistent misspellings, create a memory cue (see 24f3), and enter it in the log along with the correct spelling.

25

Using Dictionaries

IN THE OPENING SCENE OF REX STOUT'S NOVEL GAMBIT, *master sleuth Nero Wolfe is "in the middle of a fit," solemnly tearing the pages out of a large leather-bound book and dropping them one by one into a fire. What is the book that Wolfe finds "subversive and intolerably offensive"? It is a dictionary—specifically, the third edition of* Webster's New International Dictionary. *Guilty of thousands of "crimes" and threatening the very "integrity of the English language," this dictionary must be destroyed, Wolfe declares, down to its very fine binding.*

You may not have thought of dictionaries as the cause of violent controversy, but very often they have been. Such controversy usually relates to a tension between two basic and competing aims for dictionaries. One aim is to fix a standard of the language so that its users can know what is "right" and what is "wrong." Before the advent of the printing press, English spelling in particular was far from fixed, and with good reason; few people had occasion to write words down. Even more than one hundred years later, the author we know as Shakespeare spelled his own name in several different ways. By the eighteenth century, however, writers such as Alexander Pope urged a codification of the language, which they felt had reached perfection. Enter Samuel Johnson, whose Dictionary of the English Language *(1755) established an authoritative right and wrong for a long time.*

The second and competing aim of a dictionary was articulated forcefully about one hundred years after Johnson: to record a full inventory of the language as it is used, without prescribing "right" and "wrong." What enraged Wolfe was a particular dictionary's focus on this second aim rather than on the first. These dual aims persist in our dictionaries and may in fact influence your choice of which dictionary to use on which occasion. This chapter will map the territory covered by dictionaries and provide you with a means of choosing the dictionaries you want to work with.

Everyday Use

A dictionary can be particularly handy when you are faced with signing—or preparing to sign—a contract. For many Americans, choosing life insurance is an important decision that calls for understanding and evaluating complex and competing plans. Reading the materials calls for a sharp eye and a clear knowledge of what words mean. Materials describing one such plan, for example, contain the following terms: *semiannual, net cost, underwrite, waiver, conversion, incontestability,* and *incapacitated.* How many of these terms do you understand? Which ones are generally familiar but may hold specific legal meanings in a contract? Which ones would you want to look up in a dictionary before signing your name to the contract?

EXERCISE 25.1

Without looking them up, try your hand at defining at least two of the italicized terms in the Everyday Use box above. Compare your definitions with those of one or two other students. Then look up the terms in one of the dictionaries described in this chapter, and summarize briefly how your definitions differ from the ones in the dictionary.

25a

Exploring the dictionary

A good dictionary packs a surprising amount of information, including much more than the correct spelling, into a relatively small space. Look at this entry in *Webster's New World Dictionary,* Third College Edition:

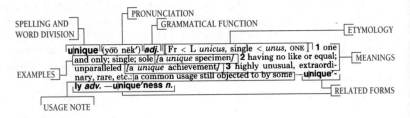

In fact, a dictionary entry may contain a dozen or more kinds of information about a word, the most common of which are listed below. The first six normally appear in all entries, the others only when relevant.

1. *Spelling,* including alternative spellings if they exist
2. *Word division,* with bars, dots, or spaces separating syllables and showing where a word may be divided at the end of a line
3. *Pronunciation,* including alternative pronunciations
4. *Grammatical functions and irregular forms* (if any), including plurals of nouns, principal parts of verbs, and comparative and superlative forms of adjectives and adverbs
5. *Etymology,* the languages and words that the word comes from
6. *Meanings,* in order of either development or frequency of use
7. *Examples* of the word in the context of a phrase or sentence
8. *Usage labels and notes* (See explanation below.)
9. *Field labels,* indicating that a word has a special meaning in a particular field of knowledge or activity
10. *Synonyms* and *antonyms*
11. *Related words* and their grammatical functions
12. *Idioms,* phrases in which the word appears and their meanings

Usage labeling and notes

For some words, many dictionaries include a kind of usage labeling, intended to let readers know that some or all meanings of the word are not considered appropriate in certain contexts. You can generally find such labels identified and described at the beginning of the dictionary. Here are some of the labels the *Webster's New World* uses.

1. *Archaic:* rarely used today except in specialized contexts
2. *Obsolete:* no longer used
3. *Colloquial:* characteristic of conversation and informal writing
4. *Slang:* extremely informal
5. *Dialect:* used mostly in a particular geographical or linguistic area, often one that is specified, such as Scotland or New England

In addition to labels, dictionaries sometimes include notes discussing usage in greater detail. In the *Webster's New World* entry for *unique,* notice that the third meaning includes a note that it is "common" but "still objected to by some."

EXERCISE 25.2

Look up the spelling, syllable division, and pronunciation of the following words in your dictionary. Note any variants in spelling and/or pronunciation.

1. process (noun)
2. heinous
3. exigency
4. schedule

5. whippet
6. crayfish
7. macabre
8. hurrah

9. greasy
10. theater

EXERCISE 25.3

Look up the etymology of the following words in your dictionary.

1. rhetoric
2. student
3. curry (noun)
4. whine

5. apple
6. sex
7. okra
8. tortilla

9. cinema
10. video

EXERCISE 25.4

Use your dictionary to find synonyms (and antonyms) of the following words.

1. coerce
2. prevaricate

3. parameter
4. odious

5. awesome
6. obfuscate

25b

Distinguishing among dictionaries

Since the time of Samuel Johnson's 1755 dictionary and Noah Webster's *American Dictionary of the English Language* (1828), the number and kinds of English-language dictionaries have multiplied many times over. While they all share the name *dictionary*, these numerous volumes differ considerably from one another. You may use a portable paperback dictionary most often, but you should be familiar with other kinds of dictionaries as well.

1

Abridged dictionaries

Abridged, or "abbreviated," **dictionaries** are the type most often used by college writers. Though they are not as complete as unabridged dictionaries, they are more affordable and more portable. Among the most helpful abridged dictionaries are *Webster's New World Dictionary, Random House Webster's College Dictionary,* and *The American Heritage Dictionary.*

Webster's New World Dictionary of American English, Third College Edition (New York: Prentice Hall, 1994), includes more than 170,000 entries; meanings are listed chronologically—in the order in which they entered the language. Geographical and biographical names appear with the regular entries, and more than 800 drawings are provided.

Random House Webster's College Dictionary (New York: Random House, 1991) has more than 180,000 entries, including many words very new to the language, from *acquaintance rape* to *zouk.* This work is notable for its attempt to eliminate sexist language from definitions, its usage notes intended to warn users when terms may be offensive or disparaging, and its appendix on "Avoiding Sexist Language."

The American Heritage Dictionary, Second College Edition (Boston: Houghton Mifflin, 1991), has more than 200,000 listings, augmented by 5,000 new scientific and technical terms and 3,000 new photographs supplementing the many photographs, drawings, and maps from the first edition. *The American Heritage* lists meanings in the order of most to least common. Notes on usage are extensive. Introductory essays provide a context for the usage notes in the form of a debate on the issue. Biographical and geographical sections, also liberally illustrated, follow the dictionary of general vocabulary, as does a section on abbreviations.

2

Unabridged dictionaries

Unabridged, or "unabbreviated," **dictionaries** are the royalty of their species—the most complete, richly detailed, and thoroughly presented dictionaries of English. Whereas good abridged dictionaries may include 175,000 items, unabridged dictionaries far more than double that figure. Because they are large and often multivolume—and hence expensive—you may not own one, but you will want and need to consult one on occasion. You can always find an unabridged dictionary in the library. Among the leading unabridged dictionaries are the *Oxford English Dictionary* and *Webster's Third New International Dictionary of the English Language.*

The Oxford English Dictionary, Second Edition, 20 volumes (New York: Oxford University Press, 1989). The grandparent of unabridged dictionaries in English, the *OED* began in Britain in the nineteenth century as an attempt to give a full history of each English word, recording its entry into the language and illustrating the development of its various meanings with dated quotations in chronological order. Volunteers all over the English-speaking world contributed quotations, and the first edition was published piecemeal over a period of more than forty years. The second edition traces more than half a million words and is unparalleled in its historical account of changes in word meanings and spellings. It is available on CD-ROM.

Webster's Third New International Dictionary of the English Language (Springfield, Mass.: Merriam-Webster, 1986). Containing more entries than any other dictionary except the *OED*—more than 450,000 in all—this one-volume work stirred considerable controversy at its publication because of its tendency, as mentioned in the introduction to this chapter, to *describe* rather than to *prescribe* usage. In all, the editors collected 6,165,000 examples of recorded usage, on which they drew for their usage notes. *Webster's Third* lists meanings in order of their entry into the language and quotes from over 14,000 different authors to provide illustrations of words in context.

Here are the *Webster's Third* entries for *unique* as an adjective and as a noun. The adjective entry lists the meaning "unusual, notable" and provides examples of the use of *most unique* but does not discuss the controversy over this usage. At the end of the entry, the notation *syn* refers to the entries for *single* and *strange*, where the shades of meaning that distinguish *unique* from its synonyms are explained. The phonetic symbols differ slightly from those in either the *OED* or the abridged dictionaries.

¹**unique** \yü'nēk, 'ₑ,ₑ\ *adj, sometimes* -ER/-EST [F, fr. L *unicus* sole, single, unique, fr. *unus* one + *-icus* -ic — more at ONE] **1 a :** being the only one **:** SOLE ⟨earning money whose ~ object could be nothing but Cyril's welfare —Arnold Bennett⟩ ⟨has thus preserved the original and often ~ records —G.B. Parks⟩ ⟨you are a miracle, a wonder, a mystery . . . one single ~ and inimitable living thing —J.C.Powys⟩ **b** *of a book* **:** known to exist in no other copy **2 :** being without a like or equal **:** single in kind or excellence **:** UNEQUALED ⟨they stand alone, ~, objects of supreme interest —A.B.Osborne⟩ ⟨as historian he knows that events, like persons, are ~ —J.M. Barzun⟩ ⟨remains singularly himself, a ~ lyrist of the first water —I.L.Salomon⟩ ⟨an almost ~ experience —Havelock Ellis⟩ ⟨tendencies present in our contemporary world which make our own times somewhat ~ —M.B.Smith⟩ ⟨story of his life is considerably more ~ than most autobiographies —Dorothy C. Fisher⟩ ⟨the more we study him, the less ~ he seems —Harry Levin⟩ — sometimes used with *to* ⟨the problem of what to do with surplus women is by no means ~ to our own society — Ralph Linton⟩ or *with* ⟨by no means ~ with the song sparrow —*Nature Mag.*⟩ **3 :** UNUSUAL, NOTABLE ⟨possessed ~ ability in the raising of funds —C.F.Thwing⟩ ⟨the wife of a career diplomat has a ~ opportunity to observe the world political scene —Ray Pierre⟩ ⟨a frankness ~ in literature —David Daiches⟩ ⟨~ peace and privacy —R.W.Hatch⟩ ⟨cheap, nourishing, and a ~ dining experience —T.H.Fielding⟩ ⟨the most ~ characteristic of that environment —R.A.Billington⟩ ⟨she's the most ~ person I ever met —Arthur Miller⟩ ⟨the most ~ theater in town —*advt*⟩ **4 :** capable of being performed in only one way ⟨the factorization of a number into its prime factors is ~⟩ **syn** see SINGLE, STRANGE
²**unique** \"\ *n* -s **:** something (as a specimen, thing, circumstance, or person) that is unique **:** the only one of its kind ⟨mistaking the ~ for the typical —W.J.Reilly⟩ ⟨the zest of the collector for possession of a ~ —Roy Bedichek⟩ ⟨a display of glass, including undercoated ~s —*Danish Foreign Office Jour.*⟩ ⟨the phoenix, the ~ of birds —Thomas De Quincey⟩

EXERCISE 25.5

See how Lewis Thomas uses *unique* in this sentence: "In a rose garden, a rose is a rose because of geraniol, a 10-carbon compound, and it's the geometric conformation of atoms and their bond angles that determine the unique fragrance." Compare the entries of *unique* on pages 394 and 398, and decide whether Thomas's usage follows the advice of either one.

EXERCISE 25.6

Look up the following words in at least one abridged and one unabridged dictionary, and compare the entries. Record any differences or disagreements you find, and bring this record to class for discussion.

1. dogmatism
2. alienate
3. discriminate
4. hopefully
5. humanism
6. culture

EXERCISE 25.7

Look up one of the following words in the *OED,* and write a paragraph describing any changes in meaning it has undergone since its entry into English.

1. cheerful
2. machine
3. vulgar
4. humor (noun)
5. honest
6. romance

25c

Consulting specialized dictionaries

Abridged and unabridged dictionaries will provide you with an enormous amount of information. Sometimes, however, you will need to turn to additional sources for more specialized information. Such sources are available in dictionaries of usage, synonyms, and slang.

Dictionaries of usage

In cases where usage is disputed or where you feel unsure of your own usage, you may wish to consult a specialized dictionary of usage. The most widely used such work, although it is much more about British than American usage, is H. W. Fowler's *Dictionary of Modern English Usage,* which was first published in 1926 and whose second edition was revised by Sir Ernest Gowers in 1965.

Dictionaries of synonyms

All writers are sometimes stuck for just the right word, and at such times, a dictionary of synonyms or a thesaurus is a friend indeed. In these works, each entry is followed by words whose meanings are similar to that of the entry. A useful source is *Webster's Dictionary of Synonyms*.

A **thesaurus** (the word comes from a word meaning "treasure" or "storehouse") provides antonyms as well as synonyms. Two thesauri are particularly helpful: *Webster's Collegiate Thesaurus* and *The New Roget's Thesaurus of the English Language in Dictionary Form*.

Remember, however, to use dictionaries of synonyms and thesauri carefully, because rarely in English are two words so close in meaning that they can be used interchangeably in radically different contexts. As Mark Twain put it, the difference between the right word and the almost right word is the difference between lightning and the lightning bug.

Dictionaries of etymology, regional English, and slang

On some occasions, you may want or need to find out all you can about the origins of a word, you may want to find out about a term used in only one area of the country, or you may want to see whether a term is considered slang. The following specialized dictionaries can help you out:

> *The Oxford Dictionary of English Etymology*. Ed. C. T. Onions. New York: Oxford University Press, 1966.
>
> *Dictionary of American Regional English*. Ed. Frederic G. Cassidy. Cambridge, Mass.: Belknap, Harvard University Press, 1985.
>
> *Dictionary of American Slang*, second supplemented edition. Ed. Harold Wentworth and Stuart Berg Flexner. New York: Crowell, 1978.
>
> *Trash Cash, Fizzbos, and Flatliners: A Dictionary of Today's Words*. Ed. Sid Lerner and Gary F. Belkin. Boston: Houghton, 1993.

▶ *FOR MULTILINGUAL WRITERS*
Using a Learner's Dictionary

In addition to using a good college dictionary, you may want to invest in one of the following dictionaries intended especially for learners of English. The *Longman Dictionary of American English* presents the English spoken in the United States; the *Oxford Advanced Learner's Dictionary of Current English* covers British English.

These dictionaries provide information about count and noncount nouns, idioms and phrasal verbs, verbs that take a gerund and those that take an infinitive, and other topics important to learners of English. You should in general avoid using a bilingual dictionary, for you'll find more accurate and idiomatic information in an English dictionary than in, for example, a Spanish-English dictionary.

EXERCISE 25.8

Look up the following words in several specialized dictionaries, and find out as much as you can about their meanings, origins, and uses.

1. wazoo	3. scam	5. whammy
2. tip	4. jazz	6. advertorial

THINKING CRITICALLY ABOUT WORDS

Reading with Attention to Words

In his autobiography, Malcolm X says that he taught himself to write by reading and copying the dictionary. Certainly you can teach yourself to be a better writer by paying careful attention to the way other writers use words that are unfamiliar to you. Choose a writer whose work you admire, and read that author's work for at least thirty minutes, noting six or seven words that you would not ordinarily have thought to use. Do a little dictionary investigative work on these words, and bring your results to class for discussion.

Thinking about Your Own Use of Words

Go back through the last several pieces of writing you have done, looking for two or three words you have used that interest you but that you know very little about. Then look up these words in at least one abridged and one unabridged dictionary and in any specialized dictionary that might give you further information. On the basis of what you have learned, check the way you have used these words in your writing. How accurately and appropriately have you used them? What synonyms could you have appropriately substituted?

26

Enriching Vocabulary

I**N ONE OF THE GREAT HEROIC TALES IN ENGLISH LITERATURE,** *Beowulf faces a series of difficult challenges. In the face of them, he calls not for weapons or for superhuman strength. Instead he says, quite simply, "I will unlock my word hoard." Beowulf regards his word hoard—his vocabulary or language—as his greatest strength. Indeed, in the history of Western culture, the connection between language and creative power has been very close. In the Bible, for instance, how does God create the world? By naming it.*

Vocabulary comes from a Latin term for "name" (vocabulum), which in turn comes from the Latin verb for "call." The connection between vocabulary and calling into being is what led a famous philosopher to declare that "the limits of my language are the limits of my world." You can recognize what the philosopher means easily enough by remembering a time in your life when you learned the name of something new. Before that time, this thing did not exist for you; yet curiously enough, once you knew its name, you began to recognize it all around you. Such is the power of vocabulary in enriching not only our personal language but our lives as well.

26a

Considering your vocabulary

At its largest, your English vocabulary includes all those words whose meanings you either recognize or can deduce from context. This, your **processing vocabulary**, allows you to interpret the meanings of many passages whose words you might not actively use yourself. Your **producing vocabulary** is more limited, made up of words you actually use in writing or speaking.

Everyday Use

Many years ago, the famous baseball player Dizzy Dean injured his leg sliding into second base. After examining the leg, the trainer announced with a serious expression that it looked as if the leg was fractured. "Fractured, hell!" cried Dean. "The damned thing's broken!" If *fractured* wasn't a part of Dizzy Dean's active vocabulary before then, he surely figured it out quickly. So it is with all of us, for we meet new words every day; and with the help of context, word roots, and dictionaries, we figure them out and make them ours. Think of times recently when you learned the name of something new—a kind of plant, for example, or a computer term like *byte,* or an unfamiliar food like *fajitas.* How exactly did you discover its meaning?

Part of what it means to mature intellectually is to broaden your mental horizons by learning how to name more things more accurately, to increase your own word hoard. Doing so involves consciously strengthening the bridges between your processing vocabulary and your producing vocabulary by beginning to use in your own speech and writing more of the words you recognize and can interpret in context. To accomplish this goal, you must become an investigative reporter of your own language and the language of others.

EXERCISE 26.1

Jot down two or three words you have heard or read lately that you would like to make part of your own vocabulary. Try defining them, and then write several sentences using each word.

Charting the history of English

Try to imagine a world without language. In fact, you probably cannot do so, for language is perhaps the most ancient heritage of the human race. Because language brings us together and indeed allows us to name and structure our experience of the world, it is well worth understanding how this heritage originated and has changed over the centuries. Knowing at least a little about the relationship of English to German, Norse, Latin, Greek, and French can help you learn more about any particular modern English word.

English has always been a hybrid language, what Daniel Defoe called "your Roman-Saxon-Danish-Norman English." Where did this hybrid come from, and how did it evolve? English, like one-third of all languages in the world, descends from Indo-European, a language spoken by a group of seminomadic peoples who almost certainly had domestic animals, worked leather, wove wool, and planted some crops. Where they lived is the subject of great controversy, though their original home must have been in some part of north-central Europe. Scholars began to argue for Indo-European as a "common source" and tried to identify its features when they noted more and more striking resemblances among words in a number of languages.

English	Latin	French	Greek	German	Dutch	Swedish	Danish
three	*tres*	*trois*	*treis*	*drei*	*drie*	*tre*	*tre*

A version of Indo-European was brought to Britain by the Germanic invasions following 449. This early language, called Anglo-Saxon or Old English, was influenced by Latin and Greek when Christianity was reintroduced into England beginning in 597, was later shaped by the Viking invasions beginning in the late 700s (the Danes feature prominently in *Beowulf*), and was transformed by French after the Norman Conquest (1066).

Although English continued to evolve in the centuries after the conquest, Latin and French were then the languages of the learned—of the church and court. (Indeed, lectures at Oxford University were delivered in Latin well into the nineteenth century.) In the late 1300s, it was Geoffrey Chaucer, writing *The Canterbury Tales* in the language of the people, who helped establish what is now called Middle English as the political, legal, and literary language of Britain. And after the advent of printing in the mid-1400s, that language became more accessible and more standardized. By about 1600, it had essentially become the Modern English we use today.

The following three versions of a biblical passage will give you an idea of how much English had evolved up to this time:

ANGLO-SAXON GOSPELS, AROUND A.D. 1000

And eft hē ongan hī æt þǣre sǣ lǣran. And him wæs mycel męnegu tō gegaderod, swā þæt hē on scip ēode, and on bǣre sǣ wæs; and eall sēo męnegu ymbe þē sǣ wæs on lande.

WYCLIFFE BIBLE, ABOUT 1380

And eft Jhesus bigan to teche at the see; and myche puple was gaderid to hym, so that he wente in to a boot, and sat in the see, and al the puple was aboute the see on the loond.

KING JAMES VERSION, 1611

And he began again to teach by the seaside: and there was gathered unto him a great multitude, so that he entered into a ship, and sat in the sea: and the whole multitude was by the sea on the land.

Note that in the Old English text, only a few words—*and, he, him, waes, on, lande*—look at all familiar. By the time of Chaucer and Wycliffe, however, many words are recognizable. And by the time of Shakespeare, the language is easily readable.

In the last four hundred years, English has continued borrowing from many languages and, as a result, now has one of the world's largest vocabularies. Modern English, then, is a plant growing luxuriously in the soil of multiple sources.

26b

Recognizing word roots

As its name suggests, a **root** is a word from which other words grow, usually through the addition of prefixes or suffixes. From the Latin root *-dic-* or *-dict-* ("speak"), for instance, grows a whole range of words in English: *contradict, dictate, dictator, diction, edict, predict, dictaphone,* and others. From the Greek root *-chrono-* ("time") come our words *chronology, synchronize, chronic,* and so on.

Here are some other Latin (L) and Greek (G) roots. Recognizing them will help you recognize networks of words.

ROOT	MEANING	EXAMPLES
-audi- (L)	to hear	audience, audio
-bene- (L)	good, well	benevolent, benefit
-bio- (G)	life	biography, biosphere
-duc(t)- (L)	to lead or to make	ductile, reproduce
-gen- (G)	race, kind	genealogy, gene
-geo- (G)	earth	geography, geometry
-graph- (G)	to write	graphic, photography
-jur-, -jus- (L)	law	justice, jurisdiction
-log(o)- (G)	word, thought	biology, logical
-luc- (L)	light	lucid, translucent
-manu- (L)	hand	manufacture, manual
-mit-, -mis- (L)	to send	permit, transmission
-path- (G)	feel, suffer	empathy, pathetic
-phil- (G)	love	philosopher, bibliophile
-photo- (G)	light	photography, telephoto
-port- (L)	to carry	transport, portable
-psych- (G)	soul	psychology, psychopath
-scrib-, -script- (L)	to write	inscribe, manuscript
-sent-, -sens- (L)	to feel	sensation, resent
-tele- (G)	far away	telegraph, telepathy

ROOT	MEANING	EXAMPLES
-tend- (L)	to stretch	extend, tendency
-terr- (L)	earth	inter, territorial
-vac- (L)	empty	vacuole, evacuation
-vid-, -vis- (L)	to see	video, envision, visit

EXERCISE 26.2

Using the list of roots above, try to figure out the meaning of each of the following words. Write a potential definition for each one, and then compare your dictionary's definition with yours.

1. terrestrial	5. beneficent	9. juridical
2. scriptorium	6. audiology	10. graphology
3. geothermal	7. vacuous	
4. lucent	8. pathogenic	

26c

Recognizing prefixes and suffixes

Originally individual words, prefixes and suffixes are groups of letters added to words or to word roots to create new words. These word additions account for much of the flexibility of English, often allowing dozens of words to be built on one root.

1
Prefixes

The word **prefix** appropriately demonstrates its own meaning: it is made up of a prefix (-*pre*-) and a root (-*fix*-) and means literally "fasten before." Fastened to the beginnings of words or roots, prefixes modify and extend meanings. Recognizing common prefixes can often help you decipher the meaning of otherwise unfamiliar words.

Prefixes of negation or opposition

PREFIX	MEANING	EXAMPLES
a-, an-	without, not	ahistorical, anemia
anti-	against	antibody, antiphonal
contra-	against	contravene, contradict

PREFIX	MEANING	EXAMPLES
de-	from, take away from	demerit, declaw
dis-	apart, away	disappear, discharge
il-, im-, in-, ir-	not	illegal, immature, indistinct, irreverent
mal-	wrong	malevolent, malpractice
mis-	wrong, bad	misapply, misanthrope
non-	not	nonentity, nonsense
un-	not	unbreakable, unable

Prefixes of quantity

PREFIX	MEANING	EXAMPLES
bi-	two	bipolar, bilateral
milli-	thousand	millimeter, milligram
mono-	one, single	monotone, monologue
omni-	all	omniscient, omnipotent
semi-	half	semicolon, semiconductor
tri-	three	tripod, trimester
uni-	one	unitary, univocal

Prefixes of time and space

PREFIX	MEANING	EXAMPLES
ante-	before	antedate, antebellum
circum-	around	circumlocution, circumnavigate
co-, col-, com-, con-, cor-	with	coequal, collaborate, commiserate, contact, correspond
e-, ex-	out of	emit, extort, expunge
hyper-	over, more than	hypersonic, hypersensitive
hypo-	under, less than	hypodermic, hypoglycemia
inter-	between	intervene, international
mega-	enlarge, large	megalomania, megaphone
micro-	tiny	micrometer, microscopic
neo-	recent	neologism, neophyte
post-	after	postwar, postscript
pre-	before	previous, prepublication
pro-	before, onward	project, propel
re-	again, back	review, re-create
sub-	under, beneath	subhuman, submarine
super-	over, above	supercargo, superimpose
syn-	at the same time	synonym, synchronize
trans-	across, over	transport, transition

EXERCISE 26.3

Using the list of prefixes above and the list of roots in 26b, try to figure out the meaning of each of the following words. Write a potential definition for each one, and then compare your dictionary's definition with yours.

1. remit	5. distend	9. inaudible
2. subterranean	6. superscript	10. apathetic
3. translucent	7. deport	
4. monograph	8. neologism	

2

Suffixes

Attached to the ends of words and word roots, **suffixes** modify and extend meanings, many times by altering the grammatical function or part of speech of the original word. Suffixes can, for example, turn the verb *create* into a noun, an adjective, or an adverb.

VERB	create
NOUNS	crea*tor*/crea*tion*/creativ*ity*/crea*ture*
ADJECTIVE	creat*ive*
ADVERB	creative*ly*

Noun suffixes

SUFFIX	MEANING	EXAMPLES
-acy	state or quality	democracy, privacy
-al	act of	rebuttal, refusal
-ance, -ence	state or quality of	maintenance, eminence
-dom	place or state of being	freedom, thralldom
-er, -or	one who	trainer, investor
-ism	doctrine or belief characteristic of	liberalism, Taoism
-ist	one who	organist, physicist
-ity	quality of	veracity, opacity
-ment	condition of	payment, argument
-ness	state of being	watchfulness, cleanliness
-ship	position held	professorship, fellowship
-sion, -tion	state of being or action	digression, transition

Verb suffixes

SUFFIX	MEANING	EXAMPLES
-ate	cause to be	concentrate, regulate
-en	cause to be or become	enliven, blacken
-ify, -fy	make or cause to be	unify, terrify, amplify
-ize	cause to become	magnetize, civilize

Adjective suffixes

SUFFIX	MEANING	EXAMPLES
-able, -ible	capable of being	assumable, edible
-al	pertaining to	regional, political
-esque	reminiscent of	picturesque, statuesque
-ful	having a notable quality	colorful, sorrowful
-ic	pertaining to	poetic, mythic
-ious, -ous	of or characterized by	famous, nutritious
-ish	having the quality of	prudish, clownish
-ive	having the nature of	festive, creative, massive
-less	without	endless, senseless

EXERCISE 26.4

Using the list of suffixes above, figure out the meaning of each of the following words. (Use your dictionary if necessary.) Then choose two of the words, and use each one in a sentence.

1. contemplative
2. fanciful
3. impairment
4. liquefy
5. barrenness
6. defiance
7. merciless
8. redden
9. standardize
10. satirist

26d

Building a word hoard

Making good use of prefixes or suffixes will increase your vocabulary, but other methods will be even more helpful in creating a word hoard that is a match for Beowulf's. These methods include analyzing contexts and reading actively.

1

Analyzing word contexts

If you have ever run into a person you knew but could not place—until you remembered the place where you normally see the person (at the grocery store, say)—you know firsthand the importance of context in helping you identify people and things. The same principle holds true for words. So if a word is at first unfamiliar to you, look carefully at its context, paying attention to all the clues that the context can give; often you will be able to deduce the meaning.

For instance, if the word *accouterments* is unfamiliar in the sentence *We stopped at a camping supply store to pick up last-minute accouterments,* the context—*a camping supply store* and *last-minute*—suggests strongly that *equipment* or some similar word fits the bill. And that is what *accouterments* means.

EXERCISE 26.5

Identify the contextual clues that help you understand any unfamiliar words in the following sentences. Then write paraphrases of three of the sentences.

1. Before Prohibition, the criminal fringe in the United States had been a self-effacing, scattered class with little popular support.

2. The ambiguity of the evidence prevented the jury from determining which parts of it were extraneous. The jury asked for clarification.

3. The community's reaction to the preternatural creature in Shelley's *Frankenstein* shows that people are often more monstrous than a monster is.

4. My fifth-grade teacher was the epitome of what I wanted to be, and I began to imitate him scrupulously.

5. Aristarchus showed that the sun is larger than the earth and proposed a heliocentric model of the solar system. In the second century A.D., however, Ptolemy challenged this theory with his geocentric model, which came to dominate astronomy for the next fourteen hundred years.

2

Becoming an active reader

As processors of information, we can read words alone, or we can read meanings. Reading meanings means filling in gaps, making connections, leaping ahead, asking questions, taking mental notes. Active readers flex their mental muscles while reading; they exercise their own understanding and thereby attain greater knowledge. Out of such activity great word hoards are born. (Chapter 1 provides guidelines to improve your reading.) Here are some additional tips for building your vocabulary.

- Make a habit of paraphrasing or summarizing unfamiliar words or phrases. Then check the dictionary to see how accurate you were.

- Practice naming the opposites of words. If you see *abbreviation,* for instance, try supplying its opposite—*enlargement, elaboration,* and so on.

- Challenge authors by trying to come up with better words than the ones they used.

- Read aloud to yourself from time to time, noting any words whose pronunciation you are unsure of. Check them in a dictionary.

- Become a collector of words, choosing those you like best and making them part of your producing vocabulary. Begin by choosing a writer you admire and reading for as long as it takes to identify several words you like but would not use in speech or writing. Your collection has started. Now analyze what you like about these words—their pronunciation, meaning, or usage.

ON VARIETIES OF ENGLISH
Learning the Vocabulary of Your Field

All occupations, professions, and disciplines rely on characteristic jargon: the vocabulary of medical fields, for example, includes technical terms such as *hematoma* and *carcinoid,* which the layperson might refer to simply as a "bruise" and a "tumor." In physics, the term *charm* indicates the quantum property assigned to the "charmed" quark. And in law, words quite often take on technical meanings associated with earlier legal decisions and precedents. In copyright law, for instance, the word *original* carries meanings and connotations that are much more highly specific and technical than those associated with the word in everyday use. You may want to keep a log of the language of your chosen field, noting both meanings and examples of each term's use. (See 46b.)

THINKING CRITICALLY ABOUT VOCABULARY

Reading with Attention to Vocabulary

Read each of the following passages, paying particular attention to the italicized words. See if you can determine the meaning of any words you don't know by using the clues suggested in this chapter—context, prefixes, roots, and suffixes. Check your understanding by looking up each word in a dictionary.

1. Now, I doubt that the imagination can be suppressed. If you truly *eradicated* it in a child, he would grow up to be an eggplant. Like all our evil *propensities,* the imagination will win out.
   – URSULA LEGUIN, "Why Are Americans Afraid of Dragons?"

2. Everything that comes alive seems to be in trade for something that dies, cell for cell. There might be some comfort in the recognition of *synchrony,* in the information that we all go down together, in the best of company.
   – LEWIS THOMAS, "Death in the Open"

3. I think it is agreed by all parties, that this *prodigious* number of children in the arms, or on the backs, or at the heels of their mothers . . . is in the present *deplorable* state of the kingdom, a very great additional *grievance.* . . .
   – JONATHAN SWIFT, "A Modest Proposal"

Thinking about Your Own Vocabulary

Read over a piece of your writing. Underline any words you think could be improved on, and then come up with several possible substitutes. If you keep a writing log, list them there as a start to your own personal word hoard.

27

Considering Diction

IN SPEAKING OF SOMEONE YOU WORK WITH, *you might choose one or more of the following words:* accomplice, ally, associate, buddy, cohort, collaborator, colleague, comrade, co-worker, mate, partner, sidekick. *The choice you make is a matter of diction, which derives from the Latin word for "say" and means literally how you say or express something. Effective diction involves many issues discussed elsewhere in this book, such as being concise (19b), using parallel structures (Chapter 21), choosing strong, precise verbs (23a), using dictionaries (Chapter 25), strengthening vocabulary (Chapter 26), using varieties of English or other languages (Chapter 28), and considering how your words can build common ground with readers (Chapter 29).*

This chapter will give you some guidance about aspects of good diction: choosing language and register appropriate to your purpose, topic, and audience; choosing words with the right denotations and connotations; balancing general and abstract words with specific and concrete ones; and using figurative language.

27a

Choosing appropriate language and register

Musing on the many possible ways to describe a face, Ford Madox Ford notes,

> That a face resembles a Dutch clock has been said too often; to say that it resembles a ham is inexact and conveys nothing; to say that it has the mournfulness of an old smashed-in meat tin, cast away on a waste building lot, would be smart—but too much of that sort of thing would become a nuisance.
> – FORD MADOX FORD

> *Everyday Use*
>
> Restaurant menus provide good examples of diction at work. See how two very different menus describe fried chicken.
>
> *Crispy-tender, finger-lickin', soul-satisfyin' good chicken. Choose regular or extra-spicy.*
>
> *Succulent poulet frit, with a subtle hint of garlic.*
> *Presented with steamed snow peas and potatoes lyonnaise.*
>
> What does the different diction tell you about the two restaurants? What do you think each of them would be like?

Ford here implies a major point about diction: effective word choice can be made only on the basis of what is appropriate to the writer's purpose, to the topic, and to the audience. What is appropriate may vary from one region to another, from one occupation to another, and from one social or ethnic group to another. In addition, the level of formality, or register, will vary depending on what is appropriate for a particular topic and audience. These levels include slang and familiar, informal, and formal diction.

1

Slang and colloquial language

Slang, or extremely informal language, is often confined to a relatively small group and usually becomes obsolete rather quickly. Some slang gains wide use (*yuppie, bummer, Big Board*); it is often colorful or amusing (why pay with a dollar bill when you can hand over a *dead president* or a *frogskin*?). **Colloquial language,** such as *a lot, in a bind,* or *snooze,* is less informal, more widely used, and longer-lasting than slang.

Slang and colloquial language can expose a writer to the risk of not being understood or of not being taken seriously. If you are writing for a general audience about arms-control negotiations, for example, and you use the term *nukes* to refer to nuclear missiles, some readers may not know what you mean, and others may be distracted or irritated by what they see as a frivolous reference to a deadly serious subject.

Consider the different language choices in these three sentences:

TO FRIENDS

I had to pull an incomplete in psych because I was barfing with that stomach flu all finals week and couldn't book it at all.

TO PARENTS

I had to take an incomplete in psychology because I had the stomach flu that was going around and couldn't study because I was throwing up all night before the final exam.

TO A COMMITTEE EVALUATING YOU FOR A SCHOLARSHIP

I was forced to request an incomplete in Psychology 102 because I had been violently ill with an intestinal virus for three days before the final examination (doctor's letter is enclosed) and was therefore unable to study.

What are the differences between these versions? Diction is the most obvious difference, but if you look closely, you will see that each version reveals that choices of diction are related to judgments about purpose and audience. Consider how strange your friends would think you if you spoke to them in the language you might use to the scholarship committee. Your distant, formal tone, created by giving such full background, would confuse them. Similarly, if you wrote to the scholarship committee in the words you would use with friends, the committee would be equally confused. They would probably think either that you were trying to be funny at a serious time or that you did not know how to address people outside your personal circle. In either case, you would be less likely to achieve your purpose—to persuade the committee to give you a scholarship.

As this example indicates, the better you know the audience, the less **context**—background information—you must specify. (Note that the three examples get progressively longer as the speaker must supply more and more context.) Your friends know you well, know about incompletes, know about finals week, know about the flu. They know your context, and thus you can use slang and informal terms that are short and telegraphic. Your parents do not know as much of your context. You must be slightly more formal with them (they have always hated the word *barf*) in addition to explaining more of the situation. For the committee, you must be even more formal, supplying a detailed explanation that will show them your seriousness. This implicit knowledge about your purpose and audience leads you to use different diction for each version. (See Chapter 2 for discussion of using language appropriate to particular audiences.)

EXERCISE 27.1

Choose something or someone to describe—a favorite cousin, a stranger on the bus, an automobile, a musical instrument, whatever strikes your fancy. Describe your subject using colloquial language and slang. Then rewrite the description, this time using neither of these. Read the two passages aloud, and note what different effects each creates.

2

Register

On the basis of a writer's relationship to the topic and the audience, we can distinguish three levels of diction, or **registers.** In order of increasing distance from the writer, these levels are *familiar, informal,* and *formal.* Formal register is the one most often appropriate for college writing.

Familiar register

Familiar register is appropriate when a very close relationship exists between writer and topic and between writer and audience. It is the language you probably use to talk to yourself or to those closest to you. It is the register found in diaries, journals, and personal letters; writers sometimes use it in essays, stories, plays, and novels to create a sense of intimacy between themselves and readers or between characters. It may include the frequent use of the first person (*I*) and first names; a lack of explicitly stated context (because the audience does not need it); and the use of sentence fragments, contractions, slang, colloquial language, regional and other "non-standard" language.

You will seldom, if ever, be called on to write in familiar register in college writing. You should, however, learn to recognize it as a reader. The following example is a letter from the English writer Virginia Stephen responding to a marriage proposal from her future husband, Leonard Woolf:

> My dear Leonard,
>   I am rushing for a train so I can only send a line in answer. There isn't anything really for me to say, except that I should like to go on as before; and that you should leave me free, and that I should be honest. As to faults, I expect mine are just as bad—less noble perhaps. But of course they are not really the question. I have decided to keep this completely secret, except for Vanessa; and I have made her promise not to tell Clive. I told Adrian that you had come up about a job which was promised you. So keep this up if he asks.
>   I am very sorry to be the cause of so much rush and worry. . . .
>   Yrs.
>   VS

Notice that Stephen assumes Woolf will know what her "line" is "in answer" to, what "this" is, and who Vanessa, Clive, and Adrian are. She uses a contraction (*isn't*) and abbreviations (*Yrs.,* her initials), as well as the colloquial expression *keep this up* to mean "pretend that this story is true." Because she was a professional writer living in a different time and a different culture, her familiar register is probably different from and more formal than yours. Nevertheless, you can see that she is writing to a very intimate audience (of one) on a very intimate topic.

Informal register

Informal register assumes a fairly close but not extremely close relationship between the writer and the audience and topic. It may use colloquial language, slang, and regional or other varieties of English, as well as contractions and other grammatical constructions that are not considered appropriate in more formal writing. The register of most conversation and of much popular media, it is often found in short stories and novels as well, especially in dialogue. Some college classes—journalism, or creative writing, for example—may call on you to use informal register. Here is an example:

> If I went through anguish in botany and economics—for different reasons—gymnasium work was even worse. I don't even like to think about it. They wouldn't let you play games or join the exercises with your glasses on and I couldn't see with mine off. I bumped into professors, horizontal bars, agricultural students, and swinging iron rings. Not being able to see, I could take it but I couldn't dish it out.
> — JAMES THURBER, "University Days"

Thurber is obviously closely involved with his topic, although the involvement is not as close as that of Virginia Stephen with Leonard Woolf's marriage proposal; Thurber is looking back at his college gymnasium work from the distance of years. Nor is he as intimately related to his audience, but his use of contractions (*don't, wouldn't, couldn't*) and the indefinite *they* and *you* create an informal tone of easy familiarity. Notice that in the last sentence he amuses the audience—a purpose for which informal register is often used—by coming up with a twist on a clichéd slang expression.

Formal register

Formal register is the language found in most academic, business, and professional writing and in serious nonfiction and magazines. Most of the writing you will do in college and probably at work will be in formal register. The following list gives its characteristics.

1. Appropriate distance between the writer and the audience: your stance should be courteous but not chummy or intimate.

2. Emotional distance between the writer and the topic: though you may know the topic very well and have strong feelings about it, your stance toward it should be somewhat restrained.

3. In general, no colloquial language, slang, or contractions.

4. Attention to the conventions of standard academic English. Other varieties—including regional, occupational, and ethnic—should be used only if appropriate to your topic, purpose, and audience (see Chapter 28).

5. Attention to the logical relationships among words and ideas: phrases and sentences should be carefully structured, not just tossed out.

Here is an example of formal register:

> "A people who mean to be their own governors," James Madison wrote, "must arm themselves with the power knowledge gives. A popular government without popular information or the means of acquiring it, is but a prologue to a farce or a tragedy, or perhaps both."
>
> Tragedy looms larger than farce in the United States today. Illiterate citizens seldom vote. Those who do are forced to cast a vote of questionable worth. They cannot make informed decisions based on serious print information. Sometimes they can be alerted to their interests by aggressive voter education. More frequently, they vote for a face, a smile, or a style, not for a mind or character or body of beliefs.
>
> – JONATHAN KOZOL, "The Human Cost of an Illiterate Society"

Notice that Kozol opens with an appeal to authority, citing a United States president who, in very strong and serious terms, warns against the effect of a populace without knowledge. Kozol repeats the key terms of Madison's warning, *tragedy* and *farce,* in the next sentence, and goes on to develop what he sees as one tragic aspect of illiteracy. His brief, straightforward sentences state the facts objectively, building up to the parallel structures of the last sentence, which contrasts voting for "a smile" with voting for "character." Though Kozol feels strongly that illiteracy is a national tragedy, his tone throughout is restrained.

ON VARIETIES OF ENGLISH
Register in Technical Writing

One kind of language frequently found in formal register is the technical discourse used in particular fields that have created special vocabularies or given common words special meaning. Businesspeople talk about *greenmail* and *upside movement,* biologists about *nucleotides* and *immunodestruction,* and baseball fans about *fielder's choices* and *suicide bunts.* Such terms may be understood by others, but they can be very confusing to those outside the field. You need, then, to judge any use of technical language very carefully, making sure that your audience will understand your terms and replacing or defining those that they will not. Technical language can be divided into two overlapping categories: neologisms and jargon.

Neologisms

New words that have not yet found their way into dictionaries, **neologisms** can be very helpful to writers, especially in the sciences and applied disciplines, where new things and concepts appear every day and need names. Terms like *byte, thermosiphon, deconstruct,* and *neutrino,* for example, could not be easily replaced except by a much longer and more complex explanation. Some neologisms, however, do not meet a real need. Words like *deaccess* and *prioritization* could be easily replaced by existing words or phrases that general readers would understand.

Jargon

Jargon is the special vocabulary of a trade or profession, enabling members to speak and write concisely to one another. It should be reserved as much as possible for a specific technical audience. Here is an example of jargon used inappropriately in writing addressed to general readers, and then revised to eliminate some of the jargon terms and define others:

JARGON

The VDT's in composition were down last week, so we had to lay out on dummies and crop and size the art with a wheel.

REVISED FOR A GENERAL AUDIENCE

The video display terminals were not working last week in the composing room, where models of the newspaper pages are made up for printing, so we had to arrange the contents of each page on a large cardboard sheet and use a wheel, a kind of circular slide rule, to figure out the size and shape of the pictures and other illustrations.

3
Pompous language, euphemisms, and doublespeak

In addition to avoiding inappropriate use of technical language, be alert to three other kinds of language sometimes found in formal register: pompous language, euphemisms, and doublespeak.

Pompous language is unnecessarily formal for the purpose, audience, or topic. Hence it often gives writing an insincere or unintentionally humorous tone, making the writer's idea seem less significant or believable.

POMPOUS

Pursuant to the August 9 memorandum regarding petroleum supply exigencies, it is incumbent upon us to endeavor to make maximal utilization of telephonic communication in lieu of personal visitation.

REVISED

As of August 9 shortages of petroleum require us to use the telephone rather than make personal visits whenever possible.

Euphemisms are terms designed to make an unpleasant idea more attractive or acceptable. *Your position is being eliminated* seeks to soften the blow of being fired or laid off; the British call this being *declared redundant,* while Canadians refer to being *made surplus.* Other euphemisms include *pass on* for *die* and *sanitation engineer* for *garbage collector.*

Use euphemisms with great care. Although they can appeal to readers by showing that the writer is considering their feelings, they can also sound pompous or suggest a wishy-washy, timid, or evasive attitude.

The name given by George Orwell to the language of Big Brother in his novel *1984,* **doublespeak** is the use of language to hide or distort the truth. During the massive layoffs and cutbacks in the corporate and business worlds in recent years, companies continued to speak of firings and layoffs as *work reengineering, employee respositioning, proactive downsizing,* and *special reprogramming.* The public—and particularly those who lost their jobs— recognized this use of doublespeak.

> ▶ *FOR MULTILINGUAL WRITERS*
> *Avoiding Fancy Diction*
>
> In writing standard academic English, which is fairly formal, you may be inclined to use the biggest and newest words in English that you know, to go for long, polysyllabic words or for fancy diction. While all of us can enrich our vocabularies— and put new words to good use—you will be well advised to resist the temptation to use flowery or high-flown diction in your college writing. Academic writing calls first of all for clear, concise prose.

EXERCISE 27.2

Revise each of these sentences to use formal register consistently.

Although be excited as soon as
  ∧ I can ~~get all enthused~~ about writing, ~~but~~ I sit down to write, ~~and~~ my mind
immediately blank.
  ∧ goes ~~right to sleep.~~

1. Desdemona's attitude is that of a wimp; she just lies down and dies, accepting her death as inevitable.

2. All candidates strive for the same results: you try to make the other guy look gross and to persuade voters that you're okay for the job.

3. Often, instead of firing an incompetent teacher, school officials will transfer the person to another school in order to avoid the hassles involved in a dismissal.

4. The more she flipped out about his actions, the more he rebelled and continued doing what he pleased.

5. My family lived in Trinidad for the first ten years of my life, and we went through a lot, but when we came to America, we thought we had it made.

27b

Denotation and connotation

Think of a stone tossed into a pool, and imagine the ripples spreading out from it, circle by circle. Or think of a note struck clear and clean, and the multiple vibrations that echo from it. In such images you can capture the distinction between **denotation**, the general meaning of a word, and **connotation**, the ripples, vibrations, and associations that accompany the word. As a writer, you want to choose words that are both denotatively and connotatively appropriate.

Words with similar denotations may have connotations that vary widely. The words *maxim, epigram, proverb, saw, saying,* and *motto,* for instance, all carry roughly the same denotation. Because of their different connotations, however, *proverb* would be the appropriate word to use in reference to a saying from the Bible; *saw* in reference to the kind of wisdom handed down anonymously; *epigram* in reference to a witty statement by someone like Dave Barry. *Dirt* and *soil* have roughly the same denotative meaning, and their connotations are close enough to allow us to use them interchangeably in most cases. *Pushy* and *assertive* also have much the same denotative meaning, but their connotations suggest different attitudes on the part of the writer, one negative, the other neutral or positive.

Because words with the wrong connotations for your intended meaning may not be as obvious as those with wrong denotations, take special care to avoid them. Good writers and readers are sensitive to the power of connotation for a number of reasons. In the first place, we do not want to be misunderstood: calling someone *skinny* rather than *slender,* for instance, might be taken as an insult or joke when such a meaning was unintended. And because connotation plays an important part in the language of politics and advertising (to name only the two most obvious fields), being alert to connotation and its power can help us read and listen more critically. Look at the differences in connotation among the following three statements:

> Students Against Racism (SAR) erected a temporary barrier on the campus oval, saying it symbolizes "the many barriers to those discriminated against by university policies."

> Left-wing agitators threw up an eyesore right on the oval to try to stampede the university into giving in to their every demand.

> Supporters of human rights for all students challenged the university's investment in racism by erecting a protest barrier on campus.

As this example demonstrates, positive and negative connotations can shift meaning significantly. The first statement is the most neutral, merely stating facts (and quoting the assertion about university policy to represent it as someone's words rather than as "facts"; the second, by using words with negative connotations (*agitators, eyesore, stampede*), is strongly critical; the third, by using words with positive connotations (*supporters of human rights*) and presenting assertions as facts (*the university's investment in racism*), gives a favorable slant to the story. You should always pay attention to the connotations of the words you read or hear—including your own words. Try to use connotation to help make your meanings clear.

Many words carry fairly general connotations, evoking similar associational responses in most listeners or readers. But connotations can be personal or distinctive to a particular audience as well. If you ever became violently ill right after eating a particular food as a child, you know the power of personal connotation. The mere mention of, say, peanut butter cookies carries powerful negative connotations for you.

The power of connotations to a particular audience was well illustrated by a meeting between Michael Dukakis and Jesse Jackson at the 1988 Democratic National Convention. Jackson was offended that Dukakis, who had clinched the party's presidential nomination, had asserted his leadership by describing himself as "the quarterback on this team," a phrase that reminded African Americans of the stereotype that they were not intelligent enough to play quarterback on football teams. For his part, Dukakis was upset by Jackson's having told the new voters he had brought into the party that they were being used to "carry bales of cotton" up to "the big house," because the connotations of this language suggested that Dukakis was like a white plantation owner profiting from the labor of African American slaves. Whenever you write for a particular audience, try to be aware of the connotations your language will hold for that group of people.

≫ Checking for wrong words

"Wrong word" errors take so many different forms that it is very difficult to name any foolproof methods of checking for them. If you often find yourself using the wrong word, however, it will be well worth your time to go through each draft looking for them.

1. Check every word you are not absolutely sure of in a dictionary to see that you're using it properly.

2. Look for homonyms, words that sound like other words (such as *to*, *too*, and *two*). Using the information in 24b, make sure you are using the correct form.

3. Keep a list of any words you use incorrectly, including example sentences showing the way you've misused them. Make a point of proofreading carefully for them.

▶ *FOR MULTILINGUAL WRITERS*
Learning Idioms

Why do you wear a diamond *on* your finger but *in* your ear (or nose)?
See 57a.

EXERCISE 27.3

Choose the word in parentheses whose denotative meaning makes sense in the
context of the sentence. Use a dictionary if necessary.

1. She listened (*apprehensively/attentively*) to the lecture and took notes.

2. Going swimming on a hot day can be a (*rapturous/ravenous*) experience.

3. Mark improved his windsurfing (*dramatically/drastically*) with lessons.

4. Franklin advised his readers to be (*feudal/frugal*) and industrious.

EXERCISE 27.4

Study the italicized words in each of the following passages, and decide what
each word's connotations contribute to your understanding of the passage. Think
of a synonym for each word, and see if you can decide what difference the new
word would make to the effect of the passage.

1. The Burmans were already *racing* past me across the mud. It was obvious
   that the elephant would never *rise* again, but he was not dead. He was
   breathing very rhythmically with long *rattling gasps,* his great *mound* of a
   side painfully rising and falling.

   – GEORGE ORWELL, "Shooting an Elephant"

2. If boxing is a sport, it is the most *tragic* of all sports because, more than
   any human activity, it *consumes* the very excellence it *displays:* Its very
   drama is this consumption.   – JOYCE CAROL OATES, "On Boxing"

3. We caught two bass, *hauling* them in *briskly* as though they were mackerel,
   pulling them over the side of the boat in a *businesslike* manner without
   any landing net, and stunning them with a *blow* on the back of the head.

   – E. B. WHITE, "Once More to the Lake"

4. Then one evening Miss Glory told me to serve the ladies on the porch.
   After I set the tray down and turned toward the kitchen, one of the women
   asked, "What's your name, *girl?*"

   – MAYA ANGELOU, *I Know Why the Caged Bird Sings*

5. The Kiowas are a summer people; they *abide* the cold and keep to themselves; but when the season *turns* and the land becomes warm and *vital,*
   they cannot *hold still.*

   – N. SCOTT MOMADAY, "The Way to Rainy Mountain"

27c

Balancing general and specific diction

Good writers move their prose along and help readers follow the meaning by balancing **general words**, those that refer to groups or classes of things, with **specific words**, those that refer to individual things. One kind of general words, **abstractions**, are words or phrases that refer to qualities or ideas, things we cannot perceive through our five senses. Specific words are often **concrete words**; they name things we can see, hear, touch, taste, or smell. Rarely can we draw a clear-cut line between general or abstract words on the one hand and specific or concrete ones on the other. Instead, most words fall somewhere between these two extremes.

GENERAL	LESS GENERAL	SPECIFIC	MORE SPECIFIC
book	dictionary	unabridged dictionary	my 1988 edition of *Webster's Dictionary*

ABSTRACT	LESS ABSTRACT	CONCRETE	MORE CONCRETE
culture	visual art	painting	Van Gogh's *Starry Night*

Because passages that contain mostly general terms or abstractions demand that readers supply most of the specific examples or concrete details with their imaginations, such writing is often hard to read. Taken to extremes, it is dull or boring. But writing that is full of specifics can also be tedious and hard to follow if the main point is not made clearly or is lost amid a flood of details. Strong writing must usually both provide readers with a general idea or overall picture and fill in that picture with specific examples or concrete details.

In the following passage, for instance, the author might have simply made a general statement—*their breakfast was always liberal and good*—or simply described the breakfast. Instead, he does both:

> There would be a brisk fire crackling in the hearth, the old smoke-gold of morning and the smell of fog, the crisp cheerful voices of the people and their ruddy competent morning look, and the cheerful smells of breakfast, which was always liberal and good, the best meal that they had: kidneys and ham and eggs and sausages and toast and marmalade and tea.
> – THOMAS WOLFE, *Of Time and the River*

Here are two student writers balancing general statements with illustrative specific details:

GENERAL	My neighbor is a nuisance.
SPECIFIC	My next-door neighbor is a nuisance, poking and prying into my life, constantly watching me as I enter and leave my house, complaining about the noise when I am having a good time, and telling my parents whenever she sees me kissing my date.
GENERAL	Central Texas has an unusual climate.
SPECIFIC	Few places in the United States display the wild climatic variations of central Texas: at one moment, the sky may be clear blue and the air balmy; at another, a racing flash flood may drown the landscape and threaten lives.

EXERCISE 27.5

Rewrite each of the following sentences to be more specific and concrete.

1. The entryway of the building was dirty.
2. The sounds at dawn are memorable.
3. Sunday dinner was good.
4. The attendant came toward my car.
5. The child played on the beach.

27d

Using figurative language

One good way to communicate with an audience is by using figurative language, or figures of speech. Such language paints pictures in our minds, allows us to "see" a point and hence understand more readily and clearly. Economists trying to explain the magnitude of the federal deficit use figurative language when they tell us how many hundred-thousand-dollar bills would have to circle the globe how many times to equal it. Scientists describing the way genetic data are transmitted use figurative language when they liken the data to a messenger that carries bits of information from one generation of cells to another and when they liken certain genetic variants to typographical errors. Far from being mere decoration, figurative language plays a crucial role in helping us follow the writer's meaning.

Particularly helpful in building understanding are figures that compare one thing to another—similes, metaphors, and analogies. Other figures include personification, hyperbole, understatement, irony, and allusion.

Similes

Similes (pronounced sim′ ə lēz) make explicit the comparison between two things by using *like, as, as if,* or *as though.*

> The fog hangs among the trees like veils of trailing lace.
> — STEPHANIE VAUGHN, "My Mother Breathing Light"

> The comb felt as if it was raking my skin off.
> — MALCOLM X, "My First Conk"

> The migraine acted as a circuit breaker, and the fuses have emerged intact.
> — JOAN DIDION, "In Bed"

Metaphors

Metaphors (pronounced met′ ə fərz) are implicit comparisons, omitting the *like, as, as if,* or *as though* of similes.

> Black women are called, in the folklore that so aptly identifies one's status in society, "the mule of the world," because we have been handed the burdens that everyone else—everyone else—refused to carry.
> — ALICE WALKER, *In Search of Our Mothers' Gardens*

> Lee was tidewater Virginia, and in his backyard were family, culture, and tradition. — BRUCE CATTON, "Grant and Lee: A Study in Contrasts"

Analogies

Analogies compare similar features of two dissimilar things and are often extended to several sentences or paragraphs in length. The following sentence, for example, uses an analogy to help us understand the rapid growth of the computer industry:

> If the aircraft industry had evolved as spectacularly as the computer industry over the past twenty-five years, a Boeing 767 would cost five hundred dollars today, and it would circle the globe in twenty minutes on five gallons of fuel.

The analogy in the next passage helps us "see" an abstract point:

> One Hundred and Twenty-fifth Street was to Harlem what the Mississippi was to the South, a long traveling river always going somewhere, carrying something. — MAYA ANGELOU, *The Heart of a Woman*

Before you use an analogy, though, make sure that the two things you are comparing have enough points of similarity to justify the comparison and make it convincing to readers. (For more on analogies, see 5g3.)

Clichés and mixed metaphors

Just as effective use of figurative language can create the impression that the writer wants to create, so *ineffective* figures of speech can create the *wrong* impression by boring, irritating, or unintentionally amusing readers. Among the most common kinds of ineffective figurative language are clichés and mixed metaphors.

Cliché (pronounced klē shā′) comes from the French word for "stereo-type," a metal plate cast from a page of type and used, before the invention of photographic printing processes, to produce multiple copies of a book or page without having to reset the type. So a **cliché** in language is an expression stamped out in duplicate to avoid the trouble of "resetting" the thought. Many clichés, like *busy as a bee* or *youth is the springtime of life,* are similes or metaphors.

By definition, we use clichés all the time, especially in speech, and many serve us quite usefully as familiar shorthand for familiar ideas. In fact, the rhythm and alliteration of some clichés continue to please, even if they are "unoriginal," for even the most brilliant among us can't be original all the time. Like anything else, however, clichés should be used in moderation: if your audience recognizes that you are using stereotyped, paint-by-numbers language to excess, they are likely to conclude that what you are saying is not very new or interesting—or true. The person who tells you that you look "pretty as a picture" uses a clichéd simile that may well sound false or insincere. Compare it with a more original compliment a grandmother once paid to her grandchildren: "You all look as pretty as brand-new red shoes."

How can you check for clichés? While one person's trite phrase may be completely new to another, one rule of thumb will serve you well: if you can predict exactly what the upcoming word(s) in a phrase will be, it stands a very good chance of being a cliché.

Mixed metaphors are comparisons that are not consistent. Instead of creating a clear and dominant impression, they confuse the reader by pulling against one another, often in unintentionally funny ways, as in the warning by a government official that "we must not drag our dirty linen through the eye of the public."

Here is a mixed metaphor revised for consistency:

MIXED

The lectures were like brilliant comets streaking through the night sky, showering the listeners with a blizzard of insight. [The conflicting images of streaking light and heavy precipitation produce humorous results.]

REVISED

The lectures were like brilliant comets streaking through the night sky, dazzling listeners with flashes of insight. [Now all images relate to light.]

Personification

Personification gives human qualities to animals, inanimate objects, or ideas, making them more vivid or understandable.

> [Television] . . . stays in one corner of the room like a horrible electronic gossip. — JONATHAN MILLER

Hyperbole

Hyperbole (pronounced hī pur´ bə lē), or **overstatement**, deliberately exaggerates to create special emphasis or humor.

> Under certain emotional circumstances, I can stand the spasms of a rich violin, but the concert piece and all wind instruments bore me in small doses and flay me in large doses. — VLADMIR NABOKOV

Understatement

Like hyperbole, **understatement**, or **litotes** (pronounced li tō´ tēz), depends on a gap between statement and fact. But while hyperbole is loud and noisy, understatement turns the volume down to a whisper. Litotes can help create a very solemn tone, as it does when one of the characters in Stephen Crane's *The Open Boat,* faced with imminent death, remarks that if he drowns, it "will be a shame." It can also create humor and other effects.

Irony

Irony, language that suggests a meaning that contrasts with or undercuts the literal meaning of the words, can create a lighthearted, spoofing tone or a serious and bitter one. In probably the most famous piece of sustained irony in English literature, "A Modest Proposal," Jonathan Swift solemnly recommends the sale and consumption of children, a proposal intended to reveal the poverty and inhuman conditions in Ireland condoned by its British rulers at the time. The following definition of *writing principles* provides an example of more lighthearted irony:

> Write hurriedly, preferably when tired. Have no plans; write down items as they occur to you. . . . Hand in your manuscript the moment it is finished. — AMBROSE BIERCE

Irony can work well to gain an audience's attention and set a definite tone, but only if the audience can be expected to recognize and appreciate the irony. (See 34d on using quotation marks to convey irony.)

Allusion

Allusions, indirect references to cultural works, people, or events, can bring an entire world of associations to the minds of readers who recognize them. If, for instance, you tell a friend in a letter that you have to return to your herculean task of writing a research essay, you are expecting that your reader will understand, by your allusion to the Labors of Hercules in classical mythology, how big a job you think the essay is. When a sports commentator said, "If Georgia Tech has an Achilles heel, it is their inexperience, their youth," he alluded to the Greek hero Achilles's one vulnerable spot, his heel.

You can draw allusions from history, from literature, from the Bible, from common wisdom, or from current events. Many current movies and popular songs are full of allusions. Remember, however, that allusions work only if your audience recognizes them.

ON VARIETIES OF ENGLISH
Signifying

One distinctive use of figurative language found extensively in African American English is **signifying**, in which a speaker cleverly and often humorously needles or insults the listener. Signifying is rhythmic, using metaphors and images drawn from everyday life. It is usually very subtle, characterized by indirection and quick verbal surprises. In the following passage, two African American men (Grave Digger and Coffin Ed) signify on their white supervisor (Anderson), who ordered them to discover the originators of a riot:

> "I take it you've discovered who started the riot," Anderson said.
> "We knew who he was all along," Grave Digger said.
> "It's just nothing we can do to him," Coffin Ed echoed.
> "Why not, for God's sake?"
> "He's dead," Coffin Ed said.
> "Who?"
> "Lincoln," Grave Digger said.
> "He hadn't ought to have freed us if he didn't want to make provisions to feed us," Coffin Ed said. "Anyone could have told him that."
> — CHESTER HIMES, *Hot Day, Hot Night*

Coffin Ed and Grave Digger demonstrate the major characteristics of effective signifying: indirection, ironic humor, fluid rhythm—and a surprising twist at the end. Rather than insulting Anderson directly by pointing out that he's asked a dumb question, they criticize the question indirectly by ultimately blaming a white man (and not just *any* white man, but one they're all supposed to revere). This twist leaves the supervisor speechless, teaching him something *and* giving Grave Digger and Coffin Ed the last word.

You will find examples of signifying in the work of many African American writers. You may also hear signifying in NBA basketball, for it is an important element of trash talking; what Grave Digger and Coffin Ed do to Anderson, Charles Barkley regularly does to his opponents on the court. As with all figurative language, it is important to recognize this verbal strategy—and to understand the meaning it adds.

EXERCISE 27.6

Identify the similes and metaphors in the following passages, and decide how each contributes to your understanding of the passage it appears in.

1. John's mother, Mom Willie, who wore her Southern background like a magnolia corsage, eternally fresh, was robust and in her sixties.
   — MAYA ANGELOU, "The Heart of a Woman"

2. I was watching everyone else and didn't see the waitress standing quietly by. Her voice was deep and soft like water moving in a cavern.
   — WILLIAM LEAST HEAT MOON, "In the Land of 'Coke-Cola' "

3. My horse, when he is in his stall or lounging about the pasture, has the same relationship to pain that I have when cuddling up with a good murder mystery—comfort and convenience have top priority.
   — VICKI HEARNE, "Horses in Partnership with Time"

EXERCISE 27.7

Read through a magazine, an essay, a story, or some reading you have been assigned and find some examples of personification, hyperbole, understatement, irony, and allusion. Bring these examples to class for discussion.

⫸ *Editing for diction*

1. First, reconsider your topic, purpose, and audience. What kind of diction is most appropriate for these?

2. Choose a couple of paragraphs from different parts of a draft, and see if the words in them hold any special connotations—optimistic? sarcastic? pessimistic? Are these appropriate to your topic, purpose, and audience?

3. Look for general and abstract terms. Are they balanced by specific and concrete ones? Do you have more of the first than the second? Would adding more specific and concrete language help bring your prose to life?

4. Look for figures of speech. Do they help create vivid images for your readers? Can they be improved?

5. Look for clichés, and replace any you find with fresher language.

6. How would you characterize the register—familiar? informal? formal? Do you include slang or colloquial language? Do you use contractions? Is the register appropriate to your audience and purpose?

7. What, finally, would you say is the general attitude your writing conveys? Is it appropriate to your audience and purpose?

EXERCISE 27.8   Revising for Diction

Return to the description you wrote in Exercise 27.1. Note any words that carry strong connotations, and identify the concrete and abstract language as well as any use of figurative language. Revise the description for better use of diction.

THINKING CRITICALLY ABOUT DICTION

Reading with Awareness of Diction

Read the following brief poem. What dominant feeling or impression does the poem produce in you? Identify the diction, those specific words and phrases that help create that impression.

> What happens to a dream deferred?
>
> Does it dry up
> Like a raisin in the sun?
> Or fester like a sore—
> And then run?
> Does it stink like rotten meat?
> Or crust and sugar over—
> Like a syrupy sweet?
>
> Maybe it just sags
> Like a heavy load.
>
> Or does it explode?   – LANGSTON HUGHES, Harlem (A Dream Deferred)

Thinking about the Diction in Your Own Writing

Read over a piece of your writing, underlining any words or phrases that are especially effective and any that could be more vivid, appropriate, concrete—improved in any way. Then ask what kind of impression you wanted to create in this piece of writing—amused? amusing? outraged? friendly? skeptical? How successful have you been? Do you see any patterns in your diction? Note down any strengths as well as any problems—in a writing log, if you keep one.

28

Considering Language Variety

A GROUP OF COLLEGE STUDENTS, all new to campus, gathers outside a diner. "I'm having a hero," says one. "I'm ordering a submarine," says another. "That's what I call a hoagie," says a third, "—and it sounds great."

You might well know this particular sandwich as a grinder, a poor boy, a cubano, or some other name. Why all the different names? This question suggests an important fact of our linguistic life: while all speakers of English share the same **language** (with common sounds, words, and word combinations), within this broad category are many differences.

Indeed, English includes many dialects, **varieties of language** that are distinguished from one another by pronunciation, vocabulary, rhetorical, and grammatical choices. Whether you order a poor boy or a hoagie reflects such differences. In this case, the difference probably is one of region. But other language differences exist as well. This chapter examines regional, occupational, and ethnic varieties of English, as well as the variety often called "standard" English. These varieties occur in both our spoken and written language, though the range of variation is generally greater in oral language than in written language.

In addition to the many varieties of English, many other languages are spoken in the United States. The Miami, Florida, school system, for instance, includes speakers of more than two hundred languages. And it would be unusual to walk down the street in any of our large cities without hearing several languages spoken and seeing written evidence of their common use. In fact, a number of teachers, scholars, and political leaders have argued for an "English plus" national-language policy to ensure that U.S. citizens develop the ability to speak more than just English. Perhaps, suggests linguist Dell Hymes, this is what the founders of our country meant by choosing a Latin motto: E pluribus unum ("Out of many, one"). "Did they not show," Hymes says, "that they expected at least a little bilingualism from all of us? E pluribus unum— bilingualism is . . . only as far away as the nearest nickel."

This chapter aims to get you thinking about the varieties of language you use—and about when you might appropriately and effectively use each one.

Everyday Use

If you attend religious services of any kind, you may have ample opportunity to observe the use of different varieties of English or, indeed, of different languages. In some religious services, Latin or Hebrew or Arabic is used in all or some parts. In others, the religious leader may use formal English for a sermon or for a reading from holy scriptures and then shift to more informal English for announcements. In the same way, the congregation may use highly formal or archaic English for a hymn, a chant, or a reading and then shift to regional English to make announcements.

If you are a member of a religious community, think about the way your group uses different varieties of English or other languages. In what part of the service is each used? What are the effects of shifting from one to the other? What cues do these shifts provide the worshipers?

28a

Recognizing different varieties of English

Everyone reading this text uses one or more varieties of English, whether they are those characteristic of particular *geographic regions,* of particular *occupations or professions,* or of particular *social, cultural, or ethnic groups.* In a given day, for example, one of the authors of this textbook might use a midwestern regional variety of English when talking with a group of students at Ohio State; an occupational variety characterized by highly specialized vocabulary when preparing a scholarly journal article; and an eastern Tennessee regional variety, which is strongly influenced by African American vernacular English, when talking on the phone with her grandmother. In each instance, the chosen language is appropriate. The question becomes, then, *when* to use a particular variety of English, or to shift from one variety to another—when to insert eastern Tennessee or African American vernacular patterns into a formal essay, for example, or when to use language from work in a conversation with friends.

Sometimes, in fact, our choices are limited or highly circumscribed by various kinds of pressures. An extreme but by no means isolated example is the tendency of many in our society to discriminate against those who fail to use an expected variety of English. Not only is there discrimination against those who don't speak "standard" English; there is also the rejection in other communities of those who sound affected or "la-di-da." Used appropriately and wisely, however, *all* varieties of English can serve many purposes. The key is to learn to use the language appropriately and effectively.

Using standard varieties of English

One variety of English, often referred to as the "standard," is that taught prescriptively in schools, used in the national media, and written and spoken widely by those thought to wield the most social and economic power. It is, in addition, the variety of English represented in this textbook (and in all textbooks). As the language used in most public institutions and in business and government, standard English is one variety you will no doubt want to be completely familiar with—all the while recognizing, however, that it is only one of many effective and powerful varieties of our language. As the linguist Steven Pinker says, "It makes sense to have a standard in the same way it makes sense for everyone to drive on the right-hand side of the road. But it's different from saying that the right side is the only true and justified side to drive on." In fact, the right-hand side of the road is not "right" in countries where the standard is to drive on the left. Similarly, what is agreed on as standard in U.S. English will not always be standard elsewhere.

But even standard English is hardly a monolith; the standard varies according to purpose and audience, from the very formal English used in academic writing and in prepared speeches to the informal English characteristic of casual conversation. Thus the notion that there is one absolutely correct and standard way to say or write something is in important ways a myth. Nevertheless, within this variation, a recognizable set of practices and conventions exists. These practices and conventions go by the shorthand name of standard English.

▶ *FOR MULTILINGUAL WRITERS*
Global English

Like other world languages, English is used in many countries around the world, resulting in many global varieties. For example, if you have studied English outside the United States, you may well have learned a British variety. British English differs somewhat from U.S. English in certain vocabulary (*bonnet* for "hood" of a car), syntax (*to hospital* rather than "to the hospital"), spelling (*centre* rather than "center"), and of course pronunciation. If you have learned a British variety of English, you will want to recognize the ways in which it differs from the U.S. standard.

28c

Using ethnic varieties of English

Whether you are a Native American or trace your ancestry to Germany, Italy, Ireland, Africa, China, Mexico, or elsewhere, you have an ethnic heritage that lives on in the English language. See how Rodney Morales uses one ethnic variety of English to paint a picture of young teens hearing a frightening, goose-bump-raising (or what he calls a "chicken skin") story about sharks from their grandmother:

> "—So, rather dan being rid of da shark, da people were stuck with many little ones, for dere mistake."
>
> Then Grandma Wong wen' pause, for dramatic effect, I guess, and she wen' add, "Dis is one of dose times. Dis is da time of da mano." She wen' look at my kid brother 'Analu and said, "Da time of da sharks."
>
> Those words ended another of Grandma's chicken skin stories. The stories she told us had been passed on to her by her grandmother, who had heard them from *her* grandmother. Always skipping a generation.
>
> "So, you boys," she said, "be careful in the water. An' watch out for men like Kawelo, who tell you not to go in the water, making you want to go in even more, den turn into sharks and—." She started coughing.
>
> She didn't finish the sentence. She didn't need to. Already 'Analu had chicken skin, and even though I was five years older and not so easily frightened, I felt one chill, too, boy. Me and 'Analu, aching for some sunlight, went out to Pilila'au Park and opted for one land sport—baseball. I had gotten a first-base glove for my 15th birthday the week before, and I couldn't wait to break it in.
>
> I dunno if those was the last words Grandma spoke, but she wen' take a nap after we left and she never got up.
>
> – RODNEY MORALES, "When the Shark Bites"

In this passage, Morales captures the sounds and rhythms of the speech characteristic of one ethnic group in the Hawaiian Islands. Notice that the narrator of the story, the brother of 'Analu, uses both standard and ethnic varieties of English—presenting information necessary to the story line mostly in more formal standard English and using a more informal, local ethnic variety to represent spoken language, which helps us "hear" the characters as they talk to one another.

This passage comes from fiction, but writers sometimes shift among varieties of English in nonfiction writing as well. Geneva Smitherman is particularly effective at using African American vernacular English to get the reader's attention, to create emphasis, and to make her point, all at the same time:

> Before about 1959 (when the first study was done to change black speech patterns), Black English had been primarily the interest of university

academics, particularly the historical linguists and cultural anthropologists. In recent years, though, the issue has become a very hot controversy, and there have been articles on Black Dialect in the national press as well as in the educational research literature. We have had pronouncements on black speech from the NAACP and the Black Panthers, from highly publicized scholars of the Arthur Jensen–William Shockley bent, from executives of national corporations such as Greyhound, and from housewives and community folk. I mean, really, it seem like everybody and they momma done had something to say on the subject!

– GENEVA SMITHERMAN, *Talkin and Testifyin*

Smitherman shifts into the African American vernacular English she is discussing in the last sentence of her paragraph, letting readers hear what she has been talking about. "Listen up," this shift says to the reader: "I'm making an important point here." And it dramatically illustrates that point by summarizing the content of the preceding academic language.

Zora Neale Hurston often mixes African American vernacular with the standard variety in her essays. In the following passage, she recounts how as a child she used to hail passing strangers and offer to ride down the road with them for a bit:

My grandmother worried about my forward ways a great deal. She had known slavery and to her my brazenness was unthinkable.

"Git down offa dat gate-post! You li'l sow, you! Git down! Setting up dere looking dem white folks right in de face! They's gowine to lynch you, yet. And don't stand in dat doorway gazing out at 'em neither. Youse too brazen to live long."

Nevertheless, I kept right on gazing at them, and "going a piece of the way" whenever I could make it. The village seemed dull to me most of the time. If the village was singing a chorus, I must have missed the tune.

– ZORA NEALE HURSTON, *Dust Tracks on a Road*

Here Hurston shifts from standard to vernacular in order to represent the pronunciation ("git," "offa," "dere"), the diction ("piece of the way"), and the syntax ("youse," "don't . . . neither") of her grandmother and to emphasize the ways in which what lay beyond her small hometown seemed very different to her young eyes.

In each of these examples, the writers have full command of standard academic English, and yet at times they choose to shift to other varieties. In each case, one important reason for the shift is to demonstrate that the writer is a member of the community whose language he or she is representing and thus to build credibility with others in the community.

Take care, however, in using the language of communities other than your own. Used inappropriately, such usage can have an opposite effect: that of destroying credibility and alienating your audience. But when used appropriately, ethnic varieties of English can build identification and understanding between writer and reader.

28d

Using occupational varieties of English

Every job has its own special variety of English. From the fast-food business to truck or taxi driving to summer recreational jobs—in fact, from architecture to zoology—each occupation uses English in somewhat different ways. Examples abound, from specialized words (*hermeneutics* and *dialogism* in literary studies) to invented words and ordinary words given a special meaning (*quark* and *charm* in physics).

Here is an example from an interview with a mail carrier:

> I [service] one big office building downtown and a smaller one. Each firm is a case. As you work on a case, you get to know the people who get personal mail. You throw it to that firm. I have sixty different outfits in the building that I service. Downtown is much easier than the residential district. You could have about 540 separations in the residential.
>
> – STUDS TERKEL, *Working*

Notice that the mail carrier uses ordinary words that have special meanings: "firm," "case," and "separations," for example. In addition, the carrier's syntax (brief sentences consistently beginning with the subject; the omission of words and phrases when the meaning is clear without them) is characteristic of spoken rather than written English. Chances are he is not conscious of using an occupational variety of English at all: when he is at work, his language is natural. In quoting him, Terkel not only captures the carrier's own speech but tells us something about his occupation as well.

Even within an occupation, there is room for variety. In writing a scholarly article intended for college teachers of writing, for instance, the authors of this textbook reported the results of a large research project in the kind of formal standard English suggested by the article's title, "Frequency of Formal Errors in Current College Writing," and characteristic of most of the text. We chose to shift into a very informal style of spoken English, however, first in the subtitle of the article ("Ma and Pa Kettle Do Research") and then in all the subheadings ("The Kettles Smell a Problem," "Ma and Pa Suck Eggs," "The Kettles Say, 'Aw, Shucks,'" and so on). We hoped such shifts would get our readers' attention, amuse them, and poke a bit of fun not only at ourselves but at the sometimes overly serious attitude many scholars and teachers take to questions of grammatical "correctness" and to such research.

The language that sportscasters use also varies, depending on whether the announcer is giving "play-by-play" commentary or "color" commentary. The following snippet, from a conversation between Pat Sommerall (play-by-play) and John Madden (color) as they announce an Eagles-Giants football game, illustrates such variation:

Sommerall:	Second and nine. Cunningham to throw it. Giles ducks to about a foot short of first. It looks like Cooks and Taylor on the stop.
Madden:	Jimmie Giles says, "I've been in a lot of big games" (he's a thirteen-year veteran), and the bad news for the Eagles was that they lost Keith Jackson, of course, but the good news is that they have Jimmie Giles. I'll tell you, Randall Cunningham feels very, very comfortable with Jimmie Giles.
Sommerall:	And it's a first down by Giles from Cunningham.
Madden:	Cunningham said to us yesterday—we were talking to him about Jimmie Giles, and he said he thinks he's twenty-seven. He wanted to know what that secret is where you just stay that one age all the time. You could bottle that and sell it.

Notice that the play-by-play commentary strings together units of words that exhibit combinations not found in ordinary syntax but that here are visually and semantically meaningful to those watching the game. In addition, the play-by-play announcer provides specific technical information ("a first down") and uses technical vocabulary ("second and nine," "on the stop") consistently. The color commentator, on the other hand, speaks in nearly complete sentences, provides interesting but tangentially related information, and uses technical vocabulary only occasionally. These differences reflect the different purposes of each announcer: one tries to sketch in exactly what is happening on the field; the other to color that sketch by commenting on it and on the players involved.

28e

Using regional varieties of English

"Ever'body says words different," said Ivy. "Arkansas folks says 'em different from Oklahomy folks says 'em different. And we seen a lady from Massachusetts, an' she said 'em differentest of all. Couldn' hardly make out what she was sayin'." — JOHN STEINBECK, *The Grapes of Wrath*

Thus does Ivy point to the existence and significance of regional varieties of English. Like Ivy—and every other speaker of English—your language has been affected by region. In writing, such regional language provides an effective means of evoking a character or place.

Garrison Keillor, for instance, has become famous for his Lake Wobegon stories, which are peppered with the English spoken in parts of Minnesota. When Keillor says "Gimme a Wendy's," he refers not to a kind of hamburger but to Saint Wendell's beer, "brewed by the Dimmers family at the Old Dimmers Brewery in nearby Saint Wendell's for five generations."

In writing of her native Vermont, a student writer included the following piece of dialogue:

> "There'll be some fine music on the green tonight, don't ya know?"
> "Well, I sure do want to go."
> "So don't I!"

In both these instances, the regional English creates a homespun effect and captures some of the language used in a particular place.

Used to capture attention, to amuse, and to evoke the sounds of a particular place, the language in the following passage from a cookbook is characteristic of rural Alabama and other areas of Appalachia.

> Then there's Big Reba Culpepper, big because there's Little Reba also; Big Reba lives in Burnt Corn, Alabama. She is famous countrywide for Reba's Rainbow Icebox Cake. Not too far from Burnt Corn is a place called Flea Hop, Alabama. Big Reba said she has a relative buried "in a small family-type cemetery right out on the edge of town. He was some kind of Civil War hero and when he died he was a very rich man." His grave was richly and clearly marked with a big bronze obelisk "that went way up high," Reba said, "and all his wives (six of them), children, and grandchildren were buried within spittin' distance of his monument. The old cemetery was all growed up with pine trees and needed a whole lot of attention to make it look halfway decent," Reba said. . . . "So I took it on myself to get up a cemetery cleaning party, with rakes, shovels and hoes, fried chicken, Hoppin' John, biscuits, ice tea and, of course, my famous Rainbow Icebox Cake, enough to kill us all. We loaded down the car and took off like Moody's goose for Flea Hop, Alabama."
>
> — ERNEST MATTHEW MICKLER

In this example, the use of particular terms ("Hoppin' John," for instance), expressions ("within spittin' distance"), grammatical structures ("all growed up"), and local references ("like Moody's goose") depicts regional pronunciations and rhythms, thus helping to capture the flavor of Big Reba's language as well as of Burnt Corn, Alabama. Notice that the regional language here is all *quoted*—that is, it is all spoken language.

ON VARIETIES OF ENGLISH
The Question of Gender

When Deborah Tannen published *You Just Don't Understand: Women and Men in Conversation,* she brought to popular attention what linguists have long documented: the differences in the use of English that seem closely related to gender. Some scholars seek to describe not only differences in men's and women's use of language but also what these differences reveal about power in relationships among women and men as well as about the social roles women and men play (and are allowed to play).

Women more often than men, for example, tend to use tag questions ("It's a good idea, isn't it?" as opposed to "It's a good idea") and indirectness ("Why don't we take a break?" instead of "Let's take a break"). Men and women may also choose different words. Women, for example, tend to draw fine distinctions in distinguishing among colors (plum, cranberry, chestnut, spruce), whereas men are more likely to use the names of the primary and secondary colors (purple, red, brown, green).

Remember, then, that within *any* variety of English—standard, occupational, regional, and ethnic alike—there will be diversity, including gender-related diversity.

EXERCISE 28.1

Try revising one of this chapter's examples of ethnic, occupational, or regional English. First, try to identify the purpose and audience for the original passage. Then rewrite the passage in order to remove all evidence of any variety of English other than the formal standard. Compare your revised version with the original and with those produced by some of your classmates. What differences do you notice in tone (is it more formal? more distant? something else?) and in overall impression? Which version seems most appropriate for the intended audience and purpose? Which do you prefer—and why?

28f

Bringing in other languages

Sometimes it may be appropriate to use a language other than English. You might do so for the same reasons you would use different varieties of English: to represent the actual words of a speaker, to make a point, to connect with your audience, to get the readers' attention.

See how Gerald Haslam uses Spanish to capture his great-grandmother's words as well as to make a point about his relationship to her:

> *"Expectoran su sangre!"* exclaimed Great-grandma when I showed her the small horned toad I had removed from my breast pocket. I turned toward my mother, who translated: "They spit blood."
> *"De los ojos,"* Grandma added. "From their eyes," mother explained, herself uncomfortable in the presence of the small beast.
> I grinned, "Awwwwwww."
> But my Great-grandmother did not smile. *"Son muy toxicos,"* she nodded with finality. Mother moved back an involuntary step, her hands suddenly busy at her breast. "Put that thing down," she ordered.
> "His name's John," I said.　　— GERALD HASLAM, *California Childhood*

Gloria Anzaldúa uses both Spanish and English in her writing to make a point about the ways in which English took away the people's language just as the "Gringos" took away their land:

> The Gringo, locked into the fiction of white superiority, seized complete political power, stripping Indians and Mexicans of their land while their feet were still rooted in it. *Con el destierro y el exilo fuimos desuñados, destroncados, destripados*—we were jerked out by the roots, truncated, disemboweled, dispossessed, and separated from our identity and our history. Many, under the threat of Anglo terrorism, abandoned homes and ranches and went to Mexico. Some stayed and protested. But as the courts, law enforcement officials, and government officials not only ignored their pleas but penalized them for their efforts, *tejanos* had no other recourse but armed retaliation.   – GLORIA ANZALDÚA, *Borderlands/La Frontera*

Here the shift from English to Spanish highlights the sense of exile and the loss of identity Anzaldúa describes, emphasizing that the "Gringos" might have been able to strip the land away from the "*tejanos*," but never their language. Anzaldúa's use of Spanish thus underscores the political and personal point she wishes to make.

Even monolingual writers have occasion to use another language— when quoting someone, for example, or when using Latin names for specific legal or medical terms. On some occasions, a writer may use a particularly apt foreign phrase that doesn't seem easily translatable or one that seems appropriate untranslated. See how the novelist Michelle Herman uses Yiddish in places where English translations just don't carry the same weight. The Yiddish evokes the grandmother's world Herman seeks to describe:

> "Skip *shabes*?" Rivke chuckled. "I don't think this is possible. Once a week comes *shabes*. About this a person doesn't have a choice."
>
> "What I *mean*"—Myra's impatience was plain—"is skip the preparation. It's too much for you, it tires you out."
>
> "*Ach*," Rivke said. "Too much for me it isn't." This wasn't true. For some time she had felt that it really was too much for her. It was only for *shabes* that she cooked; the rest of the week she ate cold cereal, fruit, pot cheese, crackers.   – MICHELE HERMAN, *Missing*

In this passage, Rivke's syntax—the inversion of word order ("Once a week comes *shabes*," for example, and "Too much for me it isn't")—reflects Yiddish rhythms. In addition, the use of the Yiddish *shabes* carries a strong association with a religious institution, one that would be lost if it were translated to "sabbath." It is not "sabbath" to Rivke; it is *shabes*.

As these examples suggest, those who are able to shift languages fluently can use a second language to advantage: to reach a wider audience and even to make a strong point. The pope, for instance, regularly delivers his annual Easter message not in one language but in a number of different languages, in order to reach out to believers in many countries and to make the spiritual point that in spite of language differences, all are one in God.

EXERCISE 28.2

We all shift regularly among varieties of English, often automatically and especially in speech, in response to changing situations and audiences. Try listening to yourself talk—at work, with parents or others in authority, with close friends, and so on. Take notes on your own use of language, noting any words and patterns that are from languages other than English or that are characteristic of a region or a job or a cultural group. Which of these might you use in writing as well as in speaking? Why would you use them, and for what effect?

Using varieties of language in academic writing

The key to shifting among varieties of English and among languages is appropriateness: when will such a shift reach your audience and help you make a particular point? Certain common college writing assignments—for example, writing about a person, place, or activity; writing based on sources; and oral presentation—might provide the opportunity to bring varieties of English or other languages into your academic writing.

See how an anthropologist weaves together regional and standard academic English in writing about one Carolina community.

> For Roadville, schooling is something most folks have not gotten enough of, but everybody believes will do something toward helping an individual "get on." In the words of one oldtime resident, "Folks that ain't got no schooling don't get to be nobody nowadays."
>
> – SHIRLEY BRICE HEATH, *Ways with Words*

In this passage, the researcher takes care to let a resident of Roadville speak her mind—and in her own words. She does so to be faithful to the person she is quoting as well as to capture some of the flavor of the spoken language.

In the following passage, a linguist uses Spanish in her discussion of literacy in a Mexican community in Chicago:

> *Gracia* (grace, wit) is used to refer to wittiness in talk; people who *tiene gracia* (have grace, are witty) are seen as clever and funny. Not everyone illustrates this quality, but those who do are obvious from the moment they speak. As one middle-aged male said,
>
> . . . *cuando ellos empiezan a hablar, desde el momento que los oyes hablar, tienen gracia. Entonces, la gente que tiene gracia, se va juntando gente a oírlos. Y hay gente más desabrida, diría yo. No tiene, no le quedan sus chistes. Aunque cuente uno una charrita . . . ya no te vas a reír igual.*

(. . . when they start to speak, from the moment that you hear them speak, they are witty. So then, the people who are witty begin to have a listening crowd gather about them. And then there are people who are more boring, I would say. They don't have, their jokes just don't make it. Even though they may tell a joke . . . you're not going to laugh in the same manner.)
     – MARCIA FARR, "Essayist Literacy and Other Verbal Performances"

Here Farr provides a translation of the Spanish, for she expects that many of her readers will not know Spanish. She evokes the language of the community she describes, however, by presenting the Spanish first.

Remember that using different languages and varieties of English can be a good way to reach out to an audience, as in the pope's use of various languages, but it can also exclude and alienate listeners or readers. Such a danger is particularly great when you shift to language that your audience may not understand or that is not your own. In such cases, you might be seen as attempting to keep others out, or to speak for others rather than letting them speak for themselves.

Translating

The question of whether or not to translate words or passages from another language into English depends on your purpose and audience. In general, you should not assume that all your readers will understand the other language. So in most cases, including a translation (as Marcia Farr does) is appropriate. Occasionally, however, the words from the other language will be clear from the context (as is *shabes* in Michelle Herman's passage). A writer might at times leave something untranslated to make a point—to let readers know what it's like not to understand, for example.

To translate, as a general rule, underline or italicize foreign words, and put the translation in roman type, enclosed in parentheses or quotation marks.

≫ When you might shift among languages

- *To repeat someone's exact words,* as Rodney Morales does (28c).
- *To evoke a person, place, or activity,* as Ernest Matthew Mickler does (28e).
- *To make a strong point,* as Gloria Anzaldúa does (28f).
- *To establish your own credibility within a community,* as Geneva Smitherman does (28c).
- *To get your audience's attention,* as Ma and Pa Kettle do (28d).

THINKING CRITICALLY ABOUT LANGUAGE VARIETY

Reading with an Eye for Language Variety

Read the passage from *The Right Stuff* on the first page of Chapter 35. *The Right Stuff* is about test pilots, and this passage features characteristic language. What words and structures could be called fighter-pilot talk, and what do they contribute to the effectiveness of the narrative? Notice the shift to standard English in the last two lines; why do you think Wolfe makes this shift?

Thinking about Your Own Use of Language

The following description of a supper features English characteristic of the Florida backwoods in the 1930s. Using this passage as an example, write a description of a memorable meal or other event from your daily life. Perhaps try to include some informal dialogue. Then look at the language you used—do you use more than one variety of English, and if so, which ones? What effect does your use of language have on your description?

Jody heard nothing; saw nothing but his plate. He had never been so hungry in his life, and after a lean winter and a slow spring . . . his mother had cooked a supper good enough for the preacher. There were poke-greens with bits of white bacon buried in them; sandbuggers made of potato and onion and the cooter he had found crawling yesterday; sour orange biscuits and at his mother's elbow the sweet potato pone. He was torn between his desire for more biscuits and another sandbugger and the knowledge, born of painful experience, that if he ate them, he would suddenly have no room for pone. The choice was plain.   — MARJORIE KINNAN RAWLINGS, *The Yearling*

29

Considering Others: Building Common Ground

East is East, and West is West, and never the twain shall meet. . . .

You say to-ma-to, and I say to-mah-to. . . .

I did it my way.

United we stand, divided we fall. / We are the world.

THESE CONTRASTING STATEMENTS suggest a challenge every writer must face: many differences separate us. Each of us is unique—in genetic makeup and in total life experience. Each of us is an individual "I"—standing alone, doing it "my" way. As a result, we sometimes have difficulty understanding one another. Yet we also share common ground. We are all part of a species inhabiting the same crowded planet. And as individuals, we are also part of numerous communities.

In the United States today, we are part of a richly diverse population representing just about every social, religious, linguistic, and cultural tradition imaginable and yet all bound by a common citizenship. How can such different people ("East is East, and West is West. . . .") ever build commonalities? Fortunately, language can help us out. The words we use can and do build common ground and help us understand that with goodwill and effort East can meet West, even if one continues to say "to-ma-to" and the other "to-mah-to".

You will often be called on to appeal to people who are in some ways different from you. When expressing ideas that readers may strongly disagree with, it is all the more important to use language that does not sharpen the disagreement—and that makes readers receptive to your argument. To be successful in this effort, you need to understand as much as you can about the ways in which others differ from you and from one another. Knowing about and respecting these differences is the first step in building common ground.

Because language influences perceptions, you need to pay special attention to how words include or exclude others, how they create or destroy common ground. This chapter will get you started in thinking about how your own language can work to respect difference and to build common ground with others.

445

Everyday Use

We recently overheard a fourteen-year-old exclaim to his aunt: "I am *not* a 'kid' anymore, so please stop calling me that!" The nephew objected to a label he found both inaccurate and disrespectful, one that clearly built no common ground between him and his aunt. Can you think of situations when you've struggled to find just the right words to avoid offending someone: what salutation to use instead of "Dear Sir" when you're not sure who will read the letter, for instance, or how to describe an eighty-year-old without calling him or her "old," or what besides "mailman" to call someone who delivers your mail—especially when that person is *not* a man? These are choices we must make every day in trying to build common ground and communicate with others. Spend some time listening to people talking—or to television or radio broadcasters. Note any instances in which they seem to be making an effort to avoid language that might seem disrespectful or destroy common ground.

29a

Remembering the golden rule: considering stereotypes about gender, race, and other things

As a child, you may have learned to "do to others what you would have them do to you." To that golden rule, we could add "say to others what you would have them say to you." Language has power. It can praise, delight, inspire. It can also hurt, offend, destroy. Language that offends any readers breaks the golden rule of language use, preventing many readers from identifying with you and thus damaging your credibility as a writer.

In many instances, avoiding such language is simple enough. We can safely assume, for instance, that no readers respond well to being referred to disparagingly—for example, as "slobs" or "nerds." But other cases are more subtle and perhaps surprising. One student found, for example, that members of a group he had been referring to as "senior citizens" were irritated by that label. Similarly, a recent survey of people with physical disabilities reported that most of them resented euphemisms like "physically challenged" because they saw them as trivializing their difficulties.

Because usage changes constantly and preferences vary, few absolute guidelines exist for using language that shows respect for differences and builds common ground in every instance. Two rules, however, can help: consider carefully the sensitivities and preferences of others, and watch for words that carry stereotypes and betray unintended assumptions.

1

Watching for stereotypes and other assumptions

Children like to play; U.S. citizens value freedom; people who do not finish high school fare less well in the job market than those who graduate. These broad statements contain **stereotypes**, standardized or fixed ideas about a group. To some extent, we all think in terms of stereotypes, and sometimes they can be helpful in making a generalization. Stereotyping any individual on the basis of generalizations about a group can be dangerous, however, for it can lead to inaccurate and even hurtful conclusions.

Stereotyping becomes especially evident in language, in the words we choose to refer to or describe others. Stereotyped language can, and often does, break the links between writers and readers—or between speakers and listeners. An instructor who notes a male student's absence from class on the morning after a big fraternity party and says, "Ah, he must be a fraternity man," is stereotyping the student on the basis of assumptions about "fraternity men." But such stereotyping may be far off the mark with this particular student—and with many other fraternity members. By indulging in it, this instructor may well be alienating some of her students and undermining her effectiveness as a teacher.

In an article in the *New Yorker*, an executive recruiter points to other dangers of language that stereotypes.

> When I hear the word *dropout*, I have this image in my mind of a kid sitting across from me in the subway car: he's smoking a cigarette; he has a radio the size of a grand piano, and he keeps turning up the volume; his legs are stretched out so nobody can pass; he is staring at me with a look I can only describe as hate. I know that's not fair or accurate because I've hired many of them. Still, I can't help thinking of that kid on the subway.

Note the ways in which the executive admits he stereotypes people on the basis of a label: *dropouts* are apparently all young and male—and all rude, noisy, and hostile. Like all stereotypes, his is the result of a stock response built up and maintained by many things in his experience—songs, books, movies, television shows, and news reports, as well as personal encounters with some individuals who have dropped out of school. The mass media are particularly powerful in creating stereotypes. But as the executive recognizes and points out, stereotypes are often not accurate or fair.

Very often based on half-truths, misunderstandings, and hand-me-down prejudices, stereotypes can lead to intolerance, bias, and bigotry. Even apparently positive or neutral ones can hurt, for they inevitably ignore the uniqueness of an individual. As writers, we need to make sure that our language doesn't stereotype any group *or* individual. Other kinds of unstated assumptions that enter into our thinking and writing destroy common ground by ignoring differences between others and ourselves. For example, a student whose paper for a religion seminar uses *we* to refer to Christians and *they* to refer to members of other religions had better be sure that all the class members and the instructor are Christian, or some of them may feel left out of this discussion. In a letter to the editor of a newspaper about a current political issue, language implying that liberals are good and conservatives bad is likely to alienate some readers and prevent them from even considering the writer's argument about the specific issue.

Sometimes assumptions are so deeply ingrained that they have the effect of completely ignoring or "erasing" large groups of people. Such was the experience of African Americans not too many years ago, who failed to see themselves mentioned in public documents, represented in the mass media, or treated as an important part of the populace. This denial of their existence is described eloquently in Ralph Ellison's 1952 novel, *Invisible Man*.

> I am an invisible man. No, I am not a spook like those who haunted Edgar Allan Poe; nor am I one of your Hollywood-movie ectoplasms. I am a man of substance, of flesh and bone, fiber and liquids—and I might even be said to possess a mind. I am invisible, understand, simply because people refuse to see me. Like the bodiless heads you see sometimes in circus sideshows, it is as though I have been surrounded by mirrors of hard, distorting glass. When they approach me they see only my surroundings, themselves, or figments of their imagination—indeed, everything and anything except me. — RALPH ELLISON, *Invisible Man*

Language can also serve to "erase," as students at the University of Kansas realized when they discovered that history books routinely report only one survivor of General George Custer's Battle of Little Bighorn: Comanche, a horse (now stuffed and on display at their university). Several thousand Sioux survived that battle, yet the history books simply ignore them, making them invisible.

On the other hand, stereotypes and other assumptions often lead writers to mention a group affiliation unnecessarily when it has no relation to the point under consideration, as in "a woman bus driver" or "a Jewish doctor." Decisions about whether to make a generalization about a group or to describe an individual as a member of a group are often difficult for writers. The following sections invite you to think about how your language can build—rather than destroy—common ground.

2

Considering assumptions about gender

An elementary teacher in Toronto got increasingly tired of seeing hands go up every time the children sang the line in Canada's national anthem, "true patriot love in all thy sons command." "When do we get to the part about the daughters?" the children inevitably asked. As a result of such questions, the House of Commons voted on a bill to change the line—to "true patriot love in all our hearts command."

These children's questions point to the ways in which powerful and often invisible gender-related elements of language affect our thinking and our behavior. We now know, for instance, that many young women at one time were discouraged from pursuing careers in medicine or engineering at least partially because speakers of our language, following stereotyped assumptions about gender roles in society, always referred to hypothetical doctors or engineers as "he" (and then labeled any woman who worked as a doctor a "woman doctor," as if to say, "She's an exception; doctors are normally male"). Equally problematic is the traditional use of *man* and *mankind* to refer to people of both sexes and the use of *he, him, his,* and *himself* to refer to people of unknown sex, as in "everyone must bring his own pencils." Because such usage ignores half the human race—or at least seems to assume that the other half is more important—it hardly helps a writer build common ground. Similarly, labels like "male nurse" or "male secretary" may offend by reflecting stereotyped assumptions about proper roles for males.

Revising sexist language

Sexist language, those words and phrases that stereotype or ignore members of either sex or that unnecessarily call attention to gender, can usually be revised fairly easily. For example, here are some alternatives to the use of masculine pronouns to refer to persons of unknown sex.

- Use plural forms:
  Lawyers must pass the bar exam before *they* can begin to practice.

- Use *he or she, him or her,* and so on:
  A lawyer must pass the bar exam before *he or she* can begin to practice.

- Eliminate the pronouns:
  A lawyer must pass the bar exam before beginning to practice.

INSTEAD OF	TRY USING
anchorman, anchorwoman	anchor
chairman, chairwoman	chair, chairperson
coed	student
congressman	member of Congress, representative
mailman	mail carrier
male nurse	nurse
man, mankind	humans, human beings, humanity the human race, humankind

INSTEAD OF	TRY USING
manpower	workers, personnel
mothering	parenting
policeman, policewoman	police officer
steward, stewardess	flight attendant
woman engineer	engineer

(For more discussion of nonsexist pronouns, see 11d.)

⟫ Editing out sexist language

1. Have you used *man* or *men* or words containing one of them to refer to people who may be female? If so, consider substituting another word—instead of *fireman,* for instance, try *firefighter.*

2. If you have mentioned someone's gender, is your doing so necessary? If you identify someone as a female architect, for example, do you (or would you) refer to someone else as a "male architect"? And if you then note that the female is an attractive blond mother of two, do you mention that the male is a muscular, square-jawed father of three? Unless gender and related matters—looks, clothes, parenthood—are relevant to your point, leave them unmentioned.

3. Do you use any occupational stereotypes? Watch for the use of female pronouns for nurses, male ones for engineers, for example.

4. Do you use language that in any way patronizes either sex? Do you refer to a wife as "the little woman," for instance, or to a husband as "her old man"?

5. Have you used *he, him, his,* or *himself* to refer to people who may be female? Try revising with the help of the guidelines in 29a2.

6. Have you overused *he and she, him and her,* and so on? Frequent use of these pronoun pairs can bore or even irritate readers.

EXERCISE 29.1

The following excerpt is taken from the 1968 edition of Dr. Benjamin Spock's *Baby and Child Care.* Read it carefully, noting any language we might today consider sexist. Then try bringing it up-to-date by revising the passage, substituting nonsexist language as necessary.

399. Feeling his oats. One year old is an exciting age. Your baby is changing in lots of ways—in his eating, in how he gets around, in what he wants to do and in how he feels about himself and other people. When he was little and helpless, you could put him where you wanted him, give him the playthings you thought suitable, feed him the foods you knew were best. Most of the time he was willing to let you be the boss, and took it all in good spirit. It's more complicated now that he is around a year old. He seems to realize that he's not meant to be a baby doll the rest of his life, that he's a human being with ideas and a will of his own.

When you suggest something that doesn't appeal to him, he feels he **must** assert himself. His nature tells him to. He just says No in words or actions, even about things that he likes to do. The psychologists call it "negativism"; mothers call it "that terrible No stage." But stop and think what would happen to him if he never felt like saying No. He'd become a robot, a mechanical man. You wouldn't be able to resist the temptation to boss him all the time, and he'd stop learning and developing. When he was old enough to go out into the world, to school and later to work, everybody else would take advantage of him, too. He'd never be good for anything.

3

Considering assumptions about race and ethnicity

One good way to begin thinking about racial and ethnic stereotypes and the assumptions that accompany them is to consider the ways your life has been shaped by your own race or ethnicity. In thinking of yourself in terms of race and ethnicity, what images, qualities, ideas come to mind? What do you know about your ancestors and about their ethnic heritage? What has such a heritage meant to your own identity and to the way you typically relate to others? Have others ever made unfair or inaccurate assumptions about you or those important to you because of your ethnicity?

One Irish American student realized that she had never even thought twice about her own ethnicity until she heard herself referred to by Mexican American dormmates as an "Anglo." Before that incident, she'd always considered ethnicity something affecting other people. Recognizing how others viewed her ethnicity helped her think about assumptions she had about them.

As we all know only too well, generalizations about racial and ethnic groups can result in especially harmful stereotyping. Such assumptions can be seen in statements that suggest, for instance, that all African Americans are musically talented, that Asian Americans all excel in math and science, or that all Germans are efficiency experts. Negative stereotypes, of course, are even more damaging. In building common ground, writers must watch for any language that ignores not only differences among individual members of a race or ethnic group but among subgroups—for instance, the many nations to which Native Americans belong or the diverse places from which Americans of Spanish-speaking ancestry have emigrated.

Using preferred terms

For writers, avoiding stereotypes and other assumptions based on race or ethnicity is only a first step. Beyond that lies the task of attempting to refer to any group in terms that its members actually desire. Doing so is sometimes not an easy task, for preferences change and even vary widely.

The word *colored,* for example, was once widely used in the United States to refer to Americans of African ancestry (in fact, it still appears in the name of the NAACP, the National Association for the Advancement of Colored People). By the 1950s, the preferred term had become *Negro;* in the 1960s, however, *black* came to be preferred by most, though certainly not all, members of that community. Then, in the late 1980s, some leaders of the American black community urged that *black* be replaced by *African American.* One such leader, the Reverend Jesse Jackson, argued that *African American* has "cultural integrity" because it designates "some land base, some historical cultural base," whereas *black* is a "baseless" designation.

Similarly, the word *Oriental,* which until recently was used to refer to people of East Asian descent, is now often considered offensive. At the University of California at Berkeley, the Oriental Languages Department is now known as the East Asian Languages Department. One advocate of the change explained that *Oriental* is appropriate for objects, like rugs, but not for people.

Many of those once referred to as *American Indians* now prefer to be called *Native Americans.* In Alaska and Canada, many of the native peoples once referred to as *Eskimos* now prefer *Inuit* (which is the official designated term in Canada). And among Americans of Spanish-speaking descent, the terms are many: *Chicano/Chicana, Hispanic, Latin American, Latino/Latina, Mexican American,* and *Puerto Rican,* to name but a few.

Clearly, then, ethnic terminology changes often enough to challenge the most careful writer. The best advice may be to consider your words carefully, to *listen* for the way members of groups refer to themselves (or *ask* their preferences), and to check any term you're unsure of in a current dictionary. The 1991 *Random House Webster's College Dictionary* includes particularly helpful usage notes about racial and ethnic designations.

4

Considering other kinds of difference

Gender, race, and ethnicity are among the most frequent challenges to a writer seeking to find common ground with readers, but you will face many others as well. The following section discusses some of them.

Age

Mention age if it is relevant, but be aware that age-related terms can carry derogatory connotations (*matronly, teenybopper, well-preserved,* and so on). Although describing Mr. Fry as "elderly but still active" may sound polite to you, chances are Mr. Fry would prefer being called "an active seventy-eight-year-old"—or just "a seventy-eight-year-old," which eliminates the unstated assumption of surprise that he is active "at his age."

Class

Because you may not usually think about class as consciously as you do about age or race, for example, you should take special care to examine your words for stereotypes or assumptions about class. Such was the case in a recent *New York Times* column entitled "Young, Privileged, and Unemployed," written by a young woman who had lost her high-paying professional job. Unable to find other "meaningful work," the author wrote, she and others like her had been forced to accept "absurd" jobs like cleaning houses and baby-sitting.

The column provoked a number of angry letters to the *Times,* like this one: "So the young and privileged are learning what we of the working classes have always understood too well: there is no entitlement in life. We have always taken the jobs you label 'absurd.' Our mothers are the women who clean your mothers' houses. . . ." Thus did the writer destroy common ground with her readers by assuming that cleaning houses is an "absurd" way to make a living and that education or social standing entitles people to more "meaningful" occupations.

As a writer, then, do not assume that all your readers share your background or values—that your classmates' families all own their homes, for instance. And avoid using any words—*redneck, blue blood,* and the like— that might alienate anyone.

Geographical areas

Though stereotypes related to geographical areas are not always insulting or even unpleasant, they are very often clichéd and exaggerated. New Englanders are not all thrifty and tight-lipped; Florida offers more than retirement and tourism; Texans do not all wear cowboy boots and Stetson hats; midwesterners are not all hard-working; many Californians neither care about nor participate in the latest trends. Check your writing carefully to be sure it doesn't make these kinds of simplistic assumptions.

Check also that you use geographical terms accurately.

America, American. Although many people use these words to refer to the United States alone, you should be aware that such usage will not necessarily be acceptable to people from Canada, Mexico, and Central or South America.

British, English. British should be used to refer to the island of Great Britain, which includes England, Scotland, and Wales, or to the United Kingdom of Great Britain and Northern Ireland. In general, do not use *English* for these broader senses.

Arab. This term refers only to people of Arabic-speaking descent. Note that Iran is not an Arab nation; its people speak Farsi, not Arabic. Note also that *Arab* is not synonymous with *Muslim* or *Moslem* (a believer in Islam). Most (but not all) Arabs are Muslim, but many Muslims (those in Pakistan, for example) are not Arab.

Physical ability or health

The question to ask yourself when writing about a person with a serious illness or physical disability is whether to mention the disability at all if it is not relevant to your discussion. If you do, consider whether the words you use carry negative connotations. You might choose, for example, to say someone "uses" a wheelchair rather than to say he or she "is confined to" one. Similarly, you might note a subtle but meaningful difference between calling someone a "person with AIDS," rather than an "AIDS victim." Mentioning the person first, the disability second, such as referring to a "child with diabetes" rather than a "diabetic child" or a "diabetic," is always a good idea. On the other hand, the survey of people with disabilities that was mentioned earlier shows that you also must be careful not to minimize the importance of a disability.

Religion

Religious stereotypes are very often inaccurate and unfair. Roman Catholics hold a wide spectrum of views on abortion, for example, Muslim women do not all wear veils, and many Baptists are not fundamentalists. In fact, not all people believe in or practice a religion at all, so be careful of such assumptions. As in other cases, do not use religious labels without considering their relevance to your point, and make every effort to get them right—for example, *Reformed* churches but *Reform* synagogues.

Sexual orientation

Partly because sexual orientation is a topic that was "erased" from most public discourse until recent decades, the stereotypes and assumptions that surround it are particularly deep-seated and, often, unconscious. Writers who wish to build common ground, therefore, should not assume that readers all share any one sexual orientation—that everyone is attracted to the opposite sex, for example.

As with any label, reference to sexual orientation should be governed by context. Someone writing about Representative Barney Frank's economic views would probably have little if any reason to refer to his sexual orientation. On the other hand, a writer concerned with diversity in U.S. government might find it important to note that Frank is a member of Congress who has made his homosexuality public.

EXERCISE 29.2

Together with two or three classmates, look at the passage by James Thurber in 8c, and discuss whether you find any of its thinking or language stereotyped. If so, do you think Thurber's humorous purpose justifies inclusion of the stereotype(s)? If Thurber were a member of your class, would you advise him to make any revisions? What would they be?

Taking time to listen

Eudora Welty once wrote about the importance of listening in her development as a writer, saying that long before she wrote stories, she "listened for stories," and that this listening led her eventually to scenes full of "things to find out and know about human beings." Listening carefully to others—taking time to hear where they are (perhaps literally) coming from—is a necessary step in finding common ground.

Listen especially for what makes those you are listening to unique, and look for common ground between you. Think of ways you can use language to help create common ground—for example, by asking questions rather than making quick, possibly wrong assumptions. Finally, try to relate the experiences of the other person to your own. Look for ways, in short, not only to notice differences but also to make connections.

≫ *Editing for language that builds common ground*

1. Are your references to race, religion, gender, sexual orientation, and so on, relevant or necessary to your discussion? If not, consider leaving them out.

2. Are there unstated assumptions that might come between you and your readers? Look, for instance, for language implying approval or disapproval and for the ways you use *we, you,* and *they.*

3. Are the terms you use to refer to groups accurate and acceptable? Because group labels and preferences are always changing, take care to be sure you use the most current or widely accepted terms.

4. Does any language used to describe others carry offensive stereotypes or connotations?

USING SOURCES
Building Common Ground

Whenever you refer to other sources, you have an opportunity to build common ground with readers. Citing sources your readers will recognize and respect, for example, can help strengthen the argument you present to those readers. And citing someone from the other side of the argument can demonstrate that you've considered that side. (See 5f on using authority to demonstrate fairness and attention to counterarguments.)

THINKING CRITICALLY ABOUT HOW LANGUAGE CAN BUILD COMMON GROUND

Reading with an Eye for Common Ground

The following poem is about finding common ground. Identify those places where the poet asserts his own individuality and those where he forges common ground with readers. How does the speaker address, perhaps indirectly, issues of racism? How does he deal with issues of difference without insulting readers? Does this poem relate to your experience with others? If so, how?

Theme for English B

The instructor said,

> Go home and write
> a page tonight.
> And let that page come out of you—
> Then, it will be true.

I wonder if it's that simple?

I am twenty-two, colored, born in Winston-Salem.
I went to school there, then Durham, then here
to this college on the hill above Harlem.
I am the only colored student in my class.
The steps from the hill lead down to Harlem,
through a park, then I cross St. Nicolas,
Eighth Avenue, Seventh, and I come to the Y,
the Harlem Branch Y, where I take the elevator
up to my room, sit down, and write this page:

It's not easy to know what is true for you or me
at twenty-two, my age. But I guess I'm what
I feel and see and hear. Harlem, I hear you:
hear you, hear me—we two—you, me talk on this page.
(I hear New York, too.) Me—who?

Well, I like to eat, sleep, drink, and be in love.
I like to work, read, learn, and understand life.
I like a pipe for a Christmas present,
or records—Bessie, bop, or Bach.

I guess being colored doesn't make me not like
the same things other folks like who are other races.
So will my page be colored that I write?
Being me, it will not be white.
But it will be
a part of you, instructor.
You are white—
yet a part of me, as I am a part of you.
That's American.

Sometimes perhaps you don't want to be a part of me.
Nor do I often want to be a part of you.
But we are, that's true!
As I learn from you,
I guess you learn from me—
although you're older—and white—
and somewhat more free.

This is my page for English B.   – Langston Hughes

Thinking about How Your Language Builds Common Ground

One good way to start thinking about differences and common ground is to look around the classroom and try to describe them in writing. Like you, generations of college students have found themselves in classes filled with people both like them and different from them. Here is Eudora Welty, describing her first year (1926) at Mississippi State College for Women.

There I landed in a world to itself, and indeed it was all new to me. It was surging with twelve hundred girls. They came from every nook and corner of the state, from the Delta, the piney woods, the Gulf Coast, the black prairie, the red clay hills, and Jackson—as the capital city and the only sizeable town, a region to itself. All were clearly differentiated sections, at that time, and though we were all put into uniforms of navy blue so as to unify us, it could have been told by the girls' accents, by their bearings, the way they came into the classroom and the way they ate, where they'd grown up. This was my first chance to learn what the body of us were like and what differences in background, persuasion of mind, and resources of character there were among Mississippians—at that, among only half of us, for we were all white. I missed the significance of both what was in, and what was out of, our well-enclosed but vibrantly alive society.
     – Eudora Welty, *One Writer's Beginnings*

Take time now to examine where you've come from—your age, ethnicity, home-town, religion, and so on. Then do the same for one or more of your classmates. Write a paragraph about the differences *and* the common ground you see. Finally, study your paragraph for any assumptions your language reveals.

Part Six

Understanding Punctuation Conventions

———————— ⟨⟩ ————————

30. Using Commas   *460*

31. Using Semicolons   *480*

32. Using End Punctuation   *487*

33. Using Apostrophes   *493*

34. Using Quotation Marks   *499*

35. Using Other Punctuation Marks   *508*

30

Using Commas

THE WORD COMMA COMES FROM THE GREEK KOMMA, meaning "cut" or "segment," and commas are used to separate parts of a sentence from one another. A clause, for example, is a segment of a sentence, and it is often set off from the rest of the sentence with a comma.

Commas also mark a pause in reading. In his essay "In Praise of the Humble Comma," Pico Iyer likens a comma to a flashing yellow light that asks the reader to slow down. You can see what he means by reading through the following sentences, first with the commas and then without:

> The hangman, a gray-haired convict in the white uniform of the prison, was waiting beside his machine.
>
> And then, when the noose was fixed, the prisoner began crying out to his god.
>
> The prisoner had vanished, and the rope was twisting on itself.
>
> "Well, that's all for this morning, thank God."
>
> – GEORGE ORWELL, "A Hanging"

Because the comma is the most frequently used punctuation mark in English, commas count in your writing. In fact, the study of student writing undertaken as part of the research for this book reveals that five of the twenty most common errors involve the comma. However, reducing comma use to hard and fast rules is difficult. First, the comma can play a number of different roles in a sentence, making general rules hard to come by. More important, many decisions about commas relate to matters of purpose, rhythm, and style rather than to grammar alone. As a result, conventions for using commas differ from one English-speaking country to another, even from one professional writer to another.

Getting full control of comma usage in your own writing thus involves not only learning some rules but also practicing the use of commas in writing and concentrating on the stylistic decisions you must learn to make as a writer. This chapter presents an opportunity for you to accomplish both these goals.

EXERCISE 30.1

The following paragraph from "Homeless" by Anna Quindlen is reproduced without any of the commas Quindlen used. Add commas where you think they're necessary or would be helpful. Then look through this chapter to check if your comma usage is appropriate. Have you used any unnecessary commas? Can you see places where you need to add any? Compare your use of commas with a classmate's.

They were not pictures of family or friends or even a dog or cat its eyes brown-red in the flashbulb's light. They were pictures of a house. It was like a thousand houses in a hundred towns not suburb not city but somewhere in between with aluminum siding and a chain-link fence a narrow driveway running up to a one-car garage and a patch of backyard. The house was yellow. I looked on the back for a date or a name but neither was there. There was no need for discussion. I knew what she was trying to tell me for it was something I had often felt. She was not adrift alone anonymous although her bags and her raincoat with the grime shadowing its creases had made me believe she was. She had a house or at least once upon a time had had one. Inside were curtains a couch a stove potholders. You are where you live. She was somebody.

Everyday Use

Commas play a surprisingly important role in recipes. Study their use in the following recipe for sweet-potato pie:

1¼ c sweet potatoes, cooked and mashed	¼ t cinnamon
	1 T butter, melted
½ c brown sugar, firmly packed	2 eggs, well beaten
½ t salt	¾ c milk

Prepare pastry for a one-crust pie, and line an 8-inch pie pan; chill. Preheat oven to 400°. Combine sweet potatoes, brown sugar, salt, cinnamon, and butter. Mix together eggs and milk. Combine all ingredients. Pour into pie shell, and bake for 45 minutes.

Commas serve here to separate ingredients (sweet potatoes) from what the cook is supposed to do (cook and mash them). How else are they used? Look at some directions you use—for making pancakes, perhaps, or for operating a tape recorder—and collect some examples of comma use. Where are they necessary, and where are they just helpful?

30a

Using commas after introductory elements

A comma usually follows an introductory word, expression, phrase, or clause. These introductory elements include adverbs (see 7b5); conjunctive adverbs (see 7b7); transitional expressions (see 6d5); participles, infinitives, and prepositional phrases, and participial, infinitive, and absolute phrases (see 7c3); and adverb clauses (see 7c4).

> *Slowly,* she became conscious of her predicament. [adverb]
>
> *Nevertheless,* the hours of a typist are flexible. [conjunctive adverb]
>
> *In fact,* only you can decide. [transitional expression]
>
> *Frustrated,* he wondered whether he should change careers. [participle]
>
> *In Fitzgerald's novel,* the color green takes on great symbolic qualities. [prepositional phrase]
>
> *Sporting a pair of specially made running shoes,* Jamie prepared for the race. [participial phrase]
>
> *To win the contest,* Connor needed luck. [infinitive phrase]
>
> *Pens poised in anticipation,* the students waited for the test to be distributed. [absolute phrase]
>
> *Since her mind was not receiving enough stimulation,* she had to resort to her imagination. [adverb clause]

After certain introductory elements—adverbs, infinitives, prepositional and infinitive phrases, and adverb clauses—some writers omit the comma if the element is short and does not seem to require a pause after it.

> *At the racetrack* Henry lost nearly his entire paycheck.

If the introductory element is followed by inverted word order, with the verb preceding the subject, do not use a comma.

> *From directly behind my seat* came huge clouds of cigar smoke.

EXERCISE 30.2

In the following sentences, add any commas that are needed after the introductory element.

1. In one of his most famous poems Frost asks why people need walls.
2. Unfortunately the door to the kennel had been left open.
3. Unable to make such a decision alone I asked my brother for help.

4. If you follow the instructions you will be able to install your radio.
5. Therefore answering the seemingly simple question is very difficult.
6. With the fifth century came the fall of the Roman Empire.
7. Their bags packed they waited for the taxi to the airport.
8. To become an Olympic competitor an athlete must train for years.
9. After the hurricane moved on the citizens of the town assessed the damage.
10. Startled by the explosion the workers dropped to the ground.

30b

Using commas in compound sentences

A comma usually precedes a coordinating conjunction (*and, but, or, for, nor, so,* or *yet*) that joins two independent clauses in a compound sentence.

> The title may sound important, but *administrative clerk* is only a euphemism for *photocopier*.
>
> The climbers will reach the summit today, or they must turn back.
>
> The show started at last, and the crowd grew quiet.
>
> No one answered, so I left a message on the machine.

You may want to use a semicolon rather than a comma when the clauses are long and complex or contain other punctuation.

> When these early migrations took place, the ice was still confined to the lands in the far north; but eight hundred thousand years ago, when man was already established in the temperate latitudes, the ice moved southward until it covered large parts of Europe and Asia.
>
> — ROBERT JASTROW, *Until the Sun Dies*

With very short clauses, you can sometimes omit the comma before *and* or *or.*

> She saw her chance and she took it.

Always use the comma if there is any chance the sentence will be misread without it.

CONFUSING	The game ended in victory and pandemonium erupted.
REVISED	The game ended in victory, and pandemonium erupted.

Be careful not to use *only* a comma between independent clauses. Doing so is usually considered a serious grammatical error, called a comma splice.

(See Chapter 15.) Use either a coordinating conjunction after the comma or a semicolon.

COMMA SPLICE	Do not say luck is responsible for your new job, give yourself the credit you deserve.
REVISED	Do not say luck is responsible for your new job, *but* give yourself the credit you deserve.
REVISED	Do not say luck is responsible for your new job; give yourself the credit you deserve.

EXERCISE 30.3

Use a comma and a coordinating conjunction (*and, but, or, for, nor, so,* or *yet*) to combine each of the following pairs of sentences into one sentence. Delete or rearrange words if necessary. Example:

> I had finished studying for the test, *so* I went to bed.

1. Max Weber was not in favor of a classless society. He thought it would lead to the expansion of the power of the state over the individual.
2. Joan Didion's nonfiction is renowned. Her novels are also worthwhile.
3. I studied ten of Verdi's operas. I have only begun to appreciate the wealth of his creativity.
4. The playwright disliked arguing with directors. She avoided rehearsals.
5. Tropical fish do not bark. They are not cuddly pets.

30c

Using commas to set off nonrestrictive elements

Nonrestrictive elements—clauses, phrases, and words that do *not* limit, or "restrict," the meaning of the words they modify—are set off from the rest of the sentence with commas. **Restrictive** elements *do* limit meaning and are *not* set off with commas.

RESTRICTIVE	Drivers *who have been convicted of drunken driving* should lose their licenses.
NONRESTRICTIVE	The two drivers involved in the accident, *who have been convicted of drunken driving,* should lose their licenses.

In the first sentence, the clause *who have been convicted of drunken driving* is essential to the meaning because it limits the word it modifies, *Drivers,* to only those drivers who have been convicted of drunken driving. Therefore, it is not set off by commas. In the second sentence, the same clause is not essential to the meaning because it does not limit what it modifies, *The two drivers involved in the accident,* but merely provides additional information about these drivers. Therefore, it *is* set off with commas.

Notice how using or not using commas to set off such an element can change the meaning of a sentence.

> The bus drivers rejecting the management offer remained on strike.

> The bus drivers, rejecting the management offer, remained on strike.

In the first sentence, not using commas to set off the phrase *rejecting the management offer* makes the phrase restrictive, limiting the meaning of *The bus drivers.* This sentence says that only some of the total group of bus drivers, the ones who rejected the offer, remained on strike, implying that other drivers went back to work. In the second sentence, the commas around the phrase makes it nonrestrictive, implying that *The bus drivers* refers to all of the drivers and that all of them remained on strike.

To decide whether an element is restrictive or nonrestrictive, mentally delete the element, and then decide whether the deletion changes the meaning of the rest of the sentence or makes it unclear. If it does, the element is probably restrictive and should not be set off with commas. If it does not, the element is probably nonrestrictive and requires commas.

1

Using commas with adjective and adverb clauses

Adjective clauses begin with *who, whom, whose, which, that, when, where,* or *why.* (See 7c4.) Adverb clauses begin with subordinating conjunctions, such as *because, although,* or *before.* (See 7b7 and 7c4.) Adverb clauses are usually essential to the meaning of the sentence; in general, do not set them off with commas unless they precede the independent clause (see 30a) or begin with *although, even though, while,* or another conjunction expressing the idea of contrast.

NONRESTRICTIVE CLAUSES

I borrowed books from the rental library of Shakespeare and Company, *which was the library and bookstore of Sylvia Beach at 12 rue de l'Odeon.* [The clause describing Shakespeare and Company is not necessary to the meaning of the independent clause and therefore is set off with a comma.]
— ERNEST HEMINGWAY, *A Moveable Feast*

The Indians, *who range in color from mocha to Dentyne,* are generally under five feet tall. [The central statement is that the Indians are under five feet tall; the information about color does not limit the statement to only some of them but simply provides additional information.]

– JOHN UPDIKE, "Venezuela for Visitors"

The park soon became a popular gathering place, *although some nearby residents complained about the noise.* [The adverb clause expresses the idea of contrast; therefore, it is set off with a comma.]

RESTRICTIVE CLAUSES

I grew up in a house *where the only regular guests were my relations.* [The information in the adjective clause is essential to the meaning of the sentence and therefore should not be set off with commas.]

– RICHARD RODRIGUEZ, "Aria: Memoir of a Bilingual Childhood"

The claim *that men like seriously to battle one another to some sort of finish* is a myth. [The adjective clause is necessary to the meaning of the sentence because it explains which claim is a myth.]

– JOHN MCMURTRY, "Kill 'Em! Crush 'Em! Eat 'Em Raw!"

An adjective clause that begins with *that* is always restrictive and is not set off with commas. An adjective clause beginning with *which* may be either restrictive or nonrestrictive; however, some writers prefer to use *which* only for nonrestrictive clauses.

2

Using commas with phrases

Participial phrases may be either restrictive or nonrestrictive. Prepositional phrases are usually restrictive but sometimes are not essential to the meaning of a sentence and are therefore set off with commas.

NONRESTRICTIVE PHRASES

Stephanie, amazed, stared at the strange vehicle. [The participle does not limit the meaning of *Stephanie.*]

The "synfuels" program, *launched at the height of the energy crisis,* languished with the drop in fuel prices. [The participial phrase does not limit the meaning of *The "synfuels" program* or change the central meaning of the sentence.]

Frederic Chopin, despite ill health, composed prolifically. [The prepositional phrase does not limit the meaning of *Frederic Chopin.*]

RESTRICTIVE PHRASES

A penny *saved* is a penny *earned.* [Without the participles, the sentence has a very different meaning.]

Wood *cut from living trees* does not burn as well as dead wood. [The participial phrase is essential to the meaning.]

The wire *for the antenna* is the last one to be connected. [The prepositional phrase restricts the meaning of *wire*.]

3

Using commas with appositives

An appositive is a noun or noun substitute that renames a nearby noun or noun substitute. (See 7c3.) When an appositive is not essential to identify what it renames, it is set off with commas.

NONRESTRICTIVE APPOSITIVES

Ms. Baker, *my high school chemistry teacher,* inspired my love of science. [Ms. Baker's name identifies her; the appositive simply provides extra information.]

Beethoven's only opera, *Fidelio,* includes the famous "Prisoners' Chorus." [Beethoven wrote only one opera, so its name is not essential.]

RESTRICTIVE APPOSITIVES

The editorial cartoonist *Thomas Nast* helped bring about the downfall of the Tweed ring in New York City. [The appositive identifies *The editorial cartoonist* as a specific cartoonist.]

Mozart's opera *The Marriage of Figaro* was considered revolutionary. [The appositive is restrictive because Mozart wrote more than one opera.]

EXERCISE 30.4

Identify the restrictive and the nonrestrictive elements in the following sentences.

1. The tornado, which had spared Waterville, leveled Douglastown.
2. The man who rescued her puppy won her eternal gratitude.
3. Jacqueline Kennedy Onassis, who died in 1994, was a figure of mystery.
4. Houses made of wood can often survive earthquakes.
5. Thurgood Marshall, the first African American to serve on the U.S. Supreme Court, died in 1993.

EXERCISE 30.5

Use commas to set off nonrestrictive clauses, phrases, and appositives in any of the following sentences that contain such elements.

1. Anyone who is fourteen years old faces strong peer pressure every day.
2. Embalming is a technique that preserves a cadaver.

3. I would feel right at home in the city dump which bears a striking resemblance to my bedroom.

4. The musical *West Side Story* was a modern version of Shakespeare's play *Romeo and Juliet*.

5. A house overlooking the ocean costs $500,000.

6. The Zunis an ancient tribe live in New Mexico.

7. The president elected for a six-year term acts as head of state.

8. Karl Marx an important nineteenth-century political philosopher believed that his role as a social thinker was to change the world.

9. Birds' hearts have four chambers whereas reptiles' have three.

10. Britain and France agreed to aid each other if one of them were attacked.

30d

Using commas to separate items in a series

A comma is used between items in a series of three or more words, phrases, or clauses.

> I bumped into professors, horizontal bars, agricultural students, and swinging iron rings.   — JAMES THURBER, "University Days"

> He has plundered our seas, ravaged our coasts, burnt our towns, and destroyed the lives of our people.
> — THOMAS JEFFERSON, Declaration of Independence

You may often see a series with no comma after the next-to-last item, particularly in newspaper writing, as in *The day was cold, dark and dreary.* Occasionally, however, omitting the comma can cause confusion, and you will never be wrong if you include it.

When the items in a series contain commas of their own or other punctuation, separate them with semicolons rather than commas (see 31b).

Coordinate adjectives, those that relate equally to the noun they modify, should be separated by commas. In the sentence *They are sincere, talented, inquisitive researchers*, the three adjectives are coordinate: they each modify *researchers* and are therefore separated by commas. Here are some other examples of coordinate adjectives.

> The *long, twisting, muddy* road led to a shack in the woods.
> His *bizarre, outrageous* sense of humor endeared him to his friends.

In a sentence like *The cracked bathroom mirror reflected his face,* however, *cracked* and *bathroom* are not coordinate because *bathroom mirror* is the equivalent of a single word, which is modified by *cracked.* Hence they are *not* separated by commas.

> Byron carried an *elegant gold pocket* watch.
> *Deflated yellow rubber* rafts were piled up in the boathouse.

You can usually determine whether adjectives are coordinate by inserting *and* between them. If the sentence makes sense with the *and,* the adjectives are coordinate and should be separated by commas.

> They are sincere *and* talented *and* inquisitive researchers. [The sentence makes sense with the *and*'s, so the adjectives *sincere, talented,* and *inquisitive* should be separated by commas.]

> Byron carried an elegant *and* gold *and* pocket watch. [In this instance, the sentence does not make sense with the *and*'s, so the adjectives *elegant, gold,* and *pocket* should not be separated by commas.]

EXERCISE 30.6

Revise any of the following sentences that require commas to set off words, phrases, or clauses in a series.

1. They found employment in truck driving farming and mining.
2. We bought zucchini peppers and tomatoes at the market.
3. James Joyce wrote novels short stories and poetry.
4. The daddy longlegs's orange body resembles a colored dot amidst eight long black legs.
5. A prestigious car a large house and membership in an exclusive club are taken as signs of success.
6. Superficial observation does not provide accurate insight into people's lives—how they feel what they believe in how they respond to others.
7. The ball sailed over the fence across the road and through the Wilsons' window.
8. I timidly offered to help a loud overbearing lavishly dressed customer.
9. Ellen is an accomplished freelance writer.
10. These Cosell clones insist on calling every play judging every move and telling everyone within earshot exactly what is wrong with the team.

30e

Using commas to set off parenthetical and transitional expressions

Parenthetical expressions are added comments or information. Because they often interrupt or digress, they are usually set off with commas. Transitional expressions are also usually set off with commas. They include conjunctive adverbs like *however* and *furthermore* and other words and phrases used to connect parts of sentences. (For full lists, see 7b7 and 6d5.)

Some studies, *incidentally,* have shown that chocolate, *of all things,* helps to prevent tooth decay.

Roald Dahl's stories, *it turns out,* were often inspired by his own childhood.

Ceiling fans are, *moreover,* less expensive than air conditioners.

Ozone is a byproduct of dry cleaning, *for example.*

30f

Using commas to set off contrasting elements, interjections, direct address, and tag questions

Contrasting elements

On official business it was she, *not my father,* one would usually hear on the phone or in stores.
     — RICHARD RODRIGUEZ, "Aria: A Memoir of a Bilingual Childhood"
The story is narrated objectively at first, *subjectively toward the end.*

Interjections

My God, who wouldn't want a wife?   — JUDY BRADY, "I Want a Wife"
We had hiked for, *say,* seven miles before stopping to rest.

Direct address

Ah, swinging generation, what new delights await?
     — TOM WOLFE, "Pornoviolence"

My friends, I must say to you that we have not made a single gain in civil rights without determined legal and nonviolent pressure.
     — MARTIN LUTHER KING, JR., "Letter from Birmingham Jail"

Tag questions

The homeless are our fellow citizens, *are they not?*

The governor did not veto the unemployment bill, *did he?*

EXERCISE 30.7

Revise each of the following sentences, using commas to set off parenthetical and transitional expressions, contrasting elements, interjections, words used in direct address, and tag questions.

1. One must consider the society as a whole not just its parts.
2. The West in fact has become solidly Republican in presidential elections.
3. Her friends did not know about her illness did they?
4. The celebration will alas conclude all too soon.
5. Ladies and gentlemen I bid you farewell.

30g

Using commas with dates, addresses, titles, and numbers

Commas are used according to established rules with dates, addresses and place-names, and numbers. Commas are also used to separate personal and professional titles from the names preceding them.

Dates

For dates, use a comma between the day of the week and the month, between the day of the month and the year, and between the year and the rest of the sentence, if any.

The war began on Thursday, *January 17, 1991,* with air strikes on Iraq.

Do not use commas with dates in inverted order or with dates consisting of only the month and the year.

18 October 1989

Thousands of Germans swarmed over and through the wall in *November 1989* and effectively demolished it.

Addresses and place-names

In addresses and place-names, use a comma after each part, including the state if no ZIP code is given. A ZIP code, however, is not preceded by a comma.

> Forward my mail to the Department of English, The Ohio State University, Columbus, Ohio 43210.
>
> Portland, Oregon, is much larger than Portland, Maine.

Titles

Use commas to set off a title such as *Jr., M.D.,* and so on, from the name preceding it and from the rest of the sentence.

> Jaime Mejia, *Ph.D.*
>
> Martin Luther King, *Jr.,* was one of this century's greatest orators.

Numbers

In numbers of five digits or more, use a comma between each group of three digits, starting from the right.

> The city's population rose to *17,126* in the 1990 census.

Do not use a comma within street numbers, ZIP codes, or page numbers.

> My parents live at *11311* Wimberly Drive, Richmond, Virginia *23233.*
>
> Turn to page 1566.

The comma is optional within numbers of four digits but is never used in years with four digits. Use a comma with numbers of more than four digits.

> The college has an enrollment of *1,789* [or *1789*] this semester.
>
> The French Revolution began in *1789.*

EXERCISE 30.8

Revise each of the following sentences, using commas appropriately with page numbers, dates, addresses and place-names, titles and numbers.

1. In my dictionary, the rules of punctuation begin on page 1560.
2. Ithaca New York has a population of about 30000.
3. The ship was hit by two torpedoes on May 7 1915 and sank in minutes.

4. MLA headquarters are at 10 Astor Place New York New York 10003.
5. The nameplate read *Donald Good R.N.* and looked quite impressive.

30h

Using commas with quotations

Commas set off a quotation from words used to introduce or identify the source of the quotation. A comma following a quotation goes *inside* the closing quotation mark.

"No one becomes depraved all at once," wrote Juvenal.

A German proverb warns, "Go to law for a sheep, and lose your cow."

"All I know about grammar," said Joan Didion, "is its infinite power."

When a quoted question or exclamation is followed by explanatory words, do not use a comma after the question mark or exclamation point.

"What's a thousand dollars?" asks Groucho Marx in *Cocoanuts*. "Mere chicken feed. A poultry matter."

"Out, out, damned spot!" cries Lady Macbeth.

Do not use a comma when a quotation is introduced by *that* or when the rest of the sentence includes more than the words used to introduce or identify the source of the quotation.

The writer of Ecclesiastes concludes that "all is vanity."

People who say "Have a nice day" irritate me.

Do not use a comma before an indirect quotation, one that does not use the speaker's exact words.

Patrick Henry declared that he wanted either liberty or death.

Abigail Adams said that all men would like to be tyrants.

EXERCISE 30.9

Insert a comma in any of the following sentences that require one.

1. "The public be damned!" William Henry Vanderbilt was reported to have said. "I'm working for my stockholders."

2. Joseph Epstein admits "I prefer not to be thought vulgar in any wise."

3. Who remarked that "youth is wasted on the young"?

4. "Neat people are lazier and meaner than sloppy people" according to Suzanne Britt.

5. "Who shall decide when doctors disagree?" asked Alexander Pope.

Using commas to facilitate understanding

Sometimes a comma is necessary to make a sentence much easier to read or understand.

CONFUSING	The members of the dance troupe strutted in in matching tuxedos and top hats.
REVISED	The members of the dance troupe strutted in, in matching tuxedos and top hats.
CONFUSING	Before I had planned to major in biology.
REVISED	Before, I had planned to major in biology.

EXERCISE 30.10

Read the following passage aloud, listening for the use of commas. Then read it again, mentally deleting the commas and noting how their absence affects meaning and rhythm. Finally, choose two of the sentences to use as a model, and create a similar pair of sentences of your own.

I ran across many words whose meanings I did not know, and I either looked them up in a dictionary or, before I had a chance to do that, encountered the word in a context that made its meaning clear. But what strange world was this? I concluded the book with the conviction that I had somehow overlooked something terribly important in life. I had once tried to write, had once reveled in feeling, had let my crude imagination roam, but the impulse to dream had been slowly beaten out of me by experience. Now it surged up again and I hungered for books, new ways of looking and seeing. It was not a matter of believing or disbelieving what I read, but of feeling something new, of being affected by something that made the look of the world different.

– RICHARD WRIGHT, "The Library Card"

30j

Checking for unnecessary commas

Excessive use of commas can spoil an otherwise fine sentence.

1

Omitting commas around restrictive elements

Do not use commas to set off restrictive elements, which limit, or restrict, the meaning of the words they modify or refer to. (See 30c.)

UNNECESSARY	I don't let my children watch TV shows, that are violent.
REVISED	I don't let my children watch TV shows that are violent. [restrictive adjective clause]
UNNECESSARY	A law, requiring the use of seat belts, was passed in 1987.
REVISED	A law requiring the use of seat belts was passed in 1987. [restrictive participial phrase]
UNNECESSARY	My only defense, against my allergies, is to stay indoors.
REVISED	My only defense against my allergies is to stay indoors. [restrictive prepositional phrase]
UNNECESSARY	The actress, Rosemary Harris, has returned to Broadway.
REVISED	The actress Rosemary Harris has returned to Broadway. [restrictive appositive]

2

Omitting commas between subjects and verbs, verbs and objects or complements, and prepositions and objects

Do not use a comma between a subject and its verb, a verb and its object or complement, or a preposition and its object. This rule holds true even if the subject, object, or complement is a long phrase or clause.

UNNECESSARY	*Watching movies on my VCR late at night, has become* an important way for me to relax. [comma between subject and verb]
REVISED	Watching movies on my VCR late at night has become an important way for me to relax.
UNNECESSARY	Parents *must decide, how much TV their children may watch.* [comma between verb and object]
REVISED	Parents must decide how much TV their children may watch.

UNNECESSARY	The winner *of, the trophy for outstanding community serv-ice* stepped forward. [comma between preposition and object]
REVISED	The winner of the trophy for outstanding community service stepped forward.

3

Omitting commas in compound constructions

Do not use a comma before or after a coordinating conjunction joining the two parts of a compound construction.

UNNECESSARY	*A buildup of the U.S. military, and deregulation of major industries* were the Reagan administration's goals. [compound subject]
REVISED	A buildup of the U.S. military and deregulation of major industries were the Reagan administration's goals.
UNNECESSARY	Mark Twain *trained as a printer and, worked as a steam-boat pilot.* [compound predicate]
REVISED	Mark Twain trained as a printer and worked as a steam-boat pilot.

4

Omitting commas in a series

Do not use a comma before the first or after the last item in a series.

UNNECESSARY	The auction included, furniture, paintings, and china.
REVISED	The auction included furniture, paintings, and china.
UNNECESSARY	The swimmer took slow, powerful, strokes.
REVISED	The swimmer took slow, powerful strokes.

≫   *Editing for commas*

Research has shown that five of the most common errors in college writing involve commas. The following are some brief guidelines for each of the five common comma errors, with examples from Lewis Thomas's "On the Need for Asylums."

AFTER INTRODUCTORY ELEMENTS

- Check every sentence that doesn't begin with the subject to see whether it opens with an element that needs to be followed by a comma. In general, most introductory elements should be followed by a comma. Though some writers do not add commas after short introductory elements, you'll never be wrong if you add one. Only when an introductory element is followed directly by a verb is it wrong to add a comma. (30a)

From time to time, medical science has achieved an undisputable triumph that is pure benefit for all levels of society and deserving of such terms as "breakthrough" and "medical miracle."

IN COMPOUND SENTENCES

- Look at every sentence that contains a coordinating conjunction (*and, but, or, nor, for, so,* or *yet*). In each one, examine the words before the conjunction. Could they function as a complete sentence, with a subject and a predicate? Could the words following the conjunction function as a sentence? If the answers to these questions are yes, you've got a compound sentence. Make sure the conjunction is preceded (not followed) by a comma. (30b)

It is not a long list, but the items are solid bits of encouragement for the future.

IN A SERIES

- Check every *and* and *or.* Then look at each one to see if it comes before the last item in a series of three or more words, phrases, or clauses. Be sure that each item in a series (except the last) is followed by a comma. (30d)

The conquests of tuberculosis, smallpox, and syphilis of the central nervous sytem should be at the top of anyone's list.

TO SET OFF NONRESTRICTIVE ELEMENTS

- Identify all adjective clauses beginning with *which, who, whom, whose, when,* or *where.* Consider each one, and decide whether it is essential to the meaning of the sentence. If so, it should not be set off by commas. Apply this same criterion to participial and prepositional phrases and to appositives: any that are essential to the meaning of the sentence should not be set off by commas. (30c)

For centuries the madhouses, as they were called, served no purpose beyond keeping deranged people out of the public view. (Continued)

WITH RESTRICTIVE ELEMENTS

- Identify all adjective clauses beginning with *that,* and make sure they are *not* set off with commas. Then look for any adjective clauses beginning with *which, who, whom, whose, when,* or *where.* In each case, decide whether it is essential to the meaning of the sentence; if not, the clause should be set off with commas. Finally, look for participial and prepositional phrases and for appositives. Ask the same question of each of them, and set off with commas any that are not essential. (30j)

There was a time when many doctors were glad to volunteer their services.

EXERCISE 30.11

Revise each of the following sentences, deleting unnecessary commas.

1. The four types of nonverbal communication are, kinesic, haptic, proxemic, and dormant, communication.
2. Observers watch facial expressions and gestures, and interpret them.
3. We could see nothing, except jagged peaks, for miles around.
4. Our supper that evening, consisted of stale bologna sandwiches.
5. Clothes, that had to be ironed, were too much trouble.
6. As we sat around the campfire, we felt boredom, and disappointment.
7. Magazines, like *Modern Maturity,* are aimed at retired people.
8. The photographer, Edward Curtis, is known for his depiction of the West.
9. We all took panicked, hasty, looks at our notebooks.
10. Driving a car, and talking on the car phone at the same time demand care.

THINKING CRITICALLY ABOUT COMMAS

Reading with an Eye for Commas

The following poem uses commas to create rhythm and guide readers. Read the poem aloud, listening especially to the effect of the commas at the end of the first and fifth lines. Then read it again as if those commas were omitted, noting the difference. What is the effect of the poet's decision *not* to use a comma at the end of the third line?

Some say the world will end in fire,
Some say in ice.
From what I've tasted of desire
I hold with those who favor fire.
But if it had to perish twice,
I think I know enough of hate
To say that for destruction ice
Is also great
And would suffice.
— ROBERT FROST, "Fire and Ice"

Thinking about Your Own Use of Commas

The following passage by Mary McCarthy, from *Memories of a Catholic Girlhood*, has had all of the author's commas removed. Punctuate the passage with commas as seems appropriate to you, and then explain in writing why you put commas where you did. Finally, check over your use of commas, consulting this chapter for guidance and noting any problems or observations.

And here was another strange thing about Myers. He not only did nothing for a living but he appeared to have no history. He came from Elkhart Indiana but beyond this fact nobody seemed to know anything about him—not even how he had met my aunt Margaret. Reconstructed from his conversation a picture of Elkhart emerged for us that showed it as a flat place consisting chiefly of ball parks poolrooms and hardware stores. Aunt Margaret came from Chicago which consisted of the Loop Marshall Field's assorted priests and monsignors and the black-and-white problem. How had these two worlds impinged? Where our family spoke freely of its relations real and imaginary Myers spoke of no one not even a parent. At the very beginning when my father's old touring car which had been shipped on still remained in our garage Myers had certain seedy cronies whom he took riding in it or who simply sat in it in our driveway as if anchored in a houseboat; but when the car went they went or were banished. Uncle Myers and Aunt Margaret had no friends no couples with whom they exchanged visits— only a middle-aged black-haired small emaciated woman with a German name and a yellowed skin whom we were taken to see one afternoon because she was dying of cancer. . . .

— MARY MCCARTHY, *Memories of a Catholic Girlhood*

31

Using Semicolons

IN CLASSICAL GREEK, groups of words comparable to what we call sentences were set off and called colons. A semicolon, therefore, is literally half a colon, or half of a sentence divided by the punctuation mark we call a semicolon. Lewis Thomas demonstrates effective use of the semicolon as he defines it, noting that

> The semicolon tells you that there is still some question about the preceding full sentence; something needs to be added. . . . It is almost always a greater pleasure to come across a semicolon than a period. The period tells you that is that; if you didn't get all the meaning you wanted or expected, you got all the writer intended to parcel out and now you have to move along. But with a semicolon there you get a pleasant little feeling of expectancy; there is more to come; read on; it will get clearer.
> — LEWIS THOMAS, "Notes on Punctuation"

As Thomas suggests, semicolons have the effect of creating a pause stronger than that of a comma but not as strong as the full pause of a period. Their primary uses are to link coordinate independent clauses and to separate items in a series.

31a

Using semicolons to link independent clauses

You can join independent clauses in several ways: with a comma and a coordinating conjunction (see 30b), with a colon (see 35d), with a dash (see 35c), or with a semicolon. Semicolons provide writers with subtle ways of signaling closely related clauses. The second clause often restates an idea expressed in the first, as it does in the first sentence of the Lewis Thomas passage above, and it sometimes expands on or presents a contrast to the

---

Everyday Use

Although semicolons are among the more formal punctuation marks, you can sometimes spot them working quite well in informal settings—on bumper stickers, for example. Here are two spotted recently.

Careful! Baby on board; driver on edge.

Vote for Espy; he means business!

Try replacing these semicolons with commas and conjunctions, periods, or exclamation points, and you'll see how useful the semicolon is. Watch for everyday uses of semicolons—in ads, on billboards, wherever—and bring them to class to compare with ones discovered by your classmates.

---

first. As a writer, you must choose when and where to use semicolons to signal such relationships. Note, for instance, the following examples:

> Immigration acts were passed; newcomers had to prove, besides moral correctness and financial solvency, their ability to read.
> — MARY GORDON, "More Than Just a Shrine"

> The problem, of course, is that it is one thing to urge somebody else to take on those anxiety-producing challenges; it is quite another to get ourselves to do it.
> — JAMES LINCOLN COLLIER, "Anxiety: Challenge by Any Other Name"

In the first sentence, Gordon uses a semicolon to lead to a clause that expands on the statement made in the first clause. She might have joined the two clauses with *and* or *so*, but the lack of a conjunction gives the sentence an abrupt, clipped rhythm that suits the topic: laws that imposed strict requirements. She might also have used a period to separate the two clauses into two sentences, but then the two ideas would not be so clearly linked. In the second example, the semicolon links two contrasting clauses; the logical connection between them is far more subtle and more immediate than it would be had Collier instead used *but*.

The sentences above contain only two independent clauses, but semicolons can also join more than two such clauses.

> On Mother's Day, Good Souls conscientiously wear carnations; on St. Patrick's Day, they faithfully don boutonnieres of shamrocks; on Columbus Day, they carefully pin on miniature Italian flags.
> — DOROTHY PARKER, "Good Souls"

A semicolon can also be used to link independent clauses joined by conjunctive adverbs such as *therefore, however,* or *indeed* or transitional expressions such as *in fact, in addition,* or *for example.* (See 7b7 and 6d5.)

> The circus comes as close to being the world in microcosm as anything I know; in a way, it puts all the rest of show business in the shade.
> — E. B. WHITE, "The Ring of Time"

If two independent clauses joined by a coordinating conjunction contain commas, you may use a semicolon instead of a comma before the conjunction to make the sentence easier to read.

> Every year, whether the Republican or the Democratic Party is in office, more and more power drains away from the individual to feed vast reservoirs in far-off places; and we have less and less say about the shape of events which shape our future.
> — WILLIAM F. BUCKLEY, JR., "Why Don't We Complain?"

EXERCISE 31.1

Choose one of the five examples shown in 31a, and use it as a model for a sentence of your own. Bring your sentence to class to compare it with those written by your classmates.

EXERCISE 31.2

Combine each of the following pairs of sentences into one sentence by using a semicolon. Example:

Take the bus to Henderson Street/ Meet me under the clock.
                         ; m

1. Establishing your position in an office is an important task. Your profile will mold your relationships with other staff members.

2. City life offers many advantages. In many ways, however, life in a small town is much more pleasant.

3. Florida's mild winter climate is ideal for bicycling. In addition, the terrain is very flat.

4. Physical education forms an important part of a university's program. Nevertheless, few students and professors clearly recognize its value.

5. The debate over political correctness affects more than the curriculum. It also affects students' social relationships.

6. Voltaire was concerned about the political implications of his skepticism. He warned his friends not to discuss atheism in front of the servants.

7. Fuel oil, natural gas, and electricity are popular sources of energy for heating homes. The least polluting, however, is solar energy.

8. My high school was excessively competitive. Virtually everyone went on to college, many to the top schools in the nation.

9. Pittsburgh was once notorious for its smoke and grime. Today its skies and streets are cleaner than those of many other American cities.

10. Propaganda is defined as the spread of ideas to further a cause. Therefore, propaganda and advertisement are synonymous terms.

31b

Using semicolons to separate items in a series

Ordinarily, commas separate items in a series. (See 30d.) But when the items themselves contain commas or other punctuation, using semicolons to separate the items will make the sentence clearer and easier to read. Such a series is best placed at the *end* of a sentence.

> Anthropology encompasses archaeology, the study of ancient civilizations through artifacts; linguistics, the study of the structure and development of language; and cultural anthropology, the study of the way of life of various peoples, especially small, nonindustrialized societies.

> I recognized the film as a political document, expressing the worst sentiments of America in the cold war: its hero, a tough military man who wants only to destroy the enemy utterly; its villain, a naively liberal scientist who wants to learn more about it; the carrot and its flying saucer, a certain surrogate for the red menace; the film's famous last words—a newsman's impassioned plea to "watch the skies"—an invitation to extended fear and jingoism.
> — STEVEN JAY GOULD, *Ever Since Darwin*

Note that a semicolon never *introduces* a series. (See 31d.)

31c

Checking for overused semicolons

If semicolons are used too often, they distract readers in the same way unnecessary repetition does, by calling attention to themselves instead of to what the writer is saying. In addition, sentence upon sentence punctuated with semicolons will sound monotonous and jerky.

OVERUSED Like many people in public life, he spoke with confidence; perhaps he even spoke with arrogance; yet I noted a certain anxiety; it touched and puzzled me; he seemed too eager to demonstrate his control of a situation and his command of the necessary data.

REVISED Like many people in public life, he spoke with confidence, perhaps even with arrogance; yet I noted a certain anxiety that touched and puzzled me. He seemed too eager to demonstrate his control of a situation and his command of the necessary data.

EXERCISE 31.3

Revise the following passage, substituting other punctuation for some of the semicolons. Add or delete words if necessary.

Remember when the neighborhood kids played football out in the vacant lot; they were there every Saturday, having a good time. Whatever happened to just playing for a good time? Now uniformed coaches yell at young players to win; they put more and more pressure on them; and parents join in the chant of win, win, win; in fact, if the child is not a winner, he or she must be—that's right—a loser. The young athlete is constantly told that winning is everything; what used to be fun is now just like a job; play to win, the adults say, or do not play at all.

31d

Checking for misused semicolons

A comma, not a semicolon, should separate an independent clause from a dependent clause or a phrase.

MISUSED The police found a set of fingerprints; which they used to identify the thief.

REVISED The police found a set of fingerprints, which they used to identify the thief.

A colon, not a semicolon, should introduce a series.

MISUSED The tour includes visits to the following art museums; the Prado, in Madrid; the Louvre, in Paris; and the Rijksmuseum, in Amsterdam.

REVISED   The tour includes visits to the following art museums: the Prado, in Madrid; the Louvre, in Paris; and the Rijksmuseum, in Amsterdam.

≫ *Editing for effective use of semicolons*

1. Note any semicolons. If you find few or none, look at each sentence together with the one that follows. Are there any pairs of sentences that express closely related ideas that would be stronger if combined into one sentence using a semicolon?

2. Make sure semicolons are used only between independent clauses or between items in a series. If you have used a semicolon between an independent clause and a dependent clause or a phrase, change it to a comma. If you have used a semicolon before the *first* item in a series, change it to a colon.

3. Do semicolons separate more than three independent clauses in a sentence, or do they separate clauses in more than two consecutive sentences? If so, would making some clauses into separate sentences make the writing smoother or less monotonous?

EXERCISE 31.4

Revise each of the following sentences to correct the misuse of semicolons.

The new system would encourage high school students to take more

academic courses; thus strengthening college preparation.

1. We accept the following forms of payment; cash, check, money order, or credit card.

2. If the North had followed up its victory at Gettysburg more vigorously; the Civil War might have ended sooner.

3. He left a large estate; which was used to endow a scholarship fund.

4. We must find a plan to provide decent health care; a necessity in today's life.

5. Verbal scores have decreased more than fifty-four points; while math scores have decreased more than thirty-six.

31e

Using semicolons with quotation marks

Ordinarily, a semicolon goes *outside* closing quotation marks.

Jackson's most famous story is "The Lottery"; it is a horrifying allegory about the power of tradition and the search for scapegoats.

THINKING CRITICALLY ABOUT SEMICOLONS

Reading with an Eye for Semicolons

The author of the following paragraph describes a solar eclipse in elaborate detail, using semicolons to separate each part of her description. Read the paragraph with attention to the use of semicolons. What different effect would the paragraph have if the author had used periods instead of semicolons? Imagine also that she had used commas and coordinating conjunctions. What is the effect of all the semicolons?

You see the wide world swaddled in darkness; you see a vast breadth of hilly land, and an enormous, distant, blackened valley; you see towns' lights, a river's path, and blurred portions of your hat and scarf; you see your husband's face looking like an early black-and-white film; and you see a sprawl of black sky and blue sky together, with unfamiliar stars in it, some barely visible bands of cloud, and over there, a small white ring. The ring is as small as one goose in a flock of migrating geese—if you happen to notice a flock of migrating geese. It is one 360th part of the visible sky. The sun we see is less than half the diameter of a dime held at arm's length.

– ANNIE DILLARD, "Solar Eclipse"

Thinking about Your Own Use of Semicolons

Think of something you might take five or ten minutes to observe—a football game, a brewing storm, an ant awkwardly carrying a crumb—and write a paragraph describing your observations point by point and using semicolons to separate each point, as Annie Dillard does in the paragraph above. When you have finished, look at the way you used semicolons. Are there places where a period or a comma and a coordinating conjunction would better serve your meaning? Revise appropriately. What can you conclude about effective ways of using semicolons? If you keep a writing log, record your thoughts there, along with any interesting examples you found.

32

Using End Punctuation

A PERIOD, QUESTION MARK, OR EXCLAMATION POINT *tells readers they have reached the end of one unit of thought and can pause and take a mental breath before moving on to the next one. As a writer, you are most often guided by meaning in your choice of end punctuation. Sometimes, however, you can use it for special effect. Look, for instance, at the way end punctuation guides readers in the following three sentences:*

> Am I tired.
>
> Am I tired?
>
> Am I tired!

The end punctuation tells us how to read each sentence: the first as a dry, matter-of-fact statement; the second as a puzzled or perhaps ironic query; the last as a note of exasperation. This chapter will explain how you can use these three kinds of end punctuation.

EXERCISE 32.1

Imagine that you work for a company that is preparing to launch a new product. First decide what the product is—some sort of food or drink, an automobile, the latest lap-top computer, or something else—and what its name should be. Then write a headline and some copy for the product's first advertisement. Note the way you have used end punctuation—where you have placed periods, question marks, and exclamation points, and compare your advertisement with those of several classmates.

Everyday Use

We see periods, question marks, and exclamation points constantly in advertising, often used to create special effects. Look at the following ads, and consider how each one would be different without these marks:

Toshiba laptops: the desktop alternative.

Get Microsoft Word now, and receive this kit FREE!

So you think you can't afford a new PC?

Look for some ads that use these marks of punctuation for special effect, and bring them to class to compare with those of your classmates.

32a

Using periods

Use a period to close sentences that make statements or give mild commands.

Books are like mountaintops jutting out of the sea.
– Jerome Bruner, Acts of Meaning

Never use a foreign phrase, a scientific word or a jargon word if you can think of an everyday English equivalent.
– George Orwell, "Politics and the English Language"

A period also closes indirect questions, which report rather than ask questions.

I asked how old the child was.

We all wonder who will win the election.

Many parents ask if autism is an inherited disorder.

In American English, periods are also used with most abbreviations:

Mr.	Jr.	Ph.D.
Ms.	B.C.	M.D.
Mrs.	A.D.	M.B.A.
A.M./a.m.	ibid.	R.N.
P.M./p.m.	Dr.	Sen.

Some abbreviations do not require periods. Among them are the postal abbreviations of state names, such as *FL* and *TN* (though the traditional abbreviations of state names, such as *Fla.* and *Tenn.*, do call for periods), and most groups of initials (*GE, CIA, PCB, AIDS, SALT, UNICEF*). If you are not sure whether a particular abbreviation should include periods, check a dictionary. (See Chapter 37 for more about abbreviations.)

EXERCISE 32.2

Revise each of the following sentences, inserting periods in the appropriate places. Example:

> *Ms. Maria Jordan received both a Ph.D. in chemistry and an M.Ed.*

1. Please attend the meeting on Tuesday at 10:00 AM in Room 401.
2. Cicero was murdered in 43 BC
3. "Have you lost something, Charles?" I inquired
4. She asked whether Operation PUSH had been founded by Jesse Jackson
5. A voluntary effort by the AMA could help contain hospital costs

---

32b

Using question marks

A question mark closes sentences that ask direct questions.

If you own things, what's their effect on you?
                              – E. M. FORSTER, "My Wood"
Who will be left to celebrate a victory made of blood and fire?
                              – THICH NHAT HANH, "Our Green Garden"

Question marks do not close *indirect* questions, which report rather than ask questions. Indirect questions close with a period (see 32a).

She asked whether I opposed his nomination.

Do not use a comma or a period after a question mark that ends a direct quotation.

"Am I my brother's keeper?" Cain asked.
Cain asked, "Am I my brother's keeper?"

A polite request phrased as a question can be followed by a period rather than a question mark.

> Would you please close the door.

Questions in a series may have question marks even when they are not separate sentences.

> I often confronted a difficult choice: should I go to practice? finish my homework? spend time with my friends?

A question mark in parentheses can be used to indicate that a writer is unsure of a date, a figure, or a word.

> Quintilian died in A.D. 96 (?).
> The meeting is on Oleonga (?) Street.

EXERCISE 32.3

Revise each of the following sentences, adding question marks and substituting them for other punctuation where appropriate. One of the sentences does not require any question marks. Example:

> *She asked the travel agent, "What is the air fare to Greece?"*

1. Social scientists face difficult questions: should they use their knowledge to shape society, merely describe human behavior, try to do both.
2. Are people with so many possessions really happy.
3. "Can I play this" asked Manuel.
4. I looked at him and asked what his point was.
5. The judge asked, "What is your verdict."

32c

Using exclamation points

Exclamation points close sentences that show surprise or strong emotion: emphatic statements, interjections, and emphatic commands.

> In those few moments of geologic time will be the story of all that has happened since we became a nation. And what a story it will be!
> — JAMES RETTIE, "But a Watch in the Night"

Ouch!

Look out!

Use exclamation points very sparingly because they can distract your readers or suggest that you are exaggerating the importance of what you are saying. Do not, for instance, use them with mild interjections or to suggest sarcasm or criticism. In general, try to create emphasis through diction (see Chapter 27) and sentence structure (see 19a) rather than with exclamation points.

Do not use a comma or a period after an exclamation point that ends a direct quotation.

> "We shall next be told," exclaims Seneca, "that the first shoemaker was a philosopher!"
>
> — THOMAS BABINGTON MACAULAY, "Francis Bacon"

EXERCISE 32.4

Revise each of the following sentences, adding or deleting exclamation points where appropriate and removing any other unnecessary punctuation you find. Example:

Look out! The tide is coming in fast!

1. This university is so large, so varied, that attempting to tell someone everything about it would take three years!

2. I screamed at Jamie, "You rat. You tricked me."

3. "This time we're starting early!," she shouted.

4. Stop, thief.

5. Oh, no. We've lost the house.

≫ *Editing for end punctuation*

1. Go through your draft to see how many sentences end with periods. If you find that all or almost all of them do, see if any of them might be more effective phrased as questions or exclamations.

2. Have you used any exclamation points? If so, consider carefully whether they are justified. Does the sentence call for extra emphasis? If in doubt, use a period instead.

EXERCISE 32.5 Revising for End Punctuation

Look at the passage by Tom Wolfe that opens Chapter 35. You will see that Wolfe has punctuated it as one very long sentence. Revise the sentence by breaking it into several shorter ones, using periods, question marks, and exclamation points to try to achieve the same rhythm as the original. Change the wording only as necessary.

THINKING CRITICALLY ABOUT END PUNCTUATION

Reading with an Eye for End Punctuation

Consider the use of end punctuation in the following paragraph. Then experiment with the end punctuation. What would be the effect of deleting the exclamation point from the quotation by Cicero or of changing it to a question mark? What would be the effect of changing Cicero's question to a statement?

> To be admired and praised, especially by the young, is an autumnal pleasure enjoyed by the lucky ones (who are not always the most deserving). "What is more charming," Cicero observes in his famous essay *De Senectute,* "than an old age surrounded by the enthusiasm of youth! . . . Attentions which seem trivial and conventional are marks of honor—the morning call, being sought after, precedence, having people rise for you, being escorted to and from the forum. . . . What pleasures of the body can be compared to the prerogatives of influence?" But there are also pleasures of the body, or the mind, that are enjoyed by a greater number of older persons. — MALCOLM COWLEY, *The View from 80*

Thinking about Your Own Use of End Punctuation

Look through something you have written recently, noting its end punctuation. Using the guidelines on page 491, see if your use of end punctuation follows any patterns. Try revising the end punctuation in a paragraph or two to emphasize (or de-emphasize) some point. What conclusions can you draw about ways of using end punctuation to draw attention to (or away from) a sentence? If you keep a writing log, put your thoughts there for future use.

33

Using Apostrophes

As A MARK OF THE POSSESSIVE CASE, *the apostrophe has an unusual history. In Old English, the endings of nouns changed according to the noun's grammatical function—a noun used as a subject, for example, had a different ending from one used as a direct object. By the fourteenth century, Middle English had dropped most of this complicated system, yet possessive and plural endings remained: Haroldes sword was still used to mean "the sword of Harold." Then in the sixteenth century, scholars concluded that the ending -es and its variants were actually contractions of his. Believing that Haroldes sword meant "Harold his sword," they began using an apostrophe instead of the e: Harold's sword.*

Even though this theory was later discredited, the possessive ending retained the apostrophe because it was a useful way to distinguish between possessive and plural forms in writing. Today we use the apostrophe primarily to signal possessive case, contractions and other omissions of words and letters, and certain plural forms. This chapter presents the conventions governing its use.

33a

Using apostrophes to signal possessive case

The possessive case denotes ownership or possession of one thing by another. (See 8c.) Use an apostrophe to form the possessive case of nouns and indefinite pronouns—*Fran's coat, nobody's fault.*

1

Forming the possessive case of singular nouns and indefinite pronouns

Add an apostrophe and -s to form the possessive of most singular nouns, including those that end in -s, and of indefinite pronouns.

John Wayne's first westerns are considered classics.

The reading list included *Keats's* poem.

Anyone's guess is as good as mine.

Apostrophes are not used with the possessive forms of *personal* pronouns: *yours, his, hers, its, ours, theirs.*

2

Forming the possessive case of plural nouns

For plural nouns not ending in *-s*, add an apostrophe and *-s*.

Robert Bly helped to popularize the *men's* movement.

The *children's* first Christmas was spent in Wales.

For plural nouns ending in *-s*, add only the apostrophe.

The *clowns'* costumes were bright green and orange.

Fifty dollars' worth of groceries filled only two shopping bags.

3

Forming the possessive case of compound words

For compound words, make the last word in the group possessive.

The *secretary of state's* speech was televised.

Both her *daughters-in-law's* birthdays fall in July.

My *in-laws'* disapproval dampened our enthusiasm for the new house.

Everyday Use

The little apostrophe can sometimes make a big difference in meaning. A friend of ours found that out when he agreed to look after a neighbor's apartment while she was out of town. "I'll leave instructions on the kitchen counter," the neighbor said as she gave him her key. Here are the instructions he found: "(1) Please water the plants in the living room—once will be fine. (2) The cat's food is on the counter. Once a day on the patio. Thanks. I'll see you Friday."

Because the note said *cat's,* he expected one cat—and when he saw one, he put it and the food outside on the patio. When the neighbor returned, she found one healthy cat—and a second, very weak one that had hidden under the bed. The difference between *cat's* and *cats'* in this instance almost cost his neighbor a cat.

4

Forming the possessive case with two or more nouns

To signal individual possession by two or more owners, make each noun possessive.

> There are great differences between *John Wayne's* and *Henry Fonda's* westerns. [Wayne and Fonda appeared in different westerns.]

To signal joint possession, make only the last noun possessive.

> *MacNeil and Lehrer's* program focuses on current issues.

≫ *Editing for possessive apostrophes*

1. Circle all the nouns that end in -*s*. Then check each one that shows ownership or possession to see that it has an apostrophe in the right place, either before or after the -*s*.
2. Then underline all the indefinite pronouns, such as *someone* and *nobody*. (See 7b3 for a list.) Any that end in -*s* should have an apostrophe before the -*s*.

EXERCISE 33.1

Write a brief paragraph, beginning "I've always been amused by my neighbor's _____." Then note every use of an apostrophe.

EXERCISE 33.2

Complete each of the following sentences by inserting 's or an apostrophe alone to form the possessive case of the italicized words.

1. Grammar is *everybody* favorite subject.
2. *Maria Callas* opera performances are now the stuff of legend.
3. I was having a good time at *P.J.,* but my friends wanted to go to *Sunny.*
4. *Carol and Jim* income dropped drastically after Jim lost his job.
5. Parents often question their *children* choice of friends.
6. Many smokers disregard the *surgeon general* warnings.
7. How the economy will recover is *anyone* guess.
8. The *governors* attitudes changed after the convention.

9. This dog has a *beagle* ears and a *St. Bernard* nose and feet.
10. *My friend and my brother* cars have the same kind of stereo system.

33b

Using apostrophes to signal contractions and other omissions

Contractions are two-word combinations formed by leaving out certain letters, which are indicated by an apostrophe. For example:

it is/it's	I would/I'd	will not/won't
was not/wasn't	he would/he'd	let us/let's
I am/I'm	would not/wouldn't	who is, who has/who's
he is, he has/he's	do not/don't	cannot/can't
you will/you'll	does not/doesn't	

Contractions are common in conversation and informal writing. Most academic work, however, calls for greater formality.

Distinguishing it's *and* its

Do not confuse the possessive pronoun *its* with the contraction *it's*. *Its* is the possessive form of *it*. *It's* is a contraction for *it is*.

> This disease is unusual; *its* symptoms vary from person to person.
>
> *It's* a difficult disease to diagnose.

(See 24b for other commonly confused pairs of possessive pronouns and contractions—*their/they're, whose/who's,* and *your/you're.*)

⋙ *Editing for misuse of* its *and* it's

1. Check each *its*. If it does not show possession, add an apostrophe before the *s*.
2. Check each *it's*. Does it mean "it is"? If not, remove the apostrophe.

Signaling omissions

An apostrophe signals omissions in some common phrases:

ten of the clock	rock and roll	class of 1992
ten o'clock	rock 'n' roll	class of '92

In addition, writers can use an apostrophe to signal omitted letters in approximating the sound of speech or some specific dialect. Note the way Mark Twain uses the apostrophe to form contractions and signal omitted letters in the following passage, in which Huckleberry Finn tells Jim about King Henry VIII:

> S'pose people left money laying around where he was—what did he do? He collared it. S'pose he contracted to do a thing; and you paid him, and didn't set down there and see that he done it—what did he do? He always done the other thing. S'pose he opened his mouth—what then? If he didn't shut it up powerful quick, he'd lose a lie, every time. That's the kind of a bug Henry was; and if we'd 'a' had him along 'stead of our kings, he'd 'a' fooled that town a heap worse than ourn done.
>
> – MARK TWAIN, *The Adventures of Huckleberry Finn*

33c

Using apostrophes to form the plural of numbers, letters, symbols, and words used as terms

An apostrophe and -*s* are used to form the plural of numbers, letters, symbols, and words referred to as such.

The gymnasts need marks of 8's and 9's to qualify for the finals.

Several Cessna *150's* were lined up for takeoff.

Many *Ph.D.'s* cannot find jobs as college teachers.

The computer prints *e's* whenever there is an error in the program.

I marked special passages with a series of three **'s*.

The five *Shakespeare's* in the essay were spelled five different ways.

Note that numbers, letters, and words referred to as words are usually italicized; but the plural ending is not, as in the examples above.

The plural of years can be written with or without the apostrophe (*1990's* or *1990s*). Whichever style you follow, be consistent.

EXERCISE 33.3

The following sentences, from which all apostrophes have been deleted, appear in Langston Hughes's "Salvation." Insert apostrophes where appropriate.

"Sister Reed, what is this child's name?"

1. There was a big revival at my Auntie Reeds church.
2. I heard the songs and the minister saying: "Why dont you come?"
3. Finally Westley said to me in a whisper: "Im tired o sitting here. Lets get up and be saved."
4. So I decided that maybe to save further trouble, Id better lie. . . .
5. That night, . . . I cried, in bed alone, and couldnt stop.

THINKING CRITICALLY ABOUT APOSTROPHES

Reading with an Eye for Apostrophes

In the following rhyme, Zora Neale Hurston uses apostrophes to form contractions and signal omitted letters. They help create the rhythms and cadences of African American vernacular English. To get a sense of this effect, try reading the lines aloud with the missing letters filled in.

> Ah got up 'bout half-past fo'
> Forty fo' robbers wuz 'round mah do'
> Ah got up and let 'em in
> Hit 'em ovah de head wid uh rollin' pin.
> — ZORA NEALE HURSTON, *Jonah's Gourd Vine*

Thinking about Your Own Use of Apostrophes

As a tool for presenting contractions and omitted letters, apostrophes play a larger role in informal writing than in formal writing. Many students need to learn to write with few or no contractions, a task that requires some effort because we all use contractions in conversation. To get an idea of the difference between spoken and written language, try transcribing a "paragraph" or so of your own spoken words. Use apostrophes whenever you use a contraction or otherwise omit a letter. Look over your paragraph to see how many apostrophes you used, and then revise the piece to make it more formal, eliminating all or most apostrophes. What conclusions can you draw about ways you should and should not use apostrophes?

34

Using Quotation Marks

As a way of bringing other people's words into our own, quotation can be a powerful writing tool. For example:

> Mrs. Macken urges parents to get books for their children, to read to them when they are "li'l," and when they start school to make certain they attend regularly. She holds herself up as an example of a "millhand's daughter who wanted to be a schoolteacher and did it through sheer hard work."
>
> – SHIRLEY BRICE HEATH, *Ways with Words*

The writer could have paraphrased—and said, for example, that parents should read to their children when they are young. By quoting, she lets her subject speak for herself—and lets us as readers hear that person's voice. In this case, the writer is reporting from field research, and in fact one of the most common occasions for using direct quotation is in citing research. Quotation marks are also used for other purposes as well: to mark certain titles, to set off definitions, to quote poetry, to signal dialogue, to highlight words used ironically. This chapter presents the conventions governing the use of quotation marks and provides guidelines for checking their use in your own writing.

34a

Using quotation marks to signal direct quotations

In American English, double quotation marks signal a direct quotation.

Bush called for a "kinder, gentler" America.

He smiled and said, "Son, this is one incident I will never forget."

Single quotation marks enclose a quotation within a quotation. Open and close the quoted passage with double quotation marks, and change any quotation marks that appear *within* the quotation to single quotation marks.

> In "The Uses of the Blues," Baldwin says, "The title 'The Uses of the Blues' does not refer to music; I don't know anything about music."

Do not use quotation marks for *indirect* quotations, which do not repeat someone's exact words.

> Father smiled and said that he would never forget the incident.

1

Quoting longer passages

If the passage you wish to quote exceeds four typed lines, set it off from the rest of the text by starting it on a new line and indenting each line ten spaces from the left margin. This format, known as **block quotation,** does not require quotation marks.

> In *Winged Words: American Indian Writers Speak,* Leslie Marmon Silko describes her early education:
>> I learned to love reading, and love books, and the printed page, and therefore was motivated to learn to write. The best thing . . . you can have in life is to have someone tell you a story . . . but in lieu of that . . . I learned at an early age to find comfort in a book, that a book would talk to me when no one else would.

Everyday Use

Some people seem to find quotation marks so visually appealing that they use them as a kind of verbal makeup, dabbing them in anywhere they feel a word or phrase could use a bit of sprucing up. Like cosmetics, though, quotation marks can have unfortunate effects if applied too freely. What is the effect of the quotation marks in the following advertisements?

On a movie marquee: Coming "Attractions"

In a supermarket: "Fresh" Asparagus

Look around you for similar misguided uses of quotation marks, and bring them to class for discussion.

2

Quoting poetry

The same general rules apply to quoting poetry as to quoting prose. If the quotation is brief (fewer than four lines), include it within your text, enclosed in double quotation marks. Separate the lines of the poem with slashes, each preceded and followed by a space.

> In one of his best-known poems, Robert Frost remarks, "Two roads diverged in a wood, and I— / I took the one less traveled by, / And that has made all the difference."

If the poetic quotation is longer, start it on a new line, indent each line ten spaces from the left margin, and do not use quotation marks.

> The duke in Robert Browning's "My Last Duchess" is clearly a jealous, vain person, whose arrogance is illustrated through his statement:
>> She thanked men—good! but thanked
> Somehow—I know not how—as if she ranked
> My gift of a nine-hundred-years-old name
> With anybody's gift.

When you quote poetry, take care to follow the indentation, spacing, capitalization, punctuation, and other features of the original passage.

EXERCISE 34.1

Quoting someone else's words can contribute authority and texture to your writing in that it adds other voices and images to your own. See how one writer uses a quotation in the following passage about Wyoming:

Most characteristic of the state's landscape is what a developer euphemistically describes as "indigenous growth right up to your front door"—a reference to waterless stands of salt sage, snakes, jackrabbits, deerflies, red dust, a brief respite of wildflowers, dry washes, and no trees.

– GRETEL EHRLICH, *The Solace of Open Spaces*

Spend a few minutes reading an article on a topic you know something about. Then write a paragraph of your own on that topic, quoting the article at least once. Choose something worded in a memorable way or someone whose voice will lend weight to your own words. Finally, check your use of quotation marks against the guidelines in this chapter.

34b

Using quotation marks to signal dialogue

When you write dialogue or quote a conversation, enclose the words of each speaker in quotation marks, and mark each shift in speaker by beginning a new paragraph, no matter how brief the quoted remark may be.

> "Star light, star bright, the first star I see tonight, I wish I may, I wish I might . . . "
>
> At first Nick wouldn't look up. "I don't see no star," he said.
>
> I pointed; "See right up there, it's the North Star."
>
> "How you know?"
>
> "My mother showed it to me."
>
> Then he looked. "Bet that ain't it."
>
> "Bet it is. When it gets all the way dark, it'll be on the handle of the Little Dipper."
>
> "If it's on the handle by the time the nine o'clock whistle blows, you get to ride my bike tomorrow all day. If it ain't, I get a kiss."
>
> "Uh-uh, Nick," I said. "Let's just bet a hot pickle."
>
> – MAXINE CLAIR, "Cherry Bomb"

Beginning a new paragraph with each change in speaker helps readers follow the dialogue. In the example above, we know when Nick is speaking and when the narrator is speaking without the author's having to repeat "I said," "Nick said," and so on.

34c

Using quotation marks to signal titles and definitions

Quotation marks are used to enclose the titles of short poems, short stories, articles, essays, songs, sections of books, and episodes of television and radio programs.

"Dover Beach" moves from calmness to sadness. [poem]

Alice Walker's "Everyday Use" is about more than just quilts. [short story]

In "Photography," Susan Sontag considers the role of photography in our society. [essay]

The *Atlantic* published an article entitled "Illiberal Education." [article]

In the chapter called "Complexion," Rodriguez describes his sensitivity about his skin color. [section of book]

Use italics rather than quotation marks for the titles of longer works, such as books and magazines (see 38a). Do not use either in titling your own writing unless your title is or includes another title or a quotation.

Definitions are sometimes set off with quotation marks.

> The French phrase *idée fixe* means literally "fixed idea."

34d

Using quotation marks to signal irony and coinages

One way of showing readers that you are using a word or a phrase ironically is to enclose it in quotation marks.

> The "banquet" consisted of dried-out chicken and canned vegetables. [The quotation marks suggest that the meal was anything but a banquet.]

Quotation marks are also used to enclose words or phrases made up by the writer, as is *forebirth* in the following example:

> Your whole first paragraph or first page may have to be guillotined in any case after your piece is finished: it is a kind of "forebirth."
> – JACQUES BARZUN, "A Writer's Discipline"

EXERCISE 34.2

Revise each of the following sentences, using quotation marks appropriately to signal titles, definitions, irony, or coinages.

1. Kowinski uses the term mallaise to mean physical and psychological disturbances caused by mall contact.

2. In Flannery O'Connor's short story Revelation, colors symbolize passion, violence, sadness, and even God.

3. The little that is known about gorillas certainly makes you want to know more, writes Alan Moorehead in his essay A Most Forgiving Ape.

4. The fun of surgery begins before the operation ever takes place.

5. Wolfe's article Radical Chic satirizes wealthy liberals.

6. Big Bill, a section of Dos Passos's *U.S.A.*, opens with a birth.

7. Amy Lowell challenges social conformity in her poem Patterns.

8. The Beatles song Love Me Do catapulted the band to international stardom.

9. My dictionary defines *isolation* as the quality or state of being alone.

10. In the episode Driven to Extremes, *48 Hours* takes a humorous look at driving in New York City.

34e

Checking for misused quotation marks

Use quotation marks only when there is a reason for them. Do not use them just to emphasize particular words or phrases, as in the following sentence.

MISUSED   Some of the boys, not including Travis, of course, would take "stingers" off wasps and bees and then put the insects "down" others' shirts.

REVISED   Some of the boys, not including Travis, of course, would take stingers off wasps and bees and then put the insects down others' shirts.

Do not use quotation marks with slang or colloquial language that seems inappropriate for formal register (see 27a); they create the impression that you are apologizing for using such language. Instead, try to express the idea in formal language. If you have a good reason to use a slang or colloquial term, use it without quotation marks.

MISUSED   After their twenty-mile hike, the campers were "wiped out" and ready to "hit the sack."

REVISED   After their twenty-mile hike, the campers were exhausted and ready to go to bed.

34f

Using quotation marks with other punctuation

1

Periods and commas go *inside* closing quotation marks.

"Don't compromise yourself," said Janis Joplin, "you are all you've got."

2

Colons and semicolons go *outside* closing quotation marks.

Everything is dark, and "a visionary light settles in her eyes"; this vision, this light, is her salvation.

I felt only one emotion after finishing "Eveline": pity.

3

Question marks, exclamation points, and dashes go *inside* closing quotation marks if they are part of the quotation, *outside* if they are not.

PART OF THE QUOTATION

Gently shake the injured person while asking, "Are you all right?"

"Jump!" one of the firefighters shouted.

"Watch out—watch out for—" Jessica began nervously.

NOT PART OF THE QUOTATION

What is the theme of "The Birth-Mark"?

How tired she must be of hearing "God Save the Queen"!

"Break a leg"—that phrase is supposed to bring good luck to a performer.

4

Footnote numbers go *outside* closing quotation marks.

Tragedy is defined by Aristotle as "an imitation of an action that is serious and of a certain magnitude."[1]

(For more information on footnotes and for examples of quotation marks in bibliographical references, see Chapters 44 and 45.)

≫ *Editing for quotation marks*

1. Use quotation marks around
   - direct quotations
   - titles of short works
2. Do not use quotation marks around
   - indirect quotations
   - titles of long works
   - words you want to emphasize
   - block quotations
3. Check other punctuation used with closing quotation marks:
   - periods and commas should be *inside* the quotation marks
   - colons, semicolons, and footnote numbers should be *outside*
   - question marks, exclamation points, and dashes should be inside if they are part of the quoted material, outside if they are not

EXERCISE 34.3

Revise each of the following sentences, deleting quotation marks used inappropriately, moving those placed incorrectly, and using more formal language in place of slang expressions in quotation marks. Example:

> In "Bartleby the Scrivener," Bartleby states time and again, "I would prefer not to."

1. The grandmother in O'Connor's story shows she is still misguided when she says, "You've got good blood! I know you wouldn't shoot a lady"!

2. What is Hawthorne telling the readers in "Rappaccini's Daughter?"

3. Very quietly, Chun Lee said, "I know the answer".

4. This "typical American" is Ruby Turpin, who in the course of the story receives a "message" that brings about a "change" in her life.

5. Being "overweight" is a problem because "excess pounds" are hard to lose and can be "dangerous" to a person's health.

6. One of Joyce Carol Oates's most shocking stories is "Bingo Master;" the triumph of brutality is devastating.

7. Macbeth "bumps off" Duncan to gain the throne for himself.

8. In his article "The Death of Broadway", Thomas M. Disch writes that "choreographers are, literally, a dying breed[1]".

9. "Know thyself—" this is the quest of the main characters in both Ibsen's *Peer Gynt* and Lewis's *Till We Have Faces.*

10. One thought flashed through my mind as I finished *"In Search of Our Mothers' Gardens:"* I want to read more of this writer's books.

EXERCISE 34.4 Revising for Quotation Marks

Revise the following paragraph to use quotation marks appropriately.

In his poem The Fly, William Blake uses the image of the poet as a fly to make a "profound statement" about the fragility of human life and thought. "Addressing" the fly, the poet regrets that "he has killed it as it was playing" and goes on to ask "whether he is not a fly, too": "For I dance, / And drink, & sing / Till some blind hand / Shall brush my wing." This image "echoes" Shakespeare's play *King Lear,* in which the character Gloucester says, "As flies to wanton boys are we to th' gods; / They kill us for their sport". Apparently, Blake is less "stressed out" by the thought of himself as a helpless "bug", since he concludes the poem, "Then am I / A happy fly, / If I live / Or if I die. But in his essay "Moral Vision in "The Fly"," Sylvester Pritchard argues that "Blake's closing image of death suggests a despair no less deep than that of Gloucester in his terrible blind sight[2]".

THINKING CRITICALLY ABOUT QUOTATION MARKS

Reading with an Eye for Quotation Marks

Read the following passage about the painter Georgia O'Keeffe, paying particular attention to the use of quotation marks. What effect is created by the author's use of quotation marks with *hardness, crustiness,* and *crusty*? How do the quotations by O'Keeffe help to support the author's description of her?

"Hardness" has not been in our century a quality much admired in women, nor in the past twenty years has it even been in official favor for men. When hardness surfaces in the very old we tend to transform it into "crustiness" or eccentricity, some tonic pepperiness to be indulged at a distance. On the evidence of her work and what she has said about it, Georgia O'Keeffe is neither "crusty" nor eccentric. She is simply hard, a straight shooter, a woman clean of received wisdom and open to what she sees. This is a woman who could early on dismiss most of her contemporaries as "dreamy," and would later single out one she liked as "a very poor painter." (And then add, apparently by way of softening the judgment: "I guess he wasn't a painter at all. He had no courage and I believe that to create one's own world in any of the arts takes courage.") This is a woman who in 1939 could advise her admirers that they were missing her point, that their appreciation of her famous flowers was merely sentimental. "When I paint a red hill," she observed coolly in the catalogue for an exhibition that year, "you say it is too bad that I don't always paint flowers. A flower touches almost everyone's heart. A red hill doesn't touch everyone's heart."

— JOAN DIDION, "Georgia O'Keeffe"

Thinking about Your Own Use of Quotation Marks

Choose a topic that is of interest on your campus, and interview one of your friends about it for ten or fifteen minutes. On the basis of your notes from the interview, write two or three paragraphs about your friend's views, using as many direct quotations as possible. Then look to see how closely you followed the conventions for quotation marks explained in this chapter. Note any usages that caused you problems—in your writing log, if you keep one.

35

Using Other
Punctuation Marks

PARENTHESES, BRACKETS, DASHES, COLONS, SLASHES, AND ELLIPSES *are marks that allow writers to punctuate sentences so that readers can best understand their meaning. The following is a passage that demonstrates the use of most of these punctuation marks:*

> Likewise, "hassling"—mock dogfighting—was strictly forbidden, and so naturally young fighter jocks could hardly wait to go up in, say, a pair of F-100s and start the duel by making a pass at each other at 800 miles an hour, the winner being the pilot who could slip in behind the other one and get locked in on his [never *her* or *his or her!*] tail ("wax his tail"), and it was not uncommon for some eager jock to try too tight an outside turn and have his engine flame out, whereupon, unable to restart it, he has to eject . . . and he shakes his fist at the victor as he floats down by parachute and his million-dollar aircraft goes *kaboom!* on the palmetto grass or the desert floor, and he starts thinking about how he can get together with the other guy back at the base in time for the two of them to get their stories straight before the investigation: "I don't know what happened, sir. I was pulling up after a target run, and it just flamed out on me."
>
> – TOM WOLFE, *The Right Stuff*

Here Wolfe uses dashes, parentheses, an ellipsis, and a colon to create rhythm and build momentum in a very long (178-word) sentence that starts with a definition of hassling *set off by dashes and builds to the pilot's less-than-tearful "story" after the colon: "I don't know what happened, sir." The editorial comment inserted in brackets calls attention to the fact that the "right stuff" was, in the world Wolfe describes here, always male. This chapter will guide you in deciding when you can use these marks of punctuation to signal relationships among sentence parts, to create particular rhythms, and to help readers follow your thoughts.*

EXERCISE 35.1

Try revising the punctuation in Tom Wolfe's passage on the opening page of this chapter, replacing dashes with parentheses (or vice versa). Compare the original and your revision. What conclusions can you draw about the emphasis each mark brings to the passage?

35a

Using parentheses

Parentheses enclose material that is of minor or secondary importance in a sentence—material that supplements, clarifies, comments on, or illustrates what precedes or follows it. Parentheses also enclose numbers or letters that precede items in a list.

Enclosing less important material

Normal children do not confuse reality and fantasy—they confuse them much less often than we adults do (as a certain great fantasist pointed out in a story called "The Emperor's New Clothes").
— URSULA LeGUIN, "Why Are Americans Afraid of Dragons?"

Boxing is a purely masculine world. (Though there are female boxers— the most famous is the black champion Lady Tyger Trimiar with her shaved head and tiger-striped attire—women's role in the sport is extremely marginal.) — JOYCE CAROL OATES, "On Boxing"

As the examples above demonstrate, a period may be placed either inside or outside a closing parenthesis, depending on whether the parenthetical text is part of a larger sentence. A comma, however, is always placed *outside* a closing parenthesis (and never before an opening one).

Gene Tunney's single defeat in an eleven-year career was to a flamboyant and dangerous fighter named Harry Greb ("The Human Windmill"), who seems to have been, judging from boxing literature, the dirtiest fighter in history. — JOYCE CAROL OATES, "On Boxing"

If the material in parentheses is a question or an exclamation, use a question mark or exclamation mark inside the closing parenthesis.

Our laughing (so deep was the pleasure!) became screaming.
— RICHARD RODRIGUEZ, "Aria: A Memoir of a Bilingual Childhood"

Use parentheses judiciously, for they break up the flow of a sentence or passage, forcing readers to hold the original train of thought in their minds while considering a secondary one.

Choosing among parentheses, commas, and dashes

As a writer, you often have a choice of setting off material in three ways: with commas, with parentheses, or with dashes. The choice is partially one of how interruptive the material is and partially one of personal style. In general, use commas when the material is least interruptive (see 30c and 30f), parentheses when it is more interruptive, and dashes when it is the most interruptive (see 35c). But if the material ends in an exclamation point or question mark (as does the last example above), you can use *only* parentheses or dashes.

Enclosing numbers or letters in a list

Five distinct styles can be distinguished: (1) Old New England, (2) Deep South, (3) Middle American, (4) Wild West and (5) Far West or Californian.   — ALISON LURIE, *The Language of Clothes*

35b

Using brackets

Brackets are used to enclose parenthetical elements in material that is within parentheses and to enclose explanatory words or comments that are inserted into a quotation. If your typewriter does not include keys for brackets, draw them in by hand.

Setting off material within parentheses

Eventually the investigation had to examine the major agencies (including the previously sacrosanct National Security Agency [NSA]) that were conducting covert operations.

Inserting material within quotations

In the following sentence, the bracketed words replace the words *he* and *it* in the original quotation:

As Curtis argues, "[Johnson] saw [the war] as a game or wrestling match in which he would make Ho Chi Minh cry 'uncle.' "

In the following sentence, the bracketed material explains what the *that* in the quotation means:

Everyday Use

Though you may never have paid much attention to them before, parentheses, brackets, dashes, colons, slashes, and ellipses are all around us. Pick up the *TV Guide*, for instance, and you will find all these punctuation marks in abundance, helping viewers preview programs in the most clear and efficient way possible. For example:

9 PM Movie (CC)—*Biography: 2 hrs. A thoughtful screenplay by* China Beach *creator John Sacret Young and a moving performance by Raul Julia distinguish "Romero," a fact-based 1989 film about the heroic Salvadoran archbishop. [Time approximate after baseball.]*

To see the helpfulness of these punctuation marks, take them all out, and decide how much extra work you have to do to read without them. Then look around to see where you find these marks. Which ones do you see most often? Which ones less often?

In defending his station's inferior children's programs, a network executive states, "If we were to do that [supply quality programs in the afternoon, one of the demands of ACT], a lot of people might say: 'How dare they lock the kids up for another two and a half hours.' "
    – MARIE WINN, *The Plug-In Drug: Television, Children, and the Family*

In the quotation in the following sentence, the artist Gauguin's name is misspelled. The bracketed word *sic*, which means "so," tells readers that the person being quoted—not the writer—made the mistake.

One admirer wrote, "She was the most striking woman I'd ever seen—a sort of wonderful combination of Mia Farrow and one of Gaugin's [*sic*] Polynesian nymphs."

EXERCISE 35.2

Revise the following sentences, using parentheses and brackets correctly. Example:

She was in fourth grade (or was it third?) when she became blind.

1. One incident of cruelty was brought to public attention by the Animal Liberation Front ALF.

2. During my research, I found that a flat-rate income tax a single-rate tax with no deductions has its problems.

3. The health care expert informed readers that "as we progress through middle age, we experience intimations of our own morality *sic*."

4. Many researchers used the Massachusetts Multiphasic Personality Inventory the MMPI for hypnotizability studies.

5. Some of the alternatives suggested include 1 tissue cultures, 2 mechanical models, 3 in vitro techniques, and 4 mathematical and electrical models.

35c

Using dashes

Pairs of dashes allow a writer to interrupt a sentence to insert a comment or to highlight particular material. In contrast to parentheses, dashes give more rather than less emphasis to the material they enclose. On most typewriters and with most word-processing software, a dash is made with two hyphens (and *no* spaces before, between, or after).

Inserting a comment

The pleasures of reading itself—who doesn't remember?—were like those of Christmas cake, a sweet devouring.

— EUDORA WELTY, "A Sweet Devouring"

Emphasizing explanatory material

Mr. Angell is addicted to dashes and parentheses—small pauses or digressions in a narrative like those moments when the umpire dusts off home plate or a pitcher rubs up a new ball—that serve to slow an already deliberate movement almost to a standstill.

— JOEL CONARROE, *New York Times Book Review*

A single dash sets off a comment or emphasizes material at the end of a sentence. It also marks a sudden shift in tone, introduces a summary or explanation of what has come before, and indicates hesitation in speech.

Emphasizing material at the end of a sentence

In the twentieth century it has become almost impossible to moralize about epidemics—except those which are transmitted sexually.

— SUSAN SONTAG, *AIDS and Its Metaphors*

Marking a sudden change in tone

Under democracy, one party always devotes its chief efforts to trying to prove that the other is unfit to rule—and both commonly succeed and are right. – H. L. MENCKEN, *Minority Report*

Introducing a summary or explanation

In walking, the average adult person employs a motor mechanism that weighs about eighty pounds—sixty pounds of muscle and twenty pounds of bone. – EDWARD WAY TEALE

Indicating hesitation in speech

As the officer approached his car, the driver stammered, "What—what have I done?"

In introducing a summary or explanation, the difference between a single dash and a colon is a subtle one. In general, however, a dash is less formal. In fact, you should use dashes sparingly in college writing, not only because they are somewhat informal but also because they cause an abrupt break in reading. Too many of them create a jerky, disconnected effect that makes it hard for readers to follow your thought.

> *Editing for effective use of dashes and parentheses*

1. Be sure that any material set off with dashes or enclosed in parentheses requires special emphasis.
2. Then check to see that the dashes or parentheses don't make the sentence difficult to follow.
3. Finally, decide whether the punctuation you've chosen creates the proper emphasis: parentheses tend to de-emphasize material they enclose; dashes add the most emphasis.

EXERCISE 35.3

Punctuate the following sentences with dashes where appropriate. Example:

> *He is quick, violent, and mean—they don't call him Dirty Harry for nothing—but appealing nonetheless.*

1. Many people would have ignored the children's taunts but not Ace.

2. Even if smoking is harmful and there is no real proof of this assertion it is unjust to outlaw smoking while other harmful substances remain legal.

3. Saving old theaters how many have we already lost? is a cultural necessity.

4. Union Carbide's plant in Bhopal, India, sprang a leak a leak that killed more than 2,000 people and injured an additional 200,000.

5. Fair-skinned people and especially those with red hair should use a strong sunscreen.

35d

Using colons

A colon, says Karl Kraus, "opens its mouth wide: woe to the writer who does not fill it with something nourishing." As Kraus suggests, colons are used to introduce something that "nourishes"—something that offers an explanation or an example, serves as an appositive, or introduces a series, a list, or a quotation. Colons also separate elements such as hours, minutes, and seconds; biblical chapter numbers and verses; and titles and subtitles.

Introducing an explanation, an example, or an appositive

And we are all on our own when it comes to keeping those lines open to ourselves: your notebook will never help me, nor mine you.
> – JOAN DIDION, "On Keeping a Notebook"

The men may also wear the getup known as Sun Belt Cool: a pale beige suit, open-collared shirt (often in a darker shade than the suit), cream-colored loafers and aviator sunglasses.
> – ALISON LURIE, *The Language of Clothes*

Introducing a series, a list, or a quotation

At the baby's one-month birthday party, Ah Po gave him the Four Valuable Things: ink, inkslab, paper, and brush.
> – MAXINE HONG KINGSTON, *China Men*

We began a series of workshops on nonviolence, and we repeatedly asked ourselves: "Are you able to accept blows without retaliation?"
> – MARTIN LUTHER KING, JR., "Letter from Birmingham Jail"

Separating elements

HOURS, MINUTES, AND SECONDS

4:59 P.M.

2:15:06

BIBLICAL CHAPTERS AND VERSES

Deuteronomy 17:2–7

I Chronicles 3:3–5

TITLES AND SUBTITLES

"Grant and Lee: A Study in Contrasts"

The Joy of Insight: Passions of a Physicist

Editing for colons

Except when it is used to separate the standard elements discussed in the preceding section, a colon should be used only at the end of an independent clause. Do not put a colon between a verb and its object or complement, between a preposition and its object, or after such expressions as *such as, especially,* or *including.*

MISUSED	Some natural fibers are: cotton, wool, silk, and linen.
REVISED	Some natural fibers are cotton, wool, silk, and linen.
MISUSED	In poetry, additional power may come from devices such as: simile, metaphor, and alliteration.
REVISED	In poetry, additional power may come from devices such as simile, metaphor, and alliteration.

EXERCISE 35.4

Insert a colon in each of the following items that needs one. Some of the items do not require a colon. Example:

Images: My Life in Film *includes revealing material written by Ingmar Bergman.*

1. The sonnet's structure is effective in revealing the speaker's message love has changed his life and ended his depression.
2. Another example is taken from Psalm 139 16.
3. Nixon claimed that throughout the Watergate investigation he believed it was his duty to stay on as president "to make every possible effort to complete the term of office to which you elected me."

4. Shifting into German, Kennedy declared "Ich bin ein Berliner."

5. Education can alleviate problems such as poverty, poor health, and the energy shortage.

6. Gandhi urged four rules tell the truth even in business, adopt more sanitary habits, abolish caste and religious divisions, and learn English.

7. Solid vocal technique is founded on the correct use of head position, diaphragm control, muscle relaxation, and voice placement.

8. *Signs of Trouble and Erosion A Report on Education in America* was submitted to Congress and the president in January 1984.

9. Even more important was what money represented success, prestige, and power.

10. Two buses go to Denver: one at 9 38 A.M. and one at 2 55 P.M.

35e

Using slashes

Slashes are used to mark line divisions in poetry quoted within text (see 34a2), to separate two alternative terms, and to separate the parts of fractions. When used to separate lines of poetry, the slash should be preceded and followed by a space.

Marking line divisions in poetry

In Sonnet 29, the persona states, "For thy sweet love rememb'red such wealth brings / That then I scorn to change my state with kings."

Separating alternatives

"I'm not the typical wife/girlfriend of a baseball player—those women you see on TV with their hair done up and their Rose Bowl Parade wave to the crowds." — ROGER ANGELL, "In the Country"

Separating parts of fractions

The structure is 138½ feet high.

35f

Using ellipses

Ellipses, or ellipsis points, are three equally spaced dots. Most often used to indicate that something has been omitted from a quoted passage, they can also be used to signal a pause or hesitation in speech in the same way that a dash can (see 35c).

Indicating omissions

Just as you should carefully use quotation marks around any material that you quote directly from a source, so you should carefully use an ellipsis to indicate that you have left out part of a quotation that otherwise appears to be a complete sentence. Look at the following example:

ORIGINAL TEXT

The quasi-official division of the population into three economic classes called high-, middle-, and low-income groups rather misses the point, because as a class indicator the amount of money is not as important as the source.   – PAUL FUSSELL, "Notes on Class"

WITH ELLIPSES

As Paul Fussell argues, "The quasi-official division of the population into three economic classes . . . rather misses the point. . . ."

In this example, the ellipses are used to indicate two different omissions—one in the middle of the sentence and one at the end. When you omit the last part of a quoted sentence, add a period before the ellipsis—for a total of four dots. Be sure a complete sentence comes before and after the four points. If your quotation ends with a source documentation (such as a page number, a name, or a title), follow these steps:

1. Use three ellipsis points but no period after the quotation.
2. Add the closing quotation mark, closed up to the third ellipsis point.
3. Add the source documentation in parentheses.
4. Use a period to indicate the end of the sentence.

Hawthorne writes, "My friend, whom I shall call Oberon—it was a name of fancy and friendship between him and me . . ." (575).

Indicating a pause or a hesitation

What you get is . . . the view from Oswald's rifle.

— TOM WOLFE, "Pornoviolence"

Then the voice, husky and familiar, came to wash over us—"The winnah, and still heavyweight champeen of the world . . . Joe Louis."

— MAYA ANGELOU, *I Know Why the Caged Bird Sings*

35g

Using emoticons

If you participate in any computer bulletin boards, discussion groups, or other electronic forms of communication, you will already have come in contact with **emoticons**, also known as *smileys*. These are marks made with combinations of keyboard characters that "punctuate" a passage by indicating the mood of the sender. Some commonly used emoticons include the following. (Look at them sideways!):

the smile: :-)
the frown: :-(
the wink: ;-)
the laugh: :-D

These marks are sometimes also used to express something about the sender's appearance. How, for instance, might a writer indicate that she or he wears glasses, has a mustache, or wears a turban? As these questions suggest, many emoticons are used simply for fun, to tease and puzzle readers. Their growing use, however, suggests that new punctuation marks are coming and that, in fact, some of these symbols may well become standard.

In the meantime, if you are using emoticons in your writing, follow the same rules you would use for other marks: Are they appropriate to your topic and purpose? Will they be readily understood and accepted by your audience?

EXERCISE 35.5

Complete the following sentence by incorporating two parts of one of the sentences in the passage below, using ellipsis points to indicate what you omit: "In 'Shopping and Other Spiritual Adventures,' Phyllis Rose says of Americans' attitudes toward shopping, _____."

We Americans are beyond a simple, possessive materialism. We're used to abundance and the possibility of possessing things. The things, and the possibility of possessing them, will still be there next week, next year. So today we can walk the aisles calmly.   – PHYLLIS ROSE, "Shopping and Other Spiritual Adventures"

EXERCISE 35.6

The following sentences use the punctuation marks presented in this chapter very effectively. Read the sentences carefully; then choose one, and use it as a model for writing a sentence of your own, making sure to use the punctuation marks in the same way in your sentence.

1. The dad was—how can you put this gracefully?—a real blimp, a wide load, and the white polyester stretch-pants only emphasized the cargo.
   – GARRISON KEILLOR, "Happy to Be Here"

2. I took exercise daily (as I still do), did not smoke (and still don't), and though excessively fond of wine, seldom drank spirits, not much liking the taste of them. – JAN MORRIS, "To Everest"

3. Not only are the distinctions we draw between male nature and female nature largely arbitrary and often pure superstition: they are completely beside the point. – BRIGID BROPHY, "Women"

4. One day a man would be ascending the pyramid at a terrific clip, and the next—bingo!—he would reach his own limits in the most unexpected way.
   – TOM WOLFE, *The Right Stuff*

5. A few traditions, thank heaven, remain fixed in the summer state of things—the June collapse of the Giants, Gaylord Perry throwing (or not throwing) spitballs, Hank Aaron hitting homers, and the commissioner . . . well, commissioning. – ROGER ANGELL, *Five Seasons*

EXERCISE 35.7   Revising for Parentheses and Dashes

The following paragraph uses many parentheses and dashes. Using the guidelines in this chapter, revise the paragraph to make it flow more smoothly, and emphasize appropriate elements by deleting some of the parentheses and dashes, replacing one with the other, or substituting other punctuation.

By the time we reached Geneva, we had been traveling more than seven weeks—it seemed like seven months!—and were getting rather tired of one another's company. (We had been only casual acquaintances before the trip.) Since there was not a great deal to see in the city—especially on Sunday—we decided to take the train to Chamonix (France) to see Mont Blanc—Europe's second-highest mountain (a decision that proved to be a disaster). After an argument about the map (the kind of argument we were having more and more often), we wandered around endlessly before finding the train station, only to discover that it was the wrong one. So we had to walk even farther—back to the other train station. Despite an exhausting pace, we just missed the train—or so we thought—until we learned that there was no train to Chamonix that day—because it was Sunday. I have never (for obvious reasons) gone back to Geneva.

THINKING CRITICALLY ABOUT PUNCTUATION

Reading with an Eye for Dashes

Although Emily Dickinson's poems are characteristically punctuated with dashes, the first editor of her work systematically eliminated them. Here is a brief Dickinson poem—with her original dashes restored. Read it twice, first ignoring the dashes and then using them to guide your reading. What effect does the final dash have? Finally, try composing a four-line poem that uses dashes to guide reading and meaning.

> Much Madness is divinest Sense—
> To a discerning Eye—
> Much Sense—the starkest Madness—
> 'Tis the Majority
> In this, as All, prevail—
> Assent—and you are sane—
> Demur—you're straightway dangerous—
> And handled with a Chain—
> — EMILY DICKINSON

Thinking about Your Own Use of Punctuation

Look through a draft you have recently written or are working on, and check your use of parentheses, brackets, dashes, colons, slashes, and ellipses. Have you followed the conventions presented in this chapter? If not, revise accordingly. Then read through the draft again, looking especially at all the parentheses and dashes. Are there too many? Check the material in parentheses to see if it could use more emphasis and thus be set off instead with dashes. Then check any material in dashes to see if it could do with less emphasis and thus be punctuated with commas or parentheses. If you keep a writing log, enter some examples of this work in your log.

Part Seven

Understanding Mechanical Conventions

36. Using Capitals   522

37. Using Abbreviations and Numbers   529

38. Using Italics   538

39. Using Hyphens   544

36

Using Capitals

AT ONE TIME, ALL LETTERS WERE WRITTEN AS CAPITALS, LIKE THIS. *By the time movable type was invented, a new system had evolved, and printers used a capital letter only for the first letter of any word they felt was particularly important. Today the conventions of capitalization are fairly well standardized, although they vary from language to language.*

EXERCISE 36.1

Spend a few minutes writing a letter to someone you haven't seen for some time. If nothing else comes to mind, tell him or her about your classes or about a trip you took. Then look over your letter. How many words have you capitalized— and why?

36a

Capitalizing the first word of a sentence or line of poetry

Capitalize the first word of a sentence.

Posing relatives for photographs is a challenge.
Could you move to the left a little?
Smile, and say cheese!

If you are quoting a full sentence, capitalize its first word.

Everyone was asking, "What will I do after I graduate?"

Capitalization of a sentence following a colon is optional.

> Gould cites the work of Darwin: The [or the] theory of natural selection incorporates the principle of evolutionary ties between all animals.

A sentence that is set off within another sentence by dashes or parentheses should not be capitalized. Note, however, that a sentence within parentheses that stands by itself *is* capitalized.

> Those assigned to transports were not humiliated like washouts—*somebody* had to fly those planes—nevertheless, they, too, had been *left behind* for lack of the right stuff.

> It *heaved,* it moved up and down underneath his feet, it pitched up, it pitched down, it rolled to port (this great beast *rolled!*) and it rolled to starboard, as the ship moved into the wind and, therefore, into the waves, and the wind kept sweeping across, sixty feet up in the air out in the open sea, and there were no railings whatsoever.

> Or a man could go for a routine physical one fine day, feeling like a million dollars, and be grounded for *fallen arches.* It happened!—just like that! (And try raising them.)
> — TOM WOLFE, *The Right Stuff*

The first word of each line in a poem is also traditionally capitalized.

> Loveliest of trees, the cherry now
> Is hung with bloom along the bough,
> And stands about the woodland ride
> Wearing white for Eastertide.   — A. E. HOUSMAN, "Loveliest of Trees"

Some poets do not capitalize each line. When citing poetry, therefore, be careful to follow the original capitalization.

> Morning sun heats up the young beech tree
> leaves and almost lights them into fireflies

> I wish I could dig up the earth to plant apples
> pears or peaches on a lazy dandelion lawn

> I am tired from this digging up of human bodies
> no one loved enough to save from death
> — JUNE JORDAN, "Aftermath"

36b

Capitalizing proper nouns and proper adjectives

Capitalize **proper nouns** (those naming specific persons, places, and things) and **proper adjectives** (those formed from proper nouns). In general, do not capitalize **common nouns** (those naming general classes of people,

Everyday Use

Writers often capitalize words or even whole passages to add a special emphasis (WOW! ZAP!). The writer Dave Barry uses this technique in his humorous newspaper columns: "Today, I saw a chicken driving a car. (I AM NOT MAKING THIS UP.)" Look through your own local newspaper, noting examples of capital letters used for emphasis. Bring some examples to class for comparison with those found by classmates.

places, and things) unless they begin a sentence or are used as part of a proper noun. Do not capitalize articles (*a, an,* or *the*) or prepositions preceding or within proper nouns or proper adjectives.

PROPER NOUNS	COMMON NOUNS
Alfred Hitchcock, Hitchcockian	the director, directorial
Brazil, Brazilian	the nation
Golden Gate Bridge	the bridge

≫ *Some commonly capitalized terms*

NAMES OF INDIVIDUALS

Martin Luther King, Jr.	Eleanor Roosevelt
Morgan Freeman	Willie Mays
Leonard Bernstein	Louise Erdrich
Aristotelian logic	Petrarchan sonnet form

GEOGRAPHIC NAMES

Asia	Pacific Ocean
Nepal	Sugarloaf Mountain
St. Louis	Michigan Avenue
African art	Parisian fashions

STRUCTURES AND MONUMENTS

Flatiron Building	Gateway Arch
Fort McHenry Tunnel	Coit Tower

SHIPS, TRAINS, AIRCRAFT, AND SPACECRAFT

S.S. *Titanic*	Metroliner
Spirit of St. Louis	*Challenger*

INSTITUTIONS, ORGANIZATIONS, AND BUSINESSES

Library of Congress	Kiwanis Club
St. Martin's Press	United Auto Workers
General Motors Corporation	Democratic Party

HISTORICAL EVENTS, ERAS, AND CALENDAR ITEMS

Shays's Rebellion	Saturday
Great Depression	July
Middle Ages	Memorial Day

RELIGIONS AND RELIGIOUS TERMS

Buddhism, Buddhists	Allah
Catholicism, Catholics	Jesus Christ
Islam, Muslims *or* Moslems	God
Judaism, Jews	the Bible
United Methodist Church,	the Koran
Methodists	Bhagavad Gita

ETHNIC GROUPS, NATIONALITIES, AND LANGUAGES

African American	English
Chicano/Chicana	Chinese
Slavic	Iraqi
Arab	Latin

TRADE NAMES

Reebok	Huggies
Xerox	Levi's
Cheerios	Walkman

1

Capitalizing titles of individuals

Capitalize titles used before a proper name. Used alone or following a proper name, most titles are not capitalized. The only exceptions are titles of some very powerful officials—for example, many writers capitalize the word *president* when it refers to the President of the United States.

Justice O'Connor	Sandra Day O'Connor, the justice
Governor Ann Richards	Ann Richards, governor of Texas
Professor Lisa Ede	Lisa Ede, an English professor
Doctor Edward A. Davies	Edward A. Davies, our doctor

2
Capitalizing academic institutions and courses

Capitalize the names of specific schools, departments, or courses but not the common nouns referring to institutions or subject areas.

University of California (*but* a California university)
History Department (*but* a history department)
Political Science 102 (*but* a political science course)

36c

Capitalizing titles of works

Capitalize most words in titles of books, articles, stories, essays, plays, poems, documents, films, paintings, and musical compositions. Articles (*a, an, the*), prepositions, conjunctions, and the *to* in an infinitive are not capitalized unless they are the first or last words in a title or subtitle.

Walt Whitman: A Life	"Lovely to Look At"
"June Recital"	Magna Carta
"Shooting an Elephant"	*In the Line of Fire*
Our Town	*The Magic Flute*

Remember to capitalize the titles of your own compositions.

36d

Capitalizing *I* and *O*

Always capitalize the pronoun *I* and the interjection *O*. Be careful, however, to distinguish between the interjections *O* and *oh*. *O* is an older form that is usually used for direct address in very formal speech. It is always capitalized, whereas *oh* is not unless it begins a sentence or is part of a title.

In fact, I don't know the answer.
Grant us peace, O Lord.

▶ *FOR MULTILINGUAL WRITERS*
Learning English Capitalization

Capitalization systems vary considerably among languages, and some languages (Arabic, Chinese, and Hebrew, for example) do not use capital letters at all. English may be the only language to capitalize *I*, but Dutch and German capitalize some forms of *you*. German capitalizes all nouns—and in fact, English used to capitalize more nouns than it does now (see *The Declaration of Independence* for one good example). As a result, the system of capitalization commonly used in standard academic English may pose challenges for speakers of other languages.

Checking for unnecessary capitalization

1

With compass directions, unless the word designates a specific geographical region

John Muir headed west, motivated by the need to explore.

The nation was at that time divided into three competing economic sections: the Northeast, the South, and the West.

2

With family relationships, unless the word is used as part of the name or as a substitute for the name

When she was a child, my mother shared a room with her aunt.

I could always tell when Mother was annoyed with Aunt Rose.

The train on which Uncle Charlie arrived spewed out thick black smoke.

3

With seasons of the year and parts of the academic year

spring	fall semester
winter	winter term
autumn	spring quarter

EXERCISE 36.2

Capitalize words as needed in the following sentences. Example:

> *T S E   T W   L   F   F*
> t. s. eliot, who wrote the waste land, was an editor at faber and faber.

1. the town in the south where i was raised had a statue of a civil war soldier in the center of main street.
2. we had a choice of fast-food, chinese, or italian restaurants.
3. I caught a glimpse of president bill clinton and his family.
4. the council of trent was convened to draw up the catholic response to the protestant reformation.
5. We drove east over the hudson river on the tappan zee bridge.
6. i wondered if my new levi's were faded enough.
7. accepting an award for his score for the film *the high and the mighty*, dmitri tiomkin thanked beethoven, brahms, wagner, and strauss.
8. i will cite the novels of vladimir nabokov, in particular *pnin* and *lolita*.
9. the battle of lexington and concord was fought in april 1775.
10. my favorite song by cole porter is "you'd be so nice to come home to."

THINKING CRITICALLY ABOUT CAPITALIZATION

Reading with an Eye for Capitalization

The following poem uses capitalization in an unconventional way. Read it over a few times, at least once aloud. What effect does the capitalization have on your understanding and recitation of the poem? Why do you think the poet chose to use capitals as she did?

> A little Madness in the Spring
> Is wholesome even for the King,
> But God be with the Clown—
> Who ponders this tremendous scene—
> This whole Experiment of Green—
> As if it were his own!
> — EMILY DICKINSON

Thinking about Your Own Use of Capitalization

With an eye for capitalization, read over something you have written recently. Have you capitalized all proper nouns and adjectives? Have you used capitals properly with dashes and parentheses? Have you capitalized sentences following colons, and if so, have you done so consistently? If you keep a writing log, enter notes and examples of any problems you have with capital letters.

37

Using Abbreviations and Numbers

IN HIS ESSAYS AND BY THE EXAMPLE OF HIS LIFE, Henry David Thoreau urged us to "simplify, simplify." Two of the tools that help writers reach that goal are abbreviations and numerals. Both serve to speed up prose and thus allow readers to process information efficiently. As with other elements, there are certain conventions for using abbreviations and numerals, especially in academic work. This chapter will explain these conventions to help you use abbreviations and numbers appropriately and correctly.

EXERCISE 37.1

Take a few moments to write directions to some place you know well—to your home from the edge of town, for example. Then read over what you've written, noting any use of abbreviations and numbers. Finally, check the guidelines in this chapter to see whether you've used them correctly.

ABBREVIATIONS

37a

Abbreviating titles and academic degrees

When used before or after a name, some personal and professional titles and academic degrees are abbreviated, even in academic writing.

Ms. Steinem
Mr. Guenette
Dr. C. William McCurdy

Henry Louis Gates, Jr.
Paul Irvin, M.D.
Jamie Barlow Kayes, Ph.D.

Everyday Use

Any time you use a telephone book, you see an abundance of abbreviations and numbers, which are meant to help readers find the proper information quickly and efficiently. If you look up the American Automobile Association in Chicago, for example, here's what you find.

AAA—CHICAGO MOTOR CLUB
    Emergency 24 Hr. Road Service
      Toll Free...*800-262-6327*
    Membership Services and Insurance
      68 E. Wacker Pl..*372-1818*

Abbreviations and figures obviously allow the publisher to include a great deal of information in a small amount of space—imagine the phone book without them! Look around you for some other uses of abbreviations and figures. How do *you* normally use them?

Other titles, including religious, military, academic, and government titles, should always be spelled out in academic writing. In other writing, they may be abbreviated when they appear before a full name but should be spelled out if they appear before only a surname.

Gen. H. Norman Schwarzkopf	General Schwarzkopf
Prof. Beverly Moss	Professor Moss
Sen. Barbara Mikulski	Senator Mikulski
Rev. Fleming Rutledge	the Reverend Rutledge

Academic degrees may be abbreviated when used alone, but personal or professional titles used alone are never abbreviated.

ACCEPTABLE	She received her *Ph.D.* this year.
INAPPROPRIATE	He was a rigorous *prof.,* and we worked hard.
REVISED	He was a rigorous *professor,* and we worked hard.

Use either a title or an academic degree, but not both, with a person's name.

INAPPROPRIATE	Dr. James Dillon, Ph.D.
REVISED	Dr. James Dillon
REVISED	James Dillon, Ph.D.

37b

Using abbreviations with years and hours

The following abbreviations are acceptable when used with numerals. Notice that A.D. precedes the numeral; all other abbreviations follow the numeral.

399 B.C. ("before Christ")
A.D. 49 (*anno Domini,* Latin for "year of our Lord")
210 B.C.E. ("before the common era")
49 C.E. ("common era")
11:15 A.M. *or* a.m. (*ante meridiem,* Latin for "before noon")
9:00 P.M. *or* p.m. (*post meridiem,* Latin for "after noon")

37c

Using acronyms and initial abbreviations

Abbreviations that can be pronounced as words are called **acronyms:** OPEC, for example, is the acronym for the Organization of Petroleum Exporting Countries. **Initial abbreviations** are those that are pronounced as separate initials: NRA for National Rifle Association, for instance. Many of the most common abbreviations for these types come from business, government, and science: NASA, PBS, DNA, GE, UNICEF, AIDS, SAT.

As long as you can be sure your readers will understand them, you can use such abbreviations in much of your college writing. If you are using a term only once or twice, you should spell it out; but when you need to use a term repeatedly, abbreviating it will serve as a convenience for you and your readers alike. If the abbreviation may be unfamiliar to your readers, however, you should "define" it for them. Spell out the full term at the first use, and give the abbreviation in parentheses. After that, you can use the abbreviation by itself.

The Comprehensive Test Ban (CTB) Treaty was first proposed in the 1950s. For those nations signing it, the CTB would bring to a halt all nuclear-weapons testing.

We set out to conduct field research on language differences in urban and rural areas of Texas. Our research was based on four communities but included a Phonological Survey of Texas (PST) and Grammatical Investigation of Texas Speech (GRITS).

abb

532 **37d** USING ABBREVIATIONS AND NUMBERS

37d

Using other kinds of abbreviations

The following guidelines will help you use some other common abbreviations. In general, you should not use any type of abbreviation not discussed in this chapter in an academic writing assignment. For example:

INAPPROPRIATE   The bio lab was deserted on Fri. nights.

REVISED   The biology laboratory was deserted on Friday nights.

Company names

Use such abbreviations as *Inc., Co.,* and *Corp.* and the ampersand (&) if they are part of a company's official name. You should not, however, use them in most other contexts.

Sears, Roebuck & Co. was the only store in town.

Reference information

Though it is conventional to abbreviate such words as *chapter* (ch.), *page* (p.), or *pages* (pp.) in source citations, it is not acceptable to do so in the body of a paper.

INAPPROPRIATE   The preface to the 1851 *ed.* of *Twice-Told Tales* states that the stories are not autobiographical.

REVISED   The preface to the 1851 *edition* of *Twice-Told Tales* states that the stories are not autobiographical.

Latin abbreviations

In general, avoid these abbreviations except when citing sources:

cf.   compare (*confer*)
e.g.   for example (*exempli gratia*)
et al.   and others (*et alii*)
etc.   and so forth (*et cetera*)
i.e.   that is (*id est*)
N.B.   note well (*nota bene*)

INAPPROPRIATE   Many firms have policies to help working parents—*e.g.,* flexible hours, parental leave, day care.

REVISED   Many firms have policies to help working parents—*for example,* flexible hours, parental leave, day care.

Geographical terms and months

Many place-names and most months of the year should be abbreviated in source citations, but they should always be written out within sentences.

INAPPROPRIATE   In *Aug.,* I moved from Lodi, *Calif.,* to *L.A.*

REVISED   In *August,* I moved from Lodi, *California,* to *Los Angeles.*

Common exceptions are *Washington, D.C.,* and *U.S.* The latter is acceptable as an adjective but not as a noun.

UNACCEPTABLE   The exchange student enjoyed the *U.S.*

ACCEPTABLE   The *U.S. delegation* negotiated the treaty.

Symbols

Symbols such as ¢, @, #, %, +, and = should not be used in the body of a paper, though they are commonly used in graphs and tables. One exception is the dollar sign ($), which is acceptable before specific figures.

INAPPROPRIATE   Only *50%* of applicants are accepted.

REVISED   Only *50 percent* of applicants are accepted.

Units of measure

Except in scientific and technical writing, most units of measure should not be abbreviated in the body of a paper.

INAPPROPRIATE   The ball sailed 425 *ft.* over the fence.

REVISED   The ball sailed 425 *feet* over the fence.

 Editing for appropriate use of abbreviations

1. Check all abbreviations. In each case, be sure you've used the correct form. If in doubt, check each one in this chapter or in a dictionary.
2. Do you use any abbreviation more than once? If so, be sure you use it consistently.
3. Be sure any abbreviated words shouldn't be spelled out instead.
4. Do you use any abbreviations your readers might not understand? If so, spell them out at first use, with the abbreviation following in parentheses.

EXERCISE 37.2

Revise each of the following sentences to eliminate any abbreviations that would be inappropriate in academic writing. Example:

> United States   percent
> The population of the U.S. grew about 10% in the 1980s.

1. The old NBC show is set in a fictional L.A. law firm.
2. An MX missile, which is 71 ft. long and 92 in. around, weighs 190,000 lbs.
3. The waiters prefer the A.M. shift because customers usually order just coffee, tea, doughnuts, etc.
4. In 1991, Rep. William Gray became pres. of the UNCF.
5. A large corp. like AT&T may help finance an employee's M.B.A.
6. Unfortunately, the five-¢ candy bar is a relic of the past.
7. Founded in 1966, NOW fights discrimination against women.
8. The local NPR station has a broadcast range of seventy-five mi.
9. After less than a yr. at U.Va., Poe left and joined the U.S. Army.
10. Dostoyevsky was influenced by many European writers—e.g., Dickens, Stendhal, and Balzac.

NUMBERS

37e

Spelling out numbers expressed in one or two words

If a number can be written as one or two words, spell it out.

The victim's screams were heard by *thirty-eight* people, none of whom called the police.

Police arrested the assailant *six* days later.

37f

Using figures for numbers expressed in more than two words

Numbers that cannot be written in one or two words should be expressed in figures.

Did you know that a baseball is wrapped in 174 yards of blue-gray wool yarn and is held together by 216 red stitches?

If one of several numbers of the same kind in the same sentence needs to be expressed in figures, all the numbers should be expressed that way.

INCONSISTENT   A complete audio system can range in cost from one hundred dollars to $2,599; however, a reliable system can be purchased for approximately five hundred dollars.

CONSISTENT   A complete audio system can range in cost from $100 to $2,599; however, a reliable system can be purchased for approximately $500.

37g

Spelling out numbers that begin sentences

When a sentence begins with a number, either spell out the number, or rewrite the sentence.

INAPPROPRIATE   277,000 hours (or 119 years) of CIA labor cost taxpayers sixteen million dollars.

HARD TO READ   Two hundred seventy-seven thousand hours (or 119 years) of CIA labor cost taxpayers sixteen million dollars.

REVISED   Taxpayers spend sixteen million dollars for 277,000 hours (or 119 years) of CIA labor.

37h

Using figures according to convention

ADDRESSES

23 Main Street; 175 Fifth Avenue, New York, NY 10010

DATES

September 17, 1951; 4 B.C.; the 1860s; the sixties

DECIMALS, FRACTIONS, AND PERCENTAGES

65.34; 8½; 77 percent (*or* 77%)

(Continued)

DIVISIONS OF BOOKS AND PLAYS

volume 5, pages 81–85 (*not* 81–5)
Act III, Scene ii (*or* Act 3, Scene 2), lines 3–9

SPECIFIC AMOUNTS OF MONEY

$7,348; $1.46 trillion; $2.50; thirty-five (*or* 35) cents

SCORES AND STATISTICS

an 8–3 Red Sox victory, a verbal score of 600
an average age of 22; a mean of 53; a ratio of 3 to 1

TIME OF DAY

6:00 A.M.; 5:45 P.M.; 12:01
without A.M. or P.M.: five in the morning; four o'clock; four-thirty

ON VARIETIES OF ENGLISH
Using Abbreviations and Numbers in a Particular Field

Certain occupations, professions, and disciplines make extensive use of numbers and symbols. Because a wrong number or a misunderstood expression in a mathematical formula, in a laboratory report, or in an engineering specification can have major repercussions, people in such fields use numbers with precision—and count on them to carry heavy burdens of meaning and proof. One way in which they ensure a common understanding is by expressing numbers and formulas consistently, according to specific rules. Yet these conventions vary from field to field. If you are studying in a field that uses numbers and symbols, you will want to make sure you understand the conventions of the field—and follow them closely.

For rules on using abbreviations and numbers in a particular discipline, the *MLA Handbook for Writers of Research Papers* or *The Chicago Manual of Style* is usually followed in the humanities; the *Publication Manual of the American Psychological Association,* in the social sciences; and the *CBE Style Manual: A Guide for Authors, Editors, and Publishers in the Biological Sciences,* in the natural sciences.

EXERCISE 37.3

Revise the numbers in the following sentences as necessary for correctness and consistency. If a sentence is correct, circle its number. Example:

twenty-first
Does the ~~21st~~ century begin in 2000 or 2001?

1. 307 miles long and 82 miles wide, the island offered little of interest.
2. Time will provide perspective on the economic crisis of the '80s.
3. You could travel around the city for only 65 cents.
4. The invasion of Kuwait began on August second, 1990.
5. The department received 1,633 calls and forty-three letters.
6. Cable TV is now available to seventy-two percent of the population.
7. Walker signed a three-year, $4.5-million contract.
8. In the 35-to-44 age group, the risk is estimated to be about 1 in 2,500.
9. The parents considered twenty-five cents enough for a five-year-old.
10. The amulet measured one and one-eighth by two and two-fifths inches.

THINKING CRITICALLY ABOUT ABBREVIATIONS AND NUMBERS

Reading with an Eye for Abbreviations and Numbers

Read the following passage adapted from an essay by Jean Shepherd ("Hairy Gertz and the Forty-Seven Crappies"), and revise it to make its treatment of abbreviations and numbers correct and consistent.

> And in the middle of the lake, several yds. away, are over 17,000 fishermen, in wooden rowboats rented at a buck and a ½ an hr. It is 2 A.M. The temp is 175, with humidity to match. And the smell of decayed toads, the dumps at the far end of the lake, and an occasional soupçon of Std. Oil, whose refinery is a couple of mi. away, is enough to put hair on the back of a mud turtle. 17 thousand guys clumped together in the middle fishing for the known 64 crappies in that lake. . . . Each boat contains a minimum of 9 guys and 14 cases of beer. And once in a while, in the darkness, is heard the sound of a guy falling over backward into the slime: SSSSGLUNK!

Thinking about Your Own Use of Abbreviations and Numbers

Look over an essay or two that you have written, noting all abbreviations and numbers. Check your usage for correctness, consistency, and appropriateness. If you discover anything you have done wrong, make a note of it (in your writing log, if you are keeping one) so that you will do it correctly the next time.

38

Using Italics

*A*FTER THE INVENTION OF PRINTING, *most type carvers produced letters whose vertical strokes printed straight up and down,* like this. *Today such type is called* **roman**. *Early Italian type designers, however, specialized in a slanted type, like the one you are reading now, known today as* **italic**. *Italics are now used for denoting certain material or for emphasis. As with other formal devices in writing, usage of italics is governed by conventions, and these are presented in this chapter.*

Your word-processing program and printer may allow you to print italic type. If it doesn't, or if you use a typewriter, you can indicate italics by <u>underlining</u> *the words you wish to emphasize.*

38a

Using italics for titles

In general, italics are used to signal the titles of long or complete works; shorter works or sections of works are set off with quotation marks. (See 34c.) Use italics for the following kinds of works:

BOOKS

A Tale of Two Cities   *The Color Purple*

CHOREOGRAPHIC WORKS

Martha Graham's *Frontier*   Agnes de Mille's *Rodeo*

FILMS AND VIDEOS

Black Orpheus *Gone with the Wind*

JOURNALS

New England Journal of Medicine *Written Communication*

LONG MUSICAL WORKS

Brandenburg Concertos The Who's *Tommy*

LONG POEMS

The Odyssey *Hiawatha*

MAGAZINES

Time the *New Yorker*

NEWSPAPERS

the *New York Times* the Cleveland *Plain Dealer*

PAMPHLETS

Thomas Paine's *Common Sense*

PAINTINGS AND SCULPTURE

Picasso's *Three Musicians* O'Keeffe's *Black Iris*

PLAYS

Long Day's Journey into Night *Gypsy*

TELEVISION AND RADIO PROGRAMS

Saturday Night Live *All Things Considered*

RECORDINGS

Pearl Jam's *Ten* Bonnie Raitt's *Luck of the Draw*

Note that sacred books, such as the Bible and the Koran, and public documents, such as the Constitution and the Magna Carta, are *not* italicized. Notice also with magazines and newspapers that an initial *the* is neither italicized nor capitalized, even if part of the official name.

Everyday Use

Look around, and you'll see italics used in many ways: on signs, in pamphlets, on the sides of trucks. On a recent visit to Chicago, a student looking for good, cheap food found this listing in a visitor's guide.

Gold Coast Dogs (418 North State). Chicago is serious about hot dogs. A good Chicago hot dog is an all-beef critter with natural casing, in a steamed bun and topped with your choice of the following (aka *everything*): yellow mustard, relish, raw chopped onion, tomato wedges, a dill pickle sliced lengthwise, maybe jalapeño peppers if you're perverse, and celery salt. A good Chicago hot dog *never* touches catsup, brown mustard, cooked onions, cheese, or sauerkraut.

For what purposes are the italics used? Look around you for some examples of italics in use, and bring in two or three interesting examples to compare with those discovered by your classmates.

38b

Using italics for words, letters, and numbers referred to as words

Italicize words, letters, or numbers referred to as words.

What's vulgar? Some people might say that the contraction of the words *what* and *is* itself is vulgar.

— JOSEPH EPSTEIN, "What Is Vulgar?"

One characteristic of some New York speech is the absence of postvocalic *r*, with some New Yorkers, for example, pronouncing the word *four* as "fouh."

The first four orbitals are represented by the letters *s, p, d,* and *f.*

On the back of his jersey was the famous *24.*

Italics are also sometimes used to signal a word that is being defined.

Learning to play the flute depends mostly on *embouchure*—the way in which the lips are positioned over the mouthpiece.

38c

Using italics for foreign words and phrases

Italicize words and phrases from other languages unless they are so frequently used by English speakers that they have come to be considered a part of English. The French word *bourgeois* and the Italian *pasta*, for instance, do *not* need to be italicized. If you are in doubt about a particular word, consult the guidelines offered by most dictionaries. As a rule, if the word is in the dictionary it should not be italicized.

> At last one of the phantom sleighs gliding along the street would come to a stop, and with gawky haste Mr. Burness in his fox-furred *shapka* would make for our door.
> — VLADIMIR NABOKOV, *Speak, Memory*

> I was *un católico* before I was a Catholic.
> — RICHARD RODRIGUEZ, *Hunger of Memory*

Note that Latin genus and species names are always italicized.

> The caterpillars of *Hapalia*, when attacked by the wasp *Apanteles machaeralis*, drop suddenly from their leaves and suspend themselves in air by a silken thread.
> — STEPHEN JAY GOULD, "Nonmoral Nature"

38d

Using italics for the names of vehicles

Italicize names of specific aircraft, spacecraft, ships, and trains. Do not italicize types and classes, such as Learjet, space shuttle, and Concorde.

AIRCRAFT AND SPACECRAFT

Spirit of St. Louis   *Discovery*

SHIPS

the *Santa Maria*   U.S.S. *Iowa*

TRAINS

the *Orient Express*   Amtrak's *Silver Star*

38e

Using italics for special emphasis

Italics can be used to help create emphasis in writing.

Now is the time to make real the promises of democracy.
— MARTIN LUTHER KING, JR., "I Have a Dream"

Gil's homer pulled the cork, and now there arose from all over the park a full, furious, happy shout of "Let's go, *Mets!* Let's go, *Mets!*" There were wild cries of encouragement before every pitch, boos for every called strike. . . . The fans' hopes, of course, *were* insane.
— ROGER ANGELL, *The Summer Game*

We believe we must be the family of America, recognizing that at the heart of the matter we are bound one to another, that the problems of a retired schoolteacher in Duluth are *our* problems. That the future of the child in Buffalo is *our* future. The struggle of a disabled man in Boston to survive, to live decently, is *our* struggle. The hunger of a woman in Little Rock *our* hunger. The failure anywhere to provide what reasonably we might, to avoid pain, is *our* failure.
— MARIO CUOMO, "Keynote Address,"
1984 Democratic National Convention

Italics can be useful, especially in informal writing, but use them sparingly. It is usually better to create emphasis with sentence structure and word choice.

EXERCISE 38.1

In each of the following sentences, underline any words that should be italicized and circle any italicized words that should not be. Example:

Critics debated whether <u>Thelma & Louise</u> was a feminist film.

1. Hawthorne's story My Kinsman, Major Molineux bears a striking resemblance to Shakespeare's play A Midsummer Night's Dream.
2. Is Samuel Beckett's play Endgame a sequel to Shakespeare's King Lear?
3. Georgetown offers a *potpourri* of cultures and styles.
4. The word veterinary comes from the Latin *veterinarius*.
5. Niko Tinbergen's essay The Bee-Hunters of Hulshorst is a diary of experiments on *Philanthus triangulum Fabr*, the *bee-killer wasp*.
6. Flying the Glamorous Glennis, named for his wife, Chuck Yeager was the first pilot to fly faster than the speed of sound.
7. The Washington Post provides extensive coverage of Congress.
8. The Waste Land is a long and difficult but ultimately rewarding poem.

9. If you have seen only a reproduction of Picasso's Guernica, you can scarcely imagine the impact of the original painting.

10. The White Star liner Titanic sank in the North Atlantic in 1912.

THINKING CRITICALLY ABOUT ITALICS

Reading with an Eye for Italics

The following passage about a graduate English seminar uses italics in several different ways—for emphasis, for a foreign phrase, and for a title. Read the passage carefully, particularly noting the effects created by the italics. How would it differ without any italic emphasis? What other words or phrases might the author have italicized?

To get into this seminar, you had to submit to a grilling wherein you renounced all former allegiance to the then-current literary religion, New Criticism, which considered that only the text existed, not the world. I passed the interview by lying—cunningly, and against my real convictions. I said that probably the world *did* exist—and walked triumphantly into the seminar room.

There were four big tables arranged in a square, with everyone's feet sticking out into the open middle of the square. You could tell who was nervous, and how much, by watching the pairs of feet twist around each other. The Great Man presided awesomely from the high bar of the square. His head was a majestic granite-gray, like a centurion in command; he *looked* famous. His clean shoes twitched only slightly, and only when he was angry.

It turned out he was angry at me a lot of the time. He was angry because he thought me a disrupter, a rioter, a provocateur, and a fool; also crazy. And this was twenty years ago, before these things were *de rigueur* in the universities. Everything was very quiet in those days: there were only the Cold War and Korea and Joe McCarthy and the Old Old Nixon, and the only revolutionaries around were in Henry James's *The Princess Casamassima*.

– CYNTHIA OZICK, "We Are the Crazy Lady"

Thinking about Your Own Use of Italics

Write a paragraph or two describing the most eccentric person you know. Make a point of italicizing some words for special emphasis. Read your passage aloud to hear the effect of the italics. Consider italicizing any other words you wish to emphasize. Now explain each use of italics, stating in words the reason for them. If you find yourself unable to give a reason, ask yourself whether the word should in fact be italicized at all.

Then revise the passage to eliminate *all but one* use of italics. Try revising sentences and choosing more precise words to convey emphasis without italics. Compare the two versions, and decide which is more effective. Can you make any conclusions about using italics for emphasis?

39

Using Hyphens

the lady whose odd smile is the merest hyphen   – KARL SHAPIRO

*T*HE "MEREST" HYPHEN IS USED TO DIVIDE WORDS *at the end of a line and to link words or word parts (such as* hand-me-down *or* bye-bye). *As such, it serves purposes both mechanical and rhetorical. Its mechanical uses are fairly straightforward, with simple rules that tell us when and where we can divide a word at the end of a line. The rhetorical ones, however, are somewhat more complicated, for though they are governed in some cases by rules, they are defined in other cases by the needs of readers. The rhetorical usefulness of a hyphen is pointed out in the following anecdote:*

> I came across a word I thought was a series of typos for *collaborators.* Reading it again, I realized the word was *colaborers.* But a hyphen would have [prevented] all the confusion.   – STEWART BEACH

*Indeed, had the word included a hyphen—*co-laborers—*its meaning would have been instantly clear.*

Sometimes the dictionary will tell you whether to hyphenate a word. Other times, you will have to decide. This chapter will help you with the decisions and the rules about using hyphens.

39a

Using hyphens to divide words at the end of a line

It is best not to divide words between lines, but when you must do so, break words between syllables. The word *metaphor*, for instance, is made up of three syllables (*met-a-phor*), and you could break it after either the *t* or the *a*. All dictionaries show syllable breaks, so the best advice for dividing words correctly is simply to look them up. In addition, you should follow certain other conventions.

- *Never divide one-syllable words*, even relatively long words.

- *Divide compound words only between the parts.* Words such as *anklebone* or *mother-in-law* should be broken between their parts (*ankle-bone*) or at their hyphens (*mother-in-law*).

- *Divide words with prefixes or suffixes between the parts.* The word *disappear-ance*, then, might be broken after its prefix (*dis-appearance*) or before its suffix (*disappear-ance*). Prefixed words that include a hyphen, such as *self-righteous*, should be divided at the hyphen.

- *Never divide abbreviations, contractions, or figures.* Though such "words" as *NASA*, *didn't*, and *150,000* have audible syllables, do not divide them in writing.

- *Leave at least two letters on each line when dividing a word.* Words such as *acorn* (*a-corn*) or *scratchy* (*scratch-y*) may not be divided at all, and a word such as *Americana* (*A-mer-i-can-a*) can be broken only after the *r* or *i*.

EXERCISE 39.1

Divide each of the following words into syllables, first referring to your dictionary. Then indicate with a hyphen the places where you might break each word at the end of a line. Indicate any words that cannot be divided into syllables or broken at the end of a line.

1. passable
2. retract
3. stripped
4. military
5. antechamber
6. inner-directed
7. haven't
8. dimming
9. anonymous
10. attitude

Everyday Use

Hyphens play a number of roles in our everyday lives. On any day, we might make a left-hand turn, order a medium-sized Coke, wear a Dodgers T-shirt, buy gasoline at a self-service station, drop in at the campus writing center for some one-on-one tutoring, worry about a long-term relationship, listen to some fifties rock-and-roll, or go out for Tex-Mex food. Jot down some of the hyphens you run across in a day.

39b

Using hyphens with compound words

Compound words are made up of more than one word (*rowboat, up-to-date*). Some compounds are written as one word, some as separate words, and some with hyphens.

ONE WORD	housefly, textbook, flowerpot
SEPARATE WORDS	high school, parking meter, floppy disk
WITH HYPHENS	city-state, sister-in-law, jack-of-all-trades

It is often difficult to remember whether a particular compound word is one word, separate words, or hyphenated. Even compounds that begin with the same word are often treated every which way—*blueberry, blue-ribbon*, and *blue cheese*, for instance. In general, then, consult the dictionary if you have any doubt about how to spell a compound. There are, in addition, some conventions that can guide you in using hyphens with compound words.

1

Hyphenating compound adjectives

Often you will use adjectives made up of word combinations that are not listed in a dictionary. The guiding principle then is to hyphenate most compound adjectives that precede a noun but not those that follow a noun.

a *well-liked* boss	My boss is *well liked*.
a *six-foot* plank	The plank is *six feet* long.

In general, the reason for hyphenating such compound adjectives is to facilitate reading. Notice, for example, how the hyphen affects your understanding of the following two sentences.

The designers used potted palms as living room dividers.

The designers used potted palms as *living-room* dividers.

In the first sentence, the word *living* may seem to modify *room dividers;* in the second, the hyphen makes clear that it is part of a compound adjective. But commonly used compound adjectives do not need to be hyphenated for clarity—*income tax reform* or *first class mail* would seldom if ever be misunderstood. Never hyphenate a combination of an adverb ending in *-ly* and an adjective: *a radically different approach*.

Compound adjectives formed from two proper nouns are hyphenated if the compound noun is hyphenated: *African American literature* (but *Austro-Hungarian history*).

2

Hyphenating coined compounds

You may sometimes want to use hyphens to link words that would not normally be hyphenated but that you are using in an unexpected way, especially as an adjective. Such combinations are called **coined compounds**.

It was an established Daddy-said-so fact. . . .

Before it reached the top of the porch it went off, a piece of tin shot God-is-whipping-you straight for Eddy's eye.

— Maxine Clair, "Cherry Bomb"

3

Hyphenating fractions and compound numbers

To write out fractions, use a hyphen to join the numerator and denominator. Also use hyphens to spell out whole numbers from twenty-one to ninety-nine, both when they stand alone and when they are part of larger numbers. (Usually such larger numbers should be written as numerals.)

one-seventh   thirty-seven
seven-sixteenths   three hundred fifty-four thousand

4

Using suspended hyphens

A series of compound words that share the same base word can be shortened by the use of suspended hyphens.

Each student should do the work *him-* or *herself.*

39c

Using hyphens with prefixes and suffixes

Most words with prefixes or suffixes are written without hyphens: *antiwar, gorillalike.* Only in the following cases do you need a hyphen:

WITH CAPITALIZED BASE WORDS

pro-Democratic, un-American, non-Catholic

WITH FIGURES

pre-1960, post-1945

WITH CERTAIN PREFIXES AND SUFFIXES

all-state, ex-husband, self-possessed, quasi-legislative,
mayor-elect, fifty-odd, twenty-some

Note that hyphens are used with *ex-* and *-some* only when these mean "former" and "approximately," respectively.

WITH COMPOUND WORDS

pre-high school, pro-civil rights, post-cold war

FOR CLARITY OR EASE OF READING

re-cover, anti-inflation, troll-like

Re-cover means "cover again"; the hyphen distinguishes it from *recover*, meaning "get well." In *anti-inflation* and *troll-like*, the hyphens separate confusing clusters of vowels and consonants.

EXERCISE 39.2

Using the dictionary as a reference, insert hyphens as needed.

1. deescalate
2. pre World War II
3. pre and post-Wall Berlin
4. happily married couple
5. a what me worry look
6. self important
7. president elect
8. seven hundred thirty three
9. a hard working farmer
10. a politician who is fast talking

EXERCISE 39.3

Insert or delete hyphens as necessary, and correct any incorrect word divisions in the following sentences. Use your dictionary if necessary.

1. Stress can lead to hypertension and ulcers.
2. The drum-beating and hand-clapping signaled that the parade was near.
3. The carpenter asked for a two pound bag of three quarter inch nails.
4. Suicide among teen-agers has tripled in the past thirty five years.
5. We urged him to be open minded and to temper his insensitive views.
6. Both pro and antiState Department groups registered complaints.
7. One of Mikhail Baryshnikov's favorite dancers was none other than Fred A-staire.

8. In Bizet's *Carmen*, the ill-fated Carmen is betrayed by her fickle-ness.
9. The governor elect joked about the preelection polls.
10. The beautifully-written essay earned high praise.

THINKING CRITICALLY ABOUT HYPHENATION

Reading with an Eye for Hyphenation

The following paragraph uses many hyphens. Read it carefully, and note how the hyphens make the paragraph easier to read. Why do you think *semi-pro* is hyphenated? Why is *junior-college* hyphenated in the last sentence?

All semi-pro leagues, it should be understood, are self-sustaining, and have no farm affiliation or other connection with the twenty-six major-league clubs, or with the seventeen leagues and hundred and fifty-two teams . . . that make up the National Association—the minors, that is. There is no central body of semi-pro teams, and semi-pro players are not included among the six hundred and fifty major-leaguers, the twenty-five hundred-odd minor-leaguers, plus all the managers, coaches, presidents, commissioners, front-office people, and scouts, who, taken together, constitute the great tent called organized ball. (A much diminished tent, at that; back in 1949, the minors included fifty-nine leagues, about four hundred and forty-eight teams, and perhaps ten thousand players.) Also outside the tent, but perhaps within its shade, are five college leagues, ranging across the country from Cape Cod to Alaska, where the most promising freshman, sophomore, and junior-college ballplayers . . . compete against each other. . . .   – ROGER ANGELL, "In the Country"

Thinking about Your Own Use of Hyphens

The difference between *re-sign* and *resign* is a hyphen.   – JIM PALMER

The above statement, heard on a televised baseball game, shows how important a hyphen can be. Look through some of your own writing to see if you ever use hyphens in a way that affects meaning or clarity. Have you followed the conventions governing use of hyphens in compound words, with prefixes and suffixes, with fractions and numbers? If you find you are misusing hyphens or are unclear about how to use them in certain situations, check those instances against this chapter. Note down any rules or thoughts about hyphenation for future use—in your writing log, if you keep one.

Part Eight

Doing Research and Using Sources

<>

40. Becoming a Researcher   552

41. Conducting Research   562

42. Using Sources   586

43. Writing a Research Essay   607

44. Documenting Sources: MLA Style   623

45. Documenting Sources: APA, CBE, and Chicago Styles   665

40

Becoming a Researcher

Research is formalized curiosity. It is poking and prying with a purpose.
— Zora Neale Hurston

*T*HE ENGLISH WORD research *derives not only from the French* chercher, *which means "to search," but also from the Late Latin* circare, *which means "to circle around, to explore." Research, then, is a way of exploring a subject by circling carefully around and around it, a process that the editors of the eleventh edition of the* Encyclopaedia Britannica *identify as all "investigations . . . based on sources of knowledge." Without research, they go on, "no authoritative words could have been written, no scientific discoveries or inventions made, no theories of any value propounded."*

Work in many professions—engineering, news reporting, law, medicine, criminal justice—relies heavily on research. But the process of investigating sources, compiling data, and drawing conclusions pervades our personal lives as well as our work. We find something out, and then we act on it. This chapter thus rests on the assumption that we are all researchers. From this basic assumption come five important premises.

1. *You already know how to do research.* You act as a researcher whenever you investigate something—whether a college, a course, a cosmetic, a computer, or a car—by reading up on it, discussing its features with your friends or with experts, or perhaps checking several stores to see what is in stock and how much it costs.

In addition, you already have essential research skills. You know how to combine experience, observation, and new information when you solve a problem, answer a question, make a decision, or analyze a situation. You know how to seek out pieces of information, evaluate their usefulness, fit them all together, and then use them to make an "educated guess." Such basic research skills are important for working and living. These are the skills you will build on as you become more familiar with academic research.

2. *Good research makes you a genuine expert.* If you approach your research with serious intent, you may gradually become someone who knows more than anyone else on campus about Dickinson's last poems, new uses for metal hybrids, or Jackie Robinson's place in sports history. You will be truly knowledgeable, and you will be able to add your knowledge to the educated conversation that takes place not only in college but also in the media, in community groups, and in the workplace.

3. *Research is usually driven by a purpose.* Whether for common everyday needs or in an academic setting, researchers seek out facts and opinions for a reason—to make a discovery; to answer a question, solve a problem, or prove something; to teach; or to advocate a position. Research is rarely an end in itself. Instead, it is a process or method used in many situations and fields for systematically discovering, testing, and sharing new ideas.

Your main purpose in college research will most often be to fulfill a specific assignment: for example, to compare literary texts, to trace the causes of the Civil War, or to survey and summarize students' feelings about mandatory drug testing of athletes. Sometimes, however, you may be asked to determine your own purpose for research.

4. *Your purpose influences the research you do, which in turn refines your purpose.* When you begin any research, it is impossible to know exactly what you will find out. You begin with a question you want to answer or a general idea that you want to explore, but you may find that your specific purpose shifts as you learn more about your subject. The evidence you have gathered, for example, may prove so startling that it calls for you to persuade—to advocate a solution to a problem—when you originally had meant only to explain the problem. In turn, as you refine your purpose, that purpose will help guide you in choosing additional sources and organizing material.

5. *Research rarely progresses in a neat line from start to finish.* You begin with a question that you may or may not be able to support. Then you do some background research and perhaps some writing. Your initial investigation may lead you to start all over—or to modify your idea and then refer to other sources. This additional research focuses your idea even more, leading you to more specific sources. Writing is an important part of this investigative process, for it forces you to sharpen your ideas and perhaps turn back to your sources for more information. Wherever the process takes you, however, your overriding goal remains the same: to develop a strong critical understanding of the information you are gathering.

One student's experience illustrates how ideas can change and develop during the research process. Assigned to write an essay on any topic, he began by puzzling over whether modern rock-guitar styles could be traced

---

Everyday Use

Your employer tells you that the company needs a new intercom system and asks you to recommend the best system for the money. You have an opportunity to visit Tokyo for a week. You need to plan that week—to find out where to stay, what to see, what to do. You are on a tight budget and want to find the local grocery with the lowest prices. Each of these situations calls for research. Take a few minutes to think of occasions in the last month when you conducted some kind of research. Then decide if there were any times you *didn't* do any research but might—or should—have done some.

---

to the electric-guitar styles developed in the 1940s and 1950s by Chicago blues groups. Starting with background sources about modern rock guitarists like Eric Clapton and Pete Townshend, he found repeated references to Muddy Waters, Howlin' Wolf, Buddy Guy, Albert King, and other Chicago blues artists. He listened to a number of records and found repeated riffs (musical phrases) and clear derivations. Based on the information he found and his understanding of the records themselves, he began to make notes for an essay.

This student's research might have ended here, but it did not. In several sources on the Chicago electric blues tradition, he found references to country blues and southern race records as influences on the Chicago artists. He was not sure what these terms meant, but then he discovered that blues music harks back to nineteenth-century slave songs, that country blues was nearly always played on a single acoustic guitar, and that the history of country blues guitar styles traces back to the 1920s.

Clearly the story was older and the traditions deeper than he had imagined. He got more books about southern and country blues musicians of the 1920s and 1930s to learn about the guitar styles of musicians like Charley Patton, Robert Johnson, Leadbelly, Mississippi John Hurt, and Lightnin' Hopkins. He began to consider the differences between electric and acoustic instruments. Finally, he looked for recordings by some of the early country blues musicians. To his amazement, he heard on these early recordings some of the exact riffs and techniques he so admired in the work of contemporary guitarists.

Thus did this writer arrive at a deeper idea for development, a far better grasp of music history, and more research sources. And he had accumulated enough information to begin crafting a fine essay.

Research for writing

College research may range from a couple of hours spent gathering background about a topic or evidence for an argument for a brief essay to weeks or months of full-scale exploration for a term paper. Chapters 40–45 provide guidelines to help you with *any* research done for the purpose of writing. In addition, these chapters show examples of work by Daniel Taffe, a student whose complete essay appears in Chapter 44. An additional complete essay appears in Chapter 45.

40a

Understanding research assignments and topics

In college, most research you do is in response to a writing assignment. Before you do anything else, therefore, be sure you understand the requirements and limits of the assignment. For his introductory writing course, Daniel Taffe received the following assignment:

> Choose a subject, a person, or an event that you want to know more about, and use it as the topic for a research essay that makes and substantiates a claim. *Note:* Because you have only one month to complete the essay, be sure that your topic is not too broad and that information about the topic is available.

1

Analyzing a research assignment

Pay close attention to the exact wording of the assignment. If it is not handed out in printed form, copy it carefully, word for word. Note whether it specifies a topic or asks you to choose your own. Consider any requirements for purpose, audience, scope of research, length, and deadline as you choose a topic. (See 40a2 for more on choosing topics.) Then try to map out a rough schedule for your research, consulting the one on p. 557.

Upon questioning, Daniel Taffe's instructor clarified some requirements of his research assignment: the essay should use information from multiple sources to support the claim; it should be roughly ten to fifteen pages in length; and it should be written for members of the writing class.

Identifying the purpose

Read through the assignment for **cue words,** such as *describe, survey, analyze, explain, classify, compare,* or *contrast,* that specify the pattern the essay is to follow. What do such words mean in this field? Keeping these meanings in mind as you begin researching will help you identify sources that fulfill the purpose. (See 2d for a discussion of ways to assess purpose.)

Identifying the audience

Find out whether your assignment specifies an audience other than the instructor. Then, to consider what your audience and/or your instructor will expect of you, answer the following questions:

- Who will be interested in the information you gather, and why?
- What do you know about their backgrounds?
- What will they want to know? What will they already know?
- What response do you want to elicit from them?
- What assumptions might they hold about the topic?
- What kinds of evidence will you need to present to convince them?
- What will your instructor expect in a strong essay on this topic?

See 2g for additional questions to consider about your audience.

Considering your rhetorical stance

When you have a broad topic, think about your own attitude toward it, your stance. Are you just curious about it? Do you like it? dislike it? find it bewildering? (See 2h.) What influences have shaped your stance?

Gauging the scope of your research

Next consider the kind of research you will need to do. Does the assignment specify how many or what kind of library sources you should use? Does it suggest any field research—interviewing, surveying, or observing?

Noting the length of the essay

Does your assignment specify the length of the final draft? The amount of research and writing time you need for a five-page essay differs markedly from that for a fifteen-page essay. And you may need more time if materials are not available or if you discover after a first draft that you must do more research. The best plan is to begin work as soon as possible.

Working toward the deadline

When is the project due? Are any preliminary materials—a working bibliography, a thesis, an outline, a first draft—due before this date?

Keeping a research log

You might set up a **research log** for keeping track of your work. In the log, jot down thoughts about your topic, lists of things to do, and ideas about possible sources, and keep track of library materials.

≫ *Scheduling a research project*

> Assignment date: _____   Try to complete by:
>
> Analyze assignment; decide on primary purpose and
>   audience; choose topic if necessary.
> Arrange library tour; develop search strategy.   _____
> Do background reading; narrow topic if necessary.   _____
> Decide on research question, tentative hypothesis.   _____
> Start working bibliography; track down sources.   _____
> Develop working thesis and rough outline.   _____
> If necessary, conduct interviews, make observations, or
>   distribute and collect questionnaires.   _____
> Send for materials needed by mail.   _____
> Read and evaluate sources; take notes.   _____
> Draft explicit thesis and outline.   _____
> Prepare first draft.   _____
> Obtain and evaluate critical responses.   _____
> Do more research if necessary.   _____
> Revise draft.   _____
> Prepare list of works cited.   _____
> Edit revised draft; use spell checker if available.   _____
> Prepare final draft.   _____
> Do final proofreading.   _____
>
> Final draft due: _____

2

Choosing a topic

Sometimes a research topic may choose you: it so fascinates or compels you that you simply must explore it. Other times a specific topic is assigned, or the choice is limited in some way. Even in these cases, however, you will probably have some leeway in tailoring the topic to your interests.

If your assignment does not specify a topic, you can best begin articulating one by keeping in mind any specifications about purpose, audience, scope, length, and deadline (see 40a1) and by considering the following questions:

- What subjects do you know something about?
- What subjects might you like to become an expert on?
- What subjects evoke a strong reaction from you—intense attraction, puzzlement, or skepticism?

In addition, skim through your textbooks or class notes, current magazines or journals, or standard reference works, looking for some topic or question that intrigues you. You may find the techniques presented in 3a for exploring a topic—brainstorming, freewriting, looping, clustering, and questioning—useful for discovering one. Even if your instructor has assigned a broad topic—such as animal rights or the role of the United States after the cold war—you may find these questions and methods useful in deciding on what aspect of it to research.

Daniel Taffe decided to find out about artist Diego Rivera. The library circulation computer led him to Rivera's autobiography, *My Art, My Life*. In skimming this text, what really caught his imagination were the discussions about Frida Kahlo, Rivera's wife. Because he had not progressed far in his research, he decided to shift his topic and find out more about Kahlo.

Getting response to your topic

As soon as you come up with a topic, draft several sentences that describe it. Then try to get some response—from your instructor and perhaps from some classmates. Ask them the following questions:

- Would you be interested in reading about this topic?
- Does the topic seem manageable?
- Can you suggest any interesting angles or approaches?
- Can you suggest any good sources of information on this topic?

40b

Narrowing and focusing a topic

Any topic you choose to research must be manageable—must suit the scope, audience, length, and time limits of your assignment. Making a topic manageable often requires narrowing it, but narrowing is not always sufficient in itself. "World War II" may be too general, but "The Battle of Midway" will probably not be any more manageable. Rather than simply reducing a large subject to a smaller one, then, *focus* on a particular slant, looking for a governing question to guide your research. One good way to work toward such a question is by brainstorming to generate a series of questions you might ask about your topic. You can then evaluate them and choose one or two that seem most interesting and most manageable.

Asking a research question and developing a hypothesis

The result of the focusing process is a **research question** that can be answered or considered through research data. The research question may be tentatively answered by a **hypothesis**, a statement of what you anticipate your research will show. (If the research question you pose has an obvious answer or requires technical knowledge beyond your grasp, refocus your question.)

Like a working thesis (see 3b), a hypothesis must be not only manageable but interesting and specific. In addition, it must be arguable, a debatable proposition that can be proved or disproved by research evidence (see 5c). For example, a statement like this one cannot be disproved: "Senator Joseph McCarthy attracted great attention with his anti-Communist crusade during the 1950s." No one would argue against this fact, and its statement is not a hypothesis. On the other hand, this statement is debatable: "Roy Cohn's political views and biased research while he was an assistant to Senator Joseph McCarthy were largely responsible for McCarthy's anti-Communist crusade." Such a statement would have to be proved or disproved; thus it is a hypothesis.

In most cases, before you formulate a research question or develop a hypothesis, you will want to explore your topic by doing background reading in general reference books and making notes. In moving from a general topic of interest, such as Senator Joseph McCarthy's anti-Communist crusade of the 1950s, to a useful hypothesis, such as the one in the previous paragraph, you first focus on a single manageable issue within the field, such as Roy Cohn's role in the crusade. After background reading, you then raise a question about that issue ("To what extent did Cohn's political views and research contribute to McCarthy's crusade?") and put forward a possible answer, your hypothesis. Throughout this process, you will profit by trying to articulate your thoughts.

Here is how Daniel Taffe moved from general topic to hypothesis:

TOPIC	Frida Kahlo's art
ISSUE	Influences on Kahlo's art
RESEARCH QUESTION	What were the major influences on Kahlo's work?
HYPOTHESIS	The events of her own life were the central influence on Kahlo's work.

The hypothesis that tentatively answers the research question is precise enough to be supported or challenged by a manageable amount of research.

40c

Investigating what you know about your topic

Once you have narrowed and focused a topic, you need to marshal everything you already know about it. This step calls for what computer scientists call a data dump: you dump onto paper all your immediate thoughts about the topic. Here are some strategies for doing so:

- *Brainstorming.* Take five minutes to list, in words or phrases, everything you think of or wonder about your hypothesis. You may find it helpful to do this in a group, with other students. (See 3a1.)

- *Freewriting in favor of your hypothesis.* For five minutes, write about every reason for believing your hypothesis is true. As in any freewriting (see 3a2), do not stop writing until the time is up.

- *Freewriting in* opposition *to your hypothesis.* For five minutes, write down every argument you can think of, no matter how weak or improbable, that someone opposed to your hypothesis might make.

- *Freewriting about your audience.* Write for five minutes about your readers, including your instructor. What do they currently believe about your topic? What sorts of evidence will convince them to accept your hypothesis? What sorts of sources will they respect?

- *Tapping your memory for sources.* List, in the form of short notes, everything you can remember about *where* you learned about your topic: computer bulletin boards, E-mail, books, magazines, courses, conversations, television. Much of what you know may seem like common knowledge, but common knowledge comes from somewhere, and "somewhere" can serve as a starting point for investigation.

40d

Moving from hypothesis to working thesis

As you gather information and begin reading sources, your research question is likely to be refined, and your hypothesis is likely to change significantly. Only after you have explored it, tested it, and sharpened it by reading and writing does the hypothesis become a **working thesis**.

The hypothesis mentioned in 40b, for instance, might be focused further or even completely changed once research begins. The writer might find the influences on McCarthy's crusade so difficult to trace that he or she would refocus the essay on why the crusade found such widespread public support or why it ended when it did. In Daniel Taffe's case, he found that the events of Kahlo's life as influences on her work were so well established that they could not be considered a hypothesis. Therefore, he shifted his attention to other influences and developed the following working thesis: "Frida Kahlo's unique style results not only from her life events but also from her knowledge of European and Mexican art."

In doing your own research, you may find that your interest shifts, that a whole line of inquiry is unproductive, that a work you need in order to complete an argument is not available, or that your hypothesis is simply wrong. In each case, the process of research pushes you to learn more and more about your hypothesis, to make it more focused and precise, to become an expert on your topic. You are, in short, becoming a researcher.

THINKING CRITICALLY ABOUT RESEARCH

If you have done research for an essay before, go back and evaluate the work you did as a researcher and as a writer in light of the principles developed in this chapter. What was the purpose of the research? Who was your audience? How was your topic focused? What kinds of sources did you use? What about your research and your essay pleased you most? What pleased you least? What advice would you give yourself if you were to revise the essay?

41

Conducting Research

As Indiana Jones's exploits suggest, research and adventure go hand in hand. Scientist June Goodfield speaks of research in the following way:

> The reason why [research] is so absorbing and exciting is that every new fact may be important, and so every new day may be important. As you go through the process, there is no way you can tell beforehand which fact, or which day, is going to be the golden one.

Goodfield's passage captures one of the essential pleasures of conducting research: the anticipation and excitement of learning something new. This chapter describes two kinds of research that can lead to such learning—library/database research and field research.

41a

Using primary and secondary sources

Samuel Johnson once remarked that "knowledge is of two kinds: we know a subject ourselves, or we know where we can find information upon it." In this sentence, Johnson summed up the distinction between primary sources, or firsthand knowledge, and secondary sources, knowledge available from the research of others.

Primary sources are the basic sources of raw information. Primary sources include notes you take in the field; laboratory experiments, surveys, or interviews you conduct; objects or artwork you examine; literary works you read; and performances you attend. Other primary sources are diaries, letters, eyewitness accounts of events, contemporary news reports, historical documents, and the raw data from experiments conducted by others.

Secondary sources are accounts produced by other investigators. They include scholars', experts', and researchers' reports and analyses of other people's laboratory work, field experiences, surveys, and so forth. Secondary sources also include critical writing, such as biographies and reviews.

Often what constitutes a primary or secondary source depends on your purpose or field. A critic's evaluation of a painting, for instance, serves as a secondary work if you are writing an essay on that painting, but it serves as a primary work if you are conducting a study of the critic's writings.

Most research writing depends on both primary and secondary sources. The primary sources ground the project in facts from firsthand accounts and discoveries, while the secondary sources provide background for investigation and support for conclusions. Daniel Taffe, for example, eventually refocused his research on imagery in the paintings of Frida Kahlo, which he traced to imagery in a number of Renaissance paintings and to Mexican art and culture—all primary sources. In discussing these works, he cites biographies, works of art criticism, and articles on the Kahlo Museum and recent sales of Kahlo's work—all secondary sources.

Unlike Taffe's essay, some research projects, such as a background survey or a review of the literature on a given topic, may require no primary sources at all. Secondary sources, on the other hand, are necessary for most research projects; even a report of a laboratory experiment is sometimes prefaced by a discussion of what other researchers have done previously. Research often builds on secondary sources in this way. You read to find out what is known or not known about a problem; you formulate a question based on what needs to be found out; then you devise a research method to answer that question.

Everyday Use

A few moments' thought may bring to mind some piece of everyday research you have done that required both reading and some kind of field work, like interviewing someone or taking a survey. An enterprising pair of writers with a passion for ice cream, for instance, wanted to write an article for a local magazine on the best ice cream in Pittsburgh. Their guiding research questions (who has the best ice cream, and what makes it best?) led them first to the library, where they did background reading on the history of ice cream and the way it is made. Then they went into the field, systematically tasting ice cream all over the city and interviewing ice-cream makers.

Think of a topic close to your home that you'd like to find out more about, and imagine how you'd go about doing so. Would you go to a library? ask friends? observe something directly?

41b

Exploring library and database resources

The library is one of a researcher's best friends, for the tasks of answering a research question and exploring and testing a hypothesis most often begin there. Libraries provide two necessary kinds of information: general background, which will give you an overview of your topic and place your research question in context, and particular support, which helps answer your research question and develop your hypothesis.

1

Beginning your library research

Start by reviewing your research question, your hypothesis, and the knowledge you already have about your topic (see 40b and c). Where did that knowledge come from? Do you own any books about your topic? Have you recently read any magazine articles about it? Do your textbooks help? This is the time to begin to list possible sources (see 42a).

Next turn to acquaintances who may be able to point you in useful directions. If, for instance, you are writing about computers and a student down the hall knows a lot about them, go and talk to her. What books does she recommend? Does she have any computer magazines?

Finally, talk to your instructor, who may be able to suggest where to begin looking for sources. If he or she has not arranged a library orientation tour for your class, find out about regularly scheduled tours, go along, and ask about sources for your topic.

Developing a research strategy

At this point, you are ready to begin your library research. The quick-reference checklist that follows on p. 565 will help you make up a preliminary list of sources you want to check when you arrive at the library.

Because Daniel Taffe found little about the topic he wanted to research—Frida Kahlo's life and art—in general reference books, he moved on to his college library catalog, which led him to some books about Kahlo. He also checked InfoTrac, a periodicals database on CD-ROM that he accessed through a computer terminal in the library; there he found a few recent articles about Kahlo, her paintings, and Mexican art. Noticing that a frequently cited biography was published in 1983, he checked periodical indexes for that year and in *The Readers' Guide to Periodical Literature* and *The Humanities Index* found reviews of the biography. Because he was interested in the autobiographical elements in Kahlo's work, he also checked the MLA (Modern Language Association) database as well as PsycLIT, a database of literature published in the field of psychology. These collections yielded some additional sources.

After doing some reading in the materials he found, he spoke again with his instructor, who brainstormed with him about the ideas he was exploring and then suggested that he interview an art historian. The interview helped him decide which of his ideas to pursue and which to drop. He then returned to the library and, after locating some more sources, felt he had enough material to support a working thesis.

≫ *Directory of library resources*

> Guides to reference books and databases (41b2)
> Encyclopedias (41b2)
> Biographical resources (41b2)
> Almanacs, yearbooks, and atlases (41b2)
> Book indexes (41b2)
> Periodical indexes (41b2)
> Computer databases (41b2)
> Library catalog (41b3)
> Vertical file (41b4)
> Special collections (41b4)
> Audio and video collections (41b4)
> Art collections (41b4)
> Interlibrary loans (41b4)

Identifying key words

Looking through card catalogs, indexes, or databases will go more efficiently if you have identified **key words** to look for—synonyms for your topic, broader terms that would include it, or appropriate subtopics. Information on ice cream, for instance, might appear under the heading of frozen desserts, dairy products, or sherbet.

A good place to check for key words is in the *Library of Congress Subject Headings,* which lists the headings under which books are cataloged in most libraries. As you search a particular print index or computer database, check its list of key words, or **descriptors**, because many indexes and databases use terms peculiar to their systems. Also check the glossary and index of appropriate textbooks. When Daniel Taffe searched one computer database, for example, he entered three key terms: *Frida Kahlo, Diego Rivera,* and *Mexican artists.*

Finding sources

Where to start? You may decide to begin your research with an overview, looking first at an encyclopedia, for example. This approach may be useful if you need a better focus on a research question or want to check for basic bibliographies. On the other hand, you may already have ideas about where to begin and so may go right to the library catalog and periodical indexes. Before you plunge in, however, ask yourself a few questions.

- *How much time do you have to spend?* If you have only two weeks to do your research, you will want to be selective. If you have several months, however, you can follow a broader course, perhaps even consulting materials beyond those available in your library.

- *How current do your sources need to be?* If you must investigate the very latest findings in a field, you will want to check periodicals. On the other hand, if you want broader, more detailed coverage and background information, you will look more to books.

- *Do you need to consult sources contemporary with an event or a person's life?* If your research deals with a specific time period, you may need to examine newspapers, magazines, and books written during that period.

- *What kinds of sources do you need to consult?* Check your assignment to see whether you are required to consult different kinds of sources. If you must use primary sources, find out whether they are readily available or whether you must make special arrangements to see them. If you need to locate nonprint sources or items in special collections, find out where they are kept and whether you need special permission to examine them.

- *How many sources should you consult?* You can expect to look over many more sources than you will actually end up using. Your best guideline is to make sure you have enough sources to support your hypothesis or prove your thesis. Check to see whether your assignment specifies a minimum or maximum number of sources.

Consulting the library staff

Your most valuable source at the library is the highly trained staff, especially the reference librarians. To get the most helpful advice from them, pose *specific* questions: not "Where can I find information about computers?" but "Where can I find information on the history of computers?" or "Where can I find the *Gale Directory of Databases*?" The more precise your question, the more useful an answer you will get.

If you find yourself unable to ask clear and precise questions, you probably need to do some general background research on your topic. Then work again on narrowing and focusing, defining a clearer issue, asking a more specific research question, and finding a sharper hypothesis. On your second trip to the library, you will be ready to ask more specific questions and find appropriate sources.

2

Selecting reference materials

Your library's reference collection includes two broad types of **reference materials**: those that are general in scope and those that deal with specific disciplines (music, zoology, political science, and so on). Guides to reference books can help you identify the ones that suit your purpose. Your research question can then help you choose the best sources to use. Among the types of sources most often consulted are encyclopedias, biographical dictionaries, summaries of current events, and book indexes. Many of these reference materials are available either on-line or on CD-ROM. These are noted accordingly (O or CD-ROM) in parentheses.

> *Gale Directory of Databases.* 1993–. Published yearly, this two-volume resource (one volume for on-line databases, the other for CD-ROM) is the most comprehensive index and guide to databases available.

> *Guide to Reference Books.* 10th ed. 1986. Edited by Eugene P. Sheehy, this large book is usually just called Sheehy. It supplies annotated lists of general reference works and specialized bibliographies and is divided into five sections: General Reference; Humanities; Social and Behavioral Sciences; History and Area Studies; and Science, Technology, and Medicine. Each section is further subdivided into areas and then into special approaches. Full bibliographic information, including the Library of Congress call number, is provided for each entry.

> *Walford's Guide to Reference Material.* 4th ed. 3 vols. 1980–86. *Walford's* three volumes deal with Science and Technology; Social and Historical Sciences, Philosophy, and Religion; and Generalities, Languages, the Arts, and Literature.

Encyclopedias

For general background on a subject, **encyclopedias** are a good place to begin, particularly because many include bibliographies. Though some encyclopedias do provide in-depth information, more often they serve as a place to start, not as a major source of information.

GENERAL ENCYCLOPEDIAS

> *Collier's Encyclopedia.* 24 vols. 1993. Designed to meet the needs of student research.

> *Encyclopedia Americana.* 30 vols. 1993. Pays particular attention to American public figures, institutions, and places.

> *New Encyclopaedia Britannica.* 32 vols. 1993. In three parts: the *Micropaedia,* which contains brief articles for quick reference, the *Macropaedia,* which contains longer entries that treat selected subjects in depth, and the *Propaedia,* which outlines the material covered in the *Micropaedia*

and the *Macropaedia*. For fine essays in the classics and humanities, see whether your library has the eleventh edition of the *Britannica*, published in 1911 and considered by many to be the most thoughtful and scholarly encyclopedia ever produced.

SPECIALIZED ENCYCLOPEDIAS

Compared with general encyclopedias, **specialized encyclopedias** usually provide more detailed articles by authorities in the field as well as extensive bibliographies for locating sources. Again, you should rely on these books more for background material than as major sources of information. These volumes are often located in the reference area for the particular discipline. Here are some examples:

Cambridge Ancient History. 12 vols. 1939–82, with later revisions.

Cambridge History of Africa. 8 vols. 1975–86.

Cambridge Medieval History. 9 vols. 1911–75.

Encyclopedia of Anthropology. 1976.

Encyclopedia of Asian History. 4 vols. 1988.

Encyclopedia of Banking and Finance. 1983.

Encyclopedia of Bioethics. 2 vols. 1982.

Encyclopedia of Biological Sciences. 1981.

Encyclopedia of Chemistry. 1983.

Encyclopedia of Computer Science and Technology. 21 vols. 1975–90.

Encyclopedia of Crime and Justice. 4 vols. 1983.

Encyclopedia of Education. 10 vols. 1971.

Encyclopedia of Management. 1982.

Encyclopedia of Philosophy. 8 vols. 1972.

Encyclopedia of Physical Education, Fitness, and Sports. 4 vols. 1991.

Encyclopedia of Physics. 1991.

Encyclopedia of Religion. 16 vols. 1987.

Encyclopedia of Social Work. 3 vols. 1990.

Encyclopedia of World Architecture. 2 vols. 1988.

Encyclopedia of World Art. 15 vols. 1959–68.

Encyclopedia of World History. 1972.

Harvard Guide to American History. 2 vols. 1974.

International Encyclopedia of the Social Sciences. 8 vols. 1979 and supplements.

McGraw-Hill Dictionary of Earth Sciences. 1984.

McGraw-Hill Dictionary of Modern Economics. 1983.

McGraw-Hill Encyclopedia of Economics. 1994.

McGraw-Hill Encyclopedia of Science and Technology.
   20 vols. 1993. (O, CD-ROM)

McGraw-Hill Encyclopedia of World Drama. 5 vols. 1984.

New Cambridge Modern History. 14 vols. 1957–75.

New Grove Dictionary of Music and Musicians. 20 vols. 1987.

Oxford Classical Dictionary. 1977.

Oxford Companion to American Literature. 1986.

Oxford Companion to English Literature. 1987.

Consult a reference librarian about any other specialized encyclopedias relating to the discipline you are researching.

Biographical resources

The lives and historical settings of famous people are the topics of biographical dictionaries and indexes. If the person you are researching is dead, consider whether you want to consult a current volume covering deceased people or a volume covering living people that was published during your subject's lifetime. Here are a few examples of biographical reference works; many others, particularly volumes specialized by geographic area or field, are available.

African American Biographies. 1992–. Provides current profiles of 558 notable men and women.

Biography Index. 1946–; quarterly. Lists biographical material found in current books and over 2,600 periodicals. (O, CD-ROM for July 1984–present)

Contemporary Authors. 1967–; annual. Short biographies of authors who have published works during the year. (CD-ROM)

Current Biography. 1940–; monthly, with annual cumulations. Informative articles on people in current events. Includes photographs and short bibliographies. (O, CD-ROM, 1984–)

Dictionary of American Biography. 1927–37 and supplements. Contains biographies of over 15,000 deceased Americans from all phases of public life since Colonial days. Entries include bibliographies of sources.

Dictionary of National Biography. 1885–1900 and supplements through 1985. Covers deceased notables from Great Britain and its colonies (excluding the post-Colonial United States).

International Who's Who. 1935–; annual. Contains biographies of persons of international status.

Notable American Women: 1607–1950. 3 vols. 1972. Supplement, *Notable American Women: The Modern Period.* 1980. Contains biographies (with bibliographies) of women who contributed to North American society. The supplement covers women who died between 1951 and 1975.

Webster's New Biographical Dictionary. 1983–. Provides biographical information on important deceased people of the last 5,000 years.

Who's Who. 1849–; annual. Covers well-known living British people. *Who Was Who,* with volumes covering about a decade each, lists British notables who died between 1897 and the present.

Who's Who in America. 1899–; biannual. Information about famous living North Americans. Notable Americans no longer living are in *Who Was Who in America,* covering 1607 to the present. Similar specialized works include *Who's Who of American Women, Who's Who of Black Americans, Who's Who in Government,* and so on.

Almanacs, yearbooks, and atlases

Almanacs, yearbooks, atlases, and other sources provide information on current events and statistical and geographic data. In addition to the following works, each of the general encyclopedias listed earlier in this section publishes an annual yearbook surveying events and developments of the preceding year in various fields.

ALMANACS, YEARBOOKS, NEWS DIGESTS

Facts on File: News Digest. 1941–; weekly. Summarizes and indexes facts about current events. (O, 1975–, and CD-ROM, 1980–)

Information Please Almanac. 1947–; annual. Includes many charts, facts, and lists as well as short summaries of the year's events and accomplishments in various fields.

Statesman's Year-Book. 1863–; annual. Contains facts and helpful current statistics about agriculture, government, population, development, religion, and other topics in countries of the world.

Statistical Abstracts of the United States. 1878–; annual. Published by the Bureau of the Census; presents government data on population, business, immigration, and other subjects. (CD-ROM, 1987–)

World Almanac and Book of Facts. 1868–; annual. Presents data and statistics on business, education, sports, government, population, and other topics. Includes institutional names and addresses and reviews important annual public events. (CD-ROM in Microsoft® Bookshelf™)

ATLASES

In addition to physical maps of all parts of the world, the following **atlases** contain maps showing population, food distribution, mineral concentrations, temperature and rainfall, and political borders, as well as many other facts and statistics.

> *Atlas of World Cultures: A Geographical Guide to Ethnographic Literature.* 1989.
>
> *Hammond Medallion World Atlas.* 1982.
>
> *National Geographic Atlas of the World.* 1990.
>
> *The New International World Atlas.* 1986.
>
> *The New York Times Atlas of the World.* 1983.

Book indexes

Other useful sources located in the reference room are **book indexes,** which can be helpful for quickly locating complete information on a book when you know only one piece of it--the author's last name, perhaps, or the title. These sources can also be valuable for alerting you to other works by a particular author or on a particular subject.

> *Books in Print.* 1948–; annual. Lists by author, subject, and title all books distributed in the United States that are currently in print. (O, CD-ROM)
>
> *Cumulative Book Index.* 1898–; monthly. Lists by author, subject, and title books in English distributed in the United States and internationally. (O, CD-ROM)
>
> *Paperbound Books in Print.* 1955–; semiannual. Lists by author, subject, and title all paperback books distributed in the United States that are currently in print. (CD-ROM)

Periodical indexes

Periodical indexes are guides to articles published in periodicals. Each index covers a specific group of periodicals, usually identified at the beginning of the index or volume. In addition to printed indexes, your library may own microform indexes that cover many of the same entries. Microform indexes cover only the past three or four years, however, so if you are searching for earlier material, check the printed indexes. **Microforms** are rolls of film (*microfilm*) or sheets (*microfiche*) that must be read on motorized projection machines. Ask the librarian for help in locating the microforms and using the machines.

GENERAL INDEXES

General indexes of periodicals—usually located in the periodicals reading room—list articles from current general-interest magazines (such as *Time* and *Newsweek*), newspapers, or a combination of these. General indexes will usually provide current sources on your topic, though they may not treat the topic in sufficient depth for your purposes.

Access: The Supplementary Index. 1979–; monthly. Indexes magazines not covered by the *Readers' Guide to Periodical Literature* (see below), such as regional and particular-interest magazines (the environment, women's issues).

Alternative Press Index. 1970–; monthly. Indexes alternative and radical publications.

Book Review Digest. 1905–; annual. Contains excerpts from reviews of books along with information for locating the full reviews in popular and scholarly periodicals. Be sure to check not only the year of a book's publication but also the next year. (O, CD-ROM, 1983–)

InfoTrac. Updated monthly. Includes three indexes: (1) the *General Periodicals Index* (current year and past four years), which covers over 1,100 general-interest publications, incorporating the *Magazine Index* and including the *New York Times* and *Wall Street Journal;* (2) the *Academic Index* (current year and past four years), which covers over 900 scholarly and general-interest publications, including the *New York Times;* and (3) the *National Newspaper Index* (current year and past three years). Some entries include a summary or even the entire article. Available only on CD-ROM. Here is an example of an entry from the *General Periodicals Index.*

```
                                        General Periodicals Index-A
KAHLO, FRIDA
    1.     "Women in Mexico."  (22 women artists active in Mexico in
           the 20th century) (exhibition at the National Academy of
           Design, New York) by Ronny Cohen il v29 ArtForum Jan '91
           p127(2)
```

Magazine Index. Updated monthly. Analyzes over 500 general-interest magazines. Available only on microfilm (1988–), on-line (1973–), and on CD-ROM, separately and as part of InfoTrac (see above).

National Newspaper Index. Updated monthly. Covers the *New York Times, Los Angeles Times, Wall Street Journal, Washington Post,* and *Christian Science Monitor.* Available on microfilm (1989–), on-line (1979–), and on CD-ROM, separately and as part of InfoTrac (see above).

NewsBank. 1970–; updated monthly. Includes over one million articles from 500 U.S. newspapers. Available only on microfiche and CD-ROM.

Newspaper Abstracts Ondisc. 1985–. Contains abstracts from eight major newspapers, updated monthly. (O, CD-ROM)

New York Times Index. 1851–; bimonthly with annual cumulations. Lists by subject every article that has appeared in the *New York Times.* For most articles of any length, short summaries are given as well. Also available on-line through NEXIS (1980–; see below).

NEXIS/LEXIS. 1974–. NEXIS contains full texts and abstracts of newspapers, magazines, wire services, newsletters, company and industry analyst reports, and broadcast transcripts. LEXIS contains legal, legislative, and regulatory information. (O)

Nineteenth Century Readers' Guide to Periodical Literature. 1890–99.

Periodical Abstracts Ondisc. 1986–. Contains abstracts of articles in over 1,000 periodicals and journals in science, social science, humanities, and business. (O, CD-ROM)

Poole's Index to Periodical Literature. 1802–1907. Indexes nineteenth-century British and American periodicals.

Readers' Guide to Periodical Literature. 1900–; semimonthly with quarterly and annual cumulations. Indexes articles from over 170 magazines. Particularly helpful for social trends, popular scientific questions, and contemporary political issues. Entries are arranged by author and subject with cross-references leading to related topics. Also available on-line and on CD-ROM (both 1983–). Here is a *Readers' Guide* entry for the subject heading *Frida Kahlo.*

Kahlo, Frida 1907–1954
about
Frida Kahlo: the Chicana as art heroine. B. Rose. il pors *Vogue* 173:152+ Ap '83
Making an art of pain. H. Herrera. il pors *Psychol Today* 17:86 Mr '83
A Mexican Georgia O'Keeffe. K. Karson. il por *N Y* 16:82-3 Mr 28 '83
A painter's passion. H. Herrera. il pors *House Gard* 155:98-109+ Ag '83
The ribbon around the bomb. M. Newman. bibl il pors *Art Am* 71:160-9 Ap '83

Times Index (London). 1913–; bimonthly. Lists articles and summaries of stories published in the London *Times.*

SPECIALIZED INDEXES AND ABSTRACTS

Many disciplines have **specialized indexes** and **abstracts** to help researchers find information in great depth. In general, such works list articles in scholarly journals for that discipline, but they may include other publications as well; check the beginning of the volume. To use these resources most efficiently, ask a reference librarian to help you identify those most likely to address your topic.

America: History and Life. 1955–. (O, CD-ROM)

Applied Science and Technology Index. 1958–. Formerly *Industrial Arts Index.* 1913–57.

Art Index. 1929–. (O, CD-ROM)

Arts and Humanities Citation Index. 1977–. (O, CD-ROM)

Biological Abstracts. 1926–. (O, CD-ROM)

Biological and Agricultural Index. 1964–. Formerly *Agricultural Index.* 1916–63. (O, CD-ROM)

Business Periodicals Index. 1958–. Formerly *Industrial Arts Index.* 1913–57. (O, CD-ROM)

Chemical Abstracts. 1907–. (O, CD-ROM)

Chicano Index. 1981–. Formerly *Chicano Periodical Index.* (CD-ROM)

Cumulative Index to Nursing and Allied Health Literature. 1961–. (O, CD-ROM)

Current Index to Journals in Education. 1969. (O, CD-ROM)

Dissertation Abstracts International. 1938–. (O, CD-ROM)

Education Index. 1929–. (O, CD-ROM)

Engineering Index. 1984–. (O, CD-ROM)

ERIC (Educational Resources Information Center). 1966–. (O, CD-ROM)

Essay and General Literature Index. 1900–. (O, CD-ROM)

General Science Index. 1978–. (O, CD-ROM)

Hispanic American Periodicals Index (HAPI). 1970–. (O, CD-ROM)

Historical Abstracts. 1955–. (O, CD-ROM)

Humanities Index. 1974–. Formerly *International Index.* 1907–65. Formerly *Social Sciences and Humanities Index.* 1965–74. (O, CD-ROM)

Index Medicus. 1960–; 1899–1926. Formerly *Quarterly Cumulative Index Medicus.* 1927–59. (O, CD-ROM)

Index to Legal Periodicals. 1908–. (O, CD-ROM)

Index to Periodicals by and about Blacks. 1960–.

MLA Bibliography of Books and Articles in the Modern Languages and Literature. 1921–. (O, CD-ROM)

Music Index: A Subject-Author Guide to Music Periodical Literature. 1949–. (CD-ROM)

Philosopher's Index. 1967–. (O, CD-ROM)

Physics Abstracts. 1898–. (O, CD-ROM)

PsychLIT. 1974–. (O, CD-ROM)

Psychological Abstracts. 1927–. (O, CD-ROM)

Public Affairs Information Service (PAIS). 1915–. (O, CD-ROM)

Science Citation Index. 1955–. (O, CD-ROM)

Social Sciences Citation Index. 1969. (O, CD-ROM)

Social Sciences Index. 1974–. Formerly *International Index.* 1907–65. Formerly *Social Sciences and Humanities Index.* 1965–74. (O, CD-ROM)

Sociological Abstracts. 1952–. (O, CD-ROM)

United States Government Publications. 1895–. (O, CD-ROM)

Women's Studies Index. 1989–.

3

Using the library catalog

A **library catalog** lists all the library's materials. The traditional format for the library catalog is the **card catalog.** Today some libraries have a **microfiche catalog,** and many have transferred (or are in the process of transferring) their holdings to a **circulation computer**, which allows patrons to use public computer terminals to search for material. Most libraries with circulation computers, however, maintain card catalogs as well. If your library is in the process of computerizing its catalog, ask a reference librarian which catalog to check for recently published materials.

In whatever form, library catalogs follow a standard pattern of organization. Each holding is identified by three kinds of entries: one headed by the author's name, one by the title, and one or (usually) more by the subject. If you can't find a book under one of these headings, try the others; sometimes cards are lost or misfiled.

Following are examples of author, title, and subject cards.

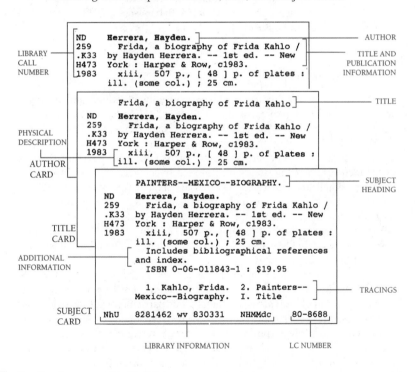

Using the circulation computer

With a circulation computer, you can easily experiment with different subject headings. Most circulation computers provide clear instructions on how and when to type in information. As with the card catalog, you search for holdings by author, title, or subject. The screen displays entries similar to those in the card catalog. Here is an example of a circulation-computer entry.

```
AUTHOR:        Herrera, Hayden
TITLE:         Frida, a biography of Frida Kahlo / by Hayden Herrera.
EDITION:       1st ed.
PUBLISHER:     New York : Harper & Row, c1983.
PHYSICAL DESC: iii, 507 p., [48] p. of plates : ill. (some col.) ; 25 cm.

NOTES:         Includes bibliographical references and index.
SUBJECTS:      Kahlo, Frida.
                 Painters - Mexico - Biography.


LOCATION          CALL#/VOL/NO/COPY              STATUS

UNH/STACK         ND259.K33 H47 1983 c.1         Available
```

Note that many circulation computers, like the one this example comes from, indicate whether a book is available or has been checked out and, if so, when it is due to be returned.

Identifying subjects

Subjects in the library catalog are usually identified and arranged according to the system presented in the *Library of Congress Subject Headings* (LCSH). This three-volume reference book may be kept at the reference desk or near the catalog. In it, you can check the exact wording of subject headings and define key terms of interest to you. You may find that the LCSH identifies headings that have not readily occurred to you. Under most headings, you'll find other subjects that are treated (identified by *UF,* "use for"), broader headings that include the subject (*BT,* "broader topic"), and narrower headings, which might be relevant (*NT,* "narrower topic"). These abbreviations are new to the most recent edition of LCSH and replace a system that used *sa* ("see also") and *xx* ("broader topic") and listed subdivisions without labels.

Searching only for subject entries is likely to be inefficient, however, because the headings are usually so broad. If the best Library of Congress heading you can identify does not match your particular needs or is so broad that your search yields many books but only a few that are useful, use other leads. Look to bibliographies, book indexes, reference books, periodical indexes, and notes in other publications for potentially useful authors and titles. Such leads are likely to be more specific and more helpful.

Using tracings

The **tracings** listed at the bottom of catalog entries identify the subject cards under which the book is listed. Keep in mind that searching only subject cards can be inefficient. Follow up on the tracings only if they seem relevant to your topic.

res

Using call numbers

Besides identifying a book's author, title, subject, and publication information, each catalog entry also lists a **call number**—the book's identification number. Most academic libraries now use the Library of Congress system, which begins call numbers with letters of the alphabet. Some libraries, however, still use the older Dewey decimal system, utilizing all numerals; the others combine systems. Once you have written down the complete call number, look for a library map or shelving plan to tell you where your book is housed. When you find it, take the time to browse through the books around it. Very often you will find the immediate area a more important treasure trove than any bibliography or index.

If your book is not on the shelf, ask about it at the circulation desk. The book may not circulate, or it may be in an area closed to the public. If someone has checked it out, the library might recall it for you. Consider the time required for the library to notify the borrower to return the book and then to notify you. Your deadline will determine whether it is realistic to request a recall.

4

Using other library resources

In addition to books and periodicals, libraries hold other useful materials that might be appropriate for your research. For example:

- *Vertical file.* Pamphlets and brochures from government and private agencies, usually kept in file cabinets
- *Special collections.* Manuscripts, rare books, local literature, memorabilia
- *Audio collections.* Records, audio cassettes, and compact discs of all kinds of music, readings, and speeches
- *Video collections.* Slides, filmstrips, and videocassettes
- *Art collections.* Drawings, paintings, engravings, and photographs
- *Interlibrary loans.* Many libraries will borrow books from another library for you; be aware that interlibrary loans often take some time and may involve some cost to you.

41c

Searching computer databases

As the preceding lists demonstrate, many important sources are now available on computer databases, either on-line or on CD-ROM. To use a database, you provide a list of authors, titles, or key words (often referred to as "descriptors"), and the computer searches the database for references to them and then prints out a list of every "match" it finds. Especially if you have to pay a fee for a database search, it is important to limit the search as much as you can.

1

Choosing key words

If you are preparing a class report on military technology in Shakespeare's plays, you can begin, for instance, by checking the *Gale Directory of Databases* to find databases that might index works related to your topic. From there, you might identify and then search the *MLA Bibliography* database for the terms *Shakespeare* and *cannon* or *firearms*, thereby picking up references to articles that mention Shakespeare in conjunction with one of these words. Doing efficient database searches thus requires that you choose your key words (descriptors) carefully. Sometimes you may search by author or title—then the key words are obvious. More often, however, you will probably be searching subject headings. Luckily, most databases include a thesaurus of key words or descriptors to help you as you start your search.

2

Using database search logic

In addition, you will need to observe the **search logic** for a particular database. For instance, using *and* usually indicates that you want two items included (Shakespeare *and* guns); both terms must be present for an article to be called up. *Or,* on the other hand, instructs the computer to include every article in which either one word *or* the other shows up. And *not* tells the computer that when a particular word appears, the article should be excluded (firearms *not* swords).

Another element of the logic of many database searches is the use of parentheses or quotation marks. These devices instruct the computer to search for the words that are enclosed in the parentheses or within the quotation marks. If you are searching for information on Lois Lane, for example, you would type in *(Lois Lane)* or *"Lois Lane."* Other similar devices enable you to call up every instance in which a key word (*Clinton,* for example) appears near another key term (*veto,* for example). Such a search would let you discover items in which the words *Clinton* and *veto* appeared within *X* number of words—say, five or ten—from each other. Understanding the search logic of the particular system you are using will make your job as a researcher more efficient and more effective.

When Daniel Taffe accessed the Modern Language Association database on CD-ROM (*MLA Bibliography of Books and Articles*), he typed on the command line *Kahlo, Frida* and *American Literature.* The database quickly reported 5 articles containing *Frida Kahlo*; 49,111 articles containing the topic *American Literature*; and 3 articles containing both key terms. Here is the information he printed out on those three articles (notice that the MLA format provides information on author, title, source, and subject, with the MLA's own descriptor words in parentheses—*sau*, for example, is the MLA descriptor for subject-author):

```
1 MLA
      AUTHOR: Salber, Linde; Stuhlmann, Gunther
      TITLE:  Artists-the Third Sex: A Few Thoughts on the
              Psychology of the Creative Age
      SOURCE: Anais: An International Journal 1993 vii p59-68

      SUBJECTS COVERED:
      --(slt) American literature (tim) 1900-1999 (sau)
      Nin, Anais (sau) Kahlo, Frida (sau) Andreas-Salome,
      Lou (sao) psychological approach
      --(slt) German literature (tim) 1800-1899

2 MLA
      AUTHOR: Gambrell, Alice Kathleen Hagood
      TITLE:  The Disquieting Muse: New World Women Artists and
              Modernist Fictions of Alterity (Dissertation
              abstract number: DA9112068; Degree granting
              institution: U of Virginia)
      SOURCE: Dissertation Abstracts International (ISSN Pt. A,
              0419-4209; Pt. B, 0419-4217; Pt. C, 1042-7279) 1991
              May v51 (11) p3738A

      SUBJECTS COVERED:
      --(slt) American literature (sic) fiction (tim)
      1900-1999 (sau) Doolittle, Hilda (sau) Rhys, Jean
      (sau) Kahlo, Frida (sau) Hurston, Zora Neale (grp)
      men artists (lfe) collaboration

3 MLA
      AUTHOR: Brennan, Karen Morley
      TITLE:  Hysteria and the Scene of Feminine
              Representation
      SOURCE: Dissertation Abstracts International (ISSN Pt. A,
              0419-4209; Pt. B, 0419-4217; Pt. C, 1042-7279)
              1990 Oct. v51(4) p1225A

      SUBJECTS COVERED:
      --(slt) American literature (sic) fiction (tim) 1900-1999 (sau)
      Nin, Anais (sau) Kahlo, Frida (sau) Acker, Kathy (lth)
      hysteria (lth) women (sap) psychoanalytical approach
```

Continuing his search, Daniel Taffe typed the key term *Frida Kahlo* into *PsychLIT*. This database reported that it contains only one reference with this key word. After looking at this reference on the screen, he printed it out (see p. 580).

Current computer technology allows you access to on-line and CD-ROM databases; to library, archival, and news resources around the world (through the Internet or various commercial services); and to people who share knowledge about some subject (through Usenet news groups or bulletin boards). For more information, see Chapter 50.

41d

Conducting research in the field

For many research projects, particularly those in the social sciences and business, you will need to collect field data. The field may be many things—a classroom, a church, an ice-cream parlor, a laboratory, or the corner grocery store. As a field researcher, you will become a detective investigating the world beyond the library. You will need to discover *where* you can find relevant information, *how* to gather it, and *who* might be your best informers.

One method of conducting field research, pioneered by anthropologists but now widely used by researchers in other disciplines as well, is **ethnography**—the study of the daily routines of ordinary people in a particular community. Ethnographic research aims to capture an insider's view of what it means to be a member of a particular group or setting.

True ethnographic research almost certainly lies beyond your grasp as an undergraduate since it requires extended observation (often over several years) and extensive, complex analysis. Nevertheless, you may be able to use several ethnographic techniques, including observation and interviewing, to very good advantage. With a limited amount of time for observing and interviewing, you won't have time to "get used to" what you are seeing and hearing and perhaps thus miss important points.

1

Observing

One of the insights of contemporary ethnographers is that observation is never neutral. Just as the camera has an angle on its subject and the person behind the camera must choose what to include and what to leave out, so an observer always has an angle on what he or she is looking at. Especially if you are a participant-observer, one who is to some degree an insider, your observations will naturally be colored by all that you know and feel about your subject and, particularly, by your participation in it. If, for instance, you decide to conduct a formal observation of your writing class, the field notes you take will reflect your status as an insider, and you will need to question or second-guess your observations accordingly to see what your participation in the class may have obscured or led you to take for granted.

In many other instances, it may be important to observe situations or phenomena in which you are not an insider and to aim for optimal objectivity, keeping yourself out of the picture and altering as little as possible the phenomena you are looking at—all the while remembering that you will always alter them somewhat. Much professional writing—for example, a doctor's diagnostic notes, a reporter's news article, or a social worker's case study—depends on such careful observation. You can observe anything in this way, from the use of bicycle paths on campus to the kinds of products advertised during Saturday-morning television shows to the growth of chicks in an agriculture lab.

"What," you might ask, "could be easier than observing something?" You just choose a subject, look at it closely, and record what you see and hear. If observing were so easy, eyewitnesses would provide reliable accounts. Yet experience shows that several people who have observed the same scene or phenomenon will most often offer contradictory "evidence." Trained observers tell us that getting down a faithful record of an observation requires intense concentration and mental agility.

Before you conduct your observation, then, decide exactly what you want to find out and anticipate what you are likely to see. Are you going to observe an action repeated by many people (such as pedestrians crossing a street), a sequence of actions (such as a medical procedure), or the interactions of a group (such as a church congregation)? Are you planning to observe a situation in which people might have many different reactions— a child crying in a grocery store, for example? Try to decide exactly what you want to record and how to do so. In the grocery store, for instance, decide whether to observe a child, his or her parents, other shoppers, or store employees, and what you want to note—what they say, what they buy, how they are dressed, and so on.

≫ *Conducting observation*

- Make plans as far in advance as possible. Brainstorm about what you are looking for and what you expect to see. Have a sense of what you are looking for, but be flexible—don't be rigidly bound to your expectations.

- Determine the purpose of the observation, and be sure it relates to your research question and hypothesis.

- If necessary, make appointments.

- Develop an appropriate system for recording your data. For field notes taken during observation, consider using a "split" notebook or page: on one side, record your observations directly; on the other, record your own thoughts and interpretations.

- Gather plenty of materials for note-taking: notebooks, pencils, a camera, tape recorder, or videocassette recorder.

- Review the steps you plan to take, going through the motions of observing and note-taking. Then conduct a trial run, taking field notes throughout. These activities will help you identify and solve potential problems before your formal observation.

- Be aware that your way of recording data will inevitably affect your final report, if only in respect to what you include in your notes and what you leave out.

- After taking field notes, go back and question your observations, remaining open to various interpretations.

2

Interviewing

Some information is best obtained by **interviewing,** or asking direct questions of other people. If you can talk with an expert, in person or on the telephone, you might get information you could not have obtained through any other kind of research. In addition to getting "expert opinion," you might ask for firsthand accounts, biographical information, or suggestions of other places to look or other people to consult. You also may wish to conduct follow-up interviews with some people you've observed.

Finding people to interview

Check first to see whether your research names any people you might contact directly. Next brainstorm for names. In addition to authorities on your topic, consider people in your community—faculty members, lawyers, librarians, government officials, or alumni of your college. Once you identify some promising possibilities, either write or telephone to see whether an interview might be arranged.

Composing questions

To prepare useful questions, you need to know your topic well, and you need to know a fair amount about your interviewee. Try to learn as much as you can about his or her experience and opinions. You will probably want to ask several kinds of questions. **Factual questions** elicit specific answers, ones that do not invite expansion or opinion.

> What flavors of ice cream does your company produce?
>
> How many people contributed to this year's United Way campaign?

In contrast, **open-ended questions** lead the interviewee to think out loud, to go in directions that interest him or her, and to give additional details.

> How would you characterize the atmosphere of the Watergate hearings?
>
> How do you feel now about your decision to go to Canada in 1968 rather than be drafted?

Avoid questions that encourage vague or rambling answers ("What do you think of youth today?") or yes/no answers ("Should the Indian Point reactor be closed?"). Instead, ask questions that must be answered with supporting details ("Why should the Indian Point reactor be closed?").

≫ Planning an interview

- Determine your exact purpose, and be sure it relates to your research question and hypothesis.
- Set up the interview in advance. Specify how long it will take, and if you wish to tape-record the session, ask permission to do so.
- Prepare a written list of questions you can use to structure the interview. Brainstorming or freewriting techniques can help you come up with questions. (3a)
- If possible, try out your questions on one or two people to determine how best to sequence them, how clear and precise they are, and how long answers will take.
- Prepare a final copy of your questions, leaving plenty of space for notes after each one.
- Check out all equipment beforehand—pens, notebook, tape recorder, and so on. Record the subject, date, time, and place of interview at the beginning of all tapes and on all handwritten notes.

Conducting an interview

Be prompt, and dress appropriately. Have your questions ready, and even if you use a tape recorder, write down the answers and any other notes you wish to make. Do not feel bound to your prepared questions as long as the interview proceeds in a direction that seems fruitful. Be flexible. Note the time, and be careful not to take up more time than you said you would. End the interview with a thank you—and follow up with a letter thanking the person for taking the time to meet with you. After you leave the interview, spend some time reviewing your notes, clarifying them and adding your comments.

3

Surveying opinion

Surveys, another common field-research strategy, can take the form of interviews (see 41d2), but more often they depend on **questionnaires.** The student investigating campus parking for motorcycles surveyed his dormitory's residents to learn how many owned motorcycles and how many had difficulty finding parking spaces. Though he sent questionnaires to everyone in the dorm, such extensive surveying is often unwieldy and even unnecessary. All you need is a representative sample of people and a questionnaire whose questions will elicit the information you need.

Questions should be clear and easy to understand and designed so that you will be able to analyze the answers easily. For example, questions that ask respondents to say yes or no or to rank something on a five-point scale of most to least desirable are easy to tabulate.

≫ *Designing a questionnaire*

1. Write out your purpose, and review your research question and hypothesis to determine the kinds of questions to ask.
2. Determine the audience for your questionnaire, and figure out how you will reach the potential respondents.
3. Using brainstorming, freewriting, or another strategy from 3a, draft some potential questions.
4. Check each question to see that it calls for a short, specific answer.
5. Test the questions on several people—including your teacher, if possible. Which questions are hard to answer? How much time do the answers require? Revise the questions as necessary.

6. If the questionnaire is to be mailed, draft a covering letter explaining the questionnaire's purpose and asking the recipient to complete the questionnaire. Provide an addressed, stamped envelope.
7. Be sure to state a deadline as well as a return address.
8. Consider adding a question that asks for comments.
9. Type the questionnaire, leaving adequate space for all answers.
10. Proofread your questionnaire.

4

Analyzing data from field research

To make sense of the information you gather and determine its significance, you need to analyze your data. First determine what you want to look at: kinds of interactions? kinds of language? comparisons between men's and women's responses? The point is to find a focus, since you can't pay equal attention to everything. See if your instructor could recommend other similar research you could check to see how it was analyzed.

Study your data for recurring words or ideas; look especially for ordinary, habitual everyday things. See if they fall into any patterns. Establish a system for coding your information, labeling each pattern you identify— a "V" for every use of violent language, for example, or a " + " for every positive response. Ask one or two classmates to review your notes or data; they may notice other patterns or question your findings in helpful ways.

What conclusions can you draw about the patterns you discover? What do they mean for your research purpose? Consider showing your findings to some of your subjects; their responses might help you to revise your analysis.

THINKING CRITICALLY ABOUT RESEARCH

Return to the exercise you completed on p. 561. Add to it by examining the ways in which you conducted your research: What use did you make of primary and secondary sources? What library and field work did you carry out? What about the process of research was most satisfying? What was most disappointing or most irritating? What sources were most (and least) useful? How can you conduct research more efficiently in the future?

42

Using Sources

ALL RESEARCH BUILDS on the astute, judicious, and sometimes inspired use of sources—that research work done by others. As Isaac Newton noted, those researchers who see the farthest do so "by standing up on the shoulders of giants." And while researchers cannot always count on a giant's shoulders to stand on, the quality of their insights is often directly related to how well they have understood and used the source materials—the shoulders—they have relied on. As a reader, you will want to make the most of your sources, using the insights you gain from them in creating powerful prose of your own. This chapter will guide you in your use of sources in research.

42a

Choosing sources

Experienced researchers know that all sources are not created equally useful, that some are more helpful or more provocative than others. One of your goals, therefore, is to learn to judge, in Francis Bacon's words, which "are to be tasted," which "swallowed," and which "chewed and digested." The following sections will help you make such judgments.

1

Building a working bibliography

One important result of choosing sources for research is the creation of a **working bibliography**—a list of books, articles, and other sources that seem likely to address your research question. The emphasis here is on *working*—for this list will include materials that may end up not being useful. As you use reference books, bibliographic sources, periodical indexes,

res

Everyday Use

Every time you pick up *Consumer Reports* to check out its evaluation of an appliance you're thinking of buying or log on to the Internet to talk to owners of a software program you are interested in, you are calling on source materials for help. Spend a few minutes thinking of other everyday source materials you use—manuals or guidebooks, for instance. Make a list of these sources, and bring it to class for discussion. How do you go about evaluating these source materials? How do you know which ones to trust?

---

the card catalog, or the circulation computer, make a bibliography entry for every source you think you might use.

Before you begin a working bibliography, check your assignment or ask your instructor to determine what system you are required to follow for documenting the sources you use (see Chapters 44 and 45). If you familiarize yourself with the system now and follow it carefully, you will have, in the proper format, all the information necessary to prepare your final list of sources cited.

≫ *Keeping a working bibliography*

1. Decide on a format: use index cards (one for each source), a notebook, or a computer file. If you use cards or notebook pages, record information on one side only so that you can arrange the entries alphabetically when preparing the list of sources cited. Many word-processing programs will sort the entries for you. Whatever system you use, follow it consistently and completely.

2. For each book, record the following:
   - Call number or other location information
   - Author and/or editor
   - Title and subtitle, if any
   - Publisher's name and location
   - Year of publication
   - Other information—translator, volume number, edition, and so on
   - Inclusive page numbers for chapters or short works

   (Continued)

3. For each article, list the following:
   - Author and/or editor
   - Article title and subtitle, if any
   - Periodical name, volume number, and date
   - Inclusive page numbers for the article

4. For entries from bibliographic or periodical indexes, list the name of the index in case you need to check the information again, and add the call number or other location information when you find the source in your library catalog.

5. For entries from databases, get a printout. You will need to convert the entries of any sources you use to the correct documentation style, but the printout can save you the interim step of copying the information by hand.

6. For nonprint sources, list the information required by the documentation system you are using, and note where you found the information.

7. When you examine the sources, check the accuracy of your information by consulting the title and copyright pages of a book and the table of contents and first page of a journal or magazine article.

For his research essay on Frida Kahlo, Daniel Taffe, who was using the Modern Language Association style of documentation (see Chapter 44), decided to record his sources on index cards. Here are two of the cards he created—the first for a book and the second for a periodical article.

BOOK

ND 259. K33
H 47
1983

Herrera, Hayden. _Frida: A Biography of Frida Kahlo_. New York: Harper, 1983.

ARTICLE

Jenkins, Nicholas. "Calla Lilies and Kahlos:
The Frida Kahlo Museum in Mexico
City." <u>ARTnews</u> Mar. 1991: 104-05.

General Periodicals Index (InfoTrac)

2

Assessing the usefulness of a source

Examining the following elements with your research question and assignment in mind can help you assess its usefulness:

- *Relevance.* Is the source closely related to your research question?
- *Author's credentials and stance.* Is the author an expert on the topic? Where does the author stand on the issues involved—and does this stance support or challenge your own views?
- *Date of publication.* How current is the material? Recent sources are often more useful than older ones, particularly in the sciences. However, the most authoritative works are often older ones.
- *Level of specialization.* Is the source general or specialized? General sources may be helpful as you begin your research, but you may then need the authority or up-to-dateness of more specialized sources. Extremely specialized works may be too hard to understand.
- *Publication background.* If a book was published by a corporation, government agency, or interest group, what is the publisher's position on the topic? What kind of periodical published an article? popular? academic? alternative?
- *Audience.* For what audience was the source written? general readers? specialists? advocates or opponents of something? a particular group?
- *Cross-referencing.* Is the source cited in other works?
- *Length.* Is the source long enough to provide adequate detail?
- *Availability.* Do you have access to the source?

You can determine many of these characteristics just by quickly looking at the parts of a source that are listed below. If you then want to explore the source more thoroughly, these elements can also help you decide how to do so most efficiently.

- *Title and subtitle.* If you are investigating coeducation in the nineteenth century and find a book called *Women in Education,* the subtitle *The Challenge of the 1970s* will tell you that you probably do not need to examine the book.

- *Copyright page.* In a book, this page will show you when the book was originally published, whether it is a revised edition, and who published it.

- *Abstract.* Abstracts are concise summaries of articles or books. They routinely precede articles in some journals and are included in certain periodical or bibliographic guides. Abstracts can help you decide whether to read the entire work; use them accordingly.

- *Table of contents.* Part and chapter titles can show you what a book contains. Try to determine whether the chapter topics are specific enough to be useful. In a periodical, the table of contents often includes brief descriptions of articles and can give you a general impression of the periodical itself.

- *Preface or foreword.* Very often these preliminary pages of a book specify in detail the writer's purposes, range of interests, intended audience, topic restrictions, research limitations, and thesis.

- *Subheadings.* Subheadings in the text can give you an idea of how much detail is given on a topic and whether that detail would be helpful to you.

- *Conclusion or afterword.* Some books and articles end with a summary of the contents and a statement of significance that could help you decide how appropriate that source is for your project.

- *Note on the author.* Check the dust jacket of a book, the first and last few pages of a work, or an article itself for information about the author.

- *Index.* Check the index for words and topics key to your project; then see whether they seem to have much importance in the book. Are the listings for your key terms many or few?

- *Bibliography and/or footnotes.* Lists of references, usually at the end of a book or article, show how carefully a writer has investigated the subject. In addition, they may help you find other sources.

42b

Reading sources with a critical eye

Research calls for active, aggressive reading. Active readers engage in a conversation of sorts with the books they read, responding to them with questions and comments. The more attentively you read and the more you respond to what you read, the better your research will be. This section will help you become an active, questioning reader. For additional information on critical reading, see 1b2.

Researchers read with a strong sense of purpose: How does this source relate to my research goals? Does it support my ideas, develop them further, or challenge them? Reading with a purpose calls for examining your sources with an astute, critical eye. Because of time constraints and the wealth of material available on most topics, you probably will not have time to read completely through all of your potential material. Thus, reading with a critical eye can make your research process more efficient. The following considerations can guide your critical reading:

Reading with your research question in mind

A good way of focusing your attention on the information most necessary to your research is to read with your research question in mind. Use the index and the table of contents to zero in on the parts of a book that will help you answer your research question. Consider the following questions as you read:

- How does this material address your research question?
- In what ways does it provide support for your hypothesis?
- How might particular quotations help support your thesis?
- Does the source include counterarguments to your hypothesis that you will need to answer? If so, what answers can you provide?

Identifying the author's stance and tone

Every author holds opinions that affect his or her discussion of an issue, opinions that you as a reader must try to recognize and understand. Even the most seemingly factual report, such as an encyclopedia article, is necessarily filled with judgments, often unstated. Read with an eye for the author's overall rhetorical stance, or perspective on the topic (see 2g), as well as for facts or explicit opinions. The rhetorical stance is closely related to the author's tone, the way his or her attitude toward topic and audience is conveyed. Alertness to perspective and tone will help you more fully understand a source and better decide how (or whether) to use it. The following questions can help you read for perspective and tone:

- What is the author's stance or perspective? Is he or she an enthusiastic advocate of something, a strong opponent, a skeptical critic, an amused onlooker, a confident specialist in the field? What forces in society may have shaped or influenced this perspective?
- Are there any clues to why the author takes this stance?

- How does this stance affect the author's presentation?
- If the author has a professional affiliation, how might the affiliation affect his or her stance?
- In what ways do you share—or not share—the author's stance?
- What is the author's tone? Is it cautious, angry, flippant, serious, impassioned? What words express this tone?

In the following paragraph, which appeared in a *Parade* magazine essay about nuclear war, the author's stance is obvious from the first sentence: he sees his topic, the possibility of nuclear war, as "an unprecedented human catastrophe." His dismissal of those who disagree with him as "fools and madmen" indicates the depth of his feelings, but his overall tone is restrained and objective because he assumes ("everyone knows") that the great majority of his readers share his view.

> Except for fools and madmen, everyone knows that nuclear war would be an unprecedented human catastrophe. A more or less typical strategic warhead has a yield of 2 megatons, the explosive equivalent of 2 million tons of TNT. But 2 million tons of TNT is about the same as all the bombs exploded in World War II—a single bomb with the explosive power of the entire Second World War but compressed into a few seconds of time and an area 30 or 40 miles across. . . .
>
> – CARL SAGAN, "The Nuclear Winter"

Assessing the author's argument and evidence

Just as every author has a point of view, every piece of writing has what may be called an argument, a position it takes. Even a report of scientific data implicitly "argues" that we should accept it as reliably gathered and reported. As you read, then, try to identify the author's argument, the reasons given in support of his or her position. Then try to decide *why* the author takes this position. Considering the following questions as you read can help you recognize—and assess—the points being argued in your sources:

- What is the author's main point?
- How much and what kind of evidence supports that point?
- How persuasive do you find the evidence?
- Can you offer counterarguments to or refutations of the evidence?
- Can you detect any questionable logic or fallacious thinking? (See 5g.)

Questioning your sources

Because all sources make an explicit or implicit argument, they often disagree with one another. Disagreements among sources arise sometimes from differences about facts, sometimes from differences about how to interpret facts. For instance, if an authoritative source says that the chances of a nuclear power plant melting down are 1 in 100,000, commentators could interpret that statistic very differently. A critic of nuclear power could argue that nuclear accidents are so terrible that this chance is too great to take, while a supporter of nuclear power could argue that such a small chance is essentially no chance at all.

The point is that all knowledge is interpreted subjectively. A writer may well tell nothing but the truth, but he or she can never tell the *whole* truth because people are not all-knowing. Thus you must build your own informed opinion, your own truth, by seeking out and assessing many viewpoints as you read. Not all disputes can be solved by appealing to "neutral facts" because facts are seldom neutral. You must examine all sources critically, using them not as unquestioned authorities but as contributions to your own interpretation.

42c

Taking notes

After you have decided that a source is useful, you will need to take careful notes on it. Doing so most efficiently calls for approaching a source with some general questions in mind. What do you expect to learn about the topic? What can the source help you demonstrate? To what part of your research is the source most relevant?

Note-taking methods vary greatly from one researcher to another. Whatever method you adopt, however, your goals will include (1) getting down enough information to help you recall the major points of the source; (2) getting down the information in the form in which you are most likely to want to incorporate it into your essay (see 43d); and (3) getting down all the information you will need in order to cite the source accurately. Taking careful and complete notes will not only help you digest the source information as you read but will also help you incorporate the material into your essay without inadvertently plagiarizing the source.

⋙ *Taking accurate notes*

1. Using index cards, a notebook, or a computer file, list the author's name and a shortened title of the source. Your working bibliography entry for the source should contain full publication information (see 42a1), so you need not repeat it in your notes.

(Continued)

2. Record exact page references. If the note refers to more than one page, indicate page breaks so that if you decide to use only part of the note, you will know which page to cite.

3. Label each note with a subject heading.

4. Identify the note as a quotation, a paraphrase, a summary, a combination of these forms, or some other form—such as your own critical comment—to avoid any confusion later. Mark quotations accurately with quotation marks, and paraphrase and summarize completely in your own words to be sure you do not inadvertently plagiarize the source. (See 42d.)

5. Read over each completed note carefully to recheck the accuracy of quotations, statistics, and specific facts.

Most of your notes will take the form of direct quotation, paraphrase, or summary. Deciding what material to include and whether to quote, paraphrase, or summarize it is an outgrowth of reading with a critical eye. You may use some sources for background information and others as support for your thesis, and these different purposes may guide you to take one kind of note rather than another—summarizing background information, for example, but quoting statements that support your views. Likewise, as you read, you will want to evaluate the usefulness of each source to your project and begin to assign the role a particular source will play in your paper.

Deciding whether to quote, paraphrase, or summarize

QUOTE

- Wording that is so memorable or expresses a point so perfectly that you cannot improve or shorten it without weakening the meaning you need
- Authors' opinions you wish to emphasize
- Respected authorities whose opinions support your own ideas
- Authors whose opinions challenge or vary greatly from those of others in the field

PARAPHRASE

- Passages that you do not wish to quote but whose details you wish to note fully

SUMMARIZE

- Long passages whose main points you wish to record selectively

1

Quoting

Quoting involves noting a source's *exact words*. Direct quotations can be effective for catching your readers' attention—for example, including a well-turned phrase in your introduction or giving an eyewitness's account in arresting detail. In a research essay, quotations from respected authorities can help establish your credibility as a researcher by showing that you've sought out experts in the field. In addition, allowing authors to speak for themselves, particularly if they hold opinions counter to yours or to those of other experts, helps demonstrate your fairness. (See 5f.)

Finally, well-chosen quotations can broaden the appeal of your essay by drawing on emotion as well as logic, appealing to the reader's mind and heart. A student writing on the ethical issues of bullfighting, for example, might introduce an argument that bullfighting is not a sport by quoting Ernest Hemingway's striking comment that "the formal bull-fight is a tragedy, not a sport, and the bull is certain to be killed." (See 5g and 5h.)

Here is an example of an original passage and Daniel Taffe's note card recording a quotation from it. Notice how Taffe uses ellipses to mark author's words he omitted and brackets to show changed capitalization.

ORIGINAL SOURCE

But Frida was also the product of a bold and brilliant generation that looked back with devotion to its Mexican roots and valued the reality it found there, uncontaminated by foreign influences. She admitted to having a great admiration for her husband's work, as well as that of José Guadalupe Posada, José María Velasco, and Gerardo Murillo (Dr. Atl), and she found great beauty in the highly developed pre-Conquest indigenous arts.

– MARTHA ZAMORA, *Frida Kahlo: The Brush of Anguish* (110)

Mexican cultural influences

Zamora, <u>Frida</u>, p. 110

"... Frida was ... the product of a bold and brilliant generation that looked back with devotion to its Mexican roots and valued the reality found there, uncontaminated by foreign influences.... [S]he found great beauty in the highly developed pre-Conquest indigenous arts."

≫ *Quoting accurately*

- Copy quotations *carefully,* with punctuation, capitalization, and spelling exactly as in the original.

- Use brackets if you introduce words of your own into the quotation or make changes in it, and use ellipses if you omit material. (See 35b and 35f.) If you later incorporate the quotation into your essay, you must copy it faithfully, brackets, ellipses, and all.

- It is especially important to enclose the quotation in quotation marks; don't rely on your memory to distinguish your own words from those of the source.

- Record the author's name, shortened title, and page number(s) on which the quotation appeared.

- Make sure you have a corresponding working bibliography entry with complete source information (see 42a1).

- Label the note with a subject heading.

2

Paraphrasing

A **paraphrase** accurately states all the relevant information from a passage *in your own words and phrasing,* without any additional comments or elaborations. A paraphrase is useful when the main points of the passage, their order, and at least some details are important but—unlike passages worth quoting—the particular wording is not. Unlike a summary, a paraphrase always restates *all* the main points of the passage in the same order and in about the same number of words.

Paraphrasing material helps you digest a passage, because chances are you can't restate the passage in your own words unless you grasp its full meaning. When you incorporate an accurate paraphrase into your essay, you show readers that you understand that source.

In order to paraphrase without plagiarizing inadvertently, *use your own words and sentence structures;* do not simply substitute synonyms, and do not imitate the author's style. If you wish to cite some of the author's words within the paraphrase, enclose them in quotation marks. A good way of assuring your originality is to paraphrase without looking at the source. When you have finished, turn back to the source, and check to see that the paraphrase accurately presents the author's meaning and that you have used your own words and phrasing.

Writing acceptable paraphrases

Looking at the following examples of paraphrases that resemble the original too closely will help you understand how to write acceptable paraphrases. Be aware that even for acceptable paraphrases you must include a citation in your essay identifying the source of the information.

ORIGINAL

But Frida's outlook was vastly different from that of the Surrealists. Her art was not the product of a disillusioned European culture searching for an escape from the limits of logic by plumbing the subconscious. Instead, her fantasy was a product of her temperament, life, and place; it was a way of coming to terms with reality, not of passing beyond reality into another realm.
— HAYDEN HERRERA, *Frida: A Biography of Frida Kahlo* (258)

UNACCEPTABLE PARAPHRASE: USING THE AUTHOR'S WORDS

As Herrera explains, Frida's vision *differed vastly from* the Surrealists' outlook, which grew out of a *disillusioned European culture* hoping to *escape* the confines *of logic. Her fantasy was* due to her own personality and life, including her Mexican roots, and she used it to *come to terms with reality* rather than to move *beyond reality.* (258)

Because the italicized phrases are either borrowed from the original without quotation marks or changed only superficially, this paraphrase plagiarizes.

UNACCEPTABLE PARAPHRASE:
USING THE AUTHOR'S SENTENCE STRUCTURES

As Herrera explains, Frida's vision was completely unlike the vision of the Surrealists. Her paintings were not the result of a disenchanted European civilization looking for a release from the confines of logical thinking by probing beneath the conscious mind. Rather, her dream was the result of her personality, situation, and location; it was a means of dealing with the real world, not of moving past it to a new dimension. (258)

While this paraphrase does not rely on the words of the original, it does follow the sentence structures too closely. Substituting synonyms for the major words in a paraphrase is not enough to avoid plagiarism. The paraphrase must represent your own interpretation of the material and thus must show your own thought patterns.

Now look at two paraphrases of the same passage that express the author's ideas accurately and acceptably, the first completely in the writer's own words and the second including quotations from the original.

ACCEPTABLE PARAPHRASE: IN THE WRITER'S OWN WORDS

As Herrera explains, Frida's surrealistic vision was unlike that of the European Surrealists. While their art grew out of their disenchantment with their society and their desire to explore the subconscious mind as a refuge from rational thinking, Frida's vision was an outgrowth of her own personality and experiences in Mexico. She used her surrealistic images to understand better her actual life, not to create a dream world. (258)

ACCEPTABLE PARAPHRASE: QUOTING SOME OF THE AUTHOR'S WORDS

As Herrera explains, Frida's surrealistic vision was unlike that of the European Surrealists. While their art grew out of their "disillusioned European culture" and their desire "for an escape from the limits of logic" through an exploration of the subconscious, Frida's dream was an outgrowth of her own personality and experiences in Mexico. She used her surrealistic images to understand better her actual life, not to "[pass] beyond reality into another realm." (258)

Notice that in the last sentence of the second paraphrase, *passing* needed to be changed to *pass* for the quotation to fit smoothly into the sentence. This change is indicated by using brackets (see 35b and 43d1).

Here is an example of an original passage and Daniel Taffe's note card recording a paraphrase of the first paragraph. (Compare a summary of the full passage, p. 600.)

ORIGINAL SOURCE

Although largely self-taught, and considered by many to be a naive painter, Frida was actually very sophisticated. Intelligent, well-read, and well-informed, she was acquainted with the traditional schools of painting. More important, she recognized the vanguard of Mexican and foreign art not only through her travels but through direct contact with the artists. Direct influences show up in some cases, as in *Magnolias* (1945), reminiscent of the work of Georgia O'Keeffe, or in *Four Inhabitants of Mexico City* (1938), recalling de Chirico. Her earliest works showed an acquaintance with art books; in her first self-portrait for Gómez Arias, she described herself as "your Botticelli," and in letters to him she expressed interest in Modigliani and Piero della Francesca. Her use of suffocating background vegetation is similar to that of Henri Rousseau, the small figures in *What the Water Gave Me* (1938) like something out of Hieronymus Bosch, and the written legends in others like those of the Mexican painter Hermenegildo Bustos.

But Frida was also the product of a bold and brilliant generation that looked back with devotion to its Mexican roots and valued the reality it found there, uncontaminated by foreign influences. She admitted to having a great admiration for her husband's work, as well as that of José Guadalupe Posada, José María Velasco, and Gerardo Murillo (Dr. Atl), and she found great beauty in the highly developed pre-Conquest indigenous arts.

– MARTHA ZAMORA, *Frida Kahlo: The Brush of Anguish* (110)

> Artistic influences
>
> Zamora, Frida, p. 110
>
> Frida mostly taught herself to paint, but she was not as unsophisticated as many thought her to be. She was bright and knowledgeable, familiar with the history of painting, acquainted with contemporary Mexican and foreign artists and their work. Some of her paintings show the influence of O'Keeffe and de Chirico. She referred to her first self-portrait as "your Botticelli" and mentioned Modigliani and della Francesca in letters to Arias. She depicts flora like Rousseau, and uses small figures like Bosch and captions like Bustos.
>
> (Paraphrase)

In the research essay presented in Chapter 44, Daniel Taffe uses part of this paraphrase in a transition sentence opening the ninth paragraph: "If Kahlo's work is often personal, however, it is not untutored or untaught. In fact, Kahlo was clearly familiar with and influenced by traditional Christian and Mexican imagery."

≫ *Paraphrasing accurately*

- Include all main points and any important details from the original, in the same order in which they were presented.
- State the meaning in your own words and sentence structures. If you want to include especially memorable language from the original, enclose it in quotation marks.
- Leave out your own comments, elaborations, or reactions.
- Record the author, shortened title, and the page number(s) on which the original material appeared.
- Make sure you have a corresponding working-bibliography entry for the material.
- Label the note with a subject heading, and identify it as a paraphrase to avoid confusion with a summary.
- Recheck the paraphrase against the original to be sure that the words and sentence structures are your own and that they express the author's meaning accurately.

3

Summarizing

A **summary** is a significantly shortened version of a passage, a section, or even a whole chapter or work that *captures main ideas in your own words*. Unlike a paraphrase, a summary uses just enough information to record the main points or the points you wish to emphasize. You needn't include all the author's points or any details, but be sure not to distort his or her meaning. The length of a summary depends on the length of the original and on how much information you will need to use. Your goal is to keep the summary as brief as possible, capturing only the gist of the original.

For a short passage, try reading it carefully and, without looking at the text, writing a one- or two-sentence summary. For a long passage or an entire chapter, skim the headings and topic sentences, and make notes of each; then write your summary in a paragraph or two. For a whole book, you may want to refer to the preface and introduction as well as chapter titles, headings, and topic sentences—and your summary may take a page or more.

Following is a note card recording a summary of the passage whose first paragraph is paraphrased by Daniel Taffe on p. 599. Notice that it states the author's main points selectively—and without using her words.

Artistic influences

Zamora, Frida, p.110

Although Frida was well acquainted with historical and contemporary artists from Europe and America, whose influence is evident in her works (particularly in her images of flora and her rendering of many scenes in a painting), she was deeply aware of her Mexican heritage.

(Summary)

≫ *Summarizing accurately*

- Include just enough information to recount the main points you wish to cite. A summary is usually far shorter than the original.

- Use your own words. If you include language from the original, enclose it in quotation marks.

- Record the author, shortened title, and page number(s) on which the original material appeared.

- Make sure you have a corresponding working-bibliography entry.

- Label the note with a subject heading, and identify it as a summary to avoid confusion with a paraphrase.

- Recheck against the original any material you plan to use to be sure you have captured the author's meaning and that your words are entirely your own.

Combination notes

Often your reading will lead you to take a **combination note**—perhaps a paraphrase with some quotations, like the second one on p. 598, or a summary of an entire chapter with a paraphrase of a key paragraph. If you combine forms, be sure to follow the guidelines for each kind of note, and label clearly which material is in which form.

Other kinds of notes

Many researchers take notes that do not fall into the preceding categories. Some take **key-term notes**, which may include names, dates, short statements—anything to jog their memories when they begin drafting. Others record **personal** or **critical notes**—thoughts, questions, disagreements, criticisms—striking ideas that come to mind as they read. Still others adopt systems peculiar to their research project. Daniel Taffe kept a separate note for each of Frida Kahlo's paintings that dealt with the themes he pursued in his essay. By labeling these notes with subject headings, he could easily determine how often each theme appeared in her work. For research that is not library based, you will probably need to take **field notes**. (See 41d.)

You may find reason to keep notes of various kinds in addition to those described here. Whatever form your notes take, always list the source's title, author, and page number(s) to document the material accurately. In addition, check that you have carefully distinguished your own thoughts and comments from the source's.

Photocopying source material

Nearly all libraries provide photocopying machines that you can use to copy pages or even whole articles or chapters. You can then annotate the photocopies with your thoughts and questions and highlight interesting quotations and key terms. Try not to rely too heavily on photocopying, however. You still need to read the material carefully and should resist the temptation to treat photocopied material as notes, an action that could lead to inadvertent plagiarizing as well as to wasting time looking for information you only vaguely remember having read. If you have read and taken careful notes on your sources rather than having relied primarily on photocopies, your drafting process will be more efficient.

If you do photocopy material, note on the photocopy all the information you need to cite the material in your list of sources cited. (And check that the page numbers are clearly legible.)

Recognizing plagiarism, acknowledging sources

"There is," in the words of Ecclesiastes, "no new thing under the sun." In a way, the biblical saying is true of research as well as of life in general: whatever research we do is influenced and affected by everything we have already read and experienced. If you try, for instance, to trace the origins of every idea you have had just today, you will quickly see the extent to which we are all indebted to others as sources of information.

Giving full acknowledgment to those sources presents a challenge, but trying to do so is important for several reasons. First, acknowledging your sources allows you to thank those whose work you have built on and thus avoid plagiarism. Second, it helps readers by placing your research in the context of other thinking and research; it shows the ways in which your research is part of a larger conversation and lets readers know where they can find more information. Finally, acknowledging your sources helps you critically examine your own research and thinking. How timely and reliable are your sources? Have you used them accurately?

Acknowledging sources fully and generously, then, provides a means of establishing your *ethos* or your credibility as a researcher. (See 5f.) Failure to credit sources breaks trust with both the research "conversation" and your readers; as a sign of dishonesty, it can easily destroy the credibility of the researcher and the research.

1

Recognizing plagiarism

Plagiarism, the use of someone else's words or ideas as your own without crediting the other person, can result in serious consequences. At some colleges, students who plagiarize fail the course automatically; at others, they are expelled. Outside academic life, eminent political, business, and scientific leaders have been stripped of candidacies, positions, and awards following charges of plagiarism.

You are probably already aware of cases of deliberate plagiarism—handing in a paper that a friend wrote for a similar course, copying passages directly from source materials. In addition, however, you should be aware of unintended plagiarism—a quotation accidentally used without quotation marks, a paraphrase that too closely resembles the original, background details used without acknowledgment in the mistaken belief that none was necessary. By understanding what material you must document, taking systematic, accurate notes, and giving full credit to sources in both parenthetical citations and your list of sources cited, you can avoid unintended plagiarism. Doing so for every idea you build on, however, is impossible. Where, then, do you draw the line?

2
Knowing which material requires acknowledgment

Some of the information you use does not need to be credited to another source because it is well-known or because you gathered the data yourself. The following discussion should help you in discerning which materials you need to credit and which ones you can use without credit.

Materials not requiring acknowledgment

Common knowledge. If most readers would be likely to know something, you need not cite it. You do not need to credit a source for the statement that George Bush was elected president in 1988, for example. If, on the other hand, you give the exact number of popular votes he received in the 1988 election, you should cite the source for that figure.

Facts available in a wide variety of sources. If a number of encyclopedias, almanacs, or textbooks include a certain piece of information, you need not cite a specific source for it. For instance, you would not need to cite a source for the fact that the Japanese bombing of Pearl Harbor on December 7, 1941, destroyed most of the base except for the oil tanks and submarines. You would, however, need to credit a source that argued that the failure to destroy the submarines meant that Japan was destined to lose the Pacific war.

Your own feelings from field research. If you conduct observation, interviews, or surveys, simply announce your findings as your own.

Materials requiring acknowledgment

For material that does not fall under the above three headings, credit sources as fully as possible, using quotation marks where appropriate, citing the source in a customary fashion, and if necessary, listing it in a list of sources. (See Chapters 44 and 45.)

Direct quotations. Whenever you use another person's words directly, credit the source. If two quotations from the same source appear close together, you can use one citation after the second quotation. If you quote some of the author's words within a paraphrase or summary, you need to cite the quotation separately, after the closing quotation mark.

Facts that are not widely known or assertions that are arguable. If your readers would be unlikely to know a fact or if an author presents as fact an assertion that may or may not be true, cite the source. To claim, for instance, that Switzerland is amassing an offensive nuclear arsenal would demand the citation of a source because Switzerland has long been an officially neutral state. If you are not sure whether a fact will be familiar to your readers or a statement is debatable, citing the source is advisable.

Judgments, opinions, and claims of others. Whenever you summarize or paraphrase anyone else's opinion, give the source for that summary or paraphrase. Even though the wording should be completely your own, you need to acknowledge the source.

Statistics, charts, tables, and graphs from any source. Credit all statistical and graphic material not derived from your own field research, even if you yourself create the graph from data in another source.

Help provided by friends, instructors, or others. A conference with an instructor may give you the idea you need to clinch an argument. Give credit. Friends may help you conduct surveys, refine questionnaires, or think through problems. Credit them, too.

If your working bibliography contains complete entries that you double-checked as you examined each source and if your notes clearly identify direct quotations, paraphrases, and summaries that you double-checked for accuracy as you took the notes, the task of acknowledging the source of each piece of information you incorporate into your essay will be much easier.

≫ *Recognizing plagiarism, acknowledging your sources*

- Maintain an accurate and thorough working bibliography. (42a1)
- Establish a consistent note-taking system, listing sources and page numbers and clearly identifying all quotations, paraphrases, summaries, statistics, and graphics. (42c)

- Identify all quotations with quotation marks—both in your notes and in your essay.
- Be sure that you summarize and paraphrase using your own words and sentence structures.
- In your essay, give a citation for each quotation, paraphrase, summary, arguable assertion or opinion, statistic, and graph that is from a source. (44a and 45a, e, and f)
- Prepare an accurate and complete list of sources cited according to the required documentation style. (44c and 45c, e, and g)

42e

Interpreting sources

Your task as a reader is to identify and understand sources and sets of data as completely as possible. As a writer, your aim must be to present data and sources *to other readers* so that they can most readily understand the point you are making. Doing so calls for you to think carefully as you work to interpret sources.

Turning data into information

Computer scientists sometimes distinguish between **data**, bits of facts or strings of statements, and **information**, the meaning attached to the data. As a researcher, you will gather a great deal of data, probably more than you need or can use. But those data become information only when their meaning is made clear. You may have gathered two dozen facts about a city's finances, for example, but turning them into information calls for pointing out their significance as a group—that, for instance, the city is on the brink of bankruptcy.

Synthesizing data and drawing inferences

You can begin turning data into information by **synthesizing**—grouping similar pieces of data together, looking for patterns or trends, and identifying the gist, or main point, of the data. Most often, finding the gist of a source or set of data will call for drawing **inferences**—conclusions that are not explicitly stated but that follow logically from the data given. For example, you may have data forecasting severe drought in every midwestern state. Other data report very low levels of crop production in those states. From these data, you infer that farmers in the Midwest face financial crisis. As a researcher, you have turned data into information.

Recording your thoughts and ideas

Perhaps the most exciting part of the research process occurs when the materials you are reading spark something in your mind and new ideas take hold. As you read, your mind is busy processing all the materials you are discovering and all those you have previously discovered, seeking connections and similarities, making distinctions, synthesizing in the ways discussed above. You will have ideas that can become part of your thesis or argument. *Don't let them get away.* Jot them down, perhaps in a special section of your writing log or research log, if you are keeping one.

Do not worry about whether an idea is true or right or even useful— just get it down, and think about it later. Some ideas may be thrown away later because they do not suit the final shape your essay takes, but others will likely *provide* the shape. Disagreements among sources can provide particularly fruitful areas to consider and may provoke you to discovering new insights all your own. Consequently, you need to pay close attention to all your sources' arguments—those you agree with as well as those you do not agree with.

THINKING CRITICALLY ABOUT PARAPHRASES AND SUMMARIES

If you are working on a research essay, choose an important source, and prepare a paraphrase of two or three paragraphs, using your own words and sentence structures. Analyze your paraphrase using the guidelines on p. 599. Then try summarizing the same passage and checking to see how well you followed the guidelines on pp. 600–601. Take note of any mistakes you made in paraphrasing or summarizing, and list ways you can avoid such mistakes in the future. Record these notes along with the revised paraphrase and summary in your writing log or research log, if you are keeping one.

43

Writing a Research Essay

A NINETEENTH-CENTURY AUTHOR REMARKED *that "in research the horizon recedes as we advance. . . . And research is always incomplete." Indeed, we might slightly alter a line from Samuel Johnson and say that a person who is tired of research is tired of living. For in many ways, the process of living constantly demands research. But while you may continue to pursue a research question for a long time, there comes a time to draw the strands of research together and articulate your conclusions in writing. This chapter will help you at that point.*

The process of research and writing are intimately linked. While you conduct research, you will also be coming up with ideas, recognizing connections among your materials, making notes, and perhaps beginning to draft. From these thoughts, you will eventually choose the final form in which to cast your conclusions. You will probably do most of your final organizing and drafting when your research is largely complete and you have most of the facts, evidence, quotations, and other data you think you need. For most college research essays, the process of drafting a final version should begin at least two weeks before the deadline, to allow time for response to the draft, further research, revision, and editing.

43a

Refining your plans

Throughout your research, you have generated notes that answer your research question and reflect on your hypothesis. Your growing understanding of the subject has no doubt led you to gather other information, which may have altered your original question. This somewhat circular process, a kind of research spiral, is at the heart of all research-based writing.

You should by now have a fair number of notes containing facts, opinions, paraphrases, summaries, quotations, and other material. You prob-

---

Everyday Use

Everyday decisions often call for research and writing. For example, a student had to decide whether to take a full-time summer job or go to summer school and work only a few hours a week. She first gathered information on how much money she could save that summer and how that figure compared with the amount she might save if she attended summer school and thus graduated a term early, when she could get a job. She also checked out all summer course offerings and asked her adviser about whether the job experience she might gain in summer work would make her more marketable. She then drafted a list of advantages and disadvantages for each choice and discussed them with her adviser and friends. Only then did she make a final decision. Can you remember a decision you have made that called for some research and writing?

---

ably also have thoughts about the connections among these many pieces of information. And you should have some sense of whether your hypothesis has been established sufficiently to serve as the thesis of an essay. Reconsider now your purpose, audience, stance, and thesis.

1

Reconsidering your purpose, audience, stance, and thesis

Given what you now know about your research question, reconsider questions such as the following:

1. What is your central purpose? What other purposes, if any, do you have?
2. What is your stance toward your topic? Are you an advocate, a critic, a reporter, an observer or participant-observer, an experimenter, or an interviewer? (2g)
3. Are you addressing an audience other than your instructor?
4. How much about your research question does your audience know already? How much background will you need to present?
5. What sorts of supporting information are your readers likely to find convincing—examples? precedents? quotations from authorities? statistics? direct observation? data drawn from interviews? (5g)
6. What tone will most appeal to them? Should you present yourself as a colleague, an expert, or a student?
7. How can you establish common ground with them and show consideration of points of view other than your own? (5f2 and Chapter 29)
8. What is your thesis trying to establish? How likely is your audience to accept it?

2

Developing an explicit thesis

One useful way of relating your purpose, audience, and thesis before you begin a full draft is by writing out an **explicit thesis statement**. Such a statement forces you to articulate all your major lines of argument and to see how well those arguments carry out your purpose and appeal to your audience. At the drafting stage, your explicit thesis statement might take the following form:

> In this essay, I plan to (explain/argue/demonstrate/analyze, and so on)
> for an audience of _____
> that _____
> because/if (1) _____, (2) _____,
> (3) _____.

For example, Daniel Taffe developed the following explicit thesis statement:

> In this essay, I plan to demonstrate for an audience of classmates from my writing class that Frida Kahlo's unique style resulted not only from the influence of life events but also from her knowledge of earlier European art, including traditional Christian imagery and Mexican culture.

3

Testing your thesis

Writing out an explicit thesis will often confirm your research and support your hypothesis. It may, however, reveal that your hypothesis is invalid, inadequately supported, or insufficiently focused. In such cases, you must then rethink your original research question, perhaps do further research, and work toward a revised hypothesis and a revised thesis. To test your thesis, consider the following list of questions:

1. How can you state the topic of your thesis or your comment about the topic more precisely or more clearly? (3b)

2. In what ways will your thesis interest and appeal to your audience? What can you do to increase that interest? (5h)

3. How could the wording of your thesis be more specific? Could you use more concrete nouns (27c) or stronger verbs (23a)? Should you add qualifying adjectives or adverbs (Chapter 12)?

4. Is your thesis going to be manageable, given your limits of time and knowledge? If not, are there things you can do to make it more manageable?

5. What evidence from your research supports each aspect of your thesis? What additional evidence do you need?

43b

Organizing information

In discussing her own process of writing, Marie Winn talks about the challenge of transforming a tangle of ideas and information "into an orderly and logical sequence on a blank piece of paper." This is the task of organization, of grouping information effectively. Experienced writers differ considerably in the ways they go about this task, and you will want to experiment until you find an organizational method that works well for you. This section will discuss two organizing strategies—grouping material by subject headings and outlining.

1

Grouping notes by subject headings

During your research, you have been taking notes and listing ideas. To group these materials, examine them for connections, finding what might be combined with what, which notes will be more useful and which less useful, which ideas lend support to the thesis and which should be put aside. Brainstorm about your research question one last time, and add the resulting notes to your other materials, looking to see whether they fit with any of the materials you already have.

If you have been keeping notes on cards, you can arrange the cards in groups by subject headings, putting the ones with your main topics in the center and arranging any related cards around them. If you have been taking notes in a notebook, you can cut the pages apart and group the slips of paper in a similar manner. If your notes are in a computer file, see whether you can sort them by subject headings or search for particular headings.

Grouping your notes in this way will help you identify major ideas and see whether you have covered all the areas you need to cover. It will also help you decide whether you have too many ideas—or whether you need to do more research in some area. Most important, it will allow you to see how the many small pieces of your research fit together and result in the larger structure of a complete essay.

Once you have established initial groups, skim through the notes looking for connections you can use to organize your draft. Daniel Taffe noticed that the notes on one of his main topics—early European art—seemed to be related to another set of notes—on Kahlo's retablo-like paintings. He thus decided to see whether he could show how traditional European religious imagery was echoed in Kahlo's distinctly Mexican work.

2
Outlining

Outlines can be used in various ways. Some writers group their notes, write a draft, and then outline the draft to study its tentative structure. Others develop a working outline from their notes, listing the major points in a tentative order with support for each point. Such a working outline may see you through the rest of the process, or you may decide to revise it as you go along. Still other writers prefer to plot out their organization early on in a formal outline. (See 3e for further discussion of outlines.)

Because Daniel Taffe was required to submit a formal outline with his essay, he moved early on from the informal topic outline he made as he grouped his notes to a formal one. His formal outline appears on pp. 647–49.

43c

Drafting your essay

When you are ready to draft your essay, set yourself a deadline, and structure your work with that deadline in mind. Gather your notes, outline, and sources. Most writers find that some sustained work (perhaps two or three hours) pays off at this point. Begin drafting where you feel most confident. If you have an idea for an introduction, begin there. If you are not sure how you want to introduce the essay but do know how you want to approach one point, begin with that, and return to the introduction later. The most important thing is to get started.

The drafting process itself varies considerably among researchers, and much about the way you draft will be up to you. Some writers try to make the first draft as perfect as possible, working meticulously paragraph by paragraph. Others draft as fast as they can, getting all their material down in whatever form it takes and smoothing it out later. Some follow an outline from start to finish; others draft sections separately and arrange them later. Your writing process is your own, and no one else can tell you what works best for you. The tips offered in 3f, however, may help.

1
Drafting a working title and introduction

The title and introduction play special roles, for they set the context for what is to come. Ideally, the title announces the subject of the essay in an intriguing or memorable way. The introduction should draw readers into the essay and provide any background they will need to understand the discussion. You can find general advice on titles in 4f1 and on introductions in 4f2 and 6f1. Some specifics you should consider in drafting an introduction to a research essay include the following:

- It is often effective to *open with a question,* especially your research question. Next, you might explain what you will do to answer the question and then *end with your thesis* (in essence, the answer).

- Because you will be bringing together several distinct points from various sources, you will probably want to *forecast your main points,* to help readers get their bearings.

- You will want to *establish your own credibility* as a research writer by revealing your experience and demonstrating what you have done to become an expert on your topic.

- In general, you may *not* want to open with a quotation—though it can be a good attention-getter. In a research essay, you may want to quote several sources to support your ideas, and opening with a quotation from one source may give the impression that you will be presenting that writer's ideas rather than using them in support of your own.

Because Daniel Taffe knew that some of his readers may never have heard of his topic, he opened his introduction, shown on p. 650, with the question "Who is Frida Kahlo?" After briefly answering it, he piques their interest with facts about recent sales of her paintings to Madonna. He then builds his credibility as a researcher by discussing the preeminent role of Hayden Herrera in Kahlo scholarship. Finally, he forecasts one of his main points, autobiographical elements in Kahlo's work, in leading up to the other one, Christian and Mexican elements, which forms the basis of his thesis.

2

Drafting your conclusion

A good conclusion to a research essay helps readers know what they have learned. Its job is not to persuade (the body of the essay should already have done that), but it can contribute to the overall effectiveness of your argument. General advice on writing conclusions can be found in 4f3 and 6f2, but the following are some specific strategies especially appropriate for research essays:

- A specific-to-general pattern is frequently appropriate. Open with a reference to your thesis, and then expand to a more general conclusion that reminds readers of the significance of your discussion.

- If you have covered several main points, you may want to remind readers of them. Be careful, however, to provide more than a mere summary.

- Try to end with something that will have an impact—a provocative quotation or question, a vivid image, a call for action, or a warning. Remember, however, that readers generally don't like obvious preaching.

- Tailor your conclusion to the needs of your readers, in terms of both the information you include and the tone and style you adopt.

Daniel Taffe's conclusion summarizes the main points of his essay and then ends with an assertion of his topic's importance that is based on an anecdote about Kahlo's life and art. (See p. 661.) His use of the pronoun *us* invokes a kinship with his readers and the possibility that they, too, are or will become students of her work.

43d

Incorporating source materials

When you reach the point of drafting your essay, a new task awaits: weaving your source materials into your writing. The challenge is to use your sources yet remain the author—quote, paraphrase, and summarize other voices while remaining the single, dominant voice in your essay.

You tentatively decided to quote, paraphrase, or summarize material when you read your sources critically and took notes. (See 42b and 42c.) As you choose which sources to use in your essay and how to use them, however, you may want to reevaluate those decisions. For example, you may decide to summarize in your essay what you paraphrased in your notes, to use only a quotation you included in the midst of a summary, or not to use a particular quotation at all. To avoid plagiarizing, document any material you do include from a source with a citation within your text (see 44a, 45a, 45e, and 45f) and an entry in your list of sources.

1

Using direct quotations

Your essay must be your own work, and you should depend on other people's words as little as possible, limiting quotations to those *necessary* to your argument or *memorable* for your readers. Reasons to use direct quotations include the following:

- To incorporate a statement expressed so effectively by the author that it cannot be paraphrased without altering the meaning
- To allow the words of an authority on your topic to contribute to your own credibility as a writer
- To allow an author to defend his or her position in his or her own words
- To create a particular effect

Consider then how to work any quotations into your text.

Enclosing brief quotations within your text

Quotations of no more than four lines (MLA style) or fewer than forty words (APA style) should be worked into your text, enclosed by quotation marks. For example:

> In Miss Eckhart, Welty recognizes a character who shares with her "the love of her art and the love of giving it, the desire to give it until there is no more left" (10).

> In Russia, however, the men who took control had hardly any experience in military or administrative fields at all. As Edward Crankshaw explained, "They were a disciplined set of revolutionary conspirators who had spent most of their adult lives in exile in Russia or abroad" (44).

Notice that both examples alert readers to the quotations by using **signal phrases** that include the author's name. When you cite a quotation in this way, you need put only the page number in the parentheses.

When you introduce a quotation without mentioning the author's name, place the name in the parentheses before the page number. Be sure, however, that you always distinguish where someone else's words begin. For example:

> In *The Third Life of Grange Copeland,* Grange's inability to respond to his son is evident "even in private and in the dark and with his son, presumably asleep" when he "could not bear to touch his son with his hand" (Walker 121).

These are but two ways of introducing a quotation. Both the MLA and the APA styles dictate conventions for what should appear in parenthetical citations in what circumstances and how they should be punctuated. See 44a and 45a for guidelines.

Setting off long quotations

Quotations longer than four lines (MLA style) or forty words (APA style) should be set off from the regular text. Begin such a quotation on a new line, and indent every line ten spaces (MLA) or five to seven spaces (APA) from the left margin. This indentation sets off the quotation clearly, so quotation marks are unnecessary. Type the quotation to the right margin, and double-space it as you do the regular text. Long quotations are usually introduced by a signal phrase or a sentence followed by a colon.

> A good seating arrangement can prevent problems; however, "withitness," as defined by Woolfolk, works even better:
>
> > Withitness is the ability to communicate to students that you are aware of what is happening in the classroom, that you "don't miss anything." With-it teachers seem to have "eyes in the back of their

heads." They avoid becoming too absorbed with a few students, since this allows the rest of the class to wander. (359)
This technique works, however, only if students actually believe that their teacher will know everything that goes on.

While long quotations are often necessary in research essays, use them cautiously. Too many of them may suggest that you did not rely on your own thinking. In addition, long quotations can make an essay seem choppy, and they can distract from your analysis of the material. If you think you may be overusing long quotations, substitute paraphrases or summaries for some of them.

Integrating quotations into your text

Quotations have to be carefully integrated into your text so that they are smoothly and clearly linked to the surrounding sentences. In most cases, you need to use a signal phrase to provide such a link. For example:

WITHOUT A SIGNAL PHRASE

In *Death of a Salesman,* Willy Loman dreams the wrong dreams and idealizes the wrong ideals. "He has lived on his smile and on his hopes, survived from sale to sale, been sustained by the illusion that he has countless friends in his territory, that everything will be all right . . ." (Brown 97).

See how the following revision uses a signal phrase to make the link between quotation and text far easier to recognize. Note also how the shift in verb tenses from text to quotation is smoothed out in the revision.

WITH A SIGNAL PHRASE

In *Death of a Salesman,* Willy Loman dreams the wrong dreams and idealizes the wrong ideals. His misguided perceptions are well captured by Brown: "He has lived on his smile and on his hopes, survived from sale to sale, been sustained by the illusion that he has countless friends in his territory, that everything will be all right . . ." (97).

Introducing a quotation with the author's name and a **signal verb** is a clear and simple way of integrating the quotation into your text. Remember, however, that the verb must be appropriate to the idea you are expressing.

As Eudora Welty notes, "Learning stamps you with its moments. Childhood's learning," she continues, "is made up of moments. It isn't steady. It's a pulse" (9).

Two signal verbs—*notes* and *continues*—are appropriate to integrate the quotations. Here are some other possible signal verbs. Some of them, like *notes* and *continues,* can be used by themselves with the author's name; others, like *interprets* or *opposes,* require more complex phrasing.

> *Signal verbs*

acknowledges	concludes	emphasizes	replies
advises	concurs	expresses	reports
agrees	confirms	interprets	responds
allows	criticizes	lists	reveals
answers	declares	objects	says
asserts	describes	observes	states
believes	disagrees	offers	suggests
charges	discusses	opposes	thinks
claims	disputes	remarks	writes

Indicating changes with brackets and ellipses

Sometimes, for the sake of clarity or length, you will wish to alter a direct quotation in some way—to make a verb tense fit smoothly into your text, to replace a pronoun with a noun, to eliminate unnecessary detail, to change a capital letter to lowercase or vice versa. Enclose any changed or added words in brackets, and indicate any deletions with ellipsis points. Because most quotations that you integrate into your essay come from longer passages, you need not use ellipses at the beginning or end of a quotation unless the last sentence of the quotation as you cite it is incomplete.

> A farmer, Jane Lee, spoke to the Nuclear Regulatory Commission about the occurrences. "There is something wrong in the [Three Mile Island] area. It is happening within nature itself," she said, referring to human miscarriages, stillbirths, and birth defects in farm animals ("Legacy" 33).
>
> Economist John Kenneth Galbraith has pointed out that "large corporations cannot afford to compete with one another. Their survival is predicated upon . . . market segmentation. In a truly competitive market someone loses. . . . American big business has finally learned that everybody has to protect everybody else's investment" (Key 17).

Be careful that any changes you make in a quotation do not alter its essential meaning. Even if an error occurs in the original, do not correct it, but alert readers to it by inserting *sic* ("thus") in brackets after it.

> As the reviewer for *Gumshoe* remarks, "This absorbing mystery offers an attractively sardonic heroin [*sic*] and a humdinger of a plot" (31).

In any event, use brackets and ellipses sparingly, for too many of them make for difficult reading and might suggest that you have changed the meaning by removing some of the context. (For more on brackets and ellipses, see 35b and 35f.)

2

Using paraphrases and summaries

When you want to use others' ideas but have no need to quote their exact words, paraphrase or summarize. Reasons for using paraphrases and summaries include the following:

- To present background information and other facts that your readers may not know
- To explain various positions on your topic

Integrating paraphrases and summaries

As with quotations, you need to introduce paraphrases and summaries clearly, usually with a signal phrase that includes the name of the author of the source. Using the author's name also helps lend authority to the material. Sometimes, in fact, you will want to highlight the source even more prominently. Notice how the writer of the following example focuses on one authority, first introducing her by name and title and then both quoting and summarizing her work:

> On the other hand, some observers of the battle of the sexes are trying to arrange cease-fires. Professor of linguistics Deborah Tannen says that she offers her book *That's Not What I Meant!* to "women and men everywhere who are trying their best to talk to each other" (19). Tannen goes on to illustrate how communication between women and men breaks down and then to suggest that a full awareness of "genderlects" can improve relationships (297).

In the following example, on the other hand, the writer focuses more on the information paraphrased, identifying the authors only parenthetically:

> Three areas of established differences in cognitive abilities are recognized by the majority of researchers: verbal ability, mathematical ability, and spatial ability (Block 517). As shown by current research, a specific cognitive sex difference exists in verbal ability; in general, females are superior to males in this area starting in early childhood (Weitz 99).

Remember that indicating the sources of paraphrases and summaries is important. Even unintentional failure to cite sources for materials that are not in quotation marks but that you could not have known or arrived at by yourself constitutes plagiarism. Make certain that you record the sources of general background information as well as sources of specific quotations, facts, viewpoints, and so forth. If your notes are incomplete or your source is unclear, relocate and reread the original to clarify the information. If you are unable to do so, you would be wise to leave out the material rather than risk plagiarism. (See Chapters 42, 44, and 45.)

> *Incorporating quotations, paraphrases, and summaries*

1. In general, use signal phrases or other clues to indicate where the cited material begins.
2. Identify quotations by enclosing those of up to four lines (MLA style) or forty words (APA style) in quotation marks and setting off longer ones.
3. Check that you reproduced the wording, spelling, punctuation, and capitalization of quotations accurately and that you indicated changes with brackets and ellipses. If your notes are unclear, look again at the original.
4. Document every quotation, paraphrase, and summary with a citation in your text and a corresponding entry in your list of sources cited. If you use some of the author's words within a paraphrase or summary, enclose them in quotation marks, and give a separate citation for them after the closing quotation mark.

3

Checking for excessive use of source material

Exactly how much you should use sources in an essay depends on your purpose, your audience, and the section of the essay. In general, your essay should not be a patchwork of quotations, paraphrases, and summaries from other people. If it is, you will have merely accumulated data; you won't have presented information in your own way. (See 42e.) You need a rhetorical stance, a perspective that represents you as the author. If you are overquoting and overciting, your own voice will disappear. The following passage illustrates this problem:

> The United States is one of the countries with the most rapid population growth. In fact, rapid population increase has been a "prominent feature of American life since the founding of the republic" (Day 31). In the past, the cause of the high rate of population growth was the combination of large-scale immigration and a high birth rate. As Day notes, "Two facts stand out in the demographic history of the United States: first, the single position as a receiver of immigrants; second, our high rate of growth from natural increase" (31).

Nevertheless, American population density is not as high as in most European countries. Day points out that the Netherlands, with a density of 906 persons per square mile, is more crowded than even the most densely populated American states (33).

Most readers will think that the source, Day, is much too prominent here. If this passage were a background discussion or a survey of the literature on a topic, with each source being different, such a large number of citations might be acceptable. But all these citations are from the same source, and readers are likely to conclude that the source is primary and the author only secondary.

43e

Reviewing your draft

Because a research essay involves a complex mix of your thoughts and materials from outside sources, it calls for an especially careful review before you begin revising. As with most kinds of writing, however, taking a break after drafting the essay is important. Get away from the draft, and try to put it out of your mind. Stay away from it for as long as you can, so that when you reread it, you can bring a fresh eye to the task.

When you return to the draft, read it straight through, without stopping. Then read it again slowly, reconsidering four things: purpose, audience, thesis, and support. You might find that outlining your draft helps you analyze it at this point. (See 3e.)

- From your reading of the draft, what do you now see as its *purpose*? How does this compare with your original purpose? Does the draft do what your assignment requires?
- What *audience* does your essay address?
- What is your *stance* toward the topic?
- What is your *thesis*? Is it clearly stated?
- What *evidence* supports your thesis? Is the evidence sufficient?

Answer these questions as best you can, since they are the starting point for revision. Next, you need a closer reading of your essay. At this point, you might benefit from the comments of other readers. Consider asking friends or classmates to read and respond to your draft.

You may also get helpful advice if you ask questions specific to your essay. If you are unsure about whether to include a particular point, how to use a certain quotation, or where to add more examples, ask readers specifically what they think you should do. (For more on getting critical responses to a draft, see 4c.)

Revising and editing your draft

Using any responses you have gathered and your own analysis, turn now to your final revision. It is advisable to work in several steps.

- *Considering responses.* Have readers identified problems you need to solve? If so, have they made specific suggestions about ways to revise? Have they identified strengths that might suggest ways of revising? For example, if they showed great interest in one point but no interest in another, consider expanding the first and deleting the second.

- *Reconsidering your original purpose, audience, and stance.* From the above analysis, do you feel confident that you have achieved your purpose? If not, what is missing? How have you appealed to your readers? How have you established common ground with them? How have you satisfied any special concerns they may have? Has your rhetorical stance toward your topic changed in any way? If so, what effect has that change had on your essay?

- *Gathering additional material.* If you need to strengthen any points, go back to your notes to see if you have the necessary materials. If you failed to consider opposing viewpoints adequately, for instance, you may need to find more material.

- *Deciding on changes you need to make.* Figure out everything you have to do to perfect your draft, and write it out. With your deadline firmly in mind, plan your revision.

- *Rewriting your draft.* Do the major work first—changing content, adding examples or evidence, addressing paragraph-level concerns. Then turn to sentence-level work and, finally, to individual words. Revise for clarity and to sharpen the dominant impression of the essay. (4g)

- *Reconsidering your title, introduction, and conclusion.* In light of the re-evaluation and revision of your draft, reread these important parts to see whether they still serve their purpose. Does the introduction accurately predict, and the conclusion accurately restate, what the body of the final essay discusses? If not, do you need to forecast your main points in the introduction or summarize them in the conclusion? Does your introduction capture readers' attention? Does your conclusion help them see the significance of your argument? Is your title specific enough to let your readers know about your research question and engaging enough to make them want to read your answer to it?

- *Checking your documentation.* Have you included a citation in your text for every quotation, paraphrase, and summary you incorporated, following consistently the required style? (42d and Chapters 44 and 45)

- *Editing your draft.* Now is the time to attend carefully to any remaining problems in grammar, usage, spelling, punctuation, and mechanics. If you are writing on a computer, take the time to use the spell checker. Check for any patterns you have identified as problems in your own writing.

43g

Preparing a list of works cited or your references

Once you have a final draft with your source materials in place, you are ready to prepare your list of works cited (MLA) or your references (APA). Follow the guidelines for your required style carefully, creating an entry for each source used in your essay. Double-check your draft against your list of sources cited to see that you have listed every source mentioned in the parenthetical citations and that you have not listed any sources not cited in your essay. (See Chapters 44 and 45 for guidelines.)

43h

Preparing and proofreading your final copy

Your final rough draft may end up looking very rough indeed, filled with cross-outs, additions in the margins, circles, and arrows. So your next task is to create a final, carefully typed, painstakingly prepared clean copy. This is the version of the paper that you will submit, the one that will represent all your work and effort. (For information on preparing a final manuscript, see Chapter 51.)

Proofreading is a time for celebration. At this point, you are making your research essay as perfect as possible; it is your very best effort. Many writers look forward to the final reading, often taking the time to read it through once backward in order to catch every word-level typographical error. So after proofreading, congratulate yourself, and savor the rewards of a job well done. You have produced a solid piece of research, clearly written and cogently argued. You have become a researcher.

THINKING CRITICALLY ABOUT RESEARCH ESSAYS

Reading with an Eye for Research

The research essays at the end of Chapters 44 and 45 were written by two students, the first of whom you've followed since Chapter 40. The first essay, which follows MLA style, was written for a composition class; the second, which follows APA style, was written for a psychology class. Read these essays carefully, and study the marginal annotations. Compare your research essay with these, noting differences in approach, style, format, and use of sources.

Thinking about Your Own Research Essay

Pause now to reflect on the research essay you have written. How did you go about organizing your information? What would you do to improve this process? What problems did you encounter in drafting? How did you solve these problems? How many quotations did you use, and how did you integrate them into your text? When and why did you use summaries and paraphrases? What did you learn from revising?

44

Documenting Sources: MLA Style

> Adam was the only man who, when he said a good thing, knew that nobody had said it before him.
> — MARK TWAIN

*A*DAM, IN OTHER WORDS, *had the luxury of not having to document his sources, but no writer since Adam has been able to make that claim. In your writing, full and accurate documentation is important because it helps build your credibility as a writer and researcher by giving credit to those people whose works influenced your own ideas.*

Documentation styles vary among disciplines, with one format favored in the humanities, for instance, another in the social sciences, and another in engineering, but they all require the same basic information. Thus you will want to use the conventions of documentation appropriate to a particular course and field. Following these rules of punctuation and format ensures consistency and helps protect you from plagiarizing because of omitted source information. (See 42d.)

Everyday Use

"Says who?" is an insistent question we have all had to answer at one time or another. It usually follows some claim: Schwarzenegger's *True Lies* is an insult to the viewer's intelligence; a Geo isn't worth the cost of a good bicycle, let alone a car. "Says who?" calls on the speaker to document his or her sources by referring to several reviews of *True Lies*, for example, or to an article in *Consumer Reports* on the Geo—or maybe by simply relying on personal experience and replying. "Says me!" When have you needed to document your sources in this way? Has the ability to provide such documentation helped you make your points?

This chapter discusses the basic format for the **Modern Language Association (MLA) style**, widely used in literature and languages as well as other fields, and shows examples of various kinds of sources. For further reference, consult the following:

Gibaldi, Joseph. *MLA Handbook for Writers of Research Papers*. 4th ed. New York: MLA, 1995.

Directory to MLA style

44a. Parenthetical citations

Author named in a signal phrase, 626
Author named in a citation, 626
Two or three authors, 626
Four or more authors, 627
Corporate author, 627
Unknown author, 627
Author of two or more works, 627
Two or more authors with the same surname, 627

Multivolume work, 628
Literary work, 628
Bible, 628
Indirect source, 628
Two or more sources in the same citation, 629
Entire work or one-page article, 629
Nonprint or electronic source, 629

44b. Explanatory and bibliographic notes

44c. List of works cited

1. BOOKS

One author, 631
Two or three authors, 631
Four or more authors, 632
Corporate author, 632
Unknown author, 632
Two or more books by the same author(s), 632
Editor or editors, 633
Author and editor, 633
Selection in an anthology or chapter in a book with an editor, 633
Two or more items from an anthology, 634
Translation, 634

Edition other than the first, 635
One volume of a multivolume work, 635
Two or more volumes of a multivolume work, 635
Preface, foreword, introduction, or afterword, 635
Article in a reference work, 635
Book that is part of a series, 636
Republication, 636
Government document, 636

Pamphlet, 637
Published proceedings of a
  conference, 637
Book published before 1900,
  637

Publisher's imprint, 637
Title within the title, 638

2. PERIODICALS

Article in a journal paginated
  by volume, 638
Article in a journal paginated
  by issue, 639
Article in a monthly magazine,
  639
Article in a weekly magazine,
  639

Article in a newspaper, 639
Editorial or letter to the editor,
  639
Unsigned article, 640
Review, 640
Article with a title within the
  title, 640

3. ELECTRONIC SOURCES

CD-ROM, 641
On-line computer service, 641
Electronic journal, newsletter,
  or conference, 641

Publication on disc, 642

4. OTHER SOURCES

Unpublished dissertation, 642
Published dissertation, 642
Article from a microform, 642
Interview, 643
Letter or electronic
  correspondence, 643
Film or videotape, 643

Television or radio program, 644
Recording, 644
Work of art, 644
Lecture or speech, 644
Performance, 645
Map or chart, 645
Cartoon, 645

44d. A sample research essay, MLA style

44a

MLA format for parenthetical citations

MLA style uses **parenthetical citations** in the text of an essay to document every quotation, paraphrase, summary, or other material requiring documentation. (See 42d.) Parenthetical citations correspond to full bibliographic entries in a list of works cited at the end of the text. Usually the author's name is mentioned in a signal phrase introducing the material, and the page number of the original source is given in parentheses after the material. Use an author's full name the first time you cite a source. For later citations, use just the last name. In general, make your parenthetical citations short, including the information your readers need to locate the full citation in the works-cited list.

Place a parenthetical citation as near the relevant material as possible without disrupting the flow of the sentence, usually before the punctuation mark at the end of the sentence or phrase containing the material. Place any punctuation mark *after* the closing parenthesis. If your citation refers to a quotation, place the citation *after* the closing quotation mark but *before* any punctuation mark. For long quotations typed as a block, place the parenthetical citation two spaces after the final punctuation mark. Here are examples of the various ways to cite sources.

AUTHOR NAMED IN A SIGNAL PHRASE

Ordinarily, use the author's name in a signal phrase to introduce the material, and simply cite the page number(s) in parentheses.

```
Herrera indicates that Kahlo believed in a "vitalistic
form of pantheism" (328).
```

AUTHOR NAMED IN A CITATION

When you do not name the author in the text, include the author's last name before the page number(s) in the parenthetical citation. There is no punctuation separating author's name from page number.

```
In places, Beauvoir "sees Marxists as believing in sub-
jectivity as much as existentialists do" (Whitmarsh 63).
```

TWO OR THREE AUTHORS

Use all the authors' last names in a signal phrase or in the parenthetical citation.

```
Gortner, Hebrun, and Nicolson maintain that "opinion
leaders" influence other people in an organization
because they are respected, not because they hold high
positions (175).
```

FOUR OR MORE AUTHORS

Use the first author's name and *et al.* ("and others"), or name all the authors in a signal phrase or in the parenthetical citation.

```
Similarly, as Belenky, Clinchy, Goldberger, and Tarule
assert, examining the lives of women expands our
understanding of human development (7).
```

CORPORATE AUTHOR

Give the full name of a corporate author if it is brief or, if it is long, give a shortened form in a signal phrase or in the parenthetical citation.

```
In fact, one of the leading foundations in the field of
higher education supports the recent proposals for
community-run public schools (Carnegie Corporation 45).
```

UNKNOWN AUTHOR

Use the full title if it is brief or, if it is long, give a shortened version in a signal phrase or in the parenthetical citation.

```
"Hype," by one analysis, is "an artificially engendered
atmosphere of hysteria" ("Today's Marketplace" 51).
```

AUTHOR OF TWO OR MORE WORKS

For a work by an author of two or more works in your list of works cited, include a shortened version of the title in a signal phrase or in the parenthetical citation.

```
Gardner presents readers with their own silliness through
his description of a "pointless, ridiculous monster,
crouched in the shadows, stinking of dead men, murdered
children, and martyred cows" (Grendel 2).
```

TWO OR MORE AUTHORS WITH THE SAME SURNAME

If your list of works cited includes works by different authors with the same surname, always include the author's first name in the signal phrases or in the parenthetical citations for those works.

```
Children will learn to write if they are allowed to
choose their own subjects, James Britton asserts, citing
the Schools Council study of the 1960s (37-42).
```

MULTIVOLUME WORK

Name the author in a signal phrase or in the parenthetical citation. Note the volume number first and then the page number(s), with a colon and one space between them.

```
Modernist writers prized experimentation and gradually
even sought to blur the line between poetry and prose,
according to Forster (3: 150).
```

If you name only one volume of the work in your list of works cited, you need include only the page number in the parenthetical citation.

LITERARY WORK

For literary works available in many editions, cite the page number(s) from the edition you used followed by a semicolon and such information as part or chapter in a novel (175; ch. 4) or act and/or scene in a play (37; sc. 1). For poems, cite only the line number(s), using the word *line(s)* in the first reference to alert readers that the numbers do not refer to pages (lines 33–34). For verse plays, give only the act, scene, and line numbers, separated by periods.

```
As Macbeth begins, the witches greet Banquo as "Lesser
than Macbeth, and greater" (1.3.65).
```

BIBLE

Identify biblical quotations by chapter and verse (John 3:16). Spell out the names of all books mentioned in your text. In a parenthetical citation, use an abbreviation for books whose names are longer than five letters (*Gen.* for *Genesis; Matt.* for *Matthew*). If you use the King James Version, you do not need to include a works-cited entry. If you use any other version, treat it as you would a book in the works-cited list. (See 44c.)

INDIRECT SOURCE

Use the abbreviation *qtd. in* to indicate that you are quoting from an indirect source—that is, someone else's report of a conversation, statement, interview, letter, or the like.

As Arthur Miller says, "When somebody is destroyed everybody finally contributes to it, but in Willy's case, the end product would be virtually the same" (qtd. in Martin and Meyer 375).

TWO OR MORE SOURCES IN THE SAME CITATION

If you refer to more than one source in parentheses, separate the information with semicolons.

Recently, however, some economists have recommended that <u>employment</u> be redefined to include unpaid domestic labor (Clark 148; Nevins 39).

ENTIRE WORK OR ONE-PAGE ARTICLE

To cite a whole work rather than a specific passage or to cite a one-page article, include the reference in the text without any page numbers or parentheses.

Thomas Hardy's tragic vision is given full vent in his <u>Jude the Obscure</u>, a bleaker novel than <u>The Return of the Native</u>.

NONPRINT OR ELECTRONIC SOURCE

Give enough information in a signal phrase or parenthetical citation for readers to locate the source in the list of works cited. Usually use the name or title under which you list the source.

Kahlo is seated with a Judas doll, identified in the film <u>Portrait of an Artist: Frida Kahlo</u> as a papier-mâché doll stuffed with firecrackers to be exploded on the day before Easter.

44b

MLA format for explanatory and bibliographic notes

MLA style allows **explanatory notes** for information or commentary that would not readily fit into the text but is needed for clarification or further explanation. In addition, MLA style permits **bibliographic notes** for citing several sources for one point and for offering information about or evaluation of a source. Superscript numbers are used in the text to refer readers to the notes, which may appear as endnotes (typed under the heading "Notes" on a separate page after the text but before the list of works cited) or as footnotes at the bottom of the page (typed four lines below the last text line). For example:

SUPERSCRIPT NUMBER IN TEXT

Stewart emphasizes the existence of social contacts in Hawthorne's life so that the audience will accept a different Hawthorne, one more attuned to modern times than the figure in Woodberry.[3]

NOTE

[3] Woodberry does, however, show that Hawthorne <u>was</u> often an unsociable individual. He emphasizes the seclusion of Hawthorne's mother, who separated herself from her family after the death of her husband, often even taking meals alone (28). Woodberry seems to imply that Mrs. Hawthorne's isolation rubbed off onto her son.

For other examples, see the "Notes" to Daniel Taffe's essay (p. 662).

44c

MLA format for a list of works cited

A list of **Works Cited** is an alphabetical list of the sources cited in your essay. (If your instructor asks that you list everything you have read as background, call the list "Works Consulted.") Start your list on a separate page after the text of your essay and any notes (see 44b). Continue the consecutive numbering of pages. Type the heading *Works Cited,* neither underlined nor in quotation marks, centered one inch from the top of the page. Double-space, and begin your first entry. Start each entry flush with the left margin; indent any subsequent line of the entry five spaces. Double-space the entire list.

List your sources alphabetically by author's last name. If the author of a source is unknown, alphabetize the source by the first major word of the title.

On the following pages, you will find sample entries that follow the MLA specifications for various kinds of sources.

1

Books

The basic entry for a book includes the following elements:

1. *Author.* List the author by last name first followed by a comma and the first name.
2. *Title.* Underline the title and any subtitle, and capitalize all major words. (See 36c for more on capitalizing titles.)
3. *Publication information.* Give the city of publication and add a colon, a space, and a shortened version of the publisher's name—dropping *Press, Publishers, Inc.,* and so on (*St. Martin's* for *St. Martin's Press, Inc.*), using only the first surname (*Harcourt* for *Harcourt Brace*), and abbreviating *University Press* (*Oxford UP* for *Oxford University Press*)—then a comma, and the year of publication.

These elements are separated from one another by a period, and the entry ends with a period. Here is an example of a basic entry for a book.

author, last name first   title, underlined   subtitle

double-space → Secord, James A. Controversy in Victorian Geology: The Cambrian-
indent 5 spaces → Silurian Dispute. Princeton: Princeton UP. 1986.

publisher's city and name

ONE AUTHOR

Herrera, Hayden. Frida: A Biography of Frida Kahlo.
 New York: Harper, 1983.

TWO OR THREE AUTHORS

List the first author, last name first; then list the name(s) of the other author(s) in regular order, with a comma between authors and an *and* before the last one.

Appleby, Joyce, Lynn Hunt, and Margaret Jacob. Telling
 the Truth about History. New York: Norton, 1994.

FOUR OR MORE AUTHORS

Give the first author listed on the title page, followed by a comma and *et al.* ("and others"), or list all the names, since the use of *et al.* diminishes the importance of the other contributors.

```
Belenky, Mary Field, Blythe Clinchy, Jill Goldberger,
     and Nancy Tarule. Women's Ways of Knowing. New York:
     Basic, 1986.
```

CORPORATE AUTHOR

Give the name of the group listed on the title page as the author, even if the same group published the book.

```
American Chemical Society. Handbook for Authors of Papers
     in the American Chemical Society Publications.
     Washington: American Chemical Soc., 1978.
```

UNKNOWN AUTHOR

Begin the entry with the title, and list the work alphabetically by the first major word of the title after any initial *a, an,* or *the.*

```
The New York Times Atlas of the World. New York: New York
     Times Books, 1980.
```

TWO OR MORE BOOKS BY THE SAME AUTHOR(S)

If you cite two or more works by the same author(s), arrange the entries alphabetically by title. List the name(s) of the author(s) in the first entry, but in subsequent entries use three hyphens followed by a period instead.

```
Lorde, Audre. A Burst of Light. Ithaca: Firebrand,
     1988.
---. Sister Outsider. Trumansburg: Crossing, 1984.
```

If you cite a work by one author who is also listed as the first coauthor of another work you cite, list the single-author work first, and repeat the author's name in the entry for the coauthored work. Also repeat the author's name if you cite a work in which that author is listed as the first of a different set of coauthors. Use three hyphens only when the work is by *exactly* the same author(s) as the previous entry.

EDITOR OR EDITORS

Treat an editor as an author, but add a comma and *ed.* (or *eds.* for more than one editor).

> Wall, Cheryl A., ed. <u>Changing Our Own Words: Essays on</u>
>   <u>Criticism, Theory, and Writing by Black Women</u>. New
>   Brunswick: Rutgers UP, 1989.

AUTHOR AND EDITOR

To cite a book that has both an author and an editor, begin the entry with the author's name if you have cited the body of the text, and list the editor's name, introduced by *Ed.*, in regular order after the title.

> James, Henry. <u>Portrait of a Lady</u>. Ed. Leon Edel.
>   Boston: Houghton, 1963.

If you have cited the editor's contribution to the work, begin the entry with the editor's name followed by a comma and *ed.*, and list the author's name, introduced by the word *By*, in regular order after the title.

> Edel, Leon, ed. <u>Portrait of a Lady</u>. By Henry James.
>   Boston: Houghton, 1963.

**SELECTION IN AN ANTHOLOGY OR CHAPTER
IN A BOOK WITH AN EDITOR**

List the following items, separated from one another by a period and two spaces: the author(s) of the selection or chapter; its title (with titles of essays, short stories, poems, and chapters in quotation marks and those of plays and long poems underlined); the title of the book in which the selection or chapter appears (underlined); *Ed.* and the name(s) of the editor(s) in regular order; the publication information; and the inclusive page numbers of the selection.

> Gordon, Mary. "The Parable of the Cave." <u>The Writer on</u>
>   <u>Her Work</u>. Ed. Janet Sternburg. New York: Norton,
>   1980. 27-32.

If the selection was originally published in a periodical and you are asked to supply information for this original source, use the following format. (See also 44c2.) Note that *Rpt.* is the abbreviation for "Reprinted."

```
Didion, Joan. "Why I Write." New York Times Book Review.
    9 Dec. 1976: 22. Rpt. in The Writer on Her Work. Ed.
    Janet Sternburg. New York: Norton, 1980. 3-16.
```

For inclusive page numbers up to 99, note all digits in the second number. For numbers above 99, note only the last two digits and any others that change in the second number (115–18, 1378–79, 296–301).

TWO OR MORE ITEMS FROM AN ANTHOLOGY

If you cite two or more selections in an anthology, include the anthology itself in your list of works cited.

```
Spender, Dale, and Janet Todd, eds. British Women
    Writers: An Anthology from the Fourteenth Century to
    the Present. New York: Bedrick, 1989.
```

Then you can list each selection you cite by its author and title, followed by a cross-reference to the anthology. The cross-reference consists of the last name(s) of the editor(s) and the inclusive page numbers of the selection.

```
Behn, Aphra. The Rover. Spender and Todd 32-152.

Linton, Eliza Lynn. "The Mad Willoughbys." Spender and
    Todd 536-86.
```

TRANSLATION

Begin the entry with the author's name, and give the translator's name, preceded by *Trans.*, after the title.

```
Zamora, Martha. Frida Kahlo: the Brush of Anguish.
    Trans. Marilyn Sode Smith. San Francisco:
    Chronicle, 1990.
```

If you cite a translated selection in an anthology, add *Trans.* and the translator's name before the title of the anthology.

```
Horace. The Art of Poetry. Trans. Burton Raffel. The
    Critical Tradition: Classic Texts and Contemporary
    Trends. Ed. David H. Richter. New York: Bedford-St.
    Martin's, 1989. 66-77.
```

EDITION OTHER THAN THE FIRST

To cite a book identified on its title page as an edition other than the first, add the information, in abbreviated form, after the title.

```
Kelly, Alfred H., Winfred A. Harbison, and Herman Belz.

    The American Constitution: Its Origins and Develop-

    ment. 6th ed. New York: Norton, 1983.
```

ONE VOLUME OF A MULTIVOLUME WORK

Give the volume number after the title, and list the number of volumes in the complete work after the date, using the abbreviations *Vol.* and *vols*.

```
Foner, Philip S., and Ronald L. Lewis, eds. The Black

    Worker. Vol. 3. Philadelphia: Lippincott, 1980.

    8 vols.
```

TWO OR MORE VOLUMES OF A MULTIVOLUME WORK

If you cite two or more volumes of a multivolume work, give the number of volumes in the complete work after the title, using the abbreviation *vols*.

```
Foner, Philip S., and Ronald L. Lewis, eds. The Black

    Worker. 8 vols. Philadelphia: Lippincott, 1980.
```

PREFACE, FOREWORD, INTRODUCTION, OR AFTERWORD

List the author of the item, then the item title, neither underlined nor in quotation marks. After the title of the book, give its author's name in regular order, preceded by the word *By*. If the same person wrote both the book and the cited item, use just the last name after *By*. List the inclusive page numbers of the item at the end of the entry.

```
Schlesinger, Arthur M., Jr. Introduction. Pioneer Women:

    Voices from the Kansas Frontier. By Joanna L. Strat-

    ton. New York: Simon, 1981. 11-15.
```

ARTICLE IN A REFERENCE WORK

List the author of the article, if there is one. If no author is identified, begin with the title. For a well-known encyclopedia, just note any edition number and date after the name of the encyclopedia. If the encyclopedia entries are arranged in alphabetical order, no volume or page numbers are needed.

> "Traquair, Sir John Stewart." <u>Encyclopaedia Britannica</u>.
>
> > 11th ed. 1911.
>
> Johnson, Peder J. "Concept Learning." <u>Encyclopedia of</u>
> > <u>Education</u>. 1971.

BOOK THAT IS PART OF A SERIES

To cite a book that is part of a series, cite the series name as it appears on the title page followed by any series number.

> Moss, Beverly J., ed. <u>Literacy across Communities</u>.
> > Written Language Series 2. Cresskill: Hampton,
> > 1994.

REPUBLICATION

To cite a modern edition of an older book, a paperback edition, or other republication, add the original date, followed by a period, after the title. Then give the publication details for the edition you used.

> Scott, Walter. <u>Kenilworth</u>. 1821. New York: Dodd, 1956.

GOVERNMENT DOCUMENT

Begin with the author, if identified. If no author is given, start with the name of the government followed by the agency and any subdivision. Use abbreviations if they can be readily understood. Then list the title, which should be underlined. For congressional documents, cite the number, session, and house of Congress (using *S* for Senate and *HR* for House of Representatives), and the type (Report, Resolution, Document), in abbreviated form, and number of the material. If you cite the *Congressional Record*, give only the date and page number. Otherwise, end with the publication information—the publisher is often the Government Printing Office (GPO)—as you would for a book.

> New Hampshire. Dept. of Transportation. <u>Right of Way Sa-</u>
> > <u>linity Reports, Hillsborough County, 1985</u>. Concord:
> > New Hampshire Dept. of Transportation, 1986.

United States. Cong. House. <u>Report of the Joint</u>
 <u>Subcommittee on Reconstruction</u>. 39th Cong., 1st
 sess. H. Rept. 30. 1865. New York: Arno, 1969.

U.S. Bureau of the Census. <u>Historical Statistics of the</u>
 <u>United States, Colonial Times to 1870</u>. Washington:
 GPO, 1975.

PAMPHLET

Treat a pamphlet as you would a book.

<u>Why Is Central America a Conflict Area?</u> Opposing View-
 points Pamphlets. St. Paul: Greenhaven, 1984.

PUBLISHED PROCEEDINGS OF A CONFERENCE

Treat proceedings as a book, but add information about the conference
if it is not part of the title.

Martin, John Steven, and Christine Mason Sutherland, eds.
 <u>Proceedings of the Canadian Society for the History</u>
 <u>of Rhetoric</u>. Calgary, Alberta: Canadian Soc. for the
 History of Rhetoric, 1986.

BOOK PUBLISHED BEFORE 1900

Omit the publisher's name, and add a comma between the place of
publication and the date.

Randolph, Peter. <u>From Slave Cabin to the Pulpit</u>.
 Boston, 1893.

PUBLISHER'S IMPRINT

If a book was published by a publisher's imprint (indicated on the
title page), hyphenate the imprint and the publisher's name.

Rose, Phyllis. <u>Parallel Lives: Five Victorian Marriages</u>.
 New York: Vintage-Random, 1984.

TITLE WITHIN THE TITLE

Do not underline the title of a book within the title of a book you are citing. Underline and enclose in quotation marks a title of a short work within a book title.

```
Gilbert, Stuart. James Joyce's Ulysses. New York:
     Vintage-Random, 1955.
```

2

Periodicals

The basic entry for a periodical includes the following elements:

1. *Author.* List the author by last name first followed by a comma and the first name.
2. *Article title.* Enclose the title and any subtitle in quotation marks, and capitalize all major words. (See 36c for more on capitalizing titles.)
3. *Publication information.* Give the periodical title (excluding any initial *a, an,* or *the*), underlined and with all major words capitalized; the volume number and issue number if appropriate; and the date of publication. For journals, list the year in parentheses followed by a colon, a space, and the inclusive page numbers. For magazines and newspapers, list the month (abbreviated, except for May, June, and July) or the day and month before the year, and do not use parentheses. Do not use *p.* or *pp.* before the page numbers. For inclusive page numbers, note all digits for numbers 1 to 99, and note only the last two digits and any others that change for numbers above 99 (24–27, 134–45).

These elements are separated from one another by a period, and the entry ends with a period. Here is an example of a basic entry for an article in a journal.

```
                        author, last name first    article title,          periodical title,
                                                    in quotation marks      underlined

                        Ficaro, Barbara. "Canterbury's First Dean." Sixteenth Century
double-space →
indent 5 spaces →       Journal 18 (1987): 343-46.  page numbers
                                volume
                                number   date, in parentheses
```

ARTICLE IN A JOURNAL PAGINATED BY VOLUME

If a periodical's pages are numbered continuously from one issue to the next within each year, follow the title of the publication with the volume number in arabic numerals.

Norris, Margot. "Narration under a Blindfold: Reading

    Joyce's 'Clay.'" <u>PMLA</u> 102 (1987): 206-15.

ARTICLE IN A JOURNAL PAGINATED BY ISSUE

Put a period and the issue number after the volume number.

Loffy, John. "The Politics at Modernism's Funeral."

    <u>Canadian Journal of Political and Social Theory</u> 6.3

    (1987): 89-96.

ARTICLE IN A MONTHLY MAGAZINE

Put the month (or months, hyphenated) before the year. Do not include volume or issue numbers.

Weiss, Philip. "The Book Thief: A True Tale of

    Bibliomania." <u>Harper's</u> Jan. 1994: 37-56.

ARTICLE IN A WEEKLY MAGAZINE

Include the day, month, and year in that order, with no commas between them. Separate the date and page number(s) with a period. Do not include volume or issue number.

Van Biema, David. "Parodies Regained." <u>Time</u> 21 Mar. 1994:

    46.

ARTICLE IN A NEWSPAPER

After the author and article title, give the name of the newspaper, underlined, as it appears on the front page but without any initial *a, an,* or *the.* Add the city in brackets after the name if it is not part of the title. Then give the date and the edition if one is listed, and add a colon and then the page number(s). If the article appears on discontinuous pages, give the first page followed by a plus sign.

Markoff, John. "Cyberspace's Most Wanted: Hacker Eludes

    F.B.I. Pursuit." <u>New York Times</u> 4 July 1994, late

    ed.: 1+.

EDITORIAL OR LETTER TO THE EDITOR

Use the label *Editorial* or *Letter,* neither underlined nor in quotation marks, after the title or after the author's name if there is no title.

```
Magee, Doug. "Soldier's Home." Editorial. Nation 26 Mar.
     1988: 400-01.

Crews, Frederick. "Was Freud a Fraud?" Letter. New York
     Times Book Review 27 Mar. 1994: 27.
```

UNSIGNED ARTICLE

Begin with the article title, alphabetizing the entry according to the first word after any initial *a, an,* or *the.*

```
"The Odds of March." Time 15 Apr. 1985: 20+.
```

REVIEW

List the reviewer's name and the title of the review, if any, followed by *Rev. of* and the title and author or director of the work reviewed. Then add the publication information for the publication in which the review appears.

```
Solinger, Rickie. "Unsafe for Women." Rev. of Next Time,
     She'll Be Dead: Battering and How to Stop It, by Ann
     Jones. New York Times Book Review 20 Mar. 1994: 16.
```

ARTICLE WITH A TITLE WITHIN THE TITLE

Enclose in single quotation marks the title of a short work within an article title. Underline the title of a book within an article title.

```
Frey, Leonard H. "Irony and Point of View in 'That
     Evening Sun.'" Faulkner Studies 2 (1953): 33-40.
```

3

Electronic sources

Even as electronic sources of information such as bibliographies on CD-ROM and electronic journals accessed through the Internet become more and more important for researchers, documenting these sources remains tricky. Some electronic documents are fluid, changing continually without any notification, making it difficult to cite a "completed" work. Others are more fixed and can be cited much like a book. The MLA guidelines call for much detail, from publication medium to information about printed versions, but they say as well that "if you cannot find some of the information required—for example, the vendor's name—cite what is available."

For periodically revised CD-ROMs and material accessed through a computer service, include (1) name of the author (if given); (2) publication information for the print source (if you can find this information in the electronic version—include the title, date, and other details as shown in 44c1 and 44c2); (3) title of the database (underlined); (4) publication medium (*CD-ROM* or *On-line*); (5) name of the vendor or computer service used (such as SilverPlatter or Dialog); and (6) electronic publication date (for CD-ROM) or the date of access (for on-line computer services). If there is no print source, put the title of the material accessed (in quotation marks) and the date of the material (if given) between the name of the author and the title of the database.

CD-ROM

The first example is for a periodically revised CD-ROM and includes the print source information. The second is for a single-issue CD-ROM (one published a single time, with no plan to update regularly); cite this kind of CD-ROM much like a book, but add *CD-ROM* as shown here.

Natchez, Gladys. "Frida Kahlo and Diego Rivera: The

    Transformation of Catastrophe to Creativity."

    Psychotherapy-Patient 4.1 (1987): 153-74.

    Psychological Abstracts 76.4 (April 1989): 11344.

    PsychLIT. CD-ROM. SilverPlatter. Nov. 1994.

"Communion." The Oxford English Dictionary. 2nd ed. CD-

    ROM. Oxford: Oxford UP, 1992.

MATERIAL FROM AN ON-LINE COMPUTER SERVICE

The first example has print source information; the second does not.

Daly, John. "Writing Apprehension and Writing

    Competency." Journal of Educational Research 72

    (1978): 566-72. ERIC. On-line. Dialog. 10 Aug. 1994.

Natchez, Gladys, "Frida Kahlo and Diego Rivera: The

    Transformation of Catastrophe to Creativity."

    PsychINFO. On-line. Dialog. 12 July 1994.

ELECTRONIC JOURNAL, NEWSLETTER, OR CONFERENCE

Include the title of the article or document (in quotation marks); the title of the journal, newsletter, or conference (underlined); the volume or other identifying number; the year or date of publication (in parentheses); and the number of pages or paragraphs (if given) or *n.pag.* to signal no pagination after the name of the author (if given). Ask your instructor if you need an availability statement; if so, add it after the word *Available*.

```
Rosenberg, Martin E. "Dynamic and Thermodynamic Tropes of
    the Subject." Postmodern Culture 4.1 (1993): 32
    pars. On-line. Internet. 15 July 1994. Available
    Telnet: gopher.nebula.lib.vt.edu Directory:
    electronic bookshelf/ejournals/postmodern culture/
    pmcv4n1 File: rose0401.txt.
```

PUBLICATION ON DISC

Cite as you would a book, adding a description of the medium of publication (*disc*) before the city of publication.

```
Larson, Deena. Marble Springs. 1st ed. Disc. Watertown:
    Eastgate, 1994.
```

4

Other sources

UNPUBLISHED DISSERTATION

Enclose the title in quotation marks. Add the identification *Diss.*, the name of the university or professional school, a comma, and the year the dissertation was accepted.

```
LeCourt, Donna. "The Self in Motion: The Status of the
    (Student) Subject in Composition Studies." Diss.
    Ohio State U., 1993.
```

PUBLISHED DISSERTATION

Cite a published dissertation as a book, adding the identification *Diss.* and the name of the university. If the dissertation was published by University Microfilms International, add *Ann. Arbor: UMI,* and the year, and list the UMI number at the end of the entry.

```
Botts, Roderic C. Influences in the Teaching of English,
    1917-1935: An Illusion of Progress. Diss.
    Northeastern U, 1970. Ann Arbor: UMI, 1971. 71-1799.
```

ARTICLE FROM A MICROFORM

Treat the article as you would a printed work, identifying the name of the microform and information for locating it.

```
Sharpe, Lora. "A Quilter's Tribute." Boston Globe 25 Mar.
     1989. Newsbank: Social Relations 12 (1989): fiche 6,
     grids B4-6.
```

INTERVIEW

List first the person interviewed. Then list the title, if the interview has one, in quotation marks (or underlined if it is a complete work). If it has no title, use the label *Interview,* neither underlined nor in quotation marks, and identify the source. If you yourself were the interviewer, use the label *Telephone interview* or *Personal interview,* and give the date it took place.

```
Schorr, Daniel. Interview. Weekend Edition. Natl. Public
     Radio. WEVO, Concord. 26 Mar. 1988.

Merget, Astrid. Telephone interview. 16 Mar. 1994.
```

LETTER OR ELECTRONIC CORRESPONDENCE

If the letter was published, cite it as a selection in a book, noting the date and any identifying number after the title.

```
Frost, Robert. "Letter to Editor of the Independent."  28
     Mar. 1894. Selected Letters of Robert Frost. Ed.
     Lawrance Thompson. New York: Holt, 1964. 19.
```

If the correspondence was sent to you, follow the forms below.

```
Moller, Willie. Letter to the author. 10 Sept. 1994.

Diaz, Gloria. E-mail to the author. 12 Feb. 1989.
```

If the letter is from an archival collection, identify the writer and the recipient, give the date, and then give the name of the collection and the name and city of the institution that houses the collection.

```
Hones, William. Letter to John and Joseph Le Conte.
     14 Jan. 1868. Le Conte Family Papers. Bancroft
     Library, U of California, Berkeley.
```

FILM OR VIDEOTAPE

Start with the title, underlined; then name the director, the company distributing the film or videotape, and the date. Other contributors, such as writers or actors, may follow the director's name. If you cite a particular person's work, such as the director's, start the entry with that person's name.

The Night of the Hunter. Dir. Charles Laughton. Perf.
    Robert Mitchum, Shelley Winters, and Lillian Gish.
    United Artists, 1955.

TELEVISION OR RADIO PROGRAM

Begin with the title of the program, underlined. Add other details (such as narrator, director, actors) after the title, as necessary. Identify the network, the local station and city, and the broadcast date. If you cite a particular person's work, begin the entry with that person's name. If you cite a particular episode, include any title, in quotation marks, before the program's title.

Hill Street Blues. Writ. Michael Kozoll and Stephen
    Bochco. Perf. Daniel J. Travanti, Joe Spano, and
    Charles Haid. NBC. WNBC, New York. 15 Jan. 1981.

RECORDING

Your research interest determines whether the name of the composer, artist, or conductor precedes the title of the recording, which is underlined, or the title of the composition, which is not underlined. If you are not using a compact disc, give the medium before the manufacturer's name. End with the name of the manufacturer and the date.

Vega, Suzanne. Solitude Standing. A&M, 1987.

Grieg, Edvard. Concerto in A-minor, op. 16. Cond. Eugene
    Ormandy. Philadelphia Orch. RCA, 1989.

WORK OF ART

List the artist followed by the work's title, underlined. Add the name of the museum or other location, a comma, and the city.

Kahlo, Frida. Self-Portrait with Cropped Hair. Museum of
    Modern Art, New York.

LECTURE OR SPEECH

List the speaker, the title in quotation marks, the name of the sponsoring institution or group, the place, and the date. If the speech is untitled, use a descriptive label (*Lecture, Keynote speech*, etc.).

```
Stern, Virginia. "Sir Stephen Powle as Adventurer in
     the Virginia Company of London." Seminar on the
     Renaissance. Columbia University. New York,
     15 Oct. 1985.
```

PERFORMANCE

List the title, other appropriate details (such as composer, writer, director), the place, and the date. If you cite a particular person, begin the entry with that person's name.

```
Frankie and Johnny in the Clair de Lune. By Terrence
     McNally. Dir. Paul Benedict. Westside Arts Theater,
     New York. 18 Jan. 1988.
```

MAP OR CHART

Cite a map or chart as you would a book with an unknown author, adding the label *Map* or *Chart.*

```
Pennsylvania. Map. Chicago: Rand, 1985.
```

CARTOON

List the cartoonist's name, the title of the cartoon (if it has one), the word *Cartoon,* and the usual publication information.

```
Trudeau, Garry. "Doonesbury." Cartoon. Philadelphia
     Inquirer. 9 Mar. 1988: 37.
```

44d

A sample research essay, MLA style

Daniel Taffe's final essay appears on the following pages. In preparing this essay, he followed the MLA guidelines described in this chapter. He was required to prepare a title page. Had he not needed a separate title page, he would have followed MLA instructions for a heading at the top of the first page of his essay (see Chapter 51 for an example). Note that, in order to annotate this essay, we have reproduced it in a smaller space than you will have on a standard (8½ by 11 inch) sheet of paper. The lines shown here are thus considerably shorter than the lines in your essay will be.

For the first page
of an essay that
does not use a
separate cover
sheet, see 4j

Frida Kahlo: More Than a Life

Heading centered
one-third down
the page

by Daniel Taffe

Writer's name
centered three or
four lines below
the title

English 231

Professor Connors

15 May 19XX

Course number
centered three or
four lines below
the writer's name

Professor's name
and the date
centered directly
below the course
number

Taffe i

Outline

Thesis statement: Frida Kahlo's unique style results not only from autobiographical influences but also from her knowledge of earlier European art, traditional Christian imagery, and Mexican culture.

I. Autobiographical influences played a large part in Kahlo's work.

   A. The events of her life were exciting and often painful.

      1. She was stricken with polio at age six.

      2. She was almost killed in a traffic collision in 1925.

      3. She began to paint while convalescing.

      4. She married Diego Rivera in 1929.

      5. Their relationship stormy, she and Rivera divorced in 1939 but remarried in 1940.

      6. She suffered many medical problems.

      7. She died in 1954.

   B. Some of her works refer to her physical pain.

      1. The Broken Column

      2. Remembrance of an Open Wound

Taffe ii

C. Some paintings depict the pain of *Subpoint*
her marriage.
1. <u>The Two Fridas</u>
2. <u>A Few Small Nips</u>

II. Earlier European art, traditional *Second major point in support of the thesis*
Christian imagery, and Mexican culture
also strongly influenced Kahlo's work.

Subpoint followed by four supporting details

A. Her background acquainted her with a
wide range of European and Mexican
art.
1. She was educated at the elite
National Preparatory School.
2. She had access to her father's
collection of German literature
and philosophy books.
3. She studied many art books,
particularly in Italian
Renaissance painting.
4. Her relationship with Rivera and
her travels in Europe increased
her awareness of art.

B. Some of her stylistic conventions *Subpoint followed by two supporting details*
seem derived from earlier European
painters.
1. The facial "mask" in her self-
portraits echoes Bosch.
2. The landscape in <u>The Broken</u>
<u>Column</u> and <u>Tree of Hope</u> echoes
Traini.

Taffe iii

C. Religion provided her with a number
   of themes and subjects.

   1. She belonged to no organized
      religion but held pantheistic
      beliefs.

   2. Her most directly religious work
      was Moses.

   3. The Wounded Table reflects the
      Christian theme of the Last
      Supper.

   4. The Broken Column and The Little
      Deer show her identification with
      the martyrdom of Saint Sebastian.

D. Her Christian imagery often shows a
   Mexican influence.

   1. She and Rivera saw Henry Ford
      Hospital as a retablo.

   2. My Birth is based on a well-known
      Aztec sculpture.

Subpoint followed by four supporting details

Final subpoint followed by two supporting details

1″

Taffe 1

Frida Kahlo: More Than a Life

Who is Frida Kahlo? Ten or fifteen
years ago, few people would have known.
Today, however, Kahlo is being recognized
as a major figure in twentieth-century art.
Her paintings, primarily self-portraits,
continue to gain popularity in the United
States as well as in her native Mexico.
My Birth, for example, was recently pur-
chased by Madonna, and Self-Portrait with
Loose Hair sold in the spring of 1991 for
$1.65 million, a record price for any Latin
American artist (Plagens et al. 54).

Much of the scholarship on Kahlo and
her art has been produced by Hayden Herrera, author of Frida: A Biography of Frida
Kahlo and numerous periodical articles
about the artist. Indeed, it is nearly impossible to read anything about Kahlo without encountering a reference to Herrera's
research. Although her biography was published almost thirty years after Kahlo's
death, her information comes, as Angela
Carter notes in her review, from sources
remarkably close to the subject. In addition to Kahlo's journal, numerous letters,
and medical records, Herrera was able to
consult a number of lovers, friends, and
relatives, as well as former wives of

Margin annotations:

Student's last name and page number in upper right-hand corner

Title announces topic, arouses readers' interest

Title centered

Introduction invites readers to learn about Kahlo, provides background

Double-space

Facts cited— author named in citation

Major source introduced

Review of source cited

Taffe 2

Kahlo's husband, the artist Diego Rivera (33).

Paraphrase— author named in signal phrase and page numbers identified in parentheses at end of the paraphrase

Herrera's interpretation of Kahlo's painting is primarily biographical, as is that of nearly every other Kahlo critic. For example, Herrera describes Kahlo's work as "autobiography in paint" and goes on to label this autobiographical work original, specific, and personal (xii). While this view is certainly not incorrect, it seems limited in important ways. For Frida Kahlo's unique style results not only from autobiographical influences but also from her knowledge of earlier European art, traditional Christian imagery, and Mexican culture.

The autobiographical aspect of Kahlo's work is undoubtedly important and thus worth examining. Her life was eventful, exciting, and often painful. Born in 1907 in a suburb of Mexico City, she was stricken with polio at age six. After a nearly complete recovery, she entered the National Preparatory School to pursue medical training. Tragedy struck again in 1925, however, when a bus she was riding on was crushed by a trolley car. As Carter describes:

Left margin annotations:

Notes the biographical focus of most Kahlo criticism

Suggests that the focus of criticism should be expanded

Explicit thesis stated

First major point: establishes autobiographical elements in Kahlo's work

Supporting examples

Right margin annotations:

Brief quotation incorporated into text—author named in signal phrase and page numbers identified in parentheses at end of the paraphrase

Subpoint introduces events of Kahlo's life

Supporting details and examples support subpoint

Taffe 3

Long quotation
set off—ellipses
indicate omission

> She almost died, and hurt herself
> so badly she never got over it.
> Her spine, collarbone, pelvis and
> a number of ribs were broken; her
> right leg was shattered, her left
> foot crushed; and . . . the steel
> handrail of the bus . . . pierced
> her left side. (33)

While convalescing, Kahlo began to
paint, and soon painting became her career.
A few years later, in 1929, she married
Diego Rivera, who was twice her age and
already a well-known muralist. Their relationship was volatile; they fought when together and were miserable when apart. Both
carried on many well-publicized affairs,
and they divorced in 1939 only to remarry
in 1940. Throughout the years, Kahlo continued to suffer medical problems stemming
from the accident. After many operations,
in 1953 her right leg was amputated below
the knee. She was devastated, and her
health declined rapidly. She died less
than a year later, in 1954.

As Herrera details in her biography,
much of Kahlo's art grows out of these dramatic personal experiences. Self-portraits
such as The Broken Column (Herrera, pl.
XXVIII),[1] which portrays Kahlo encased in a

Second subpoint
builds on first
major point by
relating details of
Kahlo's physical
pain to particular
paintings

Explanatory note
indicates source
of paintings

Taffe 4

steel orthopedic corset, nails embedded
painfully in her body, her spine replaced
with a broken marble column, or Remembrance
of an Open Wound (fig. 40), in which a
seated Kahlo displays a bandaged left foot
and a large gash on her left thigh, refer
to the physical aftermath of her accident.

Likewise, The Two Fridas (pl. XIV) and
A Few Small Nips (pl. VIII) directly depict
the pain of her relationship with Rivera.
The first shows two self-portraits, one in
Victorian dress and the other in the Tehuana (Mexican peasant) costume that Kahlo
often wore. Each Frida has her heart exposed, and an artery connects the two. The
artery originates at a picture of Rivera
held by the Tehuana Frida, thus linking the
lives of the three. But the Victorian
Frida's heart is broken because she does
not have Rivera. She holds the other, open
end of the artery in her hand and tries to
pinch it shut with medical tweezers, but
the red blood drips onto her dress. This
portrait provides a graphic example of the
connection Kahlo felt to Rivera and of her
devastating sense of loss because of his
infidelity.

Shortly after a separation precipi-
tated by Rivera's affair with her sister,

Examines two
works in detail for
their autobio-
graphical elements

Third subpoint
builds on first
major point by
relating details of
Kahlo's personal
relationship with
her husband to
particular
paintings

Detailed
description of
one painting

Taffe 5

Kahlo completed <u>A Few Small Nips</u> (pl.
VIII). The work is her most violent, the
clearest expression of the pain she suffered in her marriage. The painting, as
Martha Zamora notes, is based on a true
story: a man stabbed his girlfriend to
death and when confronted with the murder
said, "But I only gave her a few small
nips" (50). Kahlo's painting portrays a
young woman lying in bed, naked but for one
sock and shoe. Her body is covered with
bleeding gashes, and her face has a pale,
almost bluish tint; she is clearly dead.
Splashes of blood spatter the bed, the
floor, even the frame of the painting. And
they spatter the man standing over her. A
ribbon bearing the words "<u>unos cuantos</u>
<u>piquetitos</u>" ("a few small nips") is held at
the top of the painting by two birds, one
black and one white. Although not exact
likenesses, the man's features suggest that
he represents Rivera, and the woman's suggest that she is Kahlo.

If Kahlo's work is often personal,
however, it is not untutored or untaught.
In fact, Kahlo was clearly familiar with,
and also clearly influenced by, earlier
art, including traditional Christian and
Mexican imagery (Zamora 110). Indeed, it

*Paraphrase and
brief quotation—
author identified
in signal phrase*

*Detailed
description of a
second painting*

*Reiteration of
thesis and second
major point: the
influence of
earlier art*

*Source identified
in parentheses
following a para-
phrase. For the
original passage
and Daniel Taffe's
paraphrased notes
on the passage, see
pp. 598–99*

Taffe 6

Subpoint

would be surprising, given her background, if she had not been acquainted with a wide range of art, both European and Mexican. Kahlo was well educated--the National Preparatory School she attended spawned some of Mexico's greatest minds.

Supporting details

Herrera identifies Kahlo's father as a scholarly European who emigrated to Mexico, where he became a photographer (5-7), and says that Kahlo studied her father's collection of German literature and philosophy books (19) as well as many art books, particularly those reproducing Italian Renaissance

Second source cited to corroborate main point

And Zamora notes that Kahlo referred to her first self-portrait, given to a close friend, as "your Botticelli" (110). Her relationship with Rivera and her travels in Europe no doubt served further to broaden her awareness of contemporary art and its roots in earlier styles and themes.

Subpoint: the influence of other artists

A careful study of Kahlo's art reveals both stylistic and larger thematic influences on her work. One of her striking conventions is the use of a stylized facial "mask," like that in her first self-portrait, Self-Portrait Wearing a Velvet Dress (pl. I). In this painting, the mask is simply a blank stare devoid of any evidence of emotion. As Kahlo sits facing the

Summary of long passage—author named in signal phrase and page numbers identified in parentheses at appropriate points

Taffe 7

viewer, she does not smile, but neither
does she appear overly sad. In many of her
later self-images, however, the mask is
streaked by tears, which, combined with the
expressionless face, tell far more about
the subject than would any realistic expression.

Certainly, there is an autobiographical basis for the mask; it hides the subject's pain much as Kahlo hid her pain from
her friends during her life. But as Professor Richard Honeywell points out, the mask

Information from
interview cited

also suggests the influence of a painting
by Hieronymus Bosch (1450-1516), Bearing of
the Cross (reproduced in Delavoy 59).[2] The

Bibliographic note
acknowledges
help

masks of the figures in Bosch's painting,
which depicts Christ being led to the site
of his crucifixion, are horrid grimaces.
As Delavoy explains, Bosch realized that a
mask could "never convey the human quality
of a real face treated expressively" (58).
The effect of the masks is perhaps greater
than that of actual faces, however, because
of the horror they evoke. In much the same
way, Kahlo's mask creates an effect, albeit
a different one. Her mask hides emotion,
yet in doing so shows her pain powerfully.

Another stylistic influence appears in
Kahlo's use of landscape. In both The Bro-

*The influence of
Bosch supports
the subpoint*

*"Reproduced in"
shows that the
citation is for the
painting, not for
Delavoy's text*

*Second stylistic
influence—
Traini's land-
scape supports
the subpoint*

Taffe 8

ken Column and Tree of Hope (pl. XXX),
Kahlo's physical suffering, depicted as
cuts in her chest and back and in the nails
embedded in her flesh, is mirrored in the
gouges scarred into the barren terrain in
the backdrop, which projects an aura of
pain and hopelessness. This use of landscape, according to Honeywell, is a familiar element in paintings such as The
Triumph of Death by Francesco Traini (reproduced in Gardner 59), paintings Kahlo
would have undoubtedly seen. Traini's violent, ragged landscape, featuring tall
cliffs dropping out of sight, augments the
power of his elaborate depiction of several
young aristocrats confronting three
corpses.

Another major influence on Kahlo's
work, religion, provided her with a number
of themes and subjects. Her own religious
upbringing was mixed. Herrera indicates
that her mother was devoutly Catholic and
her father, "by birth Jewish," was "by
persuasion an atheist" (6); she says that
Kahlo herself, while professing no organized religion (283), nevertheless believed
in a "vitalistic form of pantheism" (328).
Although most of her religious imagery is
specifically Christian, her most directly

Subpoint: thematic influence—religion

Taffe 9

religious subject is Moses (fig. 69), which
Zamora identifies as having been commis-
sioned by José Domingo Lavin in 1945 (102).
A complex work detailing the birth of
its subject, it resembles in composition
Bosch's Garden of Earthly Delights (reproduced in Delavoy 88-89) and Traini's The
Triumph of Death, both of which contain
many little scenes to help tell the whole
story.

The story of the Last Supper has been
depicted by many artists, the most famous
version being that of Leonardo da Vinci
(reproduced in Hartt 452-53). In 1940,
Kahlo contributed to this tradition The
Wounded Table (fig. 55), painted after her
divorce. As explained in the film Portrait
of an Artist: Frida Kahlo, it depicts, from
left to right, a young boy and girl (her
sister's children), a Judas doll (a papier-
mâché figure stuffed with firecrackers to
be exploded on the day before Easter),
Kahlo, a skeleton, and a young deer. Kahlo
thus occupies the central position of
Jesus, with a symbol of betrayal on her
right, of death on her left, and of inno-
cence at either end of the table. Blood on
the floor underneath her skirt reveals that
she has already been wounded.

Supporting
examples and
details

First religious
theme—the Last
Supper—further
supports the
subpoint

Film cited by title

Explanation of
unfamiliar term
provided in
parentheses

Taffe 10

Second religious theme—
martyrdom of Saint Sebastian—
further supports the subpoint

It is not surprising that another Christian theme explored by Kahlo is martyrdom, particularly the martyrdom of Saint Sebastian. A popular Renaissance subject, Sebastian's death was depicted by, among others, Antonio del Pollaiuolo and Antonello da Messina, both in 1475. In both portrayals, Sebastian has been tied to a post and shot full of arrows. Kahlo uses the Saint Sebastian theme in two paintings, again substituting herself for the central character. In The Broken Column, described previously, Kahlo is passive, almost fatalistically calm, as she stands bound to her column by her metal corset, her flesh pierced by nails. In The Little Deer (pl. XXXI), a deer with Kahlo's head and a body pierced with arrows runs through a wood. Together the two images suggest that Kahlo found echoes of her physical and emotional torment in the tradition of Christian martyrdom.

Final subpoint: Mexican influence—retablos

In Mexico, as Herrera notes, this tradition is powerfully influenced by the "bloodiness and self-mortification" of the Aztec tradition (283). Indeed, in much of Kahlo's work, the Christian imagery shows a Mexican influence. Rivera and Kahlo owned a collection of nineteenth-century

Taffe 11

retablos, described by Nicholas Jenkins as
"votive paintings on tin, each about the
size of a postcard, melodramatically relating the facts of an intercession by God:
here a child rescued from a burning bed,
there a man rescued from drowning" (105).
In 1932, Kahlo completed Henry Ford Hospital (pl. IV), her first work on a metal
surface. Although the painting does not
adhere to the strict characteristics of a
retablo, Herrera argues that both Rivera
and Kahlo viewed it as one (151). Instead
of a divine deliverance, the painting tells
the story of a calamity: Kahlo's miscar-
riage.

Yet another example of Christian imagery filtered through Mexican culture is
My Birth (pl. VI). In this painting, the
Virgin Mary gazes out of a framed portrait
above a bed covered in white. On the bed
is a woman giving birth, her head and
shoulders covered, suggesting that she is
dead. The child being born--Kahlo--also
appears to be dead. According to Herrera,
this painting is based on a well-known
Aztec sculpture of a woman giving birth to
a man's head, a sculpture and a tradition
with which Kahlo was well acquainted (158).

Examples support the final subpoint

Additional example of Mexican influence supports the final subpoint

Taffe 12

Conclusion: summary of argument and echo of thesis

Thus, despite a desire on the part of many critics and admirers to see her as an almost entirely original artist, evidence suggests that Kahlo's art strongly reflects a number of influences from earlier paintings and from her own Mexican culture. While her work is clearly informed by her life experience, she had a deep understanding of European and Mexican artistic traditions, an understanding that powerfully shaped her creation of what the art world has come to identify as uniquely Kahlo. Just eight days before she died, Herrera tells us, Kahlo wrote in bright red paint on her last painting "VIVA LA VIDA" (LONG LIVE LIFE) (440). Those who study her art are increasingly likely to answer, "Viva la Kahlo."

Translation of Spanish provided in parentheses

Quotation reproduced in all capital letters, just as it appeared in the source

1″

Taffe 13

Heading centered

Notes ←———————— Double-space

Indent five spaces
to superscript
number

¹ All cited Kahlo paintings are repro-   Explanatory note

duced in Herrera and identified by the

plate or figure number assigned by him.

Color plates (pl.) follow p. 162 and p.

290; black-and-white illustrations (fig.)

follow p. 130 and p. 226.

² I wish to thank Professor Honeywell,   Bibliographic note

who in our interview suggested that I con-

sult several standard histories of Western

art, such as Gardner, Janson, and Hartt.

↓ 1"

Taffe 14

Heading centered

Works Cited

Carter, Angela. "A Ribbon around a Bomb."

Rev. of <u>Frida: A Biography of Frida</u>

<u>Kahlo</u>, by Hayden Herrera. <u>New States-</u>

<u>man & Society</u> 12 May 1989: 32-33.

Double-space

Weekly periodical

First line of each
entry flush with
left margin

Delavoy, Robert L. <u>Bosch</u>. Trans. Stuart

Gilbert. Cleveland: World, 1984.

Translation

Gardner, Helen. <u>Art through the Ages</u>. 7th

ed. Vol. 2. New York: Harcourt, 1980.

· 3 vols.

One volume of
multivolume work

Hartt, Frederick. <u>History of Italian</u>

Subsequent lines →
indented five
spaces

<u>Renaissance Art</u>. Englewood Cliffs:

Prentice, 1981.

Herrera, Hayden. <u>Frida: A Biography of</u>

<u>Frida Kahlo</u>. New York: Harper, 1983.

Honeywell, Richard. Telephone interview.

15 Apr. 1991.

Interview

Janson, H. W. <u>Key Monuments in the History</u>

<u>of Art</u>. New York: Abrams, 1959.

Jenkins, Nicholas. "Calla Lilies and

Kahlos: The Frida Kahlo Museum, Mexico

City." <u>ARTnews</u> Mar. 1989: 104-05.

Monthly
periodical

Natchez, Gladys. "Frida Kahlo and Diego

Rivera: The Transformation of Catas-

trophe to Creativity." <u>PsychINFO</u>.

On-line. Dialog. 12 July 1994.

On-line computer
service

Taffe 15

Plagens, Peter, et al. "Frida on Our
　　Minds." Newsweek 27 May 1991:
　　54-55.

Portrait of an Artist: Frida Kahlo. Dir.
　　Eila Hershon. RM Arts/Hershon/WDR,
　　1983.

Zamora, Martha. Frida Kahlo: The Brush of
　　Anguish. Trans. Marilyn Sode Smith.
　　San Francisco: Chronicle, 1990.

Article by more
than four authors

Film

45

Documenting Sources: APA, CBE, and Chicago Styles

*I*T'S ALL "A MATTER OF STYLE," *as the old adage suggests, in academic disciplines as in fashion and design. Indeed, the conventions of style vary among disciplines, according to what a discipline values and how it credits work. As a prospective member of one or more academic disciplines, you will have occasion to follow various disciplinary styles, particularly when you need to use their guidelines for citing and documenting sources in your own writing. This chapter introduces three widely used and important documentation styles, those of the American Psychological Association (APA), the Council of Biology Editors (CBE), and The Chicago Manual of Style (CMS).*

APA STYLE

The current *Publication Manual of the American Psychological Association* (APA) has evolved since 1929, when it began as a seven-page article offering general guidelines for stylistic standards, to a book of well over three hundred detail-filled pages. Now followed by writers in a number of fields throughout the social sciences, the APA guidelines aim to foster clear communication and easy reference. This section illustrates **APA style** and guides you in the use of such documentation in your own writing. For further reference, consult the following:

> American Psychological Association. *Publication Manual of the American Psychological Association.* 4th ed. Washington, D.C.: APA, 1994.

⫸ *Directory to APA style*

45a. Parenthetical citations

Author named in a signal
   phrase, 667
Author named in a parentheti-
   cal citation, 668
Two authors, 668
Three to five authors, 668
Six or more authors, 668
Corporate or group author,
   669

Unknown author, 669
Two or more authors with the
   same surname, 669
Two or more sources in the
   same parenthetical citation,
   669
Specific parts of a source, 670
Personal communication, 670

45b. Content notes

45c. List of references

BOOKS

Book by one author, 672
Book by two or more authors,
   672
Book by a corporate or group
   author, 672
Book by an unknown author,
   672
Book prepared by an editor, 672
Selection in a book with an edi-
   tor, 673

Translation, 673
Edition other than the first, 673
One volume of a multivolume
   work, 673
Republication, 673
Government document, 673
Two or more works by the same
   author, 673

PERIODICALS

Article in a journal paginated by
   volume, 674
Article in a journal paginated by
   issue, 674
Article in a magazine, 674
Article in a newspaper, 674
Unsigned article, 674

Editorial or letter to the editor,
   674
Review, 674
Published interview, 675
Two or more works by the same
   author in the same year, 675

ELECTRONIC MEDIA

On-line book, 675
On-line journal article, 676

On-line abstract, 676
CD-ROM abstract, 676

Material from an information service or a database, *676*

Software or computer program, *676*

OTHER SOURCES

Technical or research reports and working papers, *677*
Paper presented at a meeting or symposium, unpublished, *677*
Dissertation, unpublished, *677*

Poster session, *677*
Film or videotape, *677*
Television program, single episode, *677*
Recording, *678*

45d. A sample research essay, APA style

45a

APA format for parenthetical citations

In APA style, **parenthetical citations** in the text feature the author and date of a source in identifying each quotation, paraphrase, summary, or other material from a source. Parenthetical citations correspond to full bibliographic entries in a list of references at the end of the text. Generally, the author's name is used in a signal phrase to introduce the cited material, and the date, in parentheses, immediately follows the author's name. For a quotation, the page number, preceded by *p.*, appears in parentheses after the quotation. Following are some examples of citations for various kinds of sources.

AUTHOR NAMED IN A SIGNAL PHRASE

Key (1983) argues that the placement of women in print
advertisements is subliminally important.

As Briggs (1970) observes, parents play an important role
in building their children's self-esteem because
"children value themselves to the degree that they have
been valued" (p. 14).

AUTHOR NAMED IN A PARENTHETICAL CITATION

When you do not name the author in your text, give the name and the date, separated by a comma, in parentheses at the end of the cited material.

```
One study has found that only 68% of letters received by
editors were actually published (Renfro, 1979).
```

TWO AUTHORS

Use both names in all citations. Join the names with *and* in a signal phrase, but use an ampersand (&) instead in a parenthetical reference.

```
Murphy and Orkow (1985) reached somewhat different
conclusions by designing a study that was less dependent
on subjective judgment than were previous studies.
```

```
A recent study that was less dependent on subjective
judgment resulted in conclusions somewhat different from
those of previous studies (Murphy & Orkow, 1985).
```

THREE TO FIVE AUTHORS

List all the authors' names in a signal phrase or parenthetical citation for the first reference.

```
Belenky, Clinchy, Goldberger, and Tarule (1986) suggest
that many women rely on observing and listening to others
as ways of learning about themselves.
```

In any subsequent references, use just the first author's name plus *et al.* ("and others"). Note that all the authors' names should appear in the entry in the list of references.

```
From this experience, observe Belenky et al. (1986),
women learn to listen to themselves think, a step toward
self-expression.
```

SIX OR MORE AUTHORS

Use only the first author's name and *et al.* ("and others") in every citation, including the first. Note that all the authors' names should appear in the entry in the list of references.

As Mueller et al. (1980) demonstrated, television holds
the potential for distorting and manipulating consumers
as free-willed decision makers.

CORPORATE OR GROUP AUTHOR

Spell out the name each time you cite it. If the name is long, spell it out the first time you use it, followed by an abbreviation in brackets. In later citations, use the abbreviation only.

FIRST CITATION

(The Centers for Disease Control [CDC], 1990)

LATER CITATIONS

(CDC, 1990)

UNKNOWN AUTHOR

Use the title or its first few words in a signal phrase or a parenthetical citation.

The school profiles for the county substantiate this
trend (Guide to secondary schools, 1983).

TWO OR MORE AUTHORS WITH THE SAME SURNAME

If your list of references includes works by different authors with the same surname, include the authors' initials in each citation.

G. Jones (1984) conducted the groundbreaking study of
retroviruses.

TWO OR MORE SOURCES IN THE SAME PARENTHETICAL CITATION

If you cite more than one source at once, list all the sources in the order in which they appear in the list of references. That is, list works in alphabetical order by author's surname (separated by semicolons), and list works by the same author in chronological order (separated by commas).

(Chodorow, 1978; Gilligan, 1982)

(Gilligan, 1977, 1982)

SPECIFIC PARTS OF A SOURCE

Use abbreviations (*chap., p.,* and so on) in a parenthetical citation to name the part of a work you are citing.

```
Montgomery (1988, chap. 9) argues that his research
yielded the opposite results.
```

PERSONAL COMMUNICATION

Cite any personal letters, E-mail, electronic-bulletin-board correspondence, telephone conversations, or interviews with the person's initial(s) and last name, the identification *personal communication,* and the date. Because your readers would probably not be able to locate these sources, you need not include them in your list of references.

```
J. L. Morin (personal communication, October 14, 1990)
supported the claims made in her recent article with new
evidence.
```

45b

APA format for content notes

APA style allows content notes for information you wish to include to expand or supplement your text. Notes are indicated in the text by superscript numerals in consecutive order throughout the text, and the notes themselves are typed on a separate page after the last page of the text, under the heading "Footnotes," centered at the top of the page. Double-space all entries. Indent the first line of each note five to seven spaces as a paragraph is indented, but begin subsequent lines at the left margin.

SUPERSCRIPT IN TEXT

```
The age of the children involved was an important factor
in the selection of items for the questionnaire.[1]
```

FOOTNOTE

```
   [1] Marjorie Youngston Forman and William Cole of the
Child Study Team provided great assistance in identifying
appropriate items.
```

45c

APA format for a list of references

The alphabetical list of the sources cited in your essay is called **References.** (If your instructor asks that you list everything you have read as background, call the list *Bibliography*.) Start your list on a separate page *after* the text of your essay but *before* any appendices that explain your research procedures or results and any notes. Continue the consecutive numbering of pages. Type the heading *References,* neither underlined nor in quotation marks, centered one inch from the top of the page. Double-space, and begin your first entry. Do not indent the first line of each entry, but indent any subsequent lines of the entry five spaces. Double-space the entire list.

List your sources alphabetically by authors' last names. If a source is by an unknown author or authors, alphabetize it by the first major word of the title.

The APA style specifies treatment and placement of four basic elements—author, publication date, title, and publication information.

1. *Author.* List all authors last name first, and use only initials for first and middle names. Separate the names of multiple authors with commas, and use an ampersand before the last author's name.

2. *Publication date.* Enclose the date in parentheses. Use only the year for books and journals; use the year, a comma, and the month or month and day for magazines. Do not abbreviate the month.

3. *Title.* Underline titles and subtitles of books and periodicals. Do not enclose titles of articles in quotation marks. For books and articles, capitalize only the first word of the title and subtitle and any proper nouns or proper adjectives. Capitalize all major words in a periodical title. (See 36c for more information on capitalization.)

4. *Publication information.* For a book, list the city of publication (and the country or postal abbreviation for the state if the city is unfamiliar), a colon, and the publisher's name, dropping any *Inc., Co.,* or *Publishers.* For a periodical, follow the periodical title with a comma, the volume number (underlined), the issue number (if appropriate) in parentheses, a comma, and the inclusive page numbers of the article. For newspapers, include the abbreviations *p.* ("page") or *pp.* ("pages").

Consult the various sample entries below for information on where in an entry you should place other information.

The following examples are in a "hanging indent" format, where the first line flushes left and the subsequent lines indent. This is the customary APA format for final copy, including student papers. Unless your instructor suggests otherwise, it is the format we recommend. Note, however, that for manuscripts being submitted to journals, APA requires the reverse (first lines indented, subsequent lines flushed left), assuming that it will be converted by a typesetting system to a hanging indent.

Books

BOOK BY ONE AUTHOR

Lightman, A. (1993). Einstein's dreams. New York: Warner.

BOOK BY TWO OR MORE AUTHORS

Newcombe, F., & Ratcliffe, G. (1978). Defining females--
The nature of women in society. New York: Wiley.

BOOK BY A CORPORATE OR GROUP AUTHOR

Institute of Financial Education. (1983). Income property
lending. Homewood, IL: Dow Jones-Irwin.

BOOK BY AN UNKNOWN AUTHOR

National Geographic atlas of the world. (1988).
Washington, DC: National Geographic Society.

BOOK PREPARED BY AN EDITOR

Solomon, A. P. (Ed.). (1980). The prospective city.
Cambridge, MA: MIT Press.

SELECTION IN A BOOK WITH AN EDITOR

West, C. (1992). The postmodern crisis of the black
intellectuals. In L. Grossberg, C. Nelson, & P.
Treichler (Eds.), Cultural studies (pp. 689-705).
New York: Routledge.

TRANSLATION

Durkheim, E. (1957). <u>Suicide</u> (J. A. Spaulding & G.
    Simpson, Trans.). Glencoe, IL: Free Press of
    Glencoe.

EDITION OTHER THAN THE FIRST

Kohn, M. L. (1977). <u>Class and conformity: A study in
    values</u> (2nd ed.). Chicago: University of Chicago
    Press.

ONE VOLUME OF A MULTIVOLUME WORK

Baltes, P., & Brim, O. G. (Eds.). (1980). <u>Life-span
    development and behavior</u> (Vol. 3). New York: Basic
    Books.

REPUBLICATION

Piaget, J. (1952). <u>The language and thought of the child.</u>
    London: Routledge & Kegan Paul. (Original work
    published 1932)

GOVERNMENT DOCUMENT

U.S. Bureau of the Census. (1975). <u>Historical statistics
    of the United States, colonial times to 1870.</u>
    Washington, DC: U.S. Government Printing Office.

TWO OR MORE WORKS BY THE SAME AUTHOR(S)

List two or more works by the same author in chronological order.
Repeat the author's name in each entry.

Macrorie, K. (1968). <u>Writing to be read.</u> New York:
    Hayden.
Macrorie, K. (1970). <u>Uptaught.</u> New York: Hayden.

Periodicals

ARTICLE IN A JOURNAL PAGINATED BY VOLUME

Shuy, R. (1981). A holistic view of language. Research in the Teaching of English, 15, 101-111.

ARTICLE IN A JOURNAL PAGINATED BY ISSUE

Maienza, J. G. (1986). The superintendency: Characteristics of access for men and women. Educational Administration Quarterly, 22(4), 59-79.

ARTICLE IN A MAGAZINE

Gralla, P. (1994, April). How to enter cyberspace. PC Computing, 60-62.

ARTICLE IN A NEWSPAPER

Browne, M. W. (1988, April 26). Lasers for the battle-field raise concern for eyesight. The New York Times, pp. C1, C8.

UNSIGNED ARTICLE

What sort of person reads creative computing? (1985, August). Creative Computing, 8, 10.

EDITORIAL OR LETTER TO THE EDITOR

Russell, J. S. (1994, March 27). The language instinct [Letter to the editor]. The New York Times Book Review, 27.

REVIEW

Larmore, C. E. (1989). [Review of the book Patterns of moral complexity]. Ethics, 99, 423-426.

PUBLISHED INTERVIEW

McCarthy, E. (1968, December 24). [Interview with <u>Boston
Globe</u> Washington staff]. <u>Boston Globe,</u> p. B27.

TWO OR MORE WORKS BY THE SAME AUTHOR IN THE SAME YEAR

List two or more works by the same author published in the same
year alphabetically, and place lowercase letters (*a, b,* etc.) after the dates.

Murray, F. B. (1983a). Equilibration as cognitive
conflict. <u>Developmental Review, 3,</u> 54-61.

Murray, F. B. (1983b). Learning and development through
social interaction. In L. Liben (Ed.), <u>Piaget and
the foundations of knowledge</u> (pp. 176-201).
Hillsdale, NJ: Erlbaum.

Electronic media

In the 1994 edition of its *Publication Manual,* the APA notes that
set standards for referencing on-line information have yet to emerge. The
association offers general guidelines, however, and recommends that writers
follow standard APA format for listing author, date, and title. The date
should consist of the year of publication or the year of the most recent
update if it is available. If the year of publication is not available, use the
exact date of the search that turned up the item. Following the title, in
brackets, should be the source (*On-line* or *CD-ROM,* for example). Then
comes an availability statement, providing a reader with information sufficient to retrieve the material (for example, Telnet, FTP, Internet, E-mail, or
a particular gopher client), followed by the directory and the file name.
Notice that no period follows any of the final three elements. (See the next
section for sources available in both print and electronic forms.)

ON-LINE BOOK

Wollstonecraft, M. (1992). <u>A vindication of the rights of
women</u> (Everyman's Library Ed. orig. pub. 1929).
[On-line]. Available: Telnet: gopher.
wiretap.spies.com Directory: Library/Classic File:
woman.txt

ON-LINE JOURNAL ARTICLE

Weintraub, I. (1994). Fighting environmental racism: A
    selected annotated bibliography [14 p.]. Electronic
    Green Journal [On-line serial], 1(1). Available:
    Telnet: gopher. uidaho.edu Directory: University of
    Idaho Electronic Publications File: egjol.txt

ON-LINE ABSTRACT

Natchez, G. (1987). Frida Kahlo and Diego Rivera: The
    transformation of catastrophe to creativity [On-
    line]. Psychotherapy-Patient, 8, 153-174. Abstract
    from: DIALOG File: PsycINFO Item: 76-11344

CD-ROM ABSTRACT

Natchez, G. (1987). Frida Kahlo and Diego Rivera: The
    transformation of catastrophe to creativity.
    [CD-ROM]. Psychotherapy-Patient, 8, 153-174.
    Abstract from: SilverPlatter File: PsychLIT Item:
    76-11344

MATERIAL FROM AN INFORMATION SERVICE OR A DATABASE

Belenky, M. F. (1984). The role of deafness in the moral
    development of hearing impaired children. In
    A. Areson & J. De Caro (Eds.), Teaching, learning
    and development. Rochester, NY: National Institute
    for the Deaf. (ERIC Document Reproduction Service
    No. ED 248 646)

SOFTWARE OR COMPUTER PROGRAM

SuperCalc3 Release 2.1 [Computer program]. (1985). San
    Jose, CA: Computer Associates, Micro Products
    Division.

Other sources

TECHNICAL OR RESEARCH REPORTS AND WORKING PAPERS

Wilson, K. S. (1986). Palenque: An interactive multimedia optical disc prototype for children (Working Paper No. 2). New York: Center for Children and Technology, Bank Street College of Education.

PAPER PRESENTED AT A MEETING OR SYMPOSIUM, UNPUBLISHED

Engelbart, D. C. (1970, April). Intellectual implications of multi-access computing. Paper presented at the meeting of the Interdisciplinary Conference on Multi-Access Computer Networks, Washington, DC.

DISSERTATION, UNPUBLISHED

Leverenz, C. A. (1994). Collaboration and difference in the composition classroom. Unpublished doctoral dissertation, Ohio State University, Columbus.

POSTER SESSION

Ulman, H. L., & Walborn, E. (1993, March). Hypertext in the composition classroom. Poster session presented at the Annual Conference on College Composition and Communication, San Diego, CA.

FILM OR VIDEOTAPE

Hitchcock, A. (Producer & Director). (1954). Rear window [Film]. Los Angeles: MGM.

TELEVISION PROGRAM, SINGLE EPISODE

Kuttner, P. K., Moran, C., & Scholl, E. (1994, July 19). Passin' it on (W. Chamberlain, Executive Director). In D. Zaccardi (Executive Producer), P.O.V. New York: Public Broadcasting Service.

RECORDING

Begin with the writer's name, followed by the date of copyright. Give the recording date if it is different from the copyright.

```
Colvin, S. (1991). I don't know why. [Recorded by A.
    Krauss and Union Station]. On Every time you say
    goodbye [Cassette]. Cambridge, MA: Rounder Records.
    (1992)
```

45d

A sample research essay, APA style

An essay by Leah Clendening appears on the following pages. She followed the APA guidelines described in 45a–45c.

Content Analysis   1

A Content Analysis of Letters   Heading centered and double-spaced

to the Editor

Leah Clendening

Professor Garrett

Psychology 201

May 20, 19XX

Content Analysis   2

Abstract

No paragraph indent

This study analyzed the content of 624 letters to the editor in two newspapers--one
published in a city of over 500,000, the
other in a city of about 15,000--in order
to explore the relationship between community size and subject matter of letters. A
researcher read all of the letters printed
in the newspapers on the weekdays of three
nonconsecutive months in late 1987 and
early 1988 and then classified them according to whether they dealt with local or
national issues and recorded the findings
on a category sheet. Results indicate a
significant difference: letters in the
smaller community concentrated almost entirely on local issues, while those in the
larger community concentrated more frequently on national than on local issues.

Key words embed-
ded in abstract to
help readers iden-
tify the article

Content Analysis   3

A Content Analysis of Letters

to the Editor

Research has indicated that the average person who writes letters to an American newspaper tends to be a conservative, well-adjusted white male who is middle-aged or older and a longtime resident of his community (Singletary & Cowling, 1979). One study concluded that 71.4% of the letters printed were written by people who wished to inform or persuade by writing their letters. Most of the remainder, 27%, wished only to use the letter as a means of self-expression; the other 1.6% wished to arouse readers to action (Lemert & Larkin, 1979).

Problem

But what are the major concerns of these letter writers? Are they more concerned about events in their local communities or about national issues? Does the size of the community have some influence on the subjects of letters its members write? These questions led to the following hypothesis: people living in a small community (with a population of about 15,000) tend to be concerned more with local than with national issues. People living in a large community (with a population

Content Analysis   4

over 500,000) show more concern for national than for local issues.

Method

Newspapers

The two newspapers that served as data
sources, the Mount Vernon News and the
Cleveland Plain Dealer, were chosen mainly
for convenience and availability. Cleveland has a population of 573,822 and a
weekly distribution of the Plain Dealer of
482,564. Mount Vernon has a population of
14,380 and a weekly distribution of the
Mount Vernon News of 10,936 (1985 IMS/Ayer
Directory, 1985). Each newspaper's letters
were read for the weekdays of October 1987,
December 1987, and February 1988. Sunday
issues were not taken into account.

A category sheet of possible subjects
for the letters to the editor was adapted
from the coding sheet of Donohew's study on
Medicare (Budd, Thorp, & Donohew, 1967, p.
41). One column recorded national issues
and a second, local issues. The sheet was
constructed with a space for the newspaper's abbreviation, the date, and the letter number(s). The Mount Vernon News was
given the abbreviation MVN and the Cleveland Plain Dealer, the abbreviation CPD.

Second-level head-
ing underlined
and flush left

Subjects of study
identified

Short title used to
identify source
with no author

Materials
described

Page noted for
specific source

Content Analysis   5

Procedure

    After the category sheet was finished
and approved, observation began. The letters were read and marked for content in a
library setting. Each letter was then
classified on the category sheet that had
been titled with the proper abbreviations,
date, and letter number. As observation
progressed, constraints of time demanded a
change from filling out a separate sheet
for each letter to recording each day's
letters on the same category sheet. The
space left for recording the letter number
was used to record the total number of letters for each particular day. After all
observation was finished, the counts for
each of the newspapers were totaled for
each month and overall.

Results

    During the three months, 60 letters
were read from the Mount Vernon News.
Fifty-three pertained to local issues,
while seven pertained to national issues.
A Chi-square test with an adjustment for
continuity was used on these data to find
whether there was a statistically significant difference between concern with local
issues and concern with national issues.

*Steps in carrying
out research
explained*

*Results from first
newspaper ana-
lyzed statistically*

Content Analysis   6

Results showed an overwhelming difference between issues, even at the .01 probability level. A graph (Figure 1) was also constructed to show the number of national and local issues for each month for the MVN.

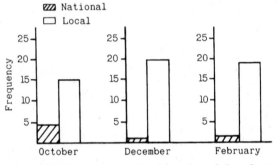

Graph used to show results

Figure 1. Frequency of national and local issues for the MVN

Of a total of 564 letters read from the Cleveland <u>Plain Dealer</u>, 248 pertained to local issues and 316 to national issues. A Chi-square test with an adjustment for continuity was also used on these data and, once again, showed a statistically significant difference. A graph (Figure 2) was constructed to show the frequency of national and local issues for each month for the CPD.

Results from second newspaper analyzed statistically

Content Analysis   7

One interesting side note is that
21.6% of the letters from the Plain Dealer
expressed grievances or appreciation, com-

Findings counter
to previous
research noted

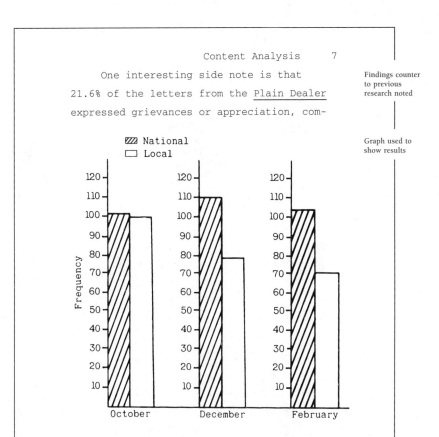

Graph used to
show results

Figure 2. Frequency of national and loca
issues for CPD

pared with 36% of the letters from the
Mount Vernon News. These findings differ
considerably from those of Lister, who
found that only 5% of letters to the editor

Content Analysis   8

were of this particular type (Lister,
1985).

Discussion

The findings of this study generally
supported the hypothesis, especially in the
smaller community, where letters concentrated overwhelmingly on local issues.
Perhaps residents of such a community do
not see themselves as strongly affected by
national politics and events. For the
larger community, the findings were not as
clear; one possibility is that many of the
letters were not from the larger community
itself but from smaller communities surrounding it.

Results
interpreted

If more time had been permitted, an
entire year's letters could have been categorized, perhaps yielding more representative information. In addition, use of a
second reader could have reduced bias on
the part of a single reader in the catego-
rization of letters. It was found as the
study progressed that a few categories
could have been added, such as religion and
local and state elections; the lack of
these categories, however, did not severely
affect the study. Another bias that would
be difficult to account for is editorial
bias: one study has found that only 68% of

Biases and possi-
ble improve-
ments in the
study listed

Content Analysis   9

letters received by editors were published
(Renfro, 1979). The only way to eliminate
this bias would be to read all the letters
received instead of only those that are
printed.

Conclusion

This study raises some interesting
questions that further study would probably
help to answer. Does gender or age influence whether people are interested in local
or national issues? What is the causal relationship between residence in small towns
and apparent greater interest in local affairs? Future studies may answer such
questions, building on the information
here.

Larger questions
noted in
conclusion

Content Analysis   10

References

Budd, R. W., Thorp, K., & Donohew, L.
(1967). Content analysis of communications. New York: Macmillan.

Lemert, J. B., & Larkin, J. P. (1979). Some
reasons why mobilizing information
fails to be in letters to the editor.
Journalism Quarterly, 56, 504-512.

Lister, L. (1985). An analysis of letters
to the editor. Social Work, 30, 77-78.

The 1985 IMS/Ayer Directory of Publications
(117th ed.). (1985). Fort Washington,
PA: IMS Press.

Renfro, P. C. (1979). Bias in selection of
letters to the editor. Journalism
Quarterly, 56, 822-826.

Singletary, M. W., & Cowling, M. (1979).
Letters to the editor of the non-daily
press. Journalism Quarterly, 56, 165-
168.

Heading centered
on new page

First line of each
entry flushes left
———→
with margin

Subsequent lines
indent five spaces

Entries listed
alphabetically by
author, last names
first; initials used
for first and
middle names

Title beginning
with a number
alphabetized as if
the number were
spelled out

CBE STYLE

45e

CBE formats for in-text citations and reference lists

Many writers in the natural sciences use the documentation style recommended in the manual of the Council of Biology Editors (CBE):

> Council of Biology Editors. *Scientific Style and Format: The CBE Manual for Authors, Editors, and Publishers.* 6th ed. New York: Cambridge UP, 1994.

The CBE Manual addresses the concerns of those working in the natural sciences. (Before following this style, however, you may wish to find out whether your instructor prefers that you use another style guide.) For an example of a student essay using CBE documentation style, see 47d.

In CBE style, citations within an essay follow one of two possible forms: a **citation-sequence** form, which calls for a superscript number or a number in parentheses following any reference to a source, or a **name-year** form, which calls for the surname of the author and the year of publication placed in parentheses following any reference to a source. Dr. Edward Huth, chairperson of the CBE Style Manual Committee, recommends either the name-and-year or the superscript system rather than the number-in-parentheses system—and further suggests that student writers check a current journal in the field or ask an instructor if in doubt about the preferred style in a particular course or discipline. Here are examples of a citation in a text, using both the citation-sequence superscript form and the name-year form.

IN-TEXT CITATION USING CITATION-SEQUENCE SUPERSCRIPT FORM

Gilman[1] provides the most complete discussion of this
phenomenon in his lengthy text.

IN-TEXT CITATION USING NAME-YEAR FORM

Gilman provides the most complete discussion of this
phenomenon in his lengthy text (Gilman 1994).

Citations in the text refer to items on a literature-cited list. Usually called **References**, this list contains only those sources referred to in the text. If you use the citation-sequence superscript form, the superscript numbers are keyed to the references *in the order in which they appear in the text,* and the sources in the references list follow the same order. If you use the name-year form, the entries in the reference list are arranged alphabetically.

The following examples illustrate both the citation-sequence and the name-year forms as they appear in the reference list. Note that the citation-sequence form calls for listing the date after the publisher's name in references to books and after the title for journal articles, while the name-year form calls for listing the date immediately after the author's name.

REFERENCE LIST USING CITATION-SEQUENCE SUPERSCRIPT FORM

[1] Freidson, Edward. Profession of medicine. New York: Dodd-Mead; 1972. 802p.

[2] Finkel, Miles J. Drugs of limited commercial value. New Engl J Med 1980; 302:643-44.

REFERENCE LIST USING NAME-YEAR FORM

Finkel, Miles J. 1980. Drugs of limited commercial value. New Engl J Med 302:643-44.

Freidson, Edward. 1972. Profession of medicine. New York: Dodd-Mead. 802p.

For electronic sources such as bulletin boards, CBE follows the National Library of Medicine guidelines, as illustrated below:

REFERENCE-LIST ENTRY FOR ENTIRE BULLETIN BOARD

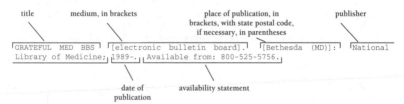

title   medium, in brackets   place of publication, in brackets, with state postal code, if necessary, in parentheses   publisher

GRATEFUL MED BBS [electronic bulletin board]. [Bethesda (MD)]: National Library of Medicine; 1989-. Available from: 800-525-5756.

date of publication   availability statement

REFERENCE-LIST ENTRY FOR CONTRIBUTION TO A BULLETIN BOARD

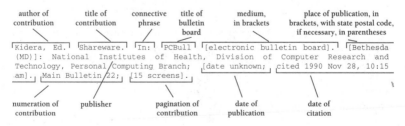

author of contribution   title of contribution   connective phrase   title of bulletin board   medium, in brackets   place of publication, in brackets, with state postal code, if necessary, in parentheses

Kidera, Ed. Shareware. In: PCBull [electronic bulletin board]. [Bethesda (MD)]: National Institutes of Health, Division of Computer Research and Technology, Personal Computing Branch; [date unknown; cited 1990 Nov 28, 10:15 am]. Main Bulletin 22; [15 screens].

numeration of contribution   publisher   pagination of contribution   date of publication   date of citation

CHICAGO STYLE

The fourteenth edition of the style guide of the University of Chicago Press, published in 1993 and called *The Chicago Manual of Style,* covers at great length two systems of documentation. One of them, referred to here as **Chicago style,** has long been used in history as well as other areas of the arts and humanities. It calls for endnotes or, less frequently, footnotes and, often, a bibliography. For further reference, consult *The Chicago Manual of Style* or the following much shorter volume intended for student writers:

> Turabian, Kate L. *A Manual for Writers of Term Papers, Theses, and Dissertations.* 5th ed. Ed. Bonnie Birtwistle Honigsblum. Chicago: U of Chicago P, 1987.

 Directory to Chicago style

45f. Notes

BOOKS

One author, *693*
More than one author, *693*
Unknown author, *693*
Editor or editors, *693*
Multivolume work, *694*

Selection in an anthology, or chapter in a book, with an editor, *693*
Edition other than the first, *693*

PERIODICALS

Article in a journal paginated by volume, *694*
Article in a journal paginated by issue, *694*

Article in a magazine, *694*
Article in a newspaper, *694*

SUBSEQUENT NOTES FOR PREVIOUSLY CITED SOURCES

45g. Bibliography

BOOKS

One author, *695*
More than one author, *695*
Unknown author, *695*
Editor or editors, *695*
Multivolume work, *696*

Selection in an anthology, or chapter in a book, with an editor, *696*
Edition other than the first, *696*

(Continued)

PERIODICALS

Article in a journal paginated by volume, *696*

Article in a journal paginated by issue, *696*

Article in a magazine, *696*

Article in a newspaper, *696*

Note: For a sample essay using Chicago style, see 47f.

45f

Chicago format for in-text citations and notes

Chicago style uses superscript numbers (^{1}) to mark citations in the text. Citations are numbered sequentially throughout the text and correspond to notes that contain complete publication information about the sources cited.

In the text, the superscript number for each note is placed near the cited material—at the end of the relevant quotation, sentence, clause, or phrase. The number is typed after any punctuation mark except the dash, and no space is left between the superscript and the preceding letter or punctuation mark.

IN THE TEXT

As Luftig notes, true friendship between the sexes may simply not be possible.[1]

IN THE NOTE

1. Victor Luftig, <u>Seeing Together: Friendship between the Sexes in English Writing</u> (Palo Alto, Calif.: Stanford University Press, 1993), 1.

Notes can be **footnotes** (typed at the bottom of the page on which the citation appears in the text) or **endnotes** (typed on a separate page under the heading "Notes"). The first line of each note is indented like a paragraph and begins with a number followed by a period and one space before the first word of the entry. All remaining lines of the entry are typed flush with the left margin. Type footnotes single-spaced with a double space between each note. Type all end notes double-spaced.

A note for a book typically begins with the author's name, in regular order, followed by a comma, the title of the source, the publication information in parentheses followed by a comma, and the page number(s). For a periodical, the article title, enclosed in quotation marks, follows the author's name and is in turn followed by a comma and the title of the journal, underlined. The format of the publication information varies according to the type of periodical. The first note for any source gives full information about the source, whereas subsequent notes are shortened.

Books

ONE AUTHOR

1. Hayden Herrera, <u>Frida: A Biography of Frida Kahlo</u> (New York: Harper and Row, 1983), 356.

MORE THAN ONE AUTHOR

2. John T. McNeill and Helena M. Gamer, <u>Medieval Handbooks of Penance</u> (New York: Octagon Books, 1965), 139.

UNKNOWN AUTHOR

3. <u>The New York Times Atlas of the World</u> (New York: New York Times Books, 1980), 67.

EDITOR OR EDITORS

4. C. Vann Woodward, ed., <u>Mary Chesnut's Civil War</u> (New Haven, Conn.: Yale University Press, 1981), 214.

SELECTION IN AN ANTHOLOGY, OR CHAPTER IN A BOOK, WITH AN EDITOR

5. Mary Gordon, "The Parable of the Cave," in <u>The Writer on Her Work</u>, ed. Janet Sternburg (New York: W. W. Norton, 1980), 30.

EDITION OTHER THAN THE FIRST

6. Alfred H. Kelly, Winfred A. Harbison, and Herman Belz, <u>The American Constitution: Its Origins and Development.</u> 6th ed. (New York: W. W. Norton, 1983), 187.

MULTIVOLUME WORK

7. Philip S. Foner and Ronald L. Lewis, eds., The Black Worker (Philadelphia: W. P. Lippincott, 1980), 3:134.

Periodicals

ARTICLE IN A JOURNAL PAGINATED BY VOLUME

8. Margot Norris, "Narration under a Blindfold: Reading Joyce's 'Clay,'" PMLA 102 (1987): 206.

ARTICLE IN A JOURNAL PAGINATED BY ISSUE

9. John Loffy, "The Politics at Modernism's Funeral," Canadian Journal of Political and Social Theory 6, no. 3 (1987): 89.

ARTICLE IN A MAGAZINE

10. Sarah Ferguson, "The Comfort of Being Sad: Kurt Cobain and the Politics of Suicide," Utne Reader, July-August 1994, 60.

ARTICLE IN A NEWSPAPER

11. Dennis Kelly, "A Financial Report Card for Colleges," USA Today, 5 July 1994, sec. D, p. 1.

Subsequent notes for previously cited sources

After providing a full citation the first time you refer to a work, any additional reference to that work need list only the author's last name followed by a comma, a shortened version of the title, a comma, and the page number.

12. Herrera, Frida, 32.
13. Foner and Lewis, Black Worker, 138-39.
14. Ferguson, "Comfort of Being Sad," 63.

45g

Chicago format for bibliography

The alphabetical list of sources for your essay is usually titled "Bibliography," according to Chicago style. If "Sources Consulted," "Works Cited," or "Selected Bibliography" better describes your list, however, any of these titles is acceptable. Begin the list on a separate page at the end, following your essay and any endnotes. Continue the consecutive numbering of pages. Type the title (without underlining or quotation marks), and center it two inches below the top of the page. Double-space, and begin each entry at the left margin. Indent the second and subsequent lines of each entry five spaces. Double-space the entire bibliography.

List sources alphabetically by authors' last names (or by the first major word in the title if the author is unknown). Separate the author, title, and fully spelled out publication information with periods. The following examples demonstrate how to arrange the elements of bibliographic entries according to Chicago style. (For a student example using Chicago style notes and bibliography in her history essay, see pp. 718–722.)

Books

ONE AUTHOR

Herrera, Hayden. <u>Frida: A Biography of Frida Kahlo</u>. New York: Harper and Row, 1983.

MORE THAN ONE AUTHOR

McNeill, John T., and Helena M. Gamer. <u>Medieval Handbooks of Penance</u>. New York: Octagon Books, 1965.

UNKNOWN AUTHOR

<u>The New York Times Atlas of the World</u>. New York: New York Times Books, 1980.

EDITOR OR EDITORS

Woodward, C. Vann, ed. <u>Mary Chesnut's Civil War</u>. New Haven, Conn.: Yale University Press, 1981.

SELECTION IN AN ANTHOLOGY, OR CHAPTER IN A BOOK, WITH AN EDITOR

Gordon, Mary. "The Parable of the Cave." In The Writer
     on Her Work, edited by Janet Sternburg, 30-45.
     New York: W. W. Norton, 1980.

EDITION OTHER THAN THE FIRST

Kelly, Alfred H., Winfred A. Harbison, and Herman Belz.
     The American Constitution: Its Origins and Devel-
     opment. 6th ed. New York: W. W. Norton, 1983.

MULTIVOLUME WORK

Foner, Philip S., and Ronald L. Lewis, eds. The Black
     Worker. Vol. 3. Philadelphia: W. P. Lippincott,
     1980.

Periodicals

ARTICLE IN A JOURNAL PAGINATED BY VOLUME

Norris, Margot. "Narration under a Blindfold: Reading
     Joyce's 'Clay.'" PMLA 102 (1987): 206-15.

ARTICLE IN A JOURNAL PAGINATED BY ISSUE

Loffy, John. "The Politics at Modernism's Funeral."
     Canadian Journal of Political and Social Theory 6,
     no. 3 (1987): 89-96.

ARTICLE IN A MAGAZINE

Ferguson, Sarah. "The Comfort of Being Sad: Kurt Cobain
     and the Politics of Suicide." Utne Reader, July-
     August 1994, 60-62.

ARTICLE IN A NEWSPAPER

Kelly, Dennis. "A Financial Report Card for Colleges."
     USA Today, 5 July 1994, sec. D, p. 1.

Part Nine

Academic Writing

<>

46. Understanding Disciplinary Discourse   698

47. Writing in the Disciplines   707

48. Writing about Literature   723

49. Writing Essay Examinations   740

46

Understanding Disciplinary Discourse

*H*OW IS WRITING USED IN VARIOUS DISCIPLINES? *A recent survey asked that question of two hundred members of professional organizations serving the following seven groups: chemists, psychologists, technical writers, city planners and managers, engineers, business executives, and teachers of language and literature. As you might guess, the great majority (98 percent) report that writing is very important to doing their jobs well. More surprising is just how much time these professionals devote to writing—an average of 46 percent of their working hours. Other surprises emerged in comparing results by profession; for instance, engineers report spending more time writing than do English teachers. But overall, this survey confirmed that good writing plays an important role in almost every profession, and in some it is crucial to success. As one MBA wrote, "Those who advance quickly in my company are those who write and speak well."*

This chapter will lead you to think about the different ways writing works in various disciplines. You may begin to get a sense of such differences as you prepare essays or other written assignments for various other courses. Certainly by the time you choose a major, you should be ready to familiarize yourself with the expectations, vocabularies, styles, methods of proof, and conventional formats used in your field.

EXERCISE 46.1

Consider how the following topics might be approached in the specified fields. What issues might each field see? What approach might each take? How might each investigate and write about the topic? Choose one topic and write a paragraph about how it might be approached by the different fields.

1. *first-grade reading abilities*—as seen by reading teachers, librarians, eye doctors, or reading-test designers

2. *soccer*—as seen by sports physicians, recreation directors, or historians

3. *ancient Egyptian mythology*—as seen by comparative literature specialists, anthropologists, archaeologists, or art historians

4. *a sunken ship*—as seen by engineers, marine biologists, economists, or journalists

46a

Analyzing academic assignments and expectations

Assignments vary widely from course to course and even from professor to professor. You may be asked to prepare one-sentence answers to study questions in history or physics, detailed laboratory reports in biology, case studies in psychology or sociology, or even film scripts in a visual media course. Thus the directions this section offers can only be general, based on experience and on discussions with professors in many disciplines. The best advice is really very simple: make sure you are in control of the assignment rather than the assignment's being in control of you. To take control, you need to understand the assignment fully and to understand what professors in the particular discipline expect in an effective response to the assignment.

When you receive an assignment in *any* discipline, your first job is to make sure you understand what that assignment is asking you to do. Some assignments may be as vague as "Write a five-page essay on one aspect of the Civil War." Others, like this psychology assignment, will be fairly specific:

Everyday Use

While you encounter the language of different fields all the time—in signing a contract or making a will (the language of law), for example, or in examining an estimate for major car repairs (the language of automotive engineering)—you probably use the language of different disciplines most often in the notes you take for your college classes. Take a minute to look carefully at the notes you have taken recently in two classes—one in the humanities or social sciences, perhaps, the other in the sciences. What words or phrases or other symbols in your notes do you associate with the language of each discipline? What other differences can you find in the two sets of class notes? Compare your findings with those of some classmates.

"Collect, summarize, and interpret data drawn from a sample of letters to the editor published in two newspapers, one in a small rural community, and one in an urban community, over a period of three months. Organize your research report according to APA requirements." (See 45d for one student's essay in response to this assignment.) In any case, you must take charge of analyzing the assignment. Answering the following questions can help you do so.

≫ *Analyzing an assignment in any discipline*

1. *What is the purpose of the assignment?* Does it serve an informal purpose—as a basis for class discussion or as a way to brainstorm about a topic? Or is the purpose more formal, a way to demonstrate your mastery of certain material and your competence as a writer?

2. *What is the assignment asking you to do?* Are you to summarize, explain, evaluate, interpret, illustrate, define? If the assignment asks you to do more than one of these things, does it specify the order in which you are to do them? (Note that the psychology assignment above does specify the activities to be carried out and the general topic to be covered in the report.)

3. *Do you need to ask for clarification of any terms?* Students responding to the psychology assignment might well ask the instructor, for instance, to discuss the meaning of *collect* or *interpret* and perhaps to give examples. Or they might want further clarification of the term *urban community* or the size of a suitable *sample*.

4. *What do you need to know or find out to do the assignment?* Students doing the psychology assignment need to develop a procedure—a way to analyze or categorize the letters to the editor. Furthermore, they need to know how to do simple statistical analyses of the data.

5. *Do you understand the expectations regarding background reading and preparation, method of organization and development, format, and length?* The psychology assignment mentions no reading, but in this field an adequate statement of a problem usually requires setting that problem in the context of other research. A student might well ask how extensive this part of the report is to be.

6. *Can you find an example of an effective response to a similar assignment?* If you can, you can analyze its parts and use it as a model for developing your own response. One psychology student, when asked to describe what constituted a "good" essay in that discipline, said, "Well, for the first two assignments I basically summarized the relevant research data as clearly and briefly as I could and then pointed out weaknesses in the research and implications of it. Since

I got A's on both papers I decided I must be doing something right."
And indeed she was. By trial and error, she had fixed on an approach
to the assignments, a method of organization, and a format that fit
into what was accepted as "good" writing in her psychology courses.

7. *Does your understanding of the assignment fit with that of other students?* Talking over an assignment with classmates is one good way
to test your understanding.

EXERCISE 46.2

Here is an assignment from a communications course. Read it carefully, and then
use the list of seven questions in 46a to analyze the assignment.

Assignment: Distribute a questionnaire to twenty people (ten male, ten
female) asking these four questions: (1) What do you expect to say and do when
you meet a stranger? (2) What don't you expect to say and do when you meet
a stranger? (3) What do you expect to say and do when you meet a very close
friend? (4) What don't you expect to say and do when you meet a very close
friend? When you have collected your twenty questionnaires, read them over
and answer the following questions:

1. What, if any, descriptions were common to all respondents' answers?
2. How do male and female responses compare?
3. What similarities and differences were found between the responses to
   the stranger and to the very close friend situations?
4. What factors (environment, time, status, gender, and so on) do you feel
   have an impact on these responses?
5. Discuss your findings, using concepts and theories explained in your text.

Understanding disciplinary vocabularies

The rhetorician Kenneth Burke describes the way people become active
participants in the "conversation of humankind" in the following way. Imagine, he says, that you enter a crowded room in which everyone is talking
and gesturing animatedly. You know no one there and cannot catch much
of what is being said. Slowly you move from group to group listening, and
finally you take a chance and interject a brief statement into the conversation.

Others listen to you and respond. Thus, slowly but surely, do you come to *participate* in, rather than to observe, the conversation.

Entering into an academic discipline or a profession is much like entering into such a conversation. At first you feel like an outsider, and you do not catch much of what you hear or read. You may be experiencing this situation right now. Indeed, everyone experiences the same thing when entering a brand-new field. Trying to enter the new "conversation" takes time and careful attention. Eventually, however, the vocabulary becomes familiar, and participating in the conversation seems easy and natural.

Of course, this chapter cannot introduce you to the vocabulary of every field. The point is that *you* must make the effort to enter into the conversation, and that again means taking charge of the situation. To get started, one of the first things you need to do is to study the vocabulary.

Determine how much of what you are hearing and reading depends on specialized or technical vocabulary. Try highlighting key terms in your reading or your notes to help you distinguish the specialized vocabulary. If you find little specialized vocabulary, try to master the new terms quickly by reading your textbook carefully, by asking questions of the instructor and other students, and by looking up a few key words or phrases.

If you find a great deal of specialized vocabulary, however, you may want to familiarize yourself with it somewhat methodically. Any of the following procedures may prove helpful.

- Keep a log of unfamiliar or confusing words *in context*. To locate definitions, check the terms in your textbook's glossary or index.

- Review your class notes each day after class. Underline important terms, review their definitions, and identify anything that is unclear. Use your textbook or ask questions to clarify anything confusing before the class moves on to a new topic.

- Check to see if your textbook has a glossary of terms or sets off definitions in italics or boldface type. Study pertinent sections to master the terms.

- Try to start using or working with key concepts. Even if they are not yet entirely clear to you, working with them will help you formulate questions that will help you come to understand them. For example, in a statistics class, try to work out (in words) how to do an analysis of covariance, step by step, even if you are not sure of the precise definition of the term. Or try to plot the narrative progression in a story even if you are still not entirely sure of the definition of *narrative progression*.

- Find the standard dictionaries or handbooks of terms for your field. Students beginning the study of literature, for instance, can turn to several guides such as *A Dictionary of Literary, Dramatic, and Cinematic Terms,* or *A Handbook to Literature.* Those entering the discipline of sociology may refer to the *Dictionary of the Social Sciences,* while students beginning statistical analysis may turn to *Statistics without Tears.* Ask your instructor or a librarian for help finding the standard references in your field.

Whatever your techniques for learning a specialized vocabulary, begin to use the new terms whenever you can—in class, in discussion with instructors and other students, and in your assignments. This ability to *use* what you learn in speaking and writing is crucial to your full understanding of and participation in the discipline.

46c

Identifying the style of a discipline

Becoming familiar with technical vocabulary is one important way of initiating yourself into a discipline or field of study. Another method is to identify stylistic features of the writing in that field. You will begin to assimilate these features automatically if you take time simply to immerse yourself in reading and thinking about the field. To speed up this process, however, study some representative pieces of writing in the field. Consider them with the following questions in mind.

- How would you describe the overall *tone* of the writing? Is it very formal, somewhat formal, informal?
- To what extent do writers in the field strive for a somewhat distanced, objective stance?
- In general, how long are the sentences? How long are the paragraphs?
- Are verbs generally active or passive—and why? Do active or passive verbs seem to be part of a characteristic manner of speaking used by writers and researchers in the field?
- Do the writers use first person (*I*) or prefer terms such as *one* or *the investigator*? What is the effect of this stylistic choice?
- Does the writing use visual elements such as graphs, tables, charts, or maps? How are these integrated into the text?
- What bibliographical styles (such as MLA, APA, CBE, or Chicago) are used? (See Chapters 44 and 45.)

Of course, writings within a single discipline may have different purposes and different styles. Although a research report is likely to follow a conventional form, a published speech greeting specialists at a convention may well be less formal and more personal no matter what the field. Furthermore, answering questions such as those above will not guarantee that you can produce a piece of writing similar to the one you are analyzing. Nevertheless, looking carefully at writing in the field brings you one step closer not only to producing similar writing but to producing more effective writing as well.

46d

Understanding the use of evidence

"Good reasons" form the core of any writing that argues a point, for they provide the *evidence* for the argument. Chapter 5 explains how to formulate good reasons. However, what is acceptable and persuasive evidence in one discipline may be more or less so in another. Observable, quantifiable data may constitute the very best evidence in, say, experimental psychology, but the same kind of data may be less appropriate—or even impossible to come by—in a historical study. As you grow familiar with any area of study, you will gather a sense of just what it takes to prove a point in that field. You can speed up this process, however, by doing some investigating and questioning of your own. As you read your textbook and other assigned materials, make a point of noticing the use of evidence. The following questions are designed to help you do so:

- How do writers in the field use precedent and authority? What or who counts as an authority in this field? How are the credentials of an authority established?

- What use is made of empirical data (things that can be observed and measured)? What kinds of data are used? How are such data gathered and presented?

- How are statistics used? How is numerical information used and presented? Are tables, charts, or graphs common? How much weight do they carry?

- How is logical reasoning used? How are definition, cause and effect, analogies, and examples used in this discipline?

- How does the field use primary and secondary sources? What are the primary materials—the firsthand sources of information—in this field? What are the secondary materials—the sources of information derived from others? How is each type of source likely to be presented?

- What other kinds of textual evidence are cited? electronic journals or databases? personal correspondence?

- How are quotations used and integrated into the text?

In addition to carrying out your own investigation of the way evidence is used in your discipline, you may want to raise this issue in class. Ask your instructor how you can best go about making a case in that field.

EXERCISE 46.3

Do some reading in books and journals associated with your prospective major or a discipline of particular interest to you, using the questions above to study the use of evidence in that discipline. If you are keeping a writing log, make an entry in it summarizing what you have learned.

Using conventional disciplinary patterns and formats

You can gather all the evidence in the world and still fail to produce effective writing in your discipline if you do not know the field's generally accepted formats for organizing and presenting evidence. Again, these formats vary widely from discipline to discipline and sometimes from instructor to instructor, but patterns do emerge. In fact, disciplines may share similar conventions for similar types of studies. The typical laboratory report, for instance, follows a fairly standard organizational framework whether it is in botany, chemistry, or parasitology. A case study in sociology or education or anthropology likewise follows a typical organizational plan. And many disciplines have similar formats for problem-solution reports, with some or all of the following: statement of problem, background for the problem's formulation, review of the literature on the subject, findings and possible solution, conclusions, and recommendations (see 47d and 47e for two examples).

Your job in any discipline is to discover its conventional formats and organizing principles so that you can practice using them. This task is easy enough to begin. Ask your instructor to recommend some excellent examples of the kind of writing you will do in the course. Then analyze these examples in terms of format and organization. You might also look at major scholarly journals in your field, checking to see what types of formats seem most common and how each is organized. Study these examples, keeping in mind these questions about organization and format.

- What types of essays or reports are common in this field? What is the purpose of each type?

- What can a reader expect to find in each type of essay or report? What does each type assume about its readers?

- How is a particular type of essay or report organized? What are its main parts? Are they labeled with conventional headings? What logic underlies this sequence of parts?

- How does a particular type of essay or report show the connections among ideas? What assumptions of the discipline does it take for granted? What points does its organization emphasize?

THINKING CRITICALLY ABOUT THE DISCOURSE OF A DISCIPLINE

Reading with an Eye for Disciplinary Discourse

Here is an introductory passage of a college textbook. Read it carefully to see what you can infer about the discourse of chemistry—about its characteristic vocabulary, style, use of evidence, and so on.

At one time it was easy to define chemistry. The traditional definition goes something like this: Chemistry is the study of the nature, properties, and composition of matter, and how these undergo changes. That served as a perfectly adequate definition as late as the 1930s, when natural science (the systematic knowledge of nature) seemed quite clearly divisible into the physical and biological sciences, with the former being comprised of physics, chemistry, geology, and astronomy and the latter consisting of botany and zoology. This classification is still used, but the emergence of important fields of study such as oceanography, paleobotany, meteorology, and biochemistry, for example, have made it increasingly clear that the dividing lines between the sciences are no longer at all sharp. Chemistry, for instance, now overlaps so much with geology (thus we have *geochemistry*), astronomy (*astrochemistry*), and physics (*physical chemistry*) that it is probably impossible to devise a really good modern definition of chemistry, except, perhaps, to fall back on the operational definition: chemistry is what chemists do. (And what chemists do is what this book is all about!)...

To make a very long story short, copper and bronze gave way to iron and steel, the latter being an iron-carbon alloy. Metals were very important in early civilization and the practice of metallurgy provided a wealth of chemical information. Egyptians, for example, learned how to obtain many different metals from their ores, and according to some experts the word *chemistry* is derived from an ancient word *khemeia,* which may refer to the Egyptians' name for their own country, *Kham.* However, some experts believe *chemistry* came from the Greek word *chyma,* which means "to melt or cast a metal." ...

– JOHN B. RUSSELL, *General Chemistry*

Thinking Critically about Your Writing in a Discipline

Choose a piece of writing you have produced for a particular discipline—a history essay, a laboratory report, a review of the literature in some particular field, or any other written assignment. Examine your writing closely for its use of that discipline's vocabulary, style, methods of proof, and conventional formats. How comfortable are you writing a piece of this kind? In what ways are you using the conventions of the discipline easily and well? What conventions give you difficulty, and why? You might interview an instructor in this field about the conventions and requirements for writing in the discipline. Make notes about what you learn about being a better writer in the field.

47

Writing in the Disciplines

W*RITE YOUR WAY TO SUCCESS!" proclaims an advertisement for a self-help booklet "guaranteed to add to your income." However inflated this claim may be, much evidence exists to suggest that if writing does not guarantee wealth, it can enhance learning. In fact, writing and learning seem to go hand-in-hand: as you strive to represent knowledge in writing, you actively learn it more thoroughly. This realization has led many colleges and universities to encourage student writing in almost all classes—from agronomy to zoology.*

47a

Writing to learn

You may already use writing to help you learn course material and to prepare for examinations. Consider the following suggestions of ways writing can help you master course material:

- Keep a course notebook for lecture notes, class discussions, and homework. Consider using left-hand pages for the major information you need to remember and right-hand pages for your own reflections and questions.
- Allow five minutes after each class to summarize what you learned and to formulate questions to ask in class.
- Try outlining information you're having trouble learning.
- Try brainstorming, clustering, or the other methods described in 3a to explore and articulate the information you're studying.
- Join with two or three other students to compare notes and discuss course material.

> *Everyday use*
>
> How many times a day do you write something down so as to remember it or understand it better? Do you jot down phone numbers? write out directions? make lists of things to do? For a day or two, make a note of every time you use writing in such ways. Most likely, you are already using writing to learn—both in and out of school.

47b

Learning to write

As the head of Hewlett Packard said recently to a group of college professors: "Just give us graduates who can write well. We'll take it from there." Indeed, learning to write is enormously important in all fields, basic to achieving, communicating, and using all knowledge. This chapter provides examples of writing in the social sciences, the natural sciences, the applied sciences, and the humanities.

47c

Writing in the social sciences: a literature survey in psychology

An introductory psychology class was given the assignment to write a brief literature review related to one aspect of child development, summarizing three journal articles addressing the topic, and drawing some conclusions based on their findings. After browsing through her textbook and thinking about the assignment, Laura Brannon decided to focus on child abuse. A trip to the library turned up many articles on this subject, and she chose three. She summarized the three articles, worked through a draft, and analyzed it, following the revision guidelines in Chapter 4. Here is the opening and closing of her essay, a **literature survey** reviewing the three articles and drawing conclusions about what they show and mean.

Note that she first presents the subject of her literature review and acknowledges the complexity of the issue—child abuse—as a means of leading in to the three articles she intends to survey. She then summarizes the first article, giving pertinent information about the subjects of the study, the size of the study, and the methods used before presenting significant results and reporting on shortcomings noted by the authors. Her summaries of the other two articles have been omitted in the excerpt printed here.

In her conclusion, she moves on to offer her own interpretation of the significance of the three articles and draws out the implications of these studies for those who seek to prevent child abuse. Note that her citations and references follow APA style guidelines throughout (see Chapter 45).

Early Detection of Child Abuse

There is no simple one-word answer to the question of what causes child abuse. The abuse of children results from a complex interaction among parent, child, and environmental factors. This complexity does not necessarily mean, however, that potential victims and abusers cannot be identified before serious damage is done. Researchers have examined methods of detecting potential or actual child abuse.

Prediction of Child Abuse: Interviews

In a study by Altemeier, O'Connor, Vietze, Sandler, and Sherrod (1984), 1,400 women between 9 and 40 weeks pregnant were interviewed to test their abusive tendencies. Four researchers were present (with an inter-rater agreement of 90% or better). The Maternal History Interview included questions about the mother's own childhood, self-image, support from others, parenting philosophy, attitudes toward pregnancy, and health-related problems (including substance abuse). Maternal and paternal stresses during the preceding year were measured with a modified Life Stress Inventory. Any information not included in the standard interview but felt by the researchers to make the mother a high risk for abuse of her child--for example, being overtly untruthful--was also recorded. When the infants were 21 to 48 months old, the Juvenile Court and the Department of Human Services were checked for reports of their abuse or neglect.

Although the interview predicted abuse (p < .0001), its ability to predict decreased with time; for example, although "six of seven families reported for abuse within the first nine months following the interview were high risk, . . . after 24 months only one of seven had been assigned to this group" (Altemeier et al., p. 395). The researchers point out some shortcomings of their study, particularly the high rate of false positives. (Only 6% of the high-risk population was reported for abuse, 22% if failure to thrive and neglect were included.) Although many incidents of abuse may go unreported (which could account for some of the false positives), this false-positive pecentage should be reduced. Also, it would be preferable if the role of subjective judgments in the method for prediction could be reduced as well.

[Brannon's review of two additional studies follows.]

Conclusions

Overall, the findings of these studies seem to indicate that tests can be devised to predict potential child abusers. The study by Murphy, Orkow, and Nicola (1985), which relies less on subjective judgments, has a significantly lower false-positive rate than the earlier study by Altemeier et al. (1984). Therefore, although such tests have not yet been perfected, they appear to be improving.

The two studies tried to integrate the complex relationships between child, parent, and environmental factors that are involved in child abuse. Ideally, if potential abusers could be identified early enough, they could undergo treatment even before the child is born. Of course, a parent could not be separated from a child on the basis of one test, and therefore, the results should remain confidential to avoid any potential for abuse of the test itself.

Whereas the tests look carefully at the parent's situation, the injury variables analyzed in the Johnson and Showers study (1985) focus attention on the child. If teachers, neighbors, relatives, or other people notice that children have frequent injuries (especially with the locations, types, and causes associated with different ages and races), abuse can be detected early and perhaps stopped.

References

Altemeier, W. A., O'Connor, S., Vietze, P., Sandler, H., & Sherrod, K. (1984). Prediction of child abuse: A prospective study of feasibility. Child Abuse and Neglect: The International Journal, 8, 393-400.

Johnson, C. F., & Showers, J. (1985). Injury variables in child abuse. Child Abuse and Neglect: The International Journal, 9, 207-215.

Murphy, S., Orkow, B., & Nicola, R. (1985). Prenatal prediction of child abuse and neglect: A prospective study. Child Abuse and Neglect: The International Journal, 9, 225-235.

47d

Writing in the natural sciences: a lab report in biology

An introductory biology class was asked to analyze an unknown cob of corn to find out the most likely genetic cross that produced it and to write a report on the findings. Excerpts from Lesley Shaffer's research report follow. Her report follows a standard format recommended in the natural sciences: an **abstract** summarizes the research and findings; the **introduction** briefly reviews other relevant research and explains the purpose of her experiment; the **methods and materials** section offers a brief description of the experiment; and the **results** section explains what the experiment produced. The lengthy **discussion and conclusions** section examines two possible dihybrid crosses and, on the basis of statistical analysis, concludes that, given the data at hand, both hypotheses are acceptable. Finally, note that her citations and **references** use CBE style (see Chapter 45).

The Determination of the Most Probable Genetic Cross

Which Produced an Unknown Cob of Corn (Zea mays)

Abstract

The analysis of an unknown cob of corn was conducted to determine the most probable genetic cross that produced it. Phenotypes for aleurone color and starch content were recognized for each of the total 460 kernels. Alleles for aleurone color were found to be dominant for purple (R) and recessive for yellow (r). Alleles for endosperm starch content were found to be dominant for starchy endosperms (Su) and recessive for sweet endosperms (su). The phenotypic ratio of the unknown cob of corn was 1.04 : 1.00 : 1.03 : 1.16 for R_ Su_, R_susu, rrSu_, and rrsusu kernels respectively. The most probable genetic cross was RrSusu rrsusu or Rrsusu rrSusu.

Introduction

The foundation of modern genetics can be attributed, in large part, to the work of Gregor Mendel. He conducted hybridization experiments on the garden pea, determining dominant and recessive alleles in peas. Using mathematics and probabilities, he also found that the genotypic ratios of the offspring from hybrid crosses could be predicted. This was based on the possible alleles that could be donated in the gametes of each parent organism (Gardner 1960).

Mendel's work can also be applied to the genetics of corn. However, there is greater complexity in hybrid crosses than Mendel's experiments reveal. In 1911, G. N. Collins and J. H. Kempton found the first clearly recognized linkage in corn, discovering that the gene for the waxy endosperm is linked to the gene for aleurone color (Gardner 1960). This discovery led to the concept of crossing-over, in which segments of homologous chromosomes break and exchange genes creating genetic recombinations. Therefore, the genotypic ratios for the offspring of hybrid crosses do not always coincide with Mendelian ratios.

The purpose of my experiment was to analyze the phenotypes expressed in the kernels of an unknown cob of corn and determine the most probable genetic cross that produced it.

Methods and Materials

A cob of corn of unknown parentage was analyzed. Analysis consisted of counting individual kernels and categorizing them according to phenotypes of aleurone color and starch content. A total of 460 kernels were counted and placed in categories of either purple aleurone / starchy endosperm, purple aleurone / sweet endosperm, yellow aleurone / starchy endosperm, or yellow aleurone / sweet endosperm.

Dominant and recessive alleles for aleurone color were determined by the analysis of a separate cob of corn. Each kernel was counted according to color. Phenotypic ratios were calculated from which the monohybrid cross was deduced. Dominant and recessive alleles for starch content were determined with the analysis of another cob of corn in which the kernels were counted for each phenotype. Phenotypic ratios were calculated, and the monohybrid cross was deduced.

A phenotypic ratio for the unknown was then calculated, and the hypothesis for the most probable genetic cross of the parent corn was deduced.

Results

The monohybrid corn cob analyzed for dominant and recessive alleles for aleurone color had 106 yellow kernels and 282 purple kernels out of a total 388 kernels. The phenotypic ratio was 1 : 2.7. The calculated Chi-square value was 1.113 for the hypothesis of a heterozygous cross.

The monohybrid corn analyzed to determine dominant and recessive alleles for starch content had 100 sweet kernels and 317 starchy kernels out of a total 427 kernels. The phenotypic ratio was 1 : 2.9. The calculated Chi-square value was 0.132 for the hypothesis of a heterozygous cross.

The unknown cob of corn analyzed had kernels which exhibited phenotypes of purple or yellow aleurones, and starchy or sweet endosperms. Of the total 460 kernels, 24.6% were purple starchy, 23.7% purple sweet, 24.3% yellow starchy, and 27.4% yellow sweet (Table 1). The phenotypic ratio was 1.04 : 1.00 : 1.03 : 1.16.

Discussion and Conclusions

The development of the endosperm starts with the initial triploid nucleus which begins rapid divisions within two to four hours after fertilization (Knowles 1990). Sixteen to thirty days after pollination, genes are activated that specify the increase of enzymes involved in the synthesis of stored products, such as

starch. From thirty-one to fifty days after pollination,
there is continued synthesis of the major storage
products. The endosperm changes as structures
specialized for the storage of starch enlarge (Walden
1978).

[Eight more paragraphs of discussion and conclusions follow.]

References

Gardner, Eldon J. 1960. Principles of genetics. New
    York: Wiley. 386 p.
Knowles, R. V.; Sprienc, F.; Phillips, R. L. 1990.
    Endoreduplication of nuclear DNA in the developing
    maize endosperm. Developmental Genetics 11:125-132.
Walden, David B. 1978. Maize breeding and genetics.
    New York: Wiley. 794 p.

[Table 1 and two figures follow.]

47e

Writing in the applied sciences: an engineering report

For a final project in systems engineering, students were asked to identify a problem, investigate it, and propose solutions. Such an assignment in the applied sciences generally results in a formal three-part project, including a **proposal**, a **progress report**, and a **final report**.

The **proposal** is often in memorandum form with the following sections: *statement of problem, proposed project and purpose, plan with deadlines,* and *evaluation* (explaining the criteria to be used in determining the success of the project).

The **progress report**, also a memo, usually contains the same heading line as those in the proposal, followed by statements about *project and purpose, progress to date,* and *practical implications* (explaining adjustments the writer must make).

The **final report** usually includes a separate *title page* and *table of contents,* which gives the page numbers of the sections of the report and any tables, figures, calculations, or illustrations; *abstract* or *executive summary,* which summarizes the project, findings, and conclusions; *introduction,* which explains what led to the project, its purpose, and any necessary background information; *methods and materials,* which describes the equipment and methodologies used; *results,* which describe the findings; *discussion and conclusions,* which explain why the results occurred, draw conclusions, and offer any appropriate recommendations; *references,* and *back matter,* including appendices of tables, figures, calculations, and so on.

Brian Hearing chose to study the problem of buses idling in Troy, New York. The following excerpts from his report, "Suggestions to Limit City Bus Idling," show his results and appendix, which includes two tables, two calculations, and a figure.

Results

Table 1 shows the results of an observational experiment conducted on October 23, 1993, at the Uncle Sam Park in downtown Troy. During the one-hour observation period, three buses spent a total of 28 minutes stationary at curbside, idling. As a rule, an engine's consumption at a bus stop amounts to 0.3 gallons per hour. For this particular test hour, 0.14 gallons were consumed. For a typical hour of a ten-hour day, 1.4 gallons were spent idling. At this rate, about 500 gallons a year are wasted on idling. (See Appendix, Calculations 1.)

Idling fuel consumption on a typical route also consumes a large amount of fuel. The bus on Route 87, from Troy to Wynantskill, made on average about 25 stops per hour. It also waited, idling for 13 minutes of the hour in the heavily residential area of Wynantskill. From Figure 1, this bus consumed 0.15 gallons per mile. From Calculations 2, this equals 4.3 gallons per hour. Dividing 0.3 gallons spent idling by 4.3 total gallons consumed, the bus spent 7 percent of its fuel just idling.

Appendix

Table 1. Stationary Idling in Downtown Troy

Test Date: October 23, 1993
Test Location: Uncle Sam Park
Start: 10:33 a.m.
Finish: 11:31 a.m.

Bus Number	Time In	Time Out	Time Idling
716	10:57	11:13	16 minutes
668	11:10	11:14	4 minutes
647	11:16	11:24	8 minutes
		Total Time:	28 minutes

Table 2. Stationary Idling on a Typical Route

Test Date: October 24, 1993
Test Location: Troy-Wynantskill Route
Start: 11:31 a.m.
Finish: 12:09 p.m.

Time	Stops	Miles
11:31 - 11:47	11	6
11:47 - 12:00	0	0 - idling
12:00 - 12:09	5	6

Total: 16 stops in 38 minutes = 25 stops/hour

Calculations 1

0.3 gallons/hour × 28 minutes / 60 minutes/hour
= 0.14 gallons per hour

0.14 gallons/hour × 10 hours/operating day × 360
operating days per year ≅ 500 gallons per year

Calculations 2

16 stops per 12 miles = 1.33 gallons per mile
(From Figure 1) = 0.15 gallons per bus mile
0.15 gallons per bus mile × 12 miles / 25 minutes
× 60 minutes/hour = 4.3 gallons per hour

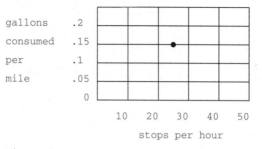

Figure 1

Relationship between gallons per mile and stops per hour

Source: C.S. Papcostas, <u>Fundamentals of Transportation Engineering</u> (Englewood Cliffs, N.J.: Prentice Hall, 1986).

47f

Writing in the humanities: a position paper in history

An introductory history course on U.S. civilization to 1877 called on students to write an essay "of no more than six pages focusing on a controversial issue related to the First Amendment. Be sure to summarize historical events, analyze the significance of the issue, and use appropriate source material from class readings or additional research you do on your own. The essay should be documented according to the Chicago system."

Kelly Darr chose to review the 1803 *Marbury v. Madison* decision and to relate that decision to the growth of the Supreme Court's powers. As is often appropriate in humanities essays, the opening paragraph introduces the subject and concludes with an explicit thesis, this one in the form of two major questions that serve as an organizational guide to the remainder of the essay and as a promise to the reader of what is to come. The middle five paragraphs provide textual evidence in response to the first question, while the two concluding paragraphs address the second question and consider the status of this decision today. Following are the first four paragraphs of the essay, excerpted, and abbreviated versions of her notes and bibliography, which follow Chicago style (see Chapter 45).

Marbury v. Madison and the
Origins of Judicial Review

The Supreme Court of the United States is a very
prestigious and powerful branch of American government
today. It has not always held this position, however.
When the government system was developed in the late 18th
century, the powers of the judicial branch were fairly
undefined. In 1803, Chief Justice John Marshall, with
his decision in Marbury v. Madison, began to define the
duties of the Court by claiming for the Supreme Court the
power of judicial review. Judicial review has been
upheld ever since, and many people take the practice for
granted. There is controversy around Marshall's decision, however, with some claiming that judicial review
was not the intent of the Framers. Two questions must be
asked: Did Marshall overstep his bounds when he declared
judicial review for the Court? If so, why has his
decision been upheld for almost two hundred years? An
examination of the actual case, Marbury v. Madison, and
of Marshall's reasons for his decision is the first step
to answering these questions.

This case was surrounded by personal and political
opposition. It was brought to Court by William Marbury,
whose commission as justice of the peace by John Adams
was withheld by Thomas Jefferson when he became
President. Jefferson's act was prompted by Adams's
attempt to fill the national judiciary with Federalist
judges on the eve before Jefferson took office. Due to a
mistake by John Marshall himself (at the time the
Secretary of State under Adams), however, the commissions
were not delivered. Jefferson, who did not appreciate
the last-minute attempt to fill the offices with
Federalists, refused to deliver the commissions after he

took office. Marbury and a few other men sued James
Madison, Secretary of State under Jefferson. Marshall,
now the Chief Justice, was eager to try the case and
attack Jefferson, his political enemy.[1]

By the time the case went to trial in 1803, two of
the five years of the term for justice of the peace had
expired. It was no longer a case over undelivered
commissions; it was a case testing the power of the
courts against the executive. . . . If Marshall issued a
writ of mandamus requiring Madison to hand over the
commissions, Jefferson could have him impeached.[2] If
Marshall ruled in favor of Jefferson, he would make the
judicial branch look even more powerless than it already
did. Marshall was in a no-win situation, and he was
aware of this predicament when he set out to make his
decision.[3]

He finally made his decision on February 24, 1803,
and it was based on two concerns: the ethics of
withholding Marbury's commission, and the right of the
Supreme Court to issue a writ of mandamus to the
President.[4] Marshall broke the issue into three
questions. The first question addressed whether Marbury
had a right to the commission. Marshall said that he did
have the right to it because it had been signed by the
President at the time and sealed with the seal of the
United States. Second, Marshall asked if Marbury then
had a right to the commission, whether the laws of the
land protected his right to the appointment? Marshall
reasoned that withholding his commission would be in
violation of his personal rights, so the laws must
protect those rights. Third, Marshall asked if the laws
protected Marbury in the form of a writ of mandamus from
the Supreme Court. Marshall reasoned that the Court

could not issue a writ of mandamus even though the Judiciary Act of 1789 said that it could. According to this law, the Supreme Court could issue writs of mandamus to people under the authority of the United States, which Marbury clearly was; however, if the Court could not issue a writ of mandamus, then this law was unconstitutional. He went on to say that the Supreme Court only had appellate jurisdiction (except in a few specific cases) and this case had been brought before the Court for original jurisdiction. Therefore he declared that the law stating that the Supreme Court could issue writs of mandamus was unconstitutional. In other words, Congress did not have the legal power to give the Court that right. He went on to say that the Constitution is the supreme law of the land, and since it was the judicial branch's duty to say what the law is, they had the power to declare acts unconstitutional. Thus Marshall denied mandamus for Marbury, and ruled in favor of Madison. At the same time, however, he took a big step toward strengthening the judicial branch by establishing judicial review for the Supreme Court.[5]

[In the next paragraph, Darr sums up the strengths and weaknesses of Marshall's decision. She then discusses the effects of Marbury v. Madison and its status today.]

Notes

1. John A. Garraty, Quarrels That Have Shaped the Constitution (New York: Harper and Row, 1987), 7–14.

2. Garraty, Quarrels, 19.

3. William C. Louthan, The United States Supreme Court. Lawmaking in the Third Branch of Government (Englewood Cliffs, N.J.: Prentice Hall, 1991), 51.

4. Thomas J. Higgins, Judicial Review Unmasked (West Hanover, Mass.: Christopher Publishing House, 1981), 40-41.

5. Marbury v. Madison, 1 Cranch, 137 (1803).

Bibliography

Garraty, John A. Quarrels That Have Shaped the Constitution. New York: Harper and Row, 1987.

Higgins, Thomas J. Judicial Review Unmasked. West Hanover, Mass.: Christopher Publishing House, 1981.

Louthan, William C. The United States Supreme Court: Lawmaking in the Third Branch of Government. Englewood Cliffs, N.J.: Prentice Hall, 1991.

Marbury v. Madison, 1 Cranch, 137 (1803).

THINKING CRITICALLY ABOUT THE WRITING IN VARIOUS DISCIPLINES

Reading in a Particular Discipline

Choose one of your textbooks, perhaps in a subject you are considering as a major. Look closely at the writing in the book, and at any study questions that ask you to write. What do you notice about the writing? For example, is there much specialized terminology? Are sentences active or passive? Is much information provided in tables and other graphs? How do these writing features affect you as a reader?

Thinking about Your Own Writing in a Discipline

Choose a piece of writing you have done for a course in the social sciences, the natural or applied sciences, or the humanities. Compare it to the appropriate example in this chapter, and make some notes about writing conventions in that particular field.

48

Writing about Literature

ARE YOU INTRIGUED BY VIRTUAL REALITY and the idea that it might enable you to broaden your own experience in heretofore hard-to-imagine ways? This chapter is about an early forerunner of virtual reality: the world's literature. Literature presents us with a range of "virtual" realities that go far beyond our own time-and-place-bound experience. Especially during a time of frenetic movement and change such as ours, literature can help us think carefully and critically about the human condition, about what it means to be human, or even to be "virtually" human. Thus does the study of literature offer a wealth of insight into human motives, character, and potential—and help us explore our own humanity.

This chapter presents three approaches to interpreting literature—text-based, context-based, and reader-based. It offers guidelines for reading and writing about literature, with examples of student writing about fiction, drama, and poetry.

Everyday Use

Literature might be called an art of story, and story might in turn be called a universal form of language, for every culture we know of has a tradition of storytelling. You no doubt do too, whether the stories you first heard were bedtime stories told by a parent, or the stories you and your friends created during play. Indeed, we might even say that a major goal of living is to create the story of our own lives, a story we can take pleasure in telling. Take a few moments to think of the earliest stories you remember. Then make a list of all the ways in which stories touch your life. Compare your notes with those of your classmates.

48a

Understanding the language of literary interpretation

In writing about literature, you may need to use a number of special terms. The following list includes terms that are frequently used in the close reading of literary works to analyze their structure and style.

≫ *A glossary of literary terms*

To analyze the sounds in a literary work, you might use the following terms:

Alliteration   the repetition of sound to create special emphasis or rhythm, as in this sentence from Eudora Welty: "Monsieur Boule inserted a *d*elicate *d*agger in Mademoiselle's left side and *d*eparted with a posed immediacy."

Meter   the rhythm of verse, as determined by the kind of rhythm—iambic, dactylic, and so on—and number of feet (groups of syllables)—pentameter, tetrameter—in a line. Iambic pentameter indicates five feet of two syllables, with the stress falling on the second of the two, as in the following line: *An aged man is but a paltry thing.*

Onomotopoeia   the use of words whose sounds call up or "echo" their meaning: *hiss* or *sizzle,* for example.

Rhythm   the beat or pattern of stresses in a line of poetry, including traditional metrical patterns or the movement of free verse, and in prose, created by repetition, parallelism, and a variation of sentence length and structure. Robert Frost's "Fire and Ice" (in Chapter 30) uses a basic iambic rhythm, with every other syllable stressed: ˘/˘/˘/.

Rhyme scheme   the pattern of end rhymes in a poem, usually designated by the letters *a, b, c.* The Emily Dickinson poem (in Chapter 36) has a rhyme scheme of *aabccd.* A Shakespearean sonnet typically follows a rhyme scheme of *abab cdcd efef gg.*

Stanza   a division of a poem: a four-line stanza is called a *quatrain;* a two-line stanza, a *couplet.* Robert Francis's poem (in Chapter 13) contains five two-line stanzas.

Literary language is sometimes distinguished from the nonliterary by its purposeful use of imagery, often to "make strange" or defamiliarize the ordinary so that we can look at it in new ways. The following terms may find use in any discussion of imagery:

Analogy a comparison of two things that are alike in some respect, often to explain one of the things or to represent it more vividly by relating it to the second. A simile is an explicit analogy, a metaphor an implied one. In "The World's Biggest Membrane" Lewis Thomas draws an analogy between earth's atmosphere and a giant membrane.

Figurative language the use of metaphor, simile, personification, and other figures of speech that enrich description and create meaning (See 5h3 and 27d.)

Imagery the vivid descriptions and figures of speech that evoke a picture in the reader's mind or appeal to the other senses. The running sore in "Harlem (A Dream Deferred)" (in Chapter 27) creates such a vivid image.

Symbolism the use of one thing to represent other things or ideas, as the flag symbolizes patriotism or as ice symbolizes hate in Frost's "Fire and Ice" (in Chapter 30).

The codes and structures of narrative are very important to literary interpretation. You might want to examine the complexities which arise from representations of the author, the characters and their relationships, or the structures of time and space in a work. Some helpful terms for doing so include the following:

Characters the people in a story, who have different motivations and who may act, react, and change accordingly during the course of a story. In Amy Dierst's essay on *The Third Life of Grange Copeland* (see 48b1), she examines the characters in the story as one way of interpreting its meaning.

Dialogism a term associated with the critic Mikhail Bakhtin, describing the rich social, cultural, and historic context surrounding any participle, word, or phrase. The word *democracy*, for instance, carries a whole history of meanings and usages that any writer using the word must contend with.

Dialogue the conversation among characters, which can show how they interact and suggest why they act as they do. The passage from Maxine Clair in 34b shows the use of dialogue in a story.

Heteroglossia a term referring to the many voices present in a work of literature. In Charles Dickins's *Hard Times,* for example, the "voice" of mass education speaks alongside the voices of many characters.

Implied author the "author" that is inferred from or implied by the text, as distinct from the real person/author. In *The Adventures of Huckleberry Finn,* for example, the real author is Samuel Clemens (or Mark Twain); the implied author is the "author" we imagine as Clemens presents himself in the text.

(Continued)

Intertextuality the system of references in one text to other texts. You might think of texts as being part of a vast intertextual conversation, with one text echoing others through quotations, allusions, parodies, or thematic references. Gary Larson's *The Far Side* Frankenstein cartoons, for example, refer intertextually to the original novel *Frankenstein* as well as to many movie versions and to other works focusing on the dangers or limits of science.

Irony the use of language to suggest the opposite, or nearly the opposite, of what the words usually mean, as in saying that being caught in a freezing downpour is "delightful." See 27d.

Narrator the person telling a story. In a short story, poem, or novel, the narrator may be a character or may be an omniscient voice with a viewpoint outside the story itself. In *The Adventures of Huckleberry Finn,* for example, the narrator is Huck Finn himself.

Parody an imitation intended for humorous or satiric effect, as in Dana Carvey's parodic imitations of George Bush. On p. 372 is an example of a student parody of Edgar Allan Poe's style.

Plot the events selected by the writer to reveal the conflicts among or within the characters, often arranged in chronological order but sometimes including flashbacks to past events. In her essay on *The Third Life of Grange Copeland* (see 48d1), Amy Dierst describes events of the plot.

Point of view the perspective from which the work is presented— in fiction, by a narrator outside the story or a character speaking in first or third person; in poetry, by the poet or a role assumed by the poet. In "Theme for English B" (in Chapter 29), the point of view is that of the student.

Protagonist the hero, heroine, or main character, often opposed by an *antagonist,* as Othello is opposed by Iago.

Setting the scene of the literary work, including the time, physical location, and social situation. "Theme for English B" (in Chapter 29) is set in Harlem during the 1950s.

Style the writer's choice of words and sentence structures. Two devices characteristic of John F. Kennedy's style are repetition and inverted word order. (See the beginning of Chapter 23 for an example from his Inaugural Address.)

Theme a major and often recurring subject or topic. Amy Dierst discusses the theme of conflict between men and women in her essay about *The Third Life of Grange Copeland* (see 48d1). The predominant theme often reveals the larger meaning of the work, including any thoughts or insights about life or people in general.

Tone the writer's attitude, conveyed through specific word choices and structures. In her essay arguing that students should consider designing their own majors (see 5i), Jennifer Georgia's tone is earnest and serious.

48b

Becoming a strong reader of literature

As a reader of literature, you are not a neutral observer, not an empty cup into which the "meaning" of a literary work is poured. If such were the case, literary works would have exactly the same meanings for all of us, and reading would be a fairly boring affair. If you have ever gone to a movie with a friend and each come away with a completely different understanding or response, you already have ample evidence that literature never has just one meaning.

Nevertheless, you may have been willing to accept the first meaning to occur to you, or to take a piece of literature at face value, failing to question or puzzle over it. The following guidelines aim to help you exercise your interpretive powers, to build your strength as a reader of literature.

≫ *For reading literature*

1. *Read the work first for an overall impression.* Read it straight through, and jot down your first impressions. How did the work make you feel? What about it is most remarkable or memorable? Are you confused about anything in it?

2. *Reread the work, annotating* the margins to "talk back," asking questions, pointing out anything that seems out of place or ineffective.

3. *What is the genre*—fiction? drama? poetry?

4. *What do you see as the major themes* of the work, the points the author seems to want to make? What evidence in the text supports these themes? Consider plot, setting, character, point of view, imagery, and sound.

5. *What may have led the author to address these points?* Consider the time and place represented in the work as well as when and where the writer wrote the work. Also consider social, political, or even personal forces that may have affected the writer.

6. *Who are the readers* the writer seems to address? Do they include you? Do you sympathize with a particular character—and if so, what causes you to do so? What is the narrator's point of view, and how does it shape your response?

7. *Review your notes,* highlighting the ideas that most interest you. Then freewrite for fifteen minutes or so about your overall response to this work and about the key point you would like to make about it.

One student's annotations of a poem

Here's my clue to
setting—a pool hall!

The Pool Players.
Seven at the Golden Shovel

We real cool. We
Left school. We

Putting "we" at the
end of the line
makes for a kind of
syncopated sound.
Cool. Jazz, maybe?

This word acts like a drumbeat.
But it makes me wonder who this
"we" is. Me? Who is talking here?

Lurk late. We
Strike straight. We

Sing sin. We
Thin gin. We

Not sure what this and the next
line mean. Look up in a slang
dictionary?

Jazz June. We
Die soon.

Yes—I was right.
Jazz for sure.

What's the link between being
"cool," jazz, and dying soon?
Leaving school is cool, maybe—
also a kind of death? Is this connection overstated? I'll have to
think some more.

– GWENDOLYN BROOKS, "We Real Cool"

This student went on to freewrite about the way the poem draws her into
the "we," in spite of the fact that she feels little connection to the pool
players at first.

48c

Considering your assignment, purpose, and audience

In most writing about literature, you will be responding to an assignment given by an instructor.

- Study the *assignment* carefully, with special attention to any key terms
  (for example, *analyze* or *discuss*.) Note any requirements about use of
  sources and length.

- The *assignment* may well imply a specific purpose. *Analyze,* for example,
  implies that your purpose will be to look at one or more parts of the
  literary work and to argue or explain their relationship to a point or theme
  of the work.

- As in all academic work, you will also want to consider the audience for your essay—your instructor, most likely, and perhaps others as well.

Developing a critical stance and a thesis

Just as all your reading is based to some extent on your personal history and knowledge and reasons for reading, so your writing about literature is based to some extent on your own **critical stance**, what you've read and where you're coming from as a writer. What perspective do you bring? How do you approach the text you're writing about? In literary studies today, such stances vary widely, and you may encounter in your professors a number of different approaches. Your critical stance will help lead you to your **thesis**, the major point or claim you wish to make about a literary work.

In general, student writers tend to adopt one of three primary stances: a *text-based stance* that builds an argument by focusing on specific features of the literary text in question; a *context-based stance* that builds an argument by focusing on the context in which a literary text exists; a *reader-based stance* that focuses on the response of a particular reader to the text and an interpretation that grows out of his or her personal response; or some combination of these approaches. The rest of this chapter introduces three student writers, each of whom takes one of these three critical stances.

1

A text-based stance

The writer of the following essay, Amy Dierst, responded to an assignment for an introductory literature class that asked her to "analyze some aspect of one of the works read this term." This is a fairly open-ended assignment, and so she checked with her instructor to make sure that her chosen focus, "the role of men," would qualify as an aspect of a work to be analyzed. Note that because the assignment called for an analysis of a work read by the entire class, she did not need to review the plot. As a student in a literature class, she could assume that analyzing characters and themes was an appropriate form of interpretation.

This kind of literary interpretation, based largely on specific evidence from the literary text itself, is the approach most students take in writing about literature. Amy Dierst makes a claim—her thesis—about the role of men in *The Third Life of Grange Copeland* that she then substantiates by citing passages from the primary source, the novel itself, as well as from secondary sources, other interpretations of the novel.

The Role of Men in

The Third Life of Grange Copeland

Many observers of American society charge that it has created a distorted definition of manhood and produced men who, in their need to assert control of their lives, release their frustration at the expense of women. In her novel <u>The Third Life of Grange Copeland</u>, Alice Walker addresses this theme from the point of view of black men and women, for whom racism heightens the distortion and its consequences. She suggests that by stifling black men's sense of freedom and control, a racist society creates frustrations that are released in family violence and inherited by their children. Because his wife and children are the only aspect of the black man's life that he can control, they become the scapegoat upon which his frustrations are released. As Walker's title suggests, she sees redemption, or spiritual rebirth into a new life, as the best defense against society's injustice. Though Walker's male characters have been labeled by some as either heartlessly cruel or pathetically weak (Steinem 89), many of them, like Grange Copeland, do change during the course of a work. Individual transformation stimulates the potential for change in the social system as a whole.

In this novel, Walker shows how the social and economic system of the 1920s offered a futile existence to Southern black families. Grange Copeland, like most Southern black men of his era, lived and worked on a farm owned and operated by a white man. This system, called sharecropping, did not allow for future planning or savings, for everything earned was returned to the white man's pocket for rent. Thus sharecropping, like slavery before it, contributed to the black man's feelings of powerlessness. In his desperation and helplessness, Grange turns to exert power in the one place he is dominant, his home. He releases his frustration by abusing his family in a weekly cycle of cruelty:

> By Thursday, Grange's gloominess reached its peak and he grimaced respectfully, with veiled eyes, at the jokes told by the man who drove the truck [the white farm owner, Mr. Shipley]. On Thursday night, he stalked the house from room to room pulled himself up and swung from the rafters. Late Saturday night Grange would come home lurching drunk, threatening to kill his wife and Brownfield [his son], stumbling and shooting his shotgun. (Walker 12)

At other times, Grange displays his frustration through neglect, a more psychologically disturbing device that later affects Brownfield's emotional stability. Grange's inability to rise above his own discontent with his life and express feeling toward his son becomes his most abusive act. Eventually, he abandons his family completely for a new life in the North. Even when he says good-bye, "even in private and in the dark and with his son, presumably asleep, Grange could not bear to touch his son with his hand" (Walker 121).

Brownfield picks up where Grange left off, giving his father's violent threats physical form by beating his own wife and children regularly. Although he, too, blames the whites for driving him to brutality, Walker suggests that his actions are not excusable on these grounds. By the time he reaches adulthood, sharecropping is not a black man's only option and cannot be used as a scapegoat. Nevertheless, he chooses to relinquish his freedom and work for Mr. Shipley.

By becoming the overseer on Mr. Shipley's plantation, Brownfield positions himself for the same failure that ruined his father. As Trudier Harris notes, over time Brownfield's loss of control of his life turns his feelings of depression and lost pride into anger, and his own destructive nature turns him toward violence and evil (240). Unable or unwilling to take responsibility for himself, Brownfield blames his own inadequacies on his wife, Mem, who bears the brunt of his anger:

> Brownfield beat his once lovely wife now, regularly, because it made him feel briefly good. Every Saturday night he beat her, trying to pin the blame for his failure on her by imprinting it on her face, and she . . . repaid him by becoming a haggard . . . witch. (Walker 55)

Brownfield demonstrates his power by stripping Mem, a former schoolteacher, of anything that would threaten his manhood. Reasoning that her knowledge is a power that he cannot have and therefore she does not deserve, he wants her to speak in her old dialect so that she will not appear to be more intelligent than he does. He also wants her to be ugly because her ugliness makes it easier for him to justify beating her. He wants her to reach a state of ultimate degradation where any strength of her character will be quickly extinguished by a blow to the face or a kick in the side. In fact, "he rather enjoyed her desolation because in it she had no hopes. She was totally weak, totally without view, without a sky" (Walker 59). In a final attempt to release his frustration, as Paul Theroux suggests, Brownfield kills Mem, literally and symbolically obliterating the remainder of her identity--her face (2).

But in the face of this brutality and degradation, Walker raises the possibility of a different fate for black men and women. While in the North, Grange undergoes a spiritual rebirth and, as Karen Gaston notes, comes to understand that white injustice is not alone responsible for the cruelty of black men toward their families (278). He also realizes that to weaken and destroy a wife and family is not a sign of manhood:

> You gits just as weak as water, no feeling of doing nothing yourself, you begins to destroy everybody around you, and you blame it on crackers [whites]. Nobody's as powerful as we make out to be, we got our own souls, don't we? (Walker 207)

Grange redeems his spirit in his "third life" with his granddaughter, Ruth. His objective now is not to destroy what he loves but to cherish it. When a judge orders Ruth to go back to live with Brownfield after his release from prison, Grange kills him before this horror becomes a reality. Although he is shot to death as he tries to escape the police, he dies a redeemed man and passes his inner strength of hope on to his granddaughter.

The impact of the racist system of the South unquestionably pervades the lives of Walker's black characters. Nevertheless, she does not portray as justifiable the destructive need of black men to exert their strength at the expense of the weak. It is necessary to be aware of societal injustices and their effects but not to use them as excuses for individual cruelty. Through her characters, Walker gives us faith that cruelty turns back on itself. Some meet tragic endings, but the redemption of Grange shows Walker's faith in change. She envisions the children of tomorrow inheriting not hatred and selfishness but compassion and honesty. Her affirmative voice demonstrates the potential for social change through individual transformation.

Here is Amy Dierst's list of works cited in her essay.

Works Cited

Gaston, Karen C. "Women in the Lives of Grange Cope-
    land." <u>College Language Association Journal</u> 24
    (1981): 276-86.

Harris, Trudier. "Violence in <u>The Third Life of Grange</u>
    <u>Copeland</u>." <u>College Language Association Journal</u> 19
    (1975): 238-47.

Steinem, Gloria. "Do You Know This Woman? She Knows
    You--A Profile on Alice Walker." <u>Ms</u>. June 1982: 89-
    94.

Theroux, Paul. Rev. of <u>The Third Life of Grange Copeland</u>,
    by Alice Walker. <u>Bookworld</u> 4 Sept. 1970: 2.

Walker, Alice. <u>The Third Life of Grange Copeland</u>. New
    York: Harcourt, 1970.

2

A context-based stance

The following essay was written for a literature class focusing on the Renaissance, and students were given a free hand in choosing topics as long as they wrote about one of the works studied in the class. Faye Purol decided to investigate some of the performance history of Shakespeare's *Othello*, and in doing so she found that this play was among the most frequently produced plays in the antebellum South. Interested to find that this play should be so popular in a time of legally sanctioned racial inequality, she decided to investigate this context for *Othello*, a decision that led her to consider elements *outside* the text of the play and to draw on other sources—like contemporary reviews and playbills—that usually do not appear in a text-based essay like the one on *Grange Copeland*. Here is the opening of Faye Purol's essay, including her thesis in the last sentence of paragraph 1.

Shakespeare's Moor in the Old South

    The first performance of a Shakespearean work in the
Old South took place in Williamsburg, Virginia, in 1751.
That play was <u>Richard III</u>, and from then until the Civil

War began in 1861, Shakespeare was the most popular
dramatist in the New World. From the first, <u>Othello</u> was
among the most frequently performed plays, somewhat
remarkable in a time and place in history where slavery
was legally sanctioned. <u>Othello</u>, with its then-shocking
theme of miscegenation, was in most every theater's
repertoire, and while sometimes altered and a few times
banned, it was usually performed just as Shakespeare
wrote it, to favorable audience receptions. I will
examine the circumstances under which <u>Othello</u> was
performed; instances when the script was altered or the
play banned completely; and possible reasons why, at a
time and place least expected, performances of <u>Othello</u>
were consistently popular events.

Like the Globe and other theaters in England, American theaters attracted all levels of people; as James H.
Dorman observes, landed gentry, who were familiar with
books and well-versed in art, enjoyed the pageantry
alongside less-educated riverboat captains and crews,
shopkeepers, laborers, bonded and free citizens, American
Indians, and strangely enough, members of that euphemistically named "peculiar institution," slaves (233).
Financial circumstances necessitated that theaters cater
to all classes, and persons of color were admitted to
theater galleries along with everyone else. Hence,
Dorman notes, black people, both slave and free, were
always a part of the audience.

> [E]vidence of theatre attendance by Negroes
> abounds in the sources of the period. A letter
> in the <u>Richmond Compiler</u> as early as November
> of 1819 complained that the theatre was likely
> to [be] a corrupting influence on slaves, not
> only because it took them from their work, but
> because of "the scenes they witness, and the
> society they mix with in the gallery." (234)

No doubt, slaves who saw <u>Othello</u> had opinions about
what they saw. No accounts have been found that describe
what any of them thought about the play, however, which
can certainly be attributed to the fact that few slaves
had been taught to read or write. . . .
The <u>Virginia Gazette</u> reported an incident that
occurred when the emperor and empress of the Cherokee
Nation attended a performance of <u>Othello</u>:

> During the performance the fighting with naked
> swords on the stage caused such great surprise
> that the empress ordered her attendants to go
> and prevent the actors from killing one an-
> other. (Dunn 74)

Presumably, the empress was impressed with the action
rather than with any racial implications, and history reveals little evidence that many American Indians attended
the theater. Still, audiences at <u>Othello</u> could be said
to be as varied in social strata as America itself. . . .

Investigating a certain context in which *Othello* was performed led
this writer to performance data, newspaper accounts, and letters to the editor.
In addition, she might have looked at many other things—contemporary
reviews, advertisements, theater programs, actors' journals. Though drama
especially lends itself to analysis of context because it's performed in various
contexts, you can investigate the context of most any literary work. Looking
at accounts of the Great Depression, for example, could yield insights into
the characters in John Steinbeck's *Grapes of Wrath*. Here is a partial list of
works cited in Faye Purol's complete essay.

Works Cited

Dorman, James H., Jr. <u>Theatre in the Ante Bellum South</u>.
Chapel Hill: U of North Carolina P, 1967.

Dunn, Esther Cloudman. <u>Shakespeare in America</u>. New
York: Macmillan, 1939.

Holbein, Woodrow L. "Shakespeare in Charleston, 1800-
1860." <u>Shakespeare in the South: An Overview</u>. Ed.
Philip C. Kolin. Jackson: UP of Mississippi, 1983.
88-111.

Shockley, Martin S. "The Richmond Theatre, 1780-1790."
    <u>Virginia Magazine of History and Biography</u> July
    1952: 421-22.

---. "Shakespeare's Plays in the Richmond Theatre, 1819-
    1838." <u>Shakespeare Association Bulletin</u> Apr. 1940:
    88-94.

3

A reader-based stance

The following excerpt by Amy Lewis was written in a class that used reading journals as a means of analyzing personal responses to the literary works studied. The assignment asked students to "choose one of the poems read in class and record in your journal your responses to the poem, beginning with your dominant or overall response, tracing the causes of that response, and moving from your response to an interpretation of the poem." Note that this journal assignment allows for a slightly more informal tone as well as for references to the reader's personal life. Note also that it does not call for any sources other than the text and the reader's own response to it.

As specified in the assignment, this essay begins with the student's personal response to the poem, looks to see what might account for this response, and then moves to her interpretation of the poem, her thesis. If a context-based analysis looks *outside* the work as a way to illuminate its meaning, a reader-based analysis looks *inside*, to the unique responses of one reader. The poem examined here is at the end of Chapter 29.

Theme for Emerson, Thoreau,

Whitman, Melville--and Me

My first response to "Theme for English B" was a
sense of empathy with the speaker's feelings of alienation from the university--specifically, from the educated white man's university. Hughes makes this alienation clear by describing the student's lonely, tedious
journey from school down the hill to his solitary room in
another world, the "Harlem Branch Y." As a woman, I suffer a similar sense of alienation at school when a middle-aged, white, male professor hands me his syllabus for
a nineteenth-century American literature course: Emerson,
Thoreau, Whitman, and Melville--no women, no people of

color, nothing but white males. I like Emerson, but the
lopsidedness of the syllabus almost makes me not <u>want</u> to
get close to any of the other authors. For whatever reason, nothing in their writing motivates <u>me</u> to write.

As the student in "Theme for English B" questions,
so do I: It's <u>not</u> that simple to "let that page come out
of you." Does the instructor really want to hear about
the pages this student might have inside him, writing in
his room at the Harlem Y? I too wonder, how can I express my isolation from those white male writers in my
responses <u>to</u> them? By thinking about who he is and what
he likes to do, Hughes's student reaches some understanding of himself and of what he might write for his English
theme. He realizes that while Harlem is a part of him,
so too is the world of New York City, which surrounds
Harlem. The student defines himself by focusing on what
he enjoys in life ("I like to eat, sleep, drink, and be
in love, / I like to work, read, learn, and understand
life.") and then recognizes these to be experiences he
and his white instructor share.

How then can I respond to the male authors, the male
professor? For me, the pages are colored by my struggle
to respond in the same way that Hughes's student says his
page "will not be white." Just as what he writes is composed of himself and of the white instructor, so it is
for me: The pages that I write for my literature course
contain parts of me <u>and</u> of my white, male professor since
I certainly internalize some of his lectures and discussion. At the same time, as I speak up in class, as I respond to those authors, so too are those around me, including the professor, touched by what I think and say.
As the student in the poem points out, we are all a part
of everyone we come into contact with--and they, a part
of us. By virtue of our interaction, we are constantly

```
learning from one another. Maybe that is what Hughes
means when he says "That's American."
```

≫ *Editing your writing about literature*

- What is your thesis? How does it reflect your interpretation of the work?
- What stance do you take toward the work: text-based, context-based, reader-based, or some combination of these? (See 48d.)
- What support do you offer for your thesis? Does this support include some specific evidence from the work?
- Do you summarize any plot or action? How does this summary support your thesis?
- How do you organize your argument? Do you move chronologically through the work? Do you consider major elements such as images or characters one by one? If you cannot discern a clear relationship among your points, ask what larger category they fit. A rough outline may help you improve your organization.
- Check all quotations. How do they each support your interpretation? Do you introduce them with appropriate signal phrases? Do you set quotations longer than four lines off from your text? Do you cite the source in parentheses at the end of the quotation? (See 43d.)
- Do you cite any secondary sources? Do you quote, paraphrase, or summarize? (See 42c.) Do you document thoroughly and accurately, following MLA guidelines? (See Chapter 44.)

THINKING CRITICALLY ABOUT LITERATURE

Reading Literature with a Critical Eye

Using this chapter, read a literary work that has been assigned to your class. Compare your notes and annotations to those done by two or three classmates. Compare your understandings of the work as well as your tentative interpretations. What do all of your readings have in common? How do they differ?

Thinking about Your Own Writing about Literature

Carefully analyze writing you have done about a literary work, using the guidelines above. What could you add to strengthen your argument? Make a list of tips you would give yourself for writing a better essay about literature.

49

Writing Essay Examinations

*I*F YOU CAN'T WRITE IT," *says author and former college dean Arthur Adams, "you don't know it." While Adams's statement is debatable in some circumstances, it certainly applies to essay examinations, where writing is the way to demonstrate what you know.*

Writing an effective essay examination requires two important abilities: recalling information and organizing the information in order to draw relevant conclusions from it. These conclusions form the thesis of the essay while the information serves as support. While this process sounds simple, writing an effective essay examination under pressure in limited time can be a daunting task. This chapter suggests ways to turn this sometimes daunting task into a perfectly manageable one.

EXERCISE 49.1

Create a question you think you might be likely to encounter on an essay examination in a class you are currently taking. Then write a paragraph or two about what you would need to know in order to write an A+ answer.

49a

Preparing for essay examinations

In getting ready for an essay examination, nothing can take the place of knowing the subject well. You can, in other words, prepare for an essay examination throughout the term by taking careful notes of lectures, texts, and other assigned reading. You may want to outline a reading assignment, list its main points, list and define its key terms, or briefly summarize its argument or main points. A particularly effective method is to divide your notes into two categories. In a notebook, label the left-hand pages "Summaries and Quotations." Label the right-hand pages "Questions and Comments." Then as you read, use the left-hand page to record brief summaries of major points, the support offered for each point, and noteworthy quotations. On the right-hand page, record questions that your reading has not answered, ideas that are unclear or puzzling, and your own comments. This form of note-taking encourages active, hardheaded reading and, combined with careful class notes, will do much to prepare you. Here are one student's notes, on Chapter 5 of this book:

Summaries and Quotations	Questions and Comments
Rhetoric—art of langauge (Aristotle) All language *is* argumentative— purpose is to persuade	Maybe all language *is* persuasive, but if I greet people warmly, I don't *consciously* try to persuade them that I'm glad to see them. I just respond naturally (unless they're having an insecure day).
To identify an *argument,* ask: 1. Does it try to persuade me? 2. Does it deal with a problem without a clear-cut answer? 3. Could I disagree with it?	Of all the statements that can be debated, I think the less absolute the possible answers, the more important the question and the harder to solve (otherwise the answer would be obvious).

In addition to taking careful, detailed notes, you can prepare for an essay examination by writing out essay answers to questions you think are likely to appear on the examination. Practicing ahead of time is much more effective than last-minute cramming. On the day of the exam, do ten to fifteen minutes of writing just before you go into the examination to "warm up" your thinking muscles.

Everyday Use

You will probably need to write the equivalent of an "essay exam" at various times in your life. Some insurance companies ask for a personal statement to accompany applications, as do many loan applications, including those for student loans. One recent graduate found herself writing a very important "exam" as part of her efforts to adopt a child when she was asked for a lengthy biographical essay that included an analysis of personal strengths and goals. Have you ever needed to write the equivalent of an essay examination?

49b

Analyzing essay examination questions

Before you begin writing, read the question over carefully several times, and *analyze* what it asks you to do. Most essay examination questions contain two kinds of terms, **strategy** terms that describe your task in writing the essay and **content** terms that define the scope and limits of the topic.

STRATEGY ┌─────── CONTENT ───────┐
Analyze Jesus's Sermon on the Mount.

STRATEGY ┌─────── CONTENT ───────────┐
Describe the major effects of reconstruction.

STRATEGY ┌──────────── CONTENT ────────────┐
Discuss the function of the river in *Huckleberry Finn*.

STRATEGY ┌──────────────── CONTENT ─────────────────┐
Explain the advantages of investing in government securities.

Words like *analyze, describe, discuss,* and *explain* tell what logical strategy to use and often set the form your answer takes. Since not all terms mean the same thing in every discipline, be sure you understand *exactly* what the term means in context of the material covered on the examination. In general, however, the most commonly used strategy terms have standard meanings, shown on the following chart:

≫ *Common strategy terms*

ANALYZE Divide an event, idea, or theory into its component elements, and examine each one in turn: *Analyze Milton Friedman's theory of permanent income.*

COMPARE AND/OR CONTRAST Demonstrate similarities or dissimilarities between two or more events or topics: *Compare the portrayal of women in* Beloved *with that in* Their Eyes Were Watching God.

DEFINE Identify and state the essential traits or characteristics of something, differentiating it clearly from other things: *Define Hegelian dialectic.*

DESCRIBE Tell about an event, person, or process in detail, creating a clear and vivid image of it: *Describe the dress of a knight.*

EVALUATE   Assess the value or significance of the topic: *Evaluate the contribution of black musicians to the development of an American musical tradition.*

EXPLAIN   Make a topic as clear and understandable as possible by offering reasons, examples, and so on: *Explain the functioning of the circulatory system.*

SUMMARIZE   State the major points concisely and comprehensively: *Summarize the major arguments against using animals in laboratory research.*

Strategy terms give you important clues for the thesis of your answer. Sometimes, however, strategy terms are not explicitly stated in an essay question. In these cases, you need to infer a strategy from the content terms. For example, a question that mentions two groups working toward the same goal may imply comparison and contrast, or a question referring to events in a given time period may imply summary. Once you understand which strategy to follow, make sure you understand the meanings of all content terms. Particularly in technical or advanced courses, specialized language may need to be clarified. *Romanticism,* for instance, means one thing in the context of eighteenth-century literature and something else in modern art. Do not hesitate to ask for such clarification.

49c

Thinking through your answer and taking notes

You may be tempted to begin writing an essay examination at once. Time is precious—but so too are organizing and planning. You will profit, therefore, by spending some time—about 10 percent of the allotted time is a good rule of thumb—thinking through your answer.

Begin by deciding which major points you need to make and in what order to present them. Jot down support for each point. Craft a clear, succinct *thesis* that satisfies the strategy term of the exam question. While in most writing situations you start from a working thesis in outlining your topic, when writing under pressure you will probably find it more efficient to outline (or simply jot down) your ideas and craft your thesis from your outline. Suppose you were asked to define the three major components of personality according to Freud. This is a clear question, and you should be able to make a brief outline as a framework for your answer.

Id
basic definition—what it *is* and *is* not
major characteristics
functions

Ego
basic definition—what it *is* and *is* not
major characteristics
functions

Superego
basic definition—what it *is* and *is* not
major characteristics
functions

From this outline, you can develop a thesis: *According to Freud, the human personality consists of the three major and interlocking elements: the id, the ego, and the superego.*

49d

Drafting your answer

Your goal in producing an essay examination answer is twofold: to demonstrate that you have mastered the course material and to communicate your ideas and information clearly, directly, and logically. During the drafting stage, follow your outline as closely as you can. Once you depart from it, you will lose time and perhaps have trouble returning to the main discussion. As a general rule, develop each major point into at least one paragraph. And make clear the connections among your main points by using transitions: *The last element of the human personality, according to Freud, is the superego.*

Besides referring to your outline for guidance, pause and read what you have written before going on to a new point. This kind of rereading may remind you of other ideas while you still have time to include them; it should also help you establish a clear connection with whatever follows. Write neatly, skip lines, and leave ample margins so you have space for changes or additions when you revise.

49e

Revising and editing your answer

Leave enough time (at least five to ten minutes) to read through your essay answer carefully. Consider the following questions:

- Is the thesis clearly stated? Does it answer the questions?
- Are all the major points covered?
- Are the major points adequately developed and supported?
- Is each sentence complete?
- Are spelling, punctuation, and syntax correct?
- Is the handwriting legible?

49f

Considering a sample essay answer

See how one student handled an essay and short-answer examination in a first-year American history course. She had fifty minutes to answer two of three essay questions and three of five short-answer questions. She chose to answer the following question first.

> Between 1870 and 1920, blacks and women both struggled to establish certain rights. What did each group want? Briefly analyze their strategies for improvement, and indicate the degree of their success.

This student began her exam with this question because she knew the most about this topic. With another essay and three short answers to write, she decided to devote *no more than twenty minutes* to this essay.

First, she analyzed what the question asked her to do, especially noting the strategy terms. She decided that the first sentence of the question strongly *implied* comparison and contrast of the two struggles. The second sentence asked for an explanation of the goals of each group, and in the third sentence, she took *analyze* and *indicate* to mean "explain what each group did and how well it succeeded." As it turned out, this was a very shrewd reading of the question. In a post-exam discussion, the instructor remarked that those who had included a comparison and contrast produced better answers than those who did not. Note that, in this instance, the strategy the instructor expected is not stated explicitly in the question. Instead, class members were expected to read between the lines to infer the strategy.

The student then identified content terms around which to develop her answer: the groups—blacks and women—and their actions—goals, strategies, and degrees of success. Using these terms, she spent about three minutes producing the following outline:

<u>Introduction</u>
goals, strategies, degree of success

Blacks

want equality
two opposing strategies: Du Bois and Washington
even with vote, great opposition

Women

many goals (economic, political, educational), but focus on vote
use male rhetoric against them
use vote to achieve other goals

Conclusion

educational and economic differences between groups

From this outline, the student crafted the following thesis: *In the years between 1870 and 1920, blacks and women were both fighting for equal rights, but in different ways.* She then wrote the following answer:

The years between 1870 and 1920 saw two major groups—blacks and women—demanding more rights, but the two groups approached the problem of inequality in different ways. Initially, women wanted the vote, equality within the family, and equal job and education opportunities. Their attempts to achieve all these goals at once were unsuccessful, as men countered by accusing them of attacking the sanctity of the family institution. (Demanding equality in the family meant confronting Christianity, which subordinated women to men.) With the lead of Carrie Chapman Catt, women narrowed their goal to a focus on the vote. They emphasized that they would vote to benefit middle-class Americans (like themselves), reduced the stridency of their rhetoric, and said that they would clean up an often corrupt government (they turned the men's strategy against them here by *emphasizing* their own purity and virtue). They also invited Wilson to talk at their conventions and won him to their side. Because of their specific focus and reorganization, women did finally receive the vote which then gave them the power to work toward their other reform goals.

Less well organized and less formally educated than middle-class women, American blacks often were unable to dedicate their full effort to the cause of equality because of severe economic problems. In addition, their leaders disagreed over strategy. Washington told the blacks to work hard and earn the vote and equality, while Du Bois maintained that blacks, like all other Americans, deserved it already. The blacks also had to overcome fierce racial prejudice. Even after they finally won the vote, whites passed laws (literacy tests and grandfather

Margin annotations: THESIS / WOMEN / GOALS / STRATEGY / DEGREE OF SUCCESS / BLACKS / GOAL / STRATEGY (SPLIT) / DEGREE OF SUCCESS

clauses) and used force (particularly through the Ku Klux Klan) to keep blacks from voting. Therefore, even after the blacks got the vote in name, they had to fight to keep and use it.

Thus both blacks and women fought for (and are still fighting for) equal rights, but the women were more successful in late nineteenth-century America. Educated, organized, and financially secure, they concentrated their efforts on getting the vote as a means to higher political objectives, and they got it. Blacks, on the other hand, had to overcome great financial barriers that reduced access to education and worked against strong organization. Even after they received the vote, prejudicial laws and practices kept these Americans subjugated. — TWO GROUPS CONTRASTED

Although this essay answer is not perfect, as the analysis in 49g makes clear, it responded accurately and fully enough to receive an A and only one criticism at the end: "No advances at all for blacks?—e.g. education."

49g

Analyzing and evaluating your answer

Although you will not have time to analyze your answers during an examination, you can improve your essay examination abilities by doing so later. When the student who wrote the answer in 49f did so, she decided to go through her answer sentence by sentence to see how well she answered the questions in 49e and what additional points she might have covered. Last, she analyzed her answer with her instructor's comments in mind.

- *Thesis.* I think my thesis worked, but it might have been clearer if I had named specific rights rather than just saying "certain rights."
- *Major points.* I included all the points in my outline, but I should have developed more the term *equality* in discussing the blacks' struggle.
- *Spelling, punctuation, usage.* Would have been better to skim essay over for spelling and punctuation errors (as in the sixth sentence).
- *Additional points.* I could have talked much more about individual women's contributions—no time.
- *Response to instructor's comments.* I should have listed black advances, which I knew—my interpretation was too negative. I also know much more about Washington and Du Bois than I showed on the exam.

Analyzing her answer in this way allows her to see whether she tends to stray from the topic and whether she could improve certain elements—such as thesis and topic sentences—in future exams.

THINKING CRITICALLY ABOUT ESSAY EXAMINATIONS

Reading an Essay Examination with a Critical Eye

Read over an essay exam you've taken recently. Using the guidelines in 49b, analyze what the exam question asked you to do. Then reread your answer carefully. Did you do what the question asked—and if not, how should you have responded differently?

Thinking about Your Own Essay Exams

Consider again the essay exam you read over for the above reading exercise. Referring to 49c–49e, reconstruct how you went about answering the question. How could you improve the content and presentation of your answer? Note any new strategies you could use for improving your success in taking essay exams.

Part Ten

Accessing and Presenting Text

50. Working On-Line   *750*

51. Designing Documents   *758*

52. Using Professional and
Business Formats   *767*

53. Making Oral Presentations   *777*

54. Assembling a Writing Portfolio   *784*

50

Working On-Line

*I*MAGINE THIS SCENE: *preparing to begin a document, you gather equipment. First a quill pen or two. Then penknives for trimming and sharpening the quill. Then ink, inkpots, blotting materials. And a stack of paper—and perhaps a stationery stand. Finally, you begin. But the ink blots and runs, the quill splits and must be mended, you misspell a word. You will have to start again.*

Until fairly recently, this scene described the plight of writers and explains why so many tended to concentrate on the neatness of the basic text, on getting the message or report or letter or story down legibly—and the first time around if possible. Producing or recopying drafts was a messy, time-consuming task that left little time for considering the overall design or appearance of a document.

The last few decades, however, have seen enormous advances in the technology of writing, most spectacularly with the advent of fairly inexpensive easy-to-use computers. As a result, writers today can modify and revise drafts with the touch of a key, turn out multiple and perfectly clean copies in a twinkling, and design as well as write their own documents. And now an inexpensive modem gives access to texts from around the world. This chapter introduces some of the basics of writing and communicating on-line.

50a

Frequent questions about writing with a computer

1

How do computers help writers?

Word-processing programs, like MacWrite, Microsoft Word, and WordPerfect, give writers the freedom to create texts efficiently and professionally, without physically erasing or retyping from scratch. With a word-processing program, you can integrate the various steps of the writing process—brainstorming, outlining, drafting, revising, editing, and proofreading. If a new idea comes to you in the middle of a draft, you can type that idea into your draft and work on it later, or you can stop to work on it and then move it to another part of your text. Or you can have several "files" open at once, "cutting" and "pasting" from one to another as you go along.

Storing your writing, notes, bibliographies, and graphics on the computer's hard disc, you'll find that your work is easier than ever to remember, organize, and keep track of. You can, in addition, keep a copy of your work on a small, easily transportable disc.

Word-processing programs also allow you to collect and organize data; keep records; and design and produce various kinds of documents; Chapter 51 discusses the particulars of document design.

2

How can a computer help me plan, organize, and draft?

Simply type in ideas as they come to you. Later on you can move them around, combine them, expand them, or delete some of them. If you have access to E-mail or electronic bulletin boards (see 50c), toss some of your ideas out to others, and elicit responses.

Outlining is especially easy. In fact, your software may contain an outlining format. If not, key in the main topics you want to cover, numbering them *I, II, III,* and so on. Then add details beneath each point. The organization you set out will not be carved in stone; if you realize a subpoint deserves more emphasis, a couple of keystrokes makes it a main topic.

Perhaps you prefer starting with a set of questions. Type in *who? what? when? where? why?* and *how?* and skip some lines between each question.

Everyday Use

It would be virtually impossible to go through even part of a day without encountering someone writing with a computer. Most offices are now computerized, and employees communicate electronically over local area networks (LANS). If you phone in an order to Pizza Hut, a clerk enters it into a computer as you speak; if you call again, a clerk can find out from the computer what you ordered, when you ordered it, and where you live. You are likely to encounter a computer even at a museum, perhaps one that invites you to ask questions—and will provide answers on the spot. For a day or two, note all your encounters with computers.

As you answer these questions, just fill in the blanks. If one answer to *why?* suggests another *how?* scroll back to *how?* and type in your thoughts.

Your ideas may come in words, in phrases, or sometimes in whole sentences or groups of sentences—even in lists or charts. Key them in as they come; just getting them on the screen will help you see where you need to do more thinking or research. You can also print out any of your work to take to the library or to class.

You might work simultaneously with notes, an outline, a draft, an old essay on a similar question, graphics, even questions for further research. At its best, a computer lets your writing process remain spontaneous.

3

How can I revise most effectively using a computer?

All word-processing programs allow you to insert, move, and delete words, sentences, and paragraphs or whole blocks of text—basic steps writers take when they revise. A word-processing program also allows you to keep different versions of your text so that you have an instantly accessible and accurate memory bank, one that will allow you to compare the effectiveness of changed and unchanged texts. You can also insert material from other files—library notes or graphics, for example, or a text you wrote for another purpose—into the body of your document without retyping it.

Some writers do all their revising on-screen, while others prefer to print out their drafts and then work on hard-copy versions. Hard copy allows you to see the entire draft spread out before you, work on it, and then return to the computer to enter revisions.

Computers also facilitate collaboration with others. If you work in a computer-laboratory classroom or if you have a computer with a modem, a computer network may permit your instructor or classmates to respond to your drafts directly on-line. Without this facility, however, you can print multiple copies of your drafts for others to respond to.

4

How can I edit and proofread using a computer?

Once you have revised your draft and are ready to edit and proofread it, a number of word-processing functions can help you make needed changes. Most writers find spell checkers invaluable. (See 24f2.) No spell checker can tell whether you've used the wrong word, however—such as *their* for *there*—or identify a word as misspelled if misplaced, added, or omitted letters have created a new word—such as *realty* for *reality*. Nothing substitutes for your own vigilance—or the eyes of a careful friend.

Computerized style checkers and grammar checkers are also available for use with word-processing programs. These can help you identify misplaced punctuation, count prepositional phrases, or recognize passive constructions or long sentences. No style checker, however, can judge shades of meaning or tone or style. Only you, the writer, can resolve these issues. The basic functions of a word-processing program can help you become your own style and spelling checker, however. The search command lets you find words or constructions you already know that you use excessively. Finding all instances of the word *of* in a text, for example, may serve as a cue to eliminating unnecessary prepositional phrases. Having the computer identify all forms of *be* or sentences that begin with *There is* or *There are* can help you identify—and replace—these sometimes weak constructions. Using your computer's search-and-replace sequence, you can correct a misspelled name throughout the text.

5

How can a computer help me present my final draft?

Many writers are now able to produce—and publish—beautifully printed essays and other materials with color, graphics, and other features once available only in commercially printed texts. Writers now have the opportunity to make decisions about their documents' design, about the way each page will look, and about how the visual rhetoric affects their credibility as writers as well as their readers' reactions. (See Chapter 51.)

6

How else can a computer help me as a writer?

Word-processing programs can let you store formats you use frequently so that you need not adjust margins, spacing, and tabs every time you write. Some programs have predesigned formats for letters, memos, and other kinds of text. If a particular course you are taking calls for a standard format for every assignment, you may be able to customize your word-processing system so that you can call up that format at the stroke of a key.

Computers can also help you in a number of other ways, particularly in gaining access to information and in communicating widely with others. For these reasons, it is important for you to get on-line as soon as possible.

50b

Getting on-line

Even if you own your own computer, you will want to become familiar with the computing facilities on your campus. If you do not already have a listing or map of these facilities, request one from the office of student affairs or from an office of academic or instructional computing. Find out the computer labs that are available for public use, noting their hours of operation and the kinds of hardware and software available. Even if you own your own computer, you may want to use a computer lab's high-quality laser printer. If you are not yet comfortable using a computer, see if there are any training programs available on campus.

In addition, check out the computing facilities in your campus library. Which of the library's resources are on-line? How many stations or terminals are available for student use? What other resources can you access from your library? If the library has orientation or training sessions, sign up for one. For more on accessing library information via computer, see 41c.

Whether or not you have your own computer, inquire about setting up a student account that will allow you to send and receive E-mail, search computer databases, and participate in other electronic arenas. Having such an account may be important if some of your classes rely on electronic assignments or distribute assignments and reading materials via computer.

50c

Communicating via the Internet

Once you are on-line, have an account with your campus computing services, and have access to a computer and a modem, you have the ability to communicate with people, groups, and institutions all over the world. The primary way to do this is through the **Internet**, a great global patchwork quilt of linked computer networks. An account on your school's host computer establishes your "address," and you are ready to communicate with anyone on the Internet or with anyone who has an account on another electronic network with access to the Internet. Although there are a variety of communication software programs connecting host computers to the Internet, all require a user to follow a similar procedure. You log on to the system by entering your user name and your password, a term that does not appear on the screen but identifies you to the system as the legitimate user of your account.

Electronic mail

One of the benefits of the Internet is that it allows you to send and receive messages almost instantly. After logging on, you can access electronic mail—**E-mail**—in your account, read and reply to it, and send new mail—all by following a fairly simple set of directions, which are supplied either by the communications software or by the computing services at your school. You may have occasion to use E-mail outside the Internet—for example, some courses use local area networks (LANS) to facilitate communication among students and teachers.

Mailing lists

Beyond allowing you to communicate with friends and colleagues, the Internet allows you to find and communicate with groups of people who share your interests, be they woodcarving, windsurfing, or whale watching. Such interest groups are called **mailing lists.** You can subscribe to mailing lists and receive and send messages to others on the list. To subscribe, you must contact the list's "administrator," sometimes a person but more often a computer program called a *listserv.* Although you may be tempted to subscribe to a number of lists, think carefully before you do. Your electronic mailbox on campus could be overrun with hundreds of messages from each list, messages you may not have time to read, much less respond to.

Usenet newsgroups

Another way to contact people who share your interest is through **Usenet,** a global network of electronic bulletin boards set up by subject and hooked in to the Internet. Once you subscribe to a group, you can post messages about the group's topic and receive answers. Through the alt.-elvis.king newsgroup, for example, you can communicate with people around the world who share a consuming interest in Elvis Presley. While **newsgroups** provide another way to communicate with others electronically, they also offer an outstanding means of accessing information. (See 50d.)

Bulletin boards

Beyond the Internet, there are a large number of local electronic **bulletin boards** (usually referred to as BBS). These are operated by local interest groups that you can connect to using a computer, modem, and telephone line. For instance, your area might have a Macintosh or IBM users group, in which members discuss the latest developments in software.

50d

Accessing information via computer

A computer also opens doors to vast information resources.

1

Browsing the Internet

A number of browsing systems allow you to search for and access information on the Internet. Two of the most friendly systems are Gopher and World Wide Web. **Gopher**, first developed at the University of Minnesota, is usually available through your Internet host. Once connected at Ohio State, for example, Gopher displays a list of items in menu format. By selecting "Other Gopher and Information Services," you can access another menu that lists all the Gopher servers in the world. Then by choosing "North America," "USA," and "all," in sequence, you can access a menu that lists in alphabetical order the Gopher servers in the United States. Using the space bar, you can then search for the source you want, or you can search for a specific word in the list you are viewing. When you find something you want, you can read it on Gopher or even send yourself an E-mail copy of it.

The **World Wide Web** (WWW) is a newer browsing resource. If you cannot tell whether you have access to WWW from your Internet host, check with the computing services office on your campus. The WWW uses "clients," programs that help you find information, and "servers," which "serve up" the information to you. Instead of getting a menu as in Gopher, your computer screen shows a document, or "home page," with formatted texts, pictures, and even sounds embedded in it. You read the text provided and select the items you wish to pursue. **Mosaic** and **MacWeb**, two multimedia programs that access the WWW, include sounds and pictures.

2

Using Archie, Veronica, WAIS, and other research resources

Part of the difficulty of working in a system as new and as much in flux as the Internet is finding the information you want; if you have no idea where in the electronic universe to find it, these three research assistants can help. **Archie** locates files for you in public archives that are available to the Internet. You simply provide a file name or partial name, and Archie searches its database and provides "finds" that match your name. **Veronica** is one of the menu items provided by Gopher. You select Veronica and provide a word or words that describe your interest; Veronica, in turn, constructs a special Gopher menu listing all the items in the database that match your word(s). You can then browse the contents just as you would any other Gopher menu. **WAIS** (Wide Area Information Server; pronounced *ways*) is a kind of super index. You choose a likely index from the choices and give WAIS the word or words you're looking for; it then provides a list of documents in that index that match or contain your word.

Most Internet locations also provide you with access to Usenet news services. (See 50c.) Through Usenet, you can call for information related to any of the interest groups you belong to by using a *news reader* program. Most Internet locations also give you automatic access to a news reader through which you can ask for information or articles of particular interest to you. In most news groups, someone continually updates a catalog of documents, which often include FAQs (frequently asked questions), answers to the most common questions the group receives. Before you put out a call or ask a question, then, it is wise to check the FAQs.

3

Using commercial sources

In addition to the vast range of sources available to you on the Internet, you may choose to subscribe to one of the pay-for-use commercial networks, such as America Online, Prodigy, CompuServe, or DIALOG. A description of these resources lies beyond the scope of this handbook, but information about them is readily available through your school's office of computing services or through your library.

4

Selected resources for working on-line

Angell, David, and Brent Heslop. *The Elements of E-mail Style*. Reading, MA: Addison-Wesley, 1994.

Butler, Mark. *How to Use the Internet*. Emeryville, CA: Ziff-Davis, 1994.

Gaffin, Adam. *Big Dummy's Guide to the Internet*. Electronic Frontier Foundation. [On-line] Available via Internet: anonymous ftp to ftp.eff.org Directory: pub/Net_info/Big_Dummy File: Big_Dummy.txt

Krol, Ed. *The Whole Internet User's Guide & Catalog*. Sebastopol, CA: O'Reilly & Associates, 1992.

Li, Xia, and Nancy B. Crane. *Electronic Style: A Guide to Citing Electronic Information*. Westport, CT: Meckler, 1994.

THINKING CRITICALLY ABOUT YOUR ON-LINE WORK

The adage about computers—"garbage in, garbage out"—continues to hold true. You can profit, therefore, from thinking about the work you currently do on-line. Start by listing all the things you currently use a computer for. Then ask yourself which of these you do most efficiently and well and which you are least accomplished at. You may find that one or two brief training sessions will allow you to use the computer more efficiently. And while you are thinking about efficiency, ask yourself what the computer helps you with *most* and what it helps you with *least;* you may improve your efficiency by giving up the tasks that do not lend themselves well to computer use.

51

Designing Documents

THE ELECTRONIC REVOLUTION HAS DRAMATICALLY AFFECTED the delivery of information. Known in the ancient Greek world as actio, delivery was an art every educated person needed to master, for how a speaker delivered a speech—tone and volume of voice, use of gestures, and so on—was of great importance to how it would be received. Today, computers have given use new ease in presenting our written texts, allowing us to use headings, lists, graphics, and other visuals. Because these visual elements can be fundamental to readability and to helping us get and keep a reader's attention, they bring a whole new dimension to writing—what some refer to as visual rhetoric. This chapter looks at some of the visual elements you might have occasion to use in your writing.

51a

Creating a visual structure

Those who study visual rhetoric tell us that effective writers use visual elements to guide readers, presenting them with documents that are easy on the eye—and easy to understand. In thinking about the overall visual structure of a document, you may well begin by considering how you use white space, how you style your first page, what kind of paper you use, and how you type or print out the final document.

1

Using white space to frame information

The white space around text acts as a frame and leads the reader through the text. For most documents, you will want to frame your page with margins of white space of between one inch and one and one-half inches—depending on the purpose of the document, its content, and its

> *Everyday Use*
>
> Many occasions call for you to prepare a document with the greatest care you can muster: a résumé for an important job interview, an application for your first mortgage, a will, a report for your boss on your productivity. Take a moment to reflect on pieces of writing—letters, applications, or other documents—you wanted to be perfectly designed. What occasioned these pieces of writing, and why was it so important that they be perfect?

audience. Since the eye takes in only so many chunks of data in one movement, very long lines can be hard to read. Wider margins help, particularly if the information is difficult or dense. In your college papers, such margins give your instructor room to make comments. Within the page, you can also use white space in other ways—around graphics or lists, for example.

Whatever the case, your goal is to make each page look inviting to your readers. Each page, therefore, should be a unit, leading the reader smoothly to the next. You would not want to put a heading at the very bottom of a page, for the reader would have to turn the page to get to the text that the heading is announcing. Nor would you want to end a page with a hyphenated word, leaving readers to guess at the second part as they turn the page.

2

Designing the first page of your document

The first page introduces your document, announcing its purpose and making an initial impression on readers. For much of the writing you will do in college, the style of the first page will be conventional: MLA format in the humanities; APA in many of the social sciences. An example of MLA format is in 44d; of APA, in 45d.

If your instructor doesn't specify a style, use the following format:

- Put your name, the course title and number, your instructor's name, and the date, each on separate lines, at the left margin about an inch from the top of the paper. Double-space between lines.
- Double-space below to the title. Center the title horizontally. Capitalize the first word of the title and all other words except articles, prepositions, and conjunctions (see 36c). Do not underline the title or put it in quotation marks. If the title is long, type it on two lines, making the first line longer than the second. Double-space the lines, and center each one.
- Double-space below the title to the first line of your text. See an example in 4i.

You may wish to use a separate title page, especially for longer works. If so, use the following format:

- Put the title about one-third of the way down the page.
- Put your name, also centered, about an inch below the title.
- An inch or so beneath the title, put the course title and number, your instructor's name, and the date, each centered and on a separate line, double-spaced. See an example in 44d.

3
Selecting appropriate paper and print

The quality of the paper you use affects the overall look and feel of your document. For most college writing, you will want to use 8½″ × 11″ good-quality white bond paper (not erasable paper). On some occasions, you may wish to use a parchment or cream-colored bond—for a résumé perhaps.

Because the print affects the readability of your document, you need to consider the overall effect you hope to achieve. If you are working on a computer, make sure the print and paper will be acceptable to your instructor. For work you want to be proud of, seek out the best-quality printer available to you. This may mean using a laser printer in one of the campus computing centers or libraries.

51b

Using consistency to lead readers through a document

Especially in longer documents, readers can be helped a great deal by consistency of design: the placement of page numbers, style of the typeface, line spacing, and margin width, for example. In every case, the regularity or consistency of the design contributes to the unity and makes it easier for a reader to process the information contained in the document.

1
Paginating your document

Except for a separate title page, which is usually left unnumbered, number every page of your document. Your instructor may ask that you follow a particular format (APA or MLA, for example); if not, number each page consecutively with arabic numerals, beginning with the first page of text. Place your last name and the page number in the upper-right-hand corner of the page, about one-half inch from the top and flush with the right margin. Do not put the number in parentheses or follow it with a period. Most word-processing systems will paginate a document for you.

2

Selecting type

Most word-processing systems allow writers to choose among a great variety of type sizes and typefaces (fonts). For most college writing, the easy-to-read ten- or eleven-point type size is best, as is a serif font (this is serif type; this is sans serif type). And although a smaller or more unusual style—such as italics or cursive—might seem attractive at first glance, readers may find such styles distracting and/or hard to read. Most important, be consistent in the size and style of typeface you choose. Unless you are striving for some special effect, shifting sizes and fonts can give an appearance of disorderliness.

3

Considering spacing and margins

Most documents you produce in college should be double-spaced. New paragraphs should be indented five spaces, with the same double-spacing between lines. Certain kinds of writing, however, or writing for certain disciplines may call for different spacing: letters and memorandums, for example, are usually single-spaced, as are lab reports in some disciplines; and some long reports may be printed with one-and-a-half-line spacing, thus saving paper. If in doubt, consult your instructor.

Word-processing programs allow you to decide whether or not you want both margins justified, or squared off—as they are on this page. You should always justify the left margin, though you may indent lists and blocks of text that are set off. However, most writers—and many instructors—prefer to leave the right margin "ragged," or unjustified.

51c

Using headings

These little words and phrases call readers to attention, announcing a new topic or segment of a topic. As such, they work with (but do not substitute for) the transitions you provide to guide readers from point to point. For brief essays and reports, you may need no headings at all. For longer documents, however, these devices serve as friendly signposts for readers, calling attention to the organization of the text and thus aiding comprehension. Some genres of reports have set headings, which readers expect (and writers therefore must provide); see 47d and 47e for some examples. If you use headings, you need to decide on type size and font, wording, and placement.

Choosing type size and style

If you look through this book, which is a long and complex document, you will note the use of various levels of headings. This chapter, for example, uses four levels of headings, distinguished by different type sizes and fonts as well as by color:

First-level heading

Second-level heading

Third-level heading

FOURTH-LEVEL HEADING

For your college writing, you might distinguish levels of headings using type—all capitals for the first-level headings, capital and lower case underlined for the second level, plain capitals and lower case for the third level, and so on. With a computer, you have even more options. For example:

ON A TYPEWRITER:	ON A COMPUTER:
FIRST-LEVEL HEADING	**FIRST-LEVEL HEADING**
<u>Second-Level Heading</u>	**Second-Level Heading**
Third-Level Heading	*Third-Level Heading*
	<u>Third-Level Heading</u>

Phrasing headings

Heading styles often follow discipline-specific conventions, but as a general rule look for the most succinct way to word your headings. Most often, this means stating the topic in a **single word**, usually a noun (*Toxicity*); in a **phrase**, usually a noun phrase (*Levels of Toxicity*) or a gerund phrase (*Measuring Toxicity*); in a **question** that will be answered in the text (*How can toxicity be measured?*); or—especially in writing about a process—in an **imperative** that tells readers what steps to take (*Measure the toxicity*).

Whichever structure you choose, make sure you use it consistently for all headings of the same level: all questions, for example, or all gerund phrases and *not* a mixture of the two. See 21d for more on maintaining parallel structure in headings.

Positioning headings

Typically, major headings are placed at the left margin. The first level of subhead may then be indented five spaces from the left, and the second level may be centered. Other positions are possible; just remember to place each level of head consistently throughout your paper.

51d

Using visuals

If a picture is worth a thousand words, then using visuals in a written composition can help make a point vividly and emphatically. As such, they can both draw readers into your argument and help persuade them to accept your claim. In some cases, visuals may even stand as the primary text you wish to present; in other cases, they will be of equal or supplemental importance to your text. In every case, they can pack extra punch by presenting information more succinctly and more clearly than words alone could.

Visuals fall into two categories: **tables,** which present information in columns and rows of numbers or words, and **figures,** which include all other visuals—pie, bar, and line charts; line and bar graphs; photographs; maps; and drawings. Many software packages offer help creating visuals.

In deciding when and where to use visuals, the best rule of thumb is simply to choose visuals that will make your points most emphatically and most help your readers understand your document. Researchers who have studied the use of visuals offer some tips about when a particular kind of visual is most appropriate:

- *Use tables* to draw readers' attention to particular numerical information.
- *Use graphs or charts* to draw readers' attention to relationships among data. *Pie charts* compare a part to the whole. *Bar charts and line graphs* compare one element to another, compare elements over time, demonstrate correlations, and/or illustrate frequency.
- *Use drawings or diagrams* to draw readers' attention to dimensions and to specific details.
- *Use maps* to draw readers' attention to location and to spatial relationships.
- *Use cartoons* to illustrate or emphasize a point dramatically or to amuse.
- *Use photographs* to draw readers' attention to a graphic scene (such as devastation following an earthquake) or to depict an object.

In choosing visuals, you will inevitably be making important rhetorical choices. Tables, for example, express information more precisely than do figures, but if they are long and complex readers will have difficulty processing the information. Figures, though less precise, can more easily be taken in at a glance. You should make your choices, then, based on your purpose and on the needs of your audience. In any case, remember that your visuals need to be numbered (*Table 1*) and given titles (*Word Choice by Race*) and perhaps captions or subtitles that provide a link to the text (Seesaw *and* Teeter-totter, *Chicago 1986*). On pages 764 through 766 are some examples of several kinds of visuals.

TABLE

Table 1
Word Choice by Race:
Seesaw and *Teeter-totter*, Chicago 1986

	Black	*White*	*Total*
Seesaw	47 (78%)	4 (15%)	51
Teeter-totter	13 (22%)	23 (85%)	36
Total	60	27	87

Source: Michael I. Miller, "How to Study Black Speech in Chicago." *Language Variation in North American English*. Ed. A. Wayne Glowka and Donald M. Lance. NY: MLA, 1993. 166.

PIE CHART

Figure 1
Racial and Ethnic Origin in the United States, 1990

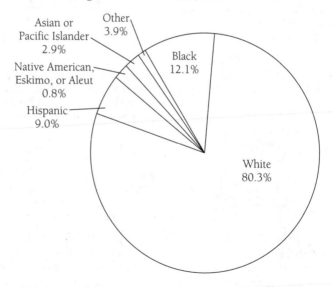

Source: U.S. Bureau of the Census, 1991.

BAR GRAPH
Figure 2
Absence of Third-person Singular -s/-es

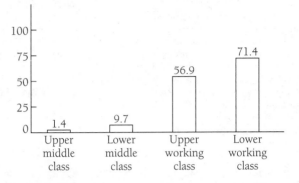

Source: Walt Wolfram, *Dialects and American English.*
Englewood Cliffs, NJ: Prentice Hall, 1991. 95.

LINE GRAPH
Figure 3
Mean Percentage of Multiple Negation by Social Class
and Gender of Speaker

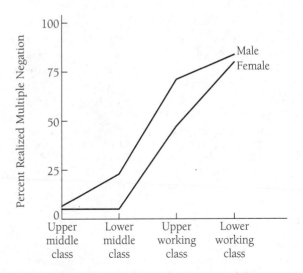

Source: Walt Wolfram, *Dialects and American English.*
Englewood Cliffs, NJ: Prentice Hall, 1991. 118.

DIAGRAM
Figure 4
Spanish-English Bilingualism and the Language Shift Process

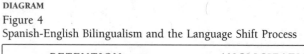

RETENTION First and second generations	ANGLICIZATION Third and fourth generations
Monolingual ⟶ Simple ⟶ English ⟶ Monolingual Spanish bilingualism bilingualism English	

Source: D. Letticia Galindo. "Bilingualism and Language Variation." *Language Variation in North American English*. Ed. A. Wayne Glowka and Donald M. Lance. NY: MLA, 1993. 166.

≫ *Some guidelines for using visuals*

- Try drafting your visuals before drafting the document they accompany. Preparing visuals in this way can be an important part of your process of inventing and planning for the complete document.

- Be sure to refer to the visual in your text before the visual itself appears, explaining the main point it makes or what it exemplifies. Say, for example, *As Table 1 demonstrates, the cost of a college education has risen dramatically in the last decade.*

- Tell readers explicitly what the visual demonstrates, especially if the visual presents complex information. Don't assume that readers will necessarily infer from it what you want them to infer.

- Number and title your visuals.

- If you did not create the visual yourself, credit your source fully.

- Use decorative touches sparingly if at all. Computer clip art is so easy to generate that you may be tempted to fancy up your visuals, but do so only if it enhances and clarifies your text.

- Get responses to your visuals in an early draft. If readers can't follow them or are distracted by them, revise accordingly.

- If you are working on a collaborative project, use every team member's talents in creating effective visuals. Two heads will almost certainly be better than one when it comes to this task.

THINKING CRITICALLY ABOUT YOUR FINAL DOCUMENT

Take a look at some writing you have recently finished. Using the guidelines in this section, assess the use of visual structure and page design, the consistent use of conventions for guiding readers through the work, and the use of emphasis in headings and visuals.

52

Using Professional and Business Formats

PRINCIPLES OF PROFESSIONAL AND BUSINESS COMMUNICATION *are rooted in ideas as old as civilization. In fact, archaeologists now believe that the very earliest forms of Western writing recorded business transactions. Today much of the world's commerce is conducted in writing—in proposals and reports and, especially, in letters and memos—electronically, by E-mail or fax, or on paper. This chapter presents guidelines for effective business and professional correspondence: letters, memos, résumés, and electronic communication.*

EXERCISE 52.1

Spend half an hour brainstorming to generate materials for your résumé, using the following headings to organize your notes: education; honors, awards, prizes; work experience; special skills; school and community activities.

52a

Writing for readers

Professional and business communications are intended to achieve specific results. An effective business letter is clear and concise, written in language its reader will readily understand. It is, in addition, polite, intended to build goodwill. Before you start writing, you should have a clear picture of your readers, your purposes for writing, and the situation in which you are writing. Only then can you decide what information you need to include and how to design your letter or memo for greatest readability.

The six C's of business and professional communication help you focus on your reader—the person you need to inform or persuade.

- *Be Clear.* Use simple words and straightforward sentences with active verbs. Use topic sentences to help readers follow your points.
- *Be Concise.* Use the words you need to make your point, but no more. Don't give readers information they don't need. Try to keep paragraphs short—in general, six lines or fewer.
- *Be Courteous.* Write in a friendly, conversational tone. Imagine how you would respond if you were the reader.
- *Be Correct.* Use a spell checker, and then proofread carefully. Just one misspelled word can make readers think you (or your ideas) are sloppy.
- *Be Consistent.* If you refer to someone as *Susan* in one sentence, don't switch to *Sue* in the next. If you use kilograms in one part of a letter, don't switch to pounds in another.
- *Be Complete.* Include all the information readers need. You don't want them to have to call or write you for important, but missing, details.

Using conventional formats

1

Writing memos

Memos are the most common form of printed correspondence sent *within an organization.* They tend to be brief because they generally deal with one subject only. Keep in mind the following guidelines:

Everyday Use

We recently asked a group of people if they had written any business or professional correspondence *outside of work* during the last couple of weeks. Here is some of the correspondence they mentioned: a letter to a credit bureau asking for a copy of the writer's credit file, a letter to the principal of a child's school, a letter asking that a credit card be canceled, and a letter thanking a community group for assisting with home care for a relative. These examples suggest that business and professional correspondence play a part in our everyday lives as well as at our jobs. Can you remember any times when you wrote some such correspondence in your everyday life? What situations required this correspondence?

- State your topic in a subject line.
- Initial your memo next to your name.
- Begin with the most important information, and move on from there.
- Try to involve readers in your opening paragraph, and make some attempt to build goodwill in your conclusion.
- Focus each paragraph on one idea.
- Emphasize specific action, making clear exactly what you want readers to do, and when.

Sample memo

```
Date:     December 10, 19XX
To:       Members of the Shipping Department
From:     Willie Smith, Supervisor WS
Subject:  Scheduling holiday time

With orders running 25% higher than average this
season, I can give everyone an opportunity to work
overtime and still enjoy the company's traditional
half day off for holiday shopping.  The schedule
must be completed by tomorrow at 5:00 pm, however;
so let me know your preferences.

Please fill out the attached form with the days and
hours you can work overtime and your first, second,
and third choices for time off.  Return it to me
before you leave today.

I will try to accommodate everybody's preferences,
relying on seniority in case of conflicts.  If we
work together, December should be good for all of
us--on and off the job.
```

2
Writing letters

Letters are generally sent outside an organization. Whether you're writing a letter of praise or asking for information, your letter should follow certain conventions. In general, it should be written to a specific person.

Begin by briefly explaining the reasons, or providing necessary background information for the letter, and close with the statement of a specific action that you are taking or want your reader to take. Consider the following tips:

- Open cordially, and maintain a polite tone—even if you have a complaint.
- State the reason for your letter clearly and specifically. Include whatever details will help your reader to see your point and respond.
- If appropriate, make clear what you hope your reader will do.
- Express appreciation for your reader's attention. Close positively, and with thanks.
- Make response as simple as possible by including your telephone or fax number or E-mail address, and, if appropriate, a self-addressed, stamped envelope.

Many organizations have a set letter format. Most frequent is the **block format**, shown on p. 771, in which all text aligns at the left margin.

52c

Applying for a job

Although a job application may contain a number of elements (writing samples, portfolios, and so on), the résumé and the letter of application are part of nearly all applications. Also a good idea, though not a requirement, is a follow-up letter, sent after a job interview.

1

Writing résumés

Résumé comes from the French word for "summary." A **résumé** summarizes your experience and qualifications and provides support for your letter. A **letter of application** or **cover letter**, on the other hand, emphasizes specific parts of the résumé, telling how your background is suited to a particular job. (See pp. 773–74.)

Sample letter and envelope block format

An effective résumé is brief, usually one or two pages. Begin by brainstorming and taking notes, answering the following questions:

- What skills have you acquired in school, at work, and from your hobbies? Try to find a common thread in all these experiences.

return address | 1432 Coventry Lane
Newton, MA 02135
date | November 7, 19XX

one space

inside address | Professor Margaret Dorner
Chair, Department of Biology
Fillmore University
Fillmore, NE 68508

one space
salutation | Dear Professor Dorner:
one space

Professor Mark Spencer, my adviser at Newton College, has suggested I write to you regarding opportunities for graduate students at Fillmore University.

I will graduate next June with a B.S. in biological sciences. My senior thesis examines the ecology of a small stream system here in Massachusetts, and I hope to continue my studies in a department with a reputation for investigating riparian communities. Professor Spencer has told me that Fillmore might be ideal.

double-space
between
paragraphs

Could you please send me an application for your graduate school and any brochures or other information about your master's program. Thank you for your attention. I look forward to hearing from you.

one space

Sincerely yours,

four spaces

Pat McIntyre

Pat McIntyre

Pat McIntyre
1432 Coventry Lane
Newton, MA 02135

Professor Margaret Dorner
Chair, Department of Biology
Fillmore University
Fillmore, NE 68508

- What can you do well: draw, write, speak other languages, organize, lead, instruct, sell, solve problems, think creatively?
- Are you good at making decisions?
- Are you good at original thinking, at taking initiative, or at following directions?
- Are you looking for experience, security, excitement, money, travel, power, prestige, or something else?

Research reports that employers usually spend less than sixty seconds scanning a résumé. Remember that they are interested not in what they can do for you, but what you can do for them. They expect a résumé to be typed or printed neatly on high-quality paper; to read easily, with clear headings, adequate spacing, and a conventional format; and to provide all the information necessary to make a decision.

Your résumé may be arranged chronologically or functionally (around skills or expertise). Either way, you will probably include the following:

1. *Name, address, and phone number,* usually centered at the top.
2. *Career objective(s).* List career goals and specific jobs for which you realistically qualify.
3. *Educational background.* Start with your most recent school, and list the others in reverse chronological order. Include degrees, diplomas, majors, and special programs or courses that pertain to your field of interest. List honors and scholarships; and your grade-point average if it is high.
4. *Work experience.* List any jobs in reverse chronological order, identifying each with dates, names of employers, and the nature of your duties. If a job is related to the one for which you are applying, give full details. Otherwise be brief. Include any military experience in this category.
5. *Personal interests, activities, awards, and skills.* If space permits, list hobbies, offices held, volunteer work, and any awards.
6. *References.* Provide the names of two or three people who know your work well first asking their permission. Give their titles, addresses, and phone or fax numbers. Or you could simply say that your references are available on request.

Look at the example of a résumé on pp. 773–74, noting in particular the use of space-saving phrases instead of full sentences. Other résumé styles are often used; you may want to ask a professor in your major field for current examples.

Andrew Saunders
837 Siuslaw Highway
Corvallis, OR 97330
(503) 555-1763

CAREER OBJECTIVE: A challenging public relations
                     position in the travel and
                     tourism industry

EDUCATION: B.A., Journalism (to be
                     awarded June 19XX)
                     Oregon State University
                     Major: Public Relations
                     Minor: Psychology
                     Major G.P.A.: 3.4/4.0

                     Core Courses:
                     - Writing for public relations
                     - Magazine production and
                       design
                     - News writing and editing

PUBLIC RELATIONS
EXPERIENCE: Public Relations Intern
                     Willamette Valley Visitor's
                       Association
                     Eugene, OR
                     April-December 19XX
                     - Wrote and placed news
                       releases.
                     - Served as liaison with West
                       Coast newspapers.
                     - Assisted in production of
                       monthly newsletter.
                     - Developed and managed
                       campaign for annual
                       Willamette Valley Winery
                       Tour.

                     Publicity Chairperson
                     Oregon State University
                       Coalition for the Homeless
                     September 19XX-June 19XX
                     - Planned successful food
                       drive.
                     - Developed public-awareness
                       campaign.

Andrew Saunders   2

OTHER WORK
EXPERIENCE: <u>Supervisor</u>
                            Sherwin-Williams Company
                            Portland, OR
                            June 19XX-June 19XX
                            ▪ Supervised warehouse
                              operations and eight-person
                              staff.
                            ▪ Worked with computerized
                              order system.

                            <u>Inside Salesperson</u>
                            Sherwin-Williams Company
                            Eugene, OR
                            Summers 19XX-XX

PROFESSIONAL
ORGANIZATIONS: Public Relations Student
                              Society of America
                            ▪ Vice President, Oregon State
                              University chapter, 19XX

                            Society of Professional
                              Journalists/Sigma Delta Chi

REFERENCES: Martin Anderson
                            Manager
                            Willamette Valley Visitor's
                              Association
                            4281 Valley River Rd.
                            Eugene, OR 97403
                            (503) 555-6333

                            Professor Shirley Sinclair
                            Department of Journalism
                            Oregon State University
                            Corvallis, OR 97330
                            (503) 555-2000 ext. 541

                            Professor Stuart Goldberg
                            Department of Journalism
                            Oregon State University
                            Corvallis, OR 97330
                            (503) 555-2000 ext. 237

2

Writing letters of application

Your letter of application is the first "version" of you that a prospective employer will see. As your personal ambassador, it should be absolutely flawless—in format, spelling, grammar, punctuation, mechanics, and usage. Whenever possible, send it to a specific individual.

A sample letter of application, modified block style

```
                                   837 Sluslaw Highway
                                   Corvallis, OR 94330
                                   February 10, 19XX

Suzanne Camdon
Director of Public Information
Northern California Bureau of Tourism
1421 Fairfax St.
San Francisco, CA 94120

Dear Ms. Camdon:

        I would like to be considered for the opening
you listed at Oregon State's placement office for a
public relations writer.  I will receive my degree in
journalism this June, and I think my education as well
as my professional experience might be appropriate for
the position.

        I recently completed an internship with the
Willamette Valley Visitor's Association.  Details of
my work there are on the enclosed résumé, but I
learned, in general, how to develop a good travel
story, meet deadlines for print and electronic media,
and work with members of the hospitality industry.

        Of special interest to you may be my work on
the Willamette Spring Winery Tour (some samples of
which are attached).  With the campaign I developed,
wineries reported a 27 percent increase over the
previous year.

        I will phone in a week or so to see if I might
talk with you more about this position.  In the
meantime, I can be reached at (503) 555-1763.  I
look forward to talking with you soon.

                           Sincerely yours,

                           Andrew Saunders
                           Andrew Saunders

enc.
```

You may want to prepare for writing a letter of application by reviewing your résumé, deciding which areas to emphasize and what information to add. Although each letter will take a somewhat different form, in most letters of application you will want to do the following:

- State your reason for writing, and name the position you seek. If appropriate, mention how you learned about the job.
- Describe, as specifically as possible, your educational and/or work experience.
- Emphasize your interest in the position, and request an interview. Say when you will follow up with a telephone call if you plan to do so.

THINKING CRITICALLY ABOUT BUSINESS AND PROFESSIONAL CORRESPONDENCE

If you have recently written a letter for business or professional reasons, evaluate it using the guidelines presented in this chapter. If not, identify a job that might interest you, and draft an application letter. Review your letter, and revise it accordingly. What would you say is the most important detail in such writing? Note your thoughts in your writing log, if you keep one.

53

Making Oral Presentations

WHEN THE GALLUP POLL REPORTS on what U.S. citizens say they fear most, the findings are always the same: public speaking is apparently more frightening to us than anything else, scarier even than an attack from outer space or nuclear holocaust. Perhaps it is not surprising, then, that students who use this handbook have asked for information on giving oral presentations.

Successful speakers point to three elements crucial to their effectiveness:

- A thorough knowledge of the subject at hand
- Careful attention to the interactive nature of speaking and thus to the needs of the audience
- Practice, practice, and more practice

This chapter offers some guidelines that can help you gain control of these crucial elements and thus help you on your way to giving successful oral presentations.

53a

Considering the assignment, purpose, and audience

You will be wise to begin preparing for an oral presentation as soon as you get the assignment. Consider the assignment carefully, noting how much time you have to prepare, how long the presentation is to be, and any requirements for the use of visual aids, handouts, or other material to accompany the presentation. Consider whether you are to make the presentation alone or as part of a group so that you can plan and practice accordingly. Particularly if you are assigned to make a group presentation, you will need time to gather information, divide duties, prepare visuals or handouts, and practice. (See Chapter 1f.) Finally, make sure that you understand the criteria for evaluation—how will the presentation be graded?

> *Everyday Use*
>
> Chances are you have recently recorded a voice-mail or telephone-answering-machine message, an oral presentation that can make a strong impression. For a few days, collect the voice-mail or answering-machine messages you hear, and bring your collection to class to compare with those of your classmates. Bring your own outgoing message as well, if you have an answering machine. What do these oral presentations suggest to you about the people who made them? What kinds of impressions do they make?

To understand your assignment fully, you must think about your purpose and your audience. In particular, consider the goal or purpose your presentation is supposed to accomplish. Are you to lead a discussion? teach a lesson? give a report? engage the class in an activity? And who will be the audience? Your instructor, almost certainly, will be an important member of the audience, and so you will want to think about what he or she expects you to do—and do well. In addition, the other class members will probably be part of the audience. In considering their needs, ask yourself what they know about your topic, what opinions they probably hold about it, and what they need to know and understand to follow your presentation and accept your point of view. For more on thinking about audience, see Chapter 2.

53b

Writing to be heard

Writing to be heard rather than read has several special requirements, among them a memorable introduction and conclusion, explicit structure and signpost language, straightforward syntax and concrete diction, and a well-prepared text.

1

Composing a memorable introduction and conclusion

Remember that listeners, like readers, tend to remember beginnings and endings most readily. Work extra hard, therefore, to make these elements memorable. Consider, for example, using a startling statement, opinion, or question; a vivid anecdote; a powerful quotation; see 6f for examples. Shifting language, especially into a variety of language that your audience will identify with, can be an effective way of catching their attention; Chapter 28 provides examples. Whenever you can link your subject to the experiences and interests of your audience, do so; listeners remember more easily that which is tied to something they relate to and care about.

2
Using structure and signpost language

Use a clear organizational structure, and give an overview of your main points toward the beginning of your presentation. (You may wish to recall these points again toward the end of the talk.) Throughout, it will be helpful to pause between major points and to use **signpost language** to mark your movement from one topic or subject to the next. Signpost language, which acts as an explicit transition in your talk, should be clear and concrete: *The second crisis point in the breakup of the Soviet Union occurred hard on the heels of the first* instead of *Another thing about the breakup of the Soviet Union . . .* For a list of transitions, see 6d5. In addition to such explicit transitions as *next, on the contrary,* or *finally,* you can offer signposts to your listeners by carefully repeating key words and ideas as well as by sticking to concrete and explicit topic sentences to introduce each new idea.

3
Considering syntax and diction

Avoid long, complicated sentences, and use straightforward syntax (subject-verb-object) as much as possible. Remember also that listeners can hold on to concrete verbs and nouns more easily than they can grasp abstractions. You will probably need to deal with abstract ideas, but try to illustrate them with concrete examples. (See 27c.) Your audience will thank you.

4
Preparing your text

You will almost certainly want to rely on some written material. Depending on the assignment, the audience, and your personal preferences, you may even decide to prepare a full text of your presentation. If so, double- or triple-space it, and use fairly large print so that it will be easy to read. Try to end each page with the end of a sentence, so you won't have to pause while you turn a page. In addition, you may decide to mark spots where you want to pause and highlight words you want to emphasize.

On the other hand, you may prefer to work from a detailed topic or outline or from note cards. If so, use the same basic techniques so that you can easily follow the material. Whatever kind of text you decide to prepare (and each kind can be highly successful), you will want to pay special attention to the task of *writing to be heard.*

53c

Sample text prepared for oral presentation

Look carefully at the following paragraphs. The first is from an essay about the importance of thinking critically before choosing a course of study; the full essay appears in 5i. The second paragraph presents the same information, this time written to be heard. See how the second text uses signpost language, repetition, vivid concrete examples, and simple syntax to make it easy to follow orally. Note also how the writer has marked her text for emphasis and pauses that will help her listeners follow the oral text.

A PARAGRAPH FROM A WRITTEN ESSAY

The decision about a major or other course of study is crucial because it determines both what we study and how we come to think about the world. The philosopher Kenneth Burke explains that we are inevitably affected not only by our experiences, but also by the terminologies through which our perceptions of those experiences are filtered. Burke calls these filters "terministic screens" and says that they affect our perception, highlighting some aspects of an experience while obscuring others. Thus the terminologies (or languages) we use influence how we see the world and how we think about what we see.

THE PARAGRAPH REVISED FOR ORAL PRESENTATION

Why is our decision about a major so crucial? I can give two important reasons. First, our major determines what we study. ∧ *Pause* Second, it determines how we come to think about the world. The philosopher Kenneth Burke explains these influences this way: our experience, he says, influences what we think about ideas and the world. But those experiences are always filtered through

language, through words and terminologies. Burke calls
these terminologies "terministic screens," a complicated-
sounding term for a pretty simple idea. Take, for example, the latest hike in student fees on our campus. The
Board of Trustees and the administration use one kind of
term to describe the hike: "modest and reasonable," they
call it. Students I know use entirely different terms:
"exorbitant and unjust," they call it. Why the difference? Because their terministic screens are entirely
different. Burke says we all have such screens made up
of language, and these screens act to screen out some
things for us and to screen in, or highlight, others.
Burke's major point is this: the terms and screens we use
have a big influence on how we see the world and how we
think about what we see.

53d

Using visuals

Visuals may be an integral part of an oral presentation, and they should
be prepared with great care. Do not think of them as add-ons but as one of
your major means of conveying information. Whatever visuals you decide
to use (charts, graphs, photographs, summary statements, or lists), they
must be large enough to be easily seen by your audience. Many speakers
use overhead projections throughout a presentation to help keep themselves
on track and to guide their audience. If you don't have an overhead projector,
you might prepare a poster or flip chart, or you could simply use a chalkboard.

Most important, make sure that they engage and help your listeners,
rather than distract them from your message. One good way to check out
the effectiveness of the visuals you plan to use is by trying them out on
classmates, friends, or roommates. If these colleagues do not clearly grasp
the meaning of the visuals, revise them and try again.

You may also want to prepare handouts for your audience: pertinent
bibliographies, for example, or text too small to be read on an overhead
projector. Unless they include material you want your audience to use while
you speak, distribute handouts at the end of the presentation.

53e

Practicing the presentation

In oral presentations as with many other things in life, practice makes perfect. Prepare a draft of your presentation, including all visuals, far enough in advance to allow for several run-throughs. Some speakers audio- or video-tape their rehearsals and then base their revisions on the tape-recorded performance. Others practice in front of a mirror or in front of friends. Do whatever works for you—just as long as you practice.

Make sure you can be heard clearly. If you are soft-spoken, concentrate on projecting your voice. If your voice tends to rise when you are in the spotlight, you may want to practice lowering your pitch. If you speak rapidly, practice slowing down and enunciating words clearly. If you practice with friends or classmates, ask them how well they can hear you and what advice they have for making your voice clearer and easier to listen to.

Once you are comfortable giving the presentation, make sure you will stay within the allotted time. One good rule of thumb is to allow roughly two and a half minutes per double-spaced eight-and-a-half- by eleven-inch page of text (or one and a half minutes per five- by seven-inch card). The only way to be sure about your time, however, is to time yourself as you practice. Knowing that your presentation is neither too short nor too long will help you to relax and gain self-confidence; and when the members of your audience sense your self-confidence, they will become increasingly receptive to your message.

53f

Making the presentation

Experienced speakers say they always expect to feel some anxiety before an oral presentation—and they develop strategies for dealing with it. In addition, they note that some nervousness can act to a speaker's advantage: adrenaline, after all, can provide a little extra jolt and help you perform well.

The best strategy seems to be to know your material well. Having confidence in your own knowledge will go a long way toward making you feel confident. In addition to doing your homework, however, you may be able to use any of the following strategies to good advantage: (1) Visualize your presentation with the aim of feeling comfortable with the idea of it; go over the scene of your presentation in your mind, and think it through completely. (2) Get some rest before the presentation, and avoid consuming an excessive amount of caffeine. (3) Consider doing some deep-breathing exercises right before the presentation. Concentrate on relaxing.

Move around the room if you are comfortable doing so. If you are more comfortable in one spot, at a table or a lectern, then stand with both feet flat on the floor. If you are standing at a lectern, rest your hands on it. Many speakers find that this stance keeps them from fidgeting.

Pause before you begin your presentation, concentrating on your opening lines. During your presentation, interact with your audience as much as possible. You can do so by facing the audience at all times and making eye contact as often as possible. You may want to choose two or three people to look at and "talk to," particularly if you are addressing a large group. Allow time for the audience to respond and ask questions. Try to keep your answers short so that others may participate in the conversation. At the conclusion of your presentation, remember to thank your audience.

> *Editing text for oral presentation*

- How does your presentation accomplish the specifications of the assignment? (53a)
- How does your presentation appeal to your audience's experiences and interests? Does it achieve your purpose? (53a)
- How does the introduction get the audience's attention? Does it provide any necessary background information? (53b1)
- What organizational structure informs your presentation? (53b2)
- Check for signpost language that can guide listeners. Are there explicit transitions? Do you repeat key words or ideas? (53b2)
- Have you used mostly straightforward sentences? Consider revising any long or complicated sentences to make your talk as easy as possible to follow. Check your words as well for too much abstraction. Substitute concrete words for abstract ones as you can. (53b3)
- Have you marked your text for pauses and emphasis? (53b4)
- Have you prepared visuals? If so, how do they contribute to your presentation? Are they large enough to be seen? If not, can you identify any information where visuals would be helpful? (53d)

THINKING CRITICALLY ABOUT ORAL PRESENTATIONS

Study the text of an oral presentation you've prepared or given. Using the editing guidelines above, see how your text appeals to your audience. Look in particular at how well you catch and hold their attention. What do you conclude about the differences between spoken and written text?

Or look over a piece of your writing. Using this chapter, revise your writing to be heard.

54

Assembling a
Writing Portfolio

*I*MAGINE THAT *L*EONARDO DA *V*INCI WERE ALIVE TODAY *and needed to show examples of his art—to get into graduate school, perhaps, or to get a job. He would begin, most likely, by assembling a portfolio of his best work. Probably he would choose one of his self-portraits and maybe a few of his architectural drawings; and no doubt he would include the* Mona Lisa. *In other words, he would include a representative sample of the kinds of work he could do, and he would choose what he considered his best work.*

Chances are that you will have occasion to put together a portfolio of your writing, and you might well be assigned to do so for your writing class. Such an assignment challenges you to think about your writing and provides the opportunity to show your best work. Like Leonardo, you will want to choose examples of the various kinds of writing you've done, and you will want to show what you consider to be your best writing. This chapter provides guidelines for assembling a representative sample of your best work in a writing portfolio.

54a

Considering the purpose and audience for your portfolio

What are the purposes for your portfolio: to fulfill course requirements? to show at a job interview? to collect examples of your writing to keep and reflect on throughout your life? Each of these purposes will lead you to make different decisions about what to include and how to arrange the portfolio. If you are fulfilling an assignment, your instructor may well specify what you need to include.

Who is your audience: your instructor? a prospective employer? a scholarship committee? What you choose to include will be affected by

Everyday Use

Portfolios come in many guises: artists develop portfolios of their work for entering competitions, for applying for jobs, or for display; investors build portfolios of investments. Think of times when you have made a point of organizing some of your work in this way. What was your purpose for doing so? Did you have an audience other than yourself? What criteria did you use for selecting things to include?

audience. If, for example, it is a writing instructor, you will need to demonstrate what you've learned; if it is a prospective employer, you may need to show what you can do.

54b

Selecting work

How many entries will you include? Unless the portfolio is strictly for personal purposes and you wish to include everything you write in it, you should probably limit yourself to five to seven examples of your writing.

Here are some kinds of writing you might include in your portfolio:

- an academic essay demonstrating your ability to argue a claim or position
- an autobiographical essay of some kind, one that shows self-insight and that demonstrates your ability to paint vivid pictures with words
- a brief report, prepared for any class or community project
- a formal essay showing your ability to analyze and solve a problem
- your favorite piece of writing
- writing based on field and library research
- an example of a collaboratively written document, accompanied by a description of how the team worked and what you contributed
- an example of your best writing on an essay examination
- correspondence, such as a letter of inquiry, a memo, or a job application
- a résumé

You should also include the assignments for this work. If your portfolio is for a writing course, you may be expected to include examples of your notes and early drafts, as well as of any response you got from other readers.

54c

Thinking about the writing you include

Regardless of how many and what kind of examples of your writing you choose to include, you need to include a written statement, perhaps in the form of a memo, that explains and reflects on your work. Such a statement should

- *describe what is in the portfolio,* explaining briefly the purpose for each work
- *explain your choices:* how did you decide these pieces of writing represented your best work?
- *reflect on your strengths and abilities as a writer:* what have you learned about writing? what problems have you encountered, and how have you solved them?

Organizing your portfolio

Prepare a table of contents, and number all pages. Label and date each piece of writing. Put a cover sheet on top with your name and the date; if the portfolio is for a class, include the course title and number. Assemble everything in a folder.

Getting response

Once you have assembled your portfolio, seek responses to it from several classmates or friends and if possible from at least one instructor. To elicit the best response, you may want to refer them to the guidelines on reviewing a draft in 4c. Revise accordingly.

If this portfolio is part of your work in a course, ask your instructor whether a few hand-done corrections are acceptable. If you intend to use it as part of a job search, however, you will want to retype or print out clean copies. Either way, the time and effort you spend revising and editing the contents of your portfolio will be time well spent.

THINKING CRITICALLY ABOUT YOUR PORTFOLIO

You can profit by analyzing your portfolio one last time before presenting it as "finished." To do so, consider how your portfolio introduces your work to readers. How do the writing samples included represent strengths as a communicator? How well have you presented the portfolio physically? What could you change, add, or delete to make your portfolio more effective?

Part Eleven

For Multilingual Writers: Mastering the Nuances of English

<>

55. Understanding Nouns and
    Noun Phrases   788

56. Understanding Verbs and
    Verb Phrases   798

57. Understanding Prepositions and
    Prepositional Phrases   810

58. Forming Clauses and Sentences   816

55

Understanding Nouns
and Noun Phrases

*I*F YOU SPOKE ANOTHER LANGUAGE *when you first started learning English, you may have felt sometimes as though you were repeating the struggles of early childhood in trying to make yourself understood. Nevertheless, as a speaker of another language you had, and continue to have, a major advantage in acquiring a command of English: since all human languages are built on the same foundation, there is a great deal in your first language that you will encounter once again as you progress in English. For example, no matter what your first language is, you are familiar with the way sentences are built up out of two primary components—nouns and verbs. This chapter will focus on some of the ways English nouns differ from those in some other languages.*

55a

Distinguishing count and noncount nouns

The nouns *tree* and *grass* differ not only in meaning but in the way they are used in sentences.

	The hill was covered with trees.
	The hill was covered with grass.
BUT NOT	The hill was covered with grasses.
	I can count twenty trees in this picture.
BUT NOT	I can count twenty grasses in this picture.
	Whitman regarded even one tree as a miracle.
	He regarded even one blade of grass as a miracle.
BUT NOT	Whitman regarded even one grass as a miracle.

> *Everyday Use*
>
> Sometimes we use noncount nouns like count nouns in the rapid-fire verbal exchanges of everyday life—for example, in coffee shops (*Two light coffees to go, please*) or supermarkets (*That's two breads and a cottage cheese*). Listen for exchanges like these and see if you run across other such examples. Then try revising them in the more expansive style of written English (*two cups of light coffee; two loaves of bread and a container of cottage cheese*).

Tree is a **count** noun and *grass* a **noncount** (or **mass**) noun. These terms do not mean that grass cannot be counted, but only that English grammar requires that if we count grass, we express it indirectly: *one blade of grass, two blades of grass,* not *one grass, two grasses.*

Count nouns usually have singular and plural forms: *tree, trees.* Noncount nouns usually have only a singular form: *grass.*

Count nouns convey the image of a distinct individual or entity or a group of distinct individuals or entities: *a doctor, a tiger, a book, a mountain, a tree; doctors, tigers, books, mountains, trees.* Noncount nouns convey the image of an indeterminate mass without distinctly separate components: *milk, ice, clay, blood, grass.* But often much the same reality can be represented either in the sharp focus of a count noun or through the hazy lens of a noncount noun.

COUNT	NONCOUNT
people (plural of *person*)	humanity
tables, chairs, beds	furniture
letters	mail
pebbles	gravel
beans	rice
oats (plural only)	wheat

Abstract nouns are likely to be noncount, but not always.

COUNT	NONCOUNT
suggestions	advice (NOT advices)
facts	information (NOT informations)
words	vocabulary

Some words can be either count or noncount, the choice of grammatical form depending on meaning.

COUNT   Before there were video games, children would spend hours playing with *marbles*.

NONCOUNT The floor of the palace was made of *marble*.

> *Some general patterns for using count and noncount nouns*

- Use a count noun to refer to a living animal, but a noncount noun to the food derived from that animal.

COUNT   The *chickens* in the yard were making a racket.

NONCOUNT I prefer *chicken* to beef.

- Things that come in different varieties are noncount, but we can make those nouns plural to talk about those varieties.

NONCOUNT We like *wine* with dinner.

COUNT   The *wines* of California are often as good as those of France.

- Abstract nouns that are noncount can often be made count to shift attention from the concept in general to specific instances of it.

NONCOUNT *Kindness* is never wasted.

COUNT   I appreciate all your *kindnesses* to me in the past.

When you learn a noun in English, you need to learn whether it is count, noncount, or both. Most dictionaries do not supply this information; among those that do are the *Oxford Advanced Learner's Dictionary* and the *Longman Dictionary of American English*. Most important, pay attention to how a word is used when you hear or read it. If it has a plural form, then it can be used as a count noun; if it occurs in the singular without a determiner (see 55c), it is noncount.

55b

Maintaining singular and plural

Look at this sentence, which might appear in a traffic report:

All four bridges into the city are crowded with cars right now.

There are three count nouns in this sentence; one is singular (*city*), and two are plural (*bridges, cars*). If you speak a language with nouns that generally have no distinct plural forms (for example, Chinese, Japanese, or Korean), you might be tempted to argue that no information would be lost if the sentence were rendered as *All four bridge into the city are crowded with car right now.* After all, the numeral *four* indicates that *bridge* is plural, and obviously there would have to be more than one car if the bridges are crowded. But each language makes its own demands, and English requires that every time you use a count noun, you ask yourself whether you are talking about one item or more than one, and that you choose a singular or a plural form accordingly. It does not matter whether that information is unimportant or obvious or has already been supplied; it must be stated explicitly again and again.

Since noncount nouns have no plural forms and are not used directly with numerals, they can be quantified only with a preceding phrase: *one quart of milk, three pounds of rice, four heads of lettuce, five blades of grass, several bits of information.* Note that the noun itself remains singular.

55c

Using determiners

A noun together with all its modifiers constitutes a **noun phrase**, and the noun around which the modifiers cluster is called the **head**. For example, in *My adventurous sister is leaving for New Zealand tomorrow*, the noun phrase *my adventurous sister* consists of two modifiers (*my* and *adventurous*) and the head *sister*. See 7b4 for more on modifiers and Chapter 17 for discussion of placing modifiers.

Both *my* and *adventurous* may be called adjectives, but *my* is a very different kind of adjective from *adventurous*, distinguished from most adjectives by several characteristics.

It is more like a pronoun, belonging to the same set of forms as *mine, me,* and *I.* It almost always comes at the beginning of the noun phrase; though you can say *my brilliant, adventurous sister,* you cannot put *brilliant* or any other adjective before *my.* In the example sentence, you cannot omit the word *my; adventurous sister* or *brilliant, adventurous sister* are not acceptable noun phrases in English. You might substitute another word for *my (our adventurous sister, this adventurous sister),* but the words that can be substituted are very limited in number; most adjectives would not qualify.

Words like *my, our,* and *this* are **determiners**. They are among the most common and important words in the English language. Using them appropriately can go a long way toward enabling you to write smooth, comprehensible English.

Unlike other adjectives, determiners do not describe the noun head; instead they identify or quantify it. They include the following:

1. *a/an, the*
2. *this, these, that, those*
3. *my, our, your, his, her, its, their;* possessive nouns and noun phrases (*Sheila's, my friend's*)
4. *whose, which, what*
5. *all, both, each, every, some, any, either, no, neither, many, much, (a) few, (a) little, several,* and *enough*
6. the numerals *one, two,* etc.

Some of these are treated in more detail in 55d.

Being careful to use determiners with singular count nouns

Every noun phrase with a singular count noun head must begin with a determiner.

NOT	adventurous sister
BUT	*my* adventurous sister
NOT	big, bad wolf
BUT	*the* big, bad wolf
OR	*a* big, bad wolf
NOT	old neighborhood
BUT	*that* old neighborhood
OR	*an* old neighborhood

If there is no reason to use a more specific determiner, use an indefinite article: *a big, bad wolf; an old neighborhood.*

Notice that every noun phrase need not begin with a determiner, only those whose head is a singular count noun. Noncount and plural count nouns sometimes have determiners, sometimes not: *This grass is green* and *Grass is green* are both acceptable, though different in meaning, as are *These trees are green* and *Trees are green.* You cannot say *Tree is green;* however; say instead *This tree is green, Every tree is green,* or at least *A tree is green.*

Remembering which determiners go with which types of noun

1. Use *this* or *that* with singular count or noncount: *this book, that milk.*
2. Use *these, (a) few, many, both,* or *several* with plural count: *these books, those plans, a few ideas, many students, both hands, several trees.*
3. Use *(a) little* or *much* with noncount: *a little milk, much affection.*
4. Use *some* or *enough* with noncount or plural count: *some milk, some books; enough trouble, enough problems.*
5. Use *a, an, every,* or *each* with singular count: *a book, every child, each word.*

55d

Working with articles

The definite article *the* and the indefinite articles *a/an* are challenging to multilingual speakers. Many languages have nothing directly comparable to them, and languages that do have articles differ from English in the details of their use.

Why do articles play such a dominant role in English when other languages manage quite well without them? Part of the answer is that many other languages can move words around in a sentence with much greater freedom than English can, and what these languages accomplish with variations in word order English does with articles. Both techniques serve to orchestrate the interaction between writer and reader (or speaker and listener), and to keep the reader alert to the flow of information.

Consider an example from 1b: *If you have ever read a book or seen a movie about Helen Keller, you will remember the electrifying moment when she first learns to "read," when she first realizes that the symbols traced in her palm contain meanings.* The sentence uses indefinite articles at the beginning (*a book* and *a movie about Helen Keller*). If the writer had used *the* instead of *a*, she would have told readers that she expected them to recognize which book and movie she meant. That might have been appropriate if the book and movie had been mentioned earlier, or if everyone could be expected to know that there was only one book and movie about Helen Keller. But in fact the writer is less demanding of her readers and does not assume they've read a book or seen a movie about Helen Keller. When the sentence shifts to definite articles (*the electrifying moment, the symbols*), the reader is drawn closer to the writer, who is essentially saying that if they have read such a book or seen such a movie, she and they share the same memories, and if not, that she's giving enough information to help them recognize the memories she has.

That is an example of what articles contribute to meaning. This section will discuss the meaning conveyed by definite articles and indefinite articles and by the absence of an article.

1

The definite article

The definite article *the* is used with nouns whose identity is known or is about to be made known to readers. The necessary information for identification can come from any of the following sources:

From the noun phrase itself

the canals *of Amsterdam*

the *new* restaurant *on M Street*

the earthquake *that devastated Mexico City in 1985*

In these examples, the information needed by the reader to make the appropriate identification is in italics.

From elsewhere in the text

Last Saturday *a fire* that started in *a restaurant* spread to a neighboring dry-goods store. *The store* was saved, although *the merchandise* suffered water damage. It was reported that there were suspicious similarities to *a fire* that had broken out nearby two days earlier.

The second mention of the word *store* is preceded by *the*, which directs our attention to the information in the previous sentence, where the store is identified. *The* before *merchandise* similarly directs us to look for identifying information; in this case we cannot find another occurrence of the same word, but we can infer that since a dry-goods store carries merchandise, it must be the merchandise of that store that is being referred to. Notice also that when a noun is repeated, the second mention does not always call for *the*. The noun *fire* occurs twice with *a*, since the second fire was not the same as the first.

From context or general knowledge

Professor to student in her office: "Please shut *the door* when you leave."

The professor is referring to the door to her office and expects the student to understand that.

The pope is expected to visit Africa in October.

The reader knows which pope is being spoken of on the basis of general knowledge: there is only one living pope.

In the above cases the use of an indefinite article rather than a definite article would convey a different meaning. However, in some cases *the* is always required:

- Before the word *same* (*the same person*)
- Usually before an ordinal number (*the third little pig*)
- Before a superlative (*the best choice*)

2

The indefinite article

Unlike the definite article, which can appear with any kind of noun, the indefinite article *a/an* occurs only with singular count nouns. *A* is used before a consonant sound: *a car, a house. An* is used before a vowel sound: *an uncle, an hour.* Pay attention to sounds rather than to spelling: *a new car, an old car.*

A/an tells readers they do not have enough information to identify the noun. The writer may or may not have a particular thing in mind, but in either case will use *a/an* if the reader lacks the information necessary for identification. Compare the following two sentences:

I need *a* new *parka* for the winter.

I saw *a parka* that I liked at Holt Renfrew, but it wasn't heavy enough.

The parka in the first sentence is hypothetical rather than actual. Since it is indefinite to the writer, it clearly is indefinite to the reader, and is used with *a,* not *the.* The second sentence refers to a very specific actual parka, but since the writer cannot expect the reader to know which one it is, it is used with *a* rather than *the.*

If you want to speak of an indefinite quantity, rather than just one indefinite thing, use the determiner *some* with a noncount noun or a plural count noun.

I need *some* more *salt* for this stew.

I saw *some plates* that I liked at Gump's, but they didn't match those I already have.

3

The zero article

If a noun appears without *the, a/an,* or any other determiner (even if it is preceded by other adjectives), it is said to have a **zero article.** The zero article is used with noncount and plural count nouns: *cheese, hot tea, crackers, ripe apples* (but not *cracker* or *ripe apple*).

Use the zero article to make generalizations.

In this world nothing is certain but *death* and *taxes.*

— BENJAMIN FRANKLIN

The zero article with *death* and *taxes* indicates that Franklin refers not to a particular death or specific taxes but to death and taxes in general.

Here English differs from many other languages that also have articles—Greek or Spanish or German, for example—and that would use the definite article to make generalizations. In English, a sentence like *The snakes are dangerous* can only refer to particular, identifiable snakes, not snakes in general.

It is sometimes possible to make general statements with *the* or *a/an* and singular count nouns.

First-year college students are confronted with a wealth of new experiences.
A first-year student is confronted with a wealth of new experiences.
The first-year student is confronted with a wealth of new experiences.

These sentences all make the same general statement, but the last two are more vivid than the first. The second focuses on a hypothetical student taken at random, and the third sentence, which is characteristic only of formal written style, projects the image of a typical student as representative of the whole class.

55e

Arranging modifiers

Some modifiers can precede the noun head and others can follow, and you need to learn what can go where. Modifiers that follow the noun head are usually phrases or clauses (*the tiles on the wall; the tiles that we bought last summer*). Modifiers that precede the head fall into two groups: cases where a specific position for a word is obligatory, and cases where a certain position may be preferred but is not obligatory.

Obligatory modifier positions

- Put determiners at the very beginning of the noun phrase: *these old-fashioned tiles*. All or both must precede, and numerals must follow, any other determiners: *all these tiles, these six tiles*.
- Put noun modifiers directly before the noun head: *these kitchen tiles*. (See 12e.)
- Put all other adjectives between determiners and noun modifiers: *these old-fashioned kitchen tiles*. If there are two or more of these adjectives, their order is variable, but there are strong preferences, described below.

Preferred modifier positions

- In general, put subjective adjectives (those that show the writer's attitude) before objective adjectives (those that merely describe): *these beautiful old-fashioned kitchen tiles*.

AMONG OBJECTIVE ADJECTIVES

- Those that indicate size generally come early: *these beautiful large old-fashioned kitchen tiles*.
- Those that indicate color generally come late: these beautiful large old-fashioned blue kitchen tiles.

- Those derived from proper nouns or from nouns that refer to materials generally come after color terms and right before noun modifiers: *these beautiful large old-fashioned blue Portuguese ceramic kitchen tiles.*
- All other objective adjectives go in the middle. Series of adjectives for which a preferred order does not exist are separated by commas: *these beautiful large decorative, heat-resistant, old-fashioned blue Portuguese ceramic kitchen tiles.*

It goes without saying that the interminable noun phrase presented as an illustration in the preceding paragraph is a monstrosity that would be out of place in almost any conceivable kind of writing. You should always budget your use of adjectives.

EXERCISE 55.1

Each of the following sentences contains an error. Rewrite each sentence correctly.

1. At an end of the eighteenth century, England and France were at war.
2. Napoleon, the French ruler, invaded Egypt with much soldiers.
3. His ultimate goal was India, which England had conquered many year before.
4. At Rosetta, near the Nile, some French soldiers were building fort.
5. They found a black large stone—the Rosetta Stone.

EXERCISE 55.2

Insert articles as necessary in the following passage from *The Silent Language*, by Edward T. Hall.

Hollywood is famous for hiring _____ various experts to teach _____ people technically what most of us learn informally. _____ case in point is _____ story about _____ children of one movie couple who noticed _____ new child in _____ neighborhood climbing _____ tree. _____ children immediately wanted to be given _____ name of his instructor in _____ tree climbing.

56

Understanding Verbs and Verb Phrases

VERBS CAN BE CALLED THE HEARTBEAT OF PROSE *in every language, but in English the metaphor is especially meaningful. With rare exceptions, you cannot deprive an English sentence of its verb without killing it. If you speak Russian or Arabic, you might wonder what is wrong with a sentence like* My teacher very intelligent. *But unlike those and many other languages, English sentences must have a verb (for example,* My teacher <u>impresses</u> me as very intelligent), *and if no other verb is chosen, a form of the verb* be *must be used:* My teacher <u>is</u> very intelligent.

56a

Forming verb phrases

Verb phrases have strict rules of order. See how verb phrases can be built up out of the main verb and one or more auxiliaries (see 9a):

My cat *drinks* milk.

My cat *is drinking* milk.

My cat *has been drinking* milk.

My cat *may have been drinking* milk.

If you try to rearrange the words in any of these sentences, you will find that most alternatives are impossible. You cannot say *My cat <u>drinking is</u> milk* or *My cat <u>been has drinking</u> milk* or *My cat <u>have may been drinking</u> milk.* The only permissible rearrangement is to move the first auxiliary to the beginning of the sentence in order to form a question.

Has my cat been drinking milk?

Everyday Use

Everyday interaction, especially in making requests, calls for a delicate balance between the need to get things done and to show consideration for other people's feelings. Modals are an important device for softening the bluntness of a message. You can ask someone to *close the window,* but it's more considerate to say *could you close the window?* Note also the difference between saying *let's go* and *shall we go?* The first is more of an order; the second, an invitation.

Pay attention to the kinds of requests people make, both those containing modals and those formed in other ways. If someone says *The phone is ringing,* is the actual meaning "Please answer the phone"? Do you notice any typical ways in which teachers make requests of students, or customers of sales personnel? Are there differences between requests between women, requests between men, and requests between women and men? How do these patterns in English compare with those in your native language?

A review of auxiliary and main verbs

In *My cat may have been drinking milk,* the main verb *drinking* is preceded by three auxiliaries: *may, have,* and *been.*

- *May* is a modal, which must be followed by the base form (*have*).

- *Have* indicates that the tense is perfect, and it must be followed by a past participle (*been*).

- *Been* (or any other form of *be*), when it is followed by a present participle (such as *drinking*), indicates that the tense is progressive.

- A form of *be* can also represent passive voice, but then the following verb form must be a past participle, as in *My cat may have been bitten by a dog.*

The main verb (MV) can be preceded by as many as four auxiliaries in sequence; however, more than three are very rare. They must be in the following order: modal + perfect *have* + progressive *be* + passive *be.*

     PERF PASS   MV
Sonya *has been invited* to stay with a family in Prague.

     PERF PROG MV
She *has been taking* an intensive course in Czech.

     MOD PROG MV
She *must be looking* forward to her trip eagerly.

Only one modal is permitted in a verb phrase.

MOD   MV
Sonya *can speak* a little Czech already.

MOD PROG   MV
She *will be studying* for three more months.

MOD MOD   MV
BUT NOT She *will can speak* Czech much better soon.

To convey the intended meaning of the last sentence, you would need to use other words: *She will be able to speak Czech much better soon.* Every time you use an auxiliary, you should be careful to put the next word in the appropriate form. Study the following pairs of example sentences; in each case, the second sentence adds an auxiliary to the first.

MODAL + BASE FORM

Alice *reads* Latin.

Alice *can read* Latin.

Paul *has* been studying.

Paul *might have* been studying.

Notice that even though sentence 1 requires *-s* at the end of the main verb *read*, sentence 2, with the modal *can*, leaves *read* in the base form. In sentence 4, the modal *might* is also followed by the base form *have*.

In many other languages the equivalent of a modal like *can* or *must* is followed by the infinitive. Be careful not to substitute an infinitive + *to* for the base form. Do not say *Alice can to read Latin.*

PERFECT *HAVE* + PAST PARTICIPLE

Everyone *went* home.

Everyone *has gone* home.

They *will be* working all day.

They *have been* working all day.

In sentence 2, the auxiliary *has* transforms the following verb into its past participle *gone* (not *has went* or *has go*). In sentence 4, where *have* has replaced the modal *will* of sentence 3, the following auxiliary *be* has become the past participle *been*.

PROGRESSIVE *BE* + PRESENT PARTICIPLE

The children *study* history in school.

The children *are studying* history in school.

A progressive form of the verb is signaled by two elements, a form of the auxiliary *be* (*are* in the second sentence) and the ending *-ing* attached to the next word. Be sure to include both elements.

NOT	The children studying in school.
OR	The children are study in school.
BUT	The children are studying in school.

PASSIVE *BE* + **PAST PARTICIPLE**

People *speak* Tagalog in the Philippines.

Tagalog *is spoken* in the Philippines.

Notice that the difference between progressive *be* and passive *be* is that the following word ends in the *-ing* of the present participle with the progressive, but with the passive the following word never ends in *-ing* and instead becomes the past participle.

If the first auxiliary in a verb phrase is *be* or *have,* it must show either present or past tense, and it must agree with the subject.

Michiko and Kyunghee *are* studying music.

Natasha *is* studying music.

Michiko and Kyunghee *were* taught by a famous violinist.

Natasha *was* taught by a famous violinist.

Michiko and Kyunghee *have* played in an orchestra.

Natasha *has* played in an orchestra.

Notice that although a modal auxiliary may also show present or past tense (for example, *can* or *could*), it never changes form to agree with the subject.

NOT	Michiko and Kyunghee cans play two instruments.
BUT	They *can* play two instruments.
NOT	Natasha cans play two instruments.
BUT	She *can* play two instruments.

56b

Using present and past tenses

Every English sentence must have at least one **finite verb** or verb phrase, one that is not an infinitive, a gerund, or a participle without any auxiliaries. Furthermore, every finite verb or verb phrase must have a tense.

In some languages, such as Chinese and Vietnamese, the verb form never changes regardless of when the action of the verb takes place, and the time of the action is simply indicated by other expressions such as *yesterday, last year,* or *next week.* In English, the time of the action must be clearly indicated by the tense form of each and every finite verb, even if the time is obvious or there are other indications of time in the sentence. Therefore, if you write a sentence like *During the Cultural Revolution millions of young people cannot go to school and are sent to the countryside,* you must change the finite verb phrases *can(not) go* and *are sent* to the past tense.

> During the Cultural Revolution millions of young people could not go to school and were sent to the countryside.

In some languages, words end in either a vowel or a single consonant, not in one consonant followed by another (Spanish, for example). If you speak such a language, remember to add the -*s* of the present tense third person singular or the -*ed* of the past tense. If you have such problems, go over your writing carefully to check whether you have added the appropriate ending to every finite verb.

NOT   Last night I call my aunt who live in Santo Domingo.

BUT   Last night I called my aunt who lives in Santo Domingo.

Understanding perfect and progressive verb phrases

The perfect and progressive auxiliaries combine with the present or past tense, or with modals, to form complex verb phrases with special meanings. In particular you should learn to recognize sentences in which the perfect or the progressive must be used and distinguish them from sentences in which a simple tense is used.

1

Distinguishing the simple present and the present perfect

Imagine writing the following sentence:

My sister *drives* a bus.

The simple present (*drives*) merely tells us about her current occupation. But if you were to add the phrase *for three years,* it would be incorrect to say *My sister* <u>*drives*</u> *a bus for three years.* You need to set up a time frame that encompasses the past and the present, and therefore you should use the present perfect or the present perfect progressive.

My sister *has driven* a bus for three years.
My sister *has been driving* a bus for three years.

2

Distinguishing the simple past and the present perfect

Consider this sentence:

Since she started working, she *has bought* a new car and a VCR.

The clause introduced by *since* sets up a time frame that runs from past to present, and requires the present perfect (*has bought*). Furthermore, the sentence does not say exactly when she bought the car or the VCR, and that indefiniteness also calls for the perfect. It would be less correct to say *Since she started working, she bought a new car and a VCR.* But what if you should go on to say when she bought the car?

She *bought* the car two years ago.

It would be incorrect to say *She has bought the car two years ago* because the perfect is incompatible with definite expressions of time. In this case, use the simple past (*bought*) rather than the present perfect (*has bought*).

3

Distinguishing the simple present and the present progressive

Return to the sentence *My sister drives a bus*. You might continue *But she is taking a vacation now.* Many languages, such as French and German, use the simple present (*drives, takes*) for both types of sentence. In English, it would be incorrect to say *But she takes a vacation now,* although you might say *But she takes a vacation every year.*

When an action is in progress at the present moment, use the present progressive. Use the simple present for actions that frequently occur during a period of time that might include the present moment (though such an assertion makes no claim that the action is taking place right now).

4

Distinguishing the simple past and the past progressive

Finally, consider this sentence:

My sister *spent* the summer in Italy.

You might be tempted into using the past progressive here instead of the simple past, since spending the summer involves a continuous stretch of time of some duration, and duration and continuousness are typically associated with the progressive. As a result, you might write *My sister was spending the summer in Italy.*

But English speakers use the past progressive infrequently, and would be unlikely to use it in this case except to convey actions that are simultaneous with other past actions. For example:

My sister *was spending* the summer in Italy when she *met* her future husband.

Use the past progressive to focus on duration, continuousness, and simultaneousness, to call attention to past action that went on at the same time as something else.

56d

Distinguishing stative and dynamic verbs

Consider the following two sentences:

Meifang *resembles* her mother.

Jorge *knows* the answer.

It would sound strange to say *Meifang is resembling her mother* or *Jorge is knowing the answer*. *Resemble* and *know* are called stative verbs, and they are rarely used with progressive forms. They can be contrasted with the majority of verbs in English, those which are called dynamic verbs and which can be used in the progressive without restriction. **Dynamic verbs** tell us about something that is happening, most typically about an action that someone is deliberately performing. **Stative verbs** tell us instead that someone or something is in a state that is unchanging, at least for a while. Dynamic verbs tell us about doing, while stative verbs tell us about being or having; the sentences about Meifang and Jorge are equivalent to the following:

Meifang is like her mother. [resemble = be]

Jorge has the answer in his mind. [know = have]

Many verbs have more than one meaning, and some of these verbs are stative with one meaning and dynamic with another. For example:

Jorge *has* the answer.
Jorge *is having* a good time at the party.

Have is stative in the first sentence but dynamic in the second. In addition to *be, have, resemble,* and *know,* verbs that are stative, at least for some of their meanings, include designations of mental states like *believe, hate, like, love, think,* and *understand,* and of other states like *belong, cost, mean, need, own,* and *weigh.*

One group of verbs calls for special attention. Imagine the following dialogue:

Helen: Listen. Do you hear anything?
Paul: Okay, I'm *listening.* Yes, I *hear* something in the hall. It *sounds* peculiar.

Listen, hear, and *sound* all have to do with sense perceptions. Yet *listen* can be used in the progressive, whereas *hear* and *sound* cannot. *Listen* indicates that Paul is deliberately doing something, whereas *hear* and *sound* refer to an experience over which Paul has no control. In other words, *hear* and *sound* are stative rather than dynamic verbs because they do not indicate voluntary action. Paul is the subject of *hear,* while the experience itself is the subject of *sound.*

With verbs of vision, *see* corresponds to *hear,* and *look* to both *listen* and *sound: I'm looking. I see something. It looks peculiar.*

But other verbs of sense perception, like *smell, taste,* and *feel,* use the same word in all three functions: *Have you tasted the soup? I'm tasting it now. I taste something strange. It tastes sour.*

One final caution: Even though stative verbs are not usually used with the -*ing* forms of the progressive aspect, they occur freely with -*ing* in non-finite participles and gerunds. For example: *Seeing is believing.*

56e

Using modals

Consider a passage from earlier in this book, beginning with the third sentence in 1f:

. . . your college course work *will* call on you to do much reading, writing, research, talking, listening, and note-taking. And as you probably have already realized, you will not—or need not—always carry out all these activities in solitude. Far from it. Instead, you can be part of a broad conversation that includes all the texts you read. . . .

This passage contains four modal auxiliaries: *will, will not, need not,* and *can.* These modals tell the reader what the writer judges to be the options available—in this case, in college work. The passage begins with *will,* which makes a firm prediction of what the reader is to expect. It continues with a firm negative prediction *(will not),* but immediately revises it to a more tentative forecast *(need not),* and finally opens up a new vista of possibilities for the reader *(can).*

The most commonly used modals

The nine basic modal auxiliaries are *can, could, will, would, shall, should, may, might,* and *must.* There are a few others as well, in particular *ought to,* which is close in meaning to *should,* and occasionally the verb *need,* which can also be a modal.

1

Using modals to refer to the past

The nine basic modals fall into the pairs *can/could, will/would, shall/ should, may/might,* as well as the loner *must.* In earlier English the second member of each pair was the past tense of the first. To a very limited degree, the second form still functions as a past tense, especially in the case of *could.*

> Ingrid *can* ski.
>
> Ingrid *could* ski when she was five.

But for the most part, in present-day English all nine modals typically refer to present or future time. This means that when you want to use a modal to refer to the past, you follow the modal with a perfect auxiliary.

> If you have a fever, you *should* see a doctor.
>
> If you had a fever, you *should have seen* a doctor.

In the case of *must,* refer to the past by using the modal substitute *had to.*

> You *must* renew your visa by the end of this week.
>
> You *had to* renew your visa by the end of last week.

2

Using modals to make requests or to give instructions

The way modals contribute to human interaction is most evident in requests and instructions. Imagine making the following request of a flight attendant:

Will you bring me a pillow?

You have expressed your request in a demanding manner, and the flight attendant might resent it. A more polite request:

Can you bring me a pillow?

This statement acknowledges that fulfilling the request may not be possible. Another way of softening the request is to use the past form of *will*, and the most discreet choice is the past form of *can*.

Would you bring me a pillow?

Could you bring me a pillow?

Using the past of modals is considered more polite than using their present forms because it makes any statement or question less assertive.

Now imagine that each of the following instructions is given by different professors to their classes:

1. You *can* submit your term paper on a floppy disc.
2. You *may* submit your term paper on a floppy disc.
3. You *should* submit your term paper on a floppy disc.
4. You *must* submit your term paper on a floppy disc.
5. You *will* submit your term paper on a floppy disc.

Instructions 1 and 2 give permission to submit the paper on disc, but do not require it; of these, 2 is more formal. Instruction 3 adds a strong recommendation; 4 allows no alternative; and 5 implies, "Don't even think of doing otherwise."

3

Using modals to reveal doubt and certainty

Modals tell the reader how confident the writer is about the likelihood that what is being asserted is true. Look at the following two sets of sentences, the first set about the present and the second about the future. Each set starts with a tentative suggestion and ends with full assurance.

Please sit down; you *might* be tired.

Please sit down; you *may* be tired.

Please sit down; you *must* be tired.

Don't lie on the grass; you *might* get Lyme disease.

Don't lie on the grass; you *may* get Lyme disease.

Don't lie on the grass; you *will* get Lyme disease.

The second set of sentences illustrates why the modal *will* (or *shall* in some varieties of English) is regarded as the marker of the future tense. It makes a prediction about what lies ahead and suppresses any sense of uncertainty.

56f

Using participial adjectives

Many verbs refer to feelings that some situation, person, or thing produces in someone's mind—for example, *bore, confuse, excite, fascinate, frighten, interest*. With most such verbs, the subject produces the feeling and the object has the feeling. For example: *The dinosaur display frightened the little boy*. This idea can be expressed in the passive as *The little boy was frightened by the dinosaur display*.

The past participle which is part of the passive formation can be used as an ordinary adjective. In such a case, it will describe the person having the feeling:

The *frightened* boy started to cry.

The same verb can form an adjective with the present participle. Then the adjective will describe the thing (or person) causing the feeling:

The *frightening* dinosaur display gave him nightmares.

Be careful not to confuse the two types of adjective. Do not write, for example, *I am interesting in African literature*. This idea should be expressed instead in one of these ways:

African literature *interests* me.

I am *interested* in African literature.

African literature is *interesting*.

You might find the following sentences helpful as a guide to using participial adjectives:

Anything can be *interesting*.

Only someone with a mind can be *interested*.

Notice that the words *anything* and *interesting* end in the same letters, as do *mind* and *interested*.

EXERCISE 56.1

Each of the following sentences contains an error. Rewrite each sentence correctly.

1. The Rosetta Stone was cover with inscriptions in two ancient languages, Greek and Egyptian.
2. Ancient Egyptian writing called hieroglyphics.
3. In the eighteenth century no one can read hieroglyphics.
4. Very soon after its discovery, the French have made copies of the stone.
5. They sent these copies to scholars who were interesting in hieroglyphics.

EXERCISE 56.2

Rewrite the following passage, adapted from "In a Jumbled Drawer" by Stephen Jay Gould, adding appropriate auxiliaries and verb endings where necessary.

As my son _____ grow _____, I _____ monitor _____ the changing fashions in kiddie culture for words expressing deep admiration—what I _____ call _____ "cool" in my day, and my father _____ designate _____ "swell." The half-life _____ seem _____ to be about six months, as "excellent" (with curious lingering emphasis on the first syllable) _____ give _____ way to "bad" (extended, like a sheep bleat, long enough to turn into its opposite), to "wicked," to "rad" (short for radical). The latest incumbent— "awesome"— _____ possess _____ more staying power, and _____ reign _____ for at least two years.

57

Understanding Prepositions and Prepositional Phrases

*A*LL LANGUAGES HAVE NOUNS AND VERBS, *but not all have prepositions. See, for instance, how the sentence* I went from Yokohama to Nagoya by car *might be rendered in Japanese:*

Yokohama	kara	Nagoya	made	kuruma	de	ikimashita.
Yokohama	from	Nagoya	to	car	by	I went

Directly below each Japanese word is its English equivalent. As you can see, both Japanese and English have words that show the relationship of a noun to the rest of the sentence (kara for "from," made for "to," de for "by"), but in Japanese they are not **prepositions,** *that is, words placed* before *noun objects, but* **postpositions,** *words placed* after *such nouns.*

English differs in various ways from other languages in the way prepositions are used. Think about whether prepositions are used differently in your native language; if so, you may need to pay special attention to the way you use prepositions in English.

57a

Using prepositions idiomatically

Even if you usually know where to use prepositions, you may have difficulty from time to time knowing which preposition to use. Each of the most common prepositions, whether in English or in other languages, has a wide range of different applications, and this range never coincides exactly from one language to another. See, for example, how English speakers use *in* and *on.*

Everyday Use

In many fields, you will find phrasal verbs that are part of their specialized vocabulary. For example: *log on* (computers), *blast off* (space exploration), *kick off* (football or soccer). Make a list of some other phrasal verbs that are used in these or other fields. How are these phrases expressed in your native language?

The peaches are *in* the refrigerator.

The peaches are *on* the table.

Is that a diamond ring *on* your finger?

If you speak Spanish, you would use one preposition (*en*) in all these sentences, which might lead you to say in English *Is that a diamond ring in your finger?*

There is no easy solution to the challenge of using English prepositions idiomatically, but there are some strategies that can make it less formidable:

> *Strategies for using prepositions idiomatically*

1. Keep in mind typical examples of the most basic sense of each preposition. For example:

   IN   The peaches are *in* the refrigerator.

   There are still some pickles *in* the jar.

   Here the object of the preposition *in* is a container that encloses something.

   ON   The peaches are *on* the table.

   The book you are looking for is *on* the top shelf.

   Here the object of the preposition *on* is a horizontal surface that supports something with which it is in direct contact.

2. Add to these examples others that show some similarities and some differences in meaning. For example:

   IN   You shouldn't drive *in* a snowstorm.

   Here there is no container, but like a container the falling snow surrounds and seems to enclose the driver.

   (Continued)

ON   Is that a diamond ring *on* your finger?

A finger is not a horizontal surface, but like such a surface it can support a ring with which it is in contact.

3. Use your imagination to create mental images that can help you remember figurative uses of prepositions. For example:

IN   Michael is *in* love.

Imagine a warm bath in which Michael is immersed (or a raging torrent, if you prefer to visualize love that way).

ON   I've just read a book *on* computer science.

Imagine a shelf labeled COMPUTER SCIENCE on which the book you have read is located.

4. Try to learn uses of prepositions not in isolation, but as part of a system. For example, in identifying the location of a place or an event, the three prepositions *in*, *on*, and *at* can be used.

The preposition *at* specifies the exact point in space or time.

AT   There will be a meeting tomorrow *at* 9:30 A.M.
     at 160 Main Street.

Expanses of space or time within which a place is located or an event takes place are treated as containers, and so require *in*.

IN   I arrived *in* the United States *in* January.

Instead of *in* or *at*, *on* must be used in two cases: with the names of streets (but not the exact address), and with days of the week or month.

ON   I visited the airlines office, which is *on* Fifth
     Avenue, *on* Wednesday.

ON   I'll be moving from my apartment *on* Park Road
     on September 30.

You might remember to use *on* in these cases if you picture in your mind the base of a building in direct contact with the pavement of a street and a 365-day appointment calendar with a date printed on the surface of each page.

57b

Using two-word verbs

Compare these two sentences:

The balloon rose off the ground.

The plane took off.

In the first sentence, the word *off* is a preposition that introduces the prepositional phrase *off the ground*. In the second sentence, on the other hand, *off* does not function as a preposition and does not introduce a prepositional phrase. Instead, it combines with *took* to form a two-word verb with its own special meaning. Such a verb is called a **phrasal verb**, and the word *off*, when used in this way, is called an **adverbial particle**. Many prepositions, as well as several other words (for example, *back* and *away*), can function as adverbial particles to form phrasal verbs.

In the first sentence, in which *off* is part of a prepositional phrase, it is possible to put other phrases between the verb and the preposition. You can say, for example:

The balloon *rose off the ground* without difficulty.

OR   The balloon *rose* without difficulty *off the ground*.

But you cannot insert such phrases in sentence 2, where *off* is not a preposition. You can say, for example:

The plane *took off* without difficulty.

BUT NOT   The plane *took* without difficulty *off*.

The verb + particle combination that makes up a phrasal verb is a tightly knit entity that usually cannot be torn apart. However, there is one major exception.

Many phrasal verbs are transitive, meaning that they take a direct object (see 7c). Take, for example, the verb + particle combination *pick up*; in the following sentence, it takes the noun phrase *my baggage* as its direct object:

I *picked up my baggage* at the terminal.

Like any other phrasal verb, it cannot easily be split apart. English speakers would never say I *picked at the terminal up my baggage*. Yet nothing prevents the direct object from being moved between the verb and the particle. The following sentence is perfectly normal:

I *picked my baggage up* at the terminal.

Furthermore, if a personal pronoun is used as the direct object, it must separate the verb from its particle:

I *picked it up* at the terminal.

In fact, it would be unacceptable for the pronoun to follow the particle, as in I *picked up it* at the terminal.

Phrasal verbs are extremely common in English. Some of them are slang (*cop out*, "fail to take responsibility"), and others, though appropriate in most conversation, are much less so in formal writing (*mess up*, "spoil"). But many phrasal verbs are normal both in speech and in most varieties of formal written English. See, for example, the quotation from Lewis Thomas at the beginning of Chapter 31 which includes two phrasal verbs: ". . .you got all the writer intended to *parcel out* and now you have to *move along*."

Thomas also uses a two-word verb of a different type: "It is almost always a greater pleasure to *come across* a semicolon than a period." *Come across* does not operate like a phrasal verb. For one thing, you can insert an additional phrase between *come* and *across*: *to come suddenly and unexpectedly across a semicolon* is acceptable if a bit unwieldy. On the other hand, the object that follows *across* cannot be moved between it and *come*; you would never say *to come a semicolon across*. *Come across* seems to consist of the verb *come* followed by the preposition *across*, which introduces the prepositional phrase *across a semicolon*. Yet *to come across a semicolon* is different from a normal verb + prepositional phrase, such as *to rise off the ground*. If you know the typical meanings of *rise* and *off*, you can interpret *to rise off the ground*. Not so with *to come across a semicolon*; the combination *come* + *across* has a special meaning ("find by chance") which could not be determined from the typical meanings of *come* and *across*. Therefore *come across* must be considered a two-word verb, but one that has much more in common with verbs followed by prepositions than with phrasal verbs. Such verbs as *come across* are called **prepositional verbs.**

Prepositional verbs include such idiomatic two-word verbs as *run into*, meaning "meet by chance," *take after*, meaning "resemble" (usually a parent or other older relative), *get over*, meaning "recover from," and *count on*, meaning "trust." They also include verb + preposition combinations in which the meaning is predictable, but the specific preposition that is required is less predictable, and must be learned together with the verb (for example, *depend on*, *look at*, *listen to*, *approve of*). There are also **phrasal-prepositional verbs,** which are verb + adverbial particle + preposition sequences (for example, *put up with*, *look forward to*, *give up on*, *get away with*).

Every comprehensive dictionary includes information about the various adverbial particles and prepositions that a verb can combine with, but only some dictionaries distinguish verb + particle from verb + preposition. *Longman Dictionary of American English* is one that does.

EXERCISE 57.1

Each of the following sentences contains a two-word verb. In some, the verb is used correctly; in some, incorrectly. Identify the two-word verb in each case, indicate whether it is a phrasal or prepositional verb, and rewrite any incorrect sentences correctly.

1. Shortly after the French invasion of Egypt, the British struck at Napoleon back.

2. By 1801, the French forces in Egypt were compelled to give up.

3. As part of the treaty of surrender, the French were required to turn the Rosetta Stone over to the British.

4. The British took back it to England.

5. The Rosetta Stone is now in the British Museum, where millions of visitors have looked at it.

EXERCISE 57.2

The poem by Langston Hughes on p. 431 includes two phrasal verbs. Identify them, and discuss with your classmates what similarities of meaning these two phrasal verbs have in the context of the poem. What phrasal verb might have been used in place of the final word *explode*? How might such a substitution have affected the impact of the poem?

58

Forming Clauses and Sentences

J UST AS THE LIVING BODY IS MADE UP OF CELLS, so most messages that we communicate are made up of sentences. But cells vary in nature from one living thing to another, and sentences are not formed in the same way in every language.

58a

Expressing subjects explicitly

English sentences consist of a subject and a predicate. This simple statement defines a gulf separating English from many other languages. Recall the Japanese sentence used at the beginning of Chapter 57: *Yokohama kara Nagoya made kuruma de ikimashita,* presented as the equivalent of "I went from Yokohama to Nagoya by car," with *ikimashita* translated as "I went." But *ikimashita* can also be rendered as "we went," "you went," "she went," "he went," or "they went." The subject is actually unexpressed but is understood from the context.

Many other languages leave out the subject when it can easily be inferred. Not English. With only limited exceptions, English demands that an explicit subject accompany an explicit predicate in every sentence. Though *Went from Yokohama to Nagoya by car* is possible on a postcard to a friend, in most varieties of spoken and written English the extra effort of explicitly stating who went is not simply an option but an obligation.

In fact every subordinate clause must have an explicit subject.

NOT   They flew to London on the Concorde because was fast.

BUT   They flew to London on the Concorde because *it* was fast.

English even requires a kind of "dummy" subject to fill the subject position in the following sentences:

Everyday Use

Signs and newspaper headlines are two types of language use that often omit sentence elements that are otherwise usually required. For instance:

NO HOT WATER TOMORROW
(*There will be no hot water tomorrow.*)
JUDGE REBUKED FOR STATEMENT TO JURY
(*A judge has been rebuked for making a statement to the jury.*)

Collect other such examples and try to formulate general rules about what elements can be omitted and what cannot (for instance, articles can but prepositions cannot). If you can find such examples in your native language, see if there are differences between those and the ones you find in English.

It is raining.
There is a strong wind.

Speakers of Spanish might be inclined to say: *Is raining* or *Has a strong wind.* In English, however, *it* and *there* are indispensable.

58b

Expressing objects explicitly

Transitive verbs typically require that objects also be explicitly stated, and in some cases even other items of information as well (see 9c). For example, it is not enough to tell someone *Give!* even if it is clear what is to be given to whom. You must say *Give it to me* or *Give her the passport* or some other such sentence. Similarly, saying *Put!* or *Put it!* is insufficient when you mean *Put it on the table.*

58c

Using English word order

You should not move subjects, verbs, or objects out of their normal positions in the sentence. In the following sentence, each element is in its appropriate place:

SUBJECT VERB OBJECT ADVERB
Omar reads books voraciously.

If you speak Turkish, Korean, or Japanese, in which the verb must come last, you may have to make a special effort never to write such a sentence as *Omar books voraciously reads,* which is not acceptable in English. If you speak Russian, which permits a great deal of freedom in word order, you must remember never to interchange the position of subject and object (*Books reads Omar voraciously* is not acceptable English) and to avoid separating the verb from its object (*Omar reads voraciously books*). See 7c and 17b.

Recognizing the sentence nucleus

This chapter began with an analogy between living cells and sentences. In English this analogy can be carried further. Just as a cell contains a nucleus that determines the essential nature of that cell, so an English sentence also contains a nucleus. Consider this brief dialogue:

A: Have Bulgaria and Brazil reached the finals in the World Cup?
B: Brazil has. Bulgaria hasn't.
A: Did Bulgaria lose to Italy?
B: Yes, it did.

When B says *Brazil has,* the combination of the subject + the auxiliary stands for the whole sentence *Brazil has reached the finals in the World Cup.* That combination can be called the **sentence nucleus.** Notice that B could not have left out more or less than those two elements; if B had said *Brazil* or *Brazil has reached,* the response would have been unacceptable English. The nucleus must be intact to represent the whole sentence.

The sentence nucleus serves many purposes, including the formation of negative statements and questions:

1. To form a negative statement, add *not* directly after the nucleus, either as a separate word or contracted with the auxiliary (*Bulgaria has not* or *Bulgaria hasn't*).

2. Form questions by reversing the order of the nucleus to auxiliary + subject, as in <u>*Have Bulgaria and Brazil*</u> reached the finals in the World Cup?

Notice that in B's second reply, *it did* stands for *Bulgaria lost to Italy.* In the full sentence, the verb *lost* has no auxiliary. In such a case, use the auxiliary *do* to form a nucleus with the subject, with *do* taking the tense form (in this case, the past tense form *did*) from the main verb.

Remember that *do* is used as an auxiliary only when no other auxiliaries are present. Note also that when it is used and the nucleus is followed by the rest of the sentence, the main verb appears in the base form.

NOT   Did Bulgaria lost to Italy?

BUT   Did Bulgaria lose to Italy?

58e

Using noun clauses, infinitives, and gerunds

Consider once again the analogy between the sentence and a cell of the living body. In one important respect, the analogy does not hold. Body tissues are made up of cells, but they are not cells themselves; sentences, on the other hand, are frequently built up (with some adjustments) out of smaller sentences, which are called **clauses**.

1

Using noun clauses

Examine the following sentence:

In my last year in high school, my adviser urged that I apply to several colleges.

This is built up out of two sentences, one of them (B) embedded in the other (A):

A. In my last year in high school, my adviser urged B.

B. I (should) apply to several colleges.

When these are combined as in the first sentence above, sentence B becomes a noun clause introduced by *that* and takes on the role of object of the verb *urged* in sentence A. Now look at the following sentence:

It made a big difference that she wrote a strong letter of recommendation.

Here the two component sentences are C and D:

C. D made a big difference.

D. She wrote a strong letter of recommendation.

In this case the noun clause formed from sentence D functions as the subject of sentence C, so that the combination reads as follows:

That she wrote a strong letter of recommendation made a big difference.

This is an acceptable sentence, but somewhat top-heavy. Usually when a lengthy noun clause is the subject of the sentence, it is moved to the end. When that is done, the result is *Made a big difference that she wrote a strong letter of recommendation.* If you speak Italian or Spanish or Portuguese, you might see nothing wrong with such a sentence. In English, however, the subject position must be filled. The "dummy" element *it* comes to the rescue and sets things right, converting the preceding example to *It made a big difference that she wrote a strong letter of recommendation.*

2

Using infinitives and gerunds

As you can see, when you construct a larger sentence out of smaller ones in English, the architecture can get complicated. In fact, you have more choices still. Not only can you use noun clauses; you can also use infinitives and gerunds. Some languages, such as Greek, do very well with just noun clauses; French and a great many other languages employ infinitives but have no equivalent to gerunds. When to use one or the other may be a challenge to multilingual writers. Though there is no simple explanation that will make it an easy task, here are some hints that will help you know when to use an infinitive or a gerund.

See how the two sentences considered above can also be stated.

In my last year in high school, my adviser urged that I apply to several colleges.

In my last year in high school, my adviser urged *me to apply* to several colleges.

It made a big difference that she wrote a strong letter of recommendation.

Her writing a strong letter of recommendation made a big difference.

In the first pair, the verb in the noun clause *that I apply to several colleges* has been changed to an infinitive (*to apply*), and the subject *I* has been put into the objective case (*me*). In the second, the verb in the noun clause *that she wrote a strong letter of recommendation* has been transformed into a gerund (*writing*), and the subject *she* has become the possessive *her*.

Why was an infinitive chosen for the first and a gerund for the second? In general, *infinitives* tend to represent intentions, desires, or expectations, while *gerunds* tend to represent facts. The gerund in the second pair calls attention to the fact that a letter was actually written; the infinitive in the first pair conveys the message that the act of applying was something desired, not an accomplished fact.

The distinction between fact and intention is not a rule but only a tendency, and it can be superseded by other rules. For instance, only a gerund, never an infinitive, can be directly preceded by a preposition. For this reason sentences like the one below must be changed as shown:

CHANGE This fruit is all right for to eat.
TO   This fruit is all right *to eat.*
OR   This fruit is all right *for eating.*
OR   This fruit is all right *for us to eat.*

The association of fact with gerunds and of intention with infinitives can help you know in the majority of cases whether to use an infinitive or a gerund when another verb immediately precedes. Consider the following examples:

Gerunds

Jerzy *enjoys going* to the theater.

We *resumed working* after our coffee break.

Caitlin *appreciated getting* chocolates from Sean.

In all of these cases the second verb is a gerund, and the gerund indicates that the action or event that it expresses actually has happened. Verbs like *enjoy, resume,* and *appreciate* can be followed only by gerunds, not by infinitives. In fact, even when these verbs do not convey clear facts, the verb that comes second must still be a gerund:

Caitlin *would appreciate getting* chocolates from Sean, but he hardly knows she exists.

Infinitives

Kumar *expected to get* a good job after graduation.

Last year, Fatima *decided to become* a math major.

The strikers have *agreed to go* back to work.

Here it is irrelevant whether the actions or events referred to by the infinitives did or did not materialize; at the moment indicated by the verbs *expect, decide,* and *agree,* those actions or events were merely intentions. These three verbs, as well as many others that specify intentions (or negative intentions, like *refuse*), must always be followed by an infinitive, never a gerund.

A few verbs can be followed by either an infinitive or a gerund; with some, such as *begin* or *continue,* the choice makes little difference in meaning, but with a handful of others, the difference in meaning is striking.

Using an infinitive to state an intention

Carlos was working as a medical technician, but he *stopped to study* English.

The infinitive indicates that Carlos intended to study English when he left his job. We are not told whether he actually did study English or not.

Using a gerund to state a fact

Carlos *stopped studying* English when he left the United States.

The gerund indicates that Carlos actually did study English, but later stopped.

Checking when to use a gerund or an infinitive

A full list of verbs that can be followed by an infinitive and verbs that can be followed by a gerund can be found in the *Index to Modern English,* by Thomas Lee Crowell, Jr. (McGraw-Hill, 1964).

58f

Using adjective clauses

Adjective clauses can be a challenge to multilingual writers. Look at the following sentence and then see what can go wrong:

The company *Mario's uncle invested in* went bankrupt.

The subject is a noun phrase in which the noun *company* is modified by the article *the* and the adjective clause *Mario's uncle invested in.* The sentence as a whole says that a certain company went bankrupt, and the adjective clause identifies the company more specifically by saying that Mario's uncle had invested in it.

One way of seeing how the adjective clause fits into the sentence is to rewrite it like this: *The company (Mario's uncle had invested in it) went bankrupt.* This is not a normal English sentence, but it helps to demonstrate a process which leads to the sentence we started with. The steps are:

1. Change the personal pronoun *it* to the relative pronoun *which: The company (Mario's uncle had invested in which) went bankrupt.* That still is not acceptable English.

2. Move either the whole prepositional phrase *in which* to the beginning of the adjective clause, or just move the relative pronoun: *The company in which Mario's uncle had invested went bankrupt* or *The company which Mario's uncle had invested in went bankrupt.* Both of these are good English sentences, the former somewhat more formal than the latter.

3. If no preposition precedes, substitute *that* for *which* or leave out the relative pronoun entirely. *The company that Mario's uncle had invested in went bankrupt* or *The company Mario's uncle had invested in went bankrupt.* Both of these are good English sentences, not highly formal but still acceptable in much formal writing.

Speakers of some languages find adjective clauses difficult in different ways. Following are some guidelines that might help.

If you speak Korean, Japanese, or Chinese

If you speak Korean, Japanese, or Chinese, the fact that the adjective clause does not precede the noun that it modifies may be disconcerting, both because that is the position of such clauses in the East Asian languages and because other modifiers, such as determiners and adjectives, do precede the noun in English.

If you speak Farsi, Arabic, or Hebrew

If you speak Farsi, Arabic, or Hebrew, you may expect the adjective clause to follow the noun as it does in English, but you might need to remind yourself to change the personal pronoun (*it*) to a relative pronoun (*which* or *that*) and then to move the relative pronoun to the beginning of the clause. You may mistakenly put a relative pronoun at the beginning but keep the personal pronoun, thus producing incorrect sentences such as *The company that Yossi's uncle invested in it went bankrupt.*

If you speak a European or Latin American language

If you are a speaker of some European or Latin American languages, you are probably acquainted with adjective clauses very much like those of English, but you may have difficulty accepting the possibility that a relative pronoun that is the object of a preposition can be moved to the beginning of the clause while leaving the preposition stranded. You might, therefore, move the preposition as well even when the relative pronoun is *that,* or you might drop the preposition altogether, generating such incorrect sentences as *The company in that Carmen's uncle invested went bankrupt* or *The company that Carmen's uncle invested went bankrupt.*

Finally, the fact that the relative pronoun can sometimes be omitted may lead to the mistaken notion that it can be omitted in all cases. Remember that you cannot omit a relative pronoun that is the subject of a verb.

NOT   Everyone invested in that company lost a great deal.

BUT   Everyone who invested in that company lost a great deal.

58g

Understanding conditional sentences

English pays special attention to whether or not something is a fact, or to the degree of confidence we have in the truth or likelihood of an assertion. It is no surprise, therefore, that English distinguishes on this basis among many different types of **conditional sentences**, that is, sentences that focus on questions of truth and that are introduced by *if* or its equivalent. The following examples illustrate a range of different conditional sentences. Each of these sentences makes different assumptions about the likelihood that what is stated in the *if*-clause is true, and then draws the corresponding conclusion in the main clause.

If you *practice* (or *have practiced*) writing frequently, you *know* (or *have learned*) what your chief problems are.

This sentence assumes that what is stated in the *if*-clause may very well be true; the alternatives in parentheses indicate that any tense that is appropriate in a simple sentence may be used in both the *if*-clause and the main clause.

If you *practice* writing for the rest of this term, you *will* (or *may*) *get* a firmer grasp of the process.

This sentence makes a prediction about the future and again assumes that what is stated may very well turn out to be true. Only the main clause uses the future tense (*will get*) or some other modal that can indicate future time (*may get*). The *if*-clause must use the present tense, even though it too refers to the future.

If you *practiced* (or *were to practice*) writing every single day, it *would* eventually *seem* much easier to you.

This sentence casts some doubt on the likelihood that what is stated will be put into effect. In the *if*-clause, the verb is either past (actually past subjunctive—see 9h) or *were to* + the base form, though it refers to future time. The main clause has *would* + the base form of the main verb.

> If you *practiced* writing on Mars, you *would find* no one to show your work to.

This sentence contemplates an impossibility at present or in the foreseeable future. As with the preceding sentence, the past subjunctive is used in the *if*-clause, although past time is not being referred to, and *would* + the base form is used in the main clause.

> If you *had practiced* writing in ancient Egypt, you *would have used* hieroglyphics.

This sentence shifts the impossibility back to the past; obviously you are not going to find yourself in ancient Egypt. But since past forms have already been used in the preceding two sentences, this one demands a form that is "more past": the past perfect in the *if*-clause, and *would* + the perfect form of the main verb in the main clause.

And so, with a feeling of gratitude that you do not have to write in hieroglyphics, you should approach the challenge of writing in English with confidence.

EXERCISE 58.1

Revise the following sentences as necessary. Not all sentences contain an error.

1. The scholar who deciphered finally hieroglyphics was Jean François Champollion.
2. Champollion enjoyed to study the languages of the Middle East.
3. By comparing the Greek and Egyptian inscriptions on the Rosetta Stone, he made a great deal of progress in understanding hieroglyphics.
4. Was of great importance that he knew Coptic, a later form of the Egyptian language.
5. In 1822 Champollion wrote a paper which he presented his decipherment of hieroglyphics in it.
6. If the Rosetta Stone was not discovered, it would have been much more difficult to decipher hieroglyphics.

EXERCISE 58.2

In his nonsense poem "The Walrus and the Carpenter," Lewis Carroll uses conditional sentences for humorous effect. Look back at the five sentence types in 58g. What sentence type is used in the following two stanzas?

The Walrus and the Carpenter
    Were walking close at hand:
They wept like anything to see
    Such quantities of sand.
"If this were only cleared away,"
    They said, "it *would* be grand."

"If seven maids with seven mops
    Swept it for half a year,
Do you suppose," the Walrus said,
    "That they could get it clear?"
"I doubt it," said the Carpenter,
    And shed a bitter tear.

Glossary of
Grammatical Terms

absolute phrase See *phrase.*

abstract noun See *noun.*

acronym A word, usually a noun, formed from the first letter(s) of several words, such as RADAR for *radio detecting and ranging.*

active voice See *voice.*

adjective A word that modifies, quantifies, identifies, or describes a word or words acting as a noun. An **attributive** adjective precedes while a **predicative** (or *predicate*) adjective follows the noun or pronoun that it modifies (*a good book, the book is good*). Of the overlapping types of adjectives, **descriptive adjectives** identify a quality that is *common,* such as a type, color, or weight (*research paper, yellow paper, heavy paper*) or *proper,* derived from a proper noun (*English history, Jacobean drama, Homeric epic*). **Demonstrative adjectives** (*this, that, these,* and *those*) specify particular nouns (*this paper, those papers*). **Indefinite adjectives** indicate quantity (*some research, any research, such research*). **Relative adjectives** qualify words bound directly to a modifying clause (*I know which research is yours*). **Interrogative adjectives** ask questions about the words they modify. *Whose research is finished? What research is she doing? Which research is in progress?* **Limiting adjectives** are the articles *a, an,* and *the.* **Numerical adjectives** modify words with *cardinal* (*two girls*) or *ordinal* numbers (*tenth year*). **Participial adjectives** are verbals that act as adjectives (*a waiting car, a damaged package*). **Possessive adjectives** include *my, your, his, her, its, one's, our, your, their* (*her research, our research*) as well as proper possessives formed by adding an *-'s* to a proper noun (*Einstein's research, America's coastline*). See 7b4, 12a, 12b, and 12c.

adjective clause See *clause.*

adjective forms Changes in an adjective from the **positive degree** (simply *tall, good*) to the **comparative** (comparing two—*taller, better*) or the **superlative** (comparing more than two—*tallest, best*). Short regular adjectives (*tall*) add *-er*

827

and -est, but irregular adjectives (*good*) do not follow this pattern. Most adjectives of two syllables or more form the comparative by adding *more* or *less* (*more beautiful, less beautiful*) and the superlative by adding *most* and *least* (*most beautiful, least beautiful*). Some adjectives (*only, forty*) do not change form.

adverb   A word that qualifies, modifies, limits, or defines a verb, an adjective, another adverb, or a clause, frequently answering the questions *where?, when?, how?, why?, to what extent?*, or *under what conditions?* Adverbs derived from adjectives and nouns commonly end in the suffix -*ly*. *She will soon travel south and probably visit her very favorite sister.* See also *conjunction.* See 7b5, 12a and c.

adverb clause   See *clause.*

adverb forms   Changes in an adverb from the **positive degree** (*eagerly*) to the **comparative** (comparing two—*more eagerly*) or the **superlative** (comparing more than two—*most eagerly*). The forms of some adverbs and adjectives are identical (*fast, faster, fastest; little, less, least*). Most adverbs, however, add *more* or *less* in the comparative and *most* or *least* in the superlative (*quickly, more quickly, most quickly*).

agreement   The correspondence of a pronoun with its antecedent in person, number, and gender or of a verb with its subject in person and number. *Tina sings, and her fans go wild; the band members play, and the crowd goes wild.* See also *antecedent, gender, number, person.* See Chapters 10 and 11.

antecedent   The specific noun that a pronoun replaces and to which it refers. The two must agree in person, number, and gender. *Fred Astaire moved his feet as no one else has.* The antecedent can sometimes follow the pronoun that refers to it. *Moving his feet as no one else has, Fred Astaire was an amazing dancer.* See 7b3, 11a, 11b, and 11c.

appositive   A noun or noun phrase that identifies or adds identifying information to a preceding noun phrase. *Magic Johnson, the best player in the NBA, scored thirty-one points. The cruelest month, April, is my favorite.* See 7c3 and 30c3.

article   *A, an,* or *the,* the most common adjectives. *A* and *an* are **indefinite** and do not specifically identify the nouns they modify. *A strange feeling came over me as an awful specter arose. The* is **definite** or specific. *The awful figure of my long-lost grandfather stood before me.*

auxiliary verb   A verb that combines with the base form or with the present or past participle of a main verb to form a verb phrase and to determine tense. The **primary** auxiliaries are *do, have,* and *be. Did he arrive? We have eaten. She is writing.* **Modal** auxiliaries such as *can, may, shall, will, could, might, should, would,* and *ought* [*to*] have only one form and show possibility, necessity, obligation, ability, capability, and so on. See 7b1 and 9a.

cardinal number   A number that answers the question *how many?—seven, one hundred fifty.* See also *ordinal number.*

case   The form of a noun or pronoun that reflects its grammatical role in a sentence. Nouns and indefinite pronouns can be **subjective, possessive,** or **objective,** but they change form only in the possessive case. *The* <u>dog</u> (subjective) *barked.* *The* <u>dog's</u> (possessive) *tail wagged. The mail carrier called the* <u>dog</u> (objective). The personal pronouns *I, he, she, we,* and *they,* as well as the relative or interrogative pronoun *who,* change form in all three cases. <u>We</u> (subjective) *will take the train to Chicago.* <u>Our</u> (possessive) *trip will last a week. Dr. Baker will meet* <u>us</u> (objective) *at the station.* See also *person, pronoun.* See Chapter 8.

clause   A group of words containing a subject and a predicate. An **independent clause** can stand alone as a sentence. *The car hit the tree.* A **dependent clause,** as the name suggests, is grammatically subordinate to an independent clause, linked to it by a subordinating conjunction or a relative pronoun. The dependent clause can function as an adjective, an adverb, or a noun. *The car hit the tree* <u>that stood at the edge of the road</u> (**adjective clause**). *The car,* <u>when it went out of control,</u> *hit the tree* (**adverb clause**). *The car hit* <u>what grew at the side of the road</u> (**noun clause**). See also *nonrestrictive element, restrictive element.* See 7c4.

collective noun   See *noun.*

comma splice   An error resulting from joining two independent clauses with only a comma. See Chapter 15 for ways of revising comma splices.

common noun   See *noun.*

comparative degree   See *adjective forms, adverb forms.*

complement   A word or group of words completing the predicate in a sentence. A **subject complement** follows a linking verb and renames or describes the subject. It can be a **predicate noun** (*Anorexia is an* <u>illness</u>) or a **predicate adjective** (*Karen Carpenter was* <u>anorexic</u>). An **object complement** renames or describes a direct object (*We considered her a* <u>baby</u> *and her behavior* <u>infantile</u>). See 7c2.

complete predicate   See *predicate.*

complete subject   See *subject.*

complex sentence   See *sentence.*

compound adjective   A combination of words (of whatever parts of speech) that function as a single adjectival unit (<u>blue-green</u> *sea,* <u>ten-story</u> *building,* <u>get-tough</u> *policy,* <u>supply side</u> *economics,* <u>north by northwest</u> *journey*). Most, but not all, compound adjectives need hyphens to separate their individual elements.

compound-complex sentence   See *sentence.*

compound noun   A combination of words forming a unit that can function as a single noun (*go-getter, in-law, Johnny-on-the-spot, oil well, southeast*).

compound predicate   See *predicate.*

compound sentence   See *sentence.*

compound subject   See *subject.*

concrete noun   See *noun*.

conjunction   A word or words that join words, phrases, clauses, or sentences. **Coordinating conjunctions** (such as *and, but, or,* or *yet*) join elements that are grammatically comparable (*Marx and Engels wrote* [two nouns]; *Marx writing one essay, but Engels writing the other* [two phrases]; *Marx wrote one essay, yet Engels wrote the other* [two independent clauses]). **Correlative conjunctions** (such as *both, and; either, or;* or *not only, but also*) are used in pairs to connect elements that are grammatically equivalent (*neither Marx nor Engels; not only Marx, but also Engels*). A **subordinating conjunction** (such as *although, because, before, if, that, when, where,* or *why*) introduces a dependent clause, which it subordinates to an independent clause. *Marx wrote at the British Museum, where he did most of his work. Before his association with Marx, Engels was already a social theorist.* A **conjunctive adverb** (such as *consequently, moreover,* or *then*) modifies one independent clause following another independent clause. A conjunctive adverb generally follows a semicolon or colon and precedes a comma. *Thoreau lived simply at Walden; however, he regularly joined his aunt for tea in Concord.* See 7b7 and 15b.

coordinating conjunction   See *conjunction*.

coordination   The grammatical equality of two or more sentence elements. When elements are coordinate, they seem to express equally significant ideas. *She wanted both to stay and to go.* See also *subordination*. See 20a.

correlative conjunction   See *conjunction*.

count noun   See *noun*.

dangling modifier   A word, phrase, or clause that cannot logically modify the sentence element to which it is syntactically related. *Studying Freud, the meaning of my dreams became clear* (incorrect; the subject of the sentence must be capable of the action represented by the participle, but *the meaning* could not have been *studying Freud*). *Studying Freud, I began to understand the meaning of my dreams* (revised; *I* was doing the studying). As the incorrect example illustrates, dangling modifiers often occur in passive sentences.

declension   See *case, inflection, number, person*.

degree   See *adjective forms, adverb forms*.

demonstrative adjective   See *adjective*.

demonstrative pronoun   See *pronoun*.

denotation   The literal meaning of a term, as opposed to its **connotation** or associations. See 27b.

dependent clause   See *clause*.

descriptive adjective   See *adjective*.

determiner   See *article*.

direct address   A construction that uses a noun or pronoun naming whoever is spoken to. *Hey, Jack. You, get moving.*

direct discourse   Quotation that reproduces a speaker's exact words, marked with quotation marks. *Jesse Jackson has often said, "I was born in the ghetto, but the ghetto wasn't born in me."* See 34a and b.

direct object   A noun or pronoun receiving the action of a **transitive verb** in an **active** construction. *McKellan recited Shakespearean soliloquies.* See also *indirect object.* See 7c2.

double comparative   The incorrect use of a comparative to modify another comparative (*more better; less longer*). See also *adjective forms, adverb forms.* See 12d3.

double negative   The incorrect use of more than one negative word to communicate a single negative idea. *Nobody couldn't do nothing; I couldn't hardly do anything.*

double superlative   The incorrect use of a superlative to modify another superlative (*most unkindest cut; least profoundest thought*). See also *adjective forms, adverb forms.* See 12d3.

expletive   A construction that introduces a sentence with *there* or *it*, usually followed by a form of *be. There are four excellent candidates for this job. It was on this day in 1952 that she was born.*

finite verb   A verb that can join with a subject to form an independent clause without adding any auxiliary verb. *I breathe.* See 7c3, 9d–g.

fused sentence   An error in which two main clauses are run together without a coordinating conjunction or suitable punctuation. Also known as a **run-on sentence.** See Chapter 15.

future tense   See *tense.*

gender   The classification of a noun or pronoun—*god, he* (masculine); *goddess, she* (feminine); *godliness, it* (neuter)—according to its sex.

gerund   A verbal identical in form to the present participle but functioning as a **noun.** *Studying is a bore* (gerund subject). *I enjoy studying* (gerund object). See 7c3.

gerund phrase   See *phrase.*

helping verb   An auxiliary verb. See *auxiliary verb.*

imperative mood   The form of a verb expressing a command or urging an action. An imperative may or may not have a stated subject. *Leave. You be quiet. Let's go.*

inconsistent structure   The joining of two or more logically and grammatically incompatible elements in a single sentence.

indefinite adjective   See *adjective.*

indefinite pronoun   See *pronoun.*

independent clause   See *clause.*

indicative mood   The form of a verb expressing a fact, questioning a fact, or voicing an opinion or probability. *Washington crossed the Delaware on Christmas Eve. Did he defeat the Hessians?* See also *mood.*

indirect discourse   A paraphrased quotation that does not repeat another's words verbatim and hence is not enclosed in quotation marks. *Coolidge said that, if nominated, he would not run.*

indirect object   A noun or pronoun identifying to or for whom or what a transitive verb's action is performed. The indirect object almost always precedes the direct object; it is usually the personal recipient of verbs of giving, showing, telling, and the like. *I handed the dean my application and told him that I needed financial aid.* See also *direct object.* See 7c2.

indirect question   A sentence pattern in which a question is the basis of a subordinate clause. *Everyone wonders why young people continue to take up smoking.* (The question, phrased directly, is "Why do young people continue to take up smoking?")

infinitive   The base form of a verb (*go, run, hit*), preceded by *to* (*to go, to run, to hit*). The *to* form is a verbal that can serve as a noun, an adverb, or occasionally, an adjective. *To go would be unthinkable* (noun, subject). *I do not wish to go* (noun, object). *I shall go to beg, to borrow, or to steal* (adverbs). *I'd like my sandwich to go* (adjective). An infinitive can be active (*to hit*) or passive (*to be hit*). Further, an infinitive can be present (*to [be] hit*) or perfect (*to have [been] hit*). An infinitive may be modified or take objects or complements as an **infinitive phrase**. See *phrase.* See 7b1 and 7c3.

inflection   Changes in word forms to indicate person, number, gender, and case in pronouns; number, gender, and case in nouns; comparative and superlative forms in adjectives and adverbs; and person, tense, voice, and mood in verbs.

intensifier   A modifier that increases the emphasis of the word or words that it modifies. *I should very much like to go. I'm so happy.* Despite their name, intensifiers are stylistically weak; they are best avoided in formal writing.

intensive pronoun   See *pronoun.*

interjection   A grammatically independent word or group of words that is usually an exclamation of surprise, shock, dismay, or the like. *Help! We're losing control. My word, what do you think you're doing?*

interrogative adjective   See *adjective.*

interrogative pronoun   See *pronoun.*

intransitive verb   A verb that does not need a direct object to complete its meaning. *The children raced up the path.* See also *verb.* See 7c2.

irregular verb   A verb with a past tense and past participle that does not follow the usual *-ed* or *-d* pattern, but marks these forms in other ways. For example, *see, saw, seen; bring, brought, brought; go, went, gone.* See also *regular verb.* See 9b.

limiting adjective   See *adjective.*

linking verb   A linking verb joins a subject with a subject complement or complements. Common linking verbs are *appear, be, become, feel,* and *seem. The argument appeared sound. It was an exercise in logic.* See also *verb.* See 7c2.

main clause   An independent clause. See *clause.*

mass noun   See *noun.*

misplaced modifier   A word, phrase, or clause confusingly positioned so that it fails to apply clearly to the expression intended. *With a credit card, the traveler paid for the motel room and opened the door. The traveler paid for the motel room and opened the door with a credit card.* Unless the writer intended to indicate that the traveler broke into a room already paid for, *with a credit card* should follow *paid* or *room.* See 17a.

modal auxiliaries   See *auxiliary verb.*

modifier   A word, phrase, or clause that acts as an adjective or an adverb and qualifies the meaning of another word, phrase, or clause. See also *adjective, adverb, clause, phrase.*

mood   The form of a verb used to indicate whether an action or a state is a possible fact or to ask a question (*indicative*), to give a command (*imperative*), or to express a wish or describe a condition contrary to fact (*subjunctive*). In other words, mood reflects the writer's or speaker's attitude toward the idea expressed by the verb. *The sea is turbulent* (indicative). *Be still, ye seas* (imperative). *Would that the sea were calm* (subjunctive). See also *imperative mood, indicative mood, subjunctive mood.* See 9g.

nominal   A word, phrase, or clause that acts as a noun.

nonfinite verb   See *verbal.*

nonrestrictive element   A word, phrase, or clause that modifies but does not limit or change the essential meaning of a sentence element. A nonrestrictive element is set off from the rest of the sentence with commas, dashes, or parentheses. *Quantum physics, a difficult subject, is fascinating. He addressed, acerbically, the failure of the system.* See also *restrictive element.* See 30c.

noun   A noun names a person, place, tangible object, concept, quality, action, or the like. Nouns serve as subjects, objects, complements, and appositives. Most nouns form the plural with the addition of *-s* or *-es* and the possessive with the addition of *'s* (see *number, case*). **Common nouns** name one (*rock, child, box*) or more (*rocks, children, boxes*) in a class or general group. **Proper nouns** begin with capital letters and name specifics such as a particular person, place, religion, time period, holiday, movement, or thing (*Angelou, Caesar, Florida, Jefferson*

Memorial, Elizabethan Age, July, Rosicrucianism, Ramadan). Some proper nouns can form plurals (*Adamses, Caesars*). **Abstract nouns** name intangible qualities, concepts, actions, or states (*virtue, Virtue, peace, violence, evil, health, haste, time, inertia*). Some abstract nouns may be common or proper, depending on the sense that the writer wishes to communicate. Many abstract nouns have plural forms (*virtues, evils*), and as plurals they become increasingly *concrete*. **Concrete nouns** name people, places, or things and may be common or proper. In addition, **collective nouns** name coherent groups. In its singular form, a collective noun names a body or group of related elements; in its plural form, it names several such bodies or groups (*pride, prides* [of lions]; *family, families; Congress, Congresses*). **Count nouns** name people, places, and things that can be counted (*one woman, two women; one park, three parks; one tree, four trees; one Smith, five Smiths*). **Mass nouns** name concrete things that are not usually counted although their plural forms may occur (*sand, sands* [of Waikiki]; *rain,* [summer] *rains*). See 7b2.

noun clause   See *clause*.

noun phrase   See *phrase*.

number   The form of a noun, pronoun, demonstrative adjective, or verb that indicates whether it is singular or plural: *oak* is singular, *oaks* plural; *I* and *me* are singular, *we* and *us* plural; *he buys* is singular, *they buy* plural; *this book* is singular, *these books* plural. See 7b1–2, Chapter 10, and Chapter 11.

object   A word or words, acting as a noun or pronoun, influenced by a transitive verb, a verbal, or a preposition. See also *direct object, indirect object, object of a preposition*. See 7c2.

object complement   See *complement*.

objective case   See *case*.

object of a preposition   A noun or pronoun connected to a sentence by a preposition, thus completing a **prepositional phrase**. *Johnson went to Pembroke College at Oxford. Thank you for coming.* See 7b6 and 7c3.

ordinal number   The form of a number that expresses order or sequence (*first, seventeenth, twenty-third, two hundredth*). See also *cardinal number*.

participial adjective   See *adjective*.

participial phrase   See *phrase*.

participle   A verbal with properties of both an adjective and a verb. Like an adjective, a participle can modify a noun or pronoun; like a verb, it has present and past tenses and can take an object. The **present** participle usually ends in -*ing*, the **past** participle in -*ed*, -*d*, -*en*, or an irregular form. Without any auxiliary verbs, the present participle is active, the past participle passive. *Reeling, Spinks hit the canvas. The torn page was a clue.* See 7c3. With auxiliary verbs, present participles form the **progressive tenses** (*I am making, I was making, I will be* *making, I have been making, I had been making, I will have been making*). Past participles form the **perfect tenses** (*I have made, I had made, I will have made*). Further, past participles, with auxiliary verbs, are used to form the passive voice (*I am beaten, I was beaten*). These compound tenses are known as verb phrases. See also *adjective, phrase, tense, verbal, voice*.

parts of speech   The eight grammatical categories into which words can be grouped depending on how they function in a sentence. Many words act as different parts of speech in different sentences. The parts of speech are *adjectives, adverbs, conjunctions, interjections, nouns, prepositions, pronouns,* and *verbs*. See 7b.

passive voice   See *voice*.

past participle   See *participle*.

past perfect tense   See *tense*.

past tense   See *tense*.

perfect tenses   See *participle, tense, verb*.

person   The relation between a subject and its corresponding verb, indicating whether the subject is speaking about itself (first person *I* or *we*), being spoken to (second person *you*), or being spoken about (third person *he, she, it,* or *they*). *Be* has several forms depending on the person (*am, is,* and *are* in the present tense plus *was* and *were* in the past). Other verbs change form in the present tense indicative with a third-person singular subject (*I fall, you fall, she falls, we fall, they fall*). See 7b1, Chapter 9, and Chapter 10. **Personal pronouns** also change form as subjects, objects, and possessives. See 7b3.

personal pronoun   See *pronoun*.

phrase   A group of words that functions as a single unit but lacks a subject, a finite verb in a predicate, or both. Phrases can be grouped not only by the parts of speech that govern or introduce them but also by their grammatical functions as adjectives, adverbs, nouns, or verbs. An **absolute phrase** modifies an entire sentence and thus is grammatically divorced from the sentence. It uses a noun or pronoun as its subject and a participle (possibly implied) or participial phrase as its predicate. *The party being over, everyone left. The party over, everyone left* (participle implied). A **gerund phrase** serves as a noun, acting as a subject, a complement, or an object. It contains a gerund, the *-ing* form of a verb acting as a noun. *Exercising regularly and sensibly is a key to good health* (subject). *I dislike exercising regularly and sensibly* (direct object). *I am bored with exercising regularly and sensibly* (object of a preposition). An **infinitive phrase** may serve as an adjective, an adverb, or a noun and is governed by an infinitive. *The Pacific Coast is the place to be* (adjective). *She went to pay her taxes* (adverb). *To be young again is all I want* (noun). A **noun phrase**, including a noun and its modifiers, may serve as a subject, a complement, or an object. *A long, rough road* (subject) *crossed the barren desert* (object). *A raccoon is a resourceful animal* (complement). A **participial phase** is governed by a present or past participle and functions as an adjective. *Breaking his leg, he stumbled. Having broken his leg, he stumbled.* A **prepositional phrase** is introduced by a preposition and may act as an adjective, an adverb, or a noun. *The gas in the laboratory is leaking* (adjective). *The firefighters went to the lab to check* (adverb). *Out of season is the least crowded time* (noun). A **verb phrase** is composed of a main verb and one or more auxiliaries, acting as a single verb in the sentence predicate. *I should have come to the review session.* See 7c3.

positive degree   See *adjective forms, adverb forms.*

possessive adjective   See *adjective, case.*

possessive case   See *case.*

predicate   The actual or implied finite verb and related words in a sentence. The predicate expresses what the subject does, experiences, or is. A **simple predicate** is the verb or verb phrase related to the subject. *For years the YMHA has been a cultural center in New York City.* A **compound predicate** has more than one simple predicate. *The athletes swam, cycled, and ran in the triathlon competition.* A **complete predicate** includes the simple predicate and any associated modifiers and objects. *I gave Sarah an engagement ring.* See 7c2.

predicate adjective   See *complement.*

predicate noun   See *complement.*

prefix   An addition (often derived from a Latin preposition or negative) to the beginning of a root word to alter its meaning (*preview, undress*). See 26c1.

preposition   A part of speech that indicates the position of a noun or pronoun in space or time and links it to other sentence elements. *He was at the top of the ladder before the other contestants had climbed to the fourth rung.* See *phrase.* See 7b6.

present participle   See *participle.*

present perfect   See *participle, tense, verb, verbal.*

present progressive   See *participle, tense, verb, verbal.*

present tense   See *tense, verb.*

progressive tenses   See *participle, tense, verb.*

pronoun   A single-word noun substitute that refers to an actual or logical antecedent. **Demonstrative pronouns** (*this, that, these,* and *those*) point out particular nouns. *This is the article I read. Those are the books I bought.* **Indefinite pronouns** do not refer to specific nouns and include *any, each, everybody, everyone, some,* and similar words. *Never in the field of human conflict was so much owed by so many to so few.* Some indefinite pronouns have a possessive case. *Everyone's best interests will be served by a cure for AIDS.* **Intensive** (or **emphatic**) **pronouns** (*myself, yourself, himself, herself, oneself, itself, ourselves, yourselves, themselves*) emphasize their antecedent nouns or personal pronouns, agreeing with them in person, number, and gender. *She herself knew that we ourselves were blameless. The fire did not damage the house itself.* **Interrogative pronouns** (*who, which,* and *what*) ask questions. *Which would you like? What is going on?* **Personal pronouns** (*I, you, he, she, it, we, you,* and *they*) observe number, gender, and case as they refer to particular people or things. *He knew what was his and also what was best for him.* See also *case, gender, number.* **Reciprocal pronouns** (*each other, one another*) refer to the individuals included in a plural antecedent. *Holmes and Frazier fought each other. The candidates debated one another.* **Reflexive pronouns,** identical in form to intensive pronouns, refer back to the subject of the sentence or clause. *I washed myself* (direct object). *I gave myself a pat on the back* (indirect object). **Relative pronouns** (*who, whom, which, that, what, whoever, whomever, whichever,* and *whatever*) connect a dependent clause to a sentence. *I wonder who will win the prize.* See 7b3.

proper adjective   See *adjective.*

proper noun   See *noun.*

reciprocal pronoun   See *pronoun.*

reflexive pronoun   See *pronoun.*

regular verb   A verb with a past tense and past participle ending in *-d* or *-ed* (*care, cared, cared; look, looked, looked*). See also *irregular verb.* See 9b.

relative adjective   See *adjective.*

relative pronoun   See *pronoun.*

restrictive element   A word, phrase, or clause that limits the essential meaning of the sentence element it modifies or provides necessary identifying information about it. The restrictive element is not set off from the element that it modifies with commas, dashes, or parentheses. *The tree that I hit was an oak. The oak at the side of the road was a hazard.* See also *nonrestrictive element.* See 30c and 30i1.

run-on sentence   See *comma splice, fused sentence.*

sentence   A group of words containing a subject and a finite verb and expressing a complete thought. In writing, a sentence begins with a capital letter and ends with a period, a question mark, or an exclamation point. A sentence may be **declarative** and make a statement (*The sun rose*), **interrogative** and ask a question (*Did the sun rise?*), **exclamatory** and indicate surprise or other strong emotion (*How beautiful the dawn is!*), or **imperative** and express a command (*Get up earlier tomorrow*). Besides having these functions, sentences are classified grammatically. A **simple** sentence is a single independent clause without dependent clauses. *I left the house.* Its subject, predicate, or both may be compound. *Sears and Roebuck founded a mail-order house and a chain of stores.* A **compound** sentence contains two or more independent clauses linked with a coordinating conjunction, a correlative conjunction, or a semicolon. *I did not wish to go, but* *she did. I did not wish to go; she did.* A **complex** sentence contains an independent clause and one or more dependent clauses. *After he had cleaned up the kitchen, Tom fell asleep in front of the television.* A **compound-complex** sentence contains at least two independent clauses and one or more dependent clauses. *We had hoped to go climbing, but the trip was postponed because she sprained her ankle.* See also *clause.* See Chapter 7.

sentence fragment   A group of words that is not a grammatically complete sentence, usually because it lacks a subject or a finite verb. Often fragments are dependent clauses, introduced by a subordinating word but punctuated as sentences. In formal writing, fragments should be revised to be complete sentences. See Chapter 16 for ways of correcting sentence fragments.

simple predicate   See *predicate.*

simple sentence   See *sentence.*

simple subject   See *subject.*

simple tense   See *tense.*

split infinitive   The often awkward intrusion of an adverb between *to* and the base form of the verb in an infinitive construction (*to better serve* rather than *to serve better*). See 17b1.

squinting   A misplaced word, phrase, or clause that could refer equally, but with different meanings, to words preceding or following it. *Playing poker often is dangerous.* The position of *often* fails to indicate whether frequent poker playing is dangerous or whether poker playing is often dangerous. See 17a3.

subject   The noun, pronoun, and related words that indicate who or what a sentence is about. A **simple** subject is a single noun or pronoun. *Owls are nocturnal birds.* A **complete** subject is the simple subject and its modifiers. *The timid gray mouse fled from the owl.* (*Mouse* is the simple subject; *the timid gray mouse* the complete subject.) Further, a subject may be **compound**: *The mouse and the owl heard the fox.*

subject complement   See *complement.*

subjective case   See *case.*

subjunctive mood   The form of a verb used to express a wish, a request, or a condition that does not exist. The *contrary-to-fact subjunctive* using *were* is the most common. *If I were president, I would change things.* The dependent *that* clause expressing a command, demand, necessity, request, requirement, or suggestion is also common. *I asked that he come.* The subjunctive also survives in many time-honored expressions. *Be that as it may. Long live the Queen!* See 9h.

subordinate clause   A dependent clause. See *clause.*

subordinating conjunction   See *conjunction.*

subordination   The grammatical dependence of one sentence element on another. *Because that town's schools are excellent, its taxes are steep.* Although a subordinate clause is grammatically dependent on the independent clause it modifies, the information it contains may be very important to the text in which it occurs. See also *clause, coordination.* See 20b.

substantive   A word, phrase, or clause that serves as a noun.

suffix   An addition to the end of a word that alters the word's meaning or part of speech—as in *migrate* (verb) and *migration* (noun) or *late* (adjective or adverb) and *lateness* (noun). See 26c2.

superlative degree   See *adjective forms, adverb forms.*

syntax   The arrangement of words in a sentence in order to reveal the relation of each to the whole and each to the other.

tense   The verb forms that indicate the time at which an action takes place or a condition exists. The times expressed by tense are basically **present, past,** and **future.** Verbs have **simple** (*I love*), **perfect** (*I have loved*), **progressive** (*I am loving*), and **perfect progressive** (*I have been loving*) forms that show tense and, used in sequences, show the time relationships of actions and events. See 9d–g.

transitive verb   A verb that directs action toward a direct object and may express action done to or for an indirect object. A transitive verb may be in the active or passive voice. *The artist gave me the sketch.* See also *verb.* See 7c2.

verb   A word or group of words, essential to a sentence, that expresses what action the subject takes or receives, what the subject is, or what the subject's state of being is. Verbs change form to show tense, number, voice, and mood. A **transitive** verb takes an object or has passive forms. *Edison invented the incandescent bulb. The incandescent bulb was invented by Edison.* An **intransitive** verb does not take an object. *The bulb glowed.* **Linking** verbs join a subject and its complement. *Edison was pleased.* Depending upon its use in a sentence, a verb may sometimes belong to all three groups. *Evans grew oranges* (transitive). *The oranges grew well* (intransitive). *The oranges grew ripe* (linking). See also *auxiliary verb, irregular verb, mood, person, regular verb, tense, verbal, voice.* See 7b1 and Chapter 9.

verbal   A **gerund, participle,** or **infinitive** serving as a noun, an adjective, or an adverb. *Running is excellent exercise* (gerund/noun). *A running athlete is an exhilarating sight* (participle/adjective). *We went to the track to run* (infinitive/ adverb). See also *gerund, infinitive, participle.* See 7c3.

verbal phrase   A phrase using a gerund, a participle, or an infinitive. See *phrase.*

verb phrase   A main verb and its auxiliary verbs. A verb phrase can act only as a predicate in a sentence. *She should have won the first race.* See *phrase.*

voice   The form of a transitive verb that indicates whether the subject is acting or being acted on. When a verb is **active,** the subject is the doer or agent. *Parker* _played_ the saxophone fantastically. When a verb is **passive**, the subject and object of the active sentence are transposed. Then the grammatical subject receives the action of the verb, action taken by the object of a preposition. _The saxophone was played fantastically by Parker._ The passive voice is formed with the appropriate tense of the verb _be_ and the past participle of the transitive verb. See also _verb._ See 9g.

Glossary of Usage

This glossary provides usage guidelines for some commonly confused words and phrases. Conventions of usage might be called the "good manners" of discourse. Just as our notions of good manners vary from culture to culture and time to time, so do conventions of usage. The word *ain't*, for instance, now considered inappropriate in formal discourse, was once widely used by the most proper British speakers and is still used normally in some spoken American dialects. So matters of usage, like other choices you must make in writing, depend on what your purpose is and what is appropriate for a particular audience at a particular time. Matters of usage, especially those that are controversial or that seem to be changing, are treated in the body of this textbook. In addition, this glossary provides you, in brief form, with a guide to generally accepted usage in college writing and with a guide for distinguishing between words whose meanings are similar or that are easily confused. For fuller discussion of these matters, you may want to consult one of the usage guides listed in 25c.

a, an   Use *a* with a word that begins with a consonant (*a forest, a book*), with a sounded *h* (*a hemisphere*), or with consonant sound such as "y" or "w" (*a euphoric moment, a one-sided match*). Use *an* with a word that begins with a vowel (*an umbrella*), with a silent *h* (*an honor*), or with a vowel sound (*an X-ray*).

accept, except   The verb *accept* means "receive" or "agree to." *Melanie will accept the job offer.* Used as a preposition, *except* means "aside from" or "excluding." *All the plaintiffs except Mr. Sneath decided to accept the settlement offered by the defendant.*

advice, advise   The noun *advice* means an "opinion" or "suggestion"; the verb *advise* means "offer or provide advice." *Charlotte's mother advised her to become a secretary, but Charlotte, who intended to become a dancer, ignored the advice.*

affect, effect   As a verb, *affect* means "influence" or "move the emotions of"; as a noun used by psychologists, it means "emotions or feelings." *Effect* is a noun meaning "result" or, less commonly, a verb meaning "bring about." *A nuclear war would have far-reaching effects. Many people are deeply affected by this realization, and some join groups aimed at effecting arms reduction.*

aggravate   Colloquially, *aggravate* means "irritate" or "annoy," but this usage should be avoided in formal writing. The formal meaning of *aggravate* is "make worse." *Having another mouth to feed aggravated their poverty.*

all ready, already   *All ready* means "fully prepared." *Already* means "previously." *We were all ready for Lucy's party when we learned that she had already left.*

all right   *All right* is always two words, not one.

all together, altogether   *All together* means "all in a group" or "gathered in one place." *Altogether* means "completely," "in all," or "everything considered." *When the students were all together in the room, it was altogether filled.*

allude, elude   *Allude* means "refer indirectly." *Elude* means "avoid" or "escape from." *The candidate frequently alluded to his immigrant grandparents who had come here to elude political oppression.*

allusion, illusion   An *allusion* indirectly refers to something, as when a writer mentions or hints at a well-known event, person, story, quotation, or other information, assuming that the reader will recognize it (*a literary allusion*). An *illusion* is a false or misleading appearance (*an optical illusion*).

a lot   *A lot* is not one word but two. Do not use it in formal writing to express "a large amount" or "a large number."

already   See *all ready, already.*

alright   See *all right.*

altogether   See *all together, altogether.*

among, between   In referring to two things or people, use *between.* In referring to three or more things or people, use *among. The relationship between the twins is different from that among the other three children.*

amount, number   Use *amount* for quantities (mass nouns) that you cannot count (singular nouns such as water, light, or power). Use *number* for quantities that you can count (usually plural nouns such as objects or people). *A small number of volunteers cleared a large amount of brush within a few hours.*

an   See *a, an.*

and/or   *And/or* should be avoided except in business or legal writing, where it is a short way of saying that one or both of two items apply. In other formal writing, take time and space to write out *X, Y, or both* rather than *X and/or Y.* If you mean *and* or *or,* use just that word.

any body, anybody, any one, anyone   *Anybody* is an indefinite pronoun, as is *anyone. Although anyone could enjoy carving wood, not just anybody could make a sculpture like that. Any body is two words, an adjective modifying a noun. Any* *body of water has its own distinctive ecology. Any one* is two adjectives or a pronoun modified by an adjective. *Customers were allowed to buy only two sale items at any one time.*

anyplace, anywhere   In formal writing, use *anywhere,* not *anyplace. She walked for an hour, not going anywhere in particular.*

anyway, anyways   Use *anyway,* not *anyways,* in writing.

anywhere   See *anyplace, anywhere.*

apt, liable, likely   *Likely to* means "probably will," and *apt to* means "inclines or tends to," but either word will do in many instances. *During an argument, he is apt to yell while she is likely to slam doors. Liable to* is often used in a more negative sense. *He is liable to get angry if he strikes out. Liable* is also a legal term meaning "obligated" or "responsible for." *The dog's owners are liable for any damage that he causes.*

as   Avoid using *as* for *because* or *when* in sentences where its meaning is not clear. For example, does *Carl left town as his father was arriving* mean *at the same time as his father was arriving* or *because his father was arriving?*

as, as if, like   These expressions are used when making comparative statements. Use *as* when comparing two qualities that people or objects possess. *The box is as wide as it is long.* Also use *as* to identify equivalent terms in a description. *Gary served as moderator at the town meeting.* Use *like* to indicate similarity but not equivalency: *Hugo, like Jane, was a detailed observer.* In such instances, *like* acts as a preposition, followed by a noun or noun phrase, while *as* may act either as a preposition or as a conjunction introducing a clause. *The dog howled like a wolf, just as if* (not *like*) *she were a wild animal.*

assure, ensure, insure   *Assure* means "convince" or "promise," and its direct object is usually a person or persons. *The candidate assured the voters he would not raise taxes. Ensure* and *insure* both mean "make certain," but *insure* is usually used in the specialized sense of protection against financial loss. *When the city began water rationing to ensure that the supply would last, the Browns found that they could no longer afford to insure their car wash business.*

as to   *As to* should not be used as a substitute for *about. Phoebe was unsure about* (not *as to*) *Bruce's intentions.*

at, where   See *where.*

awful, awfully   The formal meanings of *awful* and *awfully* are "awe-inspiring" and "in an awe-inspiring way" respectively. Colloquial speech often dilutes *awful* to mean "bad" (*I had an awful day*) and *awfully* to mean "very" (*It was awfully cold*). In formal writing, avoid these casual usages.

awhile, a while   The adverb *awhile* can be used to modify a verb. *A while,* however, is an article and a noun and can be the object of a preposition such as *for, in,* or *after. We drove awhile and then stopped for a while.*

bad, badly   *Bad* is an adjective, used to modify a subject or an object or to follow a linking verb such as *be, feel,* or *seem. Badly* is an adverb, used to modify a verb. *The hostess felt bad because the dinner was so badly prepared.*

because of, due to   Both phrases are used to describe the relationship between a cause and an effect. Use *due to* when the effect (a noun) is stated first and followed by the verb *be. His illness was due to malnutrition. (Illness,* a noun, is the effect.) Use *because of,* not *due to,* when the effect is a clause, not a noun. *He was sick because of malnutrition. (He was sick,* a clause, is the effect.)

being as, being that   These expressions are used colloquially as substitutes for *because;* avoid them in formal writing. *Because* (not *being as) Romeo killed Tybalt, he was banished to Padua.*

beside, besides   *Beside,* a preposition, means "next to." *Besides* is either a preposition meaning "other than" or "in addition to" or an adverb meaning "moreover." *No one besides Francesca knows whether the tree is still growing beside the house.*

between   See *among, between.*

breath, breathe   *Breath* is the noun, and *breathe* is the verb. *"Breathe,"* said the dentist, so June took a large *breath* of laughing gas.

bring, take   *Bring* is comparable to *come; take* is comparable to *go.* Use *bring* when an object is moved from a farther place to a nearer one; use *take* when the opposite is true. *Please take my prescription to the pharmacist, and bring my medicine back to me.*

but, yet   Use these words separately, not together. *He is strong-minded but* (not *but yet) gentle.*

but that, but what   Avoid using these as substitutes for *that* in expressions of doubt. *Hercule Poirot never doubted that* (not *but that) he would solve the case.*

can, may   *Can* refers to ability and *may* to possibility or permission to do something. *Since I can ski the slalom well, I may win the race. May* (not *can) I leave early to practice?*

can't, couldn't   These are the contractions for *cannot* and *could not.* Avoid them, like other contractions, in formal writing. *If I couldn't complete it during the break, I certainly can't now.*

can't hardly, can't scarcely   Both *hardly* and *scarcely* are negatives; therefore, the expressions *can't hardly* and *can't scarcely* are redundant double negatives. *Tim is claustrophobic and can* (not *can't) hardly breathe in elevators.*

can't help but   This expression is wordy and redundant. Use the more formal *I cannot but go* or the less formal *I can't help going* instead of *I can't help but go.*

can't scarcely   See *can't hardly, can't scarcely.*

censor, censure   *Censor* means to remove material that is considered offensive for political, moral, personal, or other reasons. *Censure* means "formally reprimand." *The public censured the newspaper for censoring negative letters to the editor.*

center around This idiom rarely if ever appears in formal writing. Use *center on* instead. *Their research centers on the disease-resistant hybrid varieties.*

compare to, compare with *Compare to* means "describe one thing as similar to another." *Hillary compared the noise to the roar of a waterfall. Compare with* is the more general activity of noting similarities and differences between objects or people. *The detective compared the latest photograph with the old one, noting how the man's appearance had changed.*

complement, compliment *Complement* means "go well with" or "enhance." *Compliment* means "praise." *Several guests complimented Julie on her marmalade, which complemented the warm, buttered scones.*

comprise, compose *Comprise* means "contain" (the whole *comprises* the parts). *Compose* means "make up" (the parts *compose* the whole). *The class comprises twenty students. Twenty students compose the class.*

conscience, conscious *Conscience,* a noun, means "a sense of right and wrong." *Conscious,* an adjective, means "awake" or "aware." *After the angry argument, Lisa was conscious of her troubled conscience.*

consensus of opinion Use *consensus* instead of this redundant phrase. *The family consensus was to sell the old house.*

consequently, subsequently *Consequently* means "as a result" or "therefore." *Subsequently* just means "afterwards." *Roger lost his job, and subsequently I lost mine. Consequently, I was unable to pay my rent.*

continual, continuous *Continual* describes an activity that is repeated at regular or frequent intervals. *Continuous* describes either an activity that is ongoing without interruption or an object that is connected without break. *The damage done by continuous erosion was increased by the continual storms.*

couple of *Couple of* is used informally to mean either "two" or "a few." Avoid it in formal writing, and say specifically what you mean.

could of See *have, of.*

criteria, criterion *Criterion* means "a standard of judgment" or "a necessary qualification." *Criteria* is the plural form. *Many people believe that public image is the wrong criterion for choosing the next president of the United States.*

data *Data* is the plural form of the Latin word *datum,* meaning "a fact" or "a result collected during research." Although *data* is used colloquially as either singular or plural, in formal writing it should be treated as plural. *These data indicate that fewer people smoke today than ten years ago.*

different from, different than *Different from* is generally preferred in formal writing although both phrases are used widely. *Her lab results were no different from his.*

differ from, differ with *Differ from* means "be unlike" in identity, appearance, or actions. *Differ with* means "disagree with" in opinion or belief. *Mr. Binns* *differs with* Ms. White *over the importance of class discussion. Therefore, the way Mr. Binns conducts his class* differs from *the way she conducts hers.*

discreet, discrete   *Discreet* means "tactful" or "prudent." *Discrete* means "distinct" or "separate." *The dean's* discreet *encouragement brought representatives of all the* discrete *factions to the meeting.*

disinterested, uninterested   *Disinterested* means "unbiased" or "impartial." *It was difficult to find* disinterested *people for the jury. Uninterested means "not interested" or "indifferent." Cecile was* uninterested *in the outcome of the trial.*

distinct, distinctive   *Distinct* means "separate" or "well defined." *The experiment involved separating the liquid into its five* distinct *elements. Distinctive means "distinguishing from others" or "characteristic." Even from a distance, everyone recognized Greg's* distinctive *way of walking.*

doesn't, don't   *Doesn't* is the contraction for *does not* and should be used with *he, she, it,* and singular nouns. *Don't* is the contraction for *do not* and should be used with *I, you, we, they,* and plural nouns. In formal writing, however, avoid these and other contractions.

due to   See *because of, due to.*

each other, one another   *Each other* is preferred in sentences involving two subjects, and *one another* in those involving more than two subjects.

effect   See *affect, effect.*

elicit, illicit   The verb *elicit* means "to draw out" or "evoke." The adjective *illicit* means "illegal." *The police tried to* elicit *from the criminal the names of others involved in his* illicit *activities.*

elude   See *allude, elude.*

emigrate from, immigrate to, migrate   *Emigrate from* means "move away from one's country." *Immigrate to* means "move to a foreign country and settle there." *My family* emigrated from *Norway in 1957. We* immigrated to *the United States. Emigration and immigration are generally permanent actions; migration suggests movement that is temporary or seasonal and either to or from a place. Every winter, whales off the Pacific coast* migrate *south from Alaska toward warmer water.*

ensure   See *assure, ensure, insure.*

enthused, enthusiastic   *Enthused* is used colloquially to mean "enthusiastic about." Avoid it in formal writing. *The students remained* enthusiastic *despite the rain and the mud that threatened to flood the excavation.*

equally as good   Replace this redundant phrase with either *equally good* or *as good as.* *The two tennis players were* equally good, *each* as good as *the other.*

especially, specially   *Especially* means "very" or "particularly." *Specially* means "for a special reason or purpose." *The audience* especially *enjoyed the new composition,* specially *written for the holiday.*

every day, everyday   *Everyday* is an adjective used to describe something as ordinary or common. *Every day* is an adjective modifying a noun, specifying which particular day. *I ride the subway every day even though pushing and shoving are everyday occurrences.*

every one, everyone   *Everyone* is an indefinite pronoun. *Every one* is a noun modified by an adjective, referring to each member of a group. *Because he began the assignment after everyone else, David knew that he could not finish every one of the selections.*

except   See *accept, except.*

explicit, implicit   *Explicit* means "directly or openly expressed." *Implicit* means "indirectly expressed or implied." *The explicit message of the ad urged consumers to buy the product while the implicit message promised popularity.*

farther, further   *Farther* refers to physical distance. *How much farther is it to Munich? Further refers to time or degree. I want to avoid further delays and further misunderstandings.*

fewer, less   Use *fewer* with objects or people that can be counted (plural nouns). Use *less* with amounts that cannot be counted (countable mass nouns). *The world would be safer with fewer bombs and less hostility.*

finalize   *Finalize* is a pretentious way of saying "end" or "make final." *We closed* (not *finalized*) *the deal.*

firstly, secondly, thirdly   These are common in British English; more common in American English are *first, second,* and *third.*

flaunt, flout   *Flaunt* means "show off." *Flout* means "mock" or "scorn." *The teens flouted convention by flaunting their multicolored wigs.*

former, latter   *Former* refers to the first and *latter* to the second of two things previously introduced. *Anna and Kim are both excellent athletes; the former plays tennis, and the latter has won several marathons.* See also *later, latter.*

further   See *farther, further.*

good, well   *Good* is an adjective and should not be used as a substitute for the adverb *well. Gabriel is a good host who cooks quite well.*

good and   *Good and* is colloquial for "very"; avoid it in formal writing. *After Peter lost his sister's camera, he was very* (not *good and*) *sorry.*

half a, a half, a half a   Both *half a* and *a half* are standard. *A half a* is wordy. *She ate half a* (or *a half* but not *a half a*) *sandwich.*

hanged, hung   Of these two past forms of the verb *hang,* only *hanged* refers to executions while *hung* is used for all other meanings. *The old woman hung her head as she passed the tree where the murderer was hanged.*

hardly   See *can't hardly, can't scarcely.*

have, of   *Have*, not *of*, should follow *could, would, should,* or *might. We should have* (not *of*) *invited them.*

herself, himself, myself, yourself   Do not use these reflexive pronouns as subjects or as objects unless they are necessary. Compare *John cut him* with *John cut himself. Jane and I* (not *myself*) *agree. They invited John and me* (not *myself*).

he/she, his/her   *He/she* and *his/her* are ungainly ways to avoid sexism in writing. Other solutions are to write out *he or she* or to alternate using *he* and *she*. Perhaps the best solutions are to eliminate the pronouns entirely or to make the subject plural (*they*), thereby avoiding all reference to gender. For instance, *Everyone should carry his/her driver's license* could be revised to *Drivers should carry driver's licenses at all times* or *People should carry their driver's licenses.*

himself   See *herself, himself, myself, yourself.*

his/her   See *he/she, his/her.*

hisself   Replace *hisself* with *himself* in formal writing.

hopefully   *Hopefully* is widely misused to mean "it is hoped," but its correct meaning is "with hope." *Sam watched the roulette wheel hopefully,* not *Hopefully, Sam will win.*

hung   See *hanged, hung.*

if, whether   Use *whether* or *whether or not* to express an alternative. *She was considering whether or not to buy the new software.* Reserve *if* for the subjunctive case. *If it rains tomorrow, our Tai Chi class will meet in the gym.*

illicit   See *elicit, illicit.*

illusion   See *allusion, illusion.*

immigrate to   See *emigrate from, immigrate to, migrate.*

impact   As a noun, *impact* means "a forceful collision." As a verb, it means "pack together." *Because they were impacted, Jason's wisdom teeth needed to be removed.* Avoid the colloquial use of *impact* or *impact on* as a weak and vague verb meaning "affect." *Population control may reduce* (not *impact*) *world hunger.*

implicit   See *explicit, implicit.*

imply, infer   To *imply* is to suggest. To *infer* is to make an educated guess. Speakers and writers *imply*; listeners and readers *infer. Beth and Peter's letter implied that they were planning a very small wedding; we inferred that we would not be invited.*

incident, instance   *Incident* refers to a specific occurrence. It should not be confused with *instance,* which is an overused, though correct, word for "example" or "case." *The violent incident was just one instance of John's fiery temper.*

incredible, incredulous   *Incredible* means "unbelievable." *Incredulous* means "not believing." *When townspeople attributed the incredible events in their town to the presence of a UFO, Marina was incredulous.*

infer   See *imply, infer.*

inside, inside of, outside, outside of   Drop *of* after the prepositions *inside* and *outside. The class regularly met* outside (not *outside of) the building.*

instance   See *incident, instance.*

insure   See *assure, ensure, insure.*

interact with, interface with   *Interact with* is a vague phrase meaning "doing something that somehow involves another person." *Interface with* is computer jargon for "discuss" or "communicate." Avoid these colloquial expressions in formal writing.

irregardless, regardless   *Regardless* is the correct word because *irregardless* is a double negative.

is when, is where   These vague and faulty shortcuts should be avoided in definitions. *Schizophrenia is a psychotic condition* in which (not *when* or *where*) *a person withdraws from reality.*

its, it's   *Its* is a possessive adjective, even though it, like *his* and *her*, does not have an apostrophe. *It's* is a contraction for *it is;* avoid *it's* and other contractions in formal writing. *It's* (more formally, *It is*) *important to begin each observation just before the rat has* its *meal.*

kind, sort, type   As singular nouns, *kind, sort,* and *type* should be modified by *this* and followed by singular nouns. The plural forms, *kinds, sorts,* and *types,* should be modified by *these* and followed by plural nouns. Write *this kind of dress* or *these kinds of dresses,* not *these kind of dress.* Use such phrases to classify or categorize, but leave them out otherwise.

kind of, sort of   Avoid using these colloquial expressions as substitutes for "rather" or "somewhat." *Laura was somewhat* (not *kind of) tired after painting for several hours in the studio.*

later, latter   *Later* means "more late" or "after some time." *Latter* refers to the last of two items mentioned and can be used to avoid repeating a subject twice. *Jackson and Chad won all their early matches, but the* latter *was injured* later *in the season.* See also *former, latter.*

latter   See *former, latter* and *later, latter.*

lay, lie   *Lay* means "place" or "put." Its forms are *lay, laid, laying, laid,* and *laid.* It generally has a direct object, specifying what has been placed. *She* laid *her books on the desk. Lie* means "recline" or "be positioned," and does not take a direct object. Its forms are *lie, lay, lain, lying. She* lay *awake until two, worrying about the exam.*

leave, let   *Leave* means "go away" or "depart." *Let* means "allow." The expressions *leave alone* and *let alone,* however, are generally considered interchangeable. *Let me* leave *now, and* leave (or *let) me* alone *from now on!*

lend, loan   In formal writing, use *loan* as a noun and *lend* as a verb. *Please lend me your pen so that I may fill out this application for a loan.*

less   See *fewer, less.*

let   See *leave, let.*

liable   See *apt, liable, likely.*

lie   See *lay, lie.*

like   See *as, as if, like.*

like, such as   Both *like* and *such as* may be used in a statement giving an example or a series of examples. *Like* means "similar to"; use *like* when comparing the subject mentioned to the examples. *A hurricane, like a flood or any other major disaster, may strain a region's emergency resources.* Use *such as* when the examples represent a general category of things or people. *Such as* is often an alternative to *for example. A destructive hurricane, such as Gilbert in 1988, may drastically alter an area's economy.*

likely   See *apt, liable, likely.*

literally   *Literally* means "actually" or "exactly as it is written" and may be used to stress the truth of a statement that might otherwise be understood as figurative. *Literally* should not be used as an intensifier in a figurative statement. *Sarah was literally at the edge of her seat* may be accurate, but *Sarah is so hungry that she could literally eat a horse* is probably not.

loan   See *lend, loan.*

loose, lose   *Lose* is a verb meaning "misplace." *Loose*, as an adjective, means "not securely attached." *Sew on that loose button before you lose it.*

lots, lots of   These informal expressions, meaning "much" or "many," should be avoided in formal writing.

man, mankind   In the past, *man* and *mankind* were used to represent all human beings, but many people now consider these terms sexist because they do not mention women. Replace such words with *people, humans, humankind, men and women,* or similar all-encompassing phrases. Replace occupational terms ending with *-man* with gender-free phrasing such as *fire fighter* for *fireman, letter carrier* for *mailman,* and *minister, clergy,* or *cleric* for *clergyman.*

may   See *can, may.*

may be, maybe   *May be* is a verb phrase. *Maybe,* the adverb, means "perhaps." *He may be the president today, but maybe he will lose the next election.*

media   *Media,* the plural form of *medium,* takes a plural verb. *The media are* (not *is*) *going to cover the council meeting.*

might of   See *have, of.*

migrate   See *emigrate from, immigrate to, migrate.*

moral, morale   A *moral* is a succinct lesson. *The unstated moral of the story is that generosity eventually is rewarded. Morale* is the spirit or mood of an individual or a group of people. *Office morale was low.*

Ms.   A term invented in the 1960s to give women a title comparable to *Mr.* for men. Formerly, a woman was called either *Miss* or *Mrs.*, each term defining her in terms of her marital status, which is a private matter. Use *Ms.* unless the woman specifies another title. *Ms.* should appear before a woman's name, not before her husband's name: *Ms. Jane Tate* or *Ms. Tate,* not *Ms. John Tate.*

myself   See *herself, himself, myself, yourself.*

nor, or   Use *either* with *or* and *neither* with *nor. Cindy hopes to study abroad either next year or the year after. Neither her mother nor her father is very encouraging.*

number   See *amount, number.*

of   See *have.*

off of   Use *off* rather than *off of. The spaghetti slipped off* (not *off of*) *the plate.*

OK, O.K., okay   All are acceptable spellings, but do not use the term in formal writing. Replace it with more exact language. *The performance was unpolished but enthusiastic* (not *OK*).

on, upon   *Upon* is an overly formal substitute for *on. My grade will depend on* (not *upon*) *how well I do on my final examination.*

on account of   Use this substitute for *because of* sparingly or not at all. See also *because of, due to.*

one another   See *each other, one another.*

or   See *nor, or.*

outside, outside of   See *inside, inside of, outside, outside of.*

owing to the fact that   Avoid this and other unnecessarily wordy expressions for *because.*

per   Use the Latin *per* only in standard technical phrases such as *miles per hour.* Otherwise, find English equivalents. *As mentioned in* (not *as per*) *the latest report, our town's average food expenses every week* (not *per week*) *are $40 per capita.*

percent, percentage   These words identify a number as a fraction of one hundred. Because they show exact statistics, these terms should not be used casually to mean "portion," "amount," or "number." *Last year, 80 percent of the club's members were female.* Use *percent* after a figure. In formal writing, spell out *percent* rather than using its symbol (%). *Percentage* is not used with a specific number. *A large percentage of sales representatives are single.*

plenty   *Plenty* means "enough" or "a great abundance." *Many immigrants consider America a land of plenty.* In formal writing, avoid its colloquial usage, meaning "very." *He was very* (not *plenty*) *tired.*

plus   *Plus,* a preposition meaning "in addition to," often is used in the context of money. *My inheritance is enough to cover my debts plus yours.* Avoid using *plus* as a transitional adverb meaning "besides," "moreover," or "in addition." *That dress does not fit me. Besides* (not *plus*), *it is the wrong color.*

precede, proceed   Both verbs, *precede* means "come before," and *proceed* means "continue" or "go forward," as in the related word *procession. Despite the storm that preceded the hallway flooding, we proceeded to class.*

pretty   Avoid using *pretty* in formal writing as a substitute for *rather, somewhat,* or *quite. Bill was quite* (not *pretty*) *disagreeable.*

principal, principle   These words are unrelated but are often confused because of their similar spellings. *Principal,* as a noun, refers to a head official or an amount of money loaned or invested. When used as an adjective, it means "most significant." The word meaning "a fundamental law, belief, or standard" is *principle. When Albert was sent to the principal, he defended himself with the principle of free speech.*

proceed   See *precede, proceed.*

quotation, quote   *Quote* is a verb, and *quotation* is a noun. In colloquial usage, *quote* is sometimes used as a short form of *quotation.* In formal writing, however, use *quotation* as the noun form. *He quoted the president, and the quotation was preserved in history books.*

raise, rise   *Raise* means "lift" or "move upward." In the case of children, it means "bring up" or "rear." As a transitive verb, it takes a direct object—someone raises something. *The guests raised their glasses in good cheer. Rise* means "go upward." It is not followed by a direct object; something rises by itself. *She saw the steam rise from the pan just as the soup bubbled into a boil.*

rarely ever   In formal writing, use *rarely* by itself, or use *hardly ever. When we were poor, we rarely went to the movies.*

real, really   The adjective *real* means "true" or "not artificial." The adverb *really,* in informal usage, means "very" or "extremely." Do not substitute *real* for *really. The old man walked really* (not *real*) *slowly.* In formal writing, avoid using *really* altogether. *The old man walked very* (not *really*) *slowly.*

reason is because   This expression mixes *the reason is that* and *because.* Use one or the other but not both together. In general, use the less wordy *because* unless you want to give a statement the air of an explanation. *The reason the copier stopped is that* (not *is because*) *the paper jammed.*

regardless   See *irregardless, regardless.*

relate to   Avoid this vague colloquial expression in formal writing. *Relate to* loosely means "understand" or "appreciate." Write *I like the Rolling Stones* and explain why rather than writing *I can relate to the Rolling Stones.*

respectfully, respectively *Respectfully* means "with respect." *Respectively* means "in the order given." *The brothers, respectively a juggler and an acrobat, respectfully greeted the audience.*

rise See *raise, rise.*

scarcely See *can't hardly, can't scarcely.*

secondly See *firstly, secondly, thirdly.*

set, sit *Set* means "put" or "place," and it is followed by a direct object—the thing that is placed. *Sit* does not take a direct object and refers to the action of taking a seat. *Amelia sat in the armchair and set her teacup on the table next to her.*

sexist language See *man/mankind; he/she, his/her.*

shall, will Today *shall* is used much more in British English than in American English. Use *shall* for polite questions in the first person (*"Shall we buy it?" "Shall I call a taxi?"*). Use *will* in all other cases involving the future tense.

should of See *have, of.*

since *Since* has two meanings. The first meaning shows the passage of time (*I have not eaten since Tuesday*); the second and more informal meaning is "because" (*Since you are in a bad mood, I will go away*). Be careful not to write sentences in which *since* is ambiguous in meaning. *Since I broke my leg, I have been doing nothing but sleeping.* (*Since* here could mean either "because" or "ever since." In order to avoid such problems some writers prefer not to use *since* to mean "because.")

sit See *set, sit.*

so, so that In formal writing, avoid using *so* by itself as an intensifier, meaning "very." Instead, follow *so* with *that* to show how the intensified condition leads to a result. *Aaron was so tired that he fell asleep at the wheel of his car.*

some body, somebody, some one, someone *Somebody* is an indefinite pronoun, as is *someone*. *When somebody comes walking down the hall, I always hope that it is someone I know. Some body* is two words, an adjective modifying a noun, while *some one* is two adjectives or a pronoun modified by an adjective. *In dealing with some body like the senate, arrange to meet consistently some one person who can represent the group.*

someplace, somewhere *Someplace* is informal for *somewhere;* use the latter in formal writing.

some time, sometime, sometimes *Some time* means "a length of time." *Please leave me some time to use the computer. Sometime* means "at some indefinite later time." *Sometime I will take you to the Orkney Islands. Sometimes* means "occasionally." *Sometimes I see him on my way to class.*

somewhere See *someplace, somewhere.*

sort See *kind, sort, type.*

sort of See *kind of, sort of.*

so that See *so, so that.*

specially See *especially, specially.*

stationary, stationery *Stationary* is an adjective meaning "standing still." *Stationery* is a noun meaning "writing paper or materials." *When the bus was <u>stationary</u> at the light, Karen took out her <u>stationery</u> and wrote a quick note to a friend.*

subsequently See *consequently, subsequently.*

such as See *like, such as.*

supposed to, used to Both of these expressions require the final *-d* indicating the past participle. *He is <u>supposed to</u> bring his calculator to class.*

sure, surely Avoid using *sure* as an intensifier in formal writing. Replace this colloquial expression with "certainly" or "without a doubt," or use the adverb *surely,* which means "it must be so." *Surely* is often used to express a hoped-for situation. *<u>Surely,</u> John will go to a doctor.* It is also used persuasively. *We cannot go on a picnic. <u>Surely,</u> it will rain.*

take See *bring, take.*

than, then Use the conjunction *than* in comparative statements. *The cat was bigger <u>than</u> the dog.* Use the adverb *then* when referring to a sequence of events or emotions. *Jim finished college, and <u>then</u> he joined the Peace Corps.*

that, which *That,* always followed by a restrictive clause, singles out or identifies the object being described. *The trip <u>that</u> you took to Japan was expensive.* ("That you took to Japan" singles out the specific trip.) *Which* may be followed by either a restrictive or a nonrestrictive clause but often is used only with the latter. The *which*-clause may simply add more information about a noun or noun clause, and it is set off by commas. *The book, <u>which</u> is on the table, is a good one.* (This *which*-clause simply adds extra, nonessential information about the book—its location. In contrast, *The book <u>that</u> is on the table is a good one* specifies or singles out the book on the table as opposed to the book on the chair or the book in some other particular place.)

their, there, they're *Their* is a pronoun, the possessive form of *they. The gardeners held onto <u>their</u> hats as the helicopter flew over. There* refers to a place. *<u>There,</u> birds sing even at night. There* also is used with the verb *be* in expletive constructions (*there is, there are*). *<u>There is</u> only a short line at the cafeteria right now. They're* is a contraction of *they* and *are* and, like all contractions, it should be avoided in formal writing. *<u>They're</u>* (more formally, *<u>they are</u>*) *living in Japan.*

theirselves, themselves Use *themselves* rather than *theirselves.*

then See *than, then.*

thirdly See *firstly, secondly, thirdly.*

'til, till, until   *Till* and *until* are both acceptable in formal writing, but some writers prefer the full word *until*. The older form *'til*, like all contractions, should be avoided in formal writing.

to, too, two   *To* is a preposition, generally showing direction or nearness. *Stan flew to Cleveland.* Avoid using *to* after *where*. *Where are you flying* (not *flying to*)? *Too* means "also." *I am flying there too. Two* is the number. *We, too, are going to the meeting in two hours.*

to, where   See *where*.

toward, towards   *Toward* is generally preferred, but either word is acceptable.

try and, try to   *Try and* is colloquial for *try to*; use *try to* in formal writing. *Try to have an expressive face.*

two   See *to, too, two*.

type   See *kind, sort, type*.

uninterested   See *disinterested, uninterested*.

unique   *Unique* means "the one and only." It describes an absolute state and therefore should not be used with adjectives that suggest degree, such as *very* or *most*. *Malcolm's hands are unique* (not *very unique*).

until   See *'til, till, until*.

upon   See *on, upon*.

used to   See *supposed to, used to*.

very   Avoid using *very* to intensify a weak adjective or adverb; instead, replace both words with one stronger, more precise, or more colorful word. Instead of *very nice*, for example, use *kind, warm, sensitive, endearing,* or *friendly*, depending on your precise meaning. Replace *very interesting* with a word such as *curious, fascinating, insightful, lively, provocative,* or *absorbing*.

way, ways   When referring to distances, use *way*, not *ways*. *The Trivia Bowl championships were a long way* (not *ways*) *off.*

well   See *good, well*.

when, where   See *is when, is where*.

where   Use *where* alone, not with prepositions such as *at* or *to*. *Where are you going?* (not *Where are you going to?*) *Where do you shop?* (not *Where do you shop at?*)

whether   See *if, whether*.

which   See *that, which*.

which, who   When referring to ideas or things, use *which* (or *that*). When referring to people, use *who*, not *which*. *My aunt, who was irritated, pushed on the door, which was still stuck.*

who, whom   In relative clauses, use *who* if the following clause begins with a verb. *Monica, who smokes incessantly, is my godmother.* (*Who* is followed by the verb *smokes.*) *Monica, who is my godmother, smokes incessantly.* (*Who* is followed by the verb *is.*) Use *whom* if the following clause begins with a noun or pronoun. *I have heard that Monica, whom I have not seen for ten years, wears only purple.* (*Whom* is followed by the pronoun *I.*) An exception occurs when a verbal phrase such as *I think* comes between *who* and the following clause. Ignore such a phrase as you decide which form to use. *Monica, who [I think] wears nothing but purple, is my godmother.* (Ignore *I think; who* is followed by the verb *wears.*)

who's, whose   *Who's* is the contraction of *who* and *is.* Avoid *who's* and other contractions in formal writing. *Who's* (more formally, *Who is*) *in the garden? Whose* is a possessive form; it may be followed by the noun it modifies. *Whose sculpture is in the garden? Whose is on the patio?*

will   See *shall, will.*

would of   See *have, of.*

yet   See *but, yet.*

your, you're   *Your* shows possession. *Bring your sleeping bags along. You're* is the contraction of *you* and *are.* Avoid it and all other contractions in formal writing. *You're* (more formally, *You are*) *in the wrong room.*

yourself   See *herself, himself, myself, yourself.*

Selected Answers
to Exercises

To help you check your progress as you work, here are answers to some exercises in Chapters 7–58. Specifically, you will find answers to even-numbered items of those exercises with predictable answers. Exercises with many possible answers—those asking you to imitate a sentence or to revise a paragraph, for example, are not answered here. You will also find here all the answers to the tutorial on using the *St. Martin's Handbook,* found on p. xviii in the Note to Students.

ANSWERS TO THE TUTORIAL ON USING THE ST. MARTIN'S HANDBOOK

1. Chapter 4.

2. Chapter 9, on using verbs, includes quick-reference guidelines on editing -*s* and -*es* verb endings. Chapter 10 covers subject-verb agreement.

3. Chapter 44 is on documenting sources in MLA style; Chapter 45 is on documenting sources in APA, CBE, and Chicago styles.

4. Part XI includes four chapters (55–58) that cover language issues of special interest to students who speak languages in addition to English. At the very end of the book is a quick reference chart that refers you to all the materials in the handbook for multilingual writers.

5. Chapter 3 offers guidelines on exploring, planning, and drafting.

6. Looking up "narrative" in the index leads you to a discussion of using narrative to support an argument in 5e, with guidelines on checking your own use of narrative on p. 87.

7. Looking up "audience" in the index leads you to 2h, about focusing on your audience, and to Chapter 29, on considering others and building common ground.

8. A look at the table of contents leads you to Chapter 53, on making oral presentations.

9. Looking up "*but*" in the index leads to 30b, which explains that a comma usually precedes a coordinating conjunction such as *but* when it joins two independent clauses in a compound sentence. You could also get to this section by turning directly to Chapter 30, on using commas, and looking for examples of how to use commas in similar sentences.

10. The table of contents tells you that Chapter 57 covers prepositions; 57a includes a set of strategies for using prepositions idiomatically, including several examples of sentences using *in* and *on.*

11. Looking up "*none*" in the index leads to 10e, where you learn that *none* can be singular or plural, depending on the noun it refers to: *none of the cake was eaten; none of the cakes were eaten.*

12. *Ref* is a revision symbol commonly used by instructors. A list of revision symbols appears on the inside back cover of the handbook. Consulting this list tells you that *ref* refers to unclear pronoun reference and that this subject is discussed in Chapter 13.

13. Skimming the table of contents leads you to Chapter 41, on conducting research, and in particular to 41b on exploring library and database resources and to 41c on searching computer databases.

14. Consulting the index under "quoting," "paraphrasing," or "summarizing" leads you to guidelines in 42c on deciding whether to quote, paraphrase, or summarize.

15. The table of contents tells you that Chapter 45 includes a section on APA documentation, with guidelines and a student essay that uses APA style.

16. The table of contents leads to Chapter 44, which provides a full discussion of MLA documentation conventions. It also lists a directory to MLA style, which leads you to section 44c3 on documenting electronic sources.

17. Scanning the table of contents leads you to Part IX, which covers academic writing in general, and to Chapter 46, which includes sections on understanding the vocabulary, style, use of evidence, and conventional formats in different disciplines.

18. Consulting the table of contents, you see that Chapter 47 contains a section on writing in the biological sciences (47d) and an excerpt from a biology paper. Turning to 47d, you find a description, an abstract and an example of one in the student excerpt.

19. A glance at the table of contents leads you to Chapter 48, on writing about literature. Section 48d discusses three ways to approach a work of literature, including an example of a student response to a poem. Checking the index under "poetry," in fact, you will find two poems by Emily Dickinson—in Chapters 35 and 36.

20. Looking up "tables" or "figures" in the index leads you to 51d, on using visuals, with examples and guidelines on constructing tables and figures.

EXERCISE 7.2: Answers

The subject is set in italics; the predicate is set in boldface.

2. *He* **was an army doctor, with a gray toothbrush moustache and a gruff voice.**

4. *The dog* **answered the sound with a whine.**

EXERCISE 7.3: Answers

2. had been leaking

4. can collect; might run; should finish

6. announced

8. will include

10. must submit

EXERCISE 7.4: Answers

Nouns are set in italics; articles are set in boldface.

2. *plagiarism*

4. *Henderson's story*; **a**; *tale*; *theft*; *violation*

EXERCISE 7.5: Answers

Pronouns are set in italics; antecedents are set in boldface.

2. **crowd**; *that*; **one**; *I*

4. *They*; *themselves*

EXERCISE 7.6: Answers

Adjectives are set in italics; adverbs are set in boldface.

2. **Hilariously**; *the*; *sly*; *the*; *the*; *first*

4. **unhappily**; *the*; *sleek*; *new*; *its*

6. *The*; **most**; *instructive*; *the*; **unfortunately**; *the*; *longest*

8. *Late*; *the*; *the*; **precipitously**

10. **seriously**; **how**; **well**; *their*; *intense*; *public*

EXERCISE 7.7: Suggested Answers

2. The beautiful, athletic heroine marries the charming, bookish prince.

4. The tall, white candles gleamed brightly on the well-scrubbed tabletop.

EXERCISE 7.8: Answers

2. through; across; into

4. During; down; between

EXERCISE 7.9: Answers

2. nevertheless; as

4. but

6. not only . . . but also

8. until

10. neither . . . nor; therefore

EXERCISE 7.10: Answers

Complete subjects are set in italics; simple subjects are set in boldface.

2. *the new* **elevator**

4. *The long, low, intricately carved* **table**

EXERCISE 7.11: Answers

Predicates are set in italics.

2. *made us a nation:* trans-made; do-us; oc-nation

4. *will never die:* intrans-will . . . never die

EXERCISE 7.12: Answers

2. in his vocabulary

4. of the dugout

EXERCISE 7.13: Suggested Answers

2. Without fear, Socrates faced death.

4. Except for a few of his followers, everyone thought Socrates was crazy.

EXERCISE 7.14: Answers

2. gerund-careful saving: n, object of prep

4. part-Raised in Idaho: adj, modifying "I"
   part-exploring nature: adj, obj compl

EXERCISE 7.15: Answers

2. inf-To listen to k. d. lang; prep-to k. d. lang

4. part-Floating on my back; prep-on my back

6. app-a sensitive child; prep-with a mixture of awe and excitement; prep-of awe and excitement

8. part-Basking in the sunlight; prep-in the sunlight; prep-in reminiscence of birch trees; prep-of birch trees

10. prep-of recreation; gerund-taking a nap

EXERCISE 7.16: Suggested Answers

2. After soaking up the sun and eating good food, she looked healthy when he saw her the second time.

4. The Sunday afternoon dragged to an absolute halt.

6. In addition to kissing babies, posing for pictures, and eating boiled chicken, the candidates shook hands with the voters.

8. A late bloomer, Ben often thought regretfully about the past.

10. A young couple and their children, they lived in a trailer, crowded together like sardines.

EXERCISE 7.17: Suggested Answers

2. Waiting to go through customs, we had our passports in our hands.

4. To annoy his parents, Michael had his ear pierced.

EXERCISE 7.18: Answers

2. dep-As a potential customer entered the store; sub conj-As; ind-Tony nervously attempted to retreat to the safety of the back room

4. dep-When she was deemed old enough to understand; sub conj-when; ind-she was told the truth; ind-she finally knew why her father had left home; rel-why

6. ind-I decided to bake a chocolate cream pie; dep-which was Lynn's favorite; rel-which

8. ind-The trip was longer; dep-than I had remembered; rel-than

10. ind-I could see that he was very tired; rel-that; ind-I had to ask him a few questions

EXERCISE 7.19: Suggested Answers

2. After many changes and upheavals, the German government dismantled the Berlin wall, which had become a symbol of oppression.

4. Rob, who was a collector of jazz records, always borrowed money from his friends.

6. We stood outside for an hour while the opening band played.

8. Because she was willing to stay home on weekends and study, Erin won the translation contest.

10. A man, whose memorial plaque hangs in the lobby, was killed in that mill in 1867.

EXERCISE 7.20: Answers

(The entire sentences are, of course, independent clauses.)

2. prep p-in our bare skins; np-our bare skins

4. prep p-in a zoo; np-a zoo; np-the ticket; prep p-for some animals and birds; np-some animals and birds

6. inf p-to read Thoreau; inf p-to enjoy him; np-his enthusiasms; np-his acute perception

8. np-no sensible writer; inf p-to develop; np-a style; vp-do have; np-distinguishing qualities; np-very evident; dep cl-when you read the words; np-the words

10. prep p-of Charlotte's descendants; vp-still live; prep p-in the barn; np-Charlotte's descendants; np-the barn; dep cl-when the warm days of spring arrive; np-the warm days; prep p-of spring; np-tiny spiders; part p-emerging into the world; np-the world

Imitation sentences will vary.

EXERCISE 7.21: Answers

2. complex, declarative, periodic

4. simple, declarative, cumulative

6. simple, imperative, periodic

8. compound-complex, declarative

EXERCISE 8.2: Answers

2. hers

4. his

EXERCISE 8.3: Answers

2. whoever: subject of *faces*

4. whom: object of preposition, *with*

EXERCISE 8.4: Answers

2. whom

4. he

6. she

8. whoever

10. whom

EXERCISE 8.5: Answers

2. I——→me

4. correct

6. him——→he

8. me——→I

10. whomever——→whoever

EXERCISE 9.2: Answers

2. have——→has

4. correct

6. be——→is

8. don't——→doesn't

10. is running

EXERCISE 9.3: Answers

2. made, found

4. lost, took

6. chooses, become

8. flung, been

10. fallen, broken, done

EXERCISE 9.4: Answers

2. sang——→sung; begun——→began

4. went——→gone

EXERCISE 9.5: Answers

2. laid

4. lying

6. sat

8. raise

10. rose

EXERCISE 9.6: Answers

2. have predicted/have been predicting—action begun in past continues

4. arrived/has arrived—started in past, may continue today

6. rode/was riding—past action, completed

8. will have watched—future action, completed by a certain time

10. rises—general truth

EXERCISE 9.8: Answers

2. *Having left* England in December, the settlers *arrived* in Virginia in May.
4. *Having cut off* all contact with family, he *did* not *know* whom to ask for help.

EXERCISE 9.9: Answers

2. Such things as elevators, subways, and closets *were avoided* by Marianne.
4. The first snow of winter *covered* the lawns and rooftops.

EXERCISE 9.11: Answers

2. was——→were   4. was——→were

EXERCISE 10.1: Suggested Answers

2. Visiting relatives *are* treacherous. ["relatives" is the subject.]

EXERCISE 10.2: Answers

2. presents   8. holds
4. supplies   10. leaves
6. were

EXERCISE 10.3: Answers

2. correct; "talking and getting up" are considered a single unit.
4. correct
6. display——→displays; "neither/nor"
8. correct; "most" refers to a quantity
10. intimidates——→intimidate; "neither/nor"
12. correct; "only one" is singular
14. was (second verb)——→were; "that" refers to "countries"

EXERCISE 11.2: Suggested Answers

2. Roommates do not always get along, but they can usually manage to tolerate each other temporarily.
4. Both Tom and Teresa are always willing to share their opinions.
6. Every house and apartment has its advantages and its drawbacks.
8. Correct
10. I often turn on the fan and the light and neglect to turn them off.

EXERCISE 12.3: Answers

2. negatively——→acts

4. really——→cold

6. badly——→hurt

8. good——→instructor

10. strictly——→brought up

EXERCISE 12.5: Suggested Answers

2. According to the article, walking is more healthful [not healthy] than jogging.

4. Women tend to live longer than men; hence, more of the elderly are women.

6. A research scientist from the Lunar and Planetary Laboratory, University of Arizona, argues that mining asteroids may well prove economically important.

8. The student cafeteria is operated by a college food service, part of a chain.

10. I think *Oedipus Rex* is a more successful play than *The Sandbox*.

EXERCISE 13.2: Suggested Answers

2. Lear divides his kingdom between the two older daughters, Goneril and Regan, whose extravagant professions of love are more flattering than the simple affection of the youngest daughter, Cordelia. The consequences of this error in judgment soon become apparent, as the older daughters prove neither grateful nor kind to him.

4. New England helped to shape many aspects of American culture, including education, religion, and government. As New Englanders moved west, they carried their institutions with them.

6. Bill broke the news to Ed of Ed's promotion. Bill broke the news of his own promotion to Ed.

8. When drug therapy is combined with psychotherapy, the patients relate better and are more responsive to their therapists, and they are less vulnerable to what disturbs them.

10. Quint trusted Smith because Smith had worked for her before. Quint trusted Smith because she had worked for Smith before.

EXERCISE 13.3: Suggested Answers

2. Texans often hear about the influence of big oil corporations.

4. After recently having a conversation with a veteran, my friend saw the Persian Gulf War differently.

6. Not only was the parcel damaged, but the delivery service said I owed postage.

8. Many employees resented smoking, so the company policy prohibited it.

10. In his lyrics, Tom Jobim often describes the beaches of Rio.

EXERCISE 14.2: Suggested Answers

2. Then, suddenly, the big day *arrived*. The children were still a bit sleepy, for their anticipation had kept them awake.

4. A cloud of snow powder rose as skis and poles *flew* in every direction.

EXERCISE 14.3: Suggested Answers

2. I think it better that Grandfather die painlessly, bravely, and with dignity than that he *continue* to live in terrible pain.

4. The coroner asked that we be quiet and *attentive.*

EXERCISE 14.4: Suggested Answers

2. No change

4. The first thing *we see* as we start down the slope is a large green banner.

EXERCISE 14.5: Suggested Answers

2. Workers with computer skills were in great demand, and a programmer could almost name *his or her* salary.

4. *All new employees* must undergo one week of observation; they must check with their *supervisors* for permission to leave.

EXERCISE 14.6: Suggested Answers

2. According to the article, the ozone layer is rapidly dwindling, *and the lives of future generations are endangered.*

4. Oscar Wilde wrote that books cannot be divided into moral and immoral categories, *and that books are either written well or badly.*

EXERCISE 15.2: Suggested Answers

2. Reporters today have no choice but to use computers.

4. My mother taught me to read, but my grandmother taught me to *love* to read.

6. Lincoln called for troops to fight the Confederacy; as a result, four more Southern states seceded.

8. E. B. White died in 1985; his work nevertheless continues to inspire readers.

10. As the music lifted her spirits, she stopped sighing and began to sing.

EXERCISE 16.2: Suggested Answers

2. Many Americans yearn to live with gusto.

4. The climbers had two choices: to go over a four-hundred-foot cliff or to turn back. They decided to make the attempt.

6. Bush promoted one tax change in particular: a reduction in the capital gains tax.

8. Offering good pay and the best equipment money can buy, organized crime has been able to attract graduates just as big business has.

10. Wollstonecraft believed in universal public education and in education that forms the heart and strengthens the body.

EXERCISE 16.3: Suggested Answers

2. *verbal-phrase fragment.* The protagonist comes to a decision to leave his family.

4. *prepositional-phrase fragment.* We were thankful for a hot shower after a week in the wilderness.

6. *appositive-phrase fragment.* Forster stopped writing novels after *A Passage to India*, one of the greatest novels of the twentieth century.

8. *compound-predicate fragment.* I loved *Beloved* and knew Toni Morrison deserved the Nobel prize.

10. *subordinate-clause fragment.* Because the younger generation often rejects the ways of its elders, one might say that rebellion is normal.

EXERCISE 17.2: Suggested Answers

2. The city spent almost $2 million on the new stadium that opened last year.

4. The clothes that I was giving away were full of holes.

6. Doctors recommend a new, painless test for cancer.

8. Before I decided to buy the stock, I knew the investment would pay off dramatically.

10. The maintenance worker shut down the turbine that was revolving out of control.

EXERCISE 17.3: Suggested Answers

2. The mayor promised that after her reelection she would not raise taxes. After her reelection, the mayor promised that she would not raise taxes.

4. Doctors can now restore limbs that have been partially severed to functioning condition. Doctors can now restore limbs that have been severed to partially functioning condition.

EXERCISE 17.4: Suggested Answers

2. The exhibit attracted large audiences because of extensive publicity.

4. Bookstores sold fifty thousand copies in the first week after publication.

EXERCISE 17.5: Suggested Answers

2. When interviewing grieving relatives, reporters show no consideration for their privacy.

4. Chosen for their looks, newscasters often have weak journalistic credentials.

EXERCISE 17.6: Suggested Answers

2. While attending a performance at Ford's Theatre, Lincoln was shot by John Wilkes Booth.

4. Dreams are somewhat like a jigsaw puzzle; when put together in the correct order, both dreams and puzzles have organization and coherence.

EXERCISE 18.2: Suggested Answers

2. To determine your rank, consult your supervisor. Ordinarily, your supervisor will advise you about your rank.

4. By not prosecuting white-collar crime as vigorously as we prosecute violent crime, we encourage white-collar criminals to ignore the law. We must prosecute white-collar crime as vigorously as violent crime unless we want to encourage white-collar criminals to ignore the law.

6. A confluence is a place where two rivers join to form one. A confluence joins two rivers to form one.

8. Oedipus has the "shock of recognition" when he suddenly realizes that he has killed his father and married his mother. The "shock of recognition" comes when Oedipus suddenly realizes that he has killed his father and married his mother.

10. Europeans discovered Australia, but the British made it into a penal colony. Although it was a European discovery, Australia became a British penal colony.

EXERCISE 18.3: Suggested Answers

2. Argentina and Peru were colonized by Spain, and Brazil was colonized by Portugal.

4. Was the dictatorship in Iraq any worse than those in many other countries?

EXERCISE 19.2: Suggested Answers

2. Also notable throughout the story is the image of chrysanthemums.

4. The presence of the Indian in these movies always conjures up destructive stereotypes of drunkenness, horse thieves, and blood-thirsty war parties.

EXERCISE 19.3: Suggested Answers

2. Many people tend to expand their sentences by adding unnecessary words.

4. I put on ten pounds immediately after I stopped exercising.

EXERCISE 20.3: Suggested Answers

2. When ticket sales were advertised for Barbra Streisand's first concert tour in years, fans lined up as many as forty-eight hours in advance.

4. *Working*, an important book by Studs Terkel, examines the situation of the American worker.

EXERCISE 21.2: Suggested Answers

2. My favorite pastimes include reading, exercising, and talking with friends.

4. I want not only hot fudge but also whipped cream.

EXERCISE 21.3: Suggested Answers

2. I will always remember how the girls dressed in green plaid skirts and the boys wore green plaid ties.

4. Needing a new pair of shoes and not being able to afford them is sad.

6. Too many students came to college to have fun, to find a husband or wife, or to put off having to go to work.

8. Her job was to show new products, to help with sales, and to participate in advertising.

10. Stress can result in low self-esteem, total frustration, sleeplessness, nervousness, or eventually suicide.

EXERCISE 22.4: Suggested Answers

2. *Periodic:* Once I mastered the problems that I had encountered at the beginning and once I became thoroughly familiar with the stock, I became the best salesperson in our store. *Cumulative:* I became the best salesperson in our store once I mastered the problems that I had encountered at the beginning and once I became thoroughly familiar with the stock.

EXERCISE 23.3: Suggested Answers

2. They started shooting pool, and before Cathy knew it, ten dollars was owed to the kid.
(Preference depends somewhat upon the context. The passive voice is unclear about who owes the kid ten dollars. Is Cathy alone? Are she and the kid the "they" of the sentence, or is someone else involved? The active is clearer if Cathy owes the kid money.)

4. I adjusted more easily to living in a dorm than to living in an apartment.
(Again, the active is preferred, since the passive adds nothing.)

EXERCISE 24.2: Answers

2. to; too

4. noticeable; until

6. believe; lose

8. affects; success; than; its

10. develop; truly; successful

12. where; and

14. businesses; dependent

16. experience; exercise

18. categories; final

20. occasion; whether; weather

22. woman's

24. It's; all right; sense

EXERCISE 24.4: Answers

2. conscience

4. leisure

6. caffeine

8. receive

10. heiress

EXERCISE 24.5: Answers

2. wholly

4. lonely

6. dyeing

8. continuous

10. outrageous

EXERCISE 24.6: Answers

2. carrying

4. studious

6. dutiful

8. obeyed

10. coyly

EXERCISE 24.7: Answers

2. fastest

4. reference

6. regrettable

8. drastically

10. weeping

EXERCISE 24.8: Answers

2. hooves

4. babies

6. spoofs

8. yourselves

10. roses

12. turkeys

14. radios

EXERCISE 25.3: Answers

2. student: from ME < L *studere,* to study

4. whine: from ME *whinen* < Indo-European *kwein,* to whiz, hiss, whistle

6. sex: from ME < L *sexus* < *secare,* to cut

8. tortilla: from Sp, diminutive of *torta,* cake

10. video: from L, I see < *videre,* to see

EXERCISE 25.4: Suggested Answers

2. *prevaricate:* (syn.) equivocate, lie, palter, fib.

4. *odious:* (syn.) disgusting, ghastly, hideous, unpleasant.

6. *obfuscate:* (syn.) darken, confuse.

EXERCISE 25.6: Suggested Answers

2. The *OED* defines *alienate* as to make strange or turn away from, to transfer ownership, and to change or alter something.

    Webster's New World Dictionary adds two slightly different meanings: to cause to be withdrawn from society, and to transfer affection.

4. The *OED* defines *hopefully* as an adverb: "In a hopeful manner, with a feeling of hope; with ground for hope, promisingly."

    Webster's New World Dictionary also lists adverb uses.

6. Both the *OED* and *Webster's New World Dictionary* define *culture* as the cultivation of the soil, the production of a particular commodity, the growth of microorganisms in a prepared substance, the development of the intellect, and the ideas or customs of a group.

   The *OED* includes two obsolete definitions: worship, and the training of the human body.

EXERCISE 26.2: Suggested Answers

2. *scriptorium:* a writing room, a room in a monastery for copying manuscripts, writing, and studying.

4. *lucent:* giving off light, shining, translucent or clear.

6. *audiology:* the science of hearing, the evaluation of hearing defects.

8. *pathogenic:* producing disease.

10. *graphology:* the study of handwriting.

EXERCISE 26.3: Suggested Answers

2. *subterranean:* beneath earth; of or relating to the area under the surface of the earth.

4. *monograph:* write a single writing; a learned treatise on a small area of learning.

6. *superscript:* write over or above; a distinguishing symbol written immediately above or above and to the right of another character.

8. *neologism:* a recent word or thought; a word, usage, or expression that is often disapproved of because of its newness or barbarousness.

10. *apathetic:* without feeling or not suffering; having or showing little or no feeling or emotion, having or showing little or no interest or concern.

EXERCISE 26.4: Suggested Answers

2. *fanciful:* full of fancy, indulging in fancies, imaginative in a playful way, whimsical.

4. *liquefy:* to change into a liquid.

6. *defiance:* the act of defying, bold resistance to authority or opposition.

8. *redden:* to make red, to become red.

10. *satirist:* a writer of satires.

EXERCISE 27.2: Suggested Answers

2. All candidates strive for the same results: to discredit their opponents and to persuade the majority of voters that they are qualified for the position.

4. The angrier she became over his actions, the more he rebelled and continued doing what he pleased.

EXERCISE 27.3: Answers

2. rapturous   4. frugal

EXERCISE 27.4: Suggested Answers

2. *tragic:* distressing, alarming, disturbing; *consumes:* defeats, feeds on, erodes; *displays:* champions, thrives on, builds up, promotes; *drama:* excitement, tension, vitality

4. *girl:* young lady, miss

EXERCISE 27.5: Suggested Answers

2. Cooing, singing, twittering—the early morning beckoning of birds outside my window makes it a treat to get up.

4. The valet stepped cautiously yet excitedly toward my Porsche.

EXERCISE 27.6: Answers will vary.

2. *deep and soft like water moving in a cavern* (simile): this simile compares the sound of her voice to water in a cavern.

EXERCISE 30.2: Answers

2. Unfortunately,

4. If you follow the instructions,

6. No comma needed.

8. No comma needed.

10. Startled by the explosion,

EXERCISE 30.3: Suggested Answers

2. Joan Didion's nonfiction is renowned, *but* her novels are also worthwhile.

4. The playwright disliked arguing with directors, *so* she avoided rehearsals.

EXERCISE 30.4: Answers

2. *Who rescued her puppy* is a restrictive clause because only the man who rescued the puppy won the gratitude. The winning of eternal gratitude is restricted to the man who rescued the puppy.

4. *Made of wood* is a restrictive participial phrase because the meaning of the sentence is not complete without it. That the houses are made of wood is what often allows them to survive earthquakes.

EXERCISE 30.5: Answers

2. No commas needed.

4. No commas needed.

6. The Zunis, an ancient tribe, live in New Mexico.

8. Karl Marx, an important nineteenth-century political philosopher, believed that his role as a social thinker was to change the world.

10. No commas needed.

EXERCISE 30.6: Answers

2. We bought zucchini, peppers, and tomatoes at the market.

4. The daddy longlegs's orange body resembles a colored dot amidst eight long, black legs.

6. Superficial observation does not provide accurate insight into people's lives—how they feel, what they believe in, how they respond to others.

8. I timidly offered to help a loud, overbearing, lavishly dressed customer.

10. These Cosell clones insist on calling every play, judging every move, and telling everyone within earshot exactly what is wrong with the team.

EXERCISE 30.7: Answers

2. The West, in fact, has become solidly Republican in presidential elections.

4. The celebration will, alas, conclude all too soon.

EXERCISE 30.8: Answers

2. Ithaca, New York, has a population of about 30,000.

4. MLA headquarters are at 10 Astor Place, New York, New York 10003.

EXERCISE 30.9: Answers

2. Joseph Epstein admits, "I prefer not to be thought vulgar in any wise."

4. "Neat people are lazier and meaner than sloppy people," according to Suzanne Britt.

EXERCISE 30.11: Answers

2. Observers watch facial expressions and gestures and interpret them.

4. Our supper that evening consisted of stale bologna sandwiches.

6. As we sat around the campfire, we felt boredom and disappointment.

8. The photographer Edward Curtis is known for his depiction of the West.

10. Driving a car and talking on the car phone at the same time demand great care.

EXERCISE 31.2: Answers

2. City life offers many advantages; in many ways, however, life in a small town is much more pleasant.

4. Physical education forms an important part of a university's program; nevertheless, few students and professors clearly recognize its value.

6. Voltaire was concerned about the political implications of his skepticism; he warned his friends not to discuss atheism in front of the servants.

8. My high school was excessively competitive; virtually everyone went on to college, many to the top schools in the nation.

10. Propaganda is defined as the spread of ideas to further a cause; therefore, propaganda and advertisement are synonymous terms.

EXERCISE 31.4: Answers

2. If the North had followed up its victory at Gettysburg more vigorously, the Civil War might have ended sooner.
4. We must find a plan to provide decent health care, a necessity in today's life.

EXERCISE 32.2: Answers

2. Cicero was murdered in 43 B.C.
4. She asked whether Operation PUSH had been founded by Jesse Jackson.

EXERCISE 32.3: Answers

2. Are people with so many possessions really happy?
4. Correct; indirect question.

EXERCISE 32.4: Suggested Answers

2. I screamed at Jamie, "You rat! You tricked me!"
4. Stop, thief!

EXERCISE 33.2: Answers

2. *Maria Callas's* opera performances are now the stuff of legend.
4. *Carol and Jim's* income dropped drastically after Jim lost his job.
6. Many smokers disregard the *surgeon general's* warnings.
8. The *governors'* attitudes changed after the convention.
10. My *friend's and my brother's* cars have the same kind of stereo system.

EXERCISE 33.3: Answers

2. I heard the songs and the minister saying: "Why *don't* you come?"
4. So I decided that maybe to save further trouble, *I'd* better lie. . . .

EXERCISE 34.2: Answers

2. In Flannery O'Connor's short story "Revelation," colors symbolize passion, violence, sadness, and even God.
4. The "fun" of surgery begins before the operation ever takes place.
6. "Big Bill," a section of Dos Passos's *U.S.A.,* opens with a birth.
8. The Beatles song "Love Me Do" catapulted the band to international stardom.
10. In the episode "Driven to Extremes," *48 Hours* takes a humorous look at driving in New York City.

EXERCISE 34.3: Suggested Answers

2. What is Hawthorne telling the readers in "Rappaccini's Daughter"?

4. This "typical American" is Ruby Turpin, who in the course of the story receives a message that brings about a change in her life.

6. One of Joyce Carol Oates's most shocking stories is "The Bingo Master"; the triumph of brutality is devastating.

8. In his article "The Death of Broadway," Thomas M. Disch writes that "choreographers are, literally, a dying breed."[1]

10. One thought flashed through my mind as I finished *In Search of Our Mothers' Gardens:* "I want to read more of this writer's books."

EXERCISE 35.2: Answers

2. During my research, I found that a flat-rate income tax (a single-rate tax with no deductions) has its problems.

4. Many researchers used the Massachusetts Multiphasic Personal Inventory (MMPI) for hypnotizability studies.

EXERCISE 35.3: Answers

2. Even if smoking is harmful—and there is no real proof of this assertion—it is unjust to outlaw smoking while other harmful substances remain legal.

4. Union Carbide's plant in Bhopal, India, sprang a leak—a leak that killed more than 2,000 people and injured an additional 200,000

EXERCISE 35.4: Answers

2. Another example is taken from Psalm 139:16.

4. Shifting into German, Kennedy declared: "Ich bin ein Berliner."

6. Ghandi urged four rules: tell the truth even in business, adopt more sanitary habits, abolish caste and religious divisions, and learn English.

8. *Signs of Trouble and Erosion: A Report on Education in America* was submitted to Congress and the president in January 1984.

10. Two buses go to Denver: one at 9:38 A.M. and one at 2:55 P.M.

EXERCISE 36.2: Answers

2. We had a choice of fast-food, Chinese, or Italian restaurants.

4. The Council of Trent was convened to draw up the Catholic response to the Protestant Reformation.

6. I wondered if my new Levi's were faded enough.

8. I will cite the novels of Vladimir Nabokov, in particular *Pnin* and *Lolita.*

10. My favorite song by Cole Porter is "You'd Be So Nice to Come Home To."

EXERCISE 37.2: Answers

2. An MX missile, which is 71 feet long and 92 inches around, weighs 190,000 pounds.

4. In 1991, Representative William Gray became president of the United Negro College Fund.

6. Unfortunately, the five-cent candy bar is a relic of the past.

8. The local National Public Radio station has a broadcast range of seventy-five miles.

10. Dostoyevsky was influenced by many European writers—for example, Dickens, Stendhal, and Balzac.

EXERCISE 37.3: Suggested Answers

2. Time will provide perspective on the economic crises of the eighties.

4. The invasion of Kuwait began on August 2, 1990.

6. Cable TV is now available to 72 percent of the population.

8. In the thirty-five to forty-four age group, the risk is estimated to be about 1 in 2,500.

10. The amulet measured 1⅛ by 2⅖ inches.

EXERCISE 38.1: Answers

2. Is Samuel Beckett's play *Endgame* a sequel to Shakespeare's *King Lear*?

4. The word *veterinary* comes from the Latin *veterinarius*.

6. Flying the *Glamorous Glennis,* named for his wife, Chuck Yeager was the first pilot to fly faster than the speed of sound.

8. *The Waste Land* is a long and difficult but ultimately rewarding poem.

10. The White Star liner *Titanic* sank in the North Atlantic in 1912.

EXERCISE 39.1: Answers

2. re*tract; re-tract

4. mil*i*tar*y; mil-i-tary

6. in*ner*di*rect*ed; inner-directed

8. dim*ming; dim-ming

10. at*ti*tude; at-ti-tude

EXERCISE 39.2: Answers

2. pre-World War II

4. Correct

6. self-important

8. seven hundred thirty-three

10. a politician who is fast-talking (Fast-talk is commonly found in dictionaries; thus hyphenation is correct even though the compound adjective comes after the noun.)

EXERCISE 39.3: Answers

2. The drumbeating and hand clapping signaled that the parade was near.
4. Suicide among teenagers has tripled in the past thirty-five years.
6. Both pro- and anti-State Department groups registered complaints.
8. In Bizet's *Carmen,* the ill-fated Carmen is betrayed by her fickleness.
10. The beautifully written essay earned high praise.

EXERCISE 55.1: Suggested Answers

2. Napoleon, the French ruler, invaded Egypt with many soldiers.
4. At Rosetta, near the Nile, some French soldiers were building a fort.

EXERCISE 56.1: Suggested Answers

2. Ancient Egyptian writing was called hieroglyphics.
4. Very soon after its discovery, the French made copies of the stone.

EXERCISE 57.1: Suggested Answers

2. give up: phrasal verb.
   Correct.
4. take back: phrasal verb.
   The British took it back to England.

EXERCISE 58.1: Suggested Answers

2. Champollion enjoyed studying the languages of the Middle East.
4. It was of great importance that he knew Coptic, a later form of the Egyptian language.
6. If the Rosetta Stone had not been discovered, it would have been much more difficult to decipher hieroglyphics.

Index

a, an, 161, 792, 794–95, 841
Abbreviations, 529–34
  in acronyms, 531
  company names, 532
  critical thinking about, 537
  editing, 533
  everyday use, 530
  geographical names, 532
  initial abbreviations, 531
  Latin, 532
  months of year, 532
  in parenthetical citations, 670
  period in, 488
  reading with eye for, 537
  reference information, 532
  in specialized writing, 536
  symbols, 533
  titles, 529–30
  units of measure, 533
  without periods, 489
  with years and hours, 531
Abridged dictionaries, 397
Absolute phrases, 179–80, 181, 835
  for sentence openings, 355
Abstractions, 424
Abstract nouns, 834
Abstracts, 573–74, 590
  evaluation of, 590
  of lab report, 712
  on-line
    APA style documentation, reference
      list, 676
    MLA style documentation, works
      cited list, 641
Academic courses, capitalization of, 526
Academic degrees, abbreviation of, 529–30
Academic writing, 698–722
  analysis of assignments, 699–700
  in applied sciences, 715–18
  characteristics of, 24
  disciplinary patterns and formats, 705
  and disciplinary vocabularies, 701–3
  evidence in, 704
  in humanities, 718–22
  language varieties in, 442–43
  in natural sciences, 711–15
  in social sciences, 708–11
  and style of discipline, 703
accept, except, 377, 841
Acronyms, 827
  abbreviation of, 531
Active voice, 224
  formation of, 224
  in prose, 367–68
A.D., 531
Addresses, commas in, 472
ad hominem charges, 90
Adjective clauses, 184, 186
  and commas, 465–66
  and multilingual writers, 822–24
  nonrestrictive, 465–66
  restrictive, 466
  words beginning, 465
Adjectives, 163–64, 249–59, 827. *See also*
    Modifiers
  adverbs modifying, 252–53
  and adverbs, 258–59
  as antecedents, 267
  comparative forms, 255–57
  coordinate adjectives, 468–69
  critical thinking about, 259
  descriptive adjectives, 163
  editing, 258–59
  everyday use, 250

Adjectives (continued)
    formation of, 249
    forms, 827–28
    functions of, 163
    infinitive phrases as, 179
    infinitives as, 250
    after linking verbs, 252
    as modifiers, 249–50
    and multilingual writers, 251
    participial adjectives, 808
    participial phrases as, 178
    participles as, 250
    past participle as, 207
    positive form, 255–56
    predicate adjectives, 173
    present participle as, 207–8
    pronouns as, 164
    proper adjectives, 164, 523–24
    quoting passages with, 259
    reading with eye for, 259
Adjective suffixes, 409
Adverb clauses, 185, 186
    and commas, 465–66
    misplaced, 302–3
    and subordinating conjunctions, 168, 465
    words beginning, 465
Adverbial particle, 813
Adverbs, 164–66, 249–59, 828. See also
    Modifiers
    adverbs modified by, 252–53
    and adjectives, 258–59
    comparative forms, 164, 255–57
    conjunctive adverbs, 164, 168–69
    critical thinking about, 259
    formation of, 250
    forms, 828
    functions of, 164
    infinitive phrases as, 179
    infinitives as, 250–51
    and language varieties, 253–54
    as modifiers, 250–51, 252–53
    placement in sentences, 165
    positive form, 255–56
    reading with eye for, 259
advice, advise, 378, 841
affect, effect, 377, 841
African American English
    African American vernacular,
        435–36
    be, use of, 209
    double negatives, 370–71
    -s and -es endings, 233
    signifying, 429–30

Afterword, MLA style documentation,
    works cited list, 635
Age, stereotypes about, 452–53
aggravate, 842
Agreement, 828. See also Pronoun-
    antecedent agreement; Subject-verb
    agreement
Aircraft
    capitalization of, 525
    italics for, 541
all, 162, 792, 796
Alliteration, 724
all ready, already, 842
all right, 842
allude, elude, 378, 842
allusion, illusion, 378, 842
Allusions, 429
-ally, 384
Almanacs, 570
a lot, 842
altar, alter, 378
Alternating method, comparison and con-
    trast, 137, 138
Alternatives, slash to separate, 516
A.M., 531
American Heritage Dictionary, The, 397
American Psychological Association. See
    APA style documentation
America Online, 757
among, between, 842
amount, number, 842
an, a, 161, 791, 794–95, 841
Analogies, 101, 426
    false, 103
    nature of, 725
Analyzing, and reading, 10
and, 167, 463
and, or, 842
Anecdotes
    in opening paragraphs, 146
    in topic development, 45
Annotating, and reading, 10
Antecedent, 828. See also Pronoun-
    antecedent agreement
    adjectives as, 267
    possessives as, 267
    of pronoun, 161
Anthology
    Chicago style documentation
        bibliography, 696
        footnotes and endnotes, 693
    MLA style documentation, works cited
        list, 633–34

Antithesis, as special effect in prose, 370
any, 792
anybody, 162
any body, anybody, 842
any one, anyone, 842
anyplace, anywhere, 843
anyway, anyways, 843
anywhere, 843
APA style documentation, 665–88
　content notes, 670
　directory to, 666–67
　example research essay, 678–88
　parenthetical citations, 666, 667–70
　quotations, 614–15
　reference list, 666–67, 671–78
　　books, 672–73
　　dissertations, 677
　　electronic media, 675–76
　　film or videotape, 677
　　government document, 673
　　interviews, 675
　　paper presented at meeting/symposium, 677
　　periodicals, 674–75
　　poster session, 677
　　recordings, 678
　　required information in, 671
　　reviews, 674
　　software, 676
　　technical reports/research reports/working papers, 677
　　television programs/episodes, 677
　　translation, 673
Apostrophes, 493–98
　common errors
　　its and *it's* confusion, I-29–I-30, 496
　　misplaced or missing apostrophe, I-21
　　possessive pronouns and contractions, 496
　in contractions, 496
　critical thinking about, 498
　everyday use, 494
　in omissions, 497
　in plurals, 497
　possessive case, 161, 493–95
　reading with eye for, 498
Applied sciences, 715–18
　writing in, 715–18
　　final report, 715–16
　　progress report, 715
　　proposal, 715
Appositive-phrase fragments, 293

Appositive phrases, 180
Appositives, 828
　and colon, 514
　commas with, 467
　nonrestrictive, 467
　pronoun case in, 202
　renaming object, 196
　renaming subject, 195
　renaming subject complement, 195
　restrictive, 467
apt, liable, likely, 843
Arabic speakers, 823
Archie, 756
are, our, 378
Argument, 78–115
　analysis of, 113–14
　appropriate situation for, 82–83
　arguable statement, characteristics of, 83
　argumentative thesis, formulation of, 84–85
　authority and testimony, 93–94
　credibility in, 87–91
　　demonstration of fairness, 89–90
　　demonstration of knowledge, 88
　　establishment of common ground, 88–89
　critical thinking about, 114–15
　emotional appeals, 100–103
　　and audience, 102
　　concrete language in, 100–101
　　description in, 100
　　emotional fallacies, 102–3
　　figurative language in, 101
　ethical fallacies, recognition of, 90–91
　example of, 107–13
　good reasons, formulation of, 86
　language, varieties of, 94
　logic of, 91–98
　　causes and effects, 94–95
　　examples and precedents, 92–93
　　inductive and deductive reasoning, 95–97
　　logical fallacies, 97–98
　and multilingual writers, 87
　narratives in support of, 86–87
　nature of, 79
　organization of
　　classical system, 105–6, 107–13
　　Toulmin system, 106
　purposes of, 81–82
　reading with an eye for, 114–15
　recognition of, 80
　using sources, 104–5

Art
    art works
        capitalization of title, 526
        MLA style documentation, works
            cited list, 644
    library collections of, 577
Articles, 793–96, 828
    definite articles, 793–94
    indefinite articles, 794–95
    as noun markers, 161
    in titles of works, 526
    zero article, 795–96
Articles from journals. *See* Periodicals
Article titles
    articles in, 526
    capitalization of, 526
    in quotation marks, 503
as, 843
as, as if, like, 843
as if, and subjunctive, 228
Assignments
    academic, analysis of, 699–701
    cue words in, 555–56
    for research project. *See* Research,
        assignments
    writing, 19–21
Assumptions. *See also* Stereotypes
    about audience, 29, 447–48
assure, ensure, insure, 843
as though, and subjunctive, 228
as to, 843
at, 166, 812
at, where, 843
Atlases, 570–71
Audience, I-8, 26–31
    building common ground with. *See*
        Common ground
    and context, 415
    critical thinking about, 30–31
    and emotional appeals, 102
    evidence offered to, 30
    freewriting about, 560
    guidelines for thinking about,
        27–28
    making assumptions about, 29
    and oral presentations, 778
    and pronoun use, 29
    and purpose for writing, 4
    reading with an eye for, 30
    for research assignment, 556
    and research essay, 608
    and reviewing draft, 57, 58
    specific audience, addressing of, 28

and use of foreign words/terms, 24–25,
    443
whole audience, appealing to, 28–30
for writing portfolio, 784
Audio collections, library, 577
Authority, in logical argument, 93–94
Author's stance, and evaluation of source,
    591–92
Auxiliary verbs, 160, 210–11, 799–801,
    828
    functions of, 210
    modal auxiliaries, 210
    most common, 210
    and present participle, 207–8
awful, awfully, 843
awhile, a while, 843

bad, badly, 844
Balanced sentence, 342–43
Bandwagon appeal, 102–3
bare, bear, 378
Base form, of verb, 207
B.C., 531
B.C.E., 531
be, 160, 210
    and faulty predication, 310
    forms as linking verbs, 173
    and passive voice, 799
    past tense forms, 209
    present tense forms, 209
    and progressive tense, 801
    third-person singular forms, 208
    varieties of English, 209
bear, bare, 378
because of, due to, 844
been, 799
Begging the question, 97
being as, being that, 844
beside, besides, 169, 844
between, among, 842
Bias. *See* Stereotypes
Bible
    colon in chapters and verse, 515
    MLA style documentation, parenthetical
        citation, 628
Bibliographic notes, MLA style for,
    629–30
Bibliography. *See also* Reference list; Refer-
        ences; Works Cited list
    Chicago style documentation, 695–96
        books, 695–96
        periodicals, 696
    working bibliography, 587–88

Biographical resources, 569–70
  types of, 569–70
Black English. *See* African American
  English
Block format, business letters, 771
Block method, comparison and contrast, 137
Block quotations, 500
board, bored, 378
Books. *See also* specific topics
  APA style documentation, reference list,
    672–74
  capitalization of title, 526
  Chicago style documentation
    bibliography, 695–96
    footnotes and endnotes, 693–94
  indexes in, 571
  italics for title, 538
  MLA style documentation, works cited
    list, 631–38
  numbers in divisions of, 536
both, 162, 792, 796
both, and, 168
Brackets, 510–11
  everyday use, 511
  for inserted material within quotations,
    510–11, 616
  to set off material within parentheses, 510
  with *sic,* 511
Brainstorming, 33–34
  and research topic, 560
brake, break, 378
breath, breathe, 844
bring, take, 844
Buildings, capitalization of, 524
Bulletin boards, electronic, 755
Business correspondence, 767–76
  block format, 771
  critical thinking about, 776
  everyday use, 768
  job application, 770–76
  letters, 769–70
  memos, 768–69
  modified block style, 775
  writing guidelines, 770
but, 167, 463
but that, but what, 844
but, yet, 844
buy, by, 378
Buzzwords, eliminating, 323

Calendar items, capitalization of, 525
Call for action, in concluding paragraphs,
  147

Call numbers, 577
can, could, 160, 210, 801, 806
can, may, 844
can't, couldn't, 844
can't hardly, can't scarcely, 844
can't help but, 844
capital, capitol, 378
Capitalization, 522–28
  commonly capitalized terms,
    524–25
  critical thinking about, 528
  everyday use, 524
  first word of line of poetry, 522–23
  first word of sentence, 522–23
  and multilingual writers, 527
  proper nouns and adjectives, 523–24
  reading with eye for, 528
  unnecessary, 527
Card catalog, 574–75
  call numbers, 577
Cardinal numbers, 828
Cartoons
  in document, 763
  MLA style documentation, works cited
    list, 645
Case, 829
  objective case, 195–96
  possessive case, 196–97
  pronouns. *See* Pronoun case
  subjective case, 194–95
Cause and effect
  in logical argument, 94–95
  paragraph development, 44, 138–39
  transitional words used for, 131
CBE style documentation, 689–90
  in-text citations, 689
    citation-sequence form, 689–90
    name-year form, 689–90
  references, 689–90
    for electronic sources, 690
CD-ROM, 577, 578
  abstracts
    APA style documentation, reference
      list, 676
    MLA style documentation, works
      cited list, 641
C.E., 531
-cede, -ceed, -sede, 385
censor, censure, 844
center around, 845
Cents sign, 533
cf., 532

Chapters of books
    APA style documentation, parenthetical
        citations, 670
    Chicago style documentation
        bibliography, 696
        footnotes and endnotes, 693
    MLA style documentation, works cited
        list, 633–34
Characters, 725
Charts
    in document, 763, 765
    MLA style documentation, works cited
        list, 645
Chicago Manual of Style, 536, 691
Chicago style documentation, 691–96
    bibliography, 691–92, 695–96
        books, 695–96
        periodicals, 696
    directory to, 691–92
    footnotes and endnotes, 691, 692–94
        books, 693–94
        periodicals, 694
        required information, 693
        subsequent notes for previously cited
            sources, 694
Chinese speakers, 790–91, 802, 823
Choreographic work, italics for title, 538
Chronological organization
    to explain process, 125
    of information, 42
    narratives, 124–25, 139
    of paragraphs, 124–25
Circulation computer, 575–76
Citation-sequence form, CBE style docu-
    mentation, 689–90
cite, sight, site, 378
Class, stereotypes about, 453
Classical system
    analysis of argument, 113
    organization of argument, 105–13
Classification
    paragraph development by, 136–37
    topic development, 43
Clauses, 183–87, 829
    adjective clauses, 184, 186, 822–24
    adverb clauses, 185, 186
    and comma splices, 283–87
    dangling, 305
    dependent clauses, 183
    and fused sentences, 283–87
    independent clauses, 183
    misplaced, 300
    and multilingual writers, 819–24

noun clauses, 184, 186, 819–90
    positioning of, 187
    to shape/expand sentences, 186
Climactic order, 320–21
    revising, 322
Climax, in narrative paragraph, 139
Clustering, 35
coarse, course, 378
Coherence of paragraphs. *See* Paragraphs,
    coherent
Coinages, quotation marks to signal, 503
Coined compounds, hyphen in, 547
Collaboration
    benefits of, 15–16
    guidelines for, 16–17
    and listening, 13
    response to draft, 57–61
    and talking, 12–13
    writing in workplace, 11
Collective nouns, 160, 833–34
    as antecedents, pronoun-antecedent
        agreement, 245
    as subject, and subject-verb agreement,
        236–37
Colloquial language, 414–15
    and quotation marks, 504
Colons, 514–15
    in biblical chapters and verse, 515
    editing, 515
    to introduce explanations, lists, etc., 514
    with quotation marks, 504
    in time, 515
    in titles and subtitles, 515
Commands
    imperative mood, 226, 227
    imperative sentences, 190, 357
    period in, 488
Commas, 460–79
    in addresses, 472
    and adjective clauses, 465–66
    and adverb clauses, 465–66
    with appositives, 467
    common errors
        comma missing in compound
            sentence, I-17–I-18
        comma missing after introductory
            element, I-16
        comma missing with nonrestrictive
            element, I-19
        comma missing in series, I-25
        unnecessary commas with restrictive
            elements, I-27

in compound sentences, 463–64, 477
and conjunctive adverbs, 169
and contrasting elements, 470
and coordinating conjunctions in
sentences, 463, 463–64
critical thinking about, 478–79
in dates, 471
and direct address, 470
editing, 477–78
everyday use, 461
to facilitate understanding, 474
with *however*, 169
and interjections, 470
after introductory elements, 462, 477
between items in a series, 468–69, 476,
477
and nonrestrictive elements, 464–65, 477
in numbers, 472
and parenthetical expressions, 470
with phrases, 466–67
and quotations, 473
reading with eye for, 478–79
and tag questions, 471
with *therefore*, 169
with *thus*, 169
in titles, 472
and transitional expressions, 470
unnecessary, 475–76
vague pronoun reference, I-17
Comma splices, I-21, 281–89, 829
checking for, 282–83
critical thinking about, 289
elimination of
linking clauses with comma and coordinating conjunction, 284–85
linking clauses with semicolon,
285–86
recasting independent clause as
dependent clause, 286–87
recasting two clauses as one independent clause, 286
separating clauses into two sentences, 283–84
everyday use, 282
and multilingual writers, 283
nature of, 281
reading with eye for, 289
revising, 288–89
as special effect, 289
Comment part, of thesis, 39
Comments, dashes for insertion of, 512
Common ground, 446–57
critical thinking about, 456–57

editing for language for, 455
everyday use, 446
and golden rule, 446
and listening, 455
reading with eye for, 456–57
and sources, use of, 456
stereotypes and assumptions, 447–55
age-related, 452–53
class-related, 453
gender-related, 448–50
and geographic areas, 453–54
racial and ethnic, 451–52
religious, 454
and sexual orientation, 454
Common nouns, 833
capitalization of, 523–24
Company names
abbreviations in, 532
capitalization of, 525
Comparative forms of adjectives and
adverbs, 255–57
double comparatives, 256
incomplete comparisons, 256–57
irregular forms, 255–56
compared to superlative forms, 256
Comparative structures, 313–14
editing, 313–14
requirements for, 313
compare to, compare with, 845
Comparing and contrasting
alternating method, 137, 138
block method, 137
paragraph development by, 137–38
topic development, 43–44
transitional words used for, 131
complement, compliment, 378, 845
Complements, 829
object complement, 174
subject complement, 173
Complete predicate, 173
Complete subject, 171
Complex sentences, 189, 357
compose, comprise, 845
Compound adjectives, 829
hyphen in, 546
Compound antecedents, pronoun-
antecedent agreement, 244–45
Compound-complex sentences, 189–90,
357, 838
Compound constructions, and commas,
476
Compound nouns, 829
plural of, 388–89

Compound predicate, 173
Compound-predicate fragments, 294
Compound prepositions, 166
Compound sentences, 189, 357, 837
 commas in, 463–64, 477
 semicolon in, 463
Compound structures, pronoun case in,
 201
Compound subjects, 172
 and subject-verb agreement, 236
Compound words
 coined compounds, 547
 hyphen in, 546, 548
 possessive case, 494
comprise, compose, 845
CompuServe, 757
Computer databases, 564–65, 577–80
 APA style documentation, reference
 list, 676
 directory of, 567, 578
 key words, 578
 MLA style documentation, works cited
 list, 641–42
 search logic, 578–79
Computers
 critical thinking about, 757
 emoticons, 518
 everyday use, 751
 on-line resources, 753–54
 Archie, 756
 browsing systems, 756
 bulletin boards, 755
 commercial networks, 757
 electronic mail, 754–55
 Gopher, 756
 information sources about, 757
 Internet, 754–56
 mailing lists, 755
 Usenet news groups, 755
 Veronica, 756
 WAIS (Wide Area Information
 Server), 756
 World Wide Web (WWW), 756
 usefulness of, 753
 writing with, 750–57
 dash in, 512
 editing and proofreading, 752–53
 final draft, 753
 and format, 71, 753
 grammar checker, 752–53
 outlines, 751
 and planning/organizing/drafting,
 751–52

 revising, 752
 spelling checker, 72, 390–91, 752–53
 usefulness of, 750–51
Concession, transitional words used for, 131
Conciseness in sentences, 322–26
 and buzzwords, 323–24
 editing, 326
 and redundant words, 323
 revising, 326–27
 and simple grammatical structure, 325
 and wordy phrases, 324–25
Concluding paragraphs, 146–49
 call for action in, 147
 question in, 147
 quotation in, 147
 specific-to-general pattern, 147
 vivid image in, 147
 warning in, 147
Conclusions
 of argument, 106
 methods of, 65
 of oral presentations, 778
 of research essay, 612–13
 and reviewing draft, 59
 revising, 65
 of source, evaluation of, 590
 transitional words used for, 131
Concrete language, in emotional appeals,
 100–101
Concrete nouns, 834
Conditional sentences, and multilingual
 writers, 229, 824–25
Conference proceedings, MLA style documentation, works cited list, 637
Conjunctions, 167–69, 830
 conjunctive adverbs, 168–69
 coordinating conjunctions, 167
 correlative conjunctions, 168
 functions of, 167
 subordinating conjunctions, 168
Conjunctive adverbs, 164, 168–69
 and comma, 169
 listing of, 169
 and semicolon, 169
Connotation, 421–22
conscience, conscious, 378, 845
consensus of opinion, 845
consequently, subsequently, 845
Consonants, adding suffixes to words
 ending in, 385, 386
Content issues, I-5–I-9
 attention to audience, I-8
 overall impression, I-8–I-9

purpose for writing, I-7–I-8
sources, use of, I-6–I-7
supporting evidence, use of, I-6
Content notes, APA style documentation, 670
Context, and knowledge of audience, 415
Context-based stance, in writing about literature, 734–37
continual, continuous, 845
Contractions
apostrophe in, 496
listing of, 496
Contrasting elements, and commas, 470
Contrasting. *See* Comparing and contrasting
Coordinate adjectives, 468–69
Coordinate structures, 328–34
critical thinking about, 339
editing, 332
everyday use, 329
reading with eye for, 339
revising, 332–33
for special effect, 331–32
Coordination, 830
Coordinating conjunctions, 167, 830
and comma in sentences, 463–64
linking clauses with, 284–85
and parallelism, 343
Copyright page, 590
Corporate author
APA style documentation
parenthetical citation, 669
reference list, 672
MLA style documentation
parenthetical citation, 627
Works Cited list, 632
Correlative conjunctions, 168, 830
and parallelism, 343
Correspondence. *See* Business correspondence; Letters
could, 160, 210, 806
Council of Biology Editors (CBE). *See* CBE style documentation
council, counsel, 378
Count nouns, 161, 788–91, 834
and determiners, 792
guidelines for use, 790
and multilingual writers, 161, 788–91
singular and plurals, 790–91
and zero article, 795
counsel, council, 378
couple of, 845
course, coarse, 378

Credibility, 87–91
attacking opponent's, 90
and demonstration of fairness, 89–90
and demonstration of knowledge, 88
and establishment of common ground, 88–89
criteria, criterion, 845
Critical notes, 601
Critical reading, guidelines for, 9–11. *See also* Reading
Critical stance, 729
Critical thinking, I-1–I-5, 78–115
about abbreviations, 537
about adjectives, 259
about adverbs, 259
about apostrophes, 498
about argument, 114–15
assessment of broad content issues, I-5–I-9
assessment of organization and presentation, I-9–I-13
about business correspondence, 776
about capitalization, 528
about commas, 478–79
about comma splices, 289
about common ground, 456–57
about computer work, 757
about coordination, 339
about diction, 431
about disciplinary discourse, 706, 722
about document design, 764
elements of, I-2–I-3, 79–80
about end punctuation, 492
errors, learning from, I-13–I-30
about essay examinations, 748
about fused sentences, 289
about grammatical structures, 315
about hyphens, 549
about italics, 543
about language variety, 444
about modifiers, 306
about numbers, 537
about oral presentations, 783
about own writing, 7–8
about paragraphs, 153
about paraphrase, 606
about pronoun-antecedent agreement, 248
about pronoun case, 205
about pronoun reference, 269–70
about prose style, 372
about punctuation, 520
about purpose and audience, 30

Critical thinking (*continued*)
about quotation marks, 507
about reading process, 11
about research, 561, 585
about research essay, 622
about revising process, 76–77
about semicolons, 486
about sentence fragments, 296
about sentences, 192
about sentence style, 327
about sentence variety, 361
about shifts, 280
about spelling, 392
about spoken and written language, 14
about subject-verb agreement, 241–42
about subordination, 339
about summaries, 606
about verbs, 231
about vocabulary, 411–12
about words, 401
about writer's attention to purpose and audience, 31
writing inventory for, I-3–I-5
writing about literature, 739
about writing portfolio, 785
about writing process, 7–8, 52–53
Cue words, in assignments, 555–56
Cumulative sentences, 359

-*d* endings. *See* -*ed* or -*d* endings
dairy, diary, 378
Dangling modifiers, I-28–I-29, 303–6, 830
editing, 305
elliptical clauses, 305
revising, 304–5
words and phrases, 304
Dashes, 512–13
editing, 513
to emphasize explanatory material, 512
to emphasize material at end of sentence, 512
to indicate hesitation in speech, 513
to insert comment, 512
to introduce summary or explanation, 513
making with word processor, 512
to mark change in tone, 513
with quotation marks, 505
reading with eye for, 520
revising, 519–20
data, 845
Data, versus information, 605
Database. *See* Computer databases

Dates, commas in, 471
Deadlines, research assignments, 556
Declarative sentences, 190, 357, 837
Deductive reasoning, 96–97
enthymeme, 96–97
major and minor premise in, 96
syllogisms, 96
Definite article, 793–94
Definitions
paragraph development by, 136
and quotation marks, 503
topic development, 43
Degrees, academic, abbreviation of, 529–30
Demonstrative pronouns, 162, 836
as adjectives, 164
Denotation, 421–22, 830
Dependent-clause fragments, 295
Dependent clauses, 183, 829
in comma splices, 286–87
in complex sentence, 189
in compound-complex sentence, 189–90
in fused sentences, 286–87
for sentence openings, 356
subject of, 194
subjunctive mood in, 228
Description
in emotional appeals, 100
in narrative paragraph, 139
Descriptive adjectives, 163
Descriptors, 565
desert, dessert, 378
Determiners, 791–92
and count nouns, 792
listing of, 791
types of nouns used with, 792
device, devise, 378
Diagrams, in document, 763, 766
Dialect. *See* Language, varieties of
DIALOG, 757
Dialogism, 725
Dialogue
in narrative, 725
in narrative paragraphs, 140
paragraphs of, 149–50
and quotation marks, 502
Diction, 413–31. *See also* Word choice
and audience, 415
colloquial language, 414–15
and context, 415
critical thinking about, 431
denotation and connotation, 421–22
editing, 430–31

everyday use, 414
figurative language, 425–30
  allusion, 429
  analogies, 426
  clichés, 426
  hyperbole, 428
  irony, 428
  metaphors, 426
  mixed metaphors, 427
  personification, 428
  signifying, 429–30
  similes, 426
  understatement, 428
general and specific words, balance in
    prose, 424–25
meaning of, 278
and multilingual writers, 420
and oral presentations, 779
reading with awareness of, 431
register, 416–19
  familiar register, 416
  formal register, 417–18
  informal register, 417
  jargon, 419
  neologisms, 418–19
  in technical writing, 418
shifts in, 279
slang, 414
Dictionaries, 393–401
  abridged dictionaries, 397
  of etymology/regional English/slang,
    400
  everyday use, 394
  exploring, 394–95
  information in entry, 394–95
  for learners of English, 400
  of synonyms, 400
  unabridged dictionaries, 397–98
  of usage, 399
  usage labeling and notes, 395
Dictionary of American Regional English,
    400
Dictionary of American Slang, 400
Dictionary of Modern English Usage, 399
die, dye, 378
different from, different than, 845
differ from, differ with, 845
Direct address, 831
  and commas, 470
Direct discourse, 831
  shifts in, 276–77
Direct object, 831
  function of, 174

and multilingual writers, 817
noun clause as, 184
and object complement, 174
and objective case, 195, 201
and transitive verbs, 174
Direct quotations. *See* Quotations
Disability, stereotypes about, 454
Disciplinary discourse, 698–706. *See also*
    Academic writing
  critical thinking about, 706, 722
  everyday use, 699
  reading with eye for, 706, 722
Discourse
  direct, 276–77
  indirect, 276–77
discreet, discrete, 846
Discussion and conclusions section,
    of natural sciences report,
    712, 714–15
disinterested, uninterested, 846
Dissertations
  APA style documentation, reference
    list, 677
  MLA style documentation, works cited
    list, 642
distinct, distinctive, 846
Dividing
  paragraph development by, 136–37
  topic development by, 43
do, 160, 210
Document design, 758–66
  critical thinking about, 766
  first page, 759
  headings, 761–62
  margins, 761
  page numbering, 760
  print, selection of, 760
  spacing, 761
  title page, 760
  typeface selection, 761
  visuals, 763–66
  white space, 758–59
Documenting sources, 623–96
  abbreviations in, 532
  APA style, 665–88
    content notes, 670
    directory to, 666–67
    example research essay, 678–88
    parenthetical citations, 666, 667–70
    reference list, 666–67, 671–78
  CBE style, 689–90
    in-text citations, 689
    references, 689–90

Documenting sources (continued)
  Chicago style, 691–96
    bibliography, 691–92, 695–96
    directory to, 691–92
    footnotes and endnotes, 691, 692–94
    and drafting essay, 621
    everyday use, 623
  MLA style, 624–64
    directory to, 624–25
    example research essay, 645–64
    explanatory/bibliographic notes,
      629–30
    list of works cited, 624–25, 630–45
    parenthetical citations, 624, 625–29
doesn't, don't, 846
Double comparatives, 256, 831
Double negatives, 370–71, 831
Doublespeak, 420
Double superlatives, 256, 831
Draft (drafting), 48–52
  answer to essay examinations, 744
  with computer, 751–52
  first, example of, 49–52
  and flexibility, 48
  guidelines for, 49
  planning of, 5, 46–48
  rereading, 56–57
  research essay, 611–13
    conclusion, 612–13
    incorporating source material,
      613–19
    introduction, 611–12
    listing sources, 621
    reviewing draft, 619–20
    revising and editing, 620–21
    title, 611
  response from others, 57–62
  reviewing, guidelines for, 58–59
  in writing process, 5–6
due to, 846
dye, die, 378
Dynamic verbs, 804–5

-e, adding suffixes to words ending in, 384
each, 162, 792
each other, 163
each other, one another, 846
-ed or -d endings
  editing, 211
  and multilingual writers, 802
  past participle, 177, 207, 211
Editing, 71–73, 191. See also Revising
  abbreviations, 533

adjectives, 258–59
colons, 515
commas, 477–78
comparative structures, 313
conciseness in sentences, 326
coordination, 332
dangling and misplaced modifiers, 305
dashes, 513
diction, 430–31
draft of research essay, 620–21
-ed or -d endings, 211
emphasis in sentences, 321
end punctuation, 491
essay examination answer, 744–45
finding pattern of errors, 72
language to build common ground,
  455
length of sentences, 353–54
oral presentations, 783
paragraphs, 151–52
parallelism, 346
parentheses, 513
possessive case, 495
process of, 7
pronoun-antecedent agreement, 247
pronoun case, 204
pronoun reference, 268
prose style, 366
quotation marks, 505
semicolons, 485
sentence fragments, 291
sentence openings, 356
-s and -es endings, 208
sexist language, 450
shifts, 272, 276
subject-verb agreement, 240
subordination, 338
verb tenses, 220
and writing with computer, 752–53
writing about literature, 739
Editions of books
  APA style documentation, reference
    list, 673
  Chicago style documentation
    bibliography, 696
    footnotes and endnotes, 693
  MLA style documentation, works cited
    list, 635, 636
Editorials
  APA style documentation, reference
    list, 674
  MLA style documentation, works cited
    list, 639

Editors
APA style documentation, reference list, 672–73
Chicago style documentation
bibliography, 695
footnote or endnotes, 693
MLA style documentation, works cited list, 633
effect, affect, 377, 841
e.g., 532
either, 792
either, or, 168
Either-or fallacy, 98
Electronic mail, 754–55
Electronic sources, 577–80
APA style documentation, reference list, 675–76
CBE style documentation, 690
MLA style documentation
parenthetical citation, 629
works cited list, 641–42
elicit, illicit, 378, 846
Ellipses, 517–18
to indicate omissions, 517
to indicate pause/hesitation, 518
in quotations, 616
Elliptical clauses, dangling, 305
Elliptical structures, 311–12
inconsistency in, 312
nature of, 202, 311
pronoun case in, 202
elude, allude, 378, 842
Embedded narration, 140–41
emigrate from, immigrate to, migrate, 846
eminent, immanent, imminent, 378
Emoticons, 518
Emotional fallacies, 102–3
bandwagon appeal, 102–3
false analogies, 103
flattery, 103
in-crowd appeal, 103
veiled threats, 103
Emphasis, 319–22
italics for, 542
in sentences, 319–22
climactic order, 320–21
closing/opening position for, 320
editing, 321
expletives for, 365
inverted word order, 371
of main idea, 320
parallel structures for, 345–46
revising, 322, 326–27

Emphatic (intensive) pronouns, 162
Encyclopedias, 567–69. *See also* Multi-volume works
general, 567–68
specialized, 568–69
Endnotes. *See* Footnotes and endnotes
End punctuation, 487–92
critical thinking about, 492
editing, 491
exclamation points, 490–91
periods, 488–89
question marks, 489–90
reading with eye for, 492
revising, 492
as special effects, 488
Engineering report, 715–18
English Prepositional Idioms, 166
enough, 792
ensure, insure, assure, 843
enthused, enthusiastic, 846
Enthymeme, 96–97
Equal (=) sign, 533
equally as good, 846
Eras, capitalization of, 525
Errors, most common, I-13–I-30
apostrophe misplaced or missing, I-21
comma missing after introductory element, I-16
comma missing with nonrestrictive element, I-19
comma missing in series, I-25
comma splice, I-21
commas with restrictive elements, I-27
commonly misspelled words, 375
fused sentences, I-27–I-28
with homonyms, 378–80
its and *it's* confusion, I-29
with *lie* and *lay, sit* and *set, rise* and *raise,* 215–17
modifiers, misplaced and dangling, I-28–I-29
preposition wrong or misplaced, I-20
in pronoun-antecedent agreement, I-26
pronoun reference, vague, I-17
pronoun shifts, I-22
sentence fragments, I-23
in subject-verb agreement, I-24–I-25
surface errors, learning from, I-13–I-15
tense shifts, I-22
verb ending wrong or missing, I-19–I-20
wrong tense or verb form, I-23–I-24
wrong word errors, I-18, 422
-es endings. *See -s* form

ESL. *See* Multilingual writers
especially, specially, 846
Essay examinations, 740–48
   analysis/evaluation of answer, 747
   analysis of questions, 742–43
   critical thinking about, 748
   drafting answer, 744
   everyday use, 741
   example of answer, 745–47
   and note-taking, 743–44
   preparing for, 740–41
   reading with eye for, 748
   revising and editing answer,
      744–45
   strategy terms, 742–43
   thinking through answer, 743–44
Essays, research. *See* Research essay
Essay titles
   capitalization of, 526
   in quotation marks, 503
et al., 532
etc., 532
Ethical fallacies, 90–91
   ad hominem charges, 90
   guilt by association, 90
Ethnic groups
   capitalization of, 525
   preferred terms related to, 452
   stereotypes about, 451–52
Ethnographic research methods, 580
Etymology
   dictionaries of, 400
   and dictionary entries, 395
Euphemisms, 419–20
every, 792
every day, everyday, 847
every one, everyone, 847
everything, 162
Evidence
   in academic writing, 704
   and audience, 30
Examples
   in argument, 92–93
   colon to introduce, 514
   in dictionary entry, 394
   in logical argument, 92–93
   transitional words used for, 131
except, accept, 377, 841
Exclamation points, 490–91
   with quotation marks, 505
Exclamatory sentences, 190, 837
Explaining
   a process, 125

and use of colon, 514
and use of dash, 513
Explanatory notes, MLA style for, 629–30
Expletives, 239, 365, 831
explicit, implicit, 847
Explicit thesis statement, 609
Exploring topic, 5, 32–46
   clustering, 35
   everyday use, 33
   freewriting, 34
   looping, 34–35
   questioning, 35–37
   use of other genres for, 37

Factual questions, in interviews, 583
fair, fare, 378
Fallacies
   emotional
      bandwagon appeal, 102–3
      false analogies, 103
      flattery, 103
      in-crowd appeal, 103
      veiled threats, 103
   ethical
      ad hominem charges, 90
      guilt by association, 90
   logical
      begging the question, 97
      either-or fallacy, 98
      hasty generalization, 98
      non sequitur, 98
      oversimplification, 98
      post hoc fallacy, 97–98
False analogies, 103
Familiar register, 416
Family relationships, capitalization of, 527
-f and *-fe* endings, plural of words ending
      in, 388
Farsi speakers, 823
farther, further, 847
Faulty predication, 309–11
few (a few), 162, 792
fewer, less, 847
Field labels, in dictionary, 395
Field notes, 601
Field research, 41, 580–85
   interviews, 582–84
   observation in, 581–82
   surveys/questionnaires, 584–85
Figurative language, 425–30, 725
   allusion, 429
   analogies, 101, 426
   cliches, 426

in emotional appeals, 101
hyperbole, 428
irony, 428
metaphors, 101, 426
mixed metaphors, 427
personification, 428
signifying, 429–30
similes, 101, 426
understatement, 428
Figures, in document, 763
Figures of speech. *See* Figurative
  language
Films
  APA style documentation, reference
    list, 677
  capitalization of title, 526
  italics for title of, 539
  MLA style documentation, works cited
    list, 643–44
Final draft. *See* Document design
finalize, 847
Final report, in applied sciences report,
  715–16
Finite verbs, 178, 801, 831
firstly, secondly, thirdly, 847
Flattery, 103
flaunt, flout, 847
Footnotes and endnotes. *See also* Notes
  APA style documentation, 670
  Chicago style documentation, 692–94
    books, 693–94
    periodicals, 694
    required information, 693
    subsequent notes for previously cited
      sources, 694
  footnote numbers, with quotation
    marks, 505
  MLA style documentation, 629–30
  of source, evaluation of, 590
for, 167, 463
Foreign words
  italics for, 541
  used with English, 24–25, 440–43
Foreword
  evaluation of, 590
  MLA style documentation, works cited
    list, 635
Formal register, 417–18
Format
  assessment of, I-12
  revising, 71
former, latter, 847
forth, fourth, 378

Fractions
  hyphen in spelled-out fractions, 547
  slash in, 516
Freewriting, 34
  and research topic, 560
French speakers, 820
Functional classification, sentences, 190,
  357–58
further, farther, 847
furthermore, 164, 169
Fused sentences, I-27–I-28, 281–89, 831
  checking for, 282–83
  critical thinking about, 289
  elimination of
    linking clauses with comma and coor-
      dinating conjunction, 284–85
    linking clauses with semicolon,
      285–86
    recasting independent clause as
      dependent clause, 286–87
    recasting two clauses as one indepen-
      dent clause, 286
    separating clauses into two sen-
      tences, 283–84
  nature of, 281
  revising, 288–89
Future tense
  future perfect, 220
  future perfect progressive, 220
  future progressive, 220
  simple, 220

Gale Directory of Databases, 567, 578
Gender, 831. *See also* Sexist language
  stereotypes about, 448–49
  and use of language, 439–40
General encyclopedias, 567–68
General indexes, 571–73
General-to-specific pattern
  paragraphs, 125–26
  opening paragraphs, 145
General words, 424–25
Generic *he,* avoiding use of, 246–47, 449
Genres of writing
  abstract, 712
  argument, 78–115
  engineering report, 715–18
  lab report, 711–15
  letters, 769–75
  literature, writing about, 723–39
  literature survey, 708–11
  meaning of, 24
  memos, 768–69

Genres of writing (*continued*)
  position paper, 718–22
  use in exploring topic, 37
Geographic names
  abbreviation of, 532
  capitalization of, 524, 527
  stereotypes about, 453–54
German speakers, 795
Gerund phrases, 178–79, 835
Gerunds, 177
  function of, 177
  vs. infinitives, 820–22
  possessive pronouns before, 197
  compared to present participles, 197
good and, 847
good, well, 847
Gopher, 756
gorilla, guerrilla, 378
Government documents
  APA style documentation, reference
    list, 673
  MLA style documentation, works cited
    list, 636–37
Grammar. *See also* Grammatical struc-
    tures; Sentences; *specific topics*
  basic grammar, understanding of,
    158
  parts of sentence, 170–87
  parts of speech, 159–70
    adjectives, 163–64
    adverbs, 164–66
    conjunctions, 167–69
    interjections, 170
    nouns, 160–61
    prepositions, 166–67
    pronouns, 161–63
    verbs, 159–60
Grammar checker, 752–53
Grammatical classification, sentences,
    189–90, 357
Grammatical structures, 307–16
  comparative structures, 313–14
  critical thinking about, 315
  elliptical structures, 311–12
  everyday use, 309
  faulty predication, 309–11
  missing words, 312
  mixed structure, 307–9
  parallel structures, 340–48
    critical thinking about, 347–48
    editing, 346
    for emphasis, 345–46
    everyday use, 342

  in headings/subheadings of reports,
    346–47
  including all necessary words in,
    344–45
  with pairs, 342–43
  reading with eye for, 347–48
  revising, 347
  in series, 340–41
  reading with eye for, 315
  revising, 314
  simplifying for conciseness, 325
Graphs, in document, 763, 765–66
Group author, APA style documentation,
    parenthetical citation, 669
Guide to Reference Books, 567
Guilt by association, 90

Habitual actions, verbs with, 209, 223
half a, a half, a half a, 847
hanged, hung, 847
Hasty generalization, 98
have
  as auxiliary verb, 210, 799–804
have, of, 848
Head, and noun phrase, 791
Headings
  in document, 761–62
  everyday use, 762
  parallelism in, 346–47
  subheadings, 590
heard, herd, 378
hear, here, 378
Hebrew speakers, 823
Helping verbs. *See* Auxiliary verbs
her, 792
herself, 162, 848
he/she, 848
Hesitation
  dashes to indicate, 513
  ellipses to indicate, 518
Heteroglossia, 725
himself, 162, 848
his, 792
his/her, 848
Historical events, capitalization of, 525
hoarse, horse, 378
Homonyms, 377–80
  most troublesome, listing of, 377
  words confused with, 378–79
  writing wrong form for, 380
hopefully, 848
Hours, abbreviations in, 531
however, 164, 169

Humanities
position paper, 718–22
writing in, 718–22
hung, hanged, 847
Hyperbole, 428
Hyphens, 544–49
in coined compounds, 547
in compound adjectives, 546
in compound words, 546, 548
critical thinking about, 549
in fractions/compound numbers, 547
with prefixes, 383, 547–48
reading with eye for, 549
with suffixes, 547–48
suspended hyphens, 547
for word division at end of line,
544–45
Hypothesis, 559–61
freewriting about, 560
moving from general topic to, 559
moving to working thesis from, 560–61

I, capitalization of, 526
i before *e* rule, 382
Ideas
coordination to relate equal ideas,
330–31
organization for coherent paragraph,
123–27
pairs of and parallel structures, 342–43
Idioms
in dictionary, 395
and multilingual writers, 423
i.e., 532
if, and subjunctive, 228
if, whether, 848
Illness, stereotypes about, 454
illusion, allusion, 378, 842
Illustration of point
paragraph development by, 135
topic development, 43
Imagery, 725
Images
in concluding paragraphs, 147
vivid, 147
impact, 848
Imperative mood, 226, 227, 831
Imperative sentences, 190, 357, 837
and subject of sentence, 172
Implied author, 725
implicit, explicit, 847
imply, infer, 848

in, 166, 811–12
incident, instance, 848
incredible, incredulous, 848
In-crowd appeal, 103
Indefinite articles, 794–95
Indefinite pronouns, 162, 836
as adjectives, 164
as antecedents, pronoun-antecedent
agreement, 246
as subject, and subject-verb agreement,
237–38
Independent clauses, 829
combining two clauses, 183
in comma splices, 286–87
in complex sentence, 189
in compound-complex sentence, 189–90
in compound sentence, 189
and conjunctive adverbs, 168–69
and coordinating conjunctions, 167
in fused sentences, 286–87
semicolons to link, 480–82
in simple sentence, 189
subject of, 194
Indexes
book indexes, 571
general indexes, 571–73
periodical indexes, 571–73
of source, evaluation of, 590
specialized indexes, 573–74
Index to Modern English, 822
Indicative mood, 226, 227, 832
Indirect discourse, 832
shifts in, 276–77
Indirect object, 832
and objective case, 195, 201
and transitive verb, 174
Indirect questions, 832
period in, 488
Indirect source, MLA style parenthetical
citation, 628–29
Inductive reasoning, 95–96
infer, imply, 848
Infinitive phrases, 179, 835
Infinitives, 177–78, 832
as adjectives, 250
as adverbs, 250–51
function of, 177
vs. gerunds, 820–22
perfect infinitive, 223
present infinitive, 222
splitting by modifier, 302
subject of, 196
Inflection, 832

Informal register, 417
Information, versus data, 605
Information gathering. *See* Research
InfoTrac, 564, 572
-*ing*
    present participle, 207–8
    verbals, 177, 197, 820–22
Initial abbreviations, 531
inside, inside of, 849
instance, incident, 848
Institutions, capitalization of, 525
Instructions, and modal auxiliaries, 807
insure, ensure, assure, 843
Intensifiers, 832
Intensive pronouns, 162, 836
interact with, interface with, 849
Interjections, 170, 832
    and commas, 470
    and exclamation point, 490–91
    functions of, 170
Interlibrary loans, 577
Internet, 754–56
Interrogative pronouns, 162, 837
    as adjectives, 164
Interrogative sentences, 190, 357, 837
Intertexuality, 726
Interviews, 582–84
    APA style documentation, reference
        list, 675
    conducting, 584
    finding subjects for, 583
    MLA style documentation, works cited
        list, 643
    planning for, 584
    types of questions, 583
Intransitive verbs, 174–75, 215–16, 832,
        839
    functions of, 174
Introduction
    of argument, 105
    content of paragraphs in, 64–65
    MLA style documentation, works cited
        list, 635
    opening paragraphs, 144–46
    of oral presentations, 778
    purposes of, 64
    of research essay, 611–12
    and reviewing draft, 58
    revising, 64–65
Introductory elements, commas after,
        I-16, 462, 477
Inversion of word order, as special effect,
        371

Irony, 428, 726
    quotation marks to signal, 503
irregardless, regardless, 849
Irregular verbs, 212–16, 833
    common irregulars, listing of, 212–14
    lie and *lay, sit* and *set, rise* and *raise,*
        215–17
    nature of, 212
is when, is where, 849
Italian speakers, 820
Italics, 538–43
    critical thinking about, 543
    for emphasis, 542
    everyday use, 540
    for foreign words/phrases, 541
    for letters as letters, 540
    for names of vehicles, 541
    for numbers as word, 540
    reading with eye for, 543
    for titles, 538–39
    titles of long works, 503
    for words as words, 540
it is, 365
itself, 162
its, it's, I-29, 377, 496, 792, 849
    and pronoun reference, 266

Japanese speakers, 816, 818, 823
Jargon, 419
    revising, 419
Job application, 770–76
    letter for, 775–76
    resume, 770, 772–74
Journals. *See also* Periodicals
    italics for title of, 539
just as . . . so, 168

Key-term notes, 601
Key words
    computer databases, 578
    in library search, 565
    in linking paragraphs, 150
    and paragraph coherence, 127
kind, sort, type, 849
kind of, sort of, 849
know, no, 378
Korean speakers, 790–91, 818, 823

Lab report, 711–15
Languages, capitalization of, 525
Language, varieties of, 433–44
    abbreviations and numbers in
        specialized writing, 536

in academic writing, 442–43
adverb use, 253–54
African American vernacular, 435–36
and argument, 94
be, 209
critical thinking about, 444
dictionaries of etymology/regional
English/slang, 400
double negatives, use of, 370–71
ethnic varieties of English, 435–36
everyday use, 433
gender differences, 439–40
global English, 434
numbers in specialized writing, 536
occupational varieties of English,
437–38
other languages used with English,
24–25, 440–43
passive voice in scientific writing,
225–26
reading with eye for, 444
recognition of, 433–34
regional varieties of English, 438–39
register in technical writing, 418
sentence variety and technical writing,
359
-s and *-es* endings, 233
signifying, 429–30
standard academic English, 434
vocabulary of professions and disciplines, 411
later, latter, 849
Latin abbreviations, 532
latter, former, 847
lay, lie, 215–17, 849
lead, led, 378
Learning, and writing, 707
leave, let, 849
Lectures
APA style documentation, reference
list, 677
MLA style documentation, works cited
list, 644–45
lend, loan, 850
less, fewer, 847
let, leave, 849
Letters
business, 769–70
block format, 771
modified block style, 775
writing guidelines, 770
for job application, 775–76
as sources

APA style documentation, parenthetical citation, 670
MLA style documentation, works
cited list, 643
Letters of the alphabet
italics for letters as letters, 540
parentheses to enclose letters in list, 510
plural of, 497
unpronounced in words, 381
Letters to the editor
APA style documentation, reference
list, 674
MLA style documentation, works cited
list, 639–40
liable, likely, apt, 843
Library, 41, 564–77
abstracts, 573–74
almanacs, 570
art collections, 577
atlases, 570–71
audio collections, 577
beginning research, 566
bibliographic resources, 569–70
book indexes, 571
call numbers, 577
card catalog, 574–75
circulation computer, 575–76
encyclopedias, 567–69
general indexes, 571–73
interlibrary loans, 577
key words, use of, 565
library catalog, 574–75, 576
microfiche catalog, 574–75
news digests, 570
periodical indexes, 571
reference materials, types of, 567
research strategy for use, 564–65
special collections, 577
specialized indexes, 573–74
staff, consulting, 566
tracings, use of, 576–77
vertical file, 577
video collections, 577
yearbooks, 570
Library catalog, 574–75, 576
identifying subjects, 576
tracings, 576
Library of Congress Subject Headings, 565,
576
lie, lay, 215–17, 849
like, as, as if, 843
like, such as, 850
likely, liable, apt, 843

likewise, 164, 169
Limiting adjectives, 827
Limiting modifiers, 298
Linking verbs, 173–74, 833, 839
  adjectives after, 252
  functions of, 173
  and subject-verb agreement, 238
Listening
  and building common ground, 455
  effective listening guidelines, 13
Lists
  colon to introduce, 514
  parentheses to enclose letters/numbers
    in, 510
literally, 850
Literary work, MLA style parenthetical
  citation, 628
Literature
  everyday use, 723
  literary terms, 724–26
  reading, guidelines for, 727
  writing about, 728–39
    assignment, 728–29
    context-based stance, 734–37
    critical thinking about, 739
    drama, 734–37
    editing, 739
    fiction, 730–34
    poetry, 737–39
    reader-based stance, 737–39
    text-based stance, 729–34
Literature cited, of natural sciences
  report, 712, 715
Literature survey, 708–11
Litotes, 428
little (a little), 792
loan, lend, 850
Logical fallacies, 97–98
  begging the question, 97
  either-or fallacy, 98
  hasty generalization, 98
  non sequitur, 98
  oversimplification, 98
  post hoc fallacy, 97–98
Logical patterns, 42–45
  cause-effect analysis, 44
  combining patterns, 45
  comparing and contrasting, 43–44
  definition, 43
  division and classification, 43
  general-to-specific pattern, 125–26
  illustration of point, 43
  narration, 44–45

paragraphs, 125–26
  problem-solution, 44
  specific-to-general pattern, 126
Longman Dictionary of American English,
  400, 790
Looping, 34–35
loose, lose, 379, 850
lots, lots of, 850
-ly, 164
  adding to words, 384–85

Magazine articles
  APA style documentation, reference
    list, 674
  Chicago style documentation
    bibliography, 696
    footnotes and endnotes, 694
  MLA style documentation, works cited
    list, 639
Magazines, italics for name of, 539
Mailing lists, 755
Main clauses. *See* Independent clauses
Main idea
  emphasis in sentences, 319–20
  and reviewing draft, 58
  and subordination in sentences, 334–35
  thesis, 38–40
Main verbs, 160, 210, 799
man, mankind, 449, 850
Manuscript preparation. *See* Document
  design
many, 792
Maps
  in document, 763
  MLA style documentation, works cited
    list, 645
Margins, in document, 761
Mass nouns, 834. *See also* Noncount nouns
may be, maybe, 850
may, can, 844
may, might, 160, 210, 799, 806
meat, meet, 379
media, 850
Memos, 768–69
Metaphors, 101, 426
  mixed, 427
Meter, 724
Methods and materials section, of natural
  sciences report, 712, 713–14
Microforms, 571
  MLA style documentation, works cited
    list, 642

Minus (−) sign, 533
Misplaced modifiers, I-28–I-29, 298–301, 833
  clauses, 300
  editing, 305
  squinting modifiers, 301
  words and phrases, 298–99
Mixed grammatical structures, 307–9
Mixed metaphors, 427
MLA Handbook for Writers of Research Papers, 536
MLA style documentation, 624–64
  directory to, 624–25
  example research essay, 645–64
  explanatory/bibliographic notes, 629–30
  parenthetical citations, 624, 625–29
  quotations, 614–15
  works cited list, 624–25, 630–45
    art works, 644
    books, 631–38
    cartoons, 645
    conference proceedings, 637
    dissertations, 642
    electronic correspondence, 643
    electronic sources, 640–42
    films/videotapes, 643–44
    government document, 636–37
    interviews, 643
    lectures or speeches, 644–45
    letters, 643
    maps or charts, 645
    microform article, 642
    pamphlets, 637
    performances, 645
    periodicals, 638–40
    recordings, 644
    software, 642
    television or radio programs, 644
Mnemonic devices, for spelling, 391
Modal auxiliaries, 210, 799–801, 805–8, 828
  everyday use, 799
  functions of, 210
  to make request/give instructions, 806–7
  to refer to past, 806
  to reveal doubt/certainty, 807–8
Modern Language Association (MLA) style. *See* MLA style documentation
Modified block style, business letters, 775
Modifiers, 297–306, 833
  adjective clauses as, 184

adjectives as, 249–50
adverb clauses as, 185
adverbs as, 250–51, 252–53
buzzwords, 323–24
critical thinking about, 306
dangling modifiers, 303–6
  editing, 306
  elliptical clauses, 305
  words and phrases, 304
disruptive modifiers, 301–3
  between parts of verb phrase, 302
  splitting infinitives, 302
  between subject and verb, 302–3
  between verb and object or subject complement, 303
everyday use, 299
limiting modifiers, 298
misplaced modifiers, 298–301
  clauses, 300
  editing, 306
  squinting modifiers, 301
  words and phrases, 298–99
nouns as, 257–58
reading with eye for, 306
sequencing, 251, 796–97
See also Adjectives; Adverbs
Money, numbers in amounts of, 536
Months of year, abbreviation of, 532
Monuments, capitalization of, 524
Mood, 226–29, 833
  imperative mood, 226, 227
  indicative mood, 226, 227
  nature of, 226
  shifts in, 273
  subjunctive mood, 226, 227–28
  of verbs, 159
moral, morale, 851
most, 162
Ms., 851
much, 792
Multilingual writers
  and adjective sequence, 251
  and adjective clauses, 822–24
  Arabic, 823
  and argument, 87
  and articles, 793–96
  audience and use of foreign words/terms, 24–25
  and capitalization, 527
  Chinese, 790–91, 802, 823
  and comma splices, 283
  and conditional sentences, 229, 824–25

Multilingual writers (continued)
and count and noncount nouns, 161, 788–91
and determiners, 791–92
and diction, 420
dictionaries for learners of English, 400, 790
Farsi, 823
French, 820
German, 795
and gerunds, 820–22
global English, 434
Greek, 795, 820
Hebrew, 823
and idioms, 423
and infinitives, 820–22
Italian, 820
Japanese, 790–91, 810, 816, 818, 823
judging sentence length, 283
Korean, 790–91, 818, 823
and modal auxiliaries, 210, 805–8
and modifiers, 796–97
and participial adjectives, 808
and prepositions, 810–12
Portuguese, 820
pronoun subjects, 268
Russian, 818
and sentence formation, 816–25
Spanish, 795, 802, 811, 817, 820
and spelling, 380
and stative and dynamic verbs, 804–5
and tenses, 802–4
and transitional words, 132
Turkish, 818
and two-word verbs, 813–14
and verb phrases, 798–801, 802–4
Vietnamese, 802
Multivolume works
APA style documentation, 673
Chicago style documentation
bibliography, 696
footnotes and endnotes, 694
MLA style documentation
parenthetical citation, 628
works cited list, 635
Musical works. See also Recordings
capitalization of title, 526
long works, italics for title of, 539
song titles, quotation marks for, 503
must, 160, 210, 799, 806, 807
my, 792
myself, 162, 848

Names of people, capitalization of, 524
Name-year form, CBE style documentation, 689–90
Narratives
chronological order of paragraphs, 124–25, 139
dialogue in, 140
embedded narration, 140–41
literary terms related to, 725–26
paragraph development by, 139–41
to support argument, 86–87
topic development by, 44–45
Narrator, 726
Nationalities, capitalization of, 525
Natural sciences, writing in, 711–15
abstract, 712
discussion and conclusions section, 712, 714–15
literature cited section, 712, 715
methods and materials section, 712, 713–14
N.B., 532
need to, 806
Negation, prefixes of, 406–7
Negatives, double, 370–71
neither, 792
neither, nor, 168
Neologisms, 418–19
New Roget's Thesaurus of the English Language in Dictionary Form, 400
Newspaper articles
APA style documentation, reference list, 674
Chicago style documentation
bibliography, 696
footnotes and endnotes, 694
MLA style documentation, works cited list, 639
Newspapers, italics for name of, 539
no, 792
no, know, 378
Nominal, 833
Nominalization, 365–66
Noncount nouns, 788–91
and determiners, 792
everyday use, 789
guidelines for use, 790
and multilingual writers, 161, 788–91
quantifying, 791
and zero article, 795
none, 162
Nonfinite verb, verbals as, 178, 839

Nonrestrictive elements, 833
  and commas, I-19, 464–65, 477
  nature of, 464
  compared to restrictive element, 464
Non sequitur, 98
nor, 167, 463
nor, or, 851
Notes. *See also* Footnotes and Endnotes
  bibliographic, MLA style for, 629–30
  content notes, APA style documenta-
    tion, 670
  footnotes and endnotes, Chicago style
    documentation, 691, 692–94
  key-term notes, 601
Note-taking, 593–602
  and accuracy, 593–94
  in classroom, guidelines for, 14–15
  combination notes, 601
  critical notes, 601
  and essay examinations, 743–44
  field notes, 601
  goals of, 593
  grouping notes, 610
  key-term notes, 601
  paraphrasing, 594, 596–600
  quoting, 594, 595–96
  summarizing, 594, 600–602
not only . . . but also, 168
Noun clauses, 184, 186, 829
  and multilingual writers, 819–20
Noun markers (determiners), articles as,
    161
Noun-phrase fragments, 293
Noun phrases, 176, 181, 790, 835
  and head, 790
  modifiers in, 796–97
Nouns, 160–61, 788–97, 833–34
  articles as noun markers, 161
  collective nouns, 160
  count and noncount nouns, 788–91
  functions of, 160
  gerund phrases as, 178
  infinitive phrases as, 179
  mass nouns, 161
  as modifiers, 257–58
  to name persons/places/things/concepts,
    160
  nominalization, 365–66
  plural form/singular meaning, 239
  plurals, 160–61
  possession, 161
  predicate nouns, 173
  proper nouns, 160

  singular, 160
  suffixes of, 408
Number (#) sign, 533
Number, 834
  and adjectives, 164
  shifts in, 275
  and verbs, 159
number, amount, 842
Numbers, 534–37
  in beginning of sentence, 535
  cardinal, 828
  commas in, 472
  critical thinking about, 537
  figures for, 534–35
  hyphen in spelled-out numbers, 547
  italics for number in text, 540
  ordinal, 834
  parentheses to enclose numbers in list,
    510
  plurals of, 497
  reading with eye for, 537
  in specialized writing, 536
  spelled out, 534, 535

O, capitalization of, 526
Object, 834
Objective case, 195–96, 829
  and compound structures, 201
  whom and *whomever,* 199, 200
Objective pronouns, 193
Object of the preposition, 176, 834
  noun clause as, 184
  and objective case, 196, 201
Objects. *See* Direct object; Indirect
    object
Observation
  in field research, 581–82
  guidelines for, 582
Occupation, and varieties of English,
    437–38
of, 848
off of, 875
OK, O.K., okay, 851
Omissions
  apostrophes for, 497
  ellipses for, 517
  of sentence elements, 817
on, 166, 811–12
on account of, 851
one, 162
one another, 163, 846
oneself, 162

On-line material. *See* Computer databases; Computers, on-line resources; Electronic sources
Onomatopoeia, 724
on, upon, 851
Open-ended questions, in interviews, 583
Opening paragraphs, 144–46
  anecdote in, 146
  general-to-specific pattern, 145
  opinion in, 146
  question in, 146
  quotation in, 145
Opinion, in opening paragraphs, 146
or, 167, 463, 851
Oral presentations, 777–783
  assignment for, 777
  critical thinking about, 783
  editing text for, 783
  everyday use, 778
  introduction and conclusion in, 778
  making presentation, 782–83
  practicing, 782
  purpose and audience, 778
  structure and signpost language in, 779
  syntax and diction in, 779
  text preparation, 779–81
  visuals, 781
Ordinal numbers, 834
Organization
  argument, 105–6
    classical system, 105–6, 107–13
    Toulmin system, 106
  assessment of, I-10–I-13
  information, 41–45
    chronological organization, 42
    logical organization, 42–45
    and reviewing draft, 58
    revising, 63
    spatial organization, 41–42
  paragraphs, 123–26
    chronological order, 124–25
    logical order, 125–26
    spatial order, 123–24
    specific-to-general, 126
Organizations, capitalization of, 525
or, nor, 851
ought to, 210, 806
our, 792
ourselves, 162
Outline, 46–48
  format for, 46–47
  full-sentence outline, 47

for research essay, 611
and writing with computer, 751
outside, outside of, 849
Oversimplification, 98
owing to the fact that, 851
Oxford Advanced Learner's Dictionary of Current English, 400, 790
Oxford Dictionary of English Etymology, 400
Oxford English Dictionary, 397–98

Page numbering, of document, 760
Paintings, italics for title of, 539
Pamphlets, italics for title of, 539
Paragraphs, 116–53
  assessment of, I-11–I-12
  coherent, 123–30
    organization of ideas, 123–27
    parallel structures, 128
    pronoun use, 129
    repetition of key words/phrases, 127
    transitional devices, 129–30
  critical thinking about, 153
  definition of, 116
  development of, 133–44
    cause and effect, 138–39
    combining patterns for, 141–42
    comparing and contrasting, 137–38
    defining word/concept, 136
    dividing and classifying, 136–37
    illustration of point, 135
    narration, 139–41
    problem-solution pattern, 139
    question-and-answer pattern, 139
    reiteration in, 141
  editing, 151–52
  everyday use, 118
  length of, 143–44
    reasons for new paragraph, 144
  linking of, 150–52
    key word repetition, 150
    parallel structure for, 150–51
    pronouns in, 151
    transitional expressions for, 151
  organization of, 123–26
    chronological order, 124–25
    logical order, 125–26
    spatial order, 123–24
    specific-to-general, 126
  purpose of, 66
  reader expectations of, 116–17
  reading with an eye for, 153
  and reviewing draft, 58

revising, 66, 133–34, 152–53
special-purpose, 144–50
    concluding paragraphs, 146–49
    opening paragraphs, 144–46
    paragraphs of dialogue, 149–50
    transitional paragraphs, 149
unified, 119–23
    position of topic sentence, 119–21
    relating each sentence to main idea,
        121–23
Parallel structures, 340–48
    antithesis, 370
    for coherence in paragraphs, 128
    critical thinking about, 347–48
    editing, 346
    for emphasis, 345–46
    everyday use, 342
    in headings, 346–47, 762
    including all necessary words in,
        344–45
    for linking paragraphs, 151
    with pairs, 342–43
    reading with eye for, 347–48
    revising, 347
    in series, 340–41
Paraphrasing, 594, 596–600
    critical thinking about, 606
    guidelines for, 599
    incorporating paraphrase in research
        essay, 617–18
    unacceptable and acceptable para-
        phrase, examples of, 597–99
Parentheses, 509–10
    editing, 513
    to enclose less important material, 509
    to enclose numbers or letters in list,
        510
    everyday use, 511
    parenthetical information and brackets,
        510
    question mark in, 490
    revising, 519
Parenthetical citations
    APA style documentation, 666, 667–70
    CBE style documentation, 689
    MLA style documentation, 624, 625–29
Parenthetical expressions, and commas, 470
Parody, 726
Participial adjectives, 808, 827
Participial phrases, 178, 181, 836
    misplaced, 299
    nonrestrictive, 466
    restrictive, 466

Participles, 177, 834
    adjectives, 250
    function of, 177
    past participle, 177, 223
    present participle, 177, 223
    present perfect participle, 223
Parts of speech, 159–70, 835. *See also spe-
    cific parts of speech*
    adjectives, 163–64
    adverbs, 164–66
    conjunctions, 167–69
    historical roots of, 159
    interjections, 170
    nouns, 160–61
    prepositions, 166–67
    pronouns, 161–63
    verbs, 159–60
passed, past, 379
Passive voice, 207, 224–26, 839–40
    appropriate use of, 225
    formation of, 224
    problem in use of, 224
    in prose, 367–68
    in scientific writing, 225–26
Past participle, 177, 207, 223, 800, 801,
    834
    irregular verbs, 212–14
Past tense, 801–4, 839
    be, 209
    irregular verbs, 212–14
    and modal auxiliaries, 806
    past perfect, 219
    past perfect progressive, 219
    past progressive, 219, 803–4
    simple, 207, 219, 803–4
    of subjunctive mood, 227–28
patience, patients, 379
peace, piece, 379
per, 851
Percentage (%) sign, 533
percent, percentage, 851
Perfect infinitive, 223
Perfect progressive tense, 839
    future, 220
    past, 219, 803–4
    present, 219, 803
Performances
    choreographic, italics for title, 538
    MLA style documentation, works cited
        list, 645
Periodicals
    APA style documentation, reference list,
        674–75

Periodicals *(continued)*
  Chicago style documentation
    bibliography, 695–96
    footnotes and endnotes, 694
  indexes to, 571–73
  MLA style documentation
    works cited list, 638–40
    on-line periodicals, 638–40
Periodic sentences, 358–59
Periods, 488–89
  with quotation marks, 504
Person, 159, 835
  shifts in, 275
  third-person singular and subject-verb
    agreement, 232–33
Personal communication. *See* Letters, sources
Personal notes, 601
personal, personnel, 379
Personal pronouns, 162, 837
  as adjectives, 164
Personification, 428
Perspective. *See* Stance
Persuasion. *See* Argument
Photocopying, source material, 601–2
Photographs, in document, 763
Phrasal verbs, 813–14
Phrase fragments
  appositive-phrase fragments, 293
  noun-phrase fragments, 293
  prepositional-phrase fragments, 293
  verbal-phrase fragments, 292
Phrases, 175–82, 835–36
  absolute phrases, 179–80, 181
  appositive phrases, 180
  commas with, 466–67
  dangling, 304
  function of, 175
  misplaced, 298–99
  nonrestrictive, 466
  noun phrases, 176, 181
  participial phrases, 181
  positioning of, 182
  prepositional phrases, 166, 176–77
  restrictive, 466–67
  for sentence openings, 355
  for shaping/expanding sentences, 181
  verbal phrases, 177–79
  verb phrases, 176
  wordy, in sentences, 324–25
Place, transitional words used for, 131
Place names. *See* Geographic names
Plagiarism, 602–5
  prevention of, 603–5
  recognition of, 602–3

plain, plane, 379
Planning a draft, 5, 46–48
  formal outline, 46–48
  writing out plan, 46–48
Plays
  capitalization of title, 526
  italics for title of, 539
    numbers in divisions of, 536
plenty, 851
Plot, 726
Plurals, 160–61
  apostrophes, 497
  count nouns, 790–91
  irregular forms, 161
  possessive case of, 494
  spelling, 387–89
    adding -*es*, 387
    adding -*s*, 387
    compound words, 388–89
    irregular plurals, 388
    words ending in *f* or *fe*, 388
    words ending in *y*, 388
Plus (+) sign, 533
plus, 852
P.M., 531
Poetry
  Brooks, Gwendolyn, "We Real Cool," 728
  capitalization of first word in line of,
    522–23
  capitalization of title, 526
  Carroll, Lewis, "Jabberwocky," 229; "The
    Walrus and the Carpenter," 825–26
  cummings, e. e., "Me up at does," 205
  Dickinson, Emily, "Much Madness is Di-
    vinest Sense," 520; "A little Mad-
    ness in the Spring," 528
  Francis, Robert, "The Pitcher," 269–70
  Frost, Robert, "Fire and Ice," 479
  Hughes, Langston, "Harlem," 431,
    "Theme for English B," 456–57
  literary terms related to, 724
  long, italics for title of, 539
  quotation marks for quoting, 500
  slash to mark division in, 516
  title in quotation marks, 503
  writing about, 737–39
Point of view, in narrative, 726
Pompous language, 419
  revising, 419
Portfolio. *See* Writing portfolio
Portuguese speakers, 820
Position paper, 718–22
Positive form
  adjectives, 255–56

adverbs, 255–56
Possessive adjectives, 196, 827
Possessive case, 196–97, 829
    apostrophes, 161, 493–95
    compound words, 494
    editing, 495
    indefinite pronouns, 493–94
    plural nouns, 161, 494
    singular nouns, 161, 493–94
    with two or more nouns, 495
Possessive pronouns, 193
    adjective forms of, 196
    before gerunds, 197
    noun forms of, 196
Poster sessions, APA style documentation,
    reference list, 677
Post hoc fallacy, 97–98
Precedents, in logical argument, 92–93
precede, proceed, 852
Predicate adjective, 173, 829
Predicate nouns, 173, 829
Predicate of sentence, 158, 173–75, 836
    complete predicate, 173
    compound predicate, 173
    and faulty predication, 309–11
    intransitive verb as, 174–75
    linking verb as, 173–74
    simple predicate, 173
    transitive verb as, 174
Preface
    evaluation of, 590
    MLA style documentation, works cited
        list, 635
Prefixes, 406–7, 836
    hyphen with, 383, 547–48
    of negation or opposition, 406–7
    of quantity, 407
    and spelling of words, 383
    of time and space, 407
Premise, major and minor, 96
Prepositional-phrase fragments, 293
Prepositional phrases, 166, 176–77, 836
    misplaced, 299
    nonrestrictive, 466
    restrictive, 467
    for sentence openings, 355
Prepositional verbs, 814
Preposition, object of. *See* Object of the
    preposition
Prepositions, 166–67, 836
    common, listing of, 166
    common errors, wrong or misplaced
        preposition, I-20
    compound prepositions, 166

functions of, 166
    idiomatic use of, 810–12
    and multilingual writers, 810–12
presence, presents, 379
Present infinitive, 222
Present participle, 177, 207–8,
    223, 800, 834
    compared to gerunds, 197
Present tense
    be, 209
    and multilingual writers, 801–2
    present perfect, 219, 802–3
    present perfect progressive, 219
    present progressive, 218, 803
    -s form, 208
    simple, 208, 218, 802, 803
    of subjunctive mood, 227
pretty, 875
Primary sources, 562
principal, principle, 379, 875
Problem-solution pattern
    paragraph development, 139
    topic development, 44
proceed, precede, 852
Process, explanation of, 125
Processing vocabulary, 402
Prodigy, 757
Producing vocabulary, 402
Progressive tense, 218–20
    elements of, 800–801
    future perfect progressive, 220
    future progressive, 220
    past perfect progressive, 219
    past progressive, 219
    present perfect progressive, 219
    present progressive, 218–19
Progress report, in applied sciences re-
    port, 715
Pronoun-antecedent agreement, 244–48
    collective-noun antecedents, 245
    common errors in, I-26
    compound antecedents, 244–45
    critical thinking about, 248
    editing, 247
    everyday use, 244
    indefinite-pronoun antecedents, 246
    and sexist pronouns, 246–47,
        449–50
Pronoun case, 194–205
    in appositives, 202
    in compound structures, 201
    critical thinking about, 205
    editing, 204
    in elliptical constructions, 202

Pronoun case (*continued*)
  everyday use, 194
  objective case, 195–96
  possessive case, 196–97
  reading with attention to, 205
  subjective case, 194–95
  we and *us* before nouns, 203
  who, whoever, whom, whomever,
    198–200
Pronoun reference, 263–70
  critical thinking about, 269–70
  editing, 268
  everyday use, 264
  keeping pronouns and antecedents
    together, 264–65
  matching pronouns to antecedents,
    263–64
  and multilingual writers, 268
  reading with attention to, 269–70
  revising, 269
  troublesome, 266–67
  vague, I-17
Pronouns, 161–63, 836
  in addressing audience, 29
  as adjectives, 164
  antecedent of, 161
  for coherence in paragraphs, 129
  demonstrative, 162
  indefinite, 162
  intensive, 162, 836–37
  interrogative, 162
  in linking paragraphs, 151
  objective, 193
  personal, 162
  possessive, 193
  reading with attention to, 248
  reciprocal, 163
  reflexive, 162
  relative, 162–63
  shifts in, 276
  subjective, 193
Pronunciation
  and dictionary, 394, 395
  and spelling, 381
Proofreading, 7, 73
  research essay, final draft, 621
  scope of, 73
  and writing with computer, 752–53
Proper adjectives, 164
  capitalization of, 523–24
Proper nouns, 160, 833
  capitalization of, 523–24
Proposal, in applied sciences report, 715

Prose style, 317–71
  active and passive voice, 367–68
  critical thinking about, 372
  editing, 366
  everyday use, 363
  general and specific words, balance of,
    424–25
  nouns changed to verbs, 365–66
  reading with eye for, 372
  revising, 366–67
  special effects, 369–72
    antithesis, 370–71
    inversion of word order, 371
    repetition, 369
  strong/precise verbs in, 364–65
Protagonist, 726
*Publication Manual of the American Psycho-
    logical Association,* 536, 665
  See also APA style documentation
Publisher's imprint, MLA style documenta-
    tion, works cited list, 637
Punctuation, 459–519. *See also* individual
    marks of punctuation
  brackets, 510–11
  colons, 514–15
  critical thinking about, 520
  dashes, 512–13
  ellipses, 517–18
  exclamation points, 490–91
  parentheses, 509–10
  periods, 488–89
  question marks, 489–90
  quotation marks, 500–507
  semicolons, 480–86
  slashes, 516
Purpose for writing, I-7–I-8, 4, 18–26
  analysis of assignment, 20–21, 22–23
  in context of academic writing, 24
  critical thinking about, 30–31
  deciding to write, 18–19
  everyday writing, 20
  and goals of instructor, 23
  identifying problem, 19
  and personal goals, 23
  reading with an eye for, 30
  research assignments, 555–56
  and reviewing draft, 58
  revising, 56
  and rhetorical stance, 25–26

Quantity, prefixes of, 407
Question-and-answer pattern, paragraph
    development by, 139

Question marks, 489–90
  with quotation marks, 505
Questionnaires, 584–85
  design of, 585
Questions
  in concluding paragraphs, 147
  indirect, period in, 488
  interrogative sentences, 190, 357
  in interviews, 583
  in opening paragraphs, 146
  in series, 490
Quotation marks, 500–507
  critical thinking about, 507
  and definitions, 503
  and dialogue, 502
  for direct quotations, 499–500
  editing, 505
  everyday use, 500
  and longer passages, 500
  misused, 503
  with other punctuation, 504–5
  for poetry, 500
  for quotation within quotation, 500
  reading with eye for, 507
  revising, 505
  semicolon with, 486
  to signal coinages, 503
  to signal irony, 503
  single, 500
  and titles, 502–3
quotation, quote, 852
Quotations, 613–16
  acknowledgement of, 604
  block quotations, 500
  bracket words in, 510–11, 616
  colon to introduce, 514
  and commas, 473
  in concluding paragraphs, 147
  ellipses in, 616
  in opening paragraphs, 145
  question mark in, 489
  in research paper, 613–16
    brief quotations, 614
    indicating changes, 616
    integrating into text, 615
    long quotations, 614–15
    reasons for use, 613
    signal phrases and signal verbs, 615–16
  shifts between direct and indirect discourse, 276–77
Quoting
  and accuracy, 596
  and note-taking, 594, 595–96

Race
  preferred terms related to, 452
  stereotypes about, 451
Radio programs
  italics for title of, 539
  MLA style documentation, works cited list, 644
  quotation marks for episode of, 503
rain, rein, reign, 379
raise, rise, 215–17, 852
Random House Webster's College Dictionary, 397
rarely ever, 852
Reader-based stance, in writing about literature, 737–39
Reader's Guide to Periodical Literature, 573
Readers. See Audience
Reading
  adverbs and adjectives, 259
  apostrophes, 498
  argument, 114–15
  with attention to words, 401
  capitalization, 528
  commas, 478–79
  comma splices, 289
  common ground, 456–57
  coordination and subordination, 339
  critical reading, guidelines for, 9–11
  critical thinking about process, 11
  dashes, 520
  diction, 431
  disciplinary discourse, 706, 722
  end punctuation, 492
  essay examinations, 748
  grammatical structures, 315
  hyphens, 549
  italics, 543
  language variety, 444
  literature, 727
  modifiers, 306
  paragraphs, 153
  pronoun case, 205
  pronoun reference, 269–70
  prose style, 372
  purpose and audience, 30
  quotation marks, 507
  relationship to writing, 9
  research essay, 622
  and revision, 76
  semicolons, 486
  sentence fragments, 296
  sentences, 192

Reading *(continued)*
  sentence style, 327
  sentence variety, 361
  shifts, 280
  sources, 590–93
  subject-verb agreement, 241–42
  verbs, 231
  vocabulary, 411–12
  and vocabulary building, 410–11
real, really, 852
Reasoning
  deductive reasoning, 96–97
  inductive reasoning, 95–96
reason is because, 852
Reciprocal pronouns, 163, 837
Recordings
  APA style documentation, reference
    list, 678
  italics for title of, 539
  MLA style documentation, works cited
    list, 644
Reference book articles, MLA style
    documentation, works cited list,
    635–36
References list
  books, 672–73
  dissertations, 677
  electronic media, 675–76
  film or videotape, 677
  government document, 673
  interviews, 675
  paper presented at meeting/symposium,
    677
  periodicals, 674–75
  poster session, 677
  recordings, 678
  reviews, 674
  software, 676
  technical reports/research reports/
    working papers, 677
  television programs/episodes, 677
  translation, 673
References. *See also* References list; works
    cited list
  CBE style documentation, 689–90
Reflexive pronouns, 162, 837
regardless, irregardless, 849
Regional English, 438–39
Register
  doublespeak, 420
  euphemisms, 419–20
  familiar register, 416
  formal register, 417–18

informal register, 417
  jargon, 419
  neologisms, 418–19
  pompous language, 419
  in technical writing, 418
Regular verbs, 211, 837
Reiterating, paragraph development by, 141
relate to, 852
Relative pronouns, 162–63, 837
  and adjective clauses, 184
  as adjectives, 164
  and noun clauses, 184
  as subject, and subject-verb agreement,
    238
Religions, capitalization of, 525
Repetition
  as effect in prose, 369
  key words in paragraphs, 127
  transitional words used for, 131
Requests, modal auxiliaries for, 806–7
Rereading, 11
  draft, 56–57
  of draft by multilingual writer, 57
Research, 10, 41, 551–695. *See also* Sources
  assignments, 11–12, 555–57
    audience for, 556
    deadlines, 556
    length of, 556
    purpose of, 555–56
    rhetorical stance, 556
    scheduling guidelines, 557
    scope of research, 556
    wording of, 555
  basic assumptions about, 552–53
  critical thinking about, 561, 585
  ethnographic methods, 580
  everyday use, 554, 608
  field research, 41, 580–85
    interviews, 582–84
    observation in, 581–82
    surveys/questionnaires, 584–85
  hermeneutic view of, 10
  hypothesis, 559–61
    moving from general topic to, 559
    moving to working thesis from, 560–61
  nature of, 552
  topic, 557–60
    choosing topic, 557–58
    narrowing topic, 558–59
    pre-writing exercises, 560
    research question related to, 559
    response to, 558
  and writing process, 40–41

Research essay, 607–22
  and audience, 608
  critical thinking about, 622
  drafting, 611–13
    conclusion, 612–13
    incorporating source material,
      613–19
    introduction, 611–12
    preparing list of sources, 621
    review of draft, 619–20
    revising and editing, 620–21
    title, 611
  incorporating source material, 613–19
    direct quotations, 613–16
    excessive, 618–19
    paraphrases, 617–18
    summaries, 617–18
  organizing information for, 610–11
    grouping notes, 610
    outlining, 611
  plan for, 607–9
  proofreading, 621
  reading with eye for, 622
  thesis, explicit, 609
Research reports, APA style documentation, reference list, 677
respectfully, respectively, 853
Responding, to reading, 11
Restrictive elements, 837
  and commas, 464, 478
  comparing to nonrestrictive element,
    464
  nature of, 464
Resumé, 770, 772–74
  example of, 773–74
  formats for, 772
  information for, 772
Reviewing a draft
  guidelines for, 619–20
  of research essay, 619–20
Reviews
  APA style documentation, reference
    list, 674
  MLA style documentation, works cited
    list, 639–40
Revising, 55–71. *See also* Editing
  and audience, 57
  climactic order, 322
  comma splices, 288–89
  conciseness in sentences, 326–27
  conclusion, 59, 65
  coordination, 332–33
  critical thinking about, 76–77

dangling modifiers, 304–5
dashes, 519–20
and distance from work, 55
draft of research essay, 620–21
emphasis in sentences, 322, 326–27
end punctuation, 492
essay examination answer, 744–45
everyday use, 55
format, 71
fused sentences, 288–89
grammatical structures, 314
guidelines for review of draft, 58–59
and instructor's response, 61–62
introduction, 58, 64–65
jargon, 419
main idea, 58
organization, 58, 63
paragraphs, 58, 66, 133–34, 152–53
parallelism, 347
parentheses, 519–20
pompous language, 419
process of, 6
pronoun reference, 269
prose style, 366–67
purpose for writing, 58
quotation marks, 505
reading with an eye for, 76
rereading draft, 56–57
and response from others, 6, 57–62
rhetorical stance, 58
sentence fragments, 291
sentence openings, 356
sentences, 59, 67–69, 191
sentence types, varying, 360–61
spelling, 391–92
subordination, 338–39
supporting points, 58, 62
thesis, 62
title, 58, 64
tone, 59, 70–71
word choice, 59, 69–70
and writing with computer, 752
Rhetorical classification, sentences, 190,
  358–59
Rhetorical stance, 25–26
  research assignments, 556
  and reviewing draft, 58
  revising, 56
  and tone, 591–92
Rhyme scheme in poetry, 724
Rhythm in poetry, 724
right, rite, write, 379
rise, raise, 215–17, 852

road, rode, 379
Run-on sentences. *See* Comma splices
Russian speakers, 818

scene, seen, 379
Schedule, for research assignments, 557
Schools, capitalization of, 526
Scientific writing. *See also* Technical
  writing
  passive voice in, 225–26
Sculpture, italics for title of, 539
Search logic, computer databases, 578–79
Seasons, and capitalization, 527
Secondary sources, 563
Semicolons, 480–86
  in compound sentences, 463
  and conjunctive adverbs, 169
  critical thinking about, 486
  editing, 485
  everyday use, 481
  with *however,* 169
  to link independent clauses, 480–82
  linking clauses with, 285–86
  misuse of, 484–85
  overuse of, 483–84
  with quotation marks, 486, 504
  reading with eye for, 486
  to separate items in series, 483
  with *therefore,* 169
  with *thus,* 169
sense, since, 379
Sentence fragments, 1-23, 290–96, 838
  compound-predicate fragments, 294
  critical thinking about, 296
  dependent-clause fragments, 295
  editing, 291
  everyday use, 292
  phrase fragments, 292–93
    appositive-phrase fragments, 293
    prepositional-phrase fragments, 293
    verbal-phrase fragments, 292
  reading with eye for, 296
  revising, 291
Sentences, 156–91, 837
  balanced sentence, 342–43
  classification of, 188–91
    functional classification, 190, 357–58
    grammatical classification, 189–90,
      357
    rhetorical classification, 190, 358–59
  clauses, 183–87
  comma splices, 281–89
  complex sentences, 189, 357, 837

compound-complex sentences, 189–90,
  357
compound sentences, 189, 357
conditional sentences, 824–25
coordination, 328–34
  critical thinking about, 339
  editing, 332
  everyday use, 329
  reading with eye for, 339
  to relate equal ideas, 330–31
  revising, 332–33
  for special effect, 331–32
critical thinking about, 192, 327
cumulative sentences, 359
declarative sentences, 190, 357, 837
definition of, 158
editing, 151, 191
everyday use, 157, 817
exclamatory sentences, 190, 357, 358,
  837
faulty construction
  comparisons, 313–14
  elliptical structures, 311–12
  faulty predication, 309–11
  missing words, 312
  mixed structure, 307–9
  reading with eye for, 315
fused sentences, 281–89
grammar of, 158–88
  basic grammar of, 158
  parts of sentence, 170–87
  parts of speech, 159–70
imperative sentences, 190, 357, 837
interrogative sentences, 190, 357, 837
and multilingual writers, 816–25
nucleus of, 818–19
parallelism in. *See* Parallel structures
parts of, 175–83
  phrases, 175–83
  predicate, 158, 173–75
  subject, 158, 171–72
patterns of, 171
periodic sentences, 358–59
reading with eye for, 192
and reviewing draft, 59
revising, 67–69, 191
  for sentence length, 67
  for sentence structure, 68
  for sentence openings, 68–69
shaping/expanding
  with clauses, 186
  with phrases, 181
simple sentences, 189, 357, 837

subordination
  critical thinking about, 339
  to distinguish main idea, 334–35
  editing, 338
  everyday use, 329
  reading with eye for, 339
  revising, 338–39
  for special effect, 336–38
topic sentence
  implied, 121
  position of, 119–21
Sentence style
  assessment of, I-11
  conciseness, 322–26
    and buzzwords, 323–24
    editing, 326
    and redundant words, 323
    revising, 326–27
    and simple grammatical structure, 325
    and wordy phrases, 324–25
  emphasis, 319–22
    climactic order, 320–21
    closing/opening position for, 320
    editing, 321
    revising, 322, 326–27
  everyday use, 319, 351
  grammatical structures, consistency of, 307–16
  lengths of sentences, 350–54
  openings, 354–56
    with dependent clauses, 356
    with phrases, 355
    revising, 356
    with transitional expressions, 355
  reading with eye for, 327
  types of sentences, 357–60
    functional types, 357–58
    revising, 360–61
    rhetorical types, 358–61
  and varieties of English, 359
  variety of sentences
    critical thinking about, 361
    editing, 353–54, 356
    reading with eye for, 361
Sequence
  of tenses, 222–23
    sequence and habitual actions, 223
    sequence with infinitives, 222–23
    sequence with participles, 223
  transitional words used for, 131
Series
  colon to introduce, 514

commas between items in, I-25, 468–69, 476, 477
  parallel structures in, 340–41
  of questions, 490
  semicolons to separate items, 483
-s and -es endings. See -s form
-s form
  African American English, 233
  editing, 208
  and multilingual writers, 802
  plurals, 387
  present tense, 208
  and singular verb form, 233
set, sit, 215–17, 853
Setting, 726
several, 792
Sexist language, 449–50
  alternative to male-oriented words, 449–50
  avoiding generic he/his/him, 246–47, 449
  dictionary section on, 397
  editing, 450
  and pronoun-antecedent agreement, 246–47
  pronouns, reading with attention to, 248
Sexual orientation, stereotypes about, 454
shall, 808
shall, should, 160, 210, 806
shall, will, 853
Shifts, 271–80
  critical thinking about, 280
  in diction, 279
  between direct and indirect discourse, 276–77
  editing, 272, 276
  everyday use, 273
  in mood, 273
  in number, 275
  in person, 275
  pronouns, 276
  in pronouns, I-22
  reading with eye for, 280
  in tense, I-22, 272
  in tone, 278–79
  in voice, 274
Ships
  capitalization of, 525
  italics for, 541
Short stories, title in quotation marks, 503
should, 160, 210, 806
sic, 511
sight, site, cite, 378

Signal verbs, before quotations, 615–16
Signifying, 429–30
Signpost language, in oral presentations, 779
Similes, 101, 426
Simple future tense, 220
Simple past tense, 207, 219, 803–4
Simple predicate, 173
Simple present tense, 208, 218, 802, 803
Simple sentences, 189, 357, 837
Simple subject, 171
since, 853
Singular nouns, 160
 count nouns, 790–91
 of plural form, 239
sit, set, 215–17, 853
site, cite, sight, 378
Slang, 414
 dictionaries of, 400
 and quotation marks, 504
Slashes, 516
 to mark line divisions in poetry, 516
 to separate alternatives, 516
 to separate parts of fractions, 516
Smileys, 518
Snapshots, in topic development, 45
so, 167, 463
Social sciences
 literature survey, 708–11
 writing in, 708–11
Software
 APA style documentation, reference list, 676
 MLA style documentation, works cited list, 641–42
some, 162, 792
somebody, 162
some body, somebody, 853
some one, someone, 853
someplace, somewhere, 853
some time, sometime, sometimes, 853
Songs, title in quotation marks, 503
so, so that, 853
sort of, kind of, 849
sort, type, kind, 849
Sources, I-6–I-7, 586–606. *See also* Documenting sources
 acknowledgement of, 603–5
 assessment of, I-13
 author's stance, 591–92
 disagreements among sources, 592–93
 main point and evidence, 592
 usefulness of sources, 589–90

building common ground, 456
choosing, 586–90
computer databases, 564–65, 577–80
 key words, 578
 search procedure, 578–79
everyday use, 563
incorporating in research essay, 613–19
 direct quotations, 613–16
 excessive source material, 618–19
 paraphrases, 617–18
 summaries, 617–18
inferences from, 605–6
interpretation of, 605–6
library, 564–77
 abstracts, 573–74
 almanacs, 570
 art collections, 577
 atlases, 570–71
 audio collections, 577
 beginning research, 566
 bibliographic resources, 569–70
 book indexes, 571
 call numbers, 577
 card catalog, 574–75
 circulation computer, 575–76
 encyclopedias, 567–69
 general indexes, 571–73
 interlibrary loans, 577
 key words, use of, 565
 library catalog, 574–75, 576
 microfiche catalog, 574–75
 news digests, 570
 periodical indexes, 571
 reference materials, types of, 567
 research strategy for use, 564–65
 special collections, 577
 specialized indexes, 573–74
 staff, consulting, 566
 tracings, use of, 576–77
 vertical file, 577
 video collections, 577
 yearbooks, 570
note-taking, 593–602
 and accuracy, 593–94
 combination notes, 601
 critical notes, 601
 field notes, 601
 goals of, 593
 key-term notes, 601
 paraphrasing, 594, 596–600
 quoting, 594, 595–96
 summarizing, 594, 600–602
and original ideas, 606

parallelism in headings, 346–47
photocopying, 601–2
and plagiarism, 602–5
primary sources, 562
and purpose and audience, 30
quoting passages with effective adjectives, 259
reading of, 590–93
secondary sources, 563
shifts between direct and indirect discourse, 276–77
support for argument, 104–5
synthesizing information from, 605–6
verbs to integrate sources, 230
working bibliography, 586–89
Space, prefixes of, 407
Spacecraft
capitalization of, 525
italics for, 541
Spacing, in document, 761
Spanish speakers, 795, 802, 811, 817, 820
Spatial organization
of information, 41–42
of paragraphs, 123–24
Special collections, library, 577
Special effects
antithesis, 370–71
comma splices as, 289
coordination for, 331–32
end punctuation, 488
inversion of word order, 371
in prose, 369–72
repetition, 369
subordination for, 336–38
Specialized encyclopedias, 568–69
Specialized indexes, 573–74
specially, especially, 872
Specific-to-general pattern
conclusions, 147
paragraphs, 126
Specific words, 424–25
Speeches, MLA style documentation, works cited list, 644–45
Spelling, 374–92
American versus British words, 380
commonly misspelled words, listing of, 375
critical thinking about, 392
and dictionary entry, 394
everyday use, 377
homonyms, 377–80
mnemonic devices for, 391

and multilingual writers, 380
plurals, 387–89
and pronunciation, 381
revising, 391–92
rules of, 382–84
adding prefixes, 383
adding suffixes, 383–84
i before *e*, 382
taking inventory, 389–91
Spelling checker, 72, 390–91, 752–53
guidelines for use, 390–91
Split infinitive, 838
Spoken language. *See also* Oral presentations
and collaboration, 12–13
comma splices in, 282
critical thinking about, 14
and indicative mood, 228
objective case in, 195
relationship to writing, 13–14
and use of *whom*, 198–99
Squinting modifiers, 301, 838
Stance
of author, 591–92
critical, 729
rhetorical, 25–26, 56, 58, 556
in writing about literature, 729–39
Standard academic English, 24, 434
Stanza, 724
State names, abbreviations, 489
stationary, stationery, 379, 854
Statistical material, acknowledgement of, 604
Stative verbs, 804–5
Stereotypes
age-related, 452–53
class-related, 453
gender-related, 448–50
and geographic areas, 453–54
racial and ethnic, 451–52
religious, 454
and sexual orientation, 454
Stories, capitalization of title, 526
Strategy terms, essay examinations, 742–43
Structure, inconsistent, 831
Style, of narrative, 726
Subheadings, 590
Subject complement, 173, 829
noun clause as, 184
and subjective case, 195, 201
Subjective case, 194–95, 829
and compound structures, 201
who and *whoever*, 199

Subjective pronouns, 193
Subject of sentence, 158, 171–72, 838
  complete subject, 171
  compound subject, 172
  and faulty predication, 309–11
  and imperative sentences, 172
  modifiers between verb and, 302–3
  and multilingual writers, 816–17, 818
  noun clause as, 184
  simple subject, 171
Subject-verb agreement, 232–41
  and collective-noun subjects, 236–37
  common errors in, I-24–I-25
  and compound subjects, 236
  critical thinking about, 241–42
  editing, 240
  everyday use, 234
  and indefinite pronoun subjects, 237–38
  and linking verbs, 238
  reading with eye to, 241–42
  and relative pronoun subjects, 238
  and subject following verb, 239
  and subject of plural form/singular
    meaning, 239
  subject/verb separated by other words,
    233–35
  third-person singular subjects, 232–33
  and titles, 240
  and words used as words, 240
Subjunctive mood, 226, 227–28, 838
  in dependent clauses, 228
  past tense of, 227–28
  present tense of, 227
Subordinate clauses. *See* Dependent
  clauses
Subordinate structures
  critical thinking about, 339
  to distinguish main idea, 334–35
  editing, 338
  everyday use, 329
  reading with eye for, 339
  revising, 338–39
  for special effect, 336–38
Subordinating conjunctions, 168, 830
  and adverb clauses, 185, 465
Subordination, 839
subsequently, consequently, 845
Substantive, 839
such as, like, 850
Suffixes, 408–9, 839
  adding to words
    -ally, 384
    -cede, -ceed, -sede, 385

    doubling final consonant, 386
    dropping final *e,* 383–84
    keeping final *e,* 384
    -ly, 384–85
    words ending in a consonant and *y,*
      385
    words ending in a vowel and *y,* 385
  of adjectives, 409
  hyphen with, 547–48
  of nouns, 408
  of verbs, 409
Summarizing
  critical thinking about, 606
  guidelines for, 600–601
  and note-taking, 600–601
  and reading, 10
Summary
  dash to introduce summary, 513
  incorporating in research essay, 617–18
  transitional words to signal, 131
Superlative forms of adjectives and
    adverbs, 255–57, 827, 828
  compared to comparative form, 256
  double superlatives, 256
  incomplete comparisons, 256–57
  irregular forms, 255–56
Supporting evidence, use of, I-6
Supporting points
  reviewing a draft for, 58
  revising, 62
supposed to, used to, 854
sure, surely, 854
Surveys, questionnaire design, 584–85
Suspended hyphens, 547
Syllables, unpronounced in words, 381
Syllogisms, 96
Symbolism, 725
Symbols
  emoticons, 518
  plurals of, 497
  use of, 533
Synonyms
  dictionaries of, 400
  and dictionary, 395
Syntax, 839
Synthesizing information, from data, 605–6

Table of contents, evaluation of, 590
Tables, in document, 763, 764
Tag questions, and commas, 471
take, bring, 844
Technical reports, APA style documenta-
  tion, reference list, 677

Technical writing
    passive voice in scientific writing, 225–26
    register in, 418
    and sentence variety, 359
Television programs
    APA style documentation, reference
        list, 677
    italics for title of, 539
    MLA style documentation, works cited
        list, 644
    quotation marks for episodes of, 503
Tenses, 217–24, 802–4
    editing, 220
    future perfect, 220
    future perfect progressive, 220
    future progressive, 220
    future, simple, 220
    past perfect progressive, 219
    past perfect tense, 207
    past progressive, 219
    past, simple, 207, 219
    present perfect, 219
    present perfect progressive, 219
    present progressive, 218–19
    present, simple, 208, 218
    sequence of, 222–23
    shifts in, I-22, 272
    simple, 217–18
Testimony, in logical argument, 94
Text-based stance, in writing about
        literature, 729–34
than, then, 379, 854
that, 162, 163, 792
    and pronoun reference, 266
    and subjunctive, 228
that, which, 854
the, 161, 793–94
their, 792
theirselves, themselves, 854
their, there, they're, 377, 854
Theme, of narrative, 726
themselves, 162
then, than, 379, 854
there are, 239, 365
there is, 239
Thesaurus, 400
these, 162, 792, 796–97
Thesis, 38–40
    argumentative thesis, formulation of,
        84–85
    evaluation of, 39–40
    explicit thesis statement, 609
    implied, 85

in opening paragraph, 145
    parts of, 39
    and reviewing draft, 58
    revising, 62
    testing of, 609
    working thesis, 38–40, 560–61
they, 267
this, 162, 792
    and pronoun reference, 266
those, 162, 792
threw, thorough, through, 379
'til, till, until, 855
Time
    A.M./P.M., 531
    colon in, 515
    numbers in, 536
    prefixes of, 407
    transitional words used for, 131
    and verbs, 159
Title page, of document, 760
Titles
    capitalization of, 526
    colon in, 515
    commas in, 472
    of individuals
        abbreviation of, 529–30
        capitalization of, 525–26
    italics for, 538–39
    and quotation marks, 502–3
    of research essay, 611
    and reviewing draft, 58
    revising, 64
    and subject-verb agreement, 240
Title within the title, MLA style documen-
        tation, works cited list, 638, 640
to, two, too, 377, 855
Tone
    dash to mark change in, 513
    meaning of, 70, 278
    of narrative, 726
    and reviewing draft, 59
    revising, 70–71
    and rhetorical stance, 591–92
    shifts in, 278–79
Topic
    exploring, 5, 32–46
        brainstorming, 33–34
        clustering, 35
        everyday use, 33
        freewriting, 34
        looping, 34–35
        questioning, 35–37
        use of other genres, 37

Topic (*continued*)
  organizing information, 41–46
  research on, 40–41
  for research project. *See* Research, topic
Topic part, of thesis, 39
Topic sentence
  editing, 151
  implied, 121
    position of, 119–21
Toulmin system
  analysis of argument, 114
  organization of argument, 106
toward, towards, 855
Tracings, 576
Trade names, capitalization of, 525
Trains
  capitalization of, 525
  italics for, 541
Transitions, 129–30
  for coherence in paragraphs, 129–32
  in linking paragraphs, 151
  and multilingual writers, 132
  transitional expressions
    and commas, 470
    for sentence openings, 355
  transitional paragraphs, 149
  words commonly used as, 131
Transitive verbs, 174, 215–16, 839
  and direct object, 174
  functions of, 174
  and indirect object, 174
Translation, 25, 443
  APA style documentation, reference
    list, 673
  MLA style documentation, works cited
    list, 634
*Trash Cash, Fizzbos, and Flatliners: A
  Dictionary of Today's Words*, 400
try and, try to, 855
Turkish speakers, 818
two, to, too, 377, 378, 855
type, kind, sort, 849
Typeface, for document, 761

Unabridged dictionaries, 397–98
Understatement, 428
uninterested, disinterested, 846
unique, 855
Units of measure, abbreviation of, 533
Unity of paragraphs. *See* Paragraphs,
  unified
until, 855
upon, on, 851

us, and pronoun case, 203
Usage, dictionaries of, 399
  Glossary of, 841–56
Usage labels, in dictionary, 394, 395
used to, supposed to, 854
Usenet news groups, 755

Vehicles
  capitalization of names of, 525
  italics for names of, 541
Verbal-phrase fragments, 292
Verbal phrases, 177–79, 839
  gerund phrases, 178–79
  infinitive phrases, 179
  participial phrases, 178
  for sentence openings, 355
Verbals, 839
  functions of, 177
  gerunds, 177, 820–22
  infinitives, 177–78, 820–22
  as nonfinite verb, 178
  object of, 195–96
  participles, 177
Verb phrases, 160, 176, 798–801, 802–4,
    836, 839
  forming, 798–801
  modifiers misplaced in, 302
  parts of, 302
  perfect and progressive, 802–4
Verbs, 159–60, 839. *See also* Auxiliary
    verbs; Predicate of sentence; Sub-
    ject-verb agreement
  adverbs modifying, 252–53
  auxiliary verbs, 160, 210–11, 799
  common errors, verb ending wrong or
    missing, I-19–I-20
  critical thinking about, 231
  dynamic verbs, 804–5
  everyday use, 207
  expletives, 365
  finite verbs, 178
  forms of, 206–9
    base form, 207
    past participle, 207
    present participle, 207–8
  functions of, 159
  to integrate sources, 230–31
  intransitive verbs, 174–75, 215–16
  irregular, 212–16
  linking verbs, 173–74
  main verbs, 160, 210, 799
  mood of, 159, 226–29
  nonfinite verbs, 178

nouns formed from, 365–66
and number, 159
and person, 159
phrasal-prepositional verbs, 814
phrasal verbs, 813–14
precise verbs in prose, 364–65
prepositional verbs, 814
reading with eye for, 231
regular, 211
-s and -es endings, 208, 233, 387, 802
-s form, 208
signal verbs, 615–16
stative verbs, 804–5
suffixes of, 409
tenses, 217–24
 editing, 220
 future perfect, 220
 future perfect progressive, 220
 future progressive, 220
 future, simple, 220
 past perfect, 207
 past perfect progressive, 219
 past progressive, 219
 past, simple, 207, 219
 present perfect, 219
 present perfect progressive, 219
 present, progressive, 218–19
 present, simple, 208, 218
 sequence of, 222–23
 simple, 217–18
and time, 159
transitive verbs, 174, 215–16
two-word verbs, 813–14
voice, 159, 224–26
 active voice, 224
 passive voice, 224–26
 varieties of language, 225–26
Veronica, 756
Vertical file, library, 577
very, 855
Videotapes
 APA style documentation, reference
  list, 677
 italics for title of, 539
 library collections, 577
 MLA style documentation, works cited
  list, 643–44
Vietnamese speakers, 802
Visuals
 in document design, 763–64
 oral presentations, 781
Vocabulary, 402–12
 context clues to meaning, 410

critical thinking about, 411–12
 everyday use, 403
 and history of English, 403–5
 prefixes, 406–7
 processing vocabulary, 402
 producing vocabulary, 402
 in professions and disciplines, 411
 and reading, 410–11
 reading with attention to, 411–12
 suffixes, 408–9
 word hoard, creating, 409–11
 word roots, 405–6
Voice, 159, 224–26, 839–40
 active voice, 224
 alternating in prose, 367–68
 passive voice, 207, 224–26
 shifts in, 274
 varieties of language, 225–26
Vowels, unstressed in words, 381

waist, waste, 379
WAIS (Wide Area Information Server),
  756
Walford's Guide to Reference Materials,
  567
Warning, in concluding paragraphs, 147
way, ways, 855
we, and pronoun case, 203
weak, week, 379
wear, were, where, 379
weather, whether, 377
Webster's Collegiate Thesaurus, 400
Webster's Dictionary of Synonyms, 400
Webster's New World Dictionary, 395, 397
Webster's Third New International Dictionary of the English Language, 398
well, good, 847
what, 162, 163, 792
whatever, 163
where, 855
whether, if, 848
whether . . . or, 168
whether, weather, 377
which, 162, 163, 792
 and pronoun reference, 266
which, that, 854
whichever, 163
which, who, 855
which, witch, 379
White space, in document design, 758–59
who, 162, 163
 pronoun case, 198–200
 and pronoun reference, 267

whoever, 163
pronoun case, 199–200
whom, pronoun case, 198–200
whomever, pronoun case, 199–200
whose, 792
who's, *whose*, 377, 856
who, *whom*, 856
who, *which*, 267, 855
will, *shall*, 853
will, *would*, 160, 806, 807
Women, use of language, 439–40
Word choice. *See also* Diction
and reviewing draft, 59
revising, 69–70
Word division
in dictionary entry, 394, 395
everyday use, 545
guidelines for, 545
hyphens in, 544–45
Word order, inversion of, 371
Word processing. *See* Computers, writing
with
Word roots, 405–6
common roots/meanings, listing of, 405
Words. *See also* Vocabulary; Word choice;
and specific types of words
abstractions, 424
buzzwords, 323
checking for wrong word errors, 422
critical thinking about, 401
dangling, 304
defining and paragraph development,
136
and dictionary, 393–401
general words, 424–25
inverted word order, 371
misplaced in sentences, 298–99
missing in grammatical structures, 312
in parallel structures, 344–45
pronunciation of, 381
reading with attention to, 401
redundant in sentences, 323
specific words, 424–25
spelling, 374–92
Words used as words
italics for, 540
plural of, 497
and subject-verb agreement, 240
Working bibliography, 586–89
preparation guidelines, 587–88
Working thesis, 38–40, 560–61
Works cited list
art works, 644

books, 631–38
cartoons, 645
conference proceedings, 637
dissertations, 642
electronic correspondence, 643
electronic sources, 640–42
films/videotapes, 643–44
government document, 636–37
interviews, 643
lectures or speeches, 644–45
letters, 643
maps or charts, 645
microform article, 642
pamphlets, 637
performances, 645
periodicals, 638–40
recordings, 644
software, 642
television or radio programs, 644
World Wide Web (WWW), 756
would, 160, 210, 806, 807
write, *right*, *rite*, 379
Writing
academic writing, 24, 698–722
best conditions for, 48–49
with computers, 750–57
essay examinations, 740–48
everyday use, 708
importance of, 2–3
and learning, 707
about literature, 723–39
relationship to talking, 13–14
relationship to reading, 9
in standard academic English, 24
Writing inventory, I-3–I-5
Writing log, I-4–I-5
purpose of, 7
research log, 557
Writing portfolio, 784–86
critical thinking about, 785
organization of, 785
purpose and audience for, 784
response to, 785
selection of work for, 785
Writing process, 71. *See also specific
topics*
and audience, 26–31
critical thinking, 7–8, 52–53
drafting in, 5–6, 48–52
editing/proofreading in, 7, 71–73
exploring in, 5, 32–46
planning in, 5, 46–48
purpose for writing, 4, 18–26

recursive activities in, 3–4
revising in, 6, 55–71

Yearbooks, 570
Years, abbreviations in, 531
yet, 167, 463, 844
you, 267
your, 792

yourself, 162, 872, 848
yourselves, 162
your, you're, 377, 856
-y
   plural of words ending in, 388
   suffix added to words ending in, 385

Zero article, 795–96

Acknowledgments (*continued from copyright page*)

e. e. cummings. "Me up at does" from *Complete Poems, 1904–1962*, edited by George J. Firmage. Copyright © 1963, 1991 by the Trustees for the E. E. Cummings Trust. Reprinted by permission of Liveright Publishing Corporation.

Emily Dickinson. "Much Madness is divinest Sense," and "A little Madness in the Spring" from *The Poems of Emily Dickinson*, Thomas H. Johnson, ed. Copyright © 1951, 1955, 1979, 1983 by the President and Fellows of Harvard College. Reprinted by permission of The Belknap Press of Harvard University: Cambridge, Mass., and the Trustees of Amherst College.

Robert Francis. "The Pitcher" from *The Orb Weaver* by Robert Francis. Copyright © 1960 by Robert Francis, Wesleyan University Press. Reprinted by permission of University Press of New England.

Robert Frost. "Fire and Ice" from *The Poetry of Robert Frost*. Copyright © 1951 by Robert Frost. Copyright © 1923, 1969 by Henry Holt and Co., Inc. Reprinted by permission of Henry Holt and Co., Inc.

A. E. Housman. "Loveliest of Trees" from *The Collected Poems of A. E. Housman*. Copyright © 1965 by Holt, Rinehart and Winston. Copyright © 1967, 1968 by Robert E. Symons. Reprinted by permission of Henry Holt and Co., Inc.

"Is Your Money Where Your Heart Is?" advertisement. Created by Chris Cornog. Reprinted by permission of Working Assets Capital Management.

"Ladies First" by Dana Owens, Simone Johnson, Mark James, Anthony Peaks, and Shane Faber. © 1989 T-Boy Music Publishing, Inc. c/o Lipservices obo itself & Queen Latifah Music, Forty-Five King Music, Forked Tongue Music/Warner Chappell Music, Inc. © 1989 Warner-Tamerlane Publishing Corp., Now & Then Music. International copyrights secured. All rights reserved. Used by kind permission.

Langston Hughes. "Dream Deferred" ("Harlem") from *The Panther and the Lash* by Langston Hughes. Copyright © 1951 by Langston Hughes. Reprinted by permission of Alfred A. Knopf Inc.

Langston Hughes. "Theme for English B" from *Montage of a Dream Deferred* by Langston Hughes. Copyright © 1951 by Langston Hughes. Copyright renewed in 1979 by George Houston/Bass. Reprinted by permission of Harold Ober Associates Incorporated.

Jeff Jarvis. "Monty" from *TV Guide*, February 5, 1994. Copyright © 1994 by News America Publications Inc. Reprinted by permission of TV Guide Magazine.

June Jordan. "Aftermath" from *Naming Our Destiny* by June Jordan. Copyright © 1989 by June Jordan. Reprinted by permission of Thunder's Mouth Press.

Readers' Guide to Periodical Literature. March 1983–February 1984, page 890, Volume 43. Copyright © 1984 by The H. W. Wilson Company. Reprinted by permission of the publisher.

Lewis Thomas. "The Attic of the Brain" from *Late Night Thoughts on Listening to Mahler's Ninth* by Lewis Thomas. Copyright © 1980 by Lewis Thomas. Used by permission of Viking Penguin, a division of Penguin Books USA Inc.

Webster's New World Dictionary, Third College Edition. The entry "unique." Copyright © 1988. Reprinted by Webster's New World Dictionaries, a Division of Simon & Schuster.

Webster's Third International Dictionary. The entry "unique." Copyright © 1986 by Merriam-Webster Inc., publisher of the Merriam-Webster dictionaries. Reprinted by permission.

Eudora Welty, from *One Writer's Beginnings*. Copyright © 1983, 1984 by Eudora Welty. Reprinted by permission of Harvard University Press: Cambridge, Mass.

FOR DOING RESEARCH AND USING SOURCES

Quick-Reference Charts and Sample Essays

Scheduling a Research Project   557

Directory of Library Resources   565

Conducting Observation   582

Planning an Interview   584

Designing a Questionnaire   585

Keeping a Working Bibliography   587

Taking Accurate Notes   593

Deciding Whether to Quote, Paraphrase, or Summarize   594

Quoting Accurately   596

Paraphrasing Accurately   599

Summarizing Accurately   600

Recognizing Plagiarism, Acknowledging Your Sources   604

Signal Verbs   616

Incorporating Quotations, Paraphrases, and Summaries   618

Directory to MLA Style   624

A Sample Research Essay, MLA Style   645

Directory to APA Style   666

A Sample Research Essay, APA Style   678

Directory to Chicago Style   691

A Sample Essay, Chicago Style   719

Guidelines on CBE Style   689

A Sample Essay, CBE Style   712

Other Special Notes on Using Sources

Thinking Critically about Their Purpose and Stance   30

Finding Support for Your Argument   104

Choosing Verbs to Integrate Sources   230

Quoting Passages with Effective Adjectives   259

Shifting between Direct and Indirect Discourse   277

Maintaining Parallelism in Headings   346

Building Common Ground   456

FOR MULTILINGUAL WRITERS

▶ **Part 11 Mastering the Nuances of English**

▶ *Chapter 55 Understanding Nouns and Noun Phrases*

55a   Distinguishing Count and Noncount Nouns   *788*
55b   Maintaining Singular and Plural   *790*
55c   Using Determiners   *791*
55d   Working with Articles   *793*
55e   Arranging Modifiers   *796*

▶ *Chapter 56 Understanding Verbs and Verb Phrases*

56a   Forming Verb Phrases   *798*
56b   Using Present and Past Tenses   *801*
56c   Understanding Perfect and Progressive Verb Phrases   *802*
56d   Distinguishing Stative and Dynamic Verbs   *804*
56e   Using Modals   *805*
56f   Using Participial Adjectives   *808*

▶ *Chapter 57 Understanding Prepositions and Prepositional Phrases*

57a   Using Prepositions Idiomatically   *810*
57b   Using Two-Word Verbs   *813*

▶ *Chapter 58 Forming Clauses and Sentences*

58a   Expressing Subjects Explicitly   *816*
58b   Expressing Objects Explicitly   *817*
58c   Using English Word Order   *817*
58d   Recognizing the Sentence Nucleus   *818*
58e   Using Noun Clauses, Infinitives, and Gerunds   *819*
58f   Using Adjective Clauses   *822*
58g   Understanding Conditional Sentences   *824*

▶ Notes in Other Sections of the Book

Bringing in Other Languages   25

Using Your Native Language to Explore Ideas   35

Asking a Native Speaker to Review Your Draft   57

Counting Your Own Experience   87

Distinguishing among Transitions   132

Count and Noncount Nouns   161

Using Modal Auxiliaries   210

Writing Conditional Sentences   229

Determining Adjective Sequence   251

Using Pronoun Subjects   268

Judging Sentence Length   283

Recognizing American Spellings   380

Using a Learner's Dictionary   400

Learning English Capitalization   527

▶ If You Speak . . .

Arabic   823

Chinese   790–91, 802, 823

Farsi   823

French   820, 823

German   795

Greek   795, 820

Hebrew   823

Italian   820, 823

Japanese   790–91, 810, 816, 818, 823

Korean   790–91, 818, 823

Portuguese   820, 823

Russian   818

Spanish   795, 802, 811, 817, 820, 823

Turkish   818

Vietnamese   802

⋙ CHECKING FOR KEY ELEMENTS IN YOUR WRITING

Broad Content Issues

1. Use of supporting evidence *I-6*
2. Use of sources *I-6*
3. Achievement of purpose *I-7*
4. Attention to audience *I-8*
5. Overall impression *I-8*

Organization and Presentation

1. Overall organization *I-10*
2. Sentence structure and style *I-11*
3. Paragraph structure *I-11*
4. Format *I-12*
5. Documentation *I-13*

The Twenty Most Common Surface Errors

1. Missing comma after an introductory element *I-16*
2. Vague pronoun reference *I-17*
3. Missing comma in a compound sentence *I-17*
4. Wrong word *I-18*
5. Missing comma(s) with a nonrestrictive element *I-19*
6. Wrong or missing verb ending *I-19*
7. Wrong or missing preposition *I-20*
8. Comma splice *I-21*
9. Missing or misplaced possessive apostrophe *I-21*
10. Unnecessary shift in tense *I-22*
11. Unnecessary shift in pronoun *I-22*
12. Sentence fragment *I-23*
13. Wrong tense or verb form *I-23*
14. Lack of agreement between subject and verb *I-24*
15. Missing comma in a series *I-25*
16. Lack of agreement between pronoun and antecedent *I-26*
17. Unnecesssary comma(s) with a restrictive element *I-27*
18. Fused sentence *I-27*
19. Dangling or misplaced modifier *I-28*
20. *Its / it's* confusion *I-29*